Examination
OF THE
COUNCIL OF TRENT

Examination
OF THE
COUNCIL OF TRENT
Part II

by
MARTIN CHEMNITZ
(1522–1586)

Fred Kramer, *Translator*

Publishing House
St. Louis

Headings in brackets have been inserted by the editor.
Some other headings were inserted by Ed. Preuss.
Some Bible texts in this publication are from the Revised
Standard Version of the Bible, copyrighted 1946, 1952, © 1971,
1973 by the Division of Christian Education of the National
Council of the Churches of Christ in the U. S. A., and used by
permission.

Concordia Publishing House, St. Louis, Missouri
Copyright © 1978 Concordia Publishing House

Manufactured in the United States of America

Library of Congress Cataloging in Publication Data (Revised)

Chemnitz, Martin, 1522-1586.
    Examination of the Council of Trent.

    1. Trent, Council of, 1545-1563. 2. Catholic
Church—Doctrinal and controversial works—
Protestant authors. 3. Lutheran Church—Doctrinal
and controversial works. I. Kramer, Fred.
II. Title.
BX8301545.C413   262'.5'2   79-143693
ISBN 0-570-03213-X (v. 1) ISBN 0-570-03272-5 (v. 2)

To my former students
who, having read Volume I of the *Examen,* assured
me that they were eagerly looking forward to the
appearance of the translation of Volume II.

CONTENTS

SEVENTH TOPIC
CONCERNING PENANCE
549—649

EIGHTH TOPIC
CONCERNING EXTREME UNCTION
651—673

TRANSLATOR'S PREFACE

The year 1971 saw the publication of Part I of the undersigned's *Examination of the Council of Trent*. The reception of this volume on the part of pastors, and particularly of theological students, was gratifyingly favorable.

When, therefore, the request came to the undersigned from the committee for Research of the Commission on Church Literature of The Lutheran Church—Missouri Synod to translate also Part II of the *Examen*, concerning the sacraments, he gladly complied, particularly because by this time his teaching load had been considerably reduced.

He was spurred on in this work by the frequent question of theological students: "When will Part II of the *Examen* be out?" He could only assure them that he would complete the translation as quickly as possible and that it would then be up to the Committee on Research to find ways and means to have the work published.

As in translating Part I, so also in his work on Part II, the translator found that the Latin text contains many errors, generally of an insignificant nature. As in Part I, he depended chiefly on the 1578 Frankfort edition, but with frequent comparisons with the 1861 Preuss edition and the 1576 German translation by Nigrinus. Many of the differences among these are indicated by footnotes.

Although Chemnitz always refers to Scripture passages only by chapter, they are given here by chapter and verse. Wherever possible, the Revised Standard Version has been used.

Many references to the church fathers are incorrect as to book and chapter, although not as to author. Most of these had to be kept as they are, for it would have been an almost impossible task to check all of these quotations.

The work of translation was finished about the time the undersigned retired from teaching in the summer of 1976. The next few months were needed for typing the completed manuscript, for which thanks are due to Mrs. Jan Akins and Mrs. Z. Eastman.

The Committee for Research found the necessary means to have the work published, and it is herewith offered to the theological world.

FRED KRAMER, *Springfield, Illinois*

PREFACE

*To the Examination of the Second Part
of the Decrees of the Council of Trent,
Concerning the Sacraments, etc.*

1 In the first Apostolic Synod (Acts 15) that part of the doctrine concerning which a disputation had been instituted at that time on account of controversies that had arisen was explained from the very sources of the prophetic Scripture and apostolic preaching. This, as Irenaeus says, was later put in writing by the will of God, in order that it might be the foundation and pillar of our faith. That part of the doctrine was explained in such a way that it showed the firm and clear basis of a true and sound understanding, in order to show the reasons why other dissenting and contrary opinions should be rejected and condemned. And this same understanding, later summed up under a few concise points (which they called dogmas, Acts 15), they placed before the churches. At the same time they also explained the basis, reasons, and proof of their decrees at length and clearly, to the end that the church might know with dependable reason from the Word of God what was to be accepted and why, and what was to be avoided.

2 That Paul and Silas did this at Antioch we know from Luke (Acts 15). And there is no doubt that what Paul treats in his epistles to the Romans and to the Galatians with great effort and many arguments he also did in other churches orally. For what they taught in words (namely, that they would not lord it over the faith of the church, 2 Cor. 1:24, but that they were always prepared to give an answer to anyone who asked a reason for the hope that was in them, 1 Peter 3:15) they confirmed by deed and examples.

3 The older synods of the fathers also followed this apostolic method, as the histories of the Nicene, Constantinopolitan, Ephesine, and Chalcedonian synods show both the decrees or canons and how the controversies were argued on both sides and on what basis they were finally decided according to the rule of Scripture. However, of many other synods only the bare canons were preserved, while the explanation of the causes and of the basis was neglected or suppressed. This has done

15

the church more harm than good. For because, according to Hilary's statement, the understanding of what is said must be taken from the causes of the speech, the canons were often understood less skillfully by later generations, and often they were, indeed, also distorted from their true and original meaning in order to establish strange and false doctrines. And finally, with the title "canon" used as a pretext, equal authority was little by little arrogated indiscriminately to all decrees and canons, without inquiry whether they had or did not have a sure, firm, and clear basis in the Word of God. And from this there was finally built up this papal tyranny which obtrudes on the church all kinds of decrees and canons in the interest of wantonness and power, without any proof from Scripture. This way of doing finally led to disgraceful shamelessness, worthy of the brow of the Babylonian harlot. For horrendous expressions are found in public writings of canonists, and these have been noted by many:

"That the power of the pope is absolute and that he may use it as he wills";

"That his will takes the place of a reason in what he wills";

"That no one should say to him, Why do you do this?"

"That he is above the law, and that he can do all things outside of the law";

"That he can give dispensation contrary to the first four councils; also against the words of the Gospel, though not against its intention";

"That he can decree against the epistles of Paul," etc.

4 The Synod of Trent indeed in the beginning pretended with a certain show of modesty that it wanted to depart from this patently monstrous impudence. For in the fifth and sixth sessions they gave some appearance as if they did not want to impose their decrees on the church with that Babylonian authority of which we have spoken but that they wanted to derive and prove them on the basis of the Word of God. However, the good fathers had experienced how great a labor and trouble it would be, even without the contradiction of any opponent, to undertake a discussion of the basis of the papalist doctrine, since indeed any such dispute whatever concerning this basis would only show more fully the weakness, or rather the hideousness and abomination, of the dogmas in the papal kingdom. Therefore when they had come to the seventh session, in which the doctrine of the sacraments was to be treated, they believed that they should refrain from this labor, since indeed those papalist materials appeared unable to sustain even the appearance of a just investigation, for the matter could be dealt with more

easily and safely with nothing more than the naked anathemas in accord with the law concerning the privileges of the Roman See (2 Thess. 2) than by showing the basis and giving reasons. For they remembered, perhaps too late, that which the prudence of our Parisian teachers in the year 1521 judged against Luther, namely, that the rule with respect to defining in the papalist church is that they explain what they mean with a few arguments, but that they do not commit to writing the reasons why they define as they do, as the manner is in court decisions. Therefore the manner of our examination in this second part will be less easy and unimpeded. Therefore the reasons and the explanations will have to be sought out of the puddles of the disputations which are found in the scholastic and papalist writers. In some things the explanations of Andrada will be able to aid our examination. But he did not treat all topics. However, I hope that it will happen that Andrada, who is so candid that he does not know how to dissemble, will on this occasion explain to us somewhat more fully what arguments were used with respect to the following articles in the public deliberations and in the private meetings of the synod. For this will be useful to all posterity. Neither Andrada nor the others who attended the council will be able to refuse this. For we have the illustrious example of Cyril at the Ephesine Council, who after the canons were published did not refuse, nor was ashamed, to publish explanations in which he gave a reason from the Word of God for the condemnations. Therefore with the kind assistance and blessing of God we shall now gird ourselves for the examination of the remaining part of the decrees of the Council of Trent.

First Topic

CONCERNING THE SACRAMENTS IN GENERAL

From the Decrees of the Seventh Session of the Council of Trent, March 3, 1547

SECTION I

Concerning the Term "Sacrament"; Also Concerning the Number and Description of the Sacraments in the New Testament

The Decree on the Sacraments of the Church, Published in the Sacred Ecumenical and General Synod of Trent, Session VII

For the completion of the salutary doctrine of justification, which was promulgated in the last preceding session, with the unanimous consent of all fathers, it seemed proper to treat of the most holy sacraments of the Church, by which all true righteousness is either begun, or if it has been begun, augmented, or recovered, if it has been lost.

Therefore the most holy, ecumenical, and general Synod of Trent, lawfully assembled in the Holy Spirit, with the same legates of the apostolic chair presiding in it, for the elimination of errors and the rooting out of heresies, with respect to the most holy sacraments, which in this our time have in part been revived from among the heresies at one time condemned by our fathers, and in part also newly invented, which are exceedingly detrimental to the purity of the Catholic Church and the salvation of souls; the council, adhering to the doctrine of Holy Scripture, the apostolic traditions, and the consensus of the other councils and of the fathers, has decided to establish and decree these present canons; others which remain for the completion of the work which has been begun will, with the assistance of the divine Spirit, be published thereafter.

CANON I

If anyone says that the sacraments of the New Law were not all instituted by our Lord Jesus Christ, or that there are either more or fewer than seven, namely, baptism, confirmation, the Eucharist, penance, extreme unction, ordination, and marriage, or also that some of these seven are not truly and properly sacraments, let him be anathema.

Examination

1 Our teachers have publicly professed in the Apology of the Augsburg Confession that they do not greatly wrangle about the term "sacrament" or about the number of sacraments, since this term is not found in Scripture. It was also understood and defined in various ways by the ancients, at times in a wider, at other times in a narrower sense. This only must be preserved, that those things which have a command and have promises of God in Scripture, whether with special rites or without them, are retained and are treated and used as they are taught in the Word of God, regardless whether they are called sacraments or not.

In the second place, that those rites which have an explicit command of God in Scripture, and added to them the clear promise of grace which is peculiar to the New Testament, are carefully distinguished from other matters which indeed have a command of God but do not have specific and sure divinely instituted rites. They also have a promise, but not the promise that through them the gratuitous reconciliation is bestowed and sealed.

In the third place, also the rites which have explicit command and clear promise of grace in the Scripture of the New Testament, but were either received from the fathers or instituted by other men, are to be distinguished from those about which we have just spoken.

In the fourth place, that a distinction be preserved between the promise of grace, which offers and bestows on believers the benefits of redemption, promised in the Gospel, solely and only through the Word, and that same promise when it is clothed in rites or ceremonies divinely instituted in the Word of God.

If in this manner the true teaching and the necessary distinction about the matters themselves were established from the teaching of Scripture, it would afterward be possible to reach agreement without great difficulty on the term, and on the number of sacraments, if the contentions concerning unwritten terms had been removed.

But when confusion and corruption is sought through the designation and number of sacraments, then it is no longer strife about words, but a necessary contest about the matters themselves. And it is in vain, yes, it is deceitful and destructive, to attempt a reconciliation about terms which is connected with danger to and corruption of the matters themselves.

2 I mention these things at the beginning of this discussion in order that no one may pervert the statement of the Augsburg Confession, when it says that one must not greatly wrangle about the term "sacrament" or about the number of sacraments, as if it wanted us simply to receive and approve the decree of the Council of Trent concerning seven sacraments in the way in which it is set forth and understood by them, without the necessary explanation and distinction of the matters themselves, yes, with manifest confusion and corruption of the matters.

Also the following declaration is necessary at the very beginning. We do not want in this dispute in any way to lessen or detract from those things which the papalists are accustomed to designate with the name "sacraments" over and above Baptism and the Lord's Supper (such as the ministry of the Word and of the sacraments, marriage, penance, the increase and confirmation of the gifts of the Holy Spirit, the comforting of the sick)—we do not, I say, want to detract from that truth, respect, worth, and usefulness, which they have and should have according to the teaching of Scripture, when we contend that these are not truly and properly sacraments instituted by Christ in the same way in which Baptism and the Lord's Supper are truly and properly sacraments. Rather, it is our aim only that we may think and speak about these things in the church in the way Scripture prescribes and teaches. For in this way they possess and retain their true worth.

ARTICLE I

1 But let us proceed to the examination of the first canon, concerning the number of sacraments of the New Testament. It has three parts. For it first takes as an axiom that which is very true, that the authority or power to institute sacraments, in order that they may be efficacious signs of grace, does not belong to any creature, but to God alone, who works that grace; therefore it is necessary that all things which ought to be truly and properly sacraments in the New Testament should have their institution from Jesus Christ our Lord because He is the "surety" of the New Testament (Heb. 7:22) and its "mediator" (Heb. 8:6; 12:24).

Secondly, it quickly adds, but without any proof, that of such sacraments in the New Testament there are neither more nor fewer than seven, although no statement of the sevenfold number can be shown either in Scripture or in the entire true and pure antiquity. Moreover, the true peculiarity of a sacrament according to Scripture can in no way fairly fit all these seven. And it is certain, as we shall show later, that, as the ancients took the term "sacrament" either in a narrower or in a wider sense, some counted fewer, some more than seven sacraments. The papalists themselves also are not ignorant of the arguments of the person who under the name of Cyprian published a discourse on foot washing and on anointing, likewise of [the writings] of Hugo and of Lombard, who are of the opinion that not all those things which they enumerate as the seven sacraments were directly instituted by Christ Himself.

In the third place, the present canon says that each one of these seven is truly and properly a sacrament. But how, I beg you, can they imagine that marriage is truly and properly a sacrament, like Baptism and the Eucharist? For what is the element instituted by Christ? What is the word which comes to the element in order that marriage may become a sacrament? Pope Syricius defines matrimony as a living according to the flesh which cannot please God. How, I say, is the righteousness of faith either begun or increased or restored through matrimony according to their own description of a sacrament as given in the decree? Durandus openly says that matrimony is not a sacrament, strictly and properly speaking, as the other sacraments of the new law. And although matters stand thus, they nevertheless boldly and proudly decree, without proofs and documentation, by sheer fiat: "If anyone says that the sacraments of the New Law were not all instituted by Jesus Christ our Lord, or that there are more or fewer than seven, or that any one of these seven is not truly and properly a sacrament, let him be anathema." Surely, if the clatter of anathemas is by itself sufficient, without sure, clear, and firm proofs of Scripture to prove dogmas, and is able to make articles of faith, the Jews will be able in this way to make their Talmudic, and the Turks their Alcoranic traditions canonical. For what is easier than to say "anathema" when you cannot prove a thing? However, lest we be intimidated by this terror, Scripture forewarns us, when it says: "They will curse; but do you bless!"

2 But this whole dispute will have to be examined somewhat more fully. It is worth our while to observe that with the ancient writers no arguments or proofs are found for numbering just seven sacraments. But in the time of Hugo and Lombard this opinion was brought into the church, from the Sorbonne, that there are neither more nor fewer sacraments in the New Testament than seven. And Lombard, though he is otherwise accustomed to prove his arguments from the fathers, does not quote even one statement from the ancients for the number seven in the matter of the sacraments. However, the scholastic writers who, in their argumentation and reasoning do not differ much among themselves, earnestly labor to prove and establish also the sevenfold number of the sacraments with arguments and reasons.

3 But it is worthy of perpetual remembrance to be made known to all posterity with what reasons and arguments the sevenfold number of sacraments was brought into the church by the scholastics and on what basis it was received. The *Compendium theologiae* gives the reasons from the teaching of the scholastics why there are neither more nor fewer than seven sacraments in the New Testament. It says: "There are seven sacraments according to the seven different kinds of people in the church. The first kind is that for those who are entering, namely baptism; the second is for those who are struggling, namely confirmation; the third for those who are resuming their place, namely the Eucharist; the fourth is for those who are rising again, namely penance; the fifth is for the departing, namely extreme unction; the sixth is for those who minister, namely ordination; the seventh is for those who bring in new soldiers, namely

matrimony." Again it says: "The sacraments are seven because they dispose men to possession of the seven virtues. For baptism is the sacrament of faith, confirmation of hope, the Eucharist of charity, penance of righteousness, extreme unction of perseverance or fortitude, ordination of prudence, matrimony of temperance." "There is also," it says, "another reason for the number of sacraments. For they are ordained against the seven spiritual sicknesses, namely, against the threefold guilt and against the fourfold punishment. Baptism against original sin, penance against mortal sin, extreme unction against venial sin, ordination against ignorance, the Eucharist against ill will, confirmation against weakness, matrimony against evil lust."

It assigns also this reason for the sevenfold number, that according to the method of bodily healing, some sacraments are curative, some preservative, some preventive, some alleviating.

But who does not see how weak, yes, how worthless these reasons are to prove so great a matter! For if these are the proofs and supports of the matter, one could with similar, yes, with the very same reasons demonstrate without difficulty either more or fewer than seven sacraments. And on account of those same reasons, if they are valid and sufficient to demonstrate this matter, it will be necessary that there were both under the law of Moses and before its promulgation neither more nor fewer than seven sacraments. For it did not first begin in the New Testament that there are seven virtues and seven spiritual sicknesses.

Equally worthless are also the remaining reasons why there are seven sacraments of the New Testament: because there are seven seals of the book (Rev. 5:1), because there are seven trumpets of the angels (Rev. 8:2), because there are seven stars in the right hand of Him who is like to the Son of man and because there are seven candlesticks (Rev. 1:12, 16), because Christ fed the multitude with seven loaves (Matt. 15:34), because there are seven eyes on the stone (Zech. 3:9), because there are seven lamps in the tabernacle (Ex. 37:23). But on this basis, and with just as strong reasoning, Dr. Brenz gathers from other numbers given in Scripture that there are both fewer and many more sacraments. I really do not see why a conclusion drawn on the basis of also other numbers noted in Scripture should not be valid, unless perhaps they think that they can blunt the power of that conclusion with this point that in Rev. 1:20, where mention is made of seven stars, the translator used the term "sacrament." Why should not therefore the proof be valid that there are seven sacraments, because in that passage where the word "sacrament" is used the number seven is set down? For these are the words: "The sacrament of the seven stars which are the angels of the seven churches." However, I will show them a passage with which the sevenfold number of the sacraments of the papal church can be shown much more properly and clearly, and that from the same abundance of proofs. For of the Babylonian harlot, that is of the Antichrist, the angel speaks thus (Rev. 17:7): "I will tell you the sacrament[1] of the woman and of the beast which bears her, which has seven heads, which are the seven hills on which the woman sits." Here you hear both the word sacrament and the number seven. Also the entire picture in that chapter does not fit badly. That is sufficient for the wise.

4 These are the proofs, these the sources on the basis of which the sevenfold number of sacraments has been brought into the church and accepted by the scholastic writers. For the scholastic writers have not even so much as attempted to prove the sevenfold number of sacraments with suitable documentation from Scripture or with testimonies from true antiquity. So manifest is, however, the worthlessness of these demonstrations, that now also the hired defenders of the papal kingdom who have any sense of shame are ashamed of it. Therefore, because they see that in the presence of the great light of the Gospel they cannot any longer delude men with these old fictions, they are now sewing together new girdles, if perhaps by means of a new patch they can give the worn-out, transparent garment some sort of appearance.

5 At the present time they employ chiefly two arguments to prove the sevenfold number of sacraments. First, they gather testimonies from certain old writers to show that these give the name "sacrament" not only to Baptism and the Eucharist, but besides also to certain other ceremonies and things, and this collection they arrange in such a way that they do not exceed the limits of the number seven. Then they prove the same from the definition of a sacrament through the rule: "To that which the definition fits also the name of that which is defined is rightly applied." Therefore we shall comment on things one by one in their order, so that the manner of our examination may oppose not only the nonsense of the older sophists but that it may also expose the disguises of the more recent orators.

6 The term "sacrament" is taken from the common and popular Latin language. For with Varro a sacrament is a pledge which litigants deposited with the high priest, and whoever won the case demanded his pledge back, but the money of those whose cause had failed was put into the public treasury. With other Latin writers a sacrament is an oath or

---

[1] Chemnitz quotes from the Vulgate, which has: *Ego tibi dicam sacramentum mulieris*, etc. The Greek word translated in the Vulgate with *sacramentum* is *mysterion*, which is usually properly translated "mystery" or "secret" in English.

pledge, confirmed by the mediation of a deity and of religion. In Vegetius[2] it is the military oath of allegiance by which the soldiers are pledged to their leader. Now the question is how and for what reason that word was taken over into the speech of the church and applied to the divinely instituted signs of grace.

The ancient interpreter, in translating the Hagiographa,[3] where the Greeks have *mysterion* at times renders it *sacramentum*, e.g., Tobit 12:7; Wisd. of Sol. 2:22; 6:24. And Dan. 2:18; 4:9, where the Greeks rendered the Aramaic *raza* with *mysterion*, he translates *sacramentum*. In the New Testament, however, he often left the Greek word *mysterion*,[4] but elsewhere he rendered it *sacramentum*. It signifies in general that which is hidden or secret, as in Tobit 12:7: "The *sacramentum* of the king must be kept secret." Ecclus. 27:16: "To reveal the secrets *(mysteria)* of a friend"; Judith 2:2: "He had a secret *(mysterium)* council with them." Thus Paul (2 Thess. 2:7), speaking of the Antichrist, says: "The mystery of iniquity is already at work." But chiefly it expresses the hidden or secret will, plan, or purpose of God, which is not known to reason by nature but is concealed from the whole world except in so far as it is divinely revealed.

Thus the doctrine concerning the redemption and reconciliation of the human race is called a mystery or sacrament of God (Col. 2:2), "the mystery of Christ" (Eph. 3:4), "the mystery of the Gospel" (Eph. 6:19), "the mystery of the faith" (1 Tim. 3:9). The incarnation of the Son of God is called "the great mystery (Vulgate: *sacramentum*) of godliness" (1 Tim. 3:16). The calling of the Gentiles is called "the *sacramentum* of the will of God" (Eph. 1:9). Paul calls the doctrine of the resurrection of the dead a *mysterium* (1 Cor. 15:51), also the conversion of the Jews (Rom. 11:25). Thus in Eph. 5:32 he calls the union of Christ with His church "a great *sacramentum*." In this sense the word *sacramentum* is used not only in the versions of Scripture but also in the language of the fathers, who often speak of a *sacramentum* "of divinity," "of the incarnation," "of Christ's suffering." Tertullian, *Contra Marcionem*, 4, calls all of Christianity "the *sacramentum* of the Christian religion."

7 However, this general meaning proves neither the twofold nor the sevenfold number of sacraments. For Paul enumerates many more such "sacraments." In 1 Cor. 13:2 he says: "If I understand all mysteries." Let us therefore get down to the kind where the meaning of the word "mys-

---

2 Flavius Vegetius Renatus, a writer on military affairs.
3 The term "Hagiographa" designated the third section of the Old Testament writings.
4 Latinized *mysterium*.

tery," or "sacrament," is narrower. Now in Greek that is called a mystery, which the Latin interpreter has rendered *sacramentum,* when something or external phenomenon means something else, beyond the appearance which it thrusts upon the external senses. Thus the vision of Nebuchadnezzar's dream is called a *sacramentum* (Dan. 2:18). And in Rev. 1:20 the phenomenon of the seven stars signifying the angels of the seven churches, and the fact that the seven candlesticks are the seven churches, is called a *sacramentum.* Thus in Rev. 17:7, where the angel explains what the seven heads of the beast bearing the harlot signify, he says: "I will tell you the *sacramentum* of the woman." So also the union of man and woman in matrimony is the *sacramentum* of the union of Christ and the church (Eph. 5:32). Related to this is what Christ says about the meaning of the parables: "To you it has been given to know the secrets (Greek: *mysteria*) of the kingdom of heaven, but to the others I speak in parables." This meaning comes somewhat closer to the question which is before us, but in this way many more sacraments will have to be counted than seven. For the fathers call all figures and allegories which signify something "sacraments." Tertullian, *Contra Marcionem,* Bk. 5, uses the terms "sacraments of figures" and "allegories of sacraments" where he speaks of the two sons of Abraham. Against the Jews he calls it "the sacrament of wood" when he disputes about the axe of Elisha and about the wood of Adam. Thus Augustine, when he weaves allegories, speaks of "the sacrament of bread," "the sacrament of the fishes," "the sacrament of the number," etc.

But our question is how and for what reason the word "sacrament" was transferred and applied to the signs of grace of the New Testament, such as are without any controversy Baptism and the Lord's Supper. I have devoted some effort to this investigation. But I have not found that Scripture applies to Baptism or to the Lord's Supper the name "mystery" or "sacrament"; yes, neither to ordination, nor to the laying on of hands (Acts 8:17 and 19:3-6), nor to the anointing of the apostles (Mark 6:13) is the appellation "mystery" or "sacrament" given in Scripture. In Eph. 3:3 not the ministry itself or ordination but the things which are proclaimed through the ministry are, and are called by Paul according to the general significance, "mysteries" or "sacraments." In Eph. 5:32, where Paul treats of matrimony, he adds: "This is a great *sacramentum.*" But he explains himself, that this great sacrament of which he speaks is not in the union of the spouses but in the union of Christ with the church. For so Ambrose and Chrysostom interpret this passage, and Paul's words are clear: "This is a great *sacramentum;* but I am speaking of Christ and the church." Theodoret interprets thus: "As Eve was formed out of Adam, so the church is born out of Christ." But if someone should argue that matrimony is called a mystery or sacrament in Scripture from this significance that as man and wife are one flesh, so also the church is flesh of the flesh of Christ, etc., we will not fight about the term. For we have already shown by examples that this use is quite widespread and that the term is applied to many other things by reason of a sign. However, our question is concerning that signification in which Baptism and the Lord's Supper are truly and properly called sacraments.

The use of the word "sacrament" in this meaning, namely, as it is applied to the efficacious signs of grace, such as are in the New Testament without controversy Baptism and the Lord's Supper, has indeed some affinity with the examples of Scripture of which we have spoken above. But it has nevertheless not been taken from Scripture but from the customary manner of speaking in the church. For Scripture never calls either Baptism or the Lord's Supper mysteries or sacraments. Therefore this is an unwritten *(agraphos)* appellation.

8 However, because it is becoming to those who are learned to give diligence that they speak after a godly fashion within the church, we shall not quarrel about the term but strive for this, that the doctrine about the matters themselves which is taught in Scripture may not be disturbed and adulterated through an unwritten word. We must therefore consider for what reason certain ecclesiastical writers applied the term "sacrament" to the New Testament signs of grace. And to this consideration belongs the fact that some used this term in a wider and others in a narrower sense. For in this way it will become clear that some of the fathers counted fewer and some more than seven sacraments.

9 Tertullian seems to transfer the term "sacrament" from the common Latin way of speaking about the military sacrament (the military oath) to Baptism in this manner. For he says to the martyrs concerning the renunciation which takes place in Baptism and concerning the other questions: "Having been called to military service, we respond to the words of the sacrament," etc. From this the whole action afterward received its name, as he says, *Adversus Praxeam:* "Faith in the Father, the Son, and the Holy Ghost, according to the sacrament of the Christians," etc. But the chief reason is this: The Greeks call Baptism and the Lord's Supper mysteries because under the visible elements spiritual grace is offered and exhibited in a hidden manner, which is not apprehended by the senses and not understood by reason, but is recognized by faith, solely from the revelation of the Word of God. And the term "mysteries" in this sense was accepted and employed in the common speech of the church also because the pagans called those peculiar rites by which they initiated their people into their idolatrous religions with the then commonly used term "mysteries." And from that the Latin writers carried over both words, mysteries and sacraments, in this usage into the speech of the church. For we have the writings of Ambrose: *De his qui initiantur mysteriis* and *De sacramentis*.

ARTICLE II

10 However, in this usage antiquity does not extend the appellation "mysteries" or "sacraments" to the number seven, but counts fewer. For the most ancient writers number only two such "mysteries" or "sacraments," Baptism and the Lord's Supper. These Justin enumerates and explains in *Apology,* 2, where he describes the rites of the church, either in Palestine, where he was born, or in Italy. For he wrote his *Apology* in Rome. Irenaeus makes mention of these things, likewise Tertullian, *Contra Marcionem,* Bks. 1 and 4, and *De corona militis.* But when, in the book *De resurrectione carnis,* he adds the laying on of hands and the anointing, he understands ceremonies then connected with the act of Baptism, not peculiar sacraments distinct from Baptism, as we shall show later. So also Cyril of Jerusalem, where he specifically describes the religious instruction and the initiation into the mysteries, speaks only of the mysteries of Baptism and the Lord's Supper. For when he argues about the anointing he understands not a special sacrament but a ceremony connected with the act of Baptism, as we shall show later under the subject of confirmation. We have the books of Ambrose concerning those who are initiated into the mysteries; likewise, under his name, some books on the sacraments. But although those books expressly promise an explanation of the doctrine of the mysteries or sacraments of the church, they nevertheless contain only a discussion of the rites of Baptism and the Lord's Supper. Therefore the oldest ecclesiastical writers did not define the mysteries or sacraments of the church as numbering seven, but as such mysteries or sacraments they acknowledge only Baptism and the Eucharist.

Those who came later did indeed begin, little by little, to extend the number more widely. Nevertheless these also count, not seven but fewer. Of this that Dionysius whom they imagine to be the Areopagite (Acts 17:34) can be a witness. He is supposed to have received the rites which he describes from the apostles as his teachers, although at the end of the *Ecclesiastica hierarchia,* where he argues about the baptism of infants, he betrays himself quite clearly, for he says: "Our holy teachers, having been trained in the early tradition, have transmitted it to us." This statement has been paraphrased as follows by a writer from Vercellae: "Our teachers, instructed by their elders, taught that it seemed good to the holy apostles," etc. This same Dionysius, I say, whoever he may really be, where he specifically describes the ecclesiastical hierarchy does not number either penance or matrimony or the anointing of the sick among the mysteries or sacraments of the church. But for the anointing of the sick he has the anointing of the dead. If our papalists will receive this into the number of sacraments, the number will not be seven but will grow to eight.

11 And not only the oldest, but also more recent ones do not know the sevenfold number of sacraments. For Gregory, ch. *Multi secularium,* numbers expressly only three sacraments to which he applies the definition: Baptism, the anointing, and the Body and Blood of the Lord. Rabanus repeats the same opinion. Paschasius says, *De coena Domini:* "The sacraments of Christ in the catholic church are Baptism, also the body and blood of the Lord." They cannot show that the number seven is expressly stated in a single one of the old writers. Lindanus adduces the sermon of Cyprian *De chrismate,* but he knows that this is not genuinely Cyprian's. And yet even that uncertain author does not count seven sacraments, but fewer.

How great is, therefore, the madness or the disgraceful worthlessness of the men of Trent, that they are not afraid to pronounce the anathema without any proofs against all who number fewer than seven sacraments of the New Testament, although the universal chorus of the most ancient antiquity has done this? But if they object that the most ancient writers nevertheless believed and taught honorably concerning ordination, matrimony, penance, etc., although they do not give them the name "sacrament," they will by their own judgment help our cause, namely, that the true worth of these things can be preserved according to the teaching of Scripture although they are not said to be truly and properly sacraments as are Baptism and the Eucharist. However, the question here is whether the most ancient church (however, I do not want spurious writings of the Romanists to be understood) fixed the number for the sacraments or mysteries of the church, which truly and properly are sacraments as are Baptism and the Lord's Supper, at seven. We have however shown that they counted fewer.

12 We shall now proceed to show that some counted more than seven. For Augustine began as almost the first to extend the term "sacrament" in this matter and to use it in a wider sense than antiquity had done. For, speaking of signs in the *Fifth Epistle to Marcellus,* he says: "Since these concern divine things they are called sacraments." And in *De civi-*

tate Dei, Bk. 10, ch. 5, he says: "A sacrament is a sacred sign." And in *Contra Faustum,* Bk. 19, ch. 11, where he describes the outward use of the sacraments, he says: "In no religion, no matter what its name, or whether it be true or false, can men be held together unless they are bound together by some community of signs or visible sacraments." In order, therefore, that a thing may be a sacrament to Augustine, it is sufficient that it is a sign of something divine or sacred, especially if it is used in certain external rites in the public assemblies of the church, either because it has a command from Christ in the New Testament, or because it is taken from the Old Testament, as the anointing, or because it was devised by churchmen, as the sign of the cross. It does not matter to Augustine whether grace is conferred by the sign, or whether it is only signified, as in marriage; likewise, whether it is the grace of reconciliation or some other gift of the Spirit, as in ordination. In this way and for this reason Augustine gives the name "sacrament" also to other and more things than antiquity had done before him. Thus in *De bono conjugali,* ch. 24, he says that the sacrament of ordination remains in the ordained. And he adds the reason for the appellation, *Contra epistolam Parmeniani,* Bk. 2, ch. 13, where he speaks of Baptism and of ordination. He says: "Each is a sacrament and is given by a certain consecration to a person, the former when he is baptized, the latter when he is ordained." And in *Contra litteras Petiliani,* Bk. 2, ch. 104, he says that in the class of visible symbols the anointing is most sacred. And a little later, as though he were giving the reason, he adds that that visible holy sacrament must be distinguished from the invisible anointing of charity. Thus he also calls marriage a sacrament. And he sets forth the reason in the book *De bono conjugali,* ch. 18: "As the sacrament of polygamy during that period signified that the multitude in all earthly tribes is subject to God, so the sacrament of monogamy in our time signifies the future unity of all of us subject to God in one heavenly commonwealth."

For this reason, because of what the sacred thing signifies, Augustine counts more than those seven sacraments for which the papalists contend. For in *De peccatorum meritis,* Bk. 2, ch. 26, he says that the catechumens are consecrated before Baptism according to a certain unique mode by the sign of Christ. So also Dionysius bestows the sign of the cross on those who are to be baptized. That sign of the cross Augustine, *Contra Faustum,* Bk. 19, ch. 14, numbers among the sacraments. And on Ps. 141: "We receive many sacraments in different ways. Some, as you know, we receive with the mouth; others we receive with our whole body, but the cross we bear on our forehead." He quickly explains the reason why it is called a sacrament. He says: "Because we blush in our forehead, He has put that disgrace, which the pagans deride, in the place where we betray shame, in order that we may not blush because of the cross." Likewise: "The cross is the sign of humility by which the pride of our soul is healed." And in discourse 19, *De sanctis,* he says: "In this figure of the cross a sacrament is contained." And he explains that, in a wider sense, the love of the neighbor is understood, etc. He also adds: "Through this sacrament of the cross the holy man Elisha through prayer revived the son of the Shunammite, applying his mouth to the mouth, and his hands to the hands of the child. Through the power of the same sacrament Moses in the desert twice struck the rock with his rod." The reader sees how widely Augustine uses the term "sacrament." For in his comments on Ps. 65 he calls all rites which were at that time employed, outside of the application of water in the act of Baptism, sacraments. For he says: "In the sacraments, and in catechizing, and in exorcising, fire is first applied." And soon he adds the reason: "Passing through fire and water you are led to consolation. For the signs of these things are in the sacraments; the things themselves are in the perfection of eternal life." But the clearest passage is in *De peccatorum meritis,* Bk. 2, ch. 26: "That which the catechumens receive, although it is not the body of Christ, is nevertheless sacred, and holier than the food by which we are nourished, since it is a sacrament." He is speaking of the *eulogia,*[5] that is, the blessed bread, which they call a substitute for Holy Communion. And that, he says expressly, is a sacrament; but he adds: "It is not a sacrament in the same way as the Eucharist." This the reader should observe well. And, *De symbolo ad catechumenos,* Bk. 4, ch. 1, he calls sacraments all the things that are done to the catechumens before Baptism. He enumerates exorcisms, prayers, chants, blowing upon them, the hair shirt, the bending of the necks, the humiliation of the feet, etc. Thus in *Epistle 23,* where he disputes about Baptism, that is about the sacrament of faith, and of the body of Christ, he adds examples about the Lord's day, and about Easter, of which it is said: "This day the Lord arose." And he explains: "We call these days by these names on account of their resemblance to those days on which these things occurred: so that it is said on account of the celebration of the sacrament that the things happen on that day which really happened, not on that day, but long before."

Bernard also, in his discourse on the Lord's Supper, maintains at some length that foot washing is a sacrament of the daily remission of sins. And at the blessing of the salt in connection with Baptism the papal

---

[5] The Latin has *sylogia,* which seems to be a misprint. Nigrinus, in the German translation of the *Examen* (1574) read *eulogia.*

church prays that through the name of the Holy Trinity a salutary sacrament may be effected for escaping the evil foe.

13 These things I have related to show on what sort of foundation the sevenfold number of sacraments is based, namely, that Augustine and certain others apply the name "sacrament" to more rites or things than to Baptism and the Lord's Supper. For we have shown that in this way the number of sacraments will far exceed the number seven, since Augustine gives the name "sacrament" to more rites or things. And it should be diligently noted that although Augustine is somewhat freer in the use of the word "sacrament," which he applies to more things than the ancients before him had done, he nevertheless shows that the other things are called sacraments for a different reason than Baptism and the Lord's Supper, and he repeatedly explains for what reason they are said to be sacraments, as we have shown by the examples we have adduced.

14 When he calls the sign of the cross a sacrament, he clearly distinguishes it from the sanctification which occurs in Baptism. And the emphasis of his words should be considered, *De peccatorum meritis,* Bk. 2, ch. 26, that "the catechumens are sanctified according to a unique mode, by the sign of Christ and the prayer at the laying on of hands." It is worthy of note that Augustine enumerates more sacraments in such a way that he nevertheless places Baptism and the Eucharist in the first, distinguished, chief, particular, and distinct place, as for instance in *De doctrina Christiana,* Bk. 3, ch. 9, where, speaking about the sacraments of the New Testament, he says: "The Lord Himself and the apostolic instruction handed down few things for many, and these very easy to do, most reverent for the understanding and most pure in their observance, such as is the sacrament of Baptism and the celebration of the body and blood of the Lord." And in *Epistola ad Januarium,* 118: "Our Lord Jesus Christ has gathered in the Gospel a community of new men through sacraments which are very few in number, very easy to observe, most excellent in their significance, such as is Baptism, observed in the name of the Trinity, the communication of His body and blood, and if anything else is recommended in the canonical Scripture."

On Ps. 103 he says: "The gift of the sacraments in Baptism, in the Eucharist, and whatever the gift is in the other holy sacraments." If in this way Baptism and the Eucharist were distinguished according to the sense of Scripture from the remaining rites, it would be easy to get together on the term "sacrament," even if it were applied also to other things through a certain extended use, for we do not seek strife about words. But the papalists simply insist that also the other rites, as many as they count, are truly and properly sacraments just as are Baptism and the Eucharist. For so that first canon which we are now treating decrees.

15 We have shown, however, that it is wrong for them to maintain that there are seven (neither more nor fewer) sacraments to be counted in the New Testament. For in all of antiquity there is not found a single testimony concerning the sevenfold number of sacraments, and that neither fewer nor more are to be counted. And those who everywhere boast about the consensus and the voice of antiquity are not able to produce even one witness. Nor can they produce the authority of any ancient council for the sevenfold number, except that about a century ago in the Council of Florence, together with purgatory and the primacy of the Roman pontiff, the sevenfold number of sacraments was tried out on the Greeks, and indeed thrust upon the Armenians. This shows the newness of the sevenfold number of the sacraments. For Bartholomew preached the Gospel to the Armenians; and under Diocletian the Armenians had the testimony that they were Christians, and zealous for godliness, according to Eusebius, Bk. 9, ch. 7. Finally, after a thousand years or more, they first received the sevenfold number of the sacraments from the Roman pontiff. Therefore the fabrication of the sevenfold number of sacraments lacks also true and firm testimonies of antiquity. For outside of the examples of Augustine, concerning which we have shown how he himself wanted them understood, they cannot produce anything from the more ancient writers which has any strength, except that they bring Dionysius, speaking through the armor of the Areopagite, onto the stage, who nevertheless also himself neither proves nor confirms the sevenfold number, as we have said above.

16 From a discourse on the foot washing, ascribed to Cyprian, Lindanus also proudly quotes a vote for the sevenfold number. But in the first place, he knows that that writing is not a genuine writing of Cyprian, but is falsely ascribed to him. Then, whoever the author is, when he wants to count up the sacraments, both those which Christ Himself instituted and those which the apostles afterwards at the dictation of the Holy Spirit handed down, he counts not seven, but only five. And he shows at the same time that it is only a lot of noise rather than a true anathema what that canon, which we are now investigating, decrees: "If anyone says that not all those seven sacraments were instituted by Christ Himself, let him be anathema." For this very thing their spurious Cyprian expressly says in that sermon which they adduce. Alexander of Hales, Part 4, quest. 8, art. 2, clearly maintains that only two sacraments were instituted by Christ, Baptism and the Eucharist. And this he proves by the fact that blood and water flowed from the side of Christ, and by what is written in 1 John 5:8, that three bear witness on earth, the Spirit, the water, and the blood. But he says that Christ had willed that the form of the remaining sacraments should be ordered by the ministers of the church; however, he expressly says that confirmation was instituted neither by Christ, nor by the apostles, but by the Council of Meaux, quest. 24, memb. 1. Also Peter a Soto, who died at the Council of Trent, uses these same words: "We have the entire sacrament of confirmation, ordination, marriage, and extreme unction, the elements, the words, and the effects, from the apostolic tradition; not that we deny that some things about these sacraments are found in Scripture; but all things which we hold with sure faith as necessary for their integrity, since they are not in Scripture, must of necessity be of apostolic tradition." This is his testimony. But although I am well aware of what he means by the term tradition, nevertheless at this point it suffices us that he confesses that the elements, the words, the effects, and the integrity of four sacraments cannot be proved from Scripture. This pretext of apostolic traditions through fabrications of this sort we have clearly removed in the earlier part of the examination.[6]

So, let them have fun with this anathema of theirs: "If anyone says that the seven sacraments were not all instituted by Christ Himself, let him be anathema."

17 This is the first argument of the papalists taken from the word "sacrament" and from the testimonies of the ancients. How strong it is is clear from what we have stated until now. Any reader who is not stupid understands with what intention and for what cause the Tridentine fathers preferred to fight with bare anathemas rather than to operate with arguments and to show proofs in this dispute.

18 The other argument for the establishment of the sevenfold number of sacraments they take from the definition. And truly such arguments which are taken from the definition are usually taken as constituting proof. But let us consider for a moment how they handle the definition of a sacrament—whether, as one says, the stone is made to conform to the ruler or whether a leaden ruler is bent to the stone. Some descriptions are found in Augustine which are not so much definitions of the thing as explanations of the term: as for instance, that a sacrament is a sign of a sacred thing; likewise, that it is the visible form of invisible grace. But these descriptions take in much territory. For they embrace more than those seven signs, as the papalists themselves confess. Therefore by various devices such limitations were sought for the definition of a sacra-

---

[6] See Chemnitz, *Examination of the Council of Trent,* Vol. I, trans. Fred Kramer (St. Louis: Concordia Publishing House, 1971), pp. 272–307.

ment that its bosom might be rendered neither narrower nor wider than the number seven, but that it might be so adjusted that it would receive into its embrace those seven which they want to have recognized as sacraments.

From Gregory, ch. *Multi secularium,* they took this definition: "A sacrament is something by which, under the cover of visible things, the divine power secretly works salvation." But this did not seem to fit the sevenfold number sufficiently, for how, according to this definition, will marriage be a sacrament? Therefore two other definitions were fashioned. One is that of Hugo: "A sacrament is a corporeal or material element set forth externally before the senses, by likeness representing, by institution signifying, and by sanctification containing some visible and spiritual grace." The other is that of Lombard: "A sacrament is the visible form of an invisible grace, so that it bears its likeness and is its cause." However they found more than a few things lacking also in these definitions. For because they teach that in the Eucharist, after the substance is destroyed, only the appearance of bread and wine remains, they saw that Hugo's definition does not fit sufficiently, namely, that a sacrament is a material and corporeal element. Likewise, because they teach that in marriage the matter of the sacrament is the words expressing the consent of the contracting parties, they see that neither the material element of Hugo nor the visible form of Lombard are sufficiently fitting. Likewise, if by grace there is understood the gratuitous reconciliation, the forgiveness of sins, and acceptance to eternal life, they see that questions could be asked about the grace which is conferred in marriage on the contracting parties, and in ordination on the ordained. For although Richard argues that through these rites also the grace which makes man acceptable is conferred, the others nevertheless acknowledge that this cannot stand.

Scotus therefore transformed the definition thus: "A sacrament is a perceptible sign, either visible or audible, efficaciously signifying the grace or the gratuitous working of God, by virtue of its divine institution, ordained for the salvation of man while he is a pilgrim." But also in this definition the words about the divine institution, and that the sacraments are said to be ordained for salvation, have offended some. Occam therefore substituted another: "A sacrament is a sign effectually signifying the gratuitous operation of God."

19 And now, dear reader, how does it look to you? Are these firm, strong, and invincible demonstrations, when definitions are changed in this way, recast and bent until they agree with our intention which we imagined should be understood without proof?

This is certainly the same as if an architect wanted to demonstrate the equability of a building and would not adjust the stones to the ruler but, on the contrary, would change and bend the ruler to the stones. Therefore it does not have the strength of a certain and sure demonstration when the sevenfold number of the sacraments is proved from definitions of this kind. And yet, no matter what these definitions are, they cause much trouble for the scholastics in defending the boundaries and limits of the province which belongs to the sacraments in the papal realm. For if a sign which effectually signifies the gratuitous work of God is a sacrament, how will not also the blessing of the monks, the consecrated water, the consecrated rose, the consecrated sword, the *Agnus Dei,* the consecration of crops, of bells, of images, the royal anointing, the dedication of a church, of a cemetery, of an altar, etc., become sacraments? For these things are done with certain consecrations and are supposed to have spiritual effects. The scholastics indeed give divergent answers, one this and another that; nevertheless they neither extricate themselves nor do they satisfy their readers, except that the frankness of Gabriel is approved, who says that the consecrated water is not a sacrament because it lacks divine institution. However, by this reasoning also not a few of the sevenfold number will fall to the ground. Therefore it is evident what sort of definitions the papalists have in this matter.

20 However, they say that they, with the same freedom, also do not accept our recent narrower definitions. Whither, therefore, shall we turn? How, and on what grounds, will we demonstrate which are truly and properly sacraments of the New Testament? I answer: "We will not quarrel about definitions, neither about this man's nor about that man's, neither about the more ancient nor about the more recent ones, but we will take that basis which is beyond controversy and confessed by all. For Baptism and the Eucharist are according to the confession of all truly and properly sacraments. From them, therefore, we shall gather what things are required as essential that a thing may be truly and properly a sacrament of the New Testament; for this will be the simplest and surest proof.

21 In order, therefore, that a thing may be a true and proper sacrament of the New Testament like Baptism and the Eucharist, the following is required: 1. That it have some external, material or corporeal and visible element or sign, which is handled, offered, and employed in a certain external rite; 2. That this element or sign and its fixed rite have an explicit divine command or divine institution; 3. That it be instituted and commanded in the New Testament; 4. That it be instituted, not for a time only, but to the end of the world, as it is written of Baptism, and until the Son of God returns to judgment, as Paul says of the Eucharist. These

things are required for the element or sign of a sacrament in the New Testament: 5. There is required for a sacrament a divine promise concerning the grace, effect, or fruit of the sacrament; 6. This promise must not simply, nakedly, and in itself have a testimony in the Word of God, but it is necessary that it be joined to the sign of the sacrament by divine ordination, and so to say be clothed with it; 7. This promise must not pertain to any and all gifts of God, spiritual or temporal, but it must be the promise of grace, or of justification, that is, of the gratuitous reconciliation, of the remission of sins, and, in sum, of the entire benefit of redemption; 8. And this promise in the sacraments is not merely either signified or announced in general, but by the power of God it is offered, displayed, applied, and sealed also to the individuals who use the sacraments in faith. These things are true, manifest, certain, and immovable. For it is in this way that Baptism and the Lord's Supper are truly and properly sacraments of the New Testament.

22 Now let us examine whether the other things in the sevenfold number are in the same way truly and properly sacraments, like Baptism and the Eucharist, concerning which there is no controversy. And because through absolution the forgiveness of sins is not only announced in general, but sins are also privately loosed and remitted to individual believers who seek this, up to this point and in this way it [absolution] agrees with the sacramental promises. And in order that the salutary use of private absolution may be the more commended to the church from the teaching of the Word of God, our teachers have often testified that they do not oppose but freely concede that absolution, because it has the application of the general promise to the individuals who use this ministry, may be numbered among the sacraments. Nevertheless this is certain, that absolution does not have by divine institution a definite external element, sign, or ceremony divinely commanded. And even if either the imposition of hands or some other external rite is employed, yet it is without a sure, specific, and express command of God. Neither is there a promise that through such an external rite God wants to be efficacious for the application of the promise of the Gospel. We do, indeed, have the promise that He wills to be efficacious through the Word in the believers; but in order that anything may be a sacrament there is required not only the bare promise in the Word, but that it be clothed with some external sign or divinely commanded ceremony by divine ordination or institution. But the announcing or reciting of the promise of the Gospel is not such a sign, for in this way also the general preaching of the Gospel would be a sacrament. For it is the power of God through which the application of the promise is made in each and every believer. Thus there would no longer be any difference between the simple promise and a sacrament. Certainly, the announcing or recitation of the words in Baptism and in the Eucharist is not the element or sign of Baptism and the Eucharist. Therefore absolution is not truly and properly a sacrament in the same way as Baptism and the Lord's Supper. However, if anyone, with this added explanation and difference, should want to call it a sacrament on account of this peculiar application of the promise, the Apology of the Augsburg Confession testifies that it does not want to object.

23 Ordination, that is, the legitimate call to the ministry of the Gospel, and the public announcement and approval of that call, has a command in Scripture; it also has the promise that God wills to equip those legitimately called with the necessary gifts for the ministry (2 Tim. 1:6-7, 14; 2 Cor. 3:5-6) and that He wills to be efficacious through their ministry, not in bodily matters but, as the ministry of the Spirit is the power of God, for the salvation of everyone who believes. And it is useful for many reasons to extol the dignity of the ministry in the church, which it has according to the intention of the Word of God, and to set it, as it were, on a high pedestal, in order to refute both the enthusiasts and the Epicurean despisers of the ministry. In this way and according to this understanding the Apology of our Confession says that it would have no difficulty calling ordination a sacrament, so long as it is distinguished from Baptism and the Eucharist, which are truly and properly sacraments. And for this reason Augustine, writing against the Donatists, calls ordination a sacrament, as we shall show at the proper place.

Ordination, therefore, has indeed a promise of the efficacy of the ministry for salvation to everyone who believes; but it does not have the promise that the blessing of the Gospel is applied for salvation to the ordained person through the ordination itself, as if it were an instrument divinely instituted for this. For many take on the ministry, which is effectual in those who believe, although they themselves who perform the ministry are not children of God. The apostles also freely used the rite of laying on of hands, which in that place and time was customary in prayers and blessings. They did not, however, teach that this rite was instituted by the Son of God in the New Testament and that it was expressly commanded, as there are commands of Christ concerning the water in Baptism and the bread and wine in the Eucharist. Later teachers added to ordination the anointing and many other ceremonies which have neither a command of Christ nor the example of the apostles. However, efficacy and the application of the divine promise must not be bound to any rite which does not have a command or word of God. Therefore ordination is not truly and properly a sacrament in the way Baptism and the Lord's

Supper are sacraments. For both the ceremony of ordination and the promise of ordination lack those qualities which are required in order that something may be truly and properly a sacrament like Baptism and the Eucharist.

24 Augustine honored matrimony with the title "sacrament" chiefly at the time when he wanted to defend marriage from the Word of God as a state or kind of life which is good, pure, and holy, against Jerome's immoderate accusations, though without mentioning Jerome by name. And because it has a certain similarity with the union of Christ and the church, Augustine readily applies the term sacrament to it, which term he is accustomed to accept and employ in a wide sense. It never entered Augustine's mind to assert that marriage is truly and properly a sacrament of the New Testament in the same way as Baptism and the Eucharist are sacraments. For, first of all, it was not first instituted in the New Testament, but immediately at the beginning, when the human race was created.

And that mystery which is in marriage did not first have its beginning in the time of the New Testament. For the ancients say that this is the mystery or sacrament, that Eve was formed out of the side of Adam while he slept, that she should be flesh of the flesh of Adam; although Augustine adds another, namely, that in the New Testament a man is to have only one wife; but also this "other" thing was so from the beginning, as the Son of God testifies. (Matt. 19:8)

In the second place, the marriage of the godly has indeed the blessing and promise of God that they may be able to dwell together in harmony, charity, and purity; but this is not that promise of the grace of justification which is peculiar to the New Testament, nor is marriage the instrument or means by which God wills to offer, exhibit, and apply the benefits of redemption, which is the true function of the sacraments. Eck concedes that also the marriage of unbelievers is a sacrament.

In the third place, marriage has clearly no external element, as is required in sacraments. For it is absurd for them to pretend that that is the *materia* when the man says: "I accept you as mine," and the *forma* when the answer is made: "And I accept you as mine."

In the fourth place a true and proper sacrament also does not follow from this, that it has a command and blessing of God and signifies something sacred. For in this way many other things would be sacraments.

25 So far as confirmation is concerned, the first apostolic church had the promise of the outpouring of the visible gifts of the Spirit on the believers. When therefore the apostles prayed over them, they added the then customary sign used in prayers, the laying on of hands. But that was

a temporary gift, for it ceased after the doctrine of the Gospel was sufficiently established. But in order that something may be a sacrament it is
necessary that it have a command and promise of God, not for a time
only, but to the end of the world. Truly it is a mockery to imitate this
ceremony without a command of God, since it is most manifest that that
gift has long ceased. But you say: "We certainly have universal and
perpetual promises of the gift of confirmation and preservation, also of
the increase of spiritual gifts." Indeed, we not only concede this, which is
full of comfort, but we add besides that there are divinely ordained means
through which the Spirit confers these gifts and confirms, increases, and
preserves them, namely, the Word, faith, prayer, and the exercise of the
gifts, as we shall explain under the topic of confirmation. But what audacity is it for this reason to devise a special sacrament without the
command and institution of God? For there are many promises and various gifts of the Spirit for which no special sacraments were divinely instituted.

I think it has happened by God's will that the laying on of hands in
confirmation has not been retained. For if it had been, the example of the
apostles could be appealed to with at least some show. But because it has
been changed into anointing with oil and the sign of the cross, it appears
all the more clearly that it is a sacrament without institution and command of Christ and also that there is no apostolic example which can be
appealed to. For the fact that the anointing with oil in the Old Testament
had been divinely instituted is not enough to establish a sacrament of the
New Testament, for otherwise also the circumcision of the Turks could be
defended as a sacrament. It is necessary therefore that it was instituted
and commanded in the New Testament. But where is the command in the
New Testament Scriptures? Where is the example that, after the abolition of the other shadows of the ancients, the use of the oil is to be
retained and that from it so many sacraments should be fashioned?
Where is the promise that by the daubing with oil the Holy Spirit is given?
Therefore there cannot be a true and proper sacrament of the New
Testament where the institution and express command of Christ is
lacking.

26 So matters stand also with respect to the anointing of the sick. For
what, according to Mark, the apostles practiced when they had received
the gift of healing is the same thing that James commanded to the church
at a time when it still had that gift. For the anointing with oil was added as
an external sign of the gift of healing. Since that has ceased, it is manifest
that also the custom of anointing with oil was temporary. For there is to
be found neither a command nor an example in Scripture that in the New

Testament it is to be applied to anything else than to the gift of healing (Mark 6:13; James 5:14). Has the church therefore now no comfort whatever for the sick? Yes indeed, it has those things which James lists, the Word, faith, prayer, etc., for these have the command and promise of God for their perpetual use. But concerning the anointing with oil, separate from the gift of healing, and for any other effect bestowed without the Word, we have no command or promise of God in the Scripture of the New Testament.

However, on these individual things more will have to be said in the proper place. Here I wanted only to show briefly, from certain and firm foundations, clear reasons why those five (penance, ordination, marriage, confirmation, and unction) neither should nor could truly and correctly be called sacraments of the New Testament in the same way as Baptism and the Eucharist. Why the papalists contend so greatly that they should simply, truly, and properly be counted among the sacraments we shall relate with respect to each one at the proper place. From the things themselves which are indicated by these terms we detract nothing. We think, however, that they cannot be honored and explained more worthily or correctly than if they are taught and explained according to the sense of the Scripture, which can be done even if we do not attribute the name "sacrament" to them in the same way as it is attributed to Baptism. Yes, the strange opinions and corruptions which the papalists have added to these things under the name sacraments cannot be fully and clearly refuted unless that lid is removed and the teaching about these matters is explained simply in the way it is transmitted in Scripture. But these things will be explained more fully and appropriately in the proper places.

27 By no means, however, are we bringing something new into the church through this disputation. For although antiquity played with the word "sacrament" in various ways (as we have shown), yet when the story comes to their mind how from the side of the dead Christ blood and water flowed forth, all say that these are the sacraments of the church, namely, the water in Baptism and the blood in the Eucharist. Augustine, *De symbolo ad catechumenos,* Bk. 2, ch. 6, says that these are the twin sacraments of the church. And, *De civitate Dei,* Bk. 15, ch. 26: "From this the sacraments flowed forth by which the believers are initiated." *In Evangelium Johannis tractatus,* 9, "When Christ had died, His side was pierced by a lance that the sacraments might flow forth by which the church is formed." The same says, on Ps. 40: "From the side of Christ the sacraments of the church flowed forth." Bede quotes from Augustine, on John 19: "He opened His side that from there in a measure the gate of life might open from which the sacraments of the church have flowed, without which one does not enter into that life which is truly life."

Chrysostom says about this passage that from these two the church was established, and he adds that from here the mysteries, that is, the sacraments, have their origin, because water and blood flowed from the side of Christ. The remaining fathers say the same thing when they explain that passage of John. And the papalists themselves sing in their churches: "From here the sacraments of salvation flow forth, in the water and the blood."

28 That this debate is not a vain strife about words but a necessary struggle this one example shows sufficiently, namely, that into the matters themselves, that is, into the doctrine of penance, of the ministry of the Word, of marriage, of confirmation and the increase of the gifts of the Spirit, of the comforting of the sick, in place of the simple purity which they ought to have and retain according to the Word of God, many strange, false, and ungodly additions were introduced, mainly because they [the papalists] seemed unable truly and properly to defend the name "sacrament" for these things if they were left in that plain simplicity in which they are handed down in Scripture. That is why our opponents fight so stubbornly about the number of sacraments. For they see that the rites and opinions which were brought into these matters beside and contrary to the Word of God, from human traditions, cannot be excused, retained, and defended under a more plausible show than with the cloak, title, and pretext of the name "sacrament." That therefore the genuine purity and simplicity may be restored to these things from the Word of God, and when restored be preserved, and that no occasion may be given to posterity again to depart from that simplicity and in its place to invent additional strange and spurious things, it is useful and necessary to discuss whether the remaining five which the papalists number are truly and properly sacraments in the same way as Baptism and the Lord's Supper.

SECTION II

Concerning the Difference Between the Sacraments of the Old and the New Testaments

CANON II

If anyone says that these same sacraments of the New Law do not differ from the sacraments of the Old Law, except that there are other ceremonies and other external rites, let him be anathema.

Examination

1 God at all times from the beginning of the world revealed His will concerning the mystery of the redemption of the human race, the gratuitous reconciliation, and the acceptance of the believers to eternal life through faith on account of the sacrifice of the Son by giving a sure Word. Moreover He added to the Word, through His own divine institution, certain sure, external signs, by which He might more excellently seal and confirm the promise of the righteousness of faith. Therefore the institution and use of sacraments did not first begin at the time of the New Testament, but the fathers during the time of the Old Testament, even before the promulgation of the Law, had certain signs or sacraments, instituted by God for this use, which were seals of the righteousness of faith (Rom. 4:11). But now, although it is the same God, the same Mediator, the same grace, righteousness, promise, faith, salvation, etc., nevertheless the external signs or seals were changed at a time when others were by divine institution substituted in their place, according as the mode of revelation afterward was rendered more glorious. This was at first like a lamp shining in a dark place; afterward the morning star arose, until finally, after the night had passed, the Sun of Righteousness rose. Thus there came after the signs of the patriarchs the institution of circumcision, and when circumcision was finally abrogated there followed, through the institution of the Son of God, the sacraments of the New Testament.

2 But because this change of the signs was violently attacked by the raillery of heretics, especially the Manichaeans, people began, not uselessly, to ask and to dispute about the agreement or similarity and about the difference between the sacraments of the Old and of the New Testament. The matter in itself, as its basis is handed down in Scripture, is plain. However, the term "sacrament," being used now in a wider, now in a narrower sense, rendered that doctrine somewhat confused. Afterward the disputations of the scholastics concerning *opere operato* confused and perverted it altogether. These disputes gave Luther occasion to begin, in the book *De captivitate Babylonica,* to inquire more diligently on the basis of Scripture about the similarity and the difference between the sacraments of the Old and of the New Testament. But lest we fight, like blindfolded gladiators, in darkness, the point at issue in this controversy must be shown.

3 But clear, and (I think) not in controversy between our papalist adversaries and ourselves, are these chief points: That to the righteous who lived during the time of the Old Testament, grace, righteousness, salvation, and eternal life were set forth, manifested, given, and conveyed by God on account of the future sacrifice of His Son, the Mediator. For that the righteous were saved at the time of the Old Testament is most certain from Scripture. However, no one is saved without the grace of God. That grace, indeed, is promised and bestowed only on account of the Blessed Seed. Also this is without controversy, that there was no other grace, also no other faith, by which the righteous were saved during the time of the Old Testament than now in the time of the New Testament. For we have the same spirit of faith. (2 Cor. 5)

The grace also by which Abraham was justified and by which David was saved is an example of the justification and salvation of all times (Rom. 4). Therefore the question will remain how, that is, through what medium, means, or instrument, God at the time of the Old Testament offered, exhibited, gave, and conferred grace for salvation to believers.

4 It is certain, however, that those fathers had the word of promise concerning the blessing on account of the Seed who was to come. They also had certain external rites added and attached by divine institution to this promise of grace.

I am not certain whether the papalists are willing to grant that that word of promise was such a means or instrument during the time of the Old Testament. Certainly we are here disputing about the sacraments, to which that promise of grace was attached by divine institution.

5 Among the old ecclesiastical writers this axiom about circumcision, which was a sacrament of the Old Testament, is general and certain, that infants at the time of the Old Testament were made free from original sin through circumcision. Bede also quotes from the fathers this statement, which is not unknown to the scholastic writers: "The sacraments of the Old Testament, observed in their time, conferred eternal life." But at the time of Lombard this opinion began to be called into question. And indeed Hugo, who lived about that time, argued very obscurely and ambiguously (as Gabriel relates) that salvation is the same for the righteous in the Old and in the New Testament; that the sacraments of the Old Testament justified indirectly and because of what followed, through mediation of the sacraments of the New Testament, which were indicated by those of the Old. However, the scholastics attribute this opinion to Lombard, that through the sacraments of the Old Testament God in no way at all bestowed grace on believers, even when they were used in faith and charity, because he thought that they had been imposed only for a burden and slavery, not for justification.

6 Through these disputations of Hugo and Lombard the apple of strife had been cast into the midst, which all of the scholastics eagerly and avidly took up, and by means of the man-made opinion of the *opus operatum* they invented this distinction between the sacraments of the two Testaments, that through the former grace was only signified but not conveyed or bestowed, even on those who received them rightly, but that through the latter grace is both signified and conveyed, even if there is in the recipient no good inner motive.

7 But because some among them saw that it is absurd to say that grace was not conferred on the just in the Old Testament, they invented the fiction that the sacraments of the Old Testament had conferred grace, not *ex opere operato* but *ex opere operante,* that is, through the measure of merit from the devotion of the one who undertakes it, which they explain thus: They say that every act of virtue which is formed by charity is meritorious; but the use of the sacraments of the Old Testament, they say, was an act of obedience. For commands had been given concerning sacraments of this kind, and therefore, they say, their use was a fulfillment of the instruction. And therefore, by reason of the virtue of obedience, through a measure of merit, the faithful then received grace through the use of the sacraments. But this opinion clashes directly and as it were head-on with Paul, who (Rom 4:10-12) expressly teaches and confirms that circumcision did not justify Abraham *ex opere operante,* through a measure of merit, but that it was a sign or seal of the righteousness of faith, of which it is characteristic that blessedness belongs to him whom God, according to His grace, because he believes, not because he works, imputes righteousness without works. (Rom. 4)

How much sense, I ask, can you expect concerning the salutary use of the sacraments from such men who outlaw from the sacraments the free promise by which grace is offered and conveyed, and the faith by which the promise is received, that is, who take the very sacraments out of the sacraments, and out of the work of God make our own work, out of grace merit, out of the promise a command? And yet the Council of Florence[7] was not ashamed to confirm these opinions of the scholastics, for it says: "The sacraments of the Old Testament did not effect grace, but only prefigured that it would have to be given through the suffering of Christ; our sacraments, however, both contain grace and confer it on those who worthily receive them." But what is this I hear? Was not grace given to the just in the time of the Old Testament by virtue of the future passion of Christ? Or did they, indeed, only have a foreshadowing that it would happen that after the birth of Christ grace should first be given to those who had come to faith after the completed passion of Christ? Certainly, the passion of Christ is that merit on account of which grace was given long ago and is still given. Nor is it true that the ancients long ago were justified by virtue of the future passion of Christ without any sure means or instrument by which it was offered and applied but that we are justified through the sacraments or by virtue of the passion of Christ.

8 I noted these things down here in order that the reader may be reminded and may understand what the particular "Helen"[8] is, for whose restoration this second canon is fighting. But that we may the more conveniently pass over to our explanation, let the reader consider this stratagem, that those who are now the hired advocates of the papalist cause, in order that they may remove the suspicion of novelty, do not in this question employ the arguments of the scholastics, because they notice how poor they are; but they endeavor to defend that opinion with the authority of Augustine through a certain statement of his which is found in his exposition of Ps. 73: "The sacraments of the New Testament give salvation; the sacraments of the Old Testament promised a Savior."

9 However, if one correctly and diligently weighs how Augustine in the passage which is adduced discusses that question, it will not only be clearly evident what his meaning was, but the true basis will also be shown from which this question can be correctly explained and decided.

We are not, however, disputing indiscriminately about all the figures and signs of the Old Testament, but about those to which a word of promise of grace was attached. For there were many figures and shadows

---

[7] The Council of Florence was a continuation of the Council of Basel, A. D. 1431–48.

[8] An allusion to Helen, the wife of Menelaus, over whom the Trojan War was fought.

in the Old Testament which indeed signified something concerning the mystery of the incarnation, redemption, and justification; but not all had joined to them an explicit divine promise that by those signs God wanted to offer, apply, and seal the promise of the righteousness of faith to the individuals who used these rites in faith. Certain ones, however, not only signified something but also had joined to them the promise that through these signs in the Word God willed to offer, apply, seal, and confirm the righteousness of faith to the individual persons who used these ceremonies in faith. Such a sign was, beyond any controversy, circumcision. Therefore the signs of the Old Testament were of two kinds: Some were only significative, but some also at the same time conveyed and sealed grace by virtue of the promise. Augustine, indeed, at times comprehends all these signs together under one and the same name of "sacraments." When he therefore calls "sacraments" the figures and shadows which are only significative signs, he says, on Ps. 73, concerning the difference between the Old and the New Testament: "The sacraments are not the same; the promises are not the same." And this he explains: "The promises are not the same, because the promised land of Canaan is a temporal kingdom, earthly happiness. The sacraments are not the same, because some are sacraments which give salvation, while others promise the Savior. The sacraments of the New Testament give salvation; the sacraments of the Old Testament promised the Savior." Will we say then that Augustine meant that the fathers in the Old Testament had only earthly promises and that they were altogether without the spiritual promise concerning righteousness before God, salvation and eternal life? Or that salvation was not given to the fathers in the Old Testament? Certainly no sane person will dare to ascribe to Augustine this manifestly wrong opinion, which he himself refutes in many passages.

10 It is therefore easy to see what Augustine intends in that passage. For he has established a comparison or rather a mutual relation, an inseparable connection between the promises and the sacraments, so that as the promises are, so are also the sacraments; and indeed that the judgment concerning the sacraments must be taken from the promises. This rule should be diligently observed. But then he says: "In the Old Testament there were certain earthly or temporal promises made to the Mosaic state, and to these promises also certain sacraments were attached." Augustine therefore concludes that as those earthly promises were figures of spiritual promises, so also the sacraments of those promises signified the future dispensation of the Savior. Therefore it is manifest that Augustine is here speaking first of the signs which are only significative, which did not have a spiritual promise attached. Thereafter Augustine also makes the distinction between the spiritual promises themselves in the Old and the New Testament—that in the Old Testament they are promises of the Christ to come, but in the New there is the announcement of the Christ who has been manifested.

However, the promise of the future Blessed Seed in the Old Testament was no less the power of God for salvation to everyone who believes than is the announcement of the manifested Christ in the New Testament. And from this ground rule, namely, concerning the distinction of the promise of grace in both Testaments, Augustine takes and establishes the difference between the sacraments which were attached by the divine Word to the promise of grace in both Testaments, for he says: "Since, therefore, you already have that which was promised, why do you seek the things which promise the Savior when you already have Him? What I am saying is that you have the things that were promised; not that we have already received eternal life, but that Christ, who was foretold by the prophets, has already come." This difference he repeats and explains in many other passages. Therefore this passage of Augustine's, upon which the papalists almost alone rely, does not help them at all, as though during the time of the Old Testament there had been simply no sacraments through which God, in His Word, offered, exhibited, and sealed grace, although it is certain that the promise of grace was then attached to certain formal rites or sacraments. That Augustine thought otherwise, we shall show later. For now I only wanted to remove and explain the objection which the papalists fashion from the passage of Augustine.

11 What they adduce from Scripture can easily be explained if the rule of Hilary is observed, that the meaning of the things that are said must be taken from the reasons why they were said. For often Scripture does not tell us what the sacraments of the Old Testament are in themselves, that is, by divine institution—seals of the promise of grace and of the righteousness of faith—but it reproves and refutes the wrong opinions which men attached to those rites while they neglected the promise and faith. For they did not teach that faith must, in the sacraments, as in the visible Word, lay hold of the promise of the future redemption through the Son, the Mediator, for whose sake God justifies those who believe, but they buried the promise and abolished the true faith and imagined that they were justified through the merit and worth of the works which they performed in those external rites. Against this opinion Paul contends when he argues about circumcision (Rom. 2:25-29; Gal. 5:2-6). And in the Epistle to the Hebrews he shows that the blood of Christ alone has the power to cleanse the conscience from sins. That, therefore, the fathers in the Old Testament were justified, he says, was accomplished, not by virtue of the blood of cattle or by other purifications, but because faith, under these figures and shadows, looked upon and apprehended another object, namely, the promise of the future sacrifice of the Son of God, the Mediator. For it is this which he treats throughout the entire Epistle to the Hebrews, where he shows at the same time the repeal or abrogation of those rites, since their fulfillment, namely Christ, has appeared and has instituted other sacraments.

12 Now that we have explained the things which they are accustomed to quote against us both from Scripture and from Augustine, the whole matter will be clear. For it is the same God, both in the Old and in the New Testament, who justifies both the circumcision and the uncircumcision. It is the same Christ, yesterday, today, and forever, for whose sake the believers have been justified and are justified both in the Old and in the New Testament. The substance of the promise (if I may use this expression) is the same, the faith is the same, the grace is the same—the same righteousness, the same salvation and eternal life, in Christ and on account of Christ, who was promised in the Old Testament as coming and is proclaimed in the New Testament as having been manifested. On these points there is and can be no controversy. But the question revolves around this—what means, instrument, and organ God willed to use in each Testament for offering, bestowing, and sealing these benefits. That in the New Testament the Word of the Gospel is the power of God for salvation to everyone who believes is not doubtful. Certain is also this, that Christ instituted the sacraments of the New Testament for this use, that through them, as through a visible Word, He might offer, convey, and seal to the believers the benefits of the Gospel. Concerning the Old Testament it is by this time also beyond controversy that the nature of the Word and promise was clearly the same there. But I ask: Was the promise of grace in the Old Testament set before the people of God as a naked word, without sacraments? I find (Gen. 17:7) that the promise of the covenant: "I will be your God, and of your seed after you," was by divine institution clothed, so to say, with the rite or sacrament of circumcision. I see also that Paul (Rom. 4:11) calls the sign of circumcision a mark or seal of the righteousness of faith. From this the fathers rightly conclude that infants under the Law were freed from original sin through circumcision. And Bede learnedly gathers from the reverse, that those who in the people of Israel received circumcision as a seal of the righteousness of faith were united through this sacrament with the church of the people of God and sealed in the covenant and communion of the benefits of Christ,

the Mediator. For God says: "Any uncircumcised male who is not circumcised in the flesh of his foreskin shall be cut off from his people; he has broken My covenant."

13 These things therefore hang together and are clear: 1. That the righteous in the Old Testament had the same Christ, received the same grace and righteousness for salvation and eternal life which the believers in the New Testament receive and have; 2. That the righteous in the Old Testament had not only the bare promise of grace, but to that promise there also were joined by divine institution certain definite rites which are called sacraments. And from this follows: 3. That the righteous in the Old Testament no less than we in the New Testament received the benefits of the Gospel which are necessary for salvation not only through the bare promise of grace on account of the coming Messiah but also through sacraments which had been joined to that promise by divine institution. Such a sacrament was, without controversy, circumcision. Therefore Paul (Col. 2:11-12) through an interchange of the words "circumcision" and "Baptism" indicates that we, who in the New Testament through Baptism have the putting off of the body of the sins of the flesh, have received and possess the same thing which the circumcised under the Old Covenant received through circumcision. For as circumcision was a seal of the righteousness of faith (Rom. 4:22), so Baptism is "an appeal to God for a clear conscience through the resurrection of Jesus Christ" (1 Peter 3:21). And that the means or instrument by which the righteousness of faith was conveyed and sealed under the Old Convenant was not only the bare promise but also its sign, namely circumcision, the institution of circumcision (Gen. 17:10-14) and the passage of Paul (Rom. 4:11) show very clearly. And in 1 Cor. 10:1-4, where he treats the story of the manna and of the water which flowed from the rock, he says that the fathers ate the same spiritual food and drank the same spiritual drink. And he expressly names Christ, who is "the same yesterday and today and for ever." (Heb. 13:8)

Augustine connects this passage of Paul with Baptism and the Lord's Supper in *In Evangelium Johannis tractatus,* 26, where he explains the preaching of Christ about the manna. He says: "Those sacraments were different in the signs; in the matter which is signified they are equal." And in *Tractatus,* 45: "The same faith is expressed in diverse signs even as in diverse words; one of them foretells the Christ to come, the other announces that Christ has come." And in *Contra Faustum Manichaeum* he argues that in the varied signs, sacraments, or ceremonies of both Testaments the matters are not different but the same. For in Bk. 19, ch. 15, he raises the question whether faith in the Christ who would suffer and rise again benefitted the righteous of old as much as faith in the Christ who has suffered and risen again now benefits us; whether the shedding of the blood of the Lamb of God, which was made for many for the remission of sins, gave anything of benefit and cleansing also to those who believed that this would happen but had departed this life before it happened. This question he indeed does not decide in this place. But elsewhere he clearly affirms from the Word of God that the righteous of the Old Testament, no matter how great their holiness, were nevertheless not saved except through faith in the Mediator, who shed His blood for the remission of sins. For these are his words.

14 Now let the reader observe what arguments Augustine weaves from this. For he says, ch. 14: "In this life no one can be righteous except he who lives by faith. For grace, righteousness, salvation, life eternal must be received by faith." But he adds: "The righteous of old who understood that through those sacraments the future revelation of faith was foretold, also themselves lived from this; for though it was still hidden and concealed, nevertheless it was understood through the observance of piety." The reader will understand the connection of the arguments. The righteous of old received the remission of sins on account of Christ the Mediator; the remission of sins, however, is not received except by faith; the faith of the ancients had for its object not only the bare Word but also the sacraments of that time; and through that faith, understood in the sacraments through the observance of piety, the just lived. All these are words of Augustine.

15 Who, therefore, will now say that the faith of the ancients received nothing through the sacraments of that time, since Augustine affirms that they lived through the faith which they understood in the sacraments? In ch. 16 he compares the Word and the sacraments. He says: "If one and the same matter is proclaimed in one way when it is to be done, for instance that fact that Christ would suffer and rise again, etc., but is proclaimed in another way when it has been done, as that Christ has suffered and risen again, etc., what is strange about it if the future passion and resurrection of Christ is promised with one kind of signs of the mysteries, and the accomplished passion and resurrection is announced with other signs? For what else are any visible sacraments except certain (as it were) sacred, visible words?" So says Augustine.

If therefore we grant that through the word of promise in the old Testament grace and salvation were offered and conveyed by God to the believers, how can we take this away from the sacraments, which are nothing else than visible words? As the reason is the same, so also is the use of the Word and of the sacraments the same.

In ch. 14 he makes them correlatives: like faith and the Word or promise, so also faith and the sacraments; what therefore faith receives, that God offers and conveys through the Word and the sacraments. Augustine's words are as follows: "At that time, therefore, faith was hidden, for all the righteous and saints also of those times believed the same things, hoped for the same things; and all those sacraments and every sacred rite were promises of things to come; now, however, faith is revealed."

In ch. 16 he says: "Against the ignorant swindle of Faustus it would have sufficed to show what an insane mistake those make who believe that if the signs and sacraments are changed, the matters themselves also are different which the prophetic rite had declared as promised and which the Gospel rite has declared fulfilled; or who think that since the matters are the same, their fulfillment should not have been announced through other sacraments than through those by which they were foretold when they were yet to be fulfilled."

16 Therefore the whole matter with respect to the comparison of the sacraments of the Old and the New Testament is very clear if only that distinction is employed which Luther teaches in *De captivitate Babylonica,* namely, that certain figures of the Old Testament were only signs which signified something but did not have joined to them a word of promise of grace. Concerning those signs we are not disputing here. But there were also in the Old Testament certain signs which had, by divine institution, the added word of the promise of grace; this word demands faith, which accepts the grace.

17 With respect to these sacraments of the ancients it is quite clear that they had, by divine institution, the same use and purpose which the sacraments of the New Testament have. For they placed before the believers one and the same Christ in the word of promise added to those sacraments; it was the same faith which sought and received, both in the word of promise and in the sacraments which were added to the promise of grace, the same grace, righteousness, remission of sins, salvation, and eternal life as now in the New Testament. Up to this point there is similarity and agreement between the sacraments of the Old and of the New Testament.

18 But is there no difference, no distinction between the sacraments of the Old and of the New Testament? There is indeed a very significant difference, as Augustine has shown in various places. 1. In the signs or external rites themselves. For when Christ had by His incarnation fulfilled those things which had been signified and promised by the sacraments of the ancients, those old sacraments were changed and abrogated, and by the institution of Christ the Mediator others were substituted for them. For Augustine says, *Contra Faustum,* Bk. 19, ch. 16: "Things that had been accomplished needed to be announced through other ceremonies than those by which they were foretold when they were still to be accomplished." 2. The sacraments of the Old Testament were predictive of the Christ who would come, but those of the New Testament are a proclamation of the manifested Christ, as Augustine says on Ps. 73 and in *In Evangelium Johannis tractatus,* 45, likewise *Contra Faustum,* Bk. 19, ch. 13. In ch. 14 he says: "Those [sacraments] in the Old Testament were promises of things to be fulfilled; these, in the New Testament, are tokens that they have been fulfilled." Augustine makes precisely the same distinction between the word of grace under the Old Covenant, concerning the Christ who should come, and in the New Testament concerning the Christ who has been manifested, *In Evangelium Johannis tractatus,* 45. In *Contra Faustum,* Bk. 19, ch. 16, Augustine says: "Therefore as in diverse words so also in diverse signs there is not a diverse but the same faith. Therefore it is also the same Christ, the same grace, for the same righteousness, the same salvation," etc.

However, also this distinction must be observed, that the same Christ, although He had been foretold in one way through the Word and the sacraments in the Old Testament (as one who would come, and the mystery of the redemption as something that must be fulfilled), is proclaimed in another way through the Word and the sacraments in the New Testament (as the Christ who has been manifested and the mystery of redemption as fulfilled), yet the power of the incarnation and redemption of Christ is the same, the same also the grace necessary for salvation. God set this forth no less during the time of the Old Testament than in the New; the faith of the ancients also received this no less certainly in the Word and in the sacraments than it is now received in the New. The fact that they did not rightly understand this distinction between the incarnation and redemption itself and its power or grace has deceived the scholastics, for when they read in Augustine that the things which were signified and promised in the Old Testament are imparted and exhibited in the New, they understand this not of the incarnation itself and of the work of redemption, but of grace and salvation, which is given and bestowed for Christ's sake, although it is most certain that the conveying and conferring of grace and salvation for Christ's sake took place no less in the Old Testament than in the New.

Therefore when Augustine says that in the Word and the sacraments of the Old Testament the truth was in the form of promise, in the New in the form of manifestation; that in the Old the signification was in the nature of a promise, while in the New the things themselves are imparted, he understands this of the incarnation of Christ and of the work of redemption, not however of its power and of grace. That these were certainly offered to the righteous in the Old Testament no one can deny who admits that they were saved.

A third distinction Augustine describes thus, *De doctrina,* Bk. 3, ch. 9: "Through sacraments, very few in number, most easy to observe, most excellent in what they signify, He gathered a community of new men." And, *Contra Faustum,* Bk. 19, ch. 13: "When Christ had by His advent fulfilled the first sacraments, then they were abolished and others were instituted, greater in power, better in usefulness, easier to perform, fewer in number." And on Ps. 73: "The sacraments have been changed; they have been made easier, more salutary, more fruitful." But will the sacraments of the Old Testament therefore be neither salutary nor fruitful at all, because the sacraments of the New Testament are said to be more salutary and more fruitful? Or because the power of the sacraments of the New Testament is declared to be greater and their usefulness better, does this mean that there will be no power or usefulness at all in the sacraments of the Old Testament? Certainly, things which are compared as to quantity, though they may differ in degree, nevertheless still belong to one and the same kind. Therefore Augustine attributes fruitfulness, usefulness, power, and salvation to the sacraments of the Old Testament by the very fact that he declares the sacraments of the New Testament to be more fruitful, more salutary, of greater power, and of better usefulness. This we freely grant, that as the mode of revelation in the New Testament is more glorious, the light of faith greater, and the measure of grace richer, so also the grace of Christ is dispensed to the believers through the sacraments of the New Testament more splendidly, more fully, more perfectly, and more richly. For now that the mystery of redemption has been consummated, reality itself has taken the place of the figures (Heb. 9), the body of the shadows (Col. 2:16-17). For the Son of God was also before His incarnation the righteousness and salvation of the believers (Is. 45:22-24) and dwelt in them (2 Cor. 6:16). But now after He became incarnate He is present as God and man with His church, and dwells in the believers. For in the human flesh which the Son of God assumed there now dwells the whole fulness of the Godhead, that from His fulness we may all receive grace upon grace (Col. 2:9; John 1:16). That was not yet accomplished in the time of the Old Testament but was promised and believed as something that would happen. But if the promise concerning the future incarnation and redemption was the power of God for salvation to the believers under the Old Covenant, certainly grace will be greater, more abundant and fuller, after the fulfillment of those things has occurred in the New Testament in Christ, who as God and man communicates Himself to the believers.

19 Therefore the sacraments of the New Testament differ from those of the Old not only in this way, that there are other ceremonies and other external rites; but there is a far more important difference, as we have said before. But the papalists are not content with these differences, but simply maintain that God did not offer and convey any grace to the believers through the sacraments of the Old Testament, even those which had a word of promise attached. That this is manifestly wrong, circumcision alone shows. However, the chief reason why they urge this dogma of the scholastics concerning the difference between the sacraments of the two Testaments so greatly is that they are trying to defend and strengthen the opinion of the *opus operatum* in every possible way. But of the *opus operatum* we shall have to speak in the examination of Canon VIII.

SECTION III

Concerning the Difference of the Sacraments Among Themselves

CANON III

If anyone says that these seven sacraments are so equal among themselves that one is in no way more worthy than the other, let him be anathema.

Examination

1 The examination of this canon we shall complete in a few words. For although they are otherwise accustomed to hurl each and every thunder of their anathemas particularly at the heads of our churches, our heads are, praise God, surely altogether free from the three-pronged thunderbolt of this third canon. For they thunder: "If anyone says that these seven sacraments are so equal among themselves that one is in no way more worthy than the other, let him be anathema."

2 We indeed are by no means the people who think and teach that those seven sacraments which they number are so equal among themselves that the other five which they count are in the same way or for the same reason truly and properly sacraments as are Baptism and the Eucharist. For this is the very thing which we discussed in the examination of the first canon, that although we do not fight about the term "sacrament," as also the ancients used it in various ways, yet those things which by divine institution have certain external rites attached to them must by all means be distinguished from those things which indeed have a command of God but not certain external rites commanded by the divine Word. And also from those rites which have an express command of God and the promise of grace or of the blessing of redemption attached by the divine Word, as do Baptism and the Eucharist, the remaining rites must be distinguished which, no matter from where they may have been received, certainly have no express command of God nor a promise attached by the divine Word concerning the application and sealing of the free reconciliation. Therefore we contend that those rites which were received from men are by no means to be put on the same level or to be

raised to an equal degree of dignity as those prior ones which were instituted by the mouth and command of the Son of God. For they are separated by a very great distance, and in the church the institutions of the Son of God must be distinguished from the inventions of men. Therefore this canon absolves us from every fault and accusation. For it pronounces the anathema on those who imagine that those seven which they count as sacraments are so equal among themselves that none is in any way of greater dignity than another.

3 Someone may perhaps think that these things were said as a joke. For it is not likely that the Tridentine fathers thunder so fearfully in this third canon about the unequal dignity of the seven sacraments because they wanted to approve our teaching, and indeed to confirm it under the bond of the anathema; nor, surely, because they wanted neither indirectly nor lightly, but with the severity of the anathema, to point out and condemn the disputations of the scholastics who imagine that, like Baptism and the Lord's Supper, so also, and with equal reason, the other five are truly and properly sacraments.

For what purpose, therefore, and in what sense, was this third canon framed? I will tell you. They wanted to repeat and establish those old affronts, namely, that the dignity of the chrism in confirmation, although it has neither a command of God nor a promise of the Son of God, is nevertheless far more excellent and glorious than that of Baptism itself, although this has an express command of God and the most certain promise attached by the mouth of the Son of God. The reason (if it please the gods in the Roman pantheon) is that Baptism can be administered also by those who are in the simple orders of priests, yes, in emergencies even by lay people, as Jerome says against the Luciferians. It has pleased them to reserve the administration of confirmation, however, to the bishops alone. They add also this reason, that Baptism is only the sacrament of initiation, but through confirmation the perfection of grace and glory is conferred. They say that also the rite of ordination is a sacrament more worthy than and superior to the sacrament of Baptism by the preeminence of its excellence and perfection (I am using their own words), because, they say: "Ordination places a man in a grace, in a position and state of dignity [that is, of fat allowances and regal preferments] which Baptism does not do." And so after they had in the first canon made the things which have no command of God but are invented by men equal to the divinely instituted ones, now, in the third canon, they demand that they should be elevated and placed in a more exalted degree of dignity than those which the Son of God Himself in the New Testament instituted by His own mouth and commended to the church. So true is the saying that he who once oversteps the limits of modesty must give diligence to be really shameless.

This is also one of the mysteries of this third canon that the dignity of the sacrament of ordination cannot bear an honorable, holy, and chaste matrimony, although they call also that a sacrament. For by so much is the sacrament of ordination worthier than matrimony that it can more readily put up with a hundred prostitutes, although in succession (as a certain man of Cologne says), than one legitimate spouse. Whether this third canon contains any other mysteries besides these, either Andrada or some other person will make known to us. However, so far as our question itself is concerned, wherein the sacraments which have the testimony of Scripture either agree or differ, this cannot be established and explained more simply and correctly than if each one is judged on the basis of its own institution and of the promise which is attached to it by the divine Word. Here that would not fit badly what they say in their decree, namely, that through the sacraments the righteousness of faith either begins, or is increased after it has begun, or is restored where it has been lost. But this is not the place to explain this more fully, for we have undertaken only an examination of the decrees and canons of the Council of Trent.

SECTION IV

Concerning the Necessity of the Sacraments

If anyone says that the sacraments of the New Law are not necessary for salvation, but superfluous, and that without them or without desire for them men obtain from God grace and justification through faith alone, though all are not necessary for every individual, let him be anathema.

Examination

1 To begin with, the cunning of the composition in this canon must be considered, for peculiar traps are hidden in almost everything that is said. They proclaim without distinction of all their sacraments which they number as such that they are necessary for salvation. For when they add: "Though all are not necessary for every individual," they understand this of ordination and marriage. However the other rites, such as confirmation, extreme unction, auricular confession, satisfaction, etc., they simply insist[9] are sacraments necessary for salvation. And it should chiefly be observed that they set the necessity of the sacraments in opposition to justification by faith alone. However, the things which are necessary for salvation must be properly distinguished, as Christ meriting it, the Father governing, the instruments or sacraments of the Word and of the sacraments through which the Holy Spirit offers, conveys, seals, increases, and confirms those benefits of the New Testament in the believers, and finally faith, which lays hold of those benefits. Each of these is ordained in its own way and in its own place for our salvation. And just as it does not follow: The sacraments are necessary for salvation, therefore Christ has not alone acquired it for us by His merit; so also it does not follow: The sacraments are necessary for salvation, therefore we do not receive the grace of justification by faith alone. Neither has any sane man ever understood justification by faith alone in such a way, as if the grace of God, the merit of Christ, and the ministry of the Word and of the sacraments were excluded from justification. No, on the contrary, in justification

---

[9] The Frankfort edition of the *Examen* of 1574 has *nolunt,* a manifest misprint, corrected by Eduard Preuss with *volunt.*

faith seeks, lays hold of, and accepts the grace of God on account of the merit of the Son, the Mediator; and these things it seeks and accepts through the ministry of the Word and of the sacraments, and it knows that through these means the Holy Spirit wills to work effectively. However, Scripture asserts that to seek, to apprehend, and to accept these benefits belongs solely to faith. It is therefore manifest how sophistical it is to set the necessity of the sacraments in opposition to justification by faith alone.

However, I think the architects of this fourth canon had something else in view with this antithesis between the necessity of the sacraments for salvation and justification by faith alone. For they do not refer the necessity of the sacraments only to this, that they are instrumental causes by which the grace of justification is offered and conveyed to us by God, but they speak of acquiring or getting the grace of justification, and this they are unwilling to ascribe to faith alone, but add the necessity of the sacraments; that is, they understand our work which we do in receiving the sacraments in such a way that faith not alone, but together with the worth or merit of this our work gets the grace of justification. And for this reason they call them "sacraments of the New Law," that there may be a mutual relation of the Law and our works also in the use of the sacraments; for this reason they also mention the vow,[10] that is, the promise of a certain work for the reception of the grace of justification. Who will therefore now say that the fathers of Trent were lacking in ingenuity, when they could in so few words conceal so many and varied snares? However, the true explanation of the question which is proposed in this fourth canon cannot be given unless we first disentangle ourselves from those snares. Therefore, when the necessity of the sacraments is debated, the question is not concerning the rites instituted by human authority, but concerning those which are truly and properly sacraments, namely, Baptism and the Lord's Supper. And in those sacraments the point is not about any magical efficacy, inherent independently in the external elements themselves, nor about the worth or merit of any work of our own, but that they are means and instruments by which God offers and faith accepts grace and salvation.

2 When the issue is shaped in this way, the explanation will not be difficult, and it will profitably remind us of many things and excite in our

---

[10] The Latin term in Canon IV is *votum*. It means first of all a solemn promise, or vow, but then also desire, wish, longing. Chemnitz understands it in Canon IV in the sense of vow. Roman Catholic translators understand it of "desire," namely for the sacraments, which under given circumstances may not be available to them. Thus they speak of "the Baptism of desire."

minds true reverence for the sacraments. However, it depends on a consideration of the teaching as to why God added sacraments to the promise of the Gospel. For God, who ordained the satisfaction of His Son, the Mediator, that it should merit and obtain our salvation; who also ordained that faith should be our hand, as it were, by which we may reach for, lay hold of, and accept the grace of God in Christ—the same God also ordained a certain means or instrument by which He wills to offer and confer the benefits of the Son, the Mediator, for our salvation, in order that faith may have and know a certain means in which it can seek and obtain grace and salvation.

3 Such a means or instrument of God is the Word of the Gospel when it is preached, heard, meditated on, and apprehended by faith. Rom. 10:17: "Justifying faith is by hearing, and hearing by the Word of God." Rom. 1:16: "The Gospel is the power of God for salvation to every one who has faith." John 5:24: "Truly I say to you, he who hears My word and believes Him who sent Me has eternal life," etc. Now surely, since God through the Word offers and conveys, faith in the word also apprehends and receives, not something that is only a half, and insufficient, but the grace which is necessary for salvation, so that the Gospel may be "the power of God for salvation to every one who has faith." There arises then the question what the use of the sacraments is, or for what reasons God by His own institution added the external rites of the sacraments to the promise of the Gospel. And indeed there are many men, some fanatics, some wicked, who both think and proclaim that the use of the sacraments is superfluous and not necessary. The souls also of the godly are often tried by thoughts like these: "Since God through the Word offers and conveys all things that are necessary for salvation, and since faith can find and lay hold of them in the Word, what need is there of sacraments? Therefore the use of the sacraments could be neglected without the loss of salvation."

Rightly do we reply from the Word of God in opposition to such temptations or clamors of the fanatics that the sacraments, which God Himself instituted that they should be aids to our salvation, are by no means to be judged either as useless or superfluous, so that they could be safely neglected or despised. For Augustine rightly says, *Contra Faustum*, Bk. 19, ch. 11: "The power of the sacraments is unspeakably great, and therefore it makes those who despise them guilty of sacrilege. For something is being wickedly despised without which godliness cannot be perfected."

4 These things must be diligently explained from the Word of God, both in order that the doctrine may be correctly understood and that the true use of the sacraments may be extolled and earnestly loved. So far therefore as God is concerned, He offers and conveys this His grace which is necessary for salvation in such a way that faith can find in that object or means whatever is necessary for salvation.

And indeed, as Chrysostom says, if we were angels no further sign would be necessary for us. But the infirmity of the flesh hinders, disturbs, distracts, and weakens faith. For it is arduous and difficult to cling with firm confidence of mind to those things which are set forth in the Word (Heb. 11:1), even though we do not see them, yes, to believe in hope against hope (Rom. 4:18), since in this life the mind always seeks the aid of the senses. Moreover, also when faith declares that the promise of God is true in general, yet it is worried chiefly about the question of whether it also pertains to me personally. Therefore God, who is rich in mercy, that He might show and commend to us the riches of His goodness, did not want to exhibit His grace to us in one way only, namely by the bare Word, but He willed to assist our infirmity through certain aids, namely through the sacraments which He instituted and joined to the promise of the Gospel, that is, through certain signs, rites, or ceremonies which meet the senses, that by means of them He might impress upon us, instruct, and make certain that what we perceive as being done outwardly in a visible manner is inwardly effected in us by the strength and power of God; for as the Word enters the ears and touches the hearts, so the rite of the sacrament enters the eyes in order that it may move the hearts, that we may not doubt that God is dealing with us and wills to be efficacious in us for salvation according to His Word. For through the Word, and through the external signs instituted by Himself, He is wont to deal with men. Moreover, the human mind not only does not of itself know the promise concerning the gratuitous reconciliation, but indeed even when that reconciliation is revealed to us through the Word, faith nevertheless finds it difficult, especially in trials, to lay hold of it and to hold it fast as something that applies also to me personally, although a pious mind does not dare to accuse it of lying in general. Therefore God instituted the sacraments to be external and visible signs and pledges of the grace and will of God toward us, by which, as through a glorous visible testimony, He testifies that the promise belongs to those individuals who embrace it by faith as they use the sacraments. In this way the sacraments are external, visible testimonies of the application of the free promise of the Gospel. For the word of the Gospel is general, but faith and the use of a sacrament apply it to individual believers.

5 In this way the sacraments are for us signs strengthening our faith in the promise of the Gospel; with respect to God they are instruments or

means through which God in the Word, by His power and working, conveys, applies, seals, confirms, increases, and preserves the grace of the Gospel promise to those who believe. However, the grace which is in the word of promise is not different from that which is conveyed in the sacraments; neither is the promise in the word of the Gospel different from that in the sacraments. The grace is the same; it is one and the same Word, except that in the sacraments, through divinely instituted signs, the Word is, so to say, rendered visible (as Augustine says) because of our infirmity. Therefore faith does not seek some other grace in the sacraments than in the Word, nor does it seek grace in the sacraments without the promise, beside or outside of the promise. For the word of promise is the object to which faith looks in the sacraments, and in it it grasps the things which are promised, offered, and conveyed by the Word in the sacraments. Thus Paul says (Eph. 5:26): "Having cleansed her [the church] by the washing of water with the Word." This teaching extols the dignity of the sacraments and kindles true reverence for their use. It is from these bases that the explanation of the question which is before us is taken. For how could pious ears bear or give heed to those profane statements that the sacraments are superfluous, and that they can safely be despised and neglected without the loss of salvation, when it is certain from the Word of God that God instituted them to aid our weakness and that, in order that He might show the riches of His goodness for procuring our salvation, He himself instituted such instruments or means that through them, by the power and working of the Holy Spirit, our faith, no matter how feeble and infirm, might be able to lay hold of grace and retain it, sealed to salvation and eternal life? The sacraments are therefore necessary both by reason of the weakness of our faith, for which aids of this kind are necessary, and by reason of the divine institution, because God instituted them for this purpose and to this end, that He might through them convey, apply, and seal the Mediator's benefits to believers for salvation. These things are certainly neither useless nor superfluous, but necessary.

6 In this sense we gladly grant that the sacraments are necessary for salvation, namely, as the instrumental cause. Nevertheless, this declaration must be added, that the sacraments are not so absolutely necessary for salvation as are faith and the Word. For without faith no one can be saved; and without the Word there can be no true faith (Rom. 10:14–17). Therefore he who does not have the Word of God cannot be saved, because he cannot receive faith. But whoever already has the true and justifying faith through the hearing of the Word, though he has by faith accepted the reconciliation, will not in any way despise the use of the sacraments for the above reasons. Or if he despises it, his faith is not true, for it does not retain its essential quality, which consists in the mutual relation of the Word and faith, namely, that faith seeks and apprehends the word of promise wherever God sets it forth by His institution. However, if someone has the true faith in Christ through hearing the Word, and opportunity is not granted to him to use the sacraments according to the divine institution, in such a case an absolute necessity of the sacraments for salvation must not be affirmed, so that salvation is denied to those to whom the ability to use the sacraments is not given although they lay hold of Christ the Mediator by faith in the Word. For to the thief on the cross, who by faith apprehended Christ in the word of promise, certainly paradise is promised although the ability was not given him to receive Baptism. Thus those who were born in the wilderness were not circumcised for 40 years on account of the continual to-and-fro of their wandering, which did not give them opportunity to receive circumcision (Joshua 5:2–7). And yet there is no doubt that some of them died during the 40 years of wandering in the wilderness, whom no one will condemn, if they were reconciled to God by faith in the promise of the coming Messiah. Therefore Augustine rightly says, *Contra Donatistas,* Bk. 4, ch. 22: "Contemplating the example of the thief again and again, I find that not only can suffering for the name of Christ supply that which was lacking with respect to Baptism, but also faith itself and the conversion of the heart, when it may not be possible to proceed to the celebration of the mystery of Baptism due to difficult times. For the aforementioned thief was not crucified for the name of Christ, but deservedly for his crimes; neither did he suffer because he was a believer, but he came to faith while he was suffering. The apostle says: 'Man believes with his heart and so is justified, and he confesses with his lips and so is saved.' How much this faith can do also without the visible sacrament of Baptism is shown by the case of this thief. But then it is fulfilled invisibly, when not contempt of religion but the case of necessity excludes the mystery of Baptism." Ch. 23: "This thief was nevertheless not altogether without the sanctification of Baptism which is received physically, because the will to receive it was not lacking, but under the circumstances he could not receive it." Ch. 24: "In that thief the goodness of the Almighty supplied what was lacking because of the absence of the sacrament of Baptism, because it was not absent from pride or contempt, but from necessity." Ch. 25: "However, when it is lacking from man's volition, it involves him in guilt, for in no way can there be said to be a conversion of the heart to God when the sacrament of God is despised." This is also what Lombard means when he says that the grace of God is not bound to the sacraments.

7 The reader should observe that it is necessary to see not only what is said by an author, but chiefly on what foundations that which is said is built. On the point of necessity in the case of the unbaptized thief Cyprian says the same thing as Augustine, but the reasons are far different. Cyprian thinks that the suffering of the thief has taken the place of Baptism, but Augustine thinks more correctly that faith of the heart which laid hold of Christ justified and saved the thief, when a case of necessity prevented Baptism. Thus antiquity, in the matter of necessity, when believers were either dragged away to martyrdom or carried off by death before they were able to be baptized, beautifully distinguished between baptism with water and baptism of the Spirit and of blood. But this they later corrupted in such a way as if the value of the work and merit in martyrdom were so great that it equalled the power of the blood of Christ in Baptism and could substitute for it. Likewise the baptism of the Spirit they interpreted in this way, that there can be in some contrite person so great a satisfaction and love that its value could take the place of the power of Baptism. These are not only strange but altogether false and wicked foundations, namely, to make the merits of our works equal the power of Baptism. Therefore, in this exception in the article of necessity, the true sources of consolation must be shown to consciences, which certainly are not that we may set our works before God instead of Baptism, but that faith, laying hold of the word of promise, even though it is kept from Baptism by necessity, nevertheless firmly declares that it accepts and possesses Christ, the grace of God, and eternal life. For the Gospel is "the power of God for salvation to every one who has faith."

8 In addition I shall add a passage of Augustine from the same book, ch. 22, which will shed light on this question of whether the sacraments are superfluous. These are his words: "It could seem superfluous in Cornelius and his friends that they should also be baptized with water, when the gift of the Holy Spirit was already in them, which otherwise none except baptized persons received, as Holy Scripture testifies. Nevertheless they were baptized. And this was done by apostolic authority, so that now no one should, because of some progress of the inner man, if perhaps before Baptism he has progressed to spiritual understanding by means of a pious heart, despise the sacrament; it is administered bodily through the office of ministers, but through it God works the consecration of man spiritually. Nor do I believe that the duty of baptizing was assigned to John for any other purpose than that the Lord Himself, who had given it, since He did not scorn to receive the baptism of a servant, might dedicate the way of humility and might by this fact most openly declare how greatly His baptism with which He Himself would baptize should be esteemed. For as a most experienced physician of eternal salvation He saw that some would be puffed up with pride, who, because they had so far progressed in understanding of the truth and in good morals, would not hesitate in the least to set themselves, so far as life and learning are concerned, above many baptized persons and would believe it was superfluous for themselves to be baptized, because they believed that they had come to that condition of mind to which many baptized persons were still trying to rise." Thus says Augustine.

SECTION V

Concerning the Efficacy and Use of the Sacraments

CANON V

If anyone says that these sacraments were instituted only for the nourishment of faith, let him be anathema.

CANON VI

If anyone says that the sacraments of the New Law do not contain the grace which they signify, or that they do not confer grace itself on those who do not place an obstacle in its way, but that they are only external signs, as it were, of the grace or righteousness accepted by faith, and certain marks of the Christian profession by which believers are distinguished from unbelievers among men, let him be anathema.

CANON VII

If anyone says that grace is not given through sacraments of this kind always and to all, as much as lies in God, even if they receive them rightly, but sometimes and to some, let him be anathema.

Examination

1 Concerning the efficacy of the sacraments, how or in what manner they offer, convey, apply, and seal grace, there have been various disputes among scholastic writers. Some indeed, like Alexander of Hales, Thomas, Durandus, etc., thought that a certain supernatural power is conferred on the external elements of the sacraments, which is not a work or ordinance of God, as though He willed, so to say, through the sacraments as through instrumental causes to confer grace through the working of the Spirit, but that it is a supernatural and spiritual power, absolutely inhering in the physical elements of the sacraments, through which they flow into and work in the soul, either effectively or by way of preparation. However, they add, in order to show that neither they themselves nor anyone else understands what they are saying, that it is an incomplete thing which in itself is not in any of the ten categories.

Hugo also says that the sacraments of the New Testament are first sanctified, consecrated, or blessed in order that through the sanctification (which is contained and included in the elements of the sacraments because of the consecration) they may sanctify when they are applied, as when a plaster is applied to a wound. To this fancy also Cyprian adhered, who declared the baptism performed by heretical or evil ministers useless, inefficacious, and invalid, because such men could not by their blessings and consecrations confer such power on the water that it would flow into and work in the soul. Out of this fancy sprang also the corrupt opinion of those who, according to Augustine, *De civitate Dei,* Bk. 21, ch. 25, promised freedom from eternal fire to all who have the sacrament of Baptism and of the body of Christ, without true faith, no matter how they have lived and in what heresy or wickedness they have been involved.

2 Indeed, this opinion that in the elements of the sacraments grace is essentially contained as medicine in a box, so that the power of the sacraments is either an essence or a quality, either complete or incomplete, inhering in the physical elements of the sacraments, was not acceptable to all among the scholastic writers, such as Bonaventura, Richard, etc. There were others who placed the power of the sacraments in the work itself by which the sacraments were either celebrated or received, so that the sacraments were said to confer grace because of the worth and merit of the work which either he who celebrates or he who receives performs. But this opinion conflicts diametrically with the true nature of the sacraments, which are actions in which it is not we who offer something that is ours, but in which God offers and conveys to us His benefits, even as He wants these accepted by us as His gifts.

3 In our time certain men, when they wanted to refute these papalist opinions vehemently, bent too far to the left. For they argued that the sacraments are nothing else than signs and marks of the Christian profession by which we may be distinguished from Jews and pagans, a use which the mysteries of Ceres and similar institutions once had among the Gentiles.

Some judged that the sacraments are only symbols of Christian fellowship, by which we are moved and obligated to help one another, as it was once the custom in concluding treaties to eat together of the things sacrificed. Others wanted to have nothing else seen in the use of the sacraments than mere allegories or signs of Christian mortification, regeneration, quickening, spiritual nourishment, etc. There are those who wish to appear to think honorably of the sacraments, and yet they teach that the sacraments are only signs of grace which is offered and conveyed already beforehand, before and outside of the use of the sacraments, so that through the sacraments God confers and conveys nothing to those who use the sacraments in faith, but that they are only signs of grace previously conferred at another time and in another way.

Related to this is also the opinion of those who think that the use of the sacraments only by way of remembrance stimulates faith, which seeks and receives grace elsewhere and in another way, not in the true use of the sacraments, just as such a reminder can be taken also from pictures. I have listed these opinions in order that the true meaning may be better understood from the anitithesis; chiefly, however, because I see that the papalists are in their disputations about this question cunningly mingling the opinions of the fanatics with the confession of our churches, although the Apology of the Augsburg Confession expressly distinguishes our understanding taken from the Word of God from the unholy opinions of the fanatics.

4 However, the testimonies of Scripture are clear, and as they cannot be denied, so they should not be evaded. In Titus 3:5 Baptism is called "the washing of regeneration and renewal of the Holy Spirit." Eph. 5:25–26: "He gave Himself up for the church, that He might sanctify her, having cleansed her by the washing of water with the Word." John 3:5: "Unless one is born of water and the Spirit, he cannot enter the kingdom of God." Acts 2:38: "Be baptized, every one of you, in the name of Jesus Christ for the forgiveness of your sins." Acts 22:16: "Be baptized, and wash away your sins, calling on His name." In 1 Peter 3:21, speaking of the water through which Noah and his family were preserved in the ark, Peter says: "Baptism, which corresponds to this, now saves you, not as a removal of dirt from the body but as an appeal to God for a clear conscience, through the resurrection of Jesus Christ." Rom. 6:3–5: "All of us who have been baptized into Christ Jesus were baptized into His death.... If we have been united with Him in a death like His, we shall certainly be united with Him in a resurrection like His." Gal. 3:27: "As many of you as were baptized . . . have put on Christ." Mark 16:16: "He who believes and is baptized will be saved."

5 These very clear statements which expressly ascribe efficacy to the sacraments and explain its nature, are not to be subverted from their simple and genuine meaning which the proper signification of the words gives by the assertion that they are figures of speech. And so the ancients understood these testimonies simply as they sound. For Augustine says concerning the sacraments, *Contra Faustum,* Bk. 19, ch. 11: "Their power avails inexpressibly much, and therefore, when they are despised, it makes men sacrilegious, for it is wicked to despise that without which piety cannot be perfected." In ch. 13 he says that the sacraments of the

New Testament are superior in power and of greater usefulness. In ch. 16 he says concerning the physical action of Baptism and the sound of the words of promise: "All these things are done and pass away; they sound and pass away: however, the power which works through them remains permanently; and the spiritual gift which is made known[11] by them is eternal." On Leviticus, quest. 84: "The Lord says: 'I will sanctify Aaron'; and to Moses He says: 'You shall sanctify him.' How then do both Moses and the Lord sanctify him? Moses does not do it instead of the Lord, but he does it by means of visible sacraments through his ministry; however, the Lord does it by the Holy Spirit through invisible grace where there is the whole fruit and the full benefit also of the visible sacraments." *In Evangelium Johannis tractatus,* 80: "Why does not Christ say, 'You are clean on account of Baptism, by which you have been washed,' but 'On account of the word which I have spoken to you,' if it is not because the Word cleanses also in the water? Take away the Word, and what is the water but water? The Word comes to the element, and it becomes a sacrament, also itself, as it were, a visible word." And soon after: "Whence is this great power of the water, that it touches the body and purifies the heart? Only the Word brings this about, not because it is spoken, but because it is believed."

6 I have added these quotations because they not only ascribe power or efficacy to the sacraments, but at the same time also explain how or in what way the sacraments are said to confer grace, as we shall now show. However, we are not treating of rites instituted without an express word of God, to which human foolhardiness ascribes spiritual efficacy equal to, yes, greater and more glorious than to those instituted by God, but of rites which are truly and properly sacraments and which have the promise of grace attached by the divine Word. And by the term "sacrament" we understand not only the external elements and the visible rites, but all those things of which we have said above, in the explanation of the first canon, that they belong to the nature of a sacrament, principally the promise of the offering and application of grace.

7 However, the explanation is neither obscure nor difficult, if that necessary distinction is added, in what way God confers grace and in what way the sacraments do not confer it. God the Father reconciles the world to Himself, accepts the believers, not imputing their sins to them. In this way, certainly, the sacraments do not confer grace like God the Father Himself. Christ is our Peace (Eph. 2:14). The death of Christ is our

---

[11] Editions of the *Examen* going back as far as 1599 have *minuatur,* which yields no acceptable sense. According to Migne, *Patrologia Latina,* Tom. 42, Col. 357, Paris, 1886, Augustine wrote *insinuatur,* which our translation follows.

reconciliation. Through His blood we are justified (Rom. 5:9). The blood of Christ cleanses us from all sin (1 John 1:7). He was raised for our justification (Rom. 4:25). In that manner, certainly, Baptism does not purge sins like Christ Himself.

The efficacy in conferring and appropriating grace belongs to the Holy Spirit. And the sacraments are certainly not to be equated with the Holy Spirit Himself, that they should be believed to confer grace equally and in entirely the same way as the Holy Spirit Himself. But is therefore nothing to be ascribed to the sacraments? Surely, what the statements of Scripture ascribe to the sacraments was recalled to our minds a little earlier in the very words of Scripture. But one must carefully and studiously beware, when we dispute about the power and efficacy of the sacraments, that we do not take away from God those things which properly belong to the grace of the Father, the efficacy of the Spirit, and the merit of the Son of God, and transfer them to the sacraments, for this would be the sin of idolatry; nor are the sacraments to be added to the merit of Christ, the grace of the Father, and the efficacy of the Holy Spirit, as auxiliary or partial causes, for this would be the same sin. For "there is no other name under heaven given among men," etc. (Acts. 4:12). And: "My glory I will not give to another" (Is. 48:11). "There is no other God besides Me, a righteous God and a Savior" (Is. 45:21).

But in what way Baptism saves us (1 Peter 3:21) and in what way it is a washing of regeneration (Titus 3:5), this Paul explains simply when he says (Eph. 5:26): "Having cleansed the church by the washing of water with the Word." And Augustine concludes the same from the statement of Christ: "You are already made clean by the word which I have spoken to you." Rightly, therefore, does the Apology of the Augsburg Confession say that both the Word and the sacraments have the same effect, the very same power or efficacy, and that the sacraments are seals of the promises. Therefore Augustine also calls them "visible words." As therefore the Gospel is the power of God for salvation to everyone who believes, not because a certain magical power inheres in the letters, the syllables, or the sound of the words, but because it is the means, organ, or instrument through which the Holy Spirit is efficacious, setting forth, offering, conveying, dispensing, and applying the merit of Christ and the grace of God for salvation to everyone who believes, so power or efficacy is attributed also to the sacraments, not because grace for salvation is to be sought in the sacraments outside of or over and beyond the merit of Christ, the compassion of the Father, and the efficacy of the Holy Spirit, but the sacraments are instrumental causes, so that through these means or instruments the Father wills to exhibit, bestow, apply His grace, the

Son to communicate His merit to the believers, the Holy Spirit to exercise His efficacy for salvation to everyone who believes.

8 In this way God retains His glory, that grace is not sought elsewhere than with God the Father, that the price and cause of the forgiveness of sins and eternal life is not sought elsewhere than in the death and resurrection of Christ, and that the efficacy of regeneration for salvation is not sought elsewhere than in the operation of the Holy Spirit. The sacraments indeed set forth, offer, convey, and seal these benefits to us in the Word, and thus they lead us to Christ, to the grace of God, to the efficacy of the Spirit. For since God wills to deal with us in the things which pertain to our salvation through certain means, and has Himself both ordained this use and instituted the Word of promise of the Gospel, this is at times proclaimed simply by itself, or nakedly, but at times clothed or made visible through certain rites or sacraments, instituted by God. Therefore the Word and the sacraments show us where faith should seek and where it can find Christ the Mediator, the Father, and the Holy Spirit in such a way that they may deal with us, convey, apply, and seal the benefits which Christ has merited and of which the Gospel tells. And in the use of the sacraments faith does not seek or look for some essential power or efficacy inhering in the external elements of the sacraments; but in the promise which is attached to the sacrament, it seeks, lays hold of, and accepts the grace of the Father, the merit of the Son, and the efficacy of the Spirit.

9 This is the simple, plain, and true teaching concerning the efficacy of the sacraments. And let the reader observe that Scripture affirms both that Baptism saves (1 Peter 3:21) and that God saves through "the washing of regeneration" (Titus 3:5). Likewise: "Baptism washes away sins" (Acts 22:16) and "Christ cleanses the church by the washing of water with the Word" (Eph. 5:26). Then let him also observe how carefully the words of Scripture are placed. Thus Peter says that Baptism saves us and that it is "an appeal to God for a clear conscience," but he adds, "through the resurrection of Jesus Christ." Paul calls it a "washing of regeneration," but this he explains thus: "God saved us in virtue of His own mercy, by the washing of regeneration." But whence has Baptism this, that it is a "washing of regeneration"? He answers: "It is the washing of regeneration and renewal in the Holy Spirit." As also Christ says (John 3): "Unless one is born of water and the Spirit," etc. But how is this accomplished? "Through Jesus Christ our Savior, so that we might be justified by His grace and become heirs in hope of eternal life" (Titus 3:6–7). For we are baptized into the death of Christ that we may be partakers of His resurrection (Rom. 6:4–5). We put on Christ when we were baptized (Gal. 3:27). For He who gave Himself for His church did not surrender the power or efficacy of sanctifying and cleansing her to another, but He Himself sanctifies and cleanses her. But does He effect this without any orderly means? Paul answers: "He sanctifies and cleanses her by the washing of water with the Word." How much simpler, plainer, surer, and safer are these teachings about the power or efficacy of the sacraments than the disputations and opinions of all men, either of the scholastics or of other fanatics!

10 Augustine also plainly thinks and speaks this way in the statements we have quoted above. For he ascribes to the sacraments strength and power; but he adds the declaration that the divine power works through the sacraments, so that Moses performs the service but the Lord, through that service, by invisible grace sanctifies through the Holy Spirit. And he affirms that in that invisible grace of sanctification through the Holy Spirit the entire fruit and the whole benefit of the visible sacraments is found.

11 To a fuller explanation belongs also this consideration, that the instrumental cause in this doctrine is a twofold one. The one is, as it were, the hand of God, by which, through the Word and sacraments, He in the Word offers, conveys, applies, and seals to the believers the benefits of the redemption. The other is, as it were, our hand, namely, that by faith we ask for, seek, lay hold of, and accept those things which God offers and presents to us through the Word and the sacraments. For the efficacy of the sacraments is not such that God through them as it were pours in or forces saving grace also on unbelievers or on those who do not accept it, as some thought also in ancient times, as Augustine relates in *De civitate Dei*, Bk. 21, ch. 25. It is rather as Paul says of the Word: "The Gospel is the power of God for salvation to everyone who has faith." And Heb. 4:2: "The message which they heard did not benefit them, because it did not meet with faith." Thus Christ says of the sacraments, because they are visible words and seals of the promise: "He who believes and is baptized will be saved; but he who does not believe will be condemned." Yes, Paul adds: "Whoever eats unworthily eats judgment upon himself." And from this the argument about this statement can be understood which was at one time used also in the schools: "Not the sacrament itself, but faith in the sacrament justifies." For the sense is not that faith justifies in such a way that it does not accept the grace which God offers and conveys in the Word and in the sacraments, or that it accepts the grace without the means or instrument of the Word and of the sacraments. For the object of faith is the Word and the sacraments, or rather, in the Word and the sacraments that true object of faith is the merit of Christ, the grace of

God, and efficacy of the Spirit. And faith justifies because it apprehends and accepts these things in the Word and in the sacraments. And in this sense, as faith in the Word, so also faith in the sacraments is said to justify.

12 Therefore when justification is ascribed to faith, the hearing of the Word and the use of the sacraments is not excluded; but in order that faith may justify, it must apprehend Christ in the Word and in the sacraments. But this understanding was contrary to the opinions of those who imagined that through the use of the sacraments, by the mere fact that the work was performed, also those receive grace for justification and salvation who use the sacraments without repentance and faith.

13 Therefore the entire teaching concerning the efficacy and use of the sacraments is clear. But if men object to this understanding and ask, for instance, what Baptism may have conferred on Cornelius, who received and had grace before Baptism (Acts 10:1–2), likewise what was the efficacy and power of circumcision in Abraham, who had the righteousness of faith before circumcision (Rom. 4:10–11), these are questions which furnish contentious minds material to harass the simple and true teaching. However, if the simple truth is sought in the fear of God, and is loved, the explanation of these questions will not be difficult, but will clarify this entire teaching. For the general rule with respect to the efficacy of the sacraments must not be taken from these extraordinary examples; it ought to be taken from the institution of the sacraments and from the promise which is attached to them. Therefore it does not follow that there is no other reason for circumcision in those who are commanded to be circumcised on the eighth day, in order that they may thus be received into the covenant, than that which was in the case of Abraham, who had already been justified. For those who are born of circumcised parents are not by nature children of the covenant. For Paul declares (Eph. 2:1–3) that not only the Gentiles, but also we who are born of circumcised parents, were by nature children of wrath. So, because in Cornelius, as a special example, spiritual sanctification preceded Baptism, it does not follow that others are not baptized for the remission of sins according to the promise, or that God does not save us by the washing of regeneration and renewal.

14 This distinction is not a recent invention. For also Augustine, *Contra Donatistas,* Bk. 4, ch. 24, makes almost the same distinction between the circumcision of Abraham and that which Isaac received on the eighth day; also between the baptism of Cornelius and that of infants. Yet circumcision was not useless in Abraham, nor Baptism in Cornelius, as if they had only been mere signs. For God does not confer and convey grace in this life just once, so that it is at once complete and perfect, so that as long as we are in this life God would will to convey and confer nothing more, and that a person would need to receive nothing more from God; but God is always giving and man is always receiving, in order that we may be joined more and more fully and perfectly to Christ, and may hold the forgiveness of sins or reconciliation more firmly, so that the benefits of redemption which have been begun in us may be preserved and strengthened and may grow and increase. These things, indeed, God confers and works, and believers seek and accept in the means instituted by God for this purpose, namely, in the use of the Word and of the sacraments. Therefore those who (Acts 2:37–41) are stung by the recognition of their sins and ask what they shall do are baptized for the remission of sins. So also God saves infants, who are by nature children of wrath, by the washing of regeneration; that is, through Baptism God offers, conveys, and applies to them the benefits of the Gospel. Abraham accepted and possessed the righteousness of faith already beforehand; Cornelius had already received the Holy Ghost. Were therefore circumcision in Abraham and Baptism in Cornelius altogether superfluous, bare, and useless signs? By no means! For the working or efficacy of the sacraments must be judged from the promise. But the promise which was attached to circumcision in the Old Testament and to Baptism in the New Testament is not useless or merely significative, but it presents what it promises. For the Father saves, Christ cleanses, the Holy Spirit regenerates through the washing of water with the Word.

But what could the sacrament confer on them, when they already previously had the righteousness of faith and the Holy Ghost? I answer: God offers, conveys, applies, and seals to Abraham through circumcision and to Cornelius through Baptism the very same grace of which they had previously received the firstlings, that they may have it more fully and richly, that they may possess and hold it more firmly, in order that the work of God begun in them may be strengthened, may grow, be increased and preserved. Thus the promise attached to the sacraments remains always and universally true and efficacious in those who use the sacraments in faith according to their institution. This the primitive church wanted to signify when it led the recently baptized adults at once from Baptism to the Communion of the body and blood of the Lord. Indeed, the reconciliation of God and the remission of sins, in whatever way it is conferred, is the same and is complete so far as God is concerned. However, because our infirmity is great and God is rich in mercy, He does not want to convey, confer, apply, and seal His grace in only one way, but through means which He has instituted for this use, and it belongs to the obedience of faith to use these means as they have been instituted and ordained by God. Thus the teaching remains firm that the sacraments are not useless or bare signs, but that God through the sacraments offers, conveys, bestows, applies, and seals His grace or the benefits of the Gospel to believers. For the promise which is attached to the sacraments by the divine Word, if it is accepted in faith, is for all and conveys the benefits.

15 Now that we have explained these things, we shall examine the three canons which are before us. The fifth canon reads: "If anyone says that the sacraments were instituted solely to nourish faith, let him be anathema." Luther's statement in the book *De captivitate Babylonica* is: "All sacraments were instituted to nourish faith."

Since they want to condemn this statement, I beg the reader to observe how deceitfully they are operating. Luther criticizes this in the papalist doctrine that, although they argue much about the power of the sacraments and about the *opus operatum*,[12] they make no mention of faith in the use of the sacraments; yes, that they teach that the sacraments confer grace without a good impulse of the heart, that is, without faith, and indeed that they even command faith to doubt with respect to the grace of the sacraments, that is, with respect to the reconciliation or the forgiveness of sins. Contrary to this Luther teaches on the basis of the Word of God that, in order that the sacraments may be profitable for salvation to those who use them, faith is altogether necessary, which accepts the grace offered in the promise of the sacraments. For a sacrament is a visible word, and the chief thing in a sacrament is the promise of grace which is added to the institution of the external rite by the divine word. However, between the word of promise and faith there is a mutual connection or relation which is so close that neither can the promise profit man without faith, nor faith without the promise. Yes, since faith is the necessary organ for accepting the grace which God offers and conveys, and since in this infirmity a weak faith can neither easily nor with assurance nor firmly apprehend and hold the promise set forth in the bare word, God made it, as it were, visible by instituting a certain rite. He did it in order that in the action with the individual users faith may in its application more readily, surely, and firmly apprehend and hold the promise. In this sense Luther says that the sacraments were instituted to quicken, nourish, confirm, increase, and preserve faith, in order that it may ap-

---

[12] On *opus operatum* see the lengthy discussion of this concept in Section VI of this topic.

prehend and receive grace and salvation in the promise, whether it comes in its bare form or clothed in a sacramental rite.

This most true doctrine, which embodies the genuine sense of Scripture, the papalist council does not want simply to condemn, but also to anathematize. But they fear the judgment of the ears of the godly, if they openly anathematize this doctrine. Therefore they deceitfully put forth a mutilated statement of Luther in such a way, as if he meant that the sacraments were not instituted to be means or instrumental causes through which God offers, conveys, applies, and seals grace to believers, but as if the sole use of the sacraments were that they should, like pictures and plays, as an external reminder, quicken and nourish faith, but that faith itself receives nothing in the use of the sacraments but wanders about elsewhere contemplating itself. This wicked opinion Luther earnestly and always disapproved in the sacramentarians. But the men of Trent concealed the true teaching of Luther and deceitfully set up this fifth canon in such a way that by this crafty trick they might render Luther's argument about the mutual relation between the sacrament and faith odious and hateful to the inexperienced.

At the same time they are after this, that they may blot out, erase, and remove faith from the true and salutary use of the sacraments. For this the reader will profitably observe in all these canons, that faith is not required by even one syllable for the salutary use of the sacraments, but all things crackle with anathemas and the proscription and removal of faith from the salutary use and efficacy of the sacraments. Therefore let us confess that the architects of the decrees of this council must have been workmen who were outstanding for sophistry.

16 In the sixth canon they arrogate the conferring of grace without distinction to all their rites which they count as sacraments. And although there are various arguments about the manner in which the sacraments confer grace, they simply, without explanation, decree that the sacraments confer grace, in order to show that they permit all opinions of the scholastics to be free, and to indicate that they do not shrink from the opinion of those who imagine that grace essentially inheres in the elements of the sacraments, as medicine in a vial. They say that the sacraments contain grace. However, they soon add that those who do not embrace this opinion make of the sacraments only bare marks of the Christian profession. This is the trick of the sixth canon. For what they say about the obstacle we shall explain in connection with the eighth canon.

17 So far as the seventh canon is concerned, "If there are any who think that by the promise attached to the sacraments God is playing with men, so that even if a person receives them rightly, God nevertheless does not convey grace always and to all who in faith use the sacraments rightly"—I hold that there is no one who is sound in piety who does not abhor that wicked opinion.

But there is trickery hidden in these words: "If they receive them rightly." For they studiously avoid any mention of faith; but in order that they may establish the human devotions and dispositions by which man makes himself worthy that God should confer the grace of the sacraments on him, they say: "If anyone receives them lawfully." And indeed we preach earnestly on the basis of Paul: "Let a man examine himself; for whoever eats unworthily eats judgment upon himself." There is no doubt, therefore, that a right disposition is required in adults, in order that the sacraments may be received worthily. This disposition the Word of God describes thus (Acts 2:38): "Repent and be baptized, every one of you, for the forgiveness of sins." Acts 8:37: "If you believe, you may be baptized."[13] Mark 16:16: "He who believes and is baptized will be saved." The papalists, indeed, are neither greatly concerned about nor do they greatly urge true inner penitence in the use of the sacraments, but they set forth other dispositions from the traditions of men, and to these they promise the conferring of grace. When these false and ungodly persuasions are censured, the papalists clamor that we deny that the grace of God is given through the sacraments, even if a person receives them rightly. But the reader now understands this deceitful sophistry.

---

[13] This verse, found in some late manuscripts, is not found in the best ancient manuscripts and has generally been omitted in modern translations of the Bible.

SECTION VI
Concerning the *Opus Operatum*

CANON VI

If anyone says that the sacraments of the New Law do not confer grace on those who do not place an obstacle, etc., let him be anathema.

CANON VIII

If anyone says that the sacraments of the New Law do not through the act performed *(ex opere operato)* confer grace, but that faith alone in the divine promise suffices to obtain grace, let him be anathema.

Examination

1 This is now finally the beautiful Helen, for the sake of whose maintenance, praise, and strengthening all the preceding canons were set up, namely, in order that the fabrication of the scholastics may be strengthened and retained, and indeed, in their own words, that the sacraments of the New Testament confer grace upon those that use them, through the act performed *(ex opere operato)*, even if a good inner impulse is not present in the recipient, provided only he does not place an obstacle. That this is indeed a new and strange doctrine the very form of the words sufficiently indicates. For it does not serve "the pattern of sound words" of which Paul speaks (2 Tim. 1:13), as for instance: "He who believes and is baptized will be saved; but he who does not believe will be condemned." Likewise: "Be baptized and wash away your sins, calling on the name of Jesus," and "He who eats unworthily eats judgment upon himself."

2 Therefore that fabrication about the *opus operans*[14] in the sacraments, which are the work of God by which He offers and conveys His

---

[14] On the expressions *opus operatum* (often found in the phrase *ex opere operato*) and *opus operans* (often found in the phrase *ex opere operante*) or *opus operantis* (often found in the phrase *ex opere operantis*) the following explanation is offered: According to the *Dictionnaire de Théologie Catholique* (Paris: Librarie Letouzey et Ané, sixth ed., 1931), Vol. 11, col. 1084, Pierre de Poitiers, a disciple of Peter Lombard, first employed the distinction between *opus operatum* and *opus operans* or, better, *opus operantis*. The distinction was

grace, which He wants to have received by faith, introduces the opinion of our works, and indeed of work performed without any good inner impulse on the part of the recipient; and it does this with strange prodigies of words, unknown both to Scripture and to antiquity. And the matter itself concerning which there is dispute is so clear and manifest that among the papalists themselves, those who want to be considered to be the foremost, like Gropper and others, shrink from the too crass abomination of this teaching. For they pretend that a wrong is being done to the scholastic teachers, as if they had taught by the opinion of the *opus operatum* that the sacraments confer grace upon someone without faith which accepts grace; but they say that the disputations concerning the *opus operatum* (the act performed) and the *opus operans* (the one performing the act) aimed at nothing else than that the genuineness of the sacraments should not be determined from the dignity or merit of the acting minister but from the institution, power, and operation of their author, who is God. For it is He who baptizes through the external ministry, so that the sacraments may be said to be valid, not from the work of the officiating minister *(ex opere operantis)* but by virtue of the act performed *(ex opere operato)*, so that the wickedness of the minister does not hinder the genuineness, integrity, and effect of the sacraments, if only they are administered according to the institution, word, and command of the Lord, so that it is the same as that which is quoted from Augustine, *De consecratione,* dist. 2, ch. *Utrum:* "Nothing more is effected by a good priest, nothing less by a bad one, because it is effected not through the merit of the one who consecrates, but through the word of its Creator and by the power of the Holy Spirit." Alphonsus says that by the opinion of the act performed *(opus operatum)* all merit of the recipient is excluded from the efficacy of the sacraments, so that the genuineness of the sacraments does not depend on the faith of the recipient and that the sacrament does not borrow its efficacy from the faith of the recipient.

Truly, "a wise remedy for a sick expression," according to a saying of Euripides. For if the papalists wanted this when they dispute about the *opus operatum,* there would be no controversy, because the statement is true; neither would we want to fight in hateful fashion about this way of speaking; or we would certainly say with Augustine: "Hold fast the meaning, correct the language!" But not even in old time have all the

---

used to show that a sacrament is valid even if it is performed by an unworthy minister, or received by an insincere person. The term *opus operatum,* "the act performed," was therefore used, e.g., for Baptism per se, as an institution of God. *Opus operans* or *opus operantis* viewed the sacrament as an action performed by a human being. *Opus operans* might therefore be translated "the one who performs the act," and *opus operantis* as "the act of him who performs it." Because the translation in either case is awkward, we retain the Latin terms as technical theological terms.

scholastics held this sense, although some argue almost this way. And not even now do the papalists want this when they contend for the opinion of the *opus operatum,* but a far different monstrosity is being nurtured and foisted on the church under those exotic words. Therefore it should first be explained what the opinion of the *opus operatum* really wants. Then the refutation will be easy.

3 All the scholastics generally make this distinction between the sacraments of the Old and of the New Testament, that the latter confer grace by the act performed *(ex opere operato),* the former, however, by the act of him who performs it *(ex opere operante).* If you now ask what they understand by the *opus operans,* to which they set the *opus operatum* in opposition, this can be understood most simply from circumcision. For they say that it conferred grace, not by the act performed, but by the act of him who performed it. However, it is beyond all controversy that circumcision in the Old Testament, also according to the teaching of the scholastics, destroyed original sin, not because of the dignity and merit of the minister who circumcised, for also women did this (Ex. 4:25; 2 Macc. 6:10), but because of the institution, power, and operation of God. Nor can it be said that the wickedness of the minister hindered the genuineness and effect of circumcision, when it was administered and received according to the institution of God. But by the expression *ex opere operante* they understand that in adults a good impulse is required, or an inner devotion in the recipient; and to this they oppose the act performed *(opus operatum).* Therefore it is manifest and certain that the scholastics did not, by the opinion of the *opus operantis* and of the *opus operatum* understand that which Gropper and others interpret (as quoted above). For the words with which they explain themselves are clear.

Gabriel (who gathered all the disputations and opinions of the masters of sentences into one work) explains the meaning of the scholastics, Bk. 4, dist. 1, quest. 3, in these words: "A sacrament is said to confer grace *ex opere operato,* so that by the very fact that it (understand sacrament) is performed, grace is conferred on the users, unless the obstacle of mortal sin prevents it," so that beyond the exhibition of the sign, outwardly conveyed, there is not required a good inner impulse in the recipient. However, the sacraments are said to confer grace *ex opere operante* through the measure of merit, namely, because the sacrament outwardly administered does not suffice for the conferring of grace, but that beyond this there is required a good impulse or an inner devotion in the recipient, according to the intention of which grace is conferred as of a worthy or suitable merit *(meritum condigni vel congrui),* exactly and not greater, on account of the giving of the sacrament.

Peter of La Palu, dist. 1, quest. 1, in the fourth of the sentences, explains the teaching of the scholastics as follows: "It is not required per se in the sacraments of the new law that a person dispose himself; therefore he is disposed through the sacrament itself, and so it is probable in every sacrament of the new law that it justifies *ex opere operato.*" Likewise: "And if it is said that the act performed is not from the sacrament, but from God in the sacrament, or with the sacrament, that is not valid, because thus the sacrament of the new law would not differ from the sacrament of the old law; because it was necessary also under the old law that a disposition should be effected in infants by God. It remains, therefore, that the sacraments of the new law effect grace and justify by the very act performed *(ex ipso opere operato).*" (Let the reader observe the antithesis by which he explains the opinion of the *opus operatum.*) Afterwards he undertakes to prove that the sacraments of the new law have the inherent and innate power to confer and cause grace *ex opere operato.* However, that power or causative virtue of grace, he says, is in Baptism in the water and in the words; in confirmation and in ordination it is in the words and in the minister, or in the mark of the bishop; in penitence it is in the ministers and in the words of absolution, and in the satisfaction imposed by the priest; in extreme unction it is in the minister in the words, in the unction, and in the oil, etc.

Marsilius, in the Fourth Sentence, quest. 2, art. 2, says: "The baptism of John we can consider in a twofold manner: the one insofar as it is an act performed, which was an outward washing of the body; the other insofar as the devotion of the recipient is concerned. Then the corresponding conclusion is that the baptism of John, insofar as it is an act performed, did not confer grace. And therefore it was not a sacrament, because that only is properly called a sacrament which confers grace *ex opere operato.*"

Mensinger quotes from Albertus, on the sixth chapter of John: "The *opus operans* is a work elicited from virtue; the *opus operatum* is the completing of an external act without an inner motive." And Mensinger adds: "Because the saints in the Old Testament received grace by faith through the use of the sacraments, therefore the sacraments of the New Testament should be of greater efficacy, so that they confer grace by the act performed, even though the *opus operans* of the recipient does not come to it, namely, faith or inner devotion."

4 I am not unaware of the fact that some argue concerning the opinion of the *opus operatum* in a slightly different manner, but for the present I only wanted to show that our teachers are not wrongfully ascribing to the scholastics the understanding set forth above. For how they understand their opinion about the *opus operatum* and explain it among themselves I have set forth not with my words but with their own. And the opinions of the common people bear witness how that teaching of the *opus operatum* was transmitted, received, and understood under the papacy. For they think that they have abundant prospect of salvation through the external giving and reception of the sacraments, regardless of what happens with respect to penitence and faith. Chiefly, however, this persuasion prevails in the saying and hearing of Masses, from which they promise themselves the effect of grace, from the administration and show of the outward act, even though no good inner impulse comes to it.

We are not speaking only of the errors of the common people, but this is how they taught in the schools concerning the Mass. Thomas, in the Fourth Sentence, dist. 11, quest. 2, says: "The Eucharist, insofar as it is a sacrament, has an effect in the living person; but insofar as it is a sacrifice, it has an effect in others for whom it is offered, in whom it does not demand spiritual life beforehand as an actuality, but as a possibility." Peter of La Palu, dist. 12: "When the Mass is celebrated for another, it destroys also mortal sin which is in the conscience of the other, not in the manner of a sacrament, which benefits the recipient only, but in the manner of a sacrifice, through the merit of Christ, by which pardon is asked for oneself, that is, for the grace of contrition. Therefore also a man can give no greater gift to another man than to give him a Mass or to celebrate it for him, for this is the unique thing in this sacrament, that it can be offered and received for another, which is not true of the other (sacraments)," etc. Gabriel, in the twelfth distinction, says: "The sacrament of the Eucharist, insofar as it is a sacrament, benefits not only those by whom it is received but also others for whom it is offered." And he adds: "It bears fruit not only in the good and just but also in sinners for whom it is offered, that they may be converted from their sins," etc.

5 Writers of our age who wish to appear as pillars in supporting the papal kingdom are wont to explain and confirm the opinion concerning the *opus operatum* with this argument, that Baptism confers grace on infants, who on account of their age are not able to believe. And indeed, at the proper place we will have to speak about infant baptism. For the moment it is sufficient to have shown that they expressly set the opinion of the *opus operatum* in opposition to faith in those who receive the sacrament, as if the case were the same in infants and adults, which Augustine expressly denies, *De baptismo,* Bk. 4, ch. 24.

6 What therefore the opinion of the *opus operatum* means in the papalist kingdom, and how it is to be understood, is clear. Gropper tries to confuse the reader in this clear matter with this piece of sophistry: "The scholastics establish a twofold *opus operans.* First, in the minister cele-

brating or administering the sacrament. Thus Gabriel, *De canone missae,* lect. 26, says: 'The Mass has power, in one way by the one who performs the act *(ex opere operante),* that is, from the personal merit of the celebrating person, on account of which God confers that which is sought by the priest on those to whom he applies the prayer and the sacrifice of the Mass. In another way, by the act performed *(ex opere operato),* that is, by the consecration, offering, and taking itself, without respect to the personal sanctity or the merit of the priest,' " etc. Then, however, they also place the *opus operans* in the person who uses the sacrament; namely, a good inner impulse as the devotion or faith of the recipient. But over against both kinds of *opus operans* they set the act performed *(opus operatum),* now in one respect, now in another. However, Gropper bravely conceals this, as if it were opposed only to the other, namely, merit in the celebrating minister, and cries out that an injustice is being done to the scholastics, as if by the opinion of the *opus operatum* they taught that for the efficacious and salutary use of the sacrament there is not required in the recipient a good inner impulse, that is, faith; although this teaching, as we have shown, is found in their writings, and in the persuasion regarding the efficacy of the Mass that opinion not only clings in the minds of the common people but is also transmitted in the writings of the teachers.

7 However, Alphonsus raises the objection that it must not at once be ascribed to the entire papalist church if one or another has argued a certain thing, because on the other side men could be brought forward who held otherwise. That therefore it may be firmly established beyond all controversy what the papalist church wants to have understood by the *opus operatum,* and that there may be no need to search this out anxiously from among moths and bookworms, we shall investigate what the assembly, sworn to the pope, decreed about the *opus operatum* at Trent. First of all, although they are not unaware that among the papalists themselves many sought mitigations of this scholastic dogma and that some interpret the *opus operatum* one way, others another way, they themselves simply approve and confirm the opinion of the *opus operatum,* without adding any clear statement by which they either approve or disapprove the explanation of the *opus operatum.* Therefore they in general approve and confirm all the arguments and opinions of the scholastics about the *opus operatum,* of whatever kind they are.

In the second place, if the reader asks whether the assembly at Trent approves of the interpretation or mitigation of the opinion concerning the *opus operatum* on the part of Gropper and certain others which we have reviewed above, the matter is not obscure. For they clearly show that when they speak of the *opus operatum* they do not want this to be understood as meaning that the genuineness and the efficacy of the sacraments do not depend either on the worthiness or the unworthiness of the minister; for about that understanding they later set down a special canon, namely, Canon 12. There is therefore no doubt that in the eighth canon they understand something else by the *opus operatum.*

Thirdly, what it is that they understand they show plainly and clearly by the antithesis. For they set these two things in opposition to each other: the *opus operatum,* and faith which accepts grace in the promise which is joined to the sacraments. Therefore they hold that through the sacraments of the new law, by the act performed *(ex opere operato),* grace is conferred in such a way that it is not necessary to receive the offered grace by faith. For the scholastics say that beside the exhibition of the publicly exhibited sign a good inner impulse in the recipient is not required; these are the words of Gabriel.

But let the reader again consider that they arranged the words in the latter part of the eighth canon so deceitfully, as if we, who attack the opinion of the *opus operatum,* held the opinion that faith alone in the divine promise suffices to obtain grace in such a way that the use of the Word and of the sacraments is not necessary, or that faith alone is sufficient in such a way that there is no need that God should offer and convey His grace to the believers through the Word and the sacraments.

8 This tumbledown, sophistical opinion concerning the *opus operatum,* an opinion utterly demolished by the Word of God, they endeavor to support, or rather to cover up before the inexperienced, although our clear explanations are extant, which testify to the contrary, as we have indicated in our explanation of the sixth canon. However, they fear with reason that if the opinion of the *opus operatum* is set forth nakedly as it is taught by the scholastics it will carry its own refutation with it. For there is invincible proof that the promise of grace, which is joined to the sacraments in such a way that for this reason Augustine calls a sacrament a "visible Word," requires faith so completely that hearing of the Word does not profit unless it meets with faith in those who hear it. (Heb. 4:2)

9 Concerning the sacraments there are express testimonies of Scripture: "He who believes and is baptized will be saved; but he who does not believe will be condemned." Yes, "He who eats unworthily eats judgment upon himself." Against these clear testimonies the papalists defend the opinion of the *opus operatum,* namely, that through the sacraments grace is so conferred on those who use them that no good inner impulse is required in the recipient. Yes, when they teach that faith ought to be in doubt concerning grace, they plainly turn everything upside down. They imagine that unbelieving persons, through the external use of the sacraments, without faith, receive and have grace; but in the believers they demand that faith should doubt whether they receive and have grace when they use the sacraments. But these things are so evident that there is no need for more words, for the matter explains itself to the children of the church. And the papalist writers themselves are now reluctant and do not dare openly to undertake the defense of this axiom, that the use of the sacraments saves those who receive them without faith. Besides it is a heresy long ago condemned by Augustine, *De civitate Dei,* Bk. 21, ch. 25, that those cannot be damned who have received the sacraments of Christ, no matter in what heresy or impiety they may have been.

10 But the scholastics (that I may add also this incidentally) appear to have taken occasion for the disputes about the *opus operatum* from what Augustine says, *Contra Donatistas,* Bk. 3, ch. 14: "It makes no difference, when one is treating of the integrity and sanctity of a sacrament, what the man believes who receives the sacrament and with what kind of faith he is imbued. It is indeed of the greatest importance for the way of salvation, but for the question of the sacrament it is of no importance. For it can happen that a man has a perfect sacrament and a false faith." And later: "It is clear that it can happen that the sacrament of Baptism remains whole in a person whose faith is not whole." He also argues that error in the faith of one who is baptized does indeed exclude the benefit of Baptism so far as the way of salvation is concerned, but that the sacrament is nevertheless not lacking to him and that it ought not to be repeated if he is converted, for then finally, when faith has been made true, the sacrament which was previously received will exercise its powers. In Bk. 4, ch. 15, and Bk. 5, ch. 8, he says: "Anyone taking the Lord's sacrament unworthily does not cause it to be evil; nor, because he does not receive it for salvation, does he receive nothing. For the body of the Lord and the blood of the Lord were there nevertheless also for those of whom the apostle said: 'He who eats unworthily eats judgment to himself.' " Because they did not consider this sufficiently, the scholastics imagined that not only the sacrament itself but also the grace and power of the sacraments is received and possessed without faith by the impenitent and unbelieving, although Augustine everywhere teaches that the sacrament is one thing and the power of the sacrament another thing; yes, in the passages already quoted he says that those who are baptized without true faith indeed receive and have Baptism, yet they do not receive and have the remission of sins, which certainly is the grace and power of Baptism. And in Bk. 5, ch. 8, he says: "The remission of sins does not follow upon Baptism, unless it is not only legitimate but is also lawfully accepted." And, *Contra Cresconium,* Bk. 1, ch. 25, when treating the saying of Paul, "He who eats unworthily . . .": "Behold, how harmful are divine and sacred things to those who use them badly!" And *Contra epistolam Parmeniani,* Bk. 2, ch. 6: "It is one and the same sacrifice on account of the name of the Lord which is invoked, and is always holy, and it will be to everyone according to the kind of heart with which he approaches to receive it, for whoever eats and drinks unworthily eats and drinks judgment upon himself. He does not say: 'To others,' but 'to himself.' Whoever therefore eats and drinks worthily eats and drinks grace to himself." So says Augustine. Therefore Augustine by no means thought that the grace of the sacraments is conferred, received, and possessed without a good impulse of the heart or without faith.

Here belongs also what Augustine says in Letter No. 23: "The infant, although he does not yet have a conscious faith, does not set against it the obstacle of contrary thinking; therefore he receives his sacrament profitably." From this statement of Augustine about infants the scholastics made the general rule that for receiving the grace of the sacraments for salvation faith is not necessary, nor a good inner impulse of the heart, but that it suffices that you do not place an obstacle. An obstacle, however, they call a mortal sin, or the intention to commit one, such as homicide and wantonness. However, they do not want to grant that unbelief or lack of faith is such an obstacle which prevents one from receiving the grace of the sacraments to salvation. But both Scripture and Augustine himself contradict this dogma, as we have noted in certain passages of his. About the baptism of infants we will speak later at the proper place. Now I only wanted to show in passing from which passages in Augustine, which they did not understand correctly nor consider diligently enough, the scholastics seem to have taken occasion for the disputation about the *opus operatum,* which expression is however found neither in Augustine nor in any other ancient writer.

SECTION VII
Concerning the Character

CANON IX

If anyone says that in three sacraments, namely, baptism, confirmation, and ordination, there is not imprinted on the soul a character, that is, a certain spiritual and indelible sign, on account of which they cannot be repeated, let him be anathema.

Examination

1 It is a great and difficult thing to pronounce the anathema on anyone, that is, to declare that he is cut off and excluded from all grace or compassion of God in Christ Jesus and that he is consigned with curses to everlasting destruction. Therefore the cause on account of which the anathema is solemnly pronounced on anyone ought not to be a light or doubtful one, but most weighty and most certain. Now, however, the men of Trent simply pronounce the anathema on all who do not approve and embrace as an article of faith the recent and uncertain fabrication of the scholastics concerning the indelible character. We shall therefore note down in a few words, of what kind, namely, how weighty, how old, how certain and true that opinion is. For this reflection will show how lightly, yes, how irresponsibly the Tridentine Synod plays with anathemas. At one time the saying was current that "kings play with pacts and oaths as boys are accustomed to play with dice." Now it would be more correct to say that the papalist councils play with anathemas no differently than boys play with dice.

2 Since Gabriel has collected the disputations of the scholastics about the character into one summary, dist. 6, quest. 2, in the fourth of his *Sententiae,* I shall briefly copy certain things from it, for from this it will be clear what it amounts to to pronounce the anathema on anyone on account of this opinion. They say that as men in a certain state sometimes receive a certain decoration or sign in the body or on the garment, by which they are recognized to be of that state or mode of life; so, they say, also through the sacraments, through which a person is placed in a certain state, God without means impresses on the soul of the recipient of the sacrament some spiritual sign by which the recipient may be recognized as being in such a state.

3 To this character they attribute many and various things. For they say that it is:

1. A sign of grace existing within, or that it would exist within if an obstacle were not placed;

2. A sign which forms man or makes him like Christ, for they imagine that through the character the recipient is enrolled in the family of Christ;

3. A sign distinguishing a man from others who do not have the character;

4. A sign which disposes a man, making him acceptable to receive the grace of the sacrament;

5. A commemorative sign, through which the recipient is caused to remember the sacrament he has received;

6. An obligative sign, which obligates a person to the divine law, as the religious garb obligates the one who wears it to observe the law of that order.

They say also that the character is something indelible in the soul, making the sacrament by which it is impressed unrepeatable. They say, therefore, that through three sacraments—Baptism, confirmation, and ordination—such a character is imprinted, but in such a way that the character of ordination is of a sixfold kind. And so the number of characters exceeds even the sevenfold number of sacraments.

4 However, they have hot arguments among themselves about the source of the indelible character, then also about what the character actually is, whether it is a restoration, or indeed an absolute quality, and what kind of quality. They say that it can be of the first, and of the second, and of the third kind of quality, likewise, that it can also be placed into the categories of relation and suffering. Also about the subject in which the character should be placed there are various opinions, whether it should be placed in the essence of the soul, or indeed into a power of the soul, likewise whether it should be placed into the power of knowing or into that of willing. Furthermore, they dispute whether circumcision imprinted the character; likewise, whether the baptism of blood and of the Spirit imprint the character; and whether such a character was imprinted also on the soul of Christ in Baptism.

5 And finally, descriptions of the character like the following are taught: The character is a spiritual sign imprinted by God alone on the soul in the reception of an unrepeatable sacrament, remaining indelibly according to common law. Or: It is a sign, imprinted upon the soul, which leads the way to grace, in the reception of an unrepeatable sacrament. Likewise: The character is a certain spiritual power for performing or receiving something in the church. This is just about the forest of the chief questions and opinions about the character.

6 Gabriel both says and proves that the term "character" in this meaning and sense is found neither in Scripture nor in the ancient ecclesiastical writers, so that even Lombard does not make mention of the character in such a meaning and sense. For when Lombard says that those who have been baptized by heretics, with the character of Christ preserved, should not be baptized again, he understands the form of the words of Baptism delivered by Christ. Then, as far as the matter itself is concerned, Gabriel adds that neither does reason show that it is necessary, nor does the authority of the fathers prove that such a character as has been described should be asserted. For the statements which are adduced from Dionysius, Augustine, John of Damascus, and Lombard concerning the character are usually and more pertinently expounded according to the mind of the authors concerning the sacrament of Baptism itself, or concerning the sacramental form, rather than about anything actually impressed on the soul, as they say of the character. And having explained these statements of the fathers, he concludes: "It is apparent therefore that neither the authority of Holy Scripture nor that of the holy fathers compel us to assert a character according to this understanding in which it is accepted by more recent teachers." He says also that there is no necessary reason which would show that such a character exists or is imprinted. For everything that is attributed to the character can be explained just as well without the character as with it. For the sacrament itself works everything without the character. Also, the things which are attributed to the character are found in the Eucharist and in the other sacraments which do not imprint the character. And finally he concludes that all reasons which are adduced are opinions, not necessary conclusions. And in the end he says: "Everything that is said about the character is in great part arbitrary and supported with scant reason."

That reason also, which principally moved the scholastics to assert the character, namely, that Baptism is not to be repeated, Gabriel shows to be unnecessary, for he says: "The principal reason for the unrepeatability of the sacraments is not the imprinting of the character, but solely the divine institution. And it is less clear that there is a character than it is that Baptism cannot be repeated, for this was certain from the time of the institution of Baptism; the matter of the character, however, is not even clearly assured today." Indeed he says there is only one authority which may do something for the character, namely, that Innocent III seems to speak about imprinting of the character in *De baptismo et eius effectu,* ch. *Majores.* But Gabriel says that also this passage can be understood differently, since even there the gloss does not say any such thing about the character.

7 But let this one reference indeed be the first and only authority by which the opinion of the character, unknown both to Scripture and to the ancients, has been foisted on the church. From the author one can surely gather what kind of dogma it is. For he is that Innocent who published the *Decretals* that the correction of rulers in secular matters should be referred to the pope, that he should be emperor whom the pope commands to be crowned. This is he who caused another emperor to be created against Philip, namely Otho, whom he favored so much that he would give the pallium to no archbishop unless he agreed with the pope against the emperor. Thus he incited deadly wars in the empire. Later, however, he endeavored to drive also Otho himself out of the empire with the thunderbolt of excommunication. This is the pope who said: "Either the pope will take away the royal diadem of Philip, or Philip will take away the apostolic insignia of the pope," so that Ursperger exclaims with just sorrow: "You have, O Rome, what you have thirsted for; sing a song, because you have conquered the world through wickedness, not through religion." Let such a man, therefore, about 1,200 years after the birth of Christ, be the author of the new fabrication about the character, which was unknown to Scripture and to the ancient church.

Indeed, it is worth the trouble to add also this, how Gabriel replies to this statement which he saw might be raised in objection: "A theologian must not set up anything, the necessity of which is not apparent from faith." However, he says also: "Believe whatever is proved either from Scripture or by conclusion of the church, although it is not definitely obtained from Scripture, because the church cannot err in the things which belong to the faith." However, because the opinion of the character does not even have a sure and express conclusion of the church, Gabriel replies: "A theologian can assert something as probable which is consonant with Scripture and the conclusion of the church, and in no way contrary, although it cannot be deduced clearly and with necessity from the things which belong to the faith. Now it seems that in the case before us it is more in harmony with the conclusion of the church to assert the character than its opposite, and so the school of theologians in common holds." And finally he says: "Let him whom this solution does not please seek another."

8 Since these things are so, let the reader gather and estimate from this one canon how much credence and authority should be given to the

Tridentine assembly, which is sworn to the Roman pontiff, because they decree about a recent fabrication which was unknown both to Scripture and to antiquity, and which rests neither on authority nor on any reason, in no other way than one would about the most certain and immovable article of faith: "If anyone says that in three sacraments, namely, baptism, confirmation, and ordination, there is not imprinted on the soul a character, that is, a certain spiritual and indelible sign, on account of which they cannot be repeated, let him be anathema." I shall add nothing more. For since this one canon sufficiently shows how much and what kind of authority this council assumes for itself, the reader who has been warned will the more diligently consider and weigh this important matter in his own mind.

9 It is meet that the true church of Christ should be all the more unfavorable to this recent, doubtful, and uncertain opinion of the imprinting of the character because it weakens the foundation of a dogma whose certainty is altogether necessary for the comforting of consciences. For in the teaching that Baptism, conferred legitimately according to Christ's institution, is not to be repeated, and for what reasons it is not to be repeated, we are dealing with an important matter, namely, on what ground, what certainty, and what proof the comfort rests that the covenant of grace which God makes with us in Baptism is perpetual, that He wills to keep it even though we depart from it, if only we return to it in true penitence through faith.

10 This so great and so necessary thing they remove from the true and solid rock of its institution and build it on shifting sand; namely, that there is no more certain consolation than the one which they have invented, that a character is imprinted on the soul through Baptism. But we have already shown how recent, uncertain, and weak the opinion about the character is, by means of the words of the scholastics themselves. But perhaps they have departed from the firmest support of this consolation, which is found in Scripture, and substituted some other slippery and fabricated thing, because they imagine that for those who lapsed after Baptism the covenant of grace into which they had been received by Baptism is no longer useful and valid because it has been dissolved and broken but that one must take refuge to the second plank, namely, our contrition and satisfaction, in order that through it we may swim out of the sea of perdition to the harbor of salvation, as the decree concerning penance will show. But the true reasons why Baptism should not be repeated will have to be explained under the Canon IX, concerning Baptism. However, that which is peculiar to Baptism, namely, that it must not be repeated, they later transferred to confirmation and to their orders, and they chiefly contend for and make greater claims for the character of these than for Baptism itself. In the other sacraments they dispute about the imprinting of a certain adornment which is almost like the character, about which there is however as yet no agreement among themselves. But perhaps God allows them to fight so stubbornly to protect the opinion of the character in confirmation and in orders so that it may be manifest with whom that character is and may be found of which frequent mention is made in Rev. 13; 14; 15; 16; 19; and 20.

SECTION VIII
Concerning the Ministers of the Sacraments

CANON X

If anyone says that all Christians have power to administer the word and all the sacraments, let him be anathema.

Examination

1 The words which they condemn in this canon they have culled from Luther's booklet *De captivitate Babylonica*. But they have both mutilated the words and corrupted the meaning, in order that they may make Luther's doctrine hateful to the inexperienced, as if it were a disturber of all divine and human order in the church. But Luther never meant that any Christian whatever either could or should indiscriminately, without a legitimate call, arrogate to himself or usurp the ministry of the Word and the administration of the sacraments in the church. On the contrary, while the papalists were either snoring or disputing only with fire and sword, Luther showed from the Word of God against the various sects of Anabaptists that no one, even if he were the most learned, ought to usurp the ministry of the Word and of the sacraments in the church without a special and legitimate call. And he earnestly admonished the church that she should not permit those to exercise the ministry of the Word and of the sacraments who do not have proof of a legitimate call, because it is written: "How can men preach unless they are sent?" (Rom. 10:15) and "I did not send the prophets, yet they ran." (Jer. 23:21)

2 And since the writings of Luther loudly proclaim throughout the world that the teaching of Scripture concerning the legitimate call of the ministers of the Word and of the sacraments was explained by him, one could wonder why they wanted in this canon to condemn it, after they had mutilated and corrupted the words of Luther and had concealed his real teaching. However, it irks them that Luther in that dispute attacks the pride, or rather the tyranny, which in the papalist kingdom is arrogated both to the mitres of the bishops and the tonsures of the priests. For on account of the prevalent opinion about the anointing of the body, the tonsure, the vestments, etc., they despised the laymen as pigs and dogs compared with themselves; yes, under this cover they commanded, changed, added, etc., whatever they pleased in the Word and the sacraments, as if they had the authority and power. And indeed they placed also the *opus operatum,* that is, the integrity and efficacy of the sacraments, in part in the character which they imagined is imprinted in ordination, as we have noted above from Peter of La Palu.

Against these tyrannical opinions Luther taught from the Word of God that Christ has given and committed the keys, that is, the ministry of the Word and of the sacraments, to the whole church, not however in such a way that everyone might usurp and appropriate this ministry to himself by his own will and personal rashness, without a legitimate call, but that, after the immediate calling ceased, God sends ministers of the Word and of the sacraments through the call and choosing of the church, if it is done according to the command of His Word, so that the highest power of the Word and of the sacraments is with God; then, that the ministry belongs to the church, so that God calls, chooses, and sends ministers through it. Thirdly, then, it is with those who are legitimately chosen and called by God through the church, therefore with the ministers to whom the use or administration of the ministry of the Word and the sacraments has been committed.

3 With this distinction, which is true and plain, Luther meant to restrain the arrogance of the priests who were puffed up by the opinion that they alone possessed all power with respect to the Word and sacraments, so that the sacraments were valid on account of the imprinting on them of some kind of character from ordination. And lest the rest of the church should dare to say by so much as a silent sigh, "What are you doing?" they pretended that the rest of the church had no power whatever in matters of the Word and the sacraments. That Luther touched this sore spot and applied the knife from the Word of God, that is truly what gives the papalists a burning pain even today, after so many years, and it sits badly. This is also the reason why they wanted to quote and condemn certain mutilated and falsified words from that disputation of Luther's in this canon.

4 Covertly, however, and as if they were after something else, they seek to establish the rule that no one, even though he has been legitimately elected and called by the church according to the precept of the Word of God, possesses any power in the administration of the Word and the sacraments unless he has been anointed and shaved by some bishop, and that sacraments administered by such a person are not true and efficacious. Let the reader understand these snares which are hidden in this canon.

5 So far indeed as the meaning of this tenth canon as the words read is concerned, I answer simply and clearly: If there are any who think that it is permitted to any and every Christian to usurp the power and to exercise the ministry of the Word and the sacraments in the church indiscriminately, without a special and legitimate call, they are rightly and deservedly condemned. For they fight against the divine rule: "How can men preach unless they are sent?" Likewise: "I did not send them, yet they ran." Likewise, against the rule of Paul: "All things should be done decently and in order in the church." However, the church has always made an exception in a case of necessity, as Jerome testifies against the Luciferians, and Augustine to Fortunatus. But what constitutes a legitimate and divine call to the ministry of the church will have to be explained later under the topic of holy orders.

SECTION IX

Concerning the Intention

If anyone says that there is not required in ministers, when they effect and confer the sacraments, at least the intention of doing what the Church does, let him be anathema.

Examination

1 The examination of this canon will clearly show that the papalists, assembled at the Council of Trent, had as their purpose not that they might correct according to the norm of the Word of God anything in the more recent inventions of the scholastics which had, after the better times of the fathers, crept into the church without the authority of Scripture and without the witness of antiquity but that all opinions which have been urged heretofore in the paplist kingdom, no matter what they are and whom they have as their authors, even if they have no appropriate testimonies either from Scripture or from antiquity, should simply be retained and confirmed. And that this might be done the more readily, they fight not with arguments and reasons but with naked anathemas. It is certainly of great concern to them that not even the appearance of change in the present form of the papalist kingdom be admitted, which would be judged to happen if they applied any correction from the rule of Scripture to the customary opinions of the scholastics. This therefore they avoid so carefully that in this canon, as also in most others, they wanted to repeat and retain the very terms of the scholastics. And unless one agrees to the naked assertion, without proofs from Scripture and testimonies from antiquity, they at once let loose the foolish clatter of their anathemas.

2 What I have said is very evident in this eleventh canon. For the dogma that for the genuineness of the sacrament there is necessary an intention on the part of the minister which looks not only to the act of conferring the sacraments according to the form of the institution but which looks also to the aim of the sacrament, namely, that in his intention the minister wills that that should happen on account of which the sacrament was instituted—that dogma, I say, has no foundation in Scripture, yes, it conflicts with the genuineness of the sacraments, which as Scripture teaches does not rest on the morals, faith, or intention of the minister but on the institution of God, if its form is preserved. Also the entire true and purer antiquity ignores that dangerous, yes, pernicious opinion of Alexander of Hales that a sacrament is not true and efficacious if the minister maliciously withholds his inner intention although in the act or administration he preserves the form of the institution.

3 But I hold that it will be agreeable and profitable if we consider how that question was debated by the ancients, and how gradually a tendency developed, until in the course of time the dogma of the papalists about the necessity of the intention of the minister was developed from it.

Augustine discusses these questions in *De baptismo*, Bk. 7, ch. 53:

1. If someone receives Baptism deceitfully, that is, with an insincere mind, in the church;

2. If someone receives it in a play with faith;

3. If someone receives Baptism from a person who is himself not baptized;

4. If the one who bestows Baptism in the church deals deceitfully.

About these questions Augustine first discusses both sides, for he says: "So far as the men themselves are concerned, there is a great difference between the one who receives Baptism in faith from an actor and the one who with an insincere mind receives Baptism in the church. But this has no bearing on the integrity of the sacrament itself. For if it has no bearing on the integrity of the sacrament in the catholic church whether men do it deceitfully or honestly, when in fact both do the same thing, I do not see how it can make a difference outside of the church when he who receives it is not cloaked in a false show but is changed by religion. Regardless whether the honest ones among whom it is performed can do more to confirm the sacrament than the deceitful ones by whom and among whom it is performed can do to frustrate it, yet, when it is afterward made known, no one repeats it. But for us it is safe that we do not proceed with some rash statement into these matters which has not originated in a catholic regional council, nor been finalized in a plenary council," etc. And soon he adds: "Nevertheless, if by chance someone should place me in a council where the question about such matters is discussed, and if none had preceded me whose opinions I would prefer to follow, and he should urge me that I should say what I myself thought, if I felt the same way as I felt when I dictated this, I would not doubt at all that those have Baptism who had anywhere and by any persons received it, consecrated with the words of the Gospel, without hypocrisy, and with some degree of faith," etc. Likewise: "Disregarding the pronouncements of our elders, I have no doubt that also those have Baptism who although they receive it deceitfully nevertheless receive it in the church, or where the church is thought to be by those in whose fellowship it is received, of whom it has been said: 'They went out from us.' However, if there were no such society of believers, and he who receives Baptism did not so believe, but all were done in fun and play and as a joke, then, on the question of whether a Baptism which is so given should be approved, I would judge that one would have to ask in prayer for a divine judgment through an oracle of some revelation. Yet I would humbly wait for those who would speak their mind after me, in case they should advance something that has already been investigated and learned." Thus writes Augustine in his usual truly Christian modesty; for the time being, however, he wants to have the genuineness and integrity of the sacraments measured by the truth and certainty of the institution, not by any quality or intention of men, either of those who give or of those who receive them, so that he does not even dare to make a pronouncement concerning a feigned or facetious action.

4 Later Lombard indicates that in his time the question concerning baptisms performed in sport or as a joke, as when some are immersed in a bath or in a river in the name of the Trinity, was discussed in such a way that it seemed to the wise to be no Baptism, because it was done without the intention of baptizing. And he adds: "For both in this and in the other sacraments, as the form must be preserved, so also the intention to celebrate it must be present." However Lombard understands the intention of the act itself of baptizing, not of the aim and effect of Baptism. For he quickly adds the statement of Augustine: "Let it not disturb you that some bring infants to Baptism not in the faith that they should be regenerated by the Spirit to eternal life but thinking that by this remedy they receive temporal health; for the infants will not fail to receive regeneration because they are not presented by them with this intention." Indeed, this statement of Lombard concerning the intention of celebrating the action of Baptism does not aim at anything else than that the institution should be preserved, in order that it may be a true sacrament. For the institution of Baptism does not aim at this, that it should be some common washing, or one which intentionally is nothing more than a game to excite laughter, or a farcical pantomime, or a profanation of the institution with a recitation of the words; but it requires that a specific action be performed, and indeed that action which Christ instituted. And this suffices for the preservation of the institution. However, what the one

who administers Baptism feels in his heart concerning this action, that does not belong to the genuineness or the integrity of Baptism, neither did Lombard aim at this. Well known is also the judgment of the bishops on the deed of Athanasius, who, as a boy, playing on the beach of the sea, pretended that he was a bishop and after the manner of a bishop wetted the playing lads in the name of the Trinity. This story Sozomen tells in Bk. 2, ch. 17, and Rufinus in [his continuation of] Eusebius, Bk. 10, ch. 14.

5 That opinion remained also after the times of Lombard. For Innocent (as Angelus maintains in his *Summa*) thought that for the genuineness or integrity of Baptism it is not necessarily required that the minister should know, think, or believe correctly concerning the substance or the effect of Baptism, yes, even if he believes the contrary and holds Baptism to be a fraud, that it is nevertheless a true Baptism if only he baptizes according to the institution; likewise, that it is not required as necessary for the genuineness of Baptism that he who baptizes either knows what the church is or that he intends to do what the church does, yes, even if he had the opposite in mind, that is, that he would not do what the church does—if only he does it, that is, if he preserves the form of the institution. He therefore argues that this only is required, that the baptizing minister intends, or at least that it appears that he intends or undertakes, not only to wash but to baptize.

6 However, not satisfied with this opinion, the scholastics went far beyond it in this debate. For they taught that for the genuineness of Baptism there is required not only the form of the institution but also the intention of the minister, and this not only with respect to the act of baptizing as its object but also with respect to the effect of Baptism, which is its end and aim. Therefore they set down three points: the act of baptizing, the words, and the intention; and they are of the opinion that these three things are required simultaneously for the genuineness or integrity of a Baptism, so that neither suffices without the other. But because they notice that in this way Baptism is rendered altogether doubtful and uncertain, they have thought out various distinctions by which they might overcome these inconveniences, namely, that one is a special intention which aims at and intends that that should happen for which Baptism was instituted; that the other is general, which aims at and intends that that should happen which the church intends in Baptism, even though the person who baptizes is either ignorant of it or does not believe it. And this again they divide into actual, habitual, and virtual intention. Thus they say that for a true Baptism there is required the general and virtual intention of the minister, with respect to the effect of

Baptism, to do that which the church does and believes. But if the minister within himself did not intend what the church intends, but what heresy intends, it would not be a true Baptism.

7 However, they themselves confess that a conscience wrestling with doubt is not consoled by these various distinctions. For since the inner intention of another cannot be known to me, if it is nevertheless necessary for the genuineness of Baptism, it will be necessary for the baptized person always to remain doubtful whether he is baptized, and so he can never be certain of his salvation. Alexander of Hales, however, replies: "Baptizing must be entrusted to a minister who is not suspect, but approved in faith, and so a strong assurance can be held, which suffices for the salvation of an adult who has the proper intention. For if by chance the minister were to withhold his inward intention, it would, indeed, not be a true sacrament, yet the adult would be saved through the baptism of the Spirit, i.e., by his penitence and charity without Baptism." However, if in the baptism of an infant the minister were to withhold his intention, and thus the child were not truly baptized, they ask whether, if the child were to die before it had attained the use of reason, it would be damned. Alexander and Thomas reply that in that case it could be piously supposed, yet without prejudice, that the Great High Priest will supply what is lacking to the sacrament. And Gabriel adds: "This is to be noted well, because it is very comforting." But why do they not hold fast the true grounds for consolation, namely, that the genuineness of the sacraments is to be determined not from the uncertain intention of the minister but from the truth and certainty of the divine institution? Yet they add that if the Great High Priest does not supply it, divine justice cannot be accused even if it does not remit sins to the infant, baptized indeed according to the institution of Christ but without the intention of the minister.

8 These are about all the things which are debated among the scholastics about the intention in the administration of the sacraments, which, lest they seem to have been imagined by us, I wanted to describe with their own words from Gabriel, that the readers, having been informed, may know and consider what the things are which are treated in these Tridentine decrees and canons, lest someone think there was no true and weighty cause why we would not and could not agree with them, and ought not if we would preserve faith and a good conscience. Now although it is certain from this account what the teaching of Scripture is with respect to this question, what the position of the ancient church, what the modest suspension of judgment of Augustine, what the disputations of the Middle Ages, and what are the opinions of more recent teachers, which are indeed most dangerous to faith and the assurance of salvation, the assembly of Trent comes together to give a specimen of that correction which has been promised under the name of a council for many years and has been awaited by the Christian world.

9 But what, I ask, does it decree about those recent opinions of the scholastics? Is such an intention of the minister as they teach necessary for the genuineness of the sacrament? Canon XI says: "If anyone says that there is not required in ministers, when they effect and confer the sacraments, at least the intention of doing what the Church does, let him be anathema." You hear that the very words of the scholastics are repeated and that their opinions are confirmed not with arguments but with anathemas. Therefore they heed neither Scripture nor antiquity; nor do they propose to correct, according to the norm of Scripture and in conformity with antiquity, the opinions which have without the authority of Scripture and without true testimonies of antiquity been brought into the church through the more recent disputations of the scholastics; but they are concerned only that all things which somehow have become customary and received in the papalist kingdom, no matter what they are and where they have originated, should be retained and established without even the least suspicion of emendation and correction.

10 Nor should the reason be passed over why they so diligently and earnestly defend that opinion about the intention, so that something which antiquity did not know, concerning which Augustine held any assertion in abeyance, is now thrust upon us to be believed without proofs, solely by the threat of the anathema, as if it were the most certain article of faith. But the dogma concerning doubt is the Helen in this case. For Sess. VI, ch. 9, they decreed that no one's sins are remitted who rests in the confidence and assurance of the remission of sins according to the promise. For they say no one can know with the certainty of faith which could not be in error that he has obtained the grace of God. For this dogma the Jesuits give this reason: Because the promise does not speak of me or of you, but is general, and faith is faith in the general pronouncements. Now, however, in the performing of the sacraments the promise of grace is not set forth in general but is applied to the individuals who use the sacraments in faith. And indeed they were instituted to the end that they should seal, confirm, and make certain the application to the individual persons.

But because they see that the true and salutary use of the sacraments conflicts directly and squarely with the dogma of doubt, they contrive various secret devices in order that, as much as lies in them, they may weaken, undermine, and overturn the solid, sure, and firm consolation which is set before the believers in the use of the sacraments. And to this end also this canon tends. For they notice that if the genuineness and efficacy of the sacraments is taught to depend on the divine institution, faith has in the use of the sacraments a safe harbor, a firm anchor, and an unshakable rock of comfort and assurance. In order to weaken, crack, and overturn these, they invent the fiction that for the genuineness of the sacraments there is required besides the divine institution also the intention of the minister, so that even if the sacraments are administered with a legitimate ceremony, according to the institution of Christ, the sacraments are nevertheless not true or efficacious if the minister either does not add his inner intention or withholds it. But since the thinking of another and his inner intention can never be known and perceived with certainty by me, it follows from this that whatever is set before faith in the sacraments for comfort is and remains in suspense, doubtful, and uncertain.

11 Let the reader diligently weigh this design of the papalists in this eleventh canon. For it is not a contention about trifles when men dispute about the intention, but they are treating of a great matter—of the comfort which is necessary for consciences, namely, whether faith should seek and place the genuineness and efficacy of the sacraments in the truth of God, who instituted them, and in the power of God, who promises and who works in the action of the sacraments in accord with His promise, or whether that divine truth and power should be made to depend on the thinking, faith, and intention of the human minister. Scripture certainly teaches that in order that the administration of the sacraments may be according to the divine institution, it has been committed to ministers as the instrumental cause, but that the power and working which makes the sacrament true and efficacious is the action and gift of God alone, for the Father saves through the washing of regeneration (Titus 3:5). Christ cleanses and sanctifies the church by the washing of water with the Word (Eph. 5:26). Baptism is the washing of regeneration and renewing, not of the minister but of the Holy Spirit (Titus 3:5). And as Paul teaches and affirms (Phil. 1:15-18), when the word of the Gospel is proclaimed as it has been divinely revealed, it is true and the power of God for salvation to everyone who believes, even if he who proclaims it either does not have or withholds the intention, that is (as Paul says), if he preaches not out of goodwill, not with a pure and sincere heart, nor out of love, but from envy, from contention, and by way of pretext. The same should certainly hold true also in the sacrament, which is the visible Word, that faith may hold the sacrament to be true and to have true efficacy when it is administered according to the institution, no matter what the minister either thinks or believes or intends, if only he preserves the institution of Christ in the administration. For as when the purity of Gospel preaching itself is vitiated and corrupted it is no longer the Gospel nor the power of God for salvation to him who believes, so when in the action or administration of the sacraments the institution itself is changed, mutilated, or corrupted, it is certain that then it is not a true sacrament. For it is the word of institution, coming to the element, which makes a sacrament. This opinion is simple, true, and certain, offering to consciences useful, firm, and necessary comfort which we shall not allow to be taken away from us, and it serves the glory of God that His truth should not be measured by the intention of a human minister, which can neither be known to us nor certain, and that faith should not depend on the human minister but should rest on the truth and power of God, who instituted the sacrament and gave the promise.

12 These two questions are, however, distinct and very different:

1. What is required and necessary for the genuineness and integrity of a sacrament?

2. What is required of a minister that, as far as his person is concerned, he may be faithful and good; with what kind of spirit, with what faith, intention, and devotion ought he to treat the sacraments lest, as St. Paul says, after preaching and ministering to others he himself should be disqualified? For that a minister who performs the sacraments with a profane, frivolous, negligent, and irreverent mind sins, is not doubtful.

However, these defects of the minister, if he administers the sacraments according to the institution of Christ, are not able to make the truth of God invalid. For neither the quality nor the faith nor the devotion of the minister belong to the essence and genuineness of the sacrament. This distinction Lombard illustrates, Bk. 4, dist. 5, with very fine statements of Augustine. "I say," declares Augustine, "and we all say, that those should be righteous by whom one is baptized, that the ministers of so great a Judge should be righteous. Let the ministers be righteous if they will; but if those who sit on the seat of Moses are not willing to be righteous, my Master Christ makes me secure, of whom the Holy Spirit says: 'This is He who baptizes.' " Likewise: "Those whom Judas baptized, Christ baptized. If therefore someone has baptized who is a drunkard, murderer, adulterer, if it was Christ's baptism, it was Christ who baptized. I do not fear the adulterer, nor the drunkard, nor the murderer, because I give attention to the dove through which it is said to me: 'This is He who baptizes.' " Likewise: "Baptism is such as He is in whose power it is given, not such as he is through whose ministry it is given." And in another place: "Therefore not only the good but also the evil have the ministry of baptizing, but neither of these has the power of Baptism. For the ministry Christ gave to His servants, but the power He retained for Himself." And he adds the reason why He did not give this power to the servants, namely, "lest a servant should place his hope in a servant."

Lombard also quotes from Isidore: "Not the man who baptizes, but the Spirit of God ministers the grace of Baptism, even if he who baptizes is a pagan."

CANON XII

If anyone says that a minister who is in mortal sin, though he observes all the essentials which belong to the effecting or conferring of a sacrament, does not effect or confer the sacrament, let him be anathema.

Concerning the statement of this canon there is no controversy between us. For this our men have defended strenuously on the basis of Scripture against the Anabaptists, who renewed the error of the Donatists, and they have solidly refuted the ravings of the Donatists. Therefore I shall add nothing here. For we have undertaken chiefly an examination of those things in the decrees of this council which are in controversy.

SECTION X

Concerning the Rites in the Administration of the Sacraments

CANON XIII

If anyone says that the received and approved rites of the Catholic Church, customarily used in the solemn administration of the sacraments, can without sin be either despised or omitted at their pleasure by the ministers, or be changed into other new ones by any pastor of the churches, let him be anathema.

Examination

1 To begin with, let the reader observe how cunningly this canon is worded. For they call all ceremonies which have been customarily employed under the papacy in the administration of the sacraments "received and approved rites of the Catholic Church," although they are not ignorant of the fact that very many of them were from the time of the apostles neither always nor everywhere in all churches received and customarily used. They know also that many of the oldest rites were abolished by later generations and changed into new ones. And although they know what liberty the Word of God grants to the church in rites of this kind, they cunningly add that this must not be done at the pleasure of every minister of the churches. And indeed, for the sake of order and decorum it should not be permitted to everyone willfully, without the decision and consent of the church, just because he desires it, either to omit or change anything even in external and indifferent things. But what this canon gives birth to is something entirely different, namely, that the pope alone, with his mitred, filleted, and horned crowd, can according to his pleasure omit ancient and indeed apostolic rites and change them into new ones, and that the church is then so bound by them that a minister, even if he lawfully observes the form of the divine institution, nevertheless sins grievously and mortally if he omits something of the papalist rites. But, on the contrary, when a minister observes only the papalist rites, even if he mutilates the Lord's Supper in one of its parts and changes the entire action of the sacrament into the different genus of a sacrifice, he does not sin at all but is thought to offer to God a most acceptable worship. And finally the sum of it is that in the administration of the sacraments more importance is attached to the ceremonies invented by and received from men than to the ceremonies instituted and commanded by the voice of the Son of God Himself, a thing which other facts besides the mutilation of the Lord's Supper proclaim. It is this which this 13th canon cunningly contrives, that that part of its Christian liberty may be taken away from the church once and for all; that, unless it seems right to the papal prelates in rites of this kind, not even the least thing dare either be omitted or changed, even if one sees from the Word of God that it either does not serve edification or that it cannot be observed without impiety.

2 But because they are not so hard of hearing that there have not come to their ears the most just complaints of almost the entire world concerning the superstition and abuse of certain ceremonies, concerning the multitude of burdensome things that should be moderated or corrected, and especially concerning the ungodly opinions which from human ordinances and long custom, particularly in these last times, have crept into the administration of the sacraments, they judged in the council that some mention of this matter should be made. But do they show any hope of moderation, of mitigation, and of emendation in those papalist rites and the superstitious opinions connected with them? Far from it! Instead they pronounce their detestable anathema unless a person believes that all those rites, with the addition of those opinions, are rites of that catholic church which the Nicene Creed defines as being apostolic. And they declare it to be a sin if even the least particle in those rites is omitted or changed. But to themselves alone they reserve full power in such matters because they have used it frequently in times past, to omit, add to, and change them.

3 But that we may come to the matter itself and that those things which in general belong to the debate concerning the rites in the administration of the sacraments may be explained simply and in orderly fashion, I shall note down certain things concerning the chief points: which rites have a command and testimony in the Word of God, which were afterwards added by the fathers and why they were added, how they began to degenerate from their first origin, and what is the rule of Christian liberty in the use of such rites in the church.

4 When therefore the question is asked whether the administration of the sacraments ought to be made without any certain and particular external rites, the answer is clear and obvious. For the very name and definition of a sacrament embraces the presence of some visible and external element to which the Word must come and includes this, that the whole action is performed and administered in a certain way and with a specific divinely instituted ceremony. How this ought to be done has been stated in Scripture and traced beforehand for the church in a sure and clear word of God, namely, that those signs and those words should be used which God Himself instituted and prescribed at the institution of each sacrament and that they should be performed and used as the institution ordains and directs. These rites are essential and necessary in the administration of the sacraments, for they carry out the institution. Furthermore, it is clear from Scripture that the apostolic church in the administration of the sacraments carefully observed this, that they should not be mute spectacles but that the doctrine concerning the essence, use, and efficacy of the sacraments should faithfully be set forth and explained to those present and about to receive the sacraments, from the Word of God and in a language to which they were accustomed and which was known to them, and that those who were about to use the sacraments, having been rightly instructed, should be diligently admonished concerning their lawful and salutary reception. The Acts of the Apostles and Paul (1 Cor. 11:23 ff.) describe the administration of Baptism and of the Lord's Supper on the basis of their institution: "Preach the Gospel!" Likewise: "Whoever believes." And: "Do this in remembrance of Me"; "You proclaim the Lord's death"; "Let a man examine himself," etc. That also prayers were used, and thanksgivings taken from the institution of the sacrament itself, Scripture clearly testifies. For the institution testifies that Christ gave thanks and that He commanded the church to do it: "Do this." And Paul says: "You proclaim the Lord's death." Likewise (Acts 22:16): "Be baptized and wash away your sins, calling on the name of Jesus."

Scripture also shows the sources from which the explanations, exhortations, prayers, and giving of thanks should be taken, namely, from the institution and from the teaching concerning the sacraments as it is handed down in the Word of God. It does not, however, prescribe a certain form in set words but leaves this free according to the circumstances for edification, so long as the foundation is preserved. These are the things which are chiefly to be observed and required in the administration of the sacraments, because they are prescribed in the institution and have the testimony and example of Scripture, that all may be done decently, in order, and for edification.

5 But let it be considered in this place what unjust demands the papalists make. For they fight for their human rites in the administration of the sacraments in such a way that they allow not even the omission of one of their ceremonies without sin and without danger of the anathema.

However, with respect to those things which are divinely commanded in the administration of the sacraments and have the testimony and example of Scripture they are by no means so diligent; on the contrary, these rigid exactors in the matter of human rites permit themselves freedom in those things which have the command and testimony of Scripture, to omit, add, change, etc., whenever they please.

Now the institution speaks of the use of the cup, and Paul adds: "Do this until He comes." The papalists, however, arbitrarily take away the cup from the administration of the Lord's Supper, and they both boast in words and now show by their action that they can give it back when they please and to whom they please. In their canon they drop these words from the words of institution: "Given for you." But, on the other hand, they add certain other things and insert them in the institution itself, as "with eyes raised to heaven," likewise, "the mystery of faith," etc. And Bonaventura, Bk. 4, dist. 8, quest. 2, asks which one should be followed when the canon differs from the evangelists or from Paul, namely, "This is the cup of My blood." He answers that the evangelists and Paul merely relate the history but that the form of consecration must be taken from the Roman Church and that therefore the words of the canon should be followed and used rather than those of the evangelists or of Paul. And these are the people who not only cry out but quickly brandish their anathemas if in their own rites even the smallest thing is omitted or changed.

It is well known and manifest that in the kingdom of the pope in the administration of the sacraments the admonitions and exhortations concerning the true and salutary use of the sacraments are either clearly neglected or are so treated in a language that is foreign, unknown to the people, that the people cannot be edified by them. Many prayers are used which are not in agreement with the institution and doctrine of the sacraments; and if there is anything good in them, solicitous care is taken that it is neither heard by the people nor understood by them. For to this end they instituted, besides the foreign language, the secret mumbling of the canon, lest by chance the people could say "Amen" to the prayers and thanksgivings (1 Cor. 14:16). These things must be said in opposition to those things which they not only plausibly preach but terribly thunder by means of their anathemas with respect to the observation of and conformity to human rites in the administration of the sacraments. For they truly strain out a gnat and swallow a camel (Matt. 23:24). For they "leave the commandment of God and hold fast the tradition of men" (Mark 7:8). Indeed, for the sake of their traditions they are not afraid to transgress the commandment of God. (Matt. 15:3)

If a legitimate reformation of the rites in the administration of the sacraments were sought according to the rule of Scripture for the edification of the church, it would have to regard chiefly those things which were prescribed by God Himself in the institution of the sacraments and which have the testimony and the example of Scripture—if anything foreign were found intermingled with them, it would be cut out; if anything had been either omitted or changed, it would be restored. This would be a true, godly, solid, and salutary reformation. However, this festering sore on the papalist body they do not even touch in this canon, yes, if any of these things has been received by long misuse, they command that it be considered an approved rite of the catholic church and forbid under threat of the anathema that anything be changed.

6 The following are the things which have the testimony and example of Scripture in the administration of the sacraments. Also after the time of the apostles, in the primitive church, there remained for a time the evangelical and apostolic simplicity that in the administration of the sacraments only those ceremonies were employed which have the command and example of Scripture. Later, however, little by little certain other things began to be added to these, at first with no evil or wicked intent, namely, that by the external rites as they met the senses of the faithful, and particularly of the more ignorant in the church, the grandeur of the sacraments might be the more commended and protected against contempt and that the power, effect, and use of the sacraments might through that action be explained more brilliantly and set forth before their eyes. Also in these added ceremonies consideration was given to what seemed to serve the preservation of order and decorum in the assemblies where the celebration of the sacraments was to be observed.

These additions were of two kinds, for they consisted either of words, or of ceremonies and gestures. I say that they consisted of words, such as exhortations, prayers, thanksgivings, readings from Scripture concerning the sacraments, the confession of faith, interrogations, and certain formulated words by which the doctrine concerning the use and efficacy either of Baptism or of the Lord's Supper is explained and as it were set before the eyes, as the exorcism, renunciation, etc. But as they administered the sacraments, they were not content only by words to set forth instruction in the doctrine concerning the worth of each sacrament and concerning its use and efficacy; but that this instruction might be more lastingly impressed on the senses and on the memory, and that it might move the spirit more strongly, they began to add to those words certain ceremonies and gestures. And indeed what once was set forth in words and instruction, they began afterward to change for the worse into many symbolic acts. So, for instance, at one time they taught in words that Baptism is spiritual enlightenment; for this there later came the great Easter candle. Yet in the beginning these ceremonies were very few in number, but later they gradually began to accumulate, so that finally those ceremonies almost turned into a theatrical production. And although this plan of the ancients is certainly not to be condemned outright, yet the masters and exacters of ceremonies exalt it far too rigidly and grandly, as if without them neither the genuineness nor the worth nor the efficacy of the sacraments would be there.

7 Because now all ceremonies, also those which are not the most ancient, are laid upon consciences as necessary under threat of the anathema, although one clearly sees into what sad misuse very many such things have degenerated, many things must be very diligently considered in this dispute about the ceremonies which are reported to have been instituted and used by the ancients in the administration of the sacraments. For, first of all, these ceremonies have no institution and command of God; therefore they should be placed in a far different and lower place than the ceremonies prescribed in the divine institution itself. In the second place, since the Son of God Himself instituted the sacraments in such a way that He commanded them to be administered with certain ceremonies instituted by Himself, it is a very important question whether men may be permitted to add other, and indeed many and various, ceremonies from any consideration whatsoever, as if those ceremonies which were divinely instituted in the administration of the sacraments were either not suitable enough or not sufficient.

Certainly, God himself ordained and prescribed in His Word those ceremonies in which He willed that the essence and administration of each sacrament may be found. And as nothing dare be taken away from the divine institution, so also nothing ought to be added. But when it is alleged that by those rites, added by men, many things are piously and usefully signified, admonished, and taught, one can reply to this that special figures belong to the Old Testament but what Christ wanted pointed out and taught in the New Testament He wanted transmitted and set forth not by means of shadows but through the light of the Word. And we have a promise of the efficacy of the Word, not however of figures invented by men. But those ceremonies which He wanted added to the Word, these He Himself instituted.

In the third place, those ceremonies which are instituted by men are judged to add more beauty to the administration of the sacraments and to commend their worth more than the ceremonies prescribed by God Himself in the institution of the sacraments. Thus the simplicity of the divine institution is thought not to possess enough beauty, nor to correspond to the worth of the sacraments. This idea, sprung from these added ceremonies, is ungodly and needs to be reproved. For we ought to estimate the beauty and dignity of the sacraments on the basis of the Word of God. It is indeed useful that in the administration of the sacraments there should be a distinction between divine actions, whose beauty and dignity is found in the Word, and the theatrical processions of the world which by their splendor commend themselves to the senses. For on this account the Son of God instituted so few and such simple ceremonies in the New Testament.

In the fourth place, the multitude, splendor, and pomp of these human rites overwhelms and obscures the ceremonies that are divinely prescribed and commanded in the administration of the sacraments. For it occupies the senses and the minds to such an extent that either no or only very little attention is given to those things which have the institution and command of God.

If the fifth place, they did not permit those rites, added little by little, to be signs impressively calling to mind the doctrine, but they attributed to each of them some special efficacy and work, without the Word and promise of God; yes, they began to divide and distribute among the ceremonies added by men even the efficacy and work of Baptism, so that exceedingly little was left to the action of Baptism itself, which has the divine institution and promise. Among the most ancient and purer writers we indeed read that those rites signify and teach something about the doctrine of the sacraments that is found in the Word of God. Indeed, it was the Montanists who first began to ascribe to them spiritual efficacy and effect, as one can see in Tertullian and Cyprian. And although these opinions were rejected in the true church at that time, yet their seeds remained in the disputes of later generations. For how often it occurs among the ancients that the unclean spirit is driven out of the persons that are to be baptized through exorcism and blowing upon them so that they may be free from the captivity of Satan before they receive Baptism, likewise that the Spirit is first given through the imposition of the hand of the bishop and through the anointing after Baptism! But if those things are collected which later generations began to attribute to their several rites, not significatively but effectively, either nothing or certainly exceedingly little will remain for the action of Baptism itself, which has the divine institution and promise. What sort of thing this is may be estimated from the consecretions, or rather the execrations, of the ointment, the salt, the wax, etc. These things must surely of necessity be censured when there is debate about ancient ceremonies.

In the sixth place, the opinion of the common people with respect to the integrity, genuineness, and efficacy of the sacraments makes the ceremonies invented by men almost as necessary as those which were instituted and commanded by God Himself. To this opinion Cyprian at one time held. And the Roman bishop Cornelius judged that Baptism, although it was administered according to the institution of Christ, yet did not have true efficacy in Novatus, because on account of his illness the other rites usually employed before and after the act of Baptism itself were lacking to him. And though this opinion was later corrected, as Lombard relates, nevertheless it clung and still clings in the minds of many. However, the men of Trent, where they impose the observance of these rites on the consciences under the threat of the anathema, do not make mention of this with so much as one word.

In the seventh place, the observance of these rites was free in the church; neither were such rites similar and the same in all churches; often also some of the most ancient rites were abrogated and omitted, such as the tasting beforehand of milk, honey, and wine, of which Tertullian and Jerome make mention. Some were changed and others newly instituted, as it was judged to serve the edification of the church. For the church used and preserved, not confused license but a godly and wholesome liberty in ecclesiastical ceremonies of this kind, instituted by men, so that by free discontinuance it abrogated, omitted, and changed also the most ancient such ceremonies when it was judged that by reason of circumstances they no longer were very important for piety, or when the cause for which they were first instituted and observed had either been removed or changed and they had thus ceased through the changed times to be useful for edification, or when they had turned aside from the purpose and use for which they had initially been instituted and had degenerated into abuse and superstition. But our opponents are delightful reformers who, when they have *ex professo* instituted a debate about ceremonies of this kind, do not with one word even make mention of these necessary reminders but only seek by their anathemas to burden the consciences, that at least the shadow of such rites, no matter what they are, which seem to have a certain pretext of custom in the Roman Church may be religiously observed, although now there is no true reason why they should be observed, no salutary purpose and use for edification; there are many such in the Canon of the Mass and in the ceremonies of Baptism, in the period of Easter and Pentecost.

In the eighth place, also this must be considered, that they mix into one chaotic mass the more recently instituted ceremonies (as the Easter candle) with the ancient ones, and these again they confuse with those that are divinely instituted. For they do not leave the added rites in the category of ceremonies which were instituted by churchmen for the sake of order, decorum, and edification, but they seek fabricated testimonies from certain spurious writings that those ceremonies were handed down by the apostles and consequently were instituted and commanded either by the Son of God or by the Holy Spirit, so that in the administration of the sacraments the authority of those ceremonies which somehow were handed down by men without the witness of Scripture is on a par with and their efficacy the equal of those which were instituted by God and which have the testimony and command of the Word of God.

8 These things I have briefly rehearsed that the reader, having been reminded, may consider how manifold and how tricky are the snares which the vagueness of this 13th canon envelopes and conceals under the venerable title of the antiquity of the catholic church. Because the hoariness of antiquity indeed seems worthy of honor and venerable also in rites of this kind, so that it may seem to be either willfulness or pride either to despise or to abrogate or to change those things which are reported to have been approved by the ancients, therefore they wanted to hurt our churches with hateful words when they say: "If anyone says that the ceremonies approved by the Catholic Church can either be despised, or arbitrarily omitted, or changed into new ones by any pastor of the churches . . ." But what the position of our churches is can easily be shown from the things we have noted down. For in the administration of the sacraments we distinguish among the ceremonies, and teach that a distinction must be made. For there are first of all certain rites which are commanded in the institution and thus are necessary and essential in the administration of the sacraments. We affirm that in these nothing is to be omitted, changed, or abrogated.

Second, there are certain things in the administration of the sacraments which have testimonies and examples in Scripture, for we read in Scripture what things the first apostolic church observed in the administration of the sacraments, e.g., explanations of the doctrine of the sacraments, exhortations, prayers, giving of thanks, etc. These things also we both observe and teach that they should be diligently observed—however, in such a way that they conform to the doctrine of the sacraments as it is handed down in Scripture, for the sacraments are not mute or idle shows, but they were instituted that they should both strengthen faith and set forth the promise of the Word more clearly.

Third, there are certain other rites which have neither the command nor the testimony of Scripture but were added by churchmen. And I judge that not even all of those should be rejected or condemned in general, but those which consist of words and interrogations that agree with the Scripture and usefully call to mind and explain something concerning the doctrine of the sacraments can be freely retained, as among us the exorcism, the renunciation, the confession of faith, etc., are retained in the administration of Baptism. However, in the things which consist of ceremonies or gestures, that liberty should be preserved which Scripture gives and which the true church has always used in human traditions of this kind, namely, that those things may be retained and used which have no admixture of ungodliness and superstition. Likewise such as have no idle games but serve either good order or decorum in the church, or can promote the edification of the people by useful and godly admonition. Finally, such as illustrate the things which belong to the essence of the sacraments but do not hide or obscure them nor transform them into an action that is plainly a different thing, as happens in the sacrifice of the Mass. However, in the case of those ecclesiastical ceremonies concerning which we teach that they may be retained, let that be observed which we have said above, namely, that these should be distinguished by a clear distinction from those which have either a command or a testimony of Scripture, lest they be made equal to them in any way, much less be preferred to them. Let no spiritual efficacy be attributed to these things without a divine promise, neither let the things which are peculiar to the sacraments be transferred to such ceremonies either in whole or in part. Nor should it be thought that such ceremonies belong to the integrity and genuineness of the sacraments, much less that they are necessary for this, but they are to be considered as indifferent rites which, if they cease to be useful for edification and if they degenerate from their salutary purpose and use into superstition and abuse, must either be corrected or changed or, after the example of the brazen serpent, be abrogated and wholly taken away. Those rites also which are retained should remain what in fact they are—indifferent ceremonies, in order that they may not become snares of consciences but be freely observed without any idea that they are necessary, so that, barring offense, they can be omitted or be changed or abrogated by the direction and consent of the church. For this should not be permitted privately to the whim of anyone. However, if this is done lawfully, it is useful to show freedom in the case of adiaphora of this kind, yet in such a way that all things are done orderly, decently, and for edification, according to the rule of Paul. Neither should churches be condemned on account of differences in rites of this kind or if, in omitting or changing them, they use their liberty according to the said rule of Paul.

9 These things are most true and also most fair with respect to ceremonies in the administration of the sacraments, for they are taken from the teaching of Scripture about indifferent things. But no matter how fair these conditions are, the papalists do not allow themselves to be satisfied; otherwise one could easily pass over and agree concerning the substance of the matter so far as ceremonies are concerned. Therefore the reader will be able to conclude from this what the papalists pursue, seek, and labor for in this 13th canon.

Second Topic

CONCERNING BAPTISM

*From the Decrees of the Seventh Session
of the Council of Trent, March 3, 1547*

SECTION I

Concerning the Baptism of John

CANON I

If anyone says that the baptism of John had the same power as the baptism of Christ, let him be anathema.

Examination

1 In all controversies the things which have a necessary use in the exercise of repentance, faith, and godliness must be distinguished from other disputes in which a difference of opinions or even some slight error of the mind does not bring about the loss of faith and salvation. Thus also with respect to the baptism of Christ, with which the church of the New Testament now baptizes, many things can profitably be said which have their necessary use: what it is, what is its power, how it is rightly dispensed and received, what is its use throughout the entire life of the baptized person, etc. The dispute concerning the baptism of John is not equally necessary, for no one is now baptized nor has been baptized with the baptism of John; but the question is only about the ceremony of that time, now long past, and practiced very briefly even then. For when John was cast into prison his baptism ceased. But that he was held in prison for more than a whole year the sequence of events in the Gospel clearly indicates. Therefore the baptism of John lasted less than one and a half years. Therefore those who argue slightly differently than some of the ancients about this question, when they had compared the statements of Scripture, should not at once be destroyed with the anathema if their argument does not militate against the truth of the doctrine of repentance, faith, and godliness.

2 The disputes of the ancients about the baptism of John are certainly not unknown to us; but they neither agree altogether among themselves nor do they condemn those who think differently.

Cyprian ascribed only an exterior washing to the baptism of John. And Lombard says: "There was only John's visible, outward act of washing, not the invisible grace of the power of God working internally. Likewise it is called the baptism of John, that is, of a man, because nothing was done there which a man might not do." This Gabriel explains thus from the understanding of the scholastics: "In the baptism of John nothing was done except what John did altogether, namely, the exterior washing of the body, so that it conferred neither repentance nor the remission of sins." And in the gloss *De consecratione,* dist. 4, ch. *Aliud est; Et non regenerabantur,* he says that God through the baptism of John did not work either repentance or the remission of sins but that it is called the baptism of repentance because he preached repentance, but that it must not be called a baptism for the remission of sins because John neither gave nor taught that. These are Gabriel's words, who mangles the text of Mark thus: "John was baptizing and preaching Baptism, namely, not his own but the future one of Christ, which would be a baptism of repentance and of the remission of sins." Chrysostom, however, weighing the words of John (Matt. 3:11), "I baptize you with water for repentance," says: "The baptism of John had nothing more than that it should lead people to repentance, for he did not say: 'In the water of remission, but of repentance.' " And later he says: "The baptism of John did not have the remission of sins, for that was the gift of that baptism which Christ instituted." Thus Chrysostom.

Augustine indeed also repeatedly speaks this way, but when he weighs more diligently what John (Mark 1:4 and Luke 3:3) preached concerning his baptism, that it was "a baptism of repentance for the remission of sins," he does not dare simply to take away the remission of sins from the baptism of John. And yet he does not simply ascribe it to it. But when it seemed to him that he could not escape from the argument of the Donatists (who attempted to defend their rebaptism by means of the act of Paul in Acts 19:1–5) in any other way, he finally embraced this opinion which lies in between. For he says, *Contra Donatistas,* Bk. 5, ch. 10: "I believe that John baptized in such a way with the water of repentance for the remission of sins that the sins of those who were baptized by him were remitted to them in hope, but that this would happen in fact in the baptism of the Lord, as the resurrection which is expected in the end has taken place in us in hope because He has 'raised us up with Him and made us sit with Him in the heavenly places.' " Likewise: "We have been saved in hope. For also John himself, when he says: 'I baptize you with the water of repentance for the remission of sins,' seeing the Lord, says: 'Behold, the Lamb of God, who takes away the sin of the world!' " And yet Augustine does not set forth this opinion of his as a necessary dogma, nor does he condemn anyone if he thinks differently. For he says thus, ch. 11: "I do not press this stubbornly, lest someone should argue that sins were forgiven also in the baptism of John but that forgiveness was bestowed through the baptism of Christ according to a fuller sanctification on those whom Paul commanded to be baptized anew (Acts 19)." So also *Contra litteras Petiliani*, Bk. 2, ch. 37, he leaves it free, if anyone brings a better and surer understanding, for he says: "Whether the cause and nature of the baptism of John is as I have explained, or whether another better and surer one is brought, this is nevertheless manifest, that the baptism of John was different from the baptism of Christ."

Ambrose, *De Spiritu Sancto,* Bk. 1, ch. 3, discussing how those twelve who denied that they knew the Holy Spirit (Acts 19:2) had been baptized with the baptism of John, says this: "John baptized for the remission of sins, not in his own name but in the name of the coming Jesus. And therefore those did not know the Spirit who had not received Baptism in the name of Christ, as John was accustomed to baptize. For though John did not baptize with the Spirit, nevertheless he preached both Christ and the Spirit. Therefore these, because they had been baptized neither in the name of Christ nor with the faith of the Spirit, were not able to receive the sacrament of Baptism; therefore they were baptized in the name of Jesus, and in them Baptism was not repeated but renewed, for there is but one Baptism. However, where there is not the full sacrament of Baptism, there is thought to be neither the beginning nor any kind of Baptism; however it is full if you confess the Father, Son, and Holy Spirit." Therefore the discussions of the ancients about the baptism of John do not all intend the same thing, and Augustine himself bears witness that they are not like articles of faith, to dissent from which is a sin worthy of the anathema.

3 However, it cannot be hidden what must be our godly conviction if the opinions of the ancients are put aside for a little while and the matter is considered and weighed more carefully from the history of John the Baptist itself. For the surest and firmest rule is that one must judge of the sacraments from the Word to which the ceremonies of the sacraments are joined and connected by the command and institution of God. It is, however, beyond controversy that John was sent both to preach and to baptize, for both are described in John 1:7, 23–33: "He came for testimony, to bear witness to the Light." "I am the voice of one crying in the wilderness." Likewise: "He sent me to baptize." Therefore the baptism of John was not a silent washing, but God wanted this ceremony to be joined and connected to the Word or preaching which the Baptist uttered and confessed. Therefore such as the Word or doctrine was, such was also the baptism in the ministry of John. But did his teaching and confession concern the putting away of impurities of the body through outward washing? Certainly not! But he preached repentance by reproving sins and by setting forth the threats of God's wrath and of unquenchable fire. But was this the sole and entire teaching of the Baptist? By no means! For Matthew says (ch. 3): "John came preaching and saying: Repent, for the kingdom of heaven is at hand." And Mark (ch. 1:1) says that that voice of one crying is "the beginning of the Gospel of Jesus Christ, the Son of God." In John 1:29–36 and 3:27–36 there are found the sweetest discourses of the Baptist concerning the person and office of Christ, the Mediator. According to Acts 19:4 he taught about faith in Christ. In Mark 1:4 he preaches about the remission of sins, as also Zacharias describes the ministry of John (Luke 1:77): "To give knowledge of salvation to His people in the forgiveness of their sins." In John 3:36 the Baptist says: "He who believes in the Son has eternal life." He also taught concerning the Father, the Son, and the Holy Ghost (John 1 and 3). Later he taught also concerning the fruits of repentance. (Luke 3 and Matt. 3)

4 Let us now proceed in our investigation, namely, whether the baptism of John was a seal for only a part of his teaching or whether it belonged to his entire teaching. This indeed is granted by all, that John himself says: "I baptize you with water for repentance" (Matt. 3:11); likewise that he baptized the people with the baptism of repentance (Acts 19:4) and that those who were baptized by him confessed their sins (Mark 1:5). But did he baptize only for repentance, without faith in Christ and forgiveness of sins? Such repentance is certainly simply a pagan thing; yes, it is the ministry of death, of the wrath of God, and of blasphemies. And Paul (Acts 19:4) expressly affirms that John baptized in such a way with the baptism of repentance that he at the same time taught those whom he baptized to believe in Christ Jesus. Mark also and Luke assert that John preached of his baptism that it was a baptism not of bare repentance only but of repentance for the remission of sins. Nor does the phrase (for the remission of sins) take away remission from the baptism of John. For it is written that he baptized also for repentance, and yet it was a "baptism of repentance" (Mark 1:4; Acts 19:4). And the same phrase is used also of the baptism of Christ (Acts 2:38): "Repent and be baptized, every one of you, for the forgiveness of your sins." Add to this that in Matt. 3:7 John himself affirms that those who sought his baptism were seeking to escape the coming wrath of God. For he receives the Pharisees and Sadducees coming to his baptism with these words: "Who warned you to flee from the wrath to come?" And in Luke 7:29–30 those who were baptized with the baptism of John are said to have justified God, but those who were not baptized are said to have rejected the purpose of God against themselves. This passage Ambrose interprets thus: "God is justified through Baptism, for he who sins and confesses his sin justifies God, believing Him, hoping for grace from Him." And in *De sacramentis,* Bk. 2, he beautifully explains that Baptism is called the purpose of God. Bede understands this purpose of God to mean that He decreed to save through the suffering and death of Christ.

Since these things are manifestly so, surely certain of the ancients did not speak circumspectly enough in former times; and now that this dispute has been explained, it is not correctly nor truly asserted by the papalists that the baptism of John was without acknowledgment of the Trinity, without faith in Christ, and without remission of sins. Nor is it true that God at that time did not work anything through the baptism of John in the believers, since repentance itself is also a gift of God (Acts 5:31; 10; [1] 2 Tim. 2:25). It is also false that the believers did not receive any spiritual gifts through the ministry of the word and baptism of John. For faith in Christ justified the believers not only after the passion of Christ but also before, that is, it accepted grace, reconciliation, remission of sins, and salvation. Of the word of his preaching John indeed affirms (John 3:36): "He who believes in the Son has eternal life." And in John 1:16 this testimony is attributed to the Baptist: "From His fulness have we all received, grace upon grace." That John set forth the same faith in Christ Jesus in his baptism to those whom he baptized Paul clearly affirms (Acts 19:4). If therefore those who were baptized with the baptism of John either died in that faith or if they died before Jesus through His disciples began to baptize, surely no one will rightly damn them, as if they had departed without the grace of God and without the forgiveness of sins.

5 Up to this point this question about the baptism of John is plain and clear, if it is explained and judged from the Word of God and the prejudices both of the ancients and of more recent writers are put aside. But the other part of the question is more difficult and obscure, namely, whether the baptism of John is clearly the same as the baptism of Christ, which is administered by the ministers of Christ after He appeared, or whether it is clearly another and different from it.

Very strong indeed are the arguments that no difference should be established between the baptism of John and that of Christ. For on both sides, as we have proved, there is the same teaching, the same Word, the same promise, the same faith, the same remission of sins, and the same rite of baptizing. And Paul (Eph. 4:4–5) shows by a series of steps that in the New Testament, where there is one body, one Spirit, one hope of our calling, one Lord, one Father, one faith, there is also one baptism. In-

---

[1] The reference should apparently be Acts 11:18.

deed, this argument, which offers very sweet consolation, moves one very greatly, that we who are members have one baptism, one and the same and in common with Christ our Head, who sanctified our baptism through contact with His most holy flesh, as the fathers speak, and by His glorious revelation has made us certain that also in our baptism there is present the Father, Son, and Holy Ghost with His grace and power, that there the Spirit is poured out, that there the Word of grace and of the goodwill of the Father is heard. All these things which offer the sweetest comfort are taken away and lost when the baptism of John, by which certainly Christ Himself was baptized, is said to be totally different in kind from the baptism of Christ. Paul says (1 Cor. 12:13) that we were all baptized into one body. But it would follow that we are not one body with Christ and with the apostles if the baptism of John and that of Christ are totally different in kind. For Christ was baptized with the baptism of John. And there is no doubt that the apostles, if not all, at least some, and particularly those of whom mention is made (John 1), were baptized with the baptism of John. For Jesus baptized no one with His own hands or by an external ministry but used for this purpose the ministry of the disciples (John 4:1–2), and certainly no one will assert that they themselves lacked Baptism. The apocryphal and uncertain fabrications of Evodius and Euthymius, in which Jesus Himself is said to have baptized Peter and Mary with His own hands, we deservedly ignore, because they conflict with the clear testimony of the evangelist John. Therefore the baptism of John neither can nor should be separated from the baptism of Christ, as if it were of a totally different kind or altogether another.

6 On the other hand, however, I also see that Augustine, who thinks that the baptism of John was one thing and that of Christ another, has certain reasons which are not to be despised. I shall not now speak about the passage in Acts 19, on which Augustine chiefly leans; yet this argument certainly carries weight, that when Christ had begun to baptize through His disciples, yes, when after the ascension of Christ people were baptized with the baptism of Christ throughout the world, nevertheless the baptism of John was always distinguished from the baptism of Christ by this appellation. For it was not according to the name of the minister called the baptism of Peter, John, Jude, Paul, etc., as was the baptism of John, which was everywhere always so called. And the sequence of the Gospel story shows that the baptism of Christ through His disciples followed after John's baptism. Neither can it be said that either Peter or any other disciple of Christ baptized with the baptism of John. For Scripture says otherwise. We read also (John 4:1–2) that Jesus Himself made disci-

ples, not however by receiving only those who had been baptized by John but by Himself baptizing, through the disciples, those whom He received into the number of His own. Nor does it seem probable that only those joined themselves to Christ who had not previously been baptized by John. Rather, John by his baptism prepared the people for the Lord in order that they should join themselves to Christ. Concerning these we read (John 3 and 4) that Christ baptized them through the disciples. And there is no doubt that the baptism of John ceased when no one was any longer baptized with the baptism of John, as Augustine shows, *In Evangelium Johannis tractatus,* 4.

7 Therefore all antiquity agrees, and Scripture itself indicates, that there is some difference between the baptism of John and that of Christ. However, concerning the nature of the difference there is debate. Augustine says, *Contra Donatistas,* Bk. 5, ch. 10, that some distinguished in this way, that the baptism of John brought no forgiveness whatever. But this opinion is not entirely approved by Augustine. Therefore he says he believes that sins were forgiven in hope to those baptized by John, but that in the baptism of Christ they are remitted in fact. But he quickly adds that he will not fight obstinately if someone defines the difference in such a way that through the baptism of John sins were indeed forgiven, but that through the baptism of Christ forgiveness was bestowed according to some fuller sanctification. And, *Contra litteras Petiliani,* Bk. 2, ch. 37, he deduces the nature of the difference learnedly from the difference of the revelation of the Word concerning Christ. For the Old Testament had a baptism into Moses (1 Cor. 10:2); it also had circumcision—these were sacraments which foretold something that was to come, that is, the Messiah who would come. The sacraments of our time are announcements of the revealed Christ who has already come. Midway between these was the ministry of John, who by teaching and baptizing went before the Messiah who was not far away but was already approaching. For on this account he is called the messenger sent before the face of Christ. And John says of Christ: "He who comes after me, His servant, is now entering upon the prepared way and is coming." However, the apostles proclaimed that Christ had already come. In this way, according to the difference of the revelation, Augustine not inappropriately distinguishes between the baptism into Moses, yes, also circumcision, and the baptism of John and the baptism of Christ. However, as, according to Augustine, John was of all who were before Him the nearest announcer of Christ, to whom alone it was granted both to proclaim Him when He was still absent and to see Him present, so also the baptism of John agrees more closely

and does not differ so greatly from the baptism of Christ as either the baptism into Moses or circumcision differed from the baptism of Christ.

8 This comparison of the Mosaic or Jewish baptism in the Old Testament, the baptism of John, and the baptism of Christ is also used by Basil, *De baptismo,* ch. 2, and by Gregory of Nazianzus in his oration *In sancta luminaria.* Cyril, *In Johannem,* Bk. 2, ch. 58, compares the Levitical purifications, the baptism of John, and the baptism of Christ and wants a distinction to be taken from the last discourse of the Baptist before his captivity, which is found in John 3. And in ch. 57 he says that the baptism of John was introductory to perfection and possessed power for preparation. But as it does not follow that the circumcised did not have the remission of sins because there is a difference between circumcision and the baptism of Christ, even so much less ought the forgiveness of sins to be taken away from the baptism of John just to establish some difference between the baptism of John and the baptism of Christ, because the baptism of John came closer to the New Testament, or rather, it was the beginning of the New Testament. But such as the difference is between the Word concerning the Christ who is to come, who is coming, and who has been revealed, such is also the difference between circumcision, the baptism of John, and the baptism of Christ. But although there is some difference with respect to the mode of revelation of the doctrine concerning Christ, yet in its essence it was the same and had the same effects in the believers at all times, whether it was in the time of the Old Testament, or at the time of John the Baptist, or after Christ had appeared, even though a certain difference in degree can be established. Therefore as is the case with the Word, so also it is with circumcision and with the baptism of John and of the apostles. These must not be distinguished too minutely. For if we were to choose to go after subtle distinctions, a difference could also be established in this way between the baptism of the apostles which they performed before the passion and resurrection of Christ and that which they performed after. This opinion I judge to be the simplest. For it agrees with the statements of Scripture and it takes away nothing from the baptism either of John or of Christ; it also holds fast the consensus of the ancient church.

9 The third question is the most difficult, namely, whether it was necessary for those who had been baptized with John's baptism to receive afterward also Christ's baptism, which was administered by His disciples; or whether, after the revealed and manifested Christ was preached, it sufficed them that they had been baptized by John. Augustine thinks that after the baptism of John it was necessary to receive the baptism of Christ.

The reason for this opinion is not a trivial one. For those who had been circumcised with a view to the coming Christ, though they already had the sign of circumcision, which was a seal of the righteousness of faith, that is, of the remission of sins, nevertheless were obliged to receive the baptism of John (Luke 7:29–30). For if they believed in the coming Christ in such a way that they refused to believe God when He showed through the ministry of John that the Messiah was already on the way, and spurned His purpose in the baptism of John, they would certainly render their faith vain and false. For the same reason those who were baptized by John and believed that the Messiah was now on the way and coming, if afterwards they refused to believe the preaching of the Christ now manifested, would certainly not have true faith. For some among our Jews believe that Christ will still come, some believe that He has been born but has not yet begun His kingdom, and yet their faith is vain and false because they are not willing to believe in the Christ who has been manifested. Now the baptism of the disciples of Christ was the seal of the doctrine concerning Christ, who was now no longer to be expected as coming into the flesh, nor was it only to be believed that He was on the way and that He would come, but that He had already come and been manifested. For this reason it seems that after the baptism of John the baptism of Christ, which was administered by His disciples, had to be received to seal the doctrine and faith concerning the now-manifested Christ.

Lombard, however, has a different opinion from that of other ancient teachers, namely, that those who had been baptized by John, if they believed in the Father, Son, and Holy Spirit, and set their hope of salvation not on John but on Christ, were not again baptized with water. Those, however, who had corrupted the baptism of John by a false and wicked doctrine (which is what the story in Acts 19:1–5 seems to intend) he judges were afterward baptized with the baptism of Christ. This opinion Ambrose clearly upholds, *De Spiritu Sancto,* Bk. 1, ch. 3, as we have quoted his opinion above. And although I do not greatly object to the opinion of Augustine, in the sense I have explained and for the reason I have stated, nevertheless I see that Scripture does not pay particularly careful or scrupulous attention to this question. For (Acts 18:24–26) Apollos knew only the baptism of John; he is received and more diligently instructed in the way of the Lord; yet we do not read that he was again baptized with water. Nor do we read that the first apostles, who had been baptized by John, were baptized with water a second time. Yes, it would follow that it would have been necessary for the Baptist himself, once Christ had begun His ministry, to be baptized with water by the apostles of Christ, if what Augustine maintains had been absolutely and universally necessary. Moreover, when the apostles make disciples of Christ (John 3:26; 4:1–2), and afterwards when they at one time baptize three thousand (Acts 2:41) and not long after five thousand (Acts 4:4), it is not reported that they inquired carefully and scrupulously lest perhaps someone in that crowd had been baptized with John's baptism, whom it would be unlawful to baptize again with water. Therefore let this question be left undecided, as one that has reasons on both sides, since in our times its use is not particularly necessary. For no matter which of the two opinions one embraces, the true and necessary foundations can be retained.

10 Now that these things have been explained in this way, it will be clear how the statements which are usually opposed from Scripture can be rightly and skillfully explained. For John himself says: "I baptize you with water for repentance, but He who is coming after me . . . will baptize you with the Holy Spirit and with fire." And because he uses the future tense, "He will baptize," he seems to intimate that Christ baptizes with the Spirit not at that time, namely, through the baptism of John, but that only after John will He baptize with the Spirit, namely, through the ministry of His disciples.

But there can be no more certain interpretation of this statement than that which was given by Christ Himself and by the apostles. For in Acts 1:5, after the Resurrection, a little while before the Ascension, Christ repeats that statement of John, and although He had already baptized for more than three years through the ministry of the apostles, He nevertheless declares that what John had said was not yet fulfilled: "He will baptize you with the Holy Spirit." And indeed He says to the apostles, who certainly had already received the Spirit of regeneration and renewal: "Before many days you shall be baptized with the Holy Spirit." This was fulfilled on the day of Pentecost, through the outpouring of the miraculous and visible gifts of the Holy Spirit. And Peter, reporting (Acts 11:16) how such gifts were poured out on Cornelius before he was baptized with water in the name of Jesus, says: "I remembered the word of the Lord, how He said, 'John baptized with water, but you shall be baptized with the Holy Spirit.' " It is clear, therefore, from the interpretation of Christ and of the apostles, concerning which baptism of the Spirit these words are to be understood. And indeed the Baptist himself adds the word "fire," in order to show that he is speaking about that visible giving of the Spirit which began on the day of Pentecost in the appearance of fire. And if it is so understood, it is true that such a baptism of the Spirit was not in the baptism of John. For the Baptist performed no sign (John 10:41); in fact, the baptism of the Spirit did not happen before the ascension of Christ, not even when Christ was baptizing through the ministry of the apostles (John 7:39). Therefore it does not follow from the statement in Matt. 3:11 that the baptism of John was altogether useless and devoid of the grace of the Father, the power of Christ, and the working of the Spirit: on the contrary, when Christ was baptized by John, then certainly the grace of the Father and the manifest bestowal of the Spirit in the baptism of John were shown in a wonderful and clear revelation.

These things, which cannot be denied, can suffice against contentious adversaries. Nevertheless I gladly grant that in that statement, that Christ baptizes with the Spirit, something more is contained than only the manifestation of those wonderful and outstanding gifts of the Spirit. For these were symbols, testifying of the inner power of Christ, of the invisible gift and working of the Spirit. And Christ must not be said to have ceased to baptize with the Spirit after those visible gifts ceased.

But I affirm that also this interpretation does not rob the baptism of John of all spiritual efficacy. For the order and context of the story in Luke and in John shows both the occasion and the true meaning of this statement. Luke writes that the people had, out of admiration for the authority of the person of the Baptist, conceived the opinion that perhaps John was the Messiah, so that they considered his baptism, of which he himself preached that it was a baptism of repentance for the remission of sins, to have that power by virtue of the person of the Baptist and on account of the outward action which he performed in baptizing. This the evangelist John explains more clearly where he writes that the men sent from Jerusalem demanded of the Baptist: "Then why are you baptizing if you are not the Christ?" For this was their objection, that he neither should nor could baptize for the remission of sins if he were not the Christ. To refute this persuasion of the common people and this objection of the Pharisees, John makes a distinction first between his own person and the person of Christ, then also between his outward ministry and the spiritual efficacy of Christ. He says: "He is stronger than I, because He was before me and is from heaven; above all, because He is the only begotten Son. I am an earthly minister, of the earth, not worthy to loose His sandals for Him. I am the voice of one crying, and I baptize with water, that is, I have, exercise, and apply the external ministry of the Word and of Baptism. But He is mightier; that is, His power, strength, and efficacy. For He is efficacious through the ministry, for through Him and on account of Him is given the forgiveness of sins, reconciliation, the Spirit, and life eternal." For thus the Baptist clearly explains in what way Christ is first, when he says: "From His fulness have we all received, grace upon grace; for grace and truth came through Christ." This the ministers do not bring about, whether it be Peter or Jude or John the Baptist or an evangelist. Therefore it is necessary to distinguish the person and efficacy of Christ from the ministers and their external ministry, yet in such a way that also the external ministry is Christ's and that we teach that it is efficacious because it is that. John does not, however, set up an antithesis like the following: "I baptize with water without the remission of sins and without the Spirit, but He shall baptize with water and the Spirit." For Christ did not apply water to anyone with His own hands (John 4:2), neither can it be said that the apostles gave the Holy Spirit by their own power when they baptized; for this belongs to Christ alone. However, He who was effective through the ministry of Peter and Paul, His was also that efficacy which was present in the ministry of John. For the ministry of John was not ineffective, for of him the angel foretold that he would convert many to God. And therefore (John 1:33) the voice of the Father says to John the Baptist concerning Christ, not in the future tense, but in the present: "This is He who baptizes with the Holy Spirit." And lest the efficacy of Christ be absolutely taken away from the ministry of the Baptist, the Holy Spirit descended upon Christ at His baptism by John in the bodily shape of a dove, that from His fulness all might receive, not only those who would afterwards be baptized by the disciples of Christ. But John speaks in the past tense, also before Christ began to baptize through the ministry of His disciples. He says: "From His fulness have we all received." For Origen rightly argues that these were words of the Baptist. And this is what the Baptist says (Matt. 3:14): "I need to be baptized by You." But he is not speaking of baptism with water, for Christ did not baptize that way (John 4:1–2); therefore he understands the baptism of the Spirit. And so the Baptist confesses that he was baptized by Christ with the Spirit, although he was not baptized with water, either by Christ or by the apostles. I do not deny that the efficacy was fuller and more glorious later in the external ministry of Christ Himself and of His apostles. For Christ Himself declares that he who is least in the kingdom of heaven, namely, now that Christ has been revealed, is greater than the Baptist (Matt. 11:11). Therefore the statement of the Baptist which we are discussing does not intend to say anything else than what Paul explains at greater length of his own ministry (1 Cor. 3:6–7 and 4:15): "I planted, Apollos watered, but God gave the growth. So neither he who plants nor he who waters is anything, but only God who gives the growth." And yet he says: "I became your father in Christ Jesus through the Gospel." Likewise: "We are servants through whom you believed." And plainly in the same manner the apostle John says of the Baptist that all were to believe through him. Therefore the ministry of the Baptist was not without the power of the Spirit, for to believe is a gift of the Spirit.

11 The other passage which was appealed to very often by the Donatists in this dispute, with which also they caused Augustine much trouble, is the story in Acts 19:1–7. This story appears to relate that certain believing disciples, who confessed that they had been baptized with John's baptism, were commanded by Paul to be baptized in the name of the Lord Jesus. But neither does this passage prove with certainty, clearly and necessarily, that it was necessary for all who had been lawfully baptized with the baptism of John to be again baptized with water by the disciples of Christ; much less does it prove that the baptism of John was without the remission of sins in believers. For from dark, ambiguous, and disputed passages nothing can be proved. However, this passage is explained in various ways by the interpreters. Some, in order to refute the Anabaptists more readily, contend that those 12 were not baptized twice with water, first by John and afterward by Paul, but that they were baptized with water only once. And among these some take the word "baptism" in the earlier part of the statement not for the application of water but for the institution and doctrine, as the whole ministry of John is called his baptism in Acts 18:25: "Apollos knew and taught only the baptism of John," so that the meaning of, "Into what were you baptized?" is, "With what doctrine were you instructed and initiated?" And these think that these 12 had indeed been instructed in the teaching of John but had not been baptized with his baptism, but that they were afterwards baptized for the first time in the name of Jesus.

Others take the word "baptism" in the earlier part of the story in its proper sense, but in the second part they take it metaphorically for those wonderful and outstanding gifts of the Spirit which Christ designates with the word "baptism" when He says (Acts 1:5): "You shall be baptized with the Spirit." And their understanding is that these had been baptized with the baptism of John but were not baptized with water by Paul, but that the particle *kai* (and), as often elsewhere so also here, is explanatory. They were baptized in the name of Jesus, that is, when Paul had laid his hands on them, the Spirit came upon them.

But both these explanations have something forced about them, and neither preserves entirely the simplicity and clarity of the text. Therefore some, considering the little Greek word *men* to which the Greek particle *de* in the following clause corresponds, do not take the clause "On hearing this they were baptized in the name of Jesus" to be words of the historian Luke concerning those 12 but as the uninterrupted context of the speech of Paul, in this sense: John indeed baptized with the baptism of repentance by faith in the Christ to come, and those who heard (namely, this teaching of the Baptist concerning faith in Christ) were baptized in the name of the Lord Jesus; that is, it was the same thing as if they had been baptized by the apostles. The Greek context readily bears and permits this explanation. An explanation that is also akin to this is found in the *Glossa* which is called *Interlinear,* although it takes those words as words of Luke the historian, namely: "When those 12 heard that there was no difference between the ministry of John and of the apostles, except that John had baptized into Him as coming, of whom the apostles testified that He had come, they at once accepted it; they were not re-baptized, but when they had heard this declaration, the baptism of John was for them baptism in the name of the Lord Jesus. For John baptized in such a way that he commanded men to believe in Christ Jesus. Therefore those whom John baptized were baptized in His name." That gloss, the entire statement of which is taken from Ambrose, *De Spiritu Sancto,* Bk. 1, ch. 3, I have quoted above. He is, however, arguing about the true and lawful baptism of John, not about those 12 of whom he thought that they had received a spurious baptism under John's name. This explanation agrees beautifully with that which is written toward the end of ch. 18 concerning Apollos, whom, because he knew only John's baptism, they indeed instructed more accurately in the way of the Lord; but we do not read that they baptized him again with water, but having instructed him more fully they commended him to the disciples that he should be received as a Christian. This statement of the *Glossa* is very simple and fitting, and Lombard also argues that those who did not place their hope in that ceremony of John but believed in the Father, Son, and Holy Spirit were not afterward again baptized with water by the disciples of Christ. But to the possible objection that without the Holy Spirit there is neither the grace of God nor the forgiveness of sins, and that although those 12 are said to have been baptized with the baptism of John yet they first received the Holy Spirit by the laying on of hands, the answer is not difficult. For Luke himself explains that he understands by the term "Spirit" the extraordinary gifts of the Spirit, as the term is understood in John 7:39. Or, if it is taken literally, it will follow that not even by the baptism of Christ was the Holy Spirit given. For it is reported that they received the Spirit after the baptism of Christ, when Paul laid his hands on them.

There are, however, those to whom the text of the story seems to convey this meaning entirely, that those 12 had first been baptized with the baptism of John and that they were afterward baptized by Paul in the name of Jesus. Ambrose, indeed, so explains this passage, *Ad Galatas,* ch. 3. For he thinks that those 12 had not been washed, but polluted by a counterfeit baptism under the name of John, and that therefore Paul commanded them to be baptized in the name of the Trinity. He argues the same way in *De Spiritu Sancto,* Bk. 1, ch. 3. And to this interpretation this could be fitted, that they do not simply confess that they had been baptized with the baptism of John but "into the baptism of John." For what this phrase means is quickly explained, where they are said to be baptized "into the name of Jesus." For this is the same as what Paul says in Rom. 6:3: "All of us who have been baptized into Christ Jesus were baptized into His death." And in 1 Cor. 1:13, 15: "You were not baptized into the name of Paul." Also it seems to follow from their confession and from the answer of Paul that they had been baptized in such a way that they neither knew the Holy Spirit nor believed in Christ, but appear to have placed their hope in that ceremony of John, so that it was a certain false zeal, yes, a manifest corruption and adulteration of the baptism of John. And so the two accounts will not hang together badly. Apollos, who had been baptized with the true and genuine baptism of John, was not again washed with water but was more fully instructed. But those 12 because they were no more baptized than those who had been washed with the baptism of the Pharisees (Mark 7:4), were not rebaptized but were truly baptized for the first time by Paul. This understanding also Lombard embraces and follows.

Augustine, however, thinks that those 12 had been baptized with the true baptism of John and that nevertheless they were afterward also baptized by Paul. For he thinks that John's baptism is one thing and Christ's another, so that anyone who had the baptism of John needed afterward also to receive the baptism of Christ. And yet he defended this his understanding against rebaptism. For anabaptism is a repetition of one and the same baptism. This understanding seems to be favored by the fact that Luke gives them the testimony that they were disciples, that is, Christians, as they were then called. And Paul ascribes faith to them when he says that they believed. For this reason also some among more recent writers think it is not unfitting if one takes the passage to mean that those 12 were first baptized with John's baptism and that they were afterward baptized by Paul in the name of the Lord Christ. For as John preached, so he also baptized into the Christ who was to come (Acts 19:4). The apostles, however, taught Christ as manifested, and joined to this teaching they had a sign—the baptism of Christ. As therefore it was necessary for the disciples of John to accept the preaching of the apostles concerning the Christ who had been manifested, so if they are said to have received the sign connected with this apostolic doctrine, this is not unfitting and there is no rebaptism; nor is the previous baptism, that of John, condemned, as the Anabaptists do. And what the text says, namely, that they were baptized in the name of the Lord Christ, this is the same as if it said: "In the name of the manifested Christ." For God made the crucified Jesus both Christ and Lord.(Acts 2:36)

I have reviewed these varying interpretations of the story in Acts 19:1–7 in order that I might show that there is no sufficient cause why he who embraces one meaning should at once condemn with the anathema those who think otherwise, and that I might wrest from the papalists this weapon in which they have great confidence. For no matter how this story is understood, one cannot draw from it a sure, clear, and necessary conclusion that there was in the baptism of John no efficacy and that the believers received neither grace nor the remission of sins from it. For by the same reasoning it would follow either that those who had been circumcised should not have been baptized or that circumcision had no efficacy in believers.

SECTION II
[Noncontroversial Canons]

CANON II

If anyone says that true and natural water is not necessary for baptism, and therefore distorts the words of our Lord Jesus Christ, "Unless one is born of the water and the Spirit," into some kind of metaphor, let him be anathema.

CANON IV

If anyone says that a baptism which is given even by heretics in the name of the Father and of the Son and of the Holy Ghost, with the intention of doing what the Church does, is not a true baptism, let him be anathema.

CANON V

If anyone says that baptism is free, that is, not necessary for salvation, let him be anathema.

Examination

What is set down in these three canons is in part not in controversy and has in part been explained previously. That water is necessarily required for the administration of baptism no one (at least so far as I know) now questions. And because Baptism is "the washing of water with the Word" (Eph. 5:26), both John and the apostles did not take other liquids but plain water for Baptism—and that not after it had previously been consecrated through special exorcisms, but without distinction simple, common water, such as is everywhere available. For they judged that Baptism was truly consecrated and hallowed by the word of institution, which in the action itself comes to the element of the water that it may be a washing of regeneration of the Holy Spirit. It is therefore not disapproved by us that the second canon says that true and natural water is a matter of necessity for Baptism. For in this way they themselves concede and confirm that the blessing of the font (as they call it) or consecrated water is not a matter of necessity in Baptism. And many idle questions about distilled waters, mixed fluids, snow, ice, etc., are thus avoided. So far as the passage John 3:5 is concerned, if anyone turns the word "water" into a metaphor in such a way that he either overthrows the doctrine of

Baptism or thinks that the sacrament of Baptism can be performed without water, he is deservedly condemned. Just the same we are not unaware that Basil interprets this passage in such a way that he understands that by water in Baptism mortification is signified, and by the Spirit vivification. What Canon IV decrees about a baptism which is performed by heretics when the form of the institution is preserved we also teach, as antiquity learnedly pointed out on the basis of this teaching in Scripture against the Donatists. Concerning the intention we have spoken in the explanation of Canon XI, even as we have spoken of the necessity of the sacraments in connection with Canon IV, "Concerning the Sacraments in General." I shall therefore add nothing, but we shall pass on to other things in which some explanation will be necessary.

SECTION III

[Whether the Roman Church Has the True Doctrine of Baptism]

CANON III

If anyone says that in the Roman Church, which is the mother and teacher of all churches, there is not the true doctrine concerning the sacrament of baptism, let him be anathema.

Examination

1 In a number of the following canons the good fathers have taken for themselves a few statements excerpted in mutilated form from Luther's booklet *De captivitate Babylonica,* not in order to refute them but (which is easier) to condemn them without arguments. Luther, who grants that the sacrament of Baptism, amid much and varied display of man-made ceremonies, nevertheless, so far as matter and form are concerned, remained unimpaired in the papalist church, very vehemently complains that the doctrine concerning the use and power of Baptism, which concerns the whole life of a Christian, was in part buried through silence and in part corrupted in the papalist kingdom. For although Scripture, in the doctrine about the salutary use of Baptism, urges and makes sweet especially these two things—the promise of salvation which is added to the rite of Baptism by the divine Word, and faith which lays hold of the promise, embraces it, retains and preserves it, Luther complains that, in so many huge wagonloads of books of questions and summaries about Baptism, hardly anywhere is mention made of this promise and of faith, but that instead of these there was brought into the church the opinion of the *opus operatum.* And although the use and the power of Baptism should endure throughout the whole life of a Christian man, the papalists teach that through sin committed after Baptism the power of Baptism is lost and, so to say, becomes ineffectual, so that in those who afterward repent there is no use for Baptism but another plank must be received by which we are carried to the harbor of salvation, namely, by our contrition, confession, and satisfaction. This Babylonian captivity of the church Luther deplores, because the teaching concerning the salutary

use and power of Baptism lies covered and buried by traditions and opinions of vows, religious orders, works, satisfactions, pilgrimages, indulgences, sects, etc. After he has shown the way and manner from the Word of God, he wishes and counsels that the true and genuine purity which is necessary for this doctrine should be restored to it. This is Luther's complaint.

2 Now indeed, after so many years, the Tridentine synod wishes to make it appear as if it wanted to apply healing hands to this festering sore on its body, which has been cut open by the sword of the Spirit. But let the diligent reader listen carefully to the kind of improvement they propose to us. Godly men complain loudly that many unsound opinions about the use and power of Baptism have crept into the Roman Church; and up to this time they fervently hoped that now at last there would be undertaken a restoration of the true and sound doctrine from the clear fountains of Christ and of the apostles, revealed in the Word of God. And the Tridentine assembly indeed assures us in many words that it has assembled to eliminate errors and to root out heresies which have grown up around the sacraments. But after they have come to the matter itself, while the minds of all are held in suspense with expectation, they pass over the living fountains and in part dig new cisterns, in part show us obsolete puddles, namely, that we should set aside the norm and rule of Scripture and that that alone and simply should be judged to be the true doctrine of the sacrament of Baptism which the Roman, that is, the papalist, church holds and observes. This is their whole reformation. Return now, Luther, and charge the papalist church from the Word of God with corrupt teaching about the use and power of Baptism! For they have learned to answer in a few words by way of that fallacy which Aristotle calls "begging the question" (*petitio principii*) and the scholastics call "trifling" (*nugatio*).

3 And so the entire Tridentine synod replies with this one very brief axiom, that the true doctrine concerning the sacrament of Baptism is found in the Roman Church. However, this is the very thing concerning which there is inquiry and controversy. But if you show them the faults and corruptions of their doctrine concerning the use and power of Baptism from the Word of God, they turn the shield of their anathemas against the sword of the Spirit. If you ask why they want the doctrine of Baptism judged according to the custom of the papalist church rather than according to the norm of Scripture, yes, why they want to defend and guard the things which dissent from Scripture and conflict with it by holding up only the authority of their church, like the head of the Gorgon,

they give this reason, that the Roman Church is the mother and teacher of all churches.

The former of these is wrong, the latter blasphemous. For the Roman Church did not bring forth the churches at Jerusalem, in Syria, Greece, and the Orient, but rather it was brought forth by them. The guardianship of faith belongs to no one save Christ alone. For to the apostles themselves it was said (Matt. 23:8, 10): "You are not to be called rabbi . . . for you have one master, the Christ." It would be somewhat more modest if they would say, even though they affirmed it falsely, that the true doctrine of the sacrament of Baptism is in the Roman Church because she holds and preserves those things which were delivered by Christ and the apostles concerning Baptism in the Word of God. But to the fathers it seemed to be the shorter way to publish nakedly and simply, under the threat of the anathema, that whatever things are transmitted in the papalist church about Baptism are true because she is the mother and teacher of all churches, to whom alone belongs the authority of prescribing, while all the rest are only under the necessity of obeying. Why, then, did they not place this concise and truly papalist canon at once at the head of the topic concerning Baptism as in a battle array, for in this way the war would have been brought to a quick end. Let the reader understand, therefore, that it was merely *pro forma* (as the saying is) that they held their daily meetings from Jan. 13 until March 3, as if they would examine the doctrine of the sacraments in general, and of Baptism, according to the norm of Scripture, when in fact they had from the beginning set before themselves this postulate, rather than the doctrine: "If anyone says that in the Roman Church, which is the mother and teacher of all churches, there is not the true doctrine concerning the sacrament of baptism, let him be anathema."

4 But what, you say, will you do, if you are not willing simply to assent to this canon? Will you condemn the baptism which is given in the papalist church? Or will you declare that those were not rightly and truly baptized who received the baptism bestowed by papalists? Or, if you cannot do this, must you concede that the doctrine of baptism which is taught in the papalist church is true? To me indeed it is not doubtful that the framers of this canon placed the words in this way with this intention, that if anyone does not simply approve everything, whatever is taught about Baptism in the papalist church, he may be declared to be an Anabaptist, who holds that no one has been rightly and truly baptized under the papacy, or, if he does not want this, that he be compelled simply to approve the entire papacy. However, we shall easily disentan-

lemma their own Canon XII under "Concerning the Sacraments in General" [p. 102], and Canon IV under "Concerning Baptism" [p. 132]. Because teaching is the principal part of the ministry, it is indeed true that when the true doctrine is corrupted and wrong opinions are established the ministry itself is altered, and that the ministry of those who corrupt the doctrine should for that reason be forsaken, because it is written: "Beware of false prophets!" Likewise: "The voice of strangers they do not hear, but flee from it." However, at the same time this also is true, that a part of the ministry, for instatnce the administration of some sacrament, may at times be in the hands even of men who in other matters embrace grave errors. Yes, often also those have, administer, and give true sacraments who patch some wrong opinions onto the sacraments, so long as they preserve the essentials which belong to the matter and the form according to the institution, as the example of circumcision by Caiaphas, the scribes, and the Pharisees testifies. But in by no means follows that, because it was a true circumcision which was given by the Pharisees, therefore also all the opinions were true which by means of their traditions beyond and contrary to the Word of God they patched on, not only to other articles of doctrine but also to circumcision itself. Therefore this example shows the true explanation of that argument which can be raised in objection with some show of right.

SECTION IV
[Whether Baptismal Grace Can Be Lost]

CANON VI

If anyone says that a baptized person cannot, even if he wanted to, lose grace, no matter how much he sins, unless he refuses to believe, let him be anathema.

Examination

1 Augustine, *De civitate Dei,* Bk. 21, quotes and refutes the fanatical disputations of certain men who promised freedom from eternal fire, either to all men or only to those who had been washed with the baptism of Christ and had become partakers of His body and blood, no matter how they lived or in what heresy or ungodliness they were found, or at least only to those who, after they have received the sacraments, retain the outward catholic profession, even though they live most wickedly. These opinions Augustine correctly and deservedly condemns and refutes. For they conflict with the statement of Paul, which he repeats a number of times (1 Cor. 6:9–10; Gal. 5:21; Eph. 5:5; and Col. 3): "Those who do such things shall not inherit the kingdom of God."

2 In our churches, if any profess either by word or by their life and deeds that grace, that is, reconciliation and salvation, is conferred and given to the baptized in such a way that they at the same time receive the privilege to live shamefully, that is, that they can and dare freely and with impunity to wallow in the greatest crimes, and nevertheless have and retain grace in the midst of such willful crimes, they are sternly reprimanded and earnestly condemned. For as grace is received and retained by faith, so by unbelief, from which follow evil fruits, that is, sins which ravage the conscience, it is lost and cast off. For "He who does not believe shall be damned." And Paul is preaching to the baptized when he says: "Those who do such things shall not inherit the kingdom of God"; "If you live according to the flesh you will die"; and, "On account of these things the wrath of God comes upon the sons of disobedience." However, we by no means teach that faith intends to reject grace and to drive out the Holy Spirit. Neither do we think that justifying faith consists only of the knowl-

143

edge of the story, or of the outward confession of the articles of faith. Much less do we teach that true and justifying faith is an Epicurean persuasion concerning grace and salvation, in impenitence and in the presence of criminal intention. In the earlier part of the *Examination* these things have been more fully explained. We therefore by no means acknowledge that those things which, in the sense I have already stated, are rightly condemned in this sixth canon are the teaching or opinion of our churches.

3 But you will say, "This is Luther's proposition, which is found in almost wholly the same words in his booklet *De captivitate Babylonica.*" But I have called attention to the fact that this canon has been so cunningly constructed that we should either imprudently condemn Luther or, if we should undertake to defend that proposition, they may be able to expose us before the whole world by a plausible show, as if our doctrine were downright shameful and blasphemous. But the matter stands well. For the lawyers have a very fine saying: "It is unjust to make a pronouncement on the basis of a small part of the law when the whole law has not been looked into." And Luther has rightly said that it is criminal, if you know that someone's meaning is godly and sound, to establish an error from words ineptly spoken. For heresy is found in the sense, not in the words, as Jerome rightly said when harassed by his detractors. But the papalists themselves knew that Luther in that passage was not arguing for or defending that Epicurean opinion which as I said in the beginning is rightly and deservedly condemned because it conflicts with the Word of God. However, in that same passage Luther expressly affirms that through sins which ravage the conscience the baptized desert the promise of the grace of Baptism, forsake the faith and its truth, and fall from the power and faith of Baptism. They are therefore not ignorant of the fact that Luther in this passage is dealing with a far different matter. And yet they have extracted from the midst of his disputation this mutilated and truncated propostion, in order that those to whom the whole debate is not known, or who do not consider what goes before and what follows, should think that Luther's doctrine is crassly and palpably ungodly and shameful. But what kind of trick this is—regardless of whether one prefers to call it sophistical or deceitful—is manifest.

Let the reader, however, consider the Tridentine technique. For Luther in that passage sharply attacks the corruption of the papalists, who teach that through the sins which are committed after Baptism the ship of Baptism is wrecked and broken up into planks, that is, that the power, strength, or grace of Baptism is totally lost and made invalid so that faith can in no way and at no time ever return and go back to it in true repentance but that now another plank must be looked for, namely, the plank of our own contrition and satisfaction, through the power of which we are carried to the harbor of salvation. This doctrine, which restricts the grace and power of Baptism to only that single moment when we are baptized, so that it has no further use later throughout our whole life, Luther shows to be false and wicked. And he explains the true meaning from the Word of God in these words: "Just as when the divine promise of Baptism has once been laid on us ('He who believes and is baptized will be saved') its truth remains until death, so faith in the same ought never to be abandoned but nourished and strengthened until death through the perpetual remembrance of the promise given to us in Baptism. Therefore when we rise from sins or repent, we do nothing else than return to the power and faith of Baptism, from which we have fallen, and to the promise then made, which we had deserted through sin. For the truth of the promise once made always remains, to receive us with outstretched hand when we return. And the heart of the penitent will be fully comforted and revived to the hope of mercy if it considers the divine promise made to it, which cannot possibly lie, which is still whole and unchanged, and which cannot be changed by any sins, as Paul says in 2 Tim. 2:13: 'If we are faithless, He remains faithful—for He cannot deny Himself.' " And he soon adds: "The grace and salvation of Baptism are not so lost through subsequent sins that there is not open a return to it in true repentance through faith. For if faith returns to the divine promise made to the baptized, in a moment the sins are swallowed up through that same faith, or rather the truth of God, because He cannot deny Himself." And finally he concludes concerning the second plank of our contrition and satisfaction: "Vanity of vanities and affliction of the spirit is everything that wearies itself outside of faith in the faithfulness of God." Thus Luther.

4 The fathers at Trent, however, proposed to condemn this understanding. But they thought that if they expressly set forth what they wanted to condemn, pious ears would not be able to bear, not even in the papalist church itself, amid so great a light of the Word, the condemnation of a statement which is true and full of necessary consolation. Therefore they invented this trick, that they would take a statement out of this disputation which, when set forth in truncated form, sounds very different, and condemn it; and in this way, as if they were doing something else, they would subject this entire treatise, which galls them no end, to the anathema.

Let the reader diligently note this. The trick lies in the word "losing" the grace of Baptism. That this losing happens through sins against the conscience and that it remains unless repentance occurs, of this there is no doubt. But they understand the loss in such a way that even if someone repents after a fall he can never, even through faith, at any time return to the grace promised in Baptism. I indeed in the beginning, when I had read through that canon once and again, did not notice that sophism, yet its consideration teaches us many things in this canon.

SECTION V

[Whether the Baptized Are Obligated to Observe the Law]

If anyone says that the baptized through baptism become debtors only of faith, and not to the observance of the whole law of Christ, let him be anathema.

Examination

1 In order that it may be seen the more readily what this canon aims at, I simply say first that if any think or teach that the baptized become through Baptism debtors only of faith alone, that is, of the historical knowledge of the articles of faith and of the outward profession, so that they believe that by a special privilege they are wholly exempt from subjection and obedience to the commandments of God and think that it is up to their own free will either to obey the commandments of God or to violate them and that they can securely indulge in sins; such, I say, are justly condemned. For they are blasphemers against Baptism itself, as if it were a license for turpitude, and they are in conflict with the teaching of Paul—Rom. 6:1–6: "Far be it from us that we should continue in sin; for we were buried with Christ by Baptism into death. . . . We know that our old self was crucified with Him so that the sinful body might be destroyed and we might no longer be enslaved to sin . . . but as Christ was raised from the dead by the glory of the Father, we too might walk in newness of life," etc. Rom. 8:12: "We are debtors, not to the flesh, to live according to the flesh." Rom. 13:8: "Owe no one anything except to love one another." 1 John 4:11: "We also ought to love one another." But do the papalists allow themselves to be satisfied by us with respect to this canon by this statement, which is true? Truly, I do not think so, for it is something else that they are striking at than appears on the face of it.

2 The promise of Baptism offers and bestows "the grace of God" (Titus 3:7), "the forgiveness of sins" (Acts 2:38), "an appeal to God for a clear conscience" (1 Peter 3:21), "regeneration in the Holy Spirit" (Titus 3:5), entrance into the kingdom of heaven (John 1),[2] salvation (Mark

---

[2] The reference should probably be John 3:5.

16:16), the inheritance "of eternal life" (Titus 3:7) through and on account of the death and resurrection of Christ (Rom. 6:3–4; 1 Peter 3:21). God wants us to accept these benefits by faith, according to the statement of Christ: "He who believes and is baptized will be saved, but he who does not believe will be condemned." On this basis our men teach that this promise and grace of Baptism is valid and firm to us, that it does not depend on the condition that the Law has been fulfilled by us, but that it requires only faith, by which we appropriate to ourselves these free gifts which are given us for Christ's sake. For faith accepts the promise of Baptism (Mark 16:16). "But the Law does not rest on faith" (Gal. 3:12). And faith would forever remain uncertain, the promise also could be neither valid nor useful, if it depended on the condition that the Law had been fulfilled by us. "For all who rely on works of the Law are under a curse" (Gal. 3:10). "That is why it depends on faith, in order that the promise may rest on grace and be guaranteed." (Rom. 4:16)

3 This teaching the papalists carp at in this seventh canon. They do not, indeed, dare to say in so many words that the efficacy of Baptism depends on the condition that the Law has been fulfilled by us, yet they do not conceal what they want. For they borrow this phrase from Gal. 5:3: "Every man who receives circumcision is bound to keep the whole Law." But Paul does not say this of the true and principal use of circumcision, of which he teaches (Rom. 4:11) that it was a seal of the righteousness of faith, to which he opposes the righteousness of the Law and of works; but he says that this follows from the opinion of the false apostles about circumcision as our own work. He adds, moreover, that if anyone is circumcised with the understanding that he becomes a debtor to keep the whole Law in order to merit grace and salvation, Christ will be of no advantage to him—that he is severed from Christ and has fallen away from grace. Let these things be compared with the words of this seventh canon, in which it is affirmed that Baptism makes us debtors to the observance of the whole law of Christ. Therefore they are covertly aiming at this, that the grace of Baptism is not received by faith alone but that also the keeping of the commandments of God is required for this.

4 In order to establish this teaching they employ a twofold sophism. Of these the first is: "In Baptism we renounce Satan and his works. There we come under obligation to mortify sin and to lead a new life that, freed from sin, we may serve God (Rom 6:3–11). Therefore the condition of faith is not all that is required, but also the condition of fulfilling the commandments of God." We indeed do not deny what Paul writes in Rom. 6 about Baptism and what they customarily set forth in the formula of renunciation in the action of Baptism, but we reply with the distinction

which Paul teaches in Titus 3:5, where he calls Baptism "the washing of regeneration and renewal." However, the chief blessings of Baptism are grace, forgiveness of sins, adoption, acceptance to salvation and to the inheritance of eternal life. For these things the condition of our works is not required, for they are given on account of the merit of the Son, the Mediator. Christ affirms that these benefits are accepted by faith (Mark 16:16). After these gifts have been received there follows the gift of renewal (Titus 3:5) and the obligation of which Paul speaks in Rom. 6. For he expressly says thus: "Having been set free from sin you have become slaves to God for righteousness." And in Titus 3:5 he says that regeneration precedes and that renewal follows. But that the object of renewal is keeping the commandments of God no one doubts. Therefore things that differ in essence must necessarily be distinguished also in teaching.

The other sophism is: "because it is most manifest that we are not baptized into Moses but into Christ, that is, not into the Law but into the Gospel." Instead of the Gospel they call it the law of Christ, that they may be able the more easily to confuse the promise of the free reconciliation for Christ's sake, which is accepted by faith, with the teaching about the commandments of God, which demand our obedience.

Thus into every canon the individual words are introduced with papalist craft and trickery. To disclose these correctly is the most important part of the explanation and refutation.

SECTION VI

[Whether the Baptized Are Obligated to Obey Church Precepts and Keep Vows]

If anyone says that the baptized are free from all precepts of holy Church, which are either written or transmitted, in such a way that they are not bound to observe them unless they want to submit to them of their own accord, let him be anathema.

If anyone says that men are to be recalled to the memory of the baptism which they have received, in such a way that they understand that all vows which they make after baptism are void by virtue of the promise already made in baptism, as though through them something were taken away both from the faith which they have professed and from baptism itself, let him be anathema.

Examination

1 I have combined these two canons. For both take the statement which they condemn from Luther's *De captivitate Babylonica,* and the basis for the explanation in both canons is the same. Let the reader observe what are the progressive steps of the council. In Canon VII they wanted to mix the commandments of God concerning our works into the gratuitous promise, and into faith they wanted to mix our observance of the commandments of God. Now in these two canons they argue that the precepts of men must be mixed with the commandments of God, and to the obligation to the divine commandments they want to join the vows of human traditions, so that in Baptism nothing may be left pure and uncontaminated by this leaven.

2 But so far as Canon VIII is concerned, Luther argues thus: "When through Baptism we have been adopted by God as children and received and enrolled into His family, then we are bound to render obedience to God—however, according to His own commandments, not according to traditions and commandments of men." For after the institution of Baptism, Christ adds (Matt. 28:20): "Teaching them to observe all that I have commanded you." And Paul (Rom. 6), where he treats of the fact that

Baptism obligates one to render the new obedience, says: "Now that you have been set free from sin, you have become slaves of God." And in the same place he explains the norm of obedience when he says: "You have become obedient from the heart to the standard of teaching to which you were committed." Scripture shows that these statements should be understood exclusively with respect to the conscience and to the worship to be rendered to God (for we are now not speaking of political and economic matters). James 4:12: "There is one lawgiver, He who is able to save and to destroy." Col. 2:20: "If with Christ you died to the elemental spirits of the universe, why do you still live as if you belonged to the world? Why do you submit to regulations . . . according to human precepts and doctrines?" For by Baptism "we have been united with Christ in a death like His" (Rom. 6:5). Therefore Baptism binds us to the commandments of God in such a way that it does not want us to be subjected to traditions according to the commandments and doctrines of men. 1 Cor. 7:21–23: Whether you are a servant or free, you are a freedman and servant of Christ. "You were bought with a price; do not become slaves of men." And to His family God says (Ezek. 20:18–20): "Do not walk in the statutes of your fathers . . . walk in My statutes . . . I the Lord am your God." Matt. 15:9: "In vain they worship Me with the precepts of men." From these principles Luther freely and rightly concludes: "Because God in His great house, which is the church, lays claim for Himself alone to the right and authority to rule by His Word over the consciences of His family, yes, of His children, and because we have in Baptism pledged ourselves to obedience to this Father who has also freed and absolved our consciences from all human traditions, commandments, and doctrines, as the statements of Scripture clearly testify, therefore neither the pope nor any other man has the right to set a single syllable over the conscience of a Christian man. Indeed, whatever is done differently is done in a tyrannical spirit, against the liberty of the church. For no law can be imposed with any right upon the consciences of Christians either by men or by angels."

3 But does this teaching absolve Christians from the obedience owed to the civil magistrate? By no means. For he is speaking expressly of things which are imposed on consciences. And the obedience which is owed to the civil magistrate is itself commanded and approved by the Word of God. But ought not the ecclesiastical ministry have reverence and authority? By all means! However, not in such a way that they have the rule in the church, either absolute or with some limitation, but that they have the ministry. Therefore when they bring the doctrine, the voice and Word of God, then we render obedience, not to men but to God

Himself. But when they lay something upon the consciences outside of, over and above, or contrary to the Word of God, then our Baptism reminds us of our obligation to render obedience to the divine Word; it reminds us also of our freedom from the commandments, doctrines, and traditions of men.

But what if the church decides something about indifferent things which makes for order, decorum, and edification? I reply: If the arrangements conflict with the Word of God, or when ungodly opinions are patched on, then obedience is simply forbidden. When, however, the matters are indifferent and are proposed without impious opinions, then the rule of Paul (1 Cor. 14:40) obtains: "All things should be done decently, in order, and for edification." Charity also, according to the example of Paul, in yielding to weak brethren does many such things which can be done without injury to the conscience. Nevertheless such things must be observed without infringing on the liberty of the conscience, without any thought that they are necessary. These things I have briefly repeated because I see that traps are being laid when the question is asked whether the baptized are entirely free from all human regulations.

4 For this reason Luther argues very strongly from the obligation of Baptism against human traditions, against doctrines and commandments of men in the church, by which they want to rule, bind, and ensnare the consciences of the baptized. And that wound which Luther inflicted on all their traditions and decrees with this weapon pains the papalists beyond measure, for they could not conceal their pain in this eighth canon. However, they bring forward nothing by which they even try to refute those most firm and most clear arguments; they merely pronounce the anathema. We, however, earnestly demand that they should first show that these arguments are empty and false. In the meantime we shall make use of the statement of Jerome: "Whatever has no authority from the canonical Scripture can be rejected with the same ease with which it is approved."

5 The case of the ninth canon is the same. For also the statement which is condemned there is taken from Luther's book on the Babylonian Captivity, and it contains a very clear and strong argument against papalist vows. For in the Old Testament the Word of God ordered the nature of vows—concerning what things and how they could be made. But in the New Testament Christ and the apostles have commanded us nothing about particular vows. However in Baptism, as a result of a prescription of the Word of God, a general profession is made, a vow or promise by which we subject ourselves to God and bind ourselves to obedience. Therefore all vows of Christians which should be considered legitimate

are rightly and deservedly to be measured against the profession in Baptism. But the rule and norm of the vow which we utter in the profession of Baptism is the statement of Christ (Matt. 28:20): "Teaching them to observe all that I have commanded you." And Rom. 6:17–18: "Having been set free from sin, you have become slaves of God . . . committed to the standard of the apostolic doctrine." Col. 2:20–21: "If with Christ you died to the elemental spirits of the universe, why do you live as still belonging to the world? Why do you submit to regulations . . . according to human precepts and doctrines?" Because these things are so, Luther complains that the consciences of the baptized are burdened, entangled in endless other laws drawn up by men in regard to vows. Some are vows of religious orders, some of pilgrimages, some of other works; and he complains that by these laws and opinions about vows both faith and Baptism are disparaged. For as if the vow of Baptism were either not excellent enough or not sufficient, they search out and heap up other things by which consciences are so occupied that the remembrance of Baptism is undermined and its dignity lessened. For it is argued and asserted that a work performed within such a vow is more excellent and worthy of much greater rewards than if it were done outside of such a vow, simply in accord with a divine command. Others add that entering a religious order is, as it were, a new baptism, which may be renewed as often thereafter as the intention of religion is again renewed. And in the midst of this din about vows hardly anyone considers his baptism worthy of remembrance. Also the laws, fetters, and chains of the vows conflict with the freedom from the commandments and doctrines of men into which we are placed through Baptism (Col. 2:16–23). And because in Baptism we solemnly promise very much—more than we can fulfill—we shall have labor enough if we want to direct our efforts throughout our whole life to this one thing. Therefore Luther thinks it is enough that all other vows should be removed and omitted, which have neither a command of God nor the example of Scripture, and all Christians be recalled to the vows of Baptism. This is Luther's argument.

6 What could be said more simply, clearly, truly, and profitably? But it grieves the papalists greatly that on the simple basis of Baptism all papalist vows should be so clearly, so solidly, and so effectually weakened and overthrown. And because in the examination of vows they have so much to fear from the rule and norm of the profession of Baptism, because they perceive that by it all their vows are annihilated, therefore they have set this long ninth canon up against it, in which they nevertheless observe anxious care lest they either confirm their opinion from Scripture or refute contrary arguments from it. But whatever irks them they simply

reject with just one word: anathema! However, the reader knows that the grounds taken from the profession of Baptism are too strong and clear, so that they cannot so easily be taken away from pious souls who have the Word of God as a lamp for their feet. It is therefore sufficient to have reminded the reader what it was that disturbed those compassionate fathers, rendered compassionate through the mercy of God, so greatly in these two canons.

SECTION VII
[Concerning the Remembrance of Baptism]

CANON X

If anyone says that all sins which are committed after baptism are either remitted or rendered venial solely through the remembrance and faith of the baptism once received, let him be anathema.

Examination

1 To begin with, we must consider what and of what kind the statement is which the papalists condemn in this tenth canon; then it will not be difficult to see with what cunning they fashion it. In his book *De captivitate Babylonica* Luther among other things reproved in the papalist doctrine also this dangerous, false, and pernicious opinion, according to which they invented the idea that the grace of Baptism is valid only for the remission of past sins, or which the time of Baptism finds in the person, so that if anyone falls into sin after Baptism, even if he repents and returns in true faith to the promise of grace and of reconciliation on account of the merit of Christ offered, given, communicated, applied, and sealed to him in Baptism, the grace of the promise in Baptism nevertheless profits him nothing further for reconciliation. But, they say, because the grace of Baptism has been so lost through the fall that, broken and dashed down, it has perished and been made invalid even if the sinner returns in earnest repentance through true faith to that covenant which God made with us in Baptism, therefore, in the case of sins committed after Baptism, faith must seek atonement and reconciliation not in the grace of that promise which is offered, communicated, and sealed to us in Baptism, but other means must be looked for, sought, and tried by which we may obtain grace, reconciliation, and remission of sins.

2 The occasion for this opinion (Luther says) was furnished by that dangerous statement of Jerome, which was either badly stated or badly understood, in which he calls penitence the second plank after the shipwreck. For in the case of sins after Baptism they despair of the first plank, or of the ship, which they consider lost, and begin to rest upon and trust in the second plank, that is, their own contrition and satisfaction. From this

155

have sprung the endless burdens of vows, religious orders, works, satisfactions, pilgrimages, indulgences, and sects—and concerning them those oceans of books, questions, opinions, human traditions, etc.

3 However, this opinion is false, dangerous, and destructive, as can surely and clearly be shown from the doctrine of Baptism. For Christ Himself declares that the act of Baptism looks not only backward, or to time past, or only to the moment when Baptism is administered, but He certainly uses the future tense when He says: "He who believes and is baptized will be saved." And it is worth noting how Scripture extends the efficacy of Baptism to all times—present, past, and future—in the believers. For Paul says (Titus 3:5): "He saved us by the washing of regeneration." Peter, writing to those who had been baptized long before, says concerning his and their baptism (1 Peter 3:21): "Baptism now saves us." And he adds the reason, because it is "an appeal to God for a clear conscience through the resurrection of Jesus Christ," which certainly is the ground of salvation at all times, whether while we are being baptized or after Baptism, either shortly or long after. And Paul, when he had said (Titus 3) concerning the past : "He saved us," lest this be restricted to past time only, adds: "Through Jesus Christ our Savior, so that we might be justified by His grace and become heirs in hope of eternal life." And in Eph. 5:26–27 he says that Christ cleanses and sanctifies the church "by the washing of water with the Word, that He might present the church to Himself in splendor, without spot or wrinkle." That this is to be perfectly fulfilled in the life to come Augustine teaches in many passages. Therefore Scripture declares that the power, efficacy, and purifying and sanctifying action of Baptism endures and is valid throughout the entire life of the Christian. Paul teaches this even more clearly, and indeed with many words, in Rom. 6.

The covenant of grace, or the treaty of peace, into which God enters with us in Baptism does not only look back to the past, or to the moment in which we are baptized, but it is an eternal covenant, as He says in Is. 54:8, 10: "With everlasting love I will have compassion on you. . . . For the mountains may depart and the hills be removed, but My steadfast love shall not depart from you, and My covenant of peace shall not be removed, says the Lord, who has compassion on you." This covenant of peace was not entered into between God and us in Baptism with the condition that if we should fall from it through sin it would be so dissolved and broken that even if we return to it in true repentance, through faith, God is nevertheless not willing to keep it valid and firm for the penitent. For the faithlessness of men cannot nullify the faithfulness of God (Rom. 3:3–4). "If we are faithless, He remains faithful—for He cannot deny

Himself" (2 Tim. 2:13). A very comforting description is found Jer. 3. It is a common saying: "If a man divorces his wife and she goes from him and becomes another man's wife, will he return to her? . . . You have played the harlot with many lovers; and would you return to Me? says the Lord. . . . Have you not just now called to Me. 'My Father, Thou art the friend of my youth . . .?' Behold, you have spoken, but you have done all the evil that you could. . . . And although she had done all these things, I said, 'Return to Me' . . . but she did not return." And the Lord said to me: "Go and proclaim these words and say, 'Return, faithless Israel . . . and I will receive you!' " etc. That this consolation is rightly applied to the covenant of Baptism is shown by the example taken from marriage. (Eph. 5)

And lest there be any doubt, Paul calls back the Galatians, who had fallen after their Baptism, and leads them back to the grace promised in Baptism (Gal. 3:27), as also the Corinthians. (1 Cor. 12:12–13).

4 The nature of the promise of grace in Baptism also proves the same thing. For the grace of Baptism promises salvation through Jesus Christ, our Savior, in order that "we might be justified by His grace and become heirs in hope of eternal life" (Titus 3:7). This is, however, the general way of justification after any lapse. Thus in 1 Peter 3:21: Baptism is "an appeal to God for a clear conscience through the resurrection of Jesus Christ." And certainly, after every fall faith in repentance seeks the reconciliation of the conscience to God, and this on account of the death and resurrection of Christ. These are the essential things in the promise of Baptism, which is offered and sealed to us once in Baptism, that it may be a perpetual seal and testimony that we have been admitted and received into communion and participation in the benefits of Christ and of the grace of God, for the remission of sins, salvation, and life eternal, if we lay hold of the promise by faith and cling to it, according to the saying: "He who believes and is baptized will be saved, but he who does not believe will be condemned." Thus the ancients not inappropriately called Baptism the first door into the church and to the kingdom of God. For from it we are sure that we have both an access and a return to the benefits of the Gospel, because we have been brought into communion with the Gospel through Baptism.

5 Therefore it is beyond controversy that for those who repent there is an access through faith, yes, a return to the grace of God in Christ Jesus. It is nothing else than that the penitent can and should return to the promise of grace given in Baptism. For Baptism is the solemn sealing and perpetual testimony that fellowship and participation in the benefits of Christ is offered and freely given us if we believe, for "he who believes and is baptized will be saved." But it is true faith not only when it lays hold of the promise of grace in the act of Baptism, but also when it retains it after Baptism; yes, it is true faith when after a fall it again in repentance lays hold of that promise. What Christ says stands fast: "He who believes and is baptized will be saved."

6 The meaning is not, however, that no one can lose the grace of Baptism, no matter how greatly he sins. For we teach that if those who had been converted commit acts against the conscience, they drive out at the same time faith, grace, and the Holy Spirit. However, the power and efficacy of Baptism is not itself destroyed on this account. For as someone can fall out of a ship while the ship itself remains unharmed, so many carelessly cast themselves out of the ark of Baptism into the sea of perdition and perish. These are the ones who desert faith in the promise and plunge into sin; but the ship itself remains whole. And if by the grace of God he who had fallen overboard can return to the ship, he will be carried to the harbor of salvation not by some new plank but by the solid ship itself from which he had fallen. But must he who had fallen be baptized again in order that he may in this way return to the ark of Baptism? We do not say this. But by the doctrine of the Law the fallen one is invited and led to repentance; the doctrine of the Gospel of the grace of God in Christ is proclaimed to him; if he believes, his sins are loosed or remitted by means of the office of the keys through the name of Christ; he is invited to the Lord's Supper, where he receives the New Testament in the blood of Christ. But this is not another, different, and new plank after the ark of Baptism has been broken and destroyed; it is the same promise, the same merit of Christ, the same grace of God, the same faith. For there is one faith according to Eph. 4:5. And Baptism is the perpetual testimony and seal that we have an entrance and a return to those benefits through faith after any lapse, not seven times but seventy times seven.

7 Therefore the preaching of repentance, the proclamation of the Gospel, the office of the keys, and the use of the Lord's Supper do not set before us even after a fall another and new plank for reconciliation with God and for salvation, different from that which was offered, given, and sealed to us in Baptism through the promise of God, but they are merely means through which we are either confirmed in the grace of Baptism or return to it after a fall. These things are simple, true, useful, and plain. So also Augustine teaches, *De nuptiis et concupiscentia*, Bk. 1, ch. 33: "What Paul says (Eph. 5:26): 'Having cleansed her by the washing of water with the Word,' is to be understood in the sense that by the same washing of regeneration and Word of sanctification all the evils of regenerate men are entirely cleansed and healed, not only the sins of the past, which are all now remitted in Baptism, but also those which are committed later through human ignorance or weakness. Not that Baptism should be repeated as often as one sins, but that by that which was once given pardon may be procured for all sins of believers, not only before but also afterward."

8 This is the teaching upon which the Tridentine fathers looked with distrust or rather with hatred and swelling pride when they set down this tenth canon. But let the reader observe that, although many of the papalist writers expressly condemn this whole teaching and defend the opposite opinion, the Tridentine assembly nevertheless did not dare to do this plainly and in so many words, fearing perhaps if not the judgment of their own conscience then at least that of pious hearers amid this light of the Gospel. So great is the power of the truth. Yet they did not see fit either to approve that doctrine or to dismiss it uncondemned. Therefore this stratagem was invented, that they misrepresent our teaching and state it differently than it is taught by our men, so that under that cover they might be able to condemn the doctrine which they oppose, and establish their own fictions. Therefore they pronounce the anathema on those who teach that sins which are committed after Baptism are remitted through the sole remembrance of the Baptism once received, that is, that to those who persevere and continue in their crimes without repentance, if only they remember perfunctorily and historically that they were at some time baptized, their sins are remitted by such remembrance, and indeed by this remembrance alone, so that there is no need for repentance and the office of the keys. Again, that all sins, however atrocious, become venial by the mere Epicurean remembrance of the Baptism once received, that is, that the baptized can persevere in them securely and with impunity. So say the Tridentine fathers. But our teachers do not acknowledge these opinions. And lest they quibble that we are hiding something, we declare: We condemn with a loud voice those Epicurean and shameful opinions, if anyone either thinks or teaches thus. Therefore it is not this but something far different which galls them; and because they do not dare to condemn it openly, they decided to condemn it under this deceitful perversion of the real point at issue. Let the reader diligently weigh this in his own mind.

SECTION VIII

[Concerning the Repeatability of Baptism]

CANON XI

If anyone says that a truly and validly conferred baptism is to be repeated in the case of someone who has denied the faith of Christ before unbelievers, when he is converted to repentance, let him be anathema.

Examination

1 We agree with the statement that no one who has been truly, validly, and legitimately baptized should be again baptized after every lapse, or even after a denial of the truth under persecution, when he is converted to repentance and desires to be reconciled to God.

2 But when the question is asked what the causes and reasons are why a legitimate Baptism should not be repeated, we find different opinions. For some who thought that when the ship or ark of Baptism is struck by sins it is so broken that it can afterwards be of no use to the baptized, even if he is again converted, judged that Baptism can be repeated and received a number of times. For Marcion taught on the basis of certain passages of the Gospel, which he twisted, that Baptism can be repeated three times to one and the same person. Others followed later who judged that because we sin daily, Baptism should also be repeated daily. These were therefore called "daily baptizers." For they judged that those who repent must not be held back from the remedy of salvation which Christ instituted; and because the earlier Baptism had been made invalid by sin, therefore it should be repeated lest the penitent sinner lack the promise: "He who believes and is baptized shall be saved." Now the papalists indeed are not strangers to the opinion that the ark of Baptism is broken through sin and altogether dissolved. Nevertheless they do not think that Baptism should be repeated. If you ask for the reason, they offer the new and uncertain fiction about the imprinting of the character, and they propose to the penitent, because his Baptism has become invalid, not this way to reconciliation with God, that he return in repentance, by faith, to the treaty of peace and the covenant of grace which

160

God entered into with us in Baptism on account of the merit of Christ; but they propose other remedies to him for regaining the grace of God.

3 Therefore a twofold explanation is necessary in the examination of this canon:

1. That Baptism is not to be repeated either after a fall or after a denial, when the sinner is converted to repentance.

2. There must also be shown true and weighty reasons from the Word of God why it is neither permitted nor necessary to repeat Baptism in the case of a baptized sinner who repents after a fall.

4 The causes or reasons are chiefly these:

I. The covenant of grace and the treaty of peace which is entered into and sealed in Baptism is not for the moment only, nor founded on the sand of the common rule: "To him who breaks faith, let faith be broken"; but it is perpetual, so that we may be able by repentance to return to it, as we have shown in the examination of the previous canon. Therefore it is not necessary to repeat Baptism. For God remains faithful forever in this His covenant. And if Baptism were repeated, an injustice would be done to the faithfulness of God Himself, as though our unfaithfulness could nullify God's faithfulness.

II. In the institution of the Eucharist Christ adds: "As often as you do this." Concerning repentance He even says: "I do not say to you seven times, but seventy times seven." Concerning Baptism, however, Scripture does not teach that as often as we fall, so often should we be baptized again. And concerning the sacraments we must judge according to the Word of God.

III. We have no example in Scripture where persons who had once been truly baptized were baptized again when, after a fall, they were converted to repentance. But to the fallen Corinthians and Galatians Paul sets forth the promise and consolation of the Baptism previously received (1 Cor. 6:11; 12:13; Gal. 3:27). We do not read in the Old Testament that those who fell after they had been circumcised were circumcised again when they repented, but that through repentance they returned to the covenant of circumcision, which was perpetual. It is the same in the New Testament with Baptism, which has taken the place of circumcision.

IV. Augustine, *In Evangelium Johannis tractatus,* 11 and 12, urges this reason: "As carnal generation is one, so also spiritual regeneration is one. As the natural birth cannot be repeated, so also not Baptism; we are born once; we are reborn once. Those, however, who either are weakened or die through sin, these are either healed or quickened again." These reasons are certain, firm, and clear. Besides these things certain others are also recorded in the discussions of the ancients, as that which Augustine says somewhere: "As Christ was crucified once, so Baptism is not to be repeated. For by His one death He redeemed all, that it might no more be necessary to die. Seeing this, the church understood that Baptism is not to be repeated." It is customary also to apply here what Christ says in John 13:10: "He who has bathed does not need to wash, except for his feet, but he is clean all over." Some also interpret Heb. 6:4 as showing that Baptism is not to be repeated, when it says: "It is impossible to renew again to repentance those who have once been enlightened," etc., for Paul calls Baptism the renewal, and the ancients called it illumination. Eph. 4:5 is also applied here: "one Baptism." But there is also "one faith," which nevertheless is repeated after a fall. The Eucharist is called "one bread," and yet it is written, "as often as," etc. Therefore the previous arguments are the surer and firmer. For this doctrine that Baptism should not be repeated must be taught in such a way that it is not merely argued that it is not to be repeated, but that Baptism is shown to be a fountain of comfort, that even after a fall, when we are again converted, even though we are not again baptized, we nevertheless have access to the treaty of peace and the covenant of grace which has been entered into with us and sealed through Baptism. For this reason I wanted to add these things concerning the explanation of the eleventh canon in this place.

SECTION IX

[Concerning the Proper Time for Baptism]

If anyone says that no one should be baptized except at the age at which Christ was baptized, or at the very moment of death, let him be anathema.

[Examination]

Concerning this opinion various things were argued in ancient times, but there is now no controversy concerning this matter. I shall therefore reply briefly that we gladly subscribe to this canon. Would that all were like this one!

[SECTION X]

[Concerning Infant Baptism]

CANON XIII

If any one says that infants, because they have not an active faith, are not to be reckoned among the believers after they have received baptism, and must therefore be baptized when they have attained to the years of discretion; or that it would be better that their baptism were omitted than that they, while not believing with their own act, should be baptized in the faith of the Church only, let him be anathema.

Examination

1 The question of the baptism of infants has been agitated with many and great contentions and disturbances by the Anabaptists, and it is profitable that the true, sure, firm, and clear foundations be shown, explained, and often repeated and inculcated from the Word of God that and why infants should be baptized. In our churches infant baptism has been diligently and learnedly defended and confirmed, and the opinions of the Anabaptists refuted. The fathers at Trent also make mention of this controversy; however, when they ought to explain the reasons why Baptism in infants should not be put off until they have reached the years of discretion, and why those are not to be rebaptized who were baptized in infancy, they omit this necessary explanation and start a dispute, which however they do not explain, concerning the faith of baptized infants, although the proof that and why Baptism also belongs to infants is not difficult, nor the arguments obscure in regard to whether and how infants believe.

2 There are other clearer and stronger arguments by which the ancients proved the baptism of infants. They appealed indeed to tradition, that is, the testimony of the first and purer church, that from apostolic times it was the universal and constant custom of the church to grant Baptism also to infants. However, the ancients do not rely either on tradition alone or on universal custom, as if infant baptism were to be received in the name of tradition although it could not be proved and established by any testimony of Scripture. Rather, they show that this tradition and custom rests on sure, firm, fitting, and harmonious testimonies of Scripture, for Christ declares in express words: "Let the children come to Me; do not hinder them, for to such belongs the kingdom of God." (Luke calls them *ta brephee,* infants who were still carried in arms.)

The kingdom of heaven does not, however, belong to infants in the same way as to the angels, who are without sin, for we are conceived and born in sin (Ps. 51:5). "That which is born of the flesh is flesh" (John 3:6), but "flesh cannot inherit the kingdom of God" (1 Cor. 15:50). "We were by nature children of wrath" (Eph. 2:3). "One man's trespass led to condemnation for all men" (Rom. 5:18). Therefore it is necessary that infants should be delivered from sin, from the wrath of God, and from damnation if they are to become heirs of the kingdom of heaven. No one can, however, be freed from those evils and come to the kingdom of heaven except by the grace of God, through the merit of Christ the Mediator. Now Christ expressly calls the little ones and wants them admitted to fellowship in His merits, for He says: "Let the children come to Me." And with respect to the will of the Father He declares: "It is not the will of My Father who is in heaven that one of these little ones should perish."

This grace God does not, however, offer, convey, give, and apply without means, but for this use He has instituted and ordained certain means or instruments. He also instituted the ministry in the church for this purpose, that it should offer and apply those means or instruments to all those for whom the promise of the Gospel, of God's grace, and of eternal life is meant.

Now that we have stated these sure, firm, and clear truths, it will be easy to answer the question before us. For because God does not want infants to perish, but declares that the kingdom of heaven is for them also, He wills that the giving and application of these benefits should be made through certain means or instruments instituted by Himself, namely, through the Word and the sacraments. It is therefore necessary that among these divinely instituted means there should be something which belongs also to infants. For the grace of God in the New Testament is not narrower, scantier, or smaller than it was in the Old Testament, where circumcision belonged also to infants. Let us therefore consider the means of application in the New Testament in order.

3 It is clear that one cannot deal with infants through the bare preaching of repentance and remission of sins, for that requires hearing (Rom. 10:17), deliberation and meditation (Ps. 119), understanding (Matt. 13:51), which are not found in infants. With regard to the Lord's Supper Paul says: "Let a man examine himself." Likewise: "Let him discern the Lord's body," a thing which cannot be ascribed to infants. Moreover, Christ instituted His Supper for such as had already become His disciples. In the Old Testament infants were circumcised on the eighth day, but they were admitted to the eating of the Passover lamb when they were able to ask: "What do you mean by this service?" (Ex. 12:26). There remains therefore of the means of grace in the New Testament only the sacrament of Baptism.

4 Now the question is whether the kingdom of heaven can and should be applied and assigned to infants through Baptism, since this cannot be done through the preaching of the Word and the Eucharist. I shall cite the arguments from Scripture which clearly confirm this.

1. Christ says of infants (Matt. 19:14): "To such belongs the kingdom of heaven." However, no one can enter the kingdom of heaven unless he is reborn (John 3:3). Baptism truly is "the washing of regeneration" (Titus 3:5). Therefore infants should be baptized in order that they may be born again and so be enabled to enter the kingdom of heaven according to Christ's promise. Yes, Christ says: "Whoever does not receive the kingdom of God like a child shall not enter it" (Mark 10:15). With respect to adults no one denies that they are born again of water and the Spirit in order to enter the kingdom of heaven (John 3:5). Therefore it must also not be denied with respect to infants, for adults receive the kingdom of God like children, according to Christ's teaching.

2. It is not the will of the heavenly Father that little children should perish (Matt. 18:14). Therefore He wills to save them. However, God does not save without means, but through "the washing of regeneration" (Titus 3:5). Therefore infants should be baptized.

3. Everyone who has sin needs forgiveness of sins, lest he perish. This, however, is conveyed through the means divinely appointed for it. Now Peter says (Acts 2:38): "Be baptized, every one of you, for the forgiveness of your sins." Therefore, lest infants perish, Baptism for the remission of sins must be given them.

4. Christ wills and commands that infants should be brought and led to Him (Matt. 18). But we cannot place infants into the arms of Christ bodily and visibly. However, Paul says of Baptism: "As many of you as were baptized have put on Christ" (Gal. 3:27) and: "All of us who have been baptized into Christ were baptized into His death" (Rom. 6:3). "We were buried with Him . . . and have been united with Him" (Rom. 6:4-5). Since therefore there is no doubt that infants should be brought to Christ, because He Himself wills and commands that this be done, the question is only by what means it can be done. Scripture shows a sure way how we can bring infants to Him, that they may put on Christ—namely, through

Baptism. It follows, therefore, that it is the will and command of Christ that infants should be baptized, that is, brought to Him, and He declares that to such as are brought to Him belongs the kingdom of heaven.

5. Christ wants to bless little children (Mark 10:16), that is, communicate His merits to them for salvation, for this is His true blessing (Gen. 22:17-18; Gal. 3:6-9; Eph. 1:3-10). Baptism is the means or instrument by which the benefits of Christ are communicated. For through Baptism Christ purifies and sanctifies (Eph. 5:26). We are baptized into His death (Rom. 6:3). Baptism saves us through the resurrection of Christ (1 Peter 3:21). Therefore infants should be baptized, in order that the blessing may be communicated to them, that is, participation in the merits of Christ.

6. When Christ says, "Let the children come to Me," He wills that infants should become His members, i.e., members of the church, whose head He is. For those who come to Christ are true members of the church (John 6:35 ff.). But we are baptized into one body (1 Cor. 12:13). Christ sanctifies His church and cleanses it "by washing of water with the Word" (Eph. 5:26). Therefore infants should be baptized in order that they may become members of the church of which Christ is the Head.

7. Those for whom Christ has given Himself that He may glorify them, them He sanctifies and cleanses by the washing of water with the Word (Eph. 5:26). But He died also for little children, because "He died for all" (2 Cor. 5:15; Heb. 7:27). And "to such belongs the kingdom of God" (Mark 10:14). It follows that He sanctifies and cleanses also infants by the washing of water with the Word. (Eph. 5:26)

8. Augustine advances a good argument when he deduces from circumcision that infants should be baptized in the New Testament, for Baptism succeeded circumcision (Col. 2:11-12). The same covenant of peace and compact of grace is for both. And because the nature of that covenant so far as infants are concerned was already known to the apostles from the manner of circumcision, therefore Christ was content with the general command concerning Baptism. He did not judge it necessary to prescribe anything in particular about infants. Neither is there any special mention concerning female children, but the statements in Matt. 28:19 and Mark 16:16 employ the masculine gender. And yet from the . . . purpose of the institution it is rightly judged that also females are to be baptized.

9. The command is universal, to baptize all who are not to be damned but saved (Matt. 28:19; Mark 16:16). Among these . . . are also little children (Matt. 18:3-4, 10). Therefore the command to baptize pertains also to infants.

10. Isaiah prophesies concerning the time of the New Testament (49:22) that it is not adults only who shall become members of the church. He says: "I will raise My signal to the peoples; and they shall bring your sons in their bosom, and your daughters shall be carried on their shoulders." In Acts 2:38-39, when Peter had said, "Be baptized, every one of you, in the name of Jesus Christ for the forgiveness of your sins, and you shall receive the gift of the Holy Spirit," he adds "for the promise is to you and to your children." In Acts 16:15, 33, and 1 Cor. 1:16 entire households are said to have been baptized, i.e., whole families, to which infants certainly also belong.

5 These demonstrations from Scripture show certainly and firmly that infants are not to be kept from Baptism. To this there comes the universal custom of the catholic church, which from the times of the apostles has always given Baptism also to infants. Therefore the basis for infant baptism is not the difficult and obscure debate about the faith of infants. But among the arguments which are usually advanced and raised against the true teaching after it has been established are principally these, that in the institution of Baptism these two things are connected: (1) teaching and baptizing; (2) believing and being baptized. But neither teaching nor believing seems to fit infants.

To the first we reply: It is true and certain that Christ connects teaching or the Word and Baptism. For Baptism is neither an ordinary nor a silent washing, but "the washing of water with the Word" (Eph. 5:26). Moreover, it is the sealing of the promise of the Gospel. Therefore Baptism neither can nor should be without the Word, as Augustine says: "Remove the Word from Baptism, and what will the water be but water?" Therefore where the Word of the Gospel is neither preached nor received, there Baptism should not be administered either to adults or to infants. For Baptism is the sealing of the doctrine of the Gospel. From this it does not, however, follow that Baptism should be denied to infants. For it is a part of the doctrine of the Gospel that also infants belong to the promise of the Gospel of the New Testament (Acts 2:39), to the church (Is. 49:22), and to the kingdom of heaven (Matt. 19:14). Therefore also that part of the doctrine is to be sealed through Baptism in little children.

Infant baptism is not a bath without the Word, but it is the washing of water with the Word, namely, of the promise of the Father's grace, of the Son's cleansing, of the Spirit's sanctification, through and on account of the merit of Christ, the Mediator. Therefore there is and remains and is preserved a connection between the Word and Baptism also in the baptism of infants; thus its institution is satisfied.

But if anyone urges that Baptism must not only be a washing of water with the Word, but that those who are baptized must also be taught, I reply: "The same was also the case in the rite of circumcision," whence it is easy to answer this objection. Before Abraham was circumcised, God instructed him (Gen. 17:1 ff.). And there is no doubt that before Abraham circumcised Ishmael and the other members of his household he first instructed them, as God says (Gen. 18:19): "I have chosen him that he may charge his children and his household after him to keep the way of the Lord." Both were commanded in the Old Testament: that they should teach their children (Deut. 4:9-10; 6:2, 20 ff.; 12:28) and that they should circumcise them (Gen. 17:12-14). In the case of adults the teaching preceded, and circumcision followed (Gen. 17:11). Infants, however, were to be circumcised on the eighth day (Gen. 17:12), but they are commanded to be instructed when they are able to ask: "What is the meaning of these testimonies?" (Deut. 6:20). Yet circumcision was "with the Word" also when infants were circumcised on the eighth day, though it was only afterward, during boyhood, that they were instructed. God Himself judged that in this way His institution was satisfied. . . .

6 This explanation is quite obvious not only on account of the similarity between circumcision and Baptism, but chiefly because in the New Testament Baptism has replaced circumcision (Col. 2:11-12). Because this was then so well known to the apostles . . . Christ did not particularly teach anything concerning the baptism of infants but was content with the general command to baptize all who were to be saved. This can be gathered also from the writings of the apostles. Paul, writing to Christian parents (Eph. 6:4) about how they should bring up their children who had already reached the age when they could obey their parents, gives a command concerning the instruction of the Lord. But he does not add that only afterward should they be baptized. Thus also in 1 John 2:12-14 he divides Christian instruction as follows: (1) for fathers; (2) for young men; (3) for children; (4) for infants, whom he calls *paidia,* when they are first able to be taught; he does not, however, add that only then or thereafter should they be baptized. Therefore they first brought their little children to Christ in their arms that they might become children of the church according to the prophecy (Is. 49:22; Luke 18:15-17), and afterward, at the proper time, Christian instruction followed. Thus they judged that the institution of Christ with respect to teaching and baptizing was satisfied.

7 A second argument, however, properly belongs to the explanation of this thirteenth cannon . . . because Christ connects believing and bapitzing: whether and in what way baptized infants believe.

I indeed, as a lover of simplicity, even though I do not understand and cannot explain how infants believe, nevertheless judge that the strong testimonies detailed above suffice to prove that infants ought to be baptized. For I ought not to disregard these if I cannot understand or explain how infants believe. Nevertheless the explanation of this canon demands that certain things be said with respect to this discussion. There are the statements of Scripture: "He that does not believe will be condemned." "He who does not believe is condemned already." "He who does not obey the Son . . . the wrath of God rests upon him." "Whoever believes in Him shall not perish but have eternal life." "Without faith it is impossible to please God," etc. Now, because infants who are baptized do not perish, but the kingdom of heaven is theirs, the question is whether infants who are baptized should be said to believe or not to believe, to have faith or not to have faith; whether they are to be numbered among the believers or the unbelievers.

8 Some simply argue that all these and similar statements of Scripture pertain only to adults, not, however, to infants, whom they hold to be saved indeed by the grace of God but without faith; nevertheless they do not want baptized infants to be numbered among the unbelievers. Therefore they are obliged to invent, without the authority of Scripture, a certain middle state between faith and unbelief, between believers and unbelievers. I cannot agree with this opinion, for the statements of Scripture are general. However, faith and unbelief, believers and unbelievers, are contradictory terms. Neither does such an interpretation agree with the passage where Baptism is commanded to be communicated to the Gentiles: "He who believes and is baptized will be saved; but he who does not believe will be condemned," that is, those who are adults; but the infants, who constitute the larger part of those who are now baptized, do not believe, and yet, although they are baptized without faith, they are not condemned but saved.

9 Therefore the statement of Augustine which he made in *De verbis apostoli, sermo* 24, is simpler, truer, and sounder. After quoting the saying of Christ, "He who does not believe will be condemned," he asks the Pelagian: "Where do you place the baptized infants? Certainly in the number of believers. For this reason the baptized infants are also according to the ancient, canonical, and well-founded custom of the church called believers. You will therefore number baptized infants among the believers; nor will you dare to judge in any other way if you do not wish openly to be a heretic." This statement Augustine often repeats elsewhere.

10 But now there arises the more difficult and obscure question: In what way do infants believe, or what kind of faith do little children have? With respect to adults the matter is clear. For in their case faith arises from hearing, thinking, meditating on, and apprehending the preached Word. It is assent in the mind and trust in the will by which the heart is raised up and set at rest. Believing, he knows that he believes; he wills and endeavors to retain faith, and then also to grow in it; he wrestles with doubt, mistrust, and fear. He shows forth its power through external signs and testimonies, etc.

If it is asked whether infants who are baptized believe altogether in this way—whether this is entirely the way faith acts in baptized infants—Augustine answers in the negative. For he says, in Letter No. 23: "Although an infant does not yet have that faith which is an act of the will, nevertheless the sacrament of this faith makes him a believer." There he is called a believer, not because he assents consciously . . . but because he receives the sacrament which transmits the faith.

In *In Evangelium Johannis tractatus*, 80, and *Contra Donatistas*, Bk. 4, ch. 24, he says: "Baptized infants cannot as yet believe with the heart to righteousness and confess with their mouth to salvation." In Letter No. 57, to Dardanus, he says: "If we wanted to demonstrate with words that infants, who do not even know human things, know divine things, I fear that we would seem to do an injustice to our senses. . . ."

In *De peccatorum meritis*, Bk. 1, ch. 19, he says that "baptized infants do not yet have a sensation of faith." This is meant in the frequent question whether infants believe by an act. If this question is understood in the manner explained by Augustine, it is clear what the answer should be. Nevertheless it should not be said that because baptized infants cannot believe by an act like adults, therefore they cannot believe in any way at all, or that faith can in no way be given them by God. Thus they do not know the Holy Spirit, says Augustine, although He is in them, just as they do not know their own mind, yes, their own life; nevertheless it must not for this reason be said that they have neither mind nor life. Augustine is at pains that he may somehow show how infants, when they are baptized, may believe, so that it is not mere make-believe when those who present an infant for Baptism reply, when asked: "He believes." Indeed, he argues in many passages that infants are baptized into a faith not their own—either that of the parents, or of those who bring them, or of the entire church, *De verbis apostoli, sermo* 14; Letters No. 23, 57, 105; *Contra Donatistas*, Bk. 4, ch. 24, etc.

11 Some interpret this as if there were clearly no action of God, as if no operation of the Spirit took place in the infant while he is baptized, but as if one were baptized while another believed, and as if the faith of another were imputed to the infant, in whom the Holy Spirit worked nothing at all for righteousness and salvation. This opinion is not in harmony with Scripture. It is indeed true that physical benefits are often procured for someone by another's faith, as in the story of the woman of Canaan. The faith of another can also sometimes by prayer obtain this, that an ungodly person is by the grace of God converted, illumined, and endowed with faith of his own. But no one who is without faith can be justified and saved by the faith of another (Rom. 1:17; 4:5). Nowhere, moreover, does Scripture teach that the faith of another is imputed to me for righteousness if I myself am without faith.

12 I do not think Augustine meant that the Holy Spirit does not work at all in infants while they are baptized. For he explains his meaning as follows, Letter No. 57: "We say therefore that the Holy Spirit dwells in baptized infants, although they do not know it. For they do not know Him, although He is in them, just as they do not know their own mind, which is in them, although they cannot as yet use it, like a dormant spark, to be aroused as they increase in age." And when he has shown that the Holy Spirit also dwells in some adults who are unconscious of it, he adds: "He is said to dwell also in such persons because He works secretly in them that they may be His temples, a work which He afterward completes in those who go forward and persevere in going forward."

In *De peccatorum meritis,* Bk. 1, ch. 33, he says: "Where, then, do we place the baptized infants if not among the believers, as the authority of the universal church everywhere demands? Therefore we place them among those who have come to faith, because this has been gained for them through the power of the sacrament and the answer of those who bring them." Ibid., ch. 25: "Infants enter into the number of the believers through the sacrament which has been divinely instituted for this purpose." In ch. 19 he says: "All this is done in hope, through the power of the sacrament and of the divine grace which the Lord has bestowed on the church."

In Letter No. 23 he explains as follows how an infant who is presented for Baptism through . . . another's will can be regenerated: "It is not written, 'Except a man be born again by the will of the parents or of those who present him, or by the faith of the ministrants' but, 'Unless one is born of water and the Spirit.' Therefore the faith of another presents the infant for Baptism, and there the water outwardly imparts the sacrament of grace; the Spirit, however, inwardly works the gift of grace. Therefore the Spirit of regeneration is present both in the adults who bring the infant and in the infant who is presented and regenerated. And through this sharing of one and the same Spirit the will of those presenting profits the infant who is presented."

This statement clearly shows that Augustine did not think that baptized infants are regenerated by another's faith, either that of the parents, or of those presenting him, or of the church, but that the faith of another, which is convinced that the promise of the Gospel belongs also to infants, presents the infant for Baptism, in which the Holy Spirit is given to the infant, working inwardly and in a hidden manner in the infant. As Augustine says in another statement, quoted by Alexander of Hales: "Faith is bestowed and nourished through Baptism."

13 This I very simply judge to be the meaning of Augustine; so also Luther explains it. Discussing in *De captivitate Babylonica* whether infants are able to have faith, he says: "Here I say what all say, that infants are aided by the faith of those who present them." This he quickly explains: "As the Word of God is powerful when it sounds forth to change even the heart of the ungodly, which is not less deaf and powerless than any infant," so he holds that through the prayer of the presenting and believing church the infant is changed, cleansed, and renewed in Baptism by infused faith, etc.

14 How this can be understood very simply is explained in the formula of agreement between the theologians of Saxony and Upper Germany, drawn up in the year 1536: "When we say that infants believe or have faith, it is not to be thought that infants understand or feel the movements of faith, but the error of those is rejected who think that baptized infants please God and are saved without any action of the Holy Spirit in them, although Christ clearly says: 'Unless one is born of water and the Spirit.' Also, the Holy Spirit is always given with the remission of sins. Neither can anyone please God without the Holy Spirit (Rom. 8:8-9). Since it is certain that baptized infants are members of the church and please God, it is also certain that the Holy Spirit is effectually working in them, and indeed working in such a way that they are able to accept the kingdom of heaven, that is, the grace of God and the forgiveness of sins. Christ expressly affirms this (Mark 10:15): 'Truly, I say to you, whoever does not receive the kingdom of God like a child shall not enter it.' Therefore it is certain from this statement of Christ that the kingdom of God is not only offered and given to little children who are presented to Christ, but also that they accept it. However, 'the unspiritual man does not receive the gifts of the Spirit' (1 Cor. 2:14). Therefore the Spirit of God must needs be efficacious in infants who are baptized, and work in them so that they are able to accept the kingdom of God, which is offered and given in Baptism—in His own manner, which is neither sufficiently known to us nor explainable. However, the Spirit of regeneration and renewal is poured out into those who are baptized (Titus 3:5-6). Therefore He is poured out also into infants. And though we do not sufficiently understand nor are able to explain in words what the nature of that action and work of the Holy Spirit is in infants who are baptized, yet that it is and is done is certain from the Word of God. This work and operation of the Holy Spirit in infants we call faith, and we say that infants believe, for the means or instrument by which the kingdom of God, which is offered in the Word and in the sacraments, is accepted Scripture calls faith, and it says that believers receive the kingdom of God. Indeed, in Mark 10:15 Christ asserts that adults receive the kingdom of God in the same way as little children receive it. And in Matt. 18:6 He says: 'Whoever causes one of these little ones who believe in Me to sin.' Among those little ones He also counts a child *(paidion)*. Moreover, circumcision is in general called a seal of the righteousness of faith (Rom. 4:11). Now, if the righteousness of faith is ascribed to circumcised infants, it follows that faith also is ascribed to them."

15 This, I judge, is the simplest understanding of this most difficult and complex question, namely, that infants are not sanctified and saved in Baptism without some act and operation of the Holy Spirit in them. That they receive the kingdom of God the Son of God Himself affirms. This cannot, however, happen without the working of the Holy Spirit. There is no doubt that the Holy Spirit can effect this in infants who do not yet use their reason, although the way and manner can neither be comprehended nor explained by us, as He has shown by a clear example in John the Baptist. For of his exultation the angel says: "He will be filled with the Holy Spirit even from his mother's womb." This singular example does not, indeed, establish a general rule; nevertheless it shows that the Holy Spirit is able to operate also in infants.

16 The scholastics and papalist writers have rendered this question, which is in itself difficult and obscure, even more complex by various arguments. For some argue that in Baptism no powers are infused in children who are not yet using their reason, neither by way of an act, nor by way of an ability, nor by way of a beginning, but that only in adulthood, which they place below the 30th year, are these conferred; or, that if they die in infancy and have been baptized, the powers are conferred on them at the separation of soul and body. Others argue that in Baptism neither abilities nor actual powers are conferred, but a root of these, which is a grace. Others make this root the mark (character) of Baptism, and say that with increase in age the branches from this root become abilities or powers out of which the acts follow at the proper time. A third group is of the opinion that a quality of powers is infused in baptized infants, not, however, acts or the use of these powers. These opinions are left hanging in air in the *Constitution of Innocent Concerning Baptism,* ch.

Majores. Afterward, at the Council of Vienna, Clement judged the last opinion to be the more probable.

What do our men of Trent say? First they condemn with the anathema anyone who says that little children who are baptized possess the act of faith. Now, if they understand the act of believing as we have explained it above in the statement of Augustine, I do not object. But if with this statement they simply want to deny to all baptized children every action and operation of the Holy Spirit, it must certainly be contradicted. Of faith as an ability they make no mention. Therefore this opinion, which was judged at the Council of Vienna to be the more probable, so displeases the Tridentine fathers that they do not consider it worthy of mention, although a discussion about infants was expressly undertaken in this 13th canon. Yet they do not think that infants are baptized without faith, but say that they are baptized only in the faith of the church. We have shown that this is wrong if they understand it as the words read, namely, that in Baptism there occurs no divine action or operation of the Holy Spirit whatever.

17 I see, however, that this entire canon was stated ambiguously and in many words with a certain amount of forethought. Therefore I wanted to explain this whole dispute in a simple way. For they appear to have aimed to censure the teaching of our churches about the faith of little children in an indirect manner, namely, that they may uphold the axiom that the sacraments confer grace without the faith of the person who uses them. If, however, they have drawn up this canon only against the opinion of the Anabaptists, we want them to know that we are farther than far removed from the sect of the Anabaptists.

SECTION XI
[Concerning Coercion to a Christian Life]

If anyone says that those who were baptized as infants should, when they grow up, be asked whether they want to hold valid what their sponsors promised in their name when they were baptized, and if they reply that they do not, that they should be allowed to have their own will and that they should not be coerced by any punishment to a Christian life, except that they be restrained from the reception of the Eucharist and of the other sacraments until they come to their senses, let him be anathema.

[Examination]

1 The statement which is censured in this canon is attributed to Erasmus. And indeed if it only demanded public and free confession from adults of that faith in which they were baptized as infants, it would contain nothing inappropriate. The form of interrogation could also be excused, for it is found, and indeed in almost sterner words, in Joshua 24:15: "Choose this day whom you will serve," etc. Nevertheless, as the statement is worded in this canon, I am not willing to defend it. For when those who were baptized in infancy have grown to adulthood, they must not be offered the free option whether they want to hold that valid which was done in their Baptism, as though the pact of grace and the covenant of peace which is offered and sealed to infants through Baptism would first begin to be valid when the consent of the adult will is added. For on this crooked basis the Anabaptists simply did away with and condemned infant baptism. But such baptized infants are to be earnestly reminded, when they have grown up, of the pact of grace and covenant of peace which God entered into with them in Baptism, and of the promise of grateful obedience to God to which they on their part obligated themselves with the renunciation of Satan. Moreover they are to be earnestly admonished to give thanks to God for this great blessing, to remain in this covenant of peace, and to be zealous to fulfill this obligation through the mortification of sin and the beginning of a new life, and that they should do this freely and from the heart. Or, if out of ingratitude they have departed from this covenant and from this obligation, [they are to be

admonished] to repent and to return to this covenant and to subject themselves again to the stipulated obedience. But to those who do otherwise the most severe threats of divine wrath and indignation are to be set forth and impressed, to which the binding key for the retaining and binding of sins and excommunication ought to be added, for these are "the weapons of our warfare." (2 Cor. 10:4)

2 The church of Christ does not, however, recognize coercion to faith through outward compulsion and corporal punishments, for it has only the sword of the Spirit. But the other sword, namely the bodily, has been committed by God to the civil magistrate. If he is pious he must use it, as for the punishment of other crimes so also for the punishment of public, external, and notorious blasphemies, especially if sedition comes to it. Thus God prescribed and commanded the magistrate of the people of Israel by a special law (Deut. 13). However, perhaps the gentle Tridentine fathers are not content with the sword of the Spirit but want to coerce those who depart from the covenant of Baptism by another punishment besides, in order that they may always have fagots ready with which they can kindle both stakes and destructive wars if anyone is not willing to swear to all their opinions.

Third Topic

CONCERNING CONFIRMATION

From the Seventh Session
of the Council of Trent, March 3, 1547

If anyone says that the confirmation of the baptized is a useless ceremony and not rather a true and proper sacrament, or that it was at one time nothing else than a certain instruction by which those approaching adolescence confessed the ground of their faith before the Church, let him be anathema.

CANON II

If anyone says that those who ascribe any power to the sacred anointing of confirmation are insulting the Holy Spirit, let him be anathema.

CANON III

If anyone says that the ordinary minister of holy confirmation is not solely the bishop, but any simple priest, let him be anathema.

Examination

1 In order that it may be possible to explain the entire debate concerning confirmation briefly and in a more suitable order, we shall first state the teaching and understanding of the papalists about confirmation. Second, we shall show how that teaching and understanding of the papalists either agrees or conflicts with Scripture. Third, we shall say certain things about the statements which are quoted from the writings of the ancients in favor of confirmation. Finally, we shall examine the canons, and show in what way our churches judge that the rite of confirmation may be observed and used in the church in a godly way and fruitfully for edification.

2 First I shall gather into a summary from their own older and more recent writers as briefly as possible what the teaching and understanding of the papalist church is concerning confirmation. I shall state it in their own words in order that my account may find greater credence. As the genuine sacraments, such as Baptism and the Lord's Supper, have a certain material and specific form (for form is what they call the word which belongs to each sacrament), so they also ascribe to their confirmation a certain material thing, namely, oil, and that not simple or common oil, nor such as the blessed oil which they call that of the catechumens and of the sick, but chrism, that is, olive oil mixed with balsam according to a certain proportion or formula. Nor indeed do they simply require a mixture of olive oil and balsam, but the chrism must be fresh, i.e., it must be consecrated every year on a certain day of the year by the bishop with certain prescribed formulas of exorcising and blessing; otherwise it is not considered a sacrament.

The form of confirmation according to their teaching is found in the words: "I sign you with the sign of the cross, and confirm you with the chrism of salvation in the name of the Father, and of the Son, and of the Holy Spirit." Confirmation itself they define as the anointing or besmearing with the consecrated chrism which is performed by the bishop with the thumb on the forehead of the baptized person, not in the act of Baptism itself but later in a special sacrament by means of the form or figure of the cross with the pronouncing of these words: "I sign you with the sign of the cross," etc. However, in that same act also other formal prayers are added, and the words: "Peace be with you" are pronounced. After this first act the bishop strikes the anointed person on the cheek with his thumb, thereupon with his whole hand. Then the forehead, which has been anointed with the ointment, is bound round about with a white cloth, which is taken off on the seventh day thereafter, that the recent anointing may not flow down or be wiped off. Finally, he is committed to his guardians. This is the act of confirmation.

3 The principal point of this controversy is the manner in which they speak of the efficacy of this confirmation of theirs. This entire dispute cannot be set forth more briefly nor be more rightly understood than if it is considered that in their teaching there is a constant antithesis between Baptism and confirmation, so that whatever effects are ascribed to confirmation are by that very fact denied to or taken away from Baptism. In what way and for what reason they suppose the sacrament of confirmation to be more excellent, worthier, and greater, so that it is to be venerated and held in greater reverence (for these are their own words) than Baptism itself, they take in part from the nature of the minister by whom it is performed or administered, who must be a bishop. But chiefly they take it from the effects, which are superior to those of Baptism itself. They quote statements like the following from apocryphal and forged writings of the oldest Roman pontiffs. Urban says: "All the faithful must receive the Holy Spirit by the laying on of hands of the bishops after Baptism, in order that they may be found full Christians." He continues to attribute to confirmation these workings of the Spirit, "that we are made spiritual, for the unspiritual man does not receive the gifts of the Spirit of God; that the heart is enlarged to prudence and constancy; that we may know how to discern between good and evil, to fight against wickedness, resist evil desires, so that fired by love of eternal life we may be able to raise our soul from earth to heavenly and divine things." This they attribute to Urban.

The reader will remember that the point of the controversy is about what confirmation confers that Baptism does not have. Their Clement says that the baptized person finally receives through confirmation the sevenfold grace of the Holy Spirit and that, if he were not sealed by the bishop with the chrism, he could be a perfect Christian in no other way, nor have a place among the perfected, even if he had been baptized.

The sevenfold grace of the Spirit they understand in the way they are accustomed to enumerate the seven gifts of the Spirit. For in the course of confirmation the bishop prays among other things thus over the confirmand: "Send upon him Thy Holy Spirit, the Paraclete of Thy sevenfold grace, from heaven, the Spirit of wisdom and knowledge, the Spirit of counsel and strength, the Spirit of understanding and piety, and fill him with the Spirit of Thy fear, and sign him with the sign of the holy cross as reconciled, and may he not lose the Holy Spirit, unto eternal life."

From a certain spurious sermon attributed to Cyprian concerning the chrism they have taken these words: "It is certain that through this fluid all the various graces descend which the Holy Spirit distributes and bestows on individuals as He wills. From the benefaction of this unction both wisdom and understanding are divinely given; counsel and strength flow from heaven; knowledge and piety and fear are poured in by heavenly inspirations. Anointed with this oil, we wrestle with spiritual wickedness in order that we, who are fragrant with the scent of spiritual balsam, cannot be contaminated with spurious and offensive smells."

They also apply to their confirmation what Cyprian says, Letter No. 12, Bk. 1: "It is necessary also that he who has been baptized be anointed, that, having received the chrism, he may be anointed by God and may be able to have in himself the grace of Christ." Also, Letter No. 1, Bk. 2: "Then finally can they be fully sanctified and be children of God when they are born again by both sacraments, namely of Baptism and of the laying on of hands."

Let the reader always remember that a contrast is made between the efficacy of Baptism and the power of confirmation, so that those things which are ascribed to confirmation are denied as being given or received in Baptism. Thus the Council of Laodicea says, Canon 48: "It is necessary that the baptized should after their baptism receive the most sacred chrism and become partakers of the heavenly kingdom." According to Eusebius, Bk. 6, ch. 46, Cornelius says: "Although Novatus had been baptized, yet, because he had not afterward been perfected with the sign of the chrism, he had never been able to obtain the Holy Spirit." Melchiades says, *De consecratione*, dist. 5: "In Baptism the Holy Spirit bestows beauty for innocence; in confirmation he gives increase for grace; in

Baptism we are regenerated to life; after Baptism we are confirmed for battle; in Baptism we are washed; in confirmation we are made strong." This Gropper explains as follows at the provincial council of Cologne: "In Baptism we are born again as children of God and receive the promise of the heavenly inheritance; but that we may retain it we orphans have need of a guardian. Therefore it is not sufficient to receive the Spirit of renewal in Baptism if we do not also through the sacrament of confirmation receive the guarding and defending Spirit. For insofar as the Holy Spirit is given in confirmation, He is the Paraclete, who is the Guardian, Comforter, and Teacher of the regenerate in Christ." Rabanus says, *De consecratione,* dist. 6: "In Baptism the Holy Spirit descends to consecrate a habitation for God; but in the anointing of confirmation the Holy Spirit comes into man with His sevenfold grace and with all the fullness of holiness, knowledge, and strength." "That is," says Durandus, "into the house which has been consecrated through Baptism," who also adds that "through Baptism the soul is betrothed to Christ, but through confirmation it is endowed and made rich." Likewise: "Through Baptism wounds are healed, but through confirmation a plenitude of graces is bestowed." He adds also: "After the confirmation we say to the confirmed: 'Peace be with you.' " This he explains thus: "The new man, who is created after God, is worthy to be greeted. In the interim, however, because he was the old man, he was not to be greeted but only to be prayed for."

The reader must always remember that the antithesis is between Baptism and confirmation. The Council of Orleans, *De consecratione,* dist. 5, says: "No one will ever be a Christian if he has not been anointed in confirmation by the bishop." A gloss says: "An infant that has been baptized but not anointed will have a lesser glory than one that has also been confirmed," and it adds: "This is to be conceded only if it is admitted that grace is conferred on the infant in Baptism." Let the reader mark this well, that grace can be taken away altogether from Baptism and ascribed to the chrism. The Council of Tours prescribes that the sacred chrism is to be guarded carefully. It adds the reason: "Lest some unbeliever touch that by which we are incorporated into Christ and by which we, who are faithful, are all sanctified." The *Compendium theologiae* says: "Confirmation arms soul and body—the soul through impression of the character against the defect of faintheartedness—the body through the shield of the cross; it gives courage against the attacks of evil spirits and against fear in confessing Christ's name; it crowns the fighter with the headband known as the *vitta,* which is bound around the head of the confirmed." Gerson quotes from Hugo: "What good does it do if, through Baptism, you rise from a fall, if you are not also, through confirmation, strengthened to stand?"

4 Here the reader should stop and weigh the matter. If all these things which up to this time we have rehearsed in the very words of the papalists are taken away from Baptism, how beggarly, bare, and poor does it leave the sacrament of Baptism! But wait a bit, kind reader, and you will hear, according to the prophecy of Daniel, a mouth speaking even greater and more hideous things. For in the *Pontificale* the bishop prays, among other things, over the balsam: "We earnestly request Thy mercy to pour out into this unguent spiritual grace, richly bestowing the fullness of sanctification, that all those regenerated through Baptism who are anointed with this fluid may attain to the fullest blessing of their bodies and souls."

When the oil is mixed with the balsam, the bishop among other things prays thus: "May the perfection of the Holy Trinity bless you, and in blessing sanctify you, and grant that whoever is externally anointed with this may be so inwardly anointed that, free from all uncleanness of bodily matter, he may gratefully acknowledge that he has been made a partaker of the kingdom of heaven." Likewise: "That all who are anointed with you may thereby receive the adoption of sons through the Holy Spirit." In the preface the bishop chants among other things: "Deign to sanctify the fatness of this substance with Thy blessing and to admix to it the power of the Holy Spirit, with the cooperation of the power of Christ, Thy Son, that it may be to those who have been born again of water and the Spirit a chrism of salvation and make them to be partakers of eternal life and heirs of the heavenly kingdom." Likewise: "May this mixture of liquids be to all who are anointed with it a propitiation and saving protection forever and ever." Likewise: "That it may be to those who are anointed with you for adoption of flesh and spirit, for the remission of sins, that their bodies may be sanctified for the reception of every spiritual grace."

After the consecration of the chrism the chanters sing among other things this verse: "Thou who art born of the heart of the Father and didst fill the womb of the Virgin, open the door of life; imprison death through the consecrated chrism."

This reminder must be repeated over and over, that there is an antithesis between Baptism and confirmation, so that whatever is ascribed to confirmation is *eo ipso* denied as belonging to or being conferred by Baptism. These by and large are the mysteries of the traditions concerning confirmation among the papalists. I have rehearsed them in their own words lest someone should think they had been forged, or claim that they had been exaggerated in a hateful manner to make the opposing party look bad. The reader will perceive that it is not about a light matter or about nothing at all when one argues with the papalists about confirmation.

It will also be understood more fully through this account what the first two canons on confirmation contain and conceal in their embrace. And now that the real point of the controversy has been recognized, the basis on which the dispute is carried on either in affirming or in refuting will be more diligently considered.

5 In the second place we must now consider what kind of basis they have and advance for their opinion. For they ascribe many and, in truth, great things to their confirmation. My friend Andrada orates verbosely: "Seeing that the infirmity of human nature is so great that the fear of imminent death can easily cause us to fall from faith, what if Christ instituted this sacrament for this reason, impressing upon it the strength and power of His blood, in order that it might make strong and perfect the faith conferred upon us in the sacred washing and anchor it as it were with the deepest roots, so that neither the tempest of peril nor the favorable breezes of glory should be able to deflect minds confirmed and made strong through the exceedingly great power of the Holy Spirit from the course of faith either through hope or through fear? Who are we that we should want to impose laws upon divine wisdom, and to measure His infinite goodness and His inmost hidden counsels with our judgment as with a norm, that we should ascribe only those blessings to Christ which we consider necessary for ourselves but that we should impiously reject, despise, and trample under foot those we cannot comprehend?" So says Andrada.

Gropper also orates that after Baptism, as after the crossing of the Red Sea, one must enter upon the vast desert of this world, in which one must battle without ceasing with foes, both internal and external, namely, with our own flesh, the world, and the devil, before we enter the Promised Land, and that the assault of these enemies is so great that anyone who enters upon this may well be terrified, cast away the treasures of Baptism, and despair, unless meanwhile he understands that Christ the Redeemer has prepared other remedies against these assaults, by which He comes to our assistance in our struggles. And since the sacrament of confirmation holds the foremost place among these means, it is a great piece of rashness and arrogance to want to repudiate this useful and necessary remedy. So says Gropper.

6 We however, my friends, are not the ones who either ignore or despise the dangers which threaten us from these enemies. . . . Nor do we trust that we can sustain and ward off their assaults by our own powers and thus remain and persevere in the faith. But we know and confess that we have need of the grace and strengthening of the Holy Spirit, who unceasingly and constantly (as Augustine says) leads, guides, confirms, strengthens, comforts, and preserves us. We know and confess also that the Holy Spirit works efficaciously in believers, not without means, but through certain means or instruments divinely instituted for this purpose. We also teach and admonish diligently that such means should be used reverently and with proper gratitude of heart. However, we know also this, that such means, to which we ascribe and for which we allege the working of the Holy Spirit, are not to be invented for us by our own will or instituted by human authority. When therefore it is asked what those means are through which we should believe that the Holy Spirit wants to work effectively, we ask above all things that an express divine command and promise be shown us. For when we have these, then we know that these means must be reverently used, because they are divinely instituted, and we know also what is to be ascribed to them.

7 Therefore I simply reply to the rhetorical declamations of Andrada and Gropper: I confess that in this life the baptized walk in great spiritual dangers in which the grace, guidance, and strengthening of the Holy Spirit is altogether necessary to them. I confess also that the Holy Spirit effects and works these things through certain means as the divine instruments instituted for this purpose. Therefore I agree wholly that these means are to be used reverently. But I add that what these means are must not be decided by human judgment, either our own or anyone else's, but that this is to be sought, learned, and shown from the Word of God. But if any such means are proposed to us which have neither a divine command of institution nor the promise of efficacy from sure, firm, and clear testimonies of Scripture, we set against them the statement of Christ: "My sheep hear My voice . . . from a stranger they will flee," and it is written: "You shall not take the name of the Lord your God in vain." However, Christ has instituted a number of means for preserving and strengthening the grace conferred in Baptism. For we find in Scripture that the Holy Spirit is poured on us abundantly in Baptism, not in order that He may work in us only in that moment when we are baptized but that He may forever preserve, guide, confirm, and strengthen us in the grace of Baptism until finally, in the next life, we are made to stand before God without spot (Eph. 5:27). We also learn from Scripture that the souls of the disciples are confirmed by the Word (Acts 14:22; 15:32; 18:23). We know also that the sacrament of the Eucharist was instituted for this use,

that the spiritual life into which we were born again through Baptism may be preserved, confirmed, and strengthened, according to the saying: "He who eats Me will live because of Me" (John 6:57). We teach that these means, which have the testimony of Scripture, should be used for strengthening in the fight against spiritual enemies, through hearing, meditation, faith, wrestling, and prayer.

But they say: "What if Christ had in addition instituted the sacrament of chrism for confirmation?" I answer: If He had judged it necessary, He would without doubt have instituted it. And if we were assured from the Word of God concerning its institution, that is, concerning a command and promise of Christ, we would want to embrace it with a grateful heart. But this, precisely, is the question in controversy. Unless they clearly prove this to us from sure, firm, and clear testimonies of Scripture, we shall not let ourselves be led away from the promise of Baptism, from the Word and the Eucharist, from faith and prayer, which means have the testimony of the Word of God, to human inventions, no matter what their pretense either of antiquity or of authority. For only He can institute a sacrament who is able to give to the sacrament spiritual efficacy, as the scholastics correctly say. Let us hear, therefore, which and what sort of grounds and arguments the papalists can bring forward from the Word of God for their chrism.

8 Three hundred years ago Alexander of Hales, par. 4, quest. 24, memb. 1, argued openly that the sacrament of papalist confirmation was neither instituted nor dispensed either by Christ or by the apostles, because this is not read in Scripture. And because neither Christ nor the apostles used these materials and this form, he says that this sacrament was instituted after the death of the apostles, at the Council of Meaux. This opinion also Bonaventura follows, who adds, Bk. 4, dist. 7, quest. 2, that the material of confirmation must of necessity first be consecrated, because Christ did not institute it and therefore also gave it no power as He did to the waters of Baptism.

Others argued that the sacrament of chrism was instituted not indeed by Christ but by the apostles. Thomas (and his followers), because he sees how harmful it is to foist something on the church under the name of a sacrament which has neither institution nor command nor promise from Christ, supposes that Christ instituted both the material and the form of confirmation and that He added also the command and promise concerning its efficacy, plainly in the manner in which it has been described above. But because he is compelled to confess that neither Christ nor the apostles made use of this material or form, he supposes further that Christ instituted it in such a way that neither He Himself nor the apostles would use it but that, when the perceptible signs of the Holy Spirit should cease, then finally there should be used in the church the anointing with the chrism, and that form of words, and that then without doubt the effect would be present, as the papalists teach and want to have believed.

But when Thomas gets to the point where he wants to prove those things which he so earnestly asserts, he confesses that there is in the Scripture not one letter indicating that, when, where, and how Christ instituted the anointing with the chrism. But because John says (20:30) that Christ did many signs which were not all written, therefore it must be believed that the chrism was instituted by Christ wholly in this way, just as the papalists say, even though it cannot be proved. What outstanding proofs! Thomas acknowledges that divine institution is necessary in order that a thing may be truly and properly a sacrament, and that it is necessary, if confirmation is to be considered a sacrament, that it be instituted by Christ. But because he is unable either to show or to prove this, he imagines and, as it were, postulates what needed first of all to be proved. He should rather have turned the argument around: Because the institution of the chrism cannot be shown and proved from the Word of God, therefore it is not truly and properly a sacrament. Thus Gabriel asks why the anointing performed in the act of Baptism, both before and after dipping, should not be a special sacrament. He gives this reason: Because it does not have divine institution.

9 The papalists, aware of the weakness and coldness of the Thomistic proof, because they could thus be judged to have a sacrament of confirmation without proof from the Word of God, spread and foisted upon the church a number of apocryphal, uncertain writings, unknown to antiquity, forged, counterfeit, and fabricated, which they attributed to certain very ancient bishops of the Roman church who were famous for steadfastness in piety, in part also for martyrdom.

In them Clement relates that he received the doctrine about the chrism from blessed Peter and that also the other apostles, taught by the Lord, taught thus. But Eusebius writes that the writings of Clement, with the exception of the one Epistle to the Corinthians, had been counterfeited already in his time. Therefore Gelasius, dist. 15, rejects them along with the apocrypha. Shall the divine institution of the chrism be proved from them?

But they say: Fabian, the famous martyr of Christ, in the epistle which is now ascribed to him, asserts that his predecessors received it from the holy apostles, who handed down the same thing also in the churches at Rome, Antioch, Jerusalem, and Ephesus, that when Christ at the Last Supper had washed the feet of His disciples, He handed down and taught the consecration of the chrism as it is described in the *Pontifical*. But this testimony is not merely uncertain, as coming from an apocryphal and forged book; it is a lie (I cannot call it anything else) and indeed unknown to all of antiquity, which was an admirer of anointing.

Tertullian says concerning Baptism that the anointing was not taken from an institution by Christ but from the early teaching of the Old Testament. The discourse concerning footwashing, which is attributed to Cyprian, reckons the chrism among those things which are believed to have been instituted not by Christ Himself but by the apostles through the Holy Spirit. And in the discourse on the chrism he asserts that the anointing with the chrism is a survival from the ceremonies of the Old Testament.

Basil also says that there is no written word concerning anointing with the chrism. Therefore he had no knowledge of that epistle of Fabian.

10 Therefore the reader hears and will diligently weigh what, what kind of, how certain, and how strong arguments and grounds of divine institution the papalists have for their confirmation. The reader will also consider how they search anywhere and everywhere for whatever testimonies they can find for their preconceived opinion. We have shown, first of all, how the scholastics argued. Second, we have recounted how they attempted to establish their confirmation from apocryphal and forged writings, and with what success. Because they realize that they have been defeated with these forged and counterfeit defenses by the light of the Word of God, that is, the sword of the Spirit, they now finally begin, in the third place, to beg from the Scriptures some testimonies which they might be able in some way to bring forward to give a semblance of right to their preconceived opinion. Let us hear these also, to see what they are and what they can accomplish.

Christ, they say, promised the apostles the power of the Spirit after Baptism (Luke 24:49; Acts 1:4-5, 8) and fulfilled this promise on the day of Pentecost, sending the Holy Spirit with the appearance of fiery tongues. Moreover, the apostles laid their hands on those who were baptized, who in this way received the Holy Spirit, (Acts 8:14-17; 19:5-6). Therefore now in the church the forehead of those who are baptized is to be anointed with the chrism, which has been consecrated in the manner described in the *Pontifical*, with the form of words which has been described above, and the effects enumerated above will follow.

There is an immense amount more in this brave conclusion than in the previously quoted passages. I hear and read what is written (Acts 1:4-

8; 8:14-17; 19:5-6). I find, however, that the visible gifts of the Spirit, such as the miracle of tongues and others, were bestowed in the primitive church through the imposition of hands. Therefore they had a promise concerning these gifts. When Ananias (Acts 9:17-19) laid hands on Paul in order that he might be filled with the Holy Spirit, he said that he had been sent for this by God. Therefore the apostles had both command and promise for what they did. And if the outpouring of the perceptible gifts still perdured in the church, also the imposition of hands would rightly be employed, which customarily was used also in connection with prayers, and chiefly when miracles were performed through the hands of apostles (Acts 5:12). But it is beyond controversy that these miracles have long ceased in the church. Therefore what is written concerning the apostles (Acts 1:4-8; 8:14-17; 19:5-6) was temporary, not universal nor for all time. For concerning the sacraments which should remain permanently in the church, and whose use is universal, Scripture adds these observations: to the close of the age (Matt. 28:20); likewise: until He comes (1 Cor. 11:26); baptize all (Matt. 28:19); by one Spirit we were all baptized into one body. (1 Cor. 12:13)

We read, however, that in the times of the apostles hands were not laid on all the baptized by the apostles, and that not all received the visible gifts of the Spirit, to whom nevertheless the necessary gifts of confirmation, growth, and perseverance were not lacking.[1] For in Acts 11:22 Barnabas is sent to the Antiochenes; without laying on of hands he exhorts them with the Word of God to constancy and perseverance in the grace they had received. God accompanies this exhortation with His blessing. The apostles confirm the souls of the disciples with the Word of God in order that they might persevere and grow in the grace they had received. (Acts 14:21-22; 15:41; 18:23)

11 Therefore it is incumbent upon the papalists to demonstrate and show a command of God, that what the apostles did (Acts 8:14-17; 19:6) is to be imitated, employed, and frequently resorted to in the church until the end of the age, until Christ comes to judgment. For no examples of the saints are to be imitated concerning which there is not a word and command of God which pertains to us. Furthermore, there must be shown a promise concerning its efficacy, if we are to imitate what the apostles did at that time. Neither can be shown or proved.

What the consequence is from this act of the apostles for the papalist confirmation is clear from the following example. Balthasar, almost the

---

[1] The text here has *deferunt*, to bring away, deliver. It appears that the reading should have been *defuerunt*, to lack. This was the understanding of Nigrinus, who translated: *Welchen es doch an notwendigen Gaben nicht mangelte.*

foremost among the Anabaptists, argued thus: "Christ bestowed a blessing on the children who were brought to Him, not by means of Baptism but by the laying on of hands (Mark 10:16). Therefore we also ought not to baptize infants but only lay hands upon them, and thus a blessing would be conferred upon them." But we have a command and promise concerning Baptism. Therefore without a command and promise we ought not to imitate what Christ indeed did and neglect that concerning which we have a clear word of God, embracing the whole church of all times. Thus Christ, by breathing upon the baptized apostles, gave them the Holy Spirit (John 20:22). Why then do we not make a special sacrament of our breathing? If you say: "Because we do not have a command and promise of God," we answer the same with respect to the example of the apostles. But when the bishop imagines that in breathing upon the richness of the chrism he is imitating what Christ did when in breathing on the disciples He said: "Receive the Holy Spirit," this is not only ridiculous but magical, superstitious, and blasphemous.

12 Nevertheless it is worth the effort to consider how clearly, how surely, and how sharply the papalists labor to prove their anointing with the chrism from these accounts: Acts 1:5; 8:17; and 19:6. For if in their confirmation they either employed fire or retained the imposition of hands, there would be some external appearance of agreement, although joined with a bad imitation, because it would be lacking a command of God. However, they want to establish their anointing with chrism from these accounts. I judge, however, that it is divinely brought about that the imposition of hands was not retained in papalist confirmation, but that anointing with chrism was substituted for it, in order that the church, noticing the palpable difference between imposition of hands and anointing on the forehead, might not so easily be misled by an appeal to Acts 1:5; 8:17; and 19:6.

But now listen carefully, good reader, for you will hear a piece of great and extraordinary subtlety. In Acts 1 the external element is fire, under the appearance of cloven tongues. In Acts 8 and 19 it is the laying on of hands. The element or material in papalist confirmation is to such an extent the same, that it is said to have the basis for its institution in these narratives. But how so? I know you will be astonished when you hear it. The oil in papalist confirmation corresponds to the fire on Pentecost. By what reasoning? Because oil nourishes fire. But a well-dried stick of oak does the same. The balsam corresponds to the appearance of tongues, because it is fragrant. But what does tongue or taste have in common with smells? Do we smell with the tongue? But perhaps these things are said among men who acknowledge only four senses—for whom smell and taste fall together in one. But hold on, dear reader. You have not yet heard all. Perhaps you desire the laying on of hands, of which mention is made in Acts 8:17 and 19:6. Look! Here it is. For in the papalist church following is the same thing as preceding; therefore when the bishop, after confirmation, taps the confirmed person on the cheek, this takes the place of the laying on of hands in Acts, which at that time preceded the giving of the Spirit. What is this I hear? Is the laying on of hands then giving a person slaps in the face? So when Christ says that they should lay hands on the sick (Mark 16:18) the meaning will be: Let them beat those who are sick well with blows; then they will be worse.

What is all this but manifest mockery of the Word of God? I have not invented these things, but have copied them from Durandus. In our time Frederick Nausea was not ashamed to repeat and maintain these things publicly. Such indeed is the proof of the material of confirmation from Scripture. The consecration, or rather enchantment, of the chrism, as it is described in the *Pontifical,* they do not attempt to prove with so much as one syllable from Scripture, because they are not able to produce even a show for it.

13 What about the formula of confirmation: "I mark you," etc? Can it be proved from Scripture, either that Christ instituted or that the apostles used this formula? Certainly, this cannot even be pretended. This form of words is expressed neither in the ancient writers nor in the canons, except that later men seem to have fabricated it or rather adulterated it out of a saying of Ambrose in *De his qui initiantur,* ch. 7. For what the priest there says after Baptism: "God the Father has marked you; the Lord Christ has confirmed you and has given the pledge of the Spirit in your heart," that a papalist dauber[2] afterward transferred to his chrism: "I mark you; I confirm you with the chrism of salvation," etc. And from this it comes that in the *Pontificals* the formula is not the same. For Gabriel says that some say: "Chrism of sanctification" instead of "chrism of salvation." Gerson has this formula: "I confirm you with the sign of the cross and with the chrism," etc. So certain are all things!

14 Therefore the material and form of confirmation has in Scripture not even seeming grounds or testimonies. Therefore those have acted more nobly and prudently who have simply confessed in accord with the facts that the papalist church has both the material and the form of her confirmation, not from Scripture but without and apart from Scripture. Papalist confirmation is exposed to ridicule rather than proved when its proof is even attempted from Scripture in this way.

15 There remains, therefore, the question about a promise of its

---

2 The text of 1574 has *delibator,* a word not found in Latin dictionaries. It is likely that Chemnitz wrote *delibutor,* from a verb meaning to smear or daub.

efficacy. Here indeed they try to befuddle the inexperienced. For they say: "Granted, the visible and miraculous gifts of the Spirit (Acts 1:5, 8; 8:6-7; 19:6) have ceased; nevertheless the promise of the grace of confirmation, of the gift of perseverance, of the preservation and increase of spiritual gifts, of strengthening through the Spirit against the flesh, the world, and the devil, etc., are for all and for all time." And after they have run through these things they at once add: "Whoever does not exclaim with the *Pontifical:* Hail, sacred chrism! tears down all these promises and tramples them underfoot."

We, however, embrace with our whole heart these sweet promises of the necessary gifts and aids of the Spirit after Baptism, and trusting in them we fight against spiritual enemies and call upon God. Here the question is not about the promises themselves, of which it is certain that they are found in the Word of God. The question is rather whether God wants these promises to be bound to the anointing with the papalist chrism in such a way that then and through this means that efficaciousness of the Spirit is given, when the bishop anoints the forehead with the episcopally enchanted chrism, adding certain words and one good slap. This is what is asked, and what cannot be proved with even one letter from Scripture. It simply does not follow: There is a promise in Scripture; therefore a sacrament must be fabricated by human judgment through which this promise may be bestowed. For such sacraments through which the application of the promises ought to be made, which Christ wants us to have in the New Testament, He Himself instituted with His own voice and promulgated to the church in Scripture.

16 But they say: "Nevertheless the apostles had a special external sign, namely, the laying on of hands, by which the Holy Spirit was conferred (Acts 8:17; 19:6), and no one will dare to say that the apostles did this without a divine command and promise; therefore there is in the New Testament a special sacrament instituted and ordained for conferring the gifts of confirmation. For the definition of a sacrament is that it is an efficacious sign of grace."

I answer: In order that something should be a sacrament there is required (as I may express it[3]) universality of the divine command and promise, embracing all ministers and all the faithful of all times in the New Testament. For Christ gave the apostles the Holy Spirit by breathing upon them (John 20:22). Handkerchiefs and the shadows of the apostles healed the sick. Why do we not make universal sacraments of these

---

[3] The edition of 1574 has *ut sit loquar,* which appears to be a misprint for *ut sic loquar.*

things, except for the reason that we do not have a command to imitate them nor, if we wanted to imitate them, a promise of efficacy? Therefore also we demand in this place that a general command be shown us that what the apostles did in Acts 8:17 and 19:6 is to be done at all times by all ministers in the church. For the apostles had many special prerogatives which are not to be imitated by other ministers of the church. Also, the apostles themselves did not want the laying on of hands to be the regular and general means without which the grace of confirmation would not be bestowed by God, for many received the grace of confirmation without the laying on of hands, e.g., the Antiochenes (Acts 11:19-26). But the apostles conferred the visible gifts of the Spirit, such as the gift of tongues, by this rite. Concerning these miracles it is manifest that they have now ceased in the church. And even if it could be granted that this rite of the apostles is (which however it is not) a universal sacrament, by what authority have the papalists been able to abolish the apostolic imposition of hands and to substitute for it the smearing of the enchanted chrism and to bind the promises to it? For the institution of the chrism in the New Testament cannot be shown and proved from Scripture.

Are there then simply no means through which God wills to bestow the gifts of confirmation and perseverance? Most certainly there are divinely ordained, sure instruments or means through which the Holy Spirit wills to confer these gifts, to confirm, increase, and preserve the Word: the Eucharist, faith, prayer, afflictions, and the exercise of the mental gifts we have received. We do not read, among these, about making a cross with the papalist chrism.

17 Therefore it has now become crystal clear that neither the material nor the consecration of the material, neither the form nor the effects of papalist confirmation have any sure, firm, clear, and sufficient testimony of Scripture. Therefore it is most truly said that the papalists hold the whole sacrament of their confirmation without testimonies and grounds of Scripture. Let the reader now reread the things which the papalists ascribe to their confirmation, as we have related them above in their own words, and let him consider how great is the audacity and how great the rashness—lest I use a harsher term—to ascribe so many and such great things to material fatness without a command, without a testimony and a promise of God's Word.

18 In addition to all this, the chrismatic confirmation of the papalists is not only without God's Word, indeed it militates against it. For when there is attributed to some material or action an efficacy of some kind, either physical or spiritual, which it does not have either from a natural cause or from a divine command, institution, and promise, this truly is a matter of superstition or of magic. And if without a command of God the name of God is employed, it is a sin against the Second Commandment. And the more excellent the effects ascribed to it without a command or promise of God, the more grievous is the sin. Let the consecration of the chrism, as found in the *Pontifical,* be compared with this axiom, and the reader will shudder.

Matters are not helped at all by the sentence of Paul (1 Tim. 4:4-5): "Everything created by God is good . . . if it is received with thanksgiving; for then it is consecrated by the Word of God and prayer." For he is not speaking there of some transmutation of creatures which we should attempt through the Word and prayer. For if the whole Gospel of John were read or the whole Psalter recited over a nettle in order that it might not sting, or over an egg in order that it might become a cannonball, nothing would be accomplished. For with the exception of the gift to perform miracles, which are done through the Word and prayer, there is a twofold sanctification of creatures: the first through the Word, of which Paul is speaking in this place, that their use is rendered holy, so that nothing should be rejected but may be used with thankfulness and a good conscience by those who believe and know the truth, in that use for which they were created; for these are the words of Paul. The other is when by virtue of the words of divine institution the water is sanctified so that it becomes a Baptism, bread and wine are sanctified that they may be the Eucharist of the body and blood of the Lord. The consecration of the chrism is done in neither of these ways, for it lacks divine institution, and neither oil nor balsam were by nature created for these effects.

19 Let what I showed in the first part be considered above all in this disputation: Nearly everything the papalists ascribe to their confirmation clearly detracts from the worth and power of Baptism. For whatever is attributed to the chrism is, by contrast, taken away from Baptism. For if Baptism were believed to bestow it, to what end would there be need for smearing with chrism? Therefore the papalist teaching concerning the chrism cannot be received and approved without harm and reproach to Baptism.

For this reason we are here gathering together in a brief summary the things set forth at greater length above: Baptism neither makes Christians nor completes Christians; this is done by confirmation. In Baptism there is not given the Spirit of wisdom, of understanding, of counsel, of courage, of knowledge, of goodness, of the fear of God, etc., but this happens in confirmation. The Holy Spirit, through whom we may resist lusts, the world, and the devil, is not given in Baptism but in confirmation. The baptized are not able to have in themselves the grace of Christ unless they are anointed. Those who are baptized are not fully the sons of God unless they are anointed. Baptism does not make partakers of the kingdom of God, but this is done by confirmation. In Baptism we do not receive the Spirit who guards, defends, governs, strengthens. In Baptism a dwelling place for God is only prepared; however, neither the Father nor the Son nor the Holy Spirit enters His home. This is first accomplished through confirmation. Baptism does not confer fullness of graces, but this is done in confirmation. Through the chrism we are incorporated into Christ and hence sanctified, etc. These are the words of the papalists. Whole sentences have been quoted in the first part.

On the other side let there be written the sayings of Scripture concerning Baptism. Mark 16:16: "He who believes and is baptized will be saved." Rom. 6:3-6: We have been baptized into His death, buried together with Him by Baptism into death. For if we have been united with Him in a death like His, we shall be also in a resurrection like His, knowing that our old man was crucified together with Him, in order that the sinful body might be destroyed. 1 Cor. 12:13: "By one Spirit we were all baptized into one body." Gal. 3:27: "As many of you as were baptized into Christ have put on Christ." John 3:5: Whoever is born of water and of the Spirit will enter the kingdom of God. Eph. 5:25-27: "Christ loved the church and gave Himself up for her, that He might sanctify her, having cleansed her by the washing of water with the Word, that He might present the church to Himself in splendor, without spot," etc. Titus 3:5-7: "He saved us . . . by the washing of regeneration and renewal in the Holy Spirit, which He poured out upon us richly through Jesus Christ our Savior, so that we might be justified by His grace and become heirs in hope of eternal life." 1 Peter 3:21: Baptism now saves us, as a result of which our conscience answers well before God through the resurrection of Christ.

20 If these are compared with each other, it will become apparent that the papalist teaching about confirmation is fraught with extraordinary harm and reproach to Baptism. And who would not have hoped that in the council if not all such things then at least some would be if not corrected then at least mitigated? But the three canons concerning confirmation, enfolding and approving as they do all opinions both of the scholastics and of the monks concerning confirmation, abundantly show what the thinking at Trent was.

This also should be considered, that the very action of Baptism is opposed to the opinion of the papalists about confirmation. For they say that in Baptism the Holy Spirit is not given for the battle against the devil. But in the act of Baptism the renunciation of Satan is demanded and made in many words. They say that in Baptism the guarding and defending Spirit is not given. Yet the baptizer prays in the course of the act of Baptism: "May He who has regenerated you preserve you to life eternal," etc.

21 As therefore we explained in the first part what kind of confirmation the papalists have, know, and understand in their church, so we have now also shown clearly what kind of sacrament it is when it is examined according to the norm of Scripture, which must by all means be done. For according to the judgment of Bede, which is found in quest. 8, ch. 1, *Nec sufficeret:* "There is prescribed for us in the sacred Scripture one rule, equally for believing and for living."

22 In the third place some things must also be said about those opinions which they are accustomed to heap up from the writings of the ancients to establish papalist chrismation. However, this neither should nor can be prejudicial to those grounds which we have shown in the second part from clear and firm testimonies of Scripture. For Augustine says rightly and truly in *Contra litteras Petiliani,* Bk. 3, ch. 6: "If anyone preaches to you about anything which pertains to faith beside what you have received in the Scripture of the Law and the Gospel, let him be anathema, whether he is a bishop or an apostle, or even an angel from heaven." "For," says he in ch. 1 of *De bono viduitatis,* "Scripture determines the rule for our doctrine." Therefore he concludes in ch. 3 of *De unitate ecclesiae:* "No matter what they bring or from where they bring it, let us rather, if we are His sheep, hear the voice of our Shepherd. Therefore let us not listen to: This I say; that you say, but to: This the Lord says."

23 Nevertheless let us not appear as though we wholly despised and trampled underfoot the judgments of the ancient church. For we reverently hold the hoary hair of antiquity in honor, but with that moderation with which they themselves wanted it done, as we showed in the first part of this *Examination*[4] from the words of the fathers themselves. We shall therefore say something about those sayings in which the ancients make mention of the chrism, all of which the papalists distort to make it apply to their confirmation as we have described it earlier.

24 Because these statements of the ancients are dissimilar we shall, in order that the explanation may be simpler and easier, bring to this heap of statements the distinction which, taken from the nature of the matter itself, will be evident.

---

[4] See Chemnitz, *Examination of the Council of Trent,* Part I, Concordia Publishing House, St. Louis, 1971, pp. 256–66.

1. The foremost statements brought forward about chrismation are taken from writings which in part were placed by the Roman church itself among the apocrypha, and in part were wholly unknown to true antiquity. There is therefore no doubt that they are forged and counterfeit, as are the decretals of certain ancient pontiffs. We showed in the earlier part of the *Examination*[5] what Cardinal Cusanus judges concerning them. Thus they are accustomed to quote pompously in this dispute from the discourse of Cyprian concerning the chrism, of which it is certain that it is a fraud. Therefore it is of no importance to dispute at length about these statements. Nevertheless the reader ought to be informed in passing what kind of cause it is for whose proof it is necessary to scrounge so many apocryphal, forged, and counterfeit testimonies.

2. Certain statements concerning anointing with the chrism have their origin from the school of the Montanist paraclete. For it is specifically Montanistic what Tertullian says concerning Baptism, namely, that those who are baptized in water do not obtain the Holy Spirit but, having been cleansed in the water, they are only prepared under the supervision of the angels for the Holy Spirit, who is finally, after they have come out of the bath, summoned and invited through the blessed anointing and laying on of the hand.

This opinion Jerome refutes with many words from Scripture in the dialog against the Luciferians. For Scripture asserts clearly that the Holy Spirit is poured out, and indeed poured out richly, through the washing of regeneration and renewal (Titus 3:5-6). For we are born again of water and the Spirit (John 3:5). Christ sanctifies and cleanses the church by the washing of water with the Word (Eph. 5:26). Cyprian has surely drawn from his teacher Tertullian when in Bk. 2, Epist. 1, he mangles the statement of Christ (John 3:5): "Unless one is born of water and the Spirit," in such a way that he gives to Baptism only the water but ascribes the Holy Spirit to the anointing and the laying on of hands. And he adds that men cannot be sons of God unless they are born through both sacraments, namely, the washing of water with the Word, and the anointing of the chrism. Therefore the other statement of Cyprian will not greatly move us, Bk. 1, Epist. 12, where he declares positively that it is necessary for one who has been baptized to be anointed in order that, having received the chrism, he may be able to have the grace of Christ in himself, etc. For it is clear from what school, namely, that of Montanus, these statements have come. It certainly is false that the baptized person does not have the grace of Christ in himself but that this is only given when the external

---

[5] *Ibid.,* pp. 300 f.

chrism has been received. For these statements of both Tertullian and Cyprian do not even acknowledge the distinction according to which some ascribe to Baptism the Spirit of regeneration and the grace of forgiveness, and to the chrism the Spirit and grace of confirmation, but they simply and in general take away the grace of Christ and the Holy Spirit from Baptism and transfer it to the anointing with the chrism. Therefore also a later age was compelled to tone down these statements. From this reminder the reader will be able to form a judgment about any other statements among those we have quoted earlier about the chrism which may smack of the school of Montanus.

Therefore we shall not permit ourselves to be led away without an investigation from the teaching of Scripture when the label of antiquity is brought forward as a pretense for timeworn abuses and errors. For what sort of thing this is can be judged from this topic.

3. However, also certain excellent writers among the fathers make mention of the anointing in their books, namely, in the same way in which they list and describe many other ceremonies which without divine command, from ecclesiastical tradition, were in use during the act of Baptism in their time. They do not, however, take away from Baptism that efficacy which Scripture ascribes to it, nor do they divide it between such ceremonies and Baptism, as papalist confirmation does. Rather they say that the efficacy of Baptism is signified and proclaimed by these super-added signs. They practiced anointing because there were many and varied uses of oil, ointment, and anointing, especially in Oriental localities, just as there also the kiss was in use, because it had been introduced into the church on account of the customs in these places as a declaration of brotherly love. We would, however, be silly if we wanted to make a universal and necessary sacrament of the kiss. Thus Augustine says concerning anointing, Bk. 15, *De Trinitate*, ch. 26: "The invisible gift of grace is signified by the visible ointment with which the church anoints the baptized."

Thus, disputing in *Contra litteras Petiliani*, Bk. 2, ch. 104, about Ps. 132, he says: "The ancient priesthood, foreshadowing the body of Christ, which comes into being through joining together in unity, had a sound anointing." He explains it as signifying spiritual sanctification and the sweet smell of spiritual love. Afterward he adds concerning the chrism: "By this anointing you[6] want to interpret the sacrament of the chrism." He does not reject this interpretation.

---

6 The statement in the *Examen* reads: *vult interpretari*, making it a statement of Augustine against Petilian. According to Migne, *Patrologia Latina*, Tom. 43, col. 34, Augustine wrote: *vultis interpretari*, "you want to interpret."

It would be possible from what older writers say about the various ceremonies of this kind to show what they wanted to signify by these ceremonies concerning the use, working, and efficacy of Baptism. This is not opposed by the fact that Augustine sometimes calls this anointing with oil or chrism a sacrament. For in his comments on Ps. 65 he also calls the catechization, the exorcism, and the fire in the act of Baptism a sacrament, as also in *De symbolo ad Catechumenos,* Bk. 4, ch. 1: "All sacraments which are performed on you by means of exorcisms, prayers, songs, breathing, haircloth, bowing of necks, humility of the feet," etc. For whatever is a sign of some sacred thing, that Augustine is accustomed to call a sacrament, as we have shown in our examination of the first canon on the sacraments.

Surely, these things about the signification of the anointing and of the remaining ceremonies are a far cry from the meaning for which the papalists contend in their confirmation. Let the reader therefore note that papalist confirmation is not at once proved when in some statement of the ancients mention is made of the chrism. For the debate is not chiefly about the word, nor about the signification or the admonition, but about the thing itself or about the efficacy which papalist confirmation ascribes to the chrism in the manner explained in the first part. Proper regard to this will show that very many testimonies of the ancients, although they make mention of the chrism, nevertheless in no way support papalist confirmation. For it is one thing to speak about the signification of ceremonies, but quite another to speak about what they effect and work.

4. But they say, by way of objection, that the ancients nevertheless often ascribe something more than merely a signification to the chrism. I answer: Apocryphal, forged, and counterfeit writings, which are falsely ascribed to some of the ancients, we rightly and deservedly refuse to receive. Neither do we want to be pressed by the authority of Tertullian and Cyprian, who in this matter clearly Montanized. Neither is it fair to prescribe to Scripture by means of more recent opinions, such as of Rabanus, Durandus, Gerson, etc.

There remains an inquiry as to the true and purer antiquity. I am not ignorant of the fact that they do not all speak in the same way; nevertheless I do not hesitate to assert that in the true and purer antiquity this papalist antithesis between Baptism and chrismation cannot be shown, which diminishes and takes away the foremost effects from Baptism and ascribes them to the chrism, as this antithesis has been explained above in the papalists' own words. This indeed is the issue in this debate, that they show from true writers of the genuine antiquity not that they make mention of oil, chrism, anointing, etc., for of this I am not ignorant, but that they teach that so many and such great effects are to be taken away from Baptism and instead ascribed to oil, chrism, and anointing and that they prove this from the Word of God as the papalists ascribe and want to have ascribed to their chrismation, whose words I have for this reason written down above. This I say and know, that this cannot be shown and proved from the genuine writings of the true fathers. In *Extra, De sacra unctione,* ch. *Ungitur,* Innocent shows that there were in ancient time some who found fault with anointings. For he says: "The church does not Judaize when she celebrates the sacrament of anointing, as those ancients lie, who know neither the Scripture nor the power of God."

Something must be said briefly about Cyril of Jerusalem, whose *Catecheses* have recently been published. For he is now compelled to be the foremost defender of the papalist chrism. We do not wish to judge unfairly concerning Cyril of Jerusalem, whose history is not unknown to us, assuming that these *Catecheses,* which were recently published, are genuine and not falsified. However, the papalists shall not take away from us that liberty in examining and judging the writings of all the fathers which Augustine often insists was given to the church, namely, that they should be examined according to the norm of the Scripture. Moreover, Jerome says that Cyril wrote this instruction in his youth. Rufinus adds that he sometimes wavered in faith, more frequently in confession. Therefore the authority of this writer is not canonical.

But let us see what he says concerning the anointing. In the second catechesis he says: "This oil, which has been exorcised, acquires such great power that it not only sweeps out the burning vestiges of sin; it even repels all visible demons." Yet Cyril anoints those who are to be baptized before Baptism. If therefore already before Baptism both the sins and the very vestiges of sins have been swept out by the oil, how can he say a little later that Baptism is the washing away of sins and that it procures adoption and the gift of the Holy Spirit?

However, he explains himself when he says: "This oil is a symbol of the richness of Christ communicated to us, and that the working of the devil has been destroyed in us, namely, in and through Baptism, of which efficacy of Baptism the oil is the symbol and the meaning." If anyone is unwilling to accept this explanation taken from the words of the author himself, he will make Cyril out as being in conflict both with himself and with Scripture itself, because he takes away the purging of sins from Baptism and gives it to the oil before Baptism.

At the beginning of the third catechesis he says that those who, having been baptized into Christ, have put on Christ have become partakers and comrades of Christ, and that the chrism exhibits the image of the Spirit with which Christ was bodily anointed. These things, symbols as it were, reminding us of the power of Baptism, can be tolerated. But presently this Cyril (whether he is genuine or a counterfeit) adds: "As the bread of the Eucharist, after invocation of the Holy Spirit, is no longer ordinary bread but is the body of Christ, so also this ointment, after it has been consecrated, is no longer mere ointment but a gift[7] of Christ which, through the advent of the Holy Spirit, has power through His divine nature, so that the body indeed is anointed with it but the soul sanctified by the life-giving Spirit." And soon thereafter: "When the gift of this sacred chrism has been received, we are deservedly called Christians. For before this grace had been given to you, you were not really worthy of that name," etc.

But Cyril himself asserts from Scripture that Baptism bestows not only the washing away of sins but also the adoption of sons and the gift of the Holy Spirit. And because the baptized have put on Christ, he asserts that through Baptism they have become partakers and comrades of Christ. How, then, does this Cyril suddenly attribute to the chrism those things which he himself, with Scripture as witness, asserts belong to Baptism, namely, the purging of sins, sanctification of the Spirit, and becoming a partaker of Christ? I simply interpret in such a way, that he understands the chrism to be a symbol, signifying and reminding what is the power and efficacy of Baptism, not that he either wants to take away this power from Baptism or to divide it, giving a part to Baptism and a part to the chrism. If the papalists are unwilling to accept this explanation, they will bring Cyril into a head-on clash with Scripture. For we are made, and are, Christians not by being anointed on the outside with some fat substance but by Christ our Lord, whom we put on in Baptism, whom we apprehend in the Word, that He may dwell in our hearts by faith. Neither were Christians first called by this name at Antioch from the fact that they had been smeared and anointed with some external fatness of oil. If therefore the authority of this Cyril is urged apart from and contrary to Scripture, we answer with the words of Augustine, Epistle 19, that a thing is not to be considered true just because the fathers thought thus, but only if they are able to persuade through the canonical authors that the thing is not at variance with the truth. Therefore we ought to judge the writings of all others on the basis of the canonical writings, and whatever in them does not agree with the divine Scriptures we can,

---

[7] The Preuss edition has changed *charisma* of the 1574 edition to *chrisma*, but erroneously. According to Migne, op. cit., Tom. 33, col. 1091, the author of the *Catecheses* wrote *charisma*, which the Latin text renders *donarium*, i.e., a votive offering or gift.

begging their pardon and preserving the honor which is due those men, disapprove and reject, even though we ourselves are incomparably inferior to the fathers, Epistle 111, and *Contra Cresconium,* Bk. 2, ch. 32; Augustine says that this is done by a just judgment, without at all despising the fathers and without rashness, *Contra Donatistas,* Bk. 7, ch. 20, and *Ad Victorem,* Bk. 2.

Let us ponder briefly therefore whether Cyril is able to persuade us from the canonical Scriptures in favor of this his statement, for he tries to do it. For he says thus: "Moses first washed the high priest with water, afterward he anointed him with ointment; thus he was called the Anointed of the Lord. Therefore those who in the New Testament want to become Christians must have the reality of that which happened to the ancients in a figure." He says that this is the truth of which John proclaims: "Ye have an unction from the Holy One, and ye know all things."[8] "Let the anointing which you have received from Him remain in you." Furthermore: "His anointing instructs you concerning all things"(1 John 2:20, 27). Up to this point Cyril does not put things together badly. But when he tries to establish his external exorcised chrism from this, it clearly does not constitute a valid logical deduction. For it is most certain that John is not speaking of some external smearing with a fat substance, but of the spiritual, inner, invisible anointing of the Spirit. And because we have in the New Testament the truth itself, we must not return to the figures of the Old Testament without a command of Christ. Therefore Cyril by no means proves the chrism from these passages of Scripture.

The other proof he offers is this: "In Is. 25: 6-7 the Greeks rendered the text thus: 'And the Lord of Sabaoth will make for all peoples in this mountain [a feast]: They shall drink wine, they shall drink joy, they shall be anointed with ointment.' " And he adds: "Transmit all these things to the peoples, for the will of the Lord is over all peoples." From this Cyril wants to prove that it is the command and will of God that in the church of the New Testament all peoples should be anointed with chrism. But I beg the reader just to consider what kind of proof this is. In the first place, Isaiah, in his language, does not state it that way but says: "On this mountain the Lord of hosts will make for all peoples a feast of fat things, a feast of wine on the lees, of fat things full of marrow, of wine on the lees well refined. And He will destroy on this mountain the covering that is cast over all peoples." It is clear, therefore, that Isaiah says nothing about

---

[8] We follow the King James version here because it agrees precisely with the Latin version, from which Cyril was quoting.

delivering the anointing to the peoples. Afterward the text itself explains that these things are allegorical, and shows how this allegory is to be understood. For he says: "He will swallow up death for ever, and the Lord God will wipe away tears from all faces, and the reproach of His people He will take away from all the earth."

How can the external smearing with material chrism be proved from an allegorical statement? Finally, if that statement were to be understood of bodily anointing, it would also follow by the same reasoning that the baptized were to be daubed with dregs[9] (perhaps as in the Lupercalia[10]) and with the fat of marrow. The reader will therefore see how cold, how forced, contorted, and strange these arguments are. The rule of Augustine is: "The authority of the statements of the fathers ought to be no greater than the quality of the arguments which they bring forward from the canonical Scriptures."

5. There is a great dissimilarity and difference between the anointing of which the ancients speak and confirmation as it is observed among the papalists. I shall briefly set down three differences which are most evident, in order that also this may become manifest, that papalist confirmation as it is now observed indeed cannot be proved or established from the genuine writings of approved fathers.

First of all, so far as the material (as they call it) or the external sign is concerned, the laying on of hands was customary among the ancients and was still in use at the time of Jerome and Augustine. But now, with the papalists, the laying on of hands has been wholly abolished. How then can it be the same sacrament, unless by chance they will persuade the peasants that giving a slap is the same thing as the laying on of hands?

Tertullian makes mention only of oil. Also Clement of Alexandria and Basil mention only oil. But the papalists contend that if the oil is not mixed with balsam it is not a true sacrament. And even though some of the scholastics argue that there is need only of oil, the Council of Florence nevertheless decrees that the material of confirmation must be chrism, prepared from oil and balsam. Therefore they do not have even this material from the ancients. I do not know whether they are able to bring forward anything from approved writings of the ancients about the mixing in of balsam. It is certain that natural balsam has become extinct along with the balsam trees. Therefore the very material of confirmation which

---

[9] Chemnitz, following the Vulgate, uses the word *faex* for the sediment which accumulates as the wine clears after fermentation.

[10] The Lupercalia was an ancient Roman festival, at which heathen priests, scantily clothed, ran through the streets, striking at passersby, especially women, whom this was supposed to render fruitful.

the papalists demand has perished from among natural products. Neither can artificial balsam fill its place, just as artificial water is not able to be the material of Baptism, or artificial wine the material of the Eucharist. Cyril anoints the baptized after Baptism with chrism, first on the forehead, second on the ears, third on the nose, fourth on the breast. Ambrose, *De his qui initiantur,* ch. 6, anoints the head of the baptized person after Baptism so that the ointment flows down from it. The papalists, however, teach that chrismation should be done on the forehead only, and that if it is done on the crown of the head, on the breast, on ears, nose, etc., it is not the sacrament of confirmation, even if the same material and form are employed. The reader will therefore see how great a dissimilarity and diversity there is between the statements of the ancients and papalist confirmation so far as the material is concerned. And when they heap up so many statements of the ancients, this diversity must be held up against them. For no matter what they bluster from the ancients about chrism, nevertheless they do not have that sacrament about which antiquity speaks. For it is not the same material, but something other and different through various changes.

In the second place: Among the ancients anointing with chrism was not a special sacrament, something different and distinct from the sacrament of Baptism. For as they had various ceremonies that went before the dipping of Baptism, so they also had various ceremonies after the dipping, connected nevertheless and joined to the act of Baptism itself. And they defined Baptism not only in terms of dipping or immersion but also included the ceremonies which went before and also those which in an almost continuous action customarily followed, so that the action of Baptism was finished and completed by the subsequent rites. This is clear everywhere in the ancients where these rites are described. Also Dionysius himself and John of Damascus do not separate anointing from Baptism but have anointing both before and immediately after Baptism.

Tertullian says: "From the day on which we have been baptized we abstain from the daily bath for one whole week." Today the papalists teach that this is to be observed not after Baptism but after confirmation. From this it is surely manifest that in ancient times there was one and the same continuous action, which has now been rent in two to make two sacraments.

The *Antididagma* of the men of Cologne asks why the priest anoints the baptized person with the chrism, seeing that he must be smeared with it later at confirmation. And it relates from the acts of the popes that Sylvester decreed that, on account of the danger of unexpected death, the priest should anoint the baptized person with chrism lest, on account of the absence of the bishop, he should depart this life without confirmation. But if the bishop were present, he should be anointed by him.

Also this account shows that in old time chrismation was joined and connected to the action of Baptism itself. Afterward, in order that the number of sacraments might be increased, they separated it from the act of Baptism. And, in order that a separate sacrament might be made of it, they willed that some measure of time should lie between, namely, 12 or 25 years, as the gloss has it, *De consecratione,* dist. 5 c, *Ut ieiun.*

Durandus judges on the basis of Rabanus that the baptized person cannot be confirmed until at least seven days after Baptism, on account of the seven gifts of the Spirit. Therefore the anointing of the ancients after Baptism was a far other and different thing from the chrismation of the papalists in confirmation. Therefore the one is neither confirmed nor established from the other.

Now let the reader judge what weight is to be attached to these witnesses which the papalists scrounge together from the ancients in behalf of their confirmation. For when cases differ, the judgment cannot be the same. Therefore, if the proof should stand, it would be necessary that both the anointing of the ancients and papalist confirmation should be clearly one and the same thing.

In the third place, the effects which the papalists today ascribe to their confirmation, these the ancients ascribe to Baptism itself. For Clement, *Paedag,* Bk.1, ch. 6, says that Baptism is called: (1) the grace by which sins are remitted; (2) the illumination through which we perceive that which is divine; (3) the perfection which lacks nothing. And he adds: "It is absurd that that should be called the grace of God which is not perfect and in every way complete. Therefore, having been dipped," he says, "we are illuminated, we are adopted as sons; having been adopted, we are made perfect; having been made perfect, we are rendered immortal." All these things Clement ascribes to the efficacy of Baptism. Cyprian, Letter No. 7, Bk. 4: "In Baptism the devil is cast out and suppressed by the faith of the believer." Hilary, *Contra Arianos:* "By the sacrament of Baptism everyone is truly made a child of God." Basil: "In Baptism a man is made an heir of the heavenly blessings." The same: "In Baptism we have confessed that we have died to sin and to the world." Gregory of Nissa: "Baptism teaches that we should not mix what remains in us of defects into the life which follows after faith." Chrysostom, in *Ad Romanos,* 6: "Baptism has power not only for this, that it wipes away prior transgressions, but also that it admonishes us to beware of future transgressions." Augustine, *De moribus Manichaeorum,* Bk. 1, ch. 35: "In that most sacred bath the renewal of a man is begun, in order that it may go forward to perfection." Hesychius says that Baptism crushes the devil, and applies here the words of the Psalm: "Thou didst break the heads of the dragons." (Ps. 74:13)

Let the reader compare these testimonies with the things the papalists take away from Baptism and ascribe to their confirmation. From this comparison it will be clear how well papalist confirmation agrees with the ancient church. In vain do they attempt to adorn it with the witnesses of antiquity, since the dissimilarity and diversity is so great. I have noted these things somewhat more at length from the statements of the ancients in order that I might tear away the disguise which they make for their confirmation out of testimonies of the ancients and that I might show clearly that papalist confirmation is not only without foundation in Scripture but also without adequate testimonies from true antiquity. For papalist confirmation is not at once proved and established when in the writings of the ancients mention is made of oil, chrism, and anointing. For this reason the difference had to be shown. For I see that the papalists are wonderfully pleased with themselves when they heap up testimonies of this kind.

6. I shall add also the following observation. Because formerly the action of Baptism was one, continuous and conjoined, with anointing and the imposition of hands, let us ask on what occasion and for what reason it first began to be torn apart and separated, until finally there was made of chrismation a distinct and separate sacrament which by way of contrast should be far superior to Baptism. I have discovered that there was chiefly a threefold reason:

First, when men who had been baptized with a true Baptism either by heretics or in a schism returned to the church, then they were not rebaptized but were received either by the laying on of hands or by anointing with chrism. There is frequent mention of this in the disputations of the ancients concerning the controversy of Cyprian. So also the Council of Laodicaea decreed, Canon 7: "Let those who return from the Novatians be taught the symbol of the faith and, having been anointed with the sacred chrism, let them so take part in the sacraments." The Council of Arles, [11] Canon 8: "If any come to the church from the heresy of the Arians, let the priests of our faith ask them the symbol. And if they discern that they were baptized into the Father, Son, and Holy Spirit, let them only lay the hand upon them in order that they may receive the Holy Spirit." Thus Leo, Epistle 77: "Let him who has been baptized among the

---

[11] Arles, in southern France, was the scene of a number of councils. The reference here is to the council of A. D. 314. The full decree is found in Mansi, *Sacrorum conciliorum nova et amplissima collectio,* II, 472.

heretics not be rebaptized, but let him be confirmed by invocation of the Holy Ghost through the laying on of hands, because he has received only the form of Baptism, without sanctification." Thus says Leo.

The ceremony was not, however, the same everywhere, as also Gregory testifies, *De consecratione,* ch. 4, *Ab antiqua.* For he reports that in the West when those who had been rightly baptized in a heresy returned to the church, they were received through the laying on of the hand, in the East through anointing with the chrism. Was this done because Baptism in itself was without sanctification and the Holy Spirit? Surely, in Eph. 5:26-27 sanctification is expressly ascribed to Baptism, as is also the rich outpouring of the Holy Spirit in Titus 3:5-6. But whoever was baptized though he did not possess the true faith was not able to receive the Holy Spirit and the sanctification of Baptism, for that we receive by faith. But when he was later converted to the true faith, then finally he rightly and salutarily laid hold of the promise of Baptism. Thus he then first accepted with true faith the sanctification of Baptism which had indeed been offered to him before but had not been accepted. In order that this might happen, the Holy Spirit was invoked upon him, to which invocation there was added the symbolic act of the laying on of hands, as Augustine says, that the laying on of hands is nothing but praying over a man, *Contra Donatistas,* Bk. 3, ch. 16. And ch. 1., quest. 1, par. *Paulianistae,* this statement is found: "If so be that they are baptized by those who administer the sacrament to them in a heresy or schism, they indeed receive the sacrament of Baptism from them, but they do not receive its power, which no one can receive without faith, even as the Lord was not able to do any sign in His fatherland on account of their unbelief." Augustine, *Contra Donatistas,* Bk. 5, ch. 23: "If the laying on of the hands were not employed with one coming out of a heresy, he would be regarded as being without any guilt. However, on account of the bond of love, the hand is laid upon heretics who have accepted correction."

The second occasion was when in an emergency someone had been baptized either by a catechumen or by a lay person. Then, in order that the Baptism might be approved and confirmed as true and legitimate, the baptized person was brought to the bishop. Thus the Council of Illiberis[12] says, Canon 18, that any believer, and in case of emergency a catechu-

---

12 Chemnitz calls this council *Eliberitanum.* Mansi, who reports this council, *op. cit.,* II, 2 ff., has at least three spellings, Liberitanum, Eliberitanum, and Illiberitanum. The name is derived from the city called in Roman times Illiberis. It stood on the site of the modern Granada. The date of this council is uncertain, but it is assumed to have been held in the first half of the fourth century A. D.

men, can baptize, in such a way that if the person who was thus baptized survives he leads him to the bishop, in order that the action might be completed through the laying on of hands. Thus the story of Novatus, found in Eusebius, Bk. 6, ch. 23, shows that in the case of those baptized lying on their beds it was not possible to employ the remaining rites which were then in use. However, lest anything be omitted, they wanted these to follow later, after health had been restored, as the history of Athanasius relates, quest. 1, ch. 1, *Spiritus Sanctus*.

The third reason and occasion was this, which Jerome describes in the dialog *Adversus Luciferianos*. He reports that in his time it was customary in the churches that the bishop would hasten forth to those in the smaller towns who had been baptized by presbyters and deacons, to invoke the Holy Spirit and to lay his hand on them. It was without doubt a good and useful custom for retaining and preserving purity of doctrine and faith that the bishop himself interrogated and examined those who had been baptized by others concerning the doctrine and faith, and when he understood that they believed rightly and had been baptized legitimately, he confirmed them with the Word, and with the laying on of hands invoked the Holy Spirit on them in order that they might persevere in this faith. But both from this custom and also from the manner of receiving those who had returned to the church from a heresy, already at the time of Jerome, yes, long before, not only the common people but also bishops formed this opinion, as if Baptism in itself were without the Holy Spirit, who was only given and received when the bishop laid his hands on the baptized for the invocation of the Holy Spirit. This opinion, which was held by the presbyter Tertullian, Pope Cornelius, and Bishop Cyprian, Jerome seriously and earnestly refutes. And he proves that Baptism is not without the Holy Spirit, because sins are not remitted to any man without the Holy Spirit; also, the soul is not cleansed in Baptism of uncleanness without the Holy Spirit.

However, Jerome asks why, in view of the fact that the Holy Spirit is bestowed in a true Baptism, it is said in the church that a baptized person receives the Holy Spirit through the hands of the bishop. Here would have been the place to say, as the papalists now do, that in Baptism the Holy Spirit is given only for regeneration, but that for the remaining necessary gifts the Holy Spirit is not given or received in Baptism but that this is finally done in confirmation by the bishop. However, Jerome does not say this, but simply answers that this observance comes by virtue of the fact that after the ascension of the Lord the Holy Spirit descended upon the apostles. He quickly shows how he wants this understood, when he says: "We find this same thing practiced in many places more for the honor of the priesthood rather than to fulfill a law. Otherwise, if the Holy Spirit descends only upon the prayer of the bishop, those are to be bewailed who, having been baptized by presbyters and deacons in chains or in prisons or in more remote places, die before they have been visited by the bishops."

This explanation of Jerome should be diligently considered, for it furnishes light for understanding many stories and statements of the ancients about receiving the Holy Spirit through the laying on of hands by the bishop. From this it can also be understood how that churchly custom later degenerated more and more, when from time to time new rites and opinions were patched on. For finally the light of the doctrine was extinguished, because it was done for the honor of the episcopacy, not because the law demanded it, and that which had been observed in the case of those who had returned from a heresy was made into a special and universal sacrament for all the baptized, and the opinions were added which are enumerated above, which manifestly detract from the dignity and power of Baptism. These are the things of which I have said that they cannot be proved from the ancients.

Also Augustine, *Contra Donatistas,* Bk. 13, ch. 16, asks why the Holy Spirit is said to be given only in the catholic church through the laying on of the hand. He answers, not in terms of the things which the papalists ascribe to their confirmation, but says: "Our forebears wanted that understood which the apostle says: 'Love has been poured into our hearts through the Holy Spirit' (Rom. 5:5). For this is the love which those do not have who have been cut off from communion with the catholic church." Likewise: "Who now expects that those on whom the hand is laid in order that they may receive the Holy Spirit will suddenly begin to speak in tongues? Rather, it is understood that invisibly and in a hidden manner through the bond of peace divine love is breathed into their hearts," etc.

He is, however, speaking expressly about returning heretics and schismatics. In what manner is love poured into them by the laying on of hands? Augustine answers: "What else is the laying on of hands but a prayer over the man? Therefore it is not, like Baptism, unrepeatable." And Gratian says about this statement of Augustine, quest. 1, ch. 1, *Arrianos:* "From the fact that he commands the laying on of hands to be repeated, it is shown that it is not a sacrament." Therefore the things they quote from the ancients are far other and different from papalist confirmation as it has been described above.

25 With these things explained in this manner, the examination of the canons on confirmation will be easy and plain. For when the first canon condemns the kind of confirmation which consists of catechetical instruction of the children and their profession of faith, it has this meaning and purpose: Our theologians have often shown that if traditions that are useless, superstitious, and in conflict with Scripture are removed, the rite of confirmation can be used in godly fashion and for the edification of the church, namely in this way, that those who were baptized in infancy (for that is now the condition of the church) would, when they have arrived at the years of discretion, be diligently instructed in the sure and simple teaching of the church's doctrine and, when it is evident that the elements of the doctrine have been sufficiently grasped, be brought afterward to the bishop and the church. There the child who was baptized in infancy would by a brief and simple admonition be reminded of his Baptism, namely, that he was baptized, how, why, and into what he was baptized, what in this Baptism the whole Trinity conferred upon and sealed to him, namely, the covenant of peace and the compact of grace, how there Satan was renounced and a profession of faith and a promise of obedience made.

Second, the child himself would give his own public profession of this doctrine and faith.

Third, he would be questioned concerning the chief parts of the Christian religion and would respond with respect to each of them or, if he should show lack of understanding in some part, he would be better instructed.

Fourth, he would be reminded and would show by his confession that he disagrees with all heathenish, heretical, fanatical, and ungodly opinions.

Fifth, there would be added an earnest and serious exhortation from the Word of God that he should persevere in his baptismal covenant and in this doctrine and faith and, by making progress in the same, might thereafter be firmly established.

Sixth, public prayer would be made for these children that God would deign, by His Holy Spirit, to govern, preserve, and strengthen them in this profession. To this prayer there could be added without superstition the laying on of hands. This prayer would not be in vain, for it relies upon the promise concerning the gift of preservation and on God's strengthening grace.

Such a rite of confirmation would surely be very useful for the edification of the young and of the whole church. It would also be in harmony with both Scripture and the purer antiquity. For the account in Acts 19: 1-7 clearly shows that when the Apostles laid their hands on someone an examination with respect to the doctrine and a profession of faith were made. Also, there are examples from the apostolic church of exhortation to perseverance and of confirming through the Word in the once-accepted doctrine and faith (Acts 14:22; 15:30-32; 18:11). And the account in Acts 8:14-17 shows that public prayer was added. Thus Canon 7 of the Council of Laodicaea and Canon 8 of the Council of Arles speak concerning an examination and profession of doctrine and faith in confirmation, as we have noted above. And for this reason a canon of a Council of Orleans[13] requires a ripe age in the confirmand.

To this fits beautifully what Dionysius says at the end of the *Ecclesiastica hierarchia* about the teacher of catechetical instruction, to whom the children who had been baptized in infancy were brought for instruction in order that they might be led through instruction and exhortations to take upon themselves and preserve the profession of faith, the renunciation of Satan, and the promise of obedience made in Baptism.

These things were proposed at the Colloquy at Ratisbon [Regensburg] in the year 1541. But Eck, in the name of the papalists, simply and proudly rejected all these things, asserting that in confirmation the use of reason is not to be expected. Therefore he thought that confirmation should be performed at a time when neither examination in doctrine nor a profession of faith nor an exhortation to perseverance can have any place in children. And so our theologians said that if these things are taken away from the rite of confirmation, even if it contained nothing superstitious, it is nevertheless only a useless ceremony.

From this account the reader understands what this first canon on confirmation is after, whence it is taken, and what it looks to, when it makes mention of a useless ceremony, instruction of children, and confession of faith. Many thought that even if the papalists wanted to retain the other customs in their confirmation, they would nevertheless add to them instruction of the children, examination in doctrine, profession of faith, a reminder of the baptism which they had received, and an exhortation to perseverance, in order that thus it might have some appearance of godliness. But all these things, though manifestly useful, are murdered with an indirect blow by the anathema of the first canon. For they want it to be the kind of sacrament which *ex opere operato,* on account of the power of the chrism, confers a grace greater than that of Baptism.

However, someone may wonder why the papalists are not willing to tolerate these things in their confirmation. The reason is because in this way confirmation would be nothing else than a reminder of the Baptism

---

[13] A number of councils were held at Orleans. We have been unable to identify either the particular council or the precise canon, and have therefore used the indefinite article.

once received and would be a strengthening in the grace which was bestowed in Baptism. This the papalists do not want, as was shown above, and therefore they banish the things which we have mentioned from their confirmation, although the canon is worded very treacherously (that confirmation is not merely instruction of children and profession of faith) even though they usually choose an age for confirmation at which instruction, examination, profession, and exhortation would clearly be out of place. These men are neither able to tolerate nor do they consider admitting so much as a single emendation, let it be ever so clearly useful.

Therefore, because nothing that is fair can be obtained from them, we state the matter the way it is, that confirmation, as it is in use in the papalist kingdom and as it has been described above, is not only a useless ceremony but is defiled with many vain, superstitious, and ungodly opinions and traditions, as has hitherto been sufficiently shown.

26 So far as the second canon is concerned, what kind of and how great a power they ascribe to their chrism without any divine command and promise, and how great is the harm and reproach to Baptism when they take away that power from Baptism and transfer it to the chrism, which has no word of God at all, has up to now been shown in many words. But to all these things they answer only with the crashing of the anathema.

Let the reader note that they want to have given to the chrism not only a certain significance and reminder of the efficacy of Baptism but a spiritual and divine power peculiar to the chrism, and distinct from Baptism, so that as in the Eucharist one can eat and drink judgment to himself, so they think that by handling the chrism with too little reverence one incurs the supreme wrath of God and more than gehenna. Thus at Vienna once upon a time Bishop Faber cried out lest the foundations of the universe collapse, when the servant who was carrying the flask with the chrism had in his simplicity smeared his shoes, which had gotten hot on the way from the summer heat, with the fat which ran out and overflowed from the mouth of the flask.

The third canon appropriates[14] the smearing of the chrism in confirmation solely to the bishop under threat of the anathema. I answer with what Luther says in *De captivitate Babylonica*:[15] The kind of bishops they are, that kind of ministry they also want to have. For because they have

---

[14] The 1574 edition of the *Examen* has *evendicat,* which appears to be a misprint. Ed. Preuss has emended this, correctly we believe, to *vindicat.*

[15] Chemnitz reproduces Luther's thought, but does not quote verbatim. We have therefore omitted the quotation marks.

cast off the preaching of the Word and the administration of the true sacraments from themselves to other, inferior men, they have, lest they themselves should have nothing to do, invented the smearing of the chrism, as being only slightly laborious and troublesome. When it comes to the performing of the lawful office of a bishop, there are very many like the noble youth who once upon a time in their assembly, when the words of Paul: *Sicut estis azymi* ("as you really are unleavened," 1 Cor. 5:7) should have been recited, chanted: *Sicut estis asini* ("as you really are asses").

However, let the reader consider the levity and prodigality of these men in the way they pour forth anathemas. Scripture knows no difference between a bishop and a presbyter. Jerome says that whatever there is of this is done more for the honor of the priesthood than from necessity based on law. It is known also that the first council of Toledo (A.D. 400), Canon 20, decreed that when the bishop is absent the presbyter can apply the chrism. And it adds that down to the time of that council in some places presbyters prepared the chrism. It is also known that Gregory, dist. 95, ch. *pervenit,* concedes to the presbyters that they should touch the baptized on their foreheads with the chrism. Neither are they ignorant of how the canonists, how Alexander, Thomas, Richard, argue this question on the basis of this canon. Yet they pronounce the anathema if anyone says that a simple priest can be the minister of confirmation. Therefore also every bishop will be anathema who has not confirmed his sheep personally with the chrism. For the canons will that no other person, but only the bishop himself, shall apply the chrism. . . .

But which age in more recent years can recall that in the richer episcopates the bishop himself smeared his sheep with the chrism? For there was thought up the mockery of the suffragans. If someone has bought a bishopric in Turkey, perhaps for Sidon, or Tripoli, or Bethlehem, and bound himself by oath that he will convert these peoples to the faith, and when the journey has scarcely been begun he quickly returns and complains about difficulty and impossibility, then the pontiff absolves him of his oath. Because, however, he has the title of a bishop, but without a church, our bishops, through this mask, afterward perform confirmation, ordinations, consecrations, and other things of this nature in their dioceses. In such an illustrious manner he satisfies the canons when the fictitious and masked suffragan signs the sheep of another, while the bishop meanwhile, after his custom, does his own thing. And still they are not afraid, also in such a case, to rattle anathemas. What is this but to make mockery of all religion!

Sessions of the Council of Trent Under Julius III

I judge it to be unnecessary to retell the history of how under Paul III, when a murderous war had been stirred up in Germany, the council was first moved to Bologna, and after the death of Paul III, interrupted; and how soon, under Julius III, when it seemed to them that they had triumphed with respect to all of Germany, it was again proclaimed that it might be continued and carried forward. For Sleidanus has told these things at length and faithfully in his history. There the reader will also find what was meanwhile done and decreed in the armed assemblies of the empire with respect to the council and what happened thereafter.

Therefore, referring these matters to their own authors, where they can and should be sought, we shall pursue the examination of those things which were decreed under Julius III in the same manner we have followed in the preceding decrees.

𝔉𝔬𝔲𝔯𝔱𝔥 𝕿𝔬𝔭𝔦𝔠

CONCERNING THE SACRAMENT
OF THE EUCHARIST

*From the Decrees of the 13th Session
of the Council of Trent*

DECREE CONCERNING THE MOST HOLY SACRAMENT
OF THE EUCHARIST

Published in the Third Session of the
Council of Trent Under Pope Julius III,
on the 11th Day of October, 1551

The most holy ecumenical and general Synod of Trent, lawfully assembled in the Holy Spirit, the same legate and nuncios of the Holy See presiding in it, although it had come together, and that not without special guidance and governance, to this end that it might set forth the true and ancient doctrine concerning the faith and the sacraments, and that it might bring forward a remedy against all the heresies and other most grievous ills by which the Church of God is now lamentably disquieted and rent into many and diverse parts, had from its very beginning above all things this as its desire, that it might utterly pluck out the accursed tares of errors and schisms which the enemy has in these our calamitous times sown in the doctrine of the faith, and in the use and worship of the most holy Eucharist, which our divine Savior left to His Church, a symbol as it were of that unity and love with which He wanted all Christians mutually linked and joined together.

Therefore this same most holy synod, handing on that sound and pure doctrine concerning this venerable and divine sacrament of the Eucharist, which the Catholic Church, instructed by Jesus Christ our Lord Himself and by His holy apostles, and taught by the Holy Spirit, who day by day brings to her mind all truth, has retained and will preserve until the end of time, forbids all believers in Christ to dare to believe, teach, or preach otherwise concerning the holy Eucharist than as it has been explained and defined in this present decree.

SECTION I

Concerning the Real Presence of Our Lord Jesus Christ in the Sacrament of the Eucharist and Concerning the Consecration

Chapter I

To begin with, the synod teaches and openly and simply professes that in the gracious sacrament of the holy Eucharist, after the bread and wine have been consecrated, our Lord Jesus Christ, true God and man, is truly, really, and substantially contained under the outward appearance of these things which can be perceived by the senses. For these things are not contradictory, that our Savior always sits at the right hand of the Father in heaven according to the natural mode of existing, and that He is nevertheless sacramentally present to us in His own substance in many other places in a manner of existing which, although we can scarcely express it in words, we can understand with thought enlightened by faith to be nevertheless possible for God, and we ought most steadfastly to believe it. For thus all our forebears, as many as were in the true Church of Jesus Christ, who treated of this most holy sacrament, most openly professed, that our Redeemer instituted this so wonderful sacrament at the Last Supper when, after He had blessed the bread and the wine, He witnessed in express and clear words that He was giving them His body and blood. Since these words, recorded by the holy evangelists, and afterward repeated by St. Paul, carry on their very face this proper and clear meaning, according to which they were understood by the fathers, it is certainly an intolerable disgrace that they are twisted by certain contentious and evil men to artificial and imaginary figures of speech by which the reality of the flesh and blood of Christ is denied, against the universal understanding of the Church, which, as a pillar and foundation of the truth, has denounced as satanical these fabrications thought out by godless men, at all times acknowledging this most excellent benefit of Christ and remembering it with a grateful mind.

CANON I

If anyone denies that in the most holy sacrament of the Eucharist the body and blood together with the soul and divinity of our Lord Jesus Christ, and therefore the whole Christ, are truly, really, and substantially contained, but says that He is in it only as in a sign or figure or power, let him be anathema.

[Examination]

1 Concerning the presence of the body and blood of our Lord Jesus Christ in His most holy Supper, or concerning the true and genuine meaning of the words of the Supper, "This is My body; this is My blood," there is at the present time a vehement and truly lamentable controversy in the church. Some contend that these words are not to be understood in that sense which their simple, proper, genuine meaning, which is commonly used in Scripture, gives but that they should be twisted by figures of speech to the point that the true and real presence of the substance of the body and blood of Christ is taken out of His Supper and removed farther from it than heaven is removed from earth, and that in the Lord's Supper there is left with us on earth only the sign and figure of the body and blood of Christ, which is itself far absent and far removed from us. Or, Christ is said to be present in the Supper only according to His divine nature, offering and supplying to the communicants not the substance itself but only the power and strength of His body and blood, which are not present but far away, farther removed from the Supper than the visible heaven is distant from earth.

I for my part confess that I disagree with these opinions. I simply confess truly and openly that I embrace and approve the judgment of those churches which acknowledge and teach the true and substantial presence of the body and blood in the Supper in that sense which the words of the Supper give in their simple, proper, and genuine meaning. I give my assent to this understanding after diligently considering the arguments of both sides. For it cannot be done without danger to the soul if one amuses himself by contriving opinions in interpreting the words of the Supper. For it is written that those who do not discern that body of the Lord which the words of the Supper declare to be offered and received there, eat judgment to themselves. But this discernment cannot be rightly made if one departs from the true and genuine sense of the words ("This is My body"). Therefore one ought not rashly to embrace any opinions whatsoever about the interpretation of those words, but the grounds ought to be diligently sought out and considered, so that we may not carry our preconceived opinions into these words but that the words themselves, and the repetitions of the Supper which are found in Scripture, may show and furnish us the true and genuine interpretation and meaning, and that not by obscure and ambiguous conjecture but by clear, sure, and firm evidence and testimonies, in order that we may be able to boast that we have the mind of Christ. (1 Cor. 2:16)

2 Because, however, Scripture is not a matter for one's private interpretation (2 Peter 1:20), this simple rule is the most certain, the safest and firmest of all, namely, that the same doctrine and sense is for this reason repeated in different places in Scripture, that the interpretation of the Holy Spirit Himself can be sought and grasped by this comparison of passages. And when the Holy Spirit wanted another meaning understood in Scripture, different from the way the words simply and properly sound, He explained and showed this either in the same or in another place in a not obscure fashion.

Now, a description of the Supper is found in Scripture from different writers, and indeed repeated at different times. But no evidence is found that the simple, proper, usual, and genuine meaning of these words ("This is My body") should be abandoned. On the contrary, many clear indications present themselves that that sense should be retained which the simple, proper, and usual meaning of the words in Scripture gives, as this has been shown more fully by us in a special booklet. This meaning does not clash with a single article of faith. For it is certain that because the whole fulness of the Godhead dwells bodily in the human nature of Christ, and the human nature of Christ has been exalted through His ascension above every name which is named, whether in this or in a future age, that therefore Christ can be present with His body wherever He wills and do whatever He wills. Therefore the presence of the body of Christ in the sacrament does not conflict with the articles of faith, either of the true human nature or of the ascension of Christ. This understanding also has the constant consensus of the ancient, true, and purer church; moreover, it is full of the sweetest consolations. If the absence of the body and blood of Christ is established, consciences are robbed of all these things. But we have explained all this in a repetition of the sound doctrine of the presence of the body and blood of Christ in the Supper in an adequate treatise.[1]

3 Therefore I do not judge it to be necessary that the whole treatment of this controversy should be repeated here. But I wanted to note down these few things here in order that I might show that I am one in confession with those churches which differ from the opinions of the sacramentarians and which hold and profess the teaching of the true and substantial presence of the body and blood of Christ in the Supper according to the true, proper, and genuine meaning of the words of institution.

4 Therefore I will not now dispute further concerning the first chapter and the first canon so far as the presence of the substance of the body

---

[1] Reference is to a book of 117 folio pages published by Chemnitz in the year 1569 under the title: *Fundamenta sanae doctrinae de vera et substantiali praesentia, exhibitione et sumptione corporis et sanguinis Domini in coena.*

and blood of Christ in the Supper is concerned, lest I go beyond the plan of this examination. Nevertheless two things must still be considered in the explanation of this chapter. The first is that it seems that by means of the words "are contained" it wants to define the mode of the presence of the body and blood of Christ in the Supper. We on our part simply believe this presence because it has the testimony of the Word of God. But we judge that one ought not to dispute about the mode of the presence, because it has not been revealed by the Word of God. Therefore we do not define an established mode of this presence, but humbly entrust it to the wisdom and omnipotence of God. We do not establish a physical or geometrical, crass and carnal manner of presence. We do not dispute about inclusion in a certain place, nor about descent or ascent of the body of Christ. Briefly, we do not hold that the body of Christ is present in the Supper in any manner that is natural to this world.

Luther also taught that the ground for the presence of the body of Christ in the Supper is not to be placed in the disputation about the ubiquity[2] but in the truth of the words of institution. Neither do we receive transubstantiation as an article of faith—a matter about which we will have to speak later. But we simply believe that presence as the words of the Supper teach; however, the mode and manner we do not define, but entrust it to the wisdom of Christ, who is both truthful and almighty.

5 The other thing I said must be noted is that they mention the consecration of the bread and wine yet do not explain what and of what kind it is, although it is an established fact that many had begged the fathers of the council that, in view of such varied disputes and opinions, they should define and prescribe a fixed form of consecration.

For some argue that the consecration consists in the soft murmuring of these four words: "This is My body" over the bread, so that neither the things which precede in the institution nor those which follow either belong to or are necessary for the consecration but that there is in the syllables and letters of these four words such power and energy that if they are pronounced by the priest over the bread they are able to convert the substance of the bread into the body of Christ.

Certain men, for instance Thomas, maintain that also certain other things from the words of institution are necessary and belong to the consecration. There is a booklet of Bessarion in which he argues this question at length, whether the consecration comes about through the

---

[2] The ubiquity or omnipresence of Christ also according to His human nature was drawn into the discussion of the real presence of the body and blood of Christ in the Lord's Supper to show that the real presence is possible.

words of institution or through the words of the canon, or whether both together are necessary for the consecration. The theologians of Cologne, in their *Antididagma*, contend earnestly and with many words that those are raving mad who think that the bread and wine are consecrated into the body and blood of Christ through the words of institution if there are not also added the words and prayers of the canon. And among the papalists many write publicly that those churches which use the words of institution of Christ in the Supper without adding the papistical canon do not have the true body and blood of Christ, as Lindanus says, only a bread-sacrament.

It is also being disputed whether consecration of the altar, priest, vessels, vestments, and of the remaining armor of the papalist Mass is necessary for the consecration of the Eucharist.

6 Though requests came from many to the Tridentine fathers, they were not willing to get in among these so very diverse opinions but, without clarifying the matter, name only the consecration of the bread and wine. Let the reader consider with what intention this is done. However, the matter in itself is plain. For some rejected the papistical consecration in such a way that they imagined the Lord's Supper could also be celebrated without the words of institution. This is manifestly false. For it is most certain that there is no sacrament without the Word, as Paul calls Baptism "the washing of water with the Word" (Eph. 5:26). The saying of Augustine has it correctly: "Let the Word come to the element, and it becomes a sacrament." Likewise: "Take the Word out of Baptism, and what will the water be but water?" In no way, therefore, can there be a Eucharist without the use of the Word. For if the Word is taken out of the Eucharist, the bread will be nothing but bread. For this reason Augustine says, *Contra Faustum,* Bk. 20, ch. 13.: "Our bread and cup becomes sacramental by a certain consecration; it does not grow that way." Therefore what is not consecrated, though it be bread and cup, is food for refreshment, not a religious sacrament. This ground is very firm, being derived from the definition of a sacrament. This addition of the Word to the element in the sacraments is called "sanctification" by the ancients. The common people call it "consecration." Paul, following the description of Mark, calls it "blessing" when he says: "The cup of blessing which we bless." (1 Cor. 10:16)

But what if someone now asks what that word of blessing is which, coming to the bread and wine, makes it the sacrament of the body and blood of Christ? Surely this is beyond controversy, that as each sacrament has some certain word of God that belongs properly and specifically to it, so also the Eucharist has a certain specific word which belongs to it, namely, the divine institution. I think among those who do not judge that what is human should either be considered equal or be preferred to things divine also this is beyond doubt, that he acts wickedly who takes away the consecration of the Eucharist from the words of divine institution and transfers it to the prayers of the canon, which have been patched together by men out of unsound and sound, or rather, mostly out of unsound materials.

And surely this blessing or consecration is not to be divided between the Word of God and words handed down by men. For it is not just any word, but the Word of God which is necessary for a sacrament. And to the Word of God, seeing it has been tried with fire, nothing is to be added (Prov. 30:6). And especially, nothing is to be added to the testament of the Son of God (Gal. 3:15-17). In short, Christ has commanded us to do in the action of the sacrament what He Himself did. He did not, however, perform a mute action, but spoke. And what He said is reported to us in Scripture, as much as the Holy Spirit judged to be necessary for us.

7 Therefore the ancient church, though it used also other exhortations and prayers in the administration of the Eucharist, nevertheless simply and correctly judged that the blessing or consecration of the Eucharist is performed with the speech of Christ, that is, with the words of institution.

The clearest statement of all is found with Ambrose, *De sacramentis* Bk. 4, ch. 4. For when he had said that the bread is the body of Christ through the consecration, he presently asks with what words and with whose speech this benediction is made. He answers: With the words and speech of the Lord Jesus, and adds that there is a difference between this and the remaining things which are spoken in that action, which are either petitions or thanksgivings; these, he says, do not belong to the consecration or blessing of the Eucharist. But when the moment has arrived for the consecration and confecting of the sacrament, then, says he, the priest no longer uses his own words but the words of Christ. What these words of Christ are he sets forth expressly, ch. 5, reciting the words of institution.

Known is also the statement of Gregory in which he declares that it was the custom of the apostles that they would consecrate the wafer only at the time of the Lord's Prayer.

It is therefore false what Lindanus ascribes to Basil, that the consecration of the Eucharist is performed with words that are not written. For in *De Spiritu Sancto*, ch. 27, Basil is not speaking about the words of consecration but about the words when the bread of the Eucharist and the cup of blessing are elevated, that is, after the blessing has taken place.

Justin also says that the priest prays and gives thanks for a long time and in many words, but not to this end, that the consecration of the Eucharist may take place in this way. For he adds that he who presides gives thanks "that He saw fit to do these things," that is, that these mysteries were instituted and handed down to us by Christ. Concerning the consecration itself he says that the food of the Eucharist is consecrated "through the word of thanks from Him," that is, through praying the word handed down by Christ Himself. Paul affirms that he received from Christ what kind of word this is (1 Cor. 11:23-25). Justin also explains himself, for he says that this is the word which the evangelists in their expositions of the institution of the Supper committed to writing.

Irenaeus says: "When to the cup with its mixture[3] and the bread which has been broken the Word of God is added, it becomes the Eucharist[4] of the body and blood of the Lord." And that he understands this of the word of institution he explains when he says that the earthly bread receives the call of God, namely, when Christ declares concerning the bread, "This is My body." Thus Ambrose says, *De his qui initiantur mysteriis*, ch. 9, that the sacrament comes into being not through the blessing of man but through the speaking of Christ.

Also Chrysostom, in his homily on the betrayal of Judas, explains this question beautifully, namely, that it is not man who sanctifies the things set before us on the Lord's Table, in order that they may be the body and blood of the Lord, but that the same Christ who sanctified His first Supper now sanctifies also our Lord's Supper. For although the words are brought forth by the mouth of the priest, nevertheless the sacraments are sanctified by the grace and power of God. For the words, "This is My body" are the words of Christ, not the words of the priest. It is through these that what is set before us is sanctified. After this he undertakes a comparison between this word of Christ and the command, "Be fruitful and multiply," which, once spoken, has efficacy in the article of creation for all time.

In *De consecratione*, dist. 2, ch. *Utrum in figura*, Augustine says that all the other things which the priest speaks or the clergy of the choir chant are nothing else than acts of praise and thanksgiving, or indeed supplications and petitions of the faithful, but that the priest, when he is about to consecrate, takes the words of the evangelists.

---

[3] In the ancient church it was customary to mix the wine for the Eucharist with water before the celebration.

[4] The 1574 edition of the *Examen* has *in Eucharistia,* which does not yield an acceptable sense. The text in Migne, *Patrologia Graeca,* VII, col. 1125, does not have *in,* and Ed. Preuss has omitted it.

And Thomas, second quest., 83, art. 4, argues in many words that the consecration is performed solely with the words of Christ, that all else in the canon belongs to the preparation of the communicants. Therefore a true blessing or consecration of the Eucharist consists in the words of institution of the Son of God Himself, through which He Himself today and even to the end of the age consecrates and hallows for us the bread and the wine in order that, through divine grace and power, they may acquire that name which by nature they do not have, namely, that they may be His body and blood.

8 Let the reader observe, however, that very many among the papalists, although they are not able to banish the words of institution entirely from the consecration of the Eucharist, have nevertheless cut off a large part, so that with the exception of these four words, "This is My body," all else in the words of institution neither belongs nor does anything with respect to the consecration. Their purpose in arguing this is that with the words, "He gave it to them saying, 'Take, eat,' " etc., removed from the consecration, they might have a sacrament *extra usum.*[5]

But when Paul was about to instruct the Corinthians how they could celebrate not a common but the Lord's Supper, he recites and prescribes the entire institution. Justin, in reminding of the word taught by Christ, with which the Eucharist is consecrated, goes back to the description of the institution which is found in the evangelists. Eusebius of Emesa,[6] *De consecratione*, dist. 2, ch. *Quia corpus*, says that the priest in the consecration says: "Take, this is My body; drink, this is My blood." So also Ambrose, *De sacramentis*, Bk. 4, ch. 5. In short, in all the ancient liturgies not only four words, but the whole and entire institution is recited in consecrating the mysteries.

9 Two things, therefore, have now been shown:
  I. That the Eucharist is sanctified or consecrated, not by the prayer of man but by the word of institution;
 II. That the institution is not to be mutilated but is to be used in its entirety for the blessing of the Eucharist and for its administration.

In the third place also this must be explained, that the recitation of these words is not to be used in the way magicians recite their incantations

---

  [5] *Extra usum*, i.e., apart from the use for which the sacrament was instituted, e.g., in the so-called still Masses, which were celebrated for the souls presumed to be in purgatory. At such Masses no communicants were present.

  [6] Chemnitz has Emissenus. Preuss has revised this to Emisenus, the name Chemnitz regularly uses for Eusebius of Emesa.

in set formulas, for instance to bring down Jupiter Elicius[7] or the moon from heaven, namely, by the strength and power of the letters and syllables, if they are recited and pronounced a certain way; but as Paul asserts, that in the preaching of the Gospel Christ Himself speaks through the mouth of the ministers (Rom. 15:18-19; 2 Cor. 13:3) and that God is "making His appeal through us" (2 Cor. 5:20). So in the action of the Eucharist the minister acts as an ambassador in the place of Christ, who is Himself there present, and through the ministers pronounces these words: "This is My body; this do," etc., and for this reason His Word is efficacious. Therefore it is not a man, the minister, who by his consecration and blessing makes bread and wine into the body and blood of Christ, but Christ Himself, by means of His Word, is present in this action, and by means of the Word of His institution, which is spoken through the mouth of the minister, He brings it about that the bread is His body and the cup His blood, clearly in the same manner as it is He Himself who baptizes, though it be through the minister, and through His Word brings it about that the Baptism is a washing of regeneration and renewal. Therefore we use the words of institution as an ordinance, command, promise, and prerogative from our Mediator Jesus Christ, in order that we may be reminded and made sure with respect to what is done and believed in the Lord's Supper. For we come together that we may receive, eat and drink, not common bread or an ordinary cup, but that bread which is the body of the Lord and that cup which is the blood of the New Testament. But by nature bread is not the body of Christ nor wine His blood. Neither can any creature but only the Son of God by virtue of His omnipotence bring it about that bread should be His body and wine His blood. Yet He brought this about in the first Supper through the Word, when He said: "This is My body."

10 Therefore the words of institution are spoken in our Lord's Supper, not merely for the sake of history but to show to the church that Christ Himself, through His Word, according to His command and promise, is present in the action of the Supper and by the power of this Word offers His body and blood to those who eat. For it is He who distributes, though it be through the minister; it is He who says: "This is My body." It is He who is efficacious through His Word, so that the bread is His body and the wine His blood. In this way, and because of this, we are sure and believe that in the Lord's Supper we eat, not ordinary bread and wine but the body and blood of Christ.

---

[7] So called because he was thought to be brought down from heaven by incantations.

Thus the priest of Dionysius,[8] as he began the administration of the Eucharist, by way of prerogative prefaced it with these words: "You have said, 'Do this in remembrance of Me.' "

Ambrose, *De sacramentis*, Bk. 4, ch. 5, makes a beautiful distinction among the words of institution. For some are the words of the evangelists, which nevertheless are not recited just for the sake of the history but are as it were a prerogative which we in the action of the Lord's Supper ought to use, such as: "He took bread, blessed, broke, gave to His disciples," etc. Others are certainly words of Christ, by virtue of which the bread is the body of Christ and the wine His blood, such as: "Take, eat, drink; this is My body, this is My blood." This is the difference between the consecration and the historical recitation of the words. For when the institution is recited but we do not do what Christ did in the Supper and commanded to be done, then it is not a consecration but merely a recitation of history. But when we recite the words and do what He commanded, then we bless the bread and the cup with these words.

11 I know very well that this question is argued in different ways by many. Some look only on the work of the one who consecrates, that is, on the external recitation of the words, as this is performed by the minister, so that they almost make something magical of the consecration. Some indeed simply remove the Word from the Eucharist, and others retain only the narration of the history of the institution, without applying it to the present action in our Lord's Supper. But I judge that this understanding concerning the blessing or consecration of the Eucharist which I have set forth is both very simple and true. If this is rightly taught, it is useful both for teaching and for strengthening the faith.

12 However, we cannot simply accept the understanding of the papalists concerning the consecration of the Eucharist. For when they dispute concerning the word through which the blessing or consecration of the Eucharist comes about, they either mutilate the greater part of the institution itself, as was said above, as though with the exception of four words all the rest in the institution either did not belong or did not do anything to the consecration, or they patch human traditions onto the Word of God, as though the consecration could not come about through the words of institution unless there are added on also the things which have been patched together in the canon of the Mass. In this way, so far as in them lies, they render the whole sacrament of the Eucharist uncertain. For Peter Comestor[9] says that the words of institution are not the words

---

[8] Apparently either Dionysius of Rome or Dionysius of Antioch, both of whom wrote during the third century of the Christian era.

[9] Peter Comestor, A.D. 1100—1180, French theologian and writer.

for the blessing, because it is not known what words Christ used when He blessed the Eucharist. But Ambrose and Chrysostom assert the opposite. A certain Proclus supposes that the apostles composed the canon between the day of the Ascension and Pentecost, in order that it might be the form of consecration. But Gregory asserts that the apostles did not use the canonical prayer but consecrated the host only in connection with the Lord's Prayer. Therefore the canonical blessing is wholly doubtful and uncertain. Therefore also that sacrament which they say is consecrated with the canonical prayer will be doubtful. We however, when we ascribe the blessing to the words of Christ in the institution, have a sure and firm foundation.

Moreover, the papalists ascribe the consecration or hallowing in part also to the work of the priest, and indeed not only to the outward recitation of the words, but also to other actions of the priest, as the spreading, folding, lifting up, and gesticulations of the hands, the bending of the neck, the turning of the body, the transferring of the book, making the sign of the cross, and other similar things, but especially to the consecration bestowed on the priest, the altar, vessels, vestments, etc.

13 These things deserve and need to be censured, in order that the true foundation may be shown on which this greatest of all mysteries rests, namely, that we believe that in the Lord's Supper there is present, offered, and received, not common bread and ordinary wine but the body and blood of Christ.

SECTION II

Concerning the Reason for the Institution of This Most Holy Sacrament

Chapter II

Therefore when our Savior was about to depart from this world to the Father, He instituted this sacrament, in which He poured out, as it were, the riches of His divine love for men, making a memorial of His wonderful works; and He commanded that, as we receive it, we should revere His memory and proclaim His death until He comes to judge the world. He wanted this sacrament to be received as spiritual food of souls, by which the living might be fed and comforted with the life of Him who said: "He who eats Me will also himself live because of Me," and as an antidote, as it were, by which we may be freed from daily faults and preserved from mortal sins. Furthermore, He wanted this to be a pledge of our future glory and everlasting happiness, and thus a symbol of that one body of which He is Himself the head and to which He wanted us, as members, to be bound by the closest bond of faith, hope, and love, that we might all speak the same thing and that there might be no divisions among us.

CANON V

If anyone says, either that the foremost fruit of the most holy Eucharist is the forgiveness of sins, or that no other effects result from it, let him be anathema.

Examination

1 A simple and true explanation from the Word of God of the teaching concerning the purpose, use, and benefit, or concerning the power and efficacy of the Eucharist is most useful. For by this teaching the minds are stirred up to a more frequent use of this sacrament; by this use minds are incited to faith, prayer, and giving of thanks; finally, the conscience of the believer is strengthened by the sweetest comfort from this teaching, that the whole treasury of all the benefits which Christ the Mediator procured by the offering up of His body and the shedding of His blood belongs also to him in the so great infirmity of the flesh, that it is certainly communicated to him, and firmly given and pledged to him. Because we are subjected to the diverse calamities of this life, this teaching also shows what a pledge we have of our future liberation at some time, of immortality and glory. Therefore the dispute is about something

great, and it is altogether necessary to preserve the purity of this teaching as it is delivered to us in the Word of God, in such a way that it is not falsified either by additions or subtractions.

2 The reader needs to be reminded again what the dispute is about, or what is the issue in this controversy between the papalists and us about this teaching. For the dogmatists at Trent do not state plainly enough what is in controversy, although it is not unknown what they wish to condemn here. Indeed, they stated the fifth canon as though the point of the controversy were that we ascribe the forgiveness of sins to the believing reception of the Eucharist in such a way that we deny that also other effects accrue to the believer from this reception, although it is really something very different which they want to condemn. In order, therefore, that those things may be explained by which the papalists hope to be able to confuse the judgment of the reader or at least to hinder it, let it be plainly and clearly shown what they want to revile and condemn in our teaching about the purpose and benefit of the Eucharist. I shall briefly recite, in the words and sentences of the fathers, some of these effects of the Eucharist about which the canon appears to speak. These we in no way take away from the Eucharist, but teach that in the reception of the sacrament faith should reverently consider and embrace with thanksgiving all the riches and the whole treasury of benefits which Christ the Mediator procured by the offering up of His body and the shedding of His blood.

3 Because in the Eucharist we receive that body of Christ which has been given for us, and the blood of the New Testament which has been shed for the remission of sins, who will deny that believers there receive the whole treasury of the benefits of Christ? For they receive that through which sins are remitted, by which death is abolished, by which life is communicated to us, by which Christ unites us to Himself as members, so that He is in us and we are in Him. Hilary says beautifully: "When these things have been taken and drunk, they bring about both that Christ is in us and that we are in Him." Cyril says: "When in the mystical benediction we eat the flesh of Christ in faith, we have from it life in ourselves, being joined to that flesh which has been made life, so that not only does the soul ascend through the Holy Spirit into a blessed life, but also this earthly body is restored by this food to immortality, to be resurrected on the last day."

Therefore we receive in the Eucharist the most certain and most excellent pledge of our reconciliation with God, of the forgiveness of sins, of immortality and future glorification. And in truth, in this sacrament Christ richly pours out the treasures of His divine love toward men. For in

His Supper He gives us as food that body which He gave into death for us, in order that from it, as solid, divine, and life-giving food we may live, be nourished, grow, be comforted, and so transformed into Him that we can never be separated from Him, as Augustine affectionately says, speaking for Christ: "'You will not transform Me into you, but you will be transformed into Me.' A sacred meal this, in which Christ is eaten, the memory of His suffering contemplated, the mind filled with grace, and a pledge of the glory to come given!"

Beautiful is the statement of Ignatius, which is found in his Epistle to the Ephesians, where he calls the Eucharist[10] *pharmakon athanasias, antidoton tou mee apothanein, alla zeen en theoo dia Ieesou Christou, katharteerion alexikakon*, that is, "a medicine of immortality, an antidote, that we may not die but live in God through Jesus Christ, a cleansing remedy through warding off[11] and driving out evils."

Very fitting is this statement of Bernard: "The body of Christ is to the sick a medicine, to pilgrims a way; it strengthens the weak, delights the strong, heals weariness, preserves health. Through it man becomes more gentle under reproof, more patient under labor, more ardent for love, wiser for caution, more ready to obey, more devoted to giving of thanks."

Cyprian says: "Those whom we exhort to do battle are not to be left unarmed and naked, but are to be armed with the protection of the body and blood of Christ. For this is the purpose of the Eucharist, that it may be a defense to those who receive it. Therefore that person cannot be fit for martyrdom who is not armed by the church for the battle, and that mind fails which is not raised up and warmed by the reception of the Eucharist."

Chrysostom says: "If those who touched the hem of His garment were properly healed, how much more shall we be strengthened if we have Him in us whole? He will quiet in us the savage law of our members, He will quench the perturbations of the mind, drive out all sicknesses, raise us up from every fall, and, when the power of the enemy has been overcome, He will incite us to true piety and indeed will transform us into His own image." He comments on 1 Corinthians: "This table is the strength of our soul, the power of our mind, the bond of our confidence, our ground, hope, salvation, light, our very life. If we will depart hence, fortified with this sacrifice, we shall ascend to the sacred court with the greatest confidence."

---

[10] The edition of 1574 has *Eucharistia*. The rules of Latin grammar demand *Eucharistiam*. Ed. Preuss has so corrected it.

[11] The edition of 1574 has *avermutationem*, an evident misprint. Ed. Preuss has corrected this to *averruncationem*, a warding off.

Ambrose, *De his qui initiantur mysteriis,* ch. 8, says: "This food which you are receiving supplies the substance of eternal life." And, *In Lucam,* he says: "We eat the body of Christ in order that we may be able to be partakers of eternal life."

Basil, *In asceticis,* says that it is a characteristic of those who receive the Eucharist that they continually preserve the memory of Him who died for us and rose again. Therefore, when we use the Lord's Supper, the benefits which have been vouched for and procured for us by the offering up of the body of Christ and the shedding of His blood should be pondered with a grateful mind, proclaimed and declared publicly, and commemorated and celebrated with public and private thanksgiving. For the Eucharist is not a mere historical reminder of the death of Christ and of His benefits, but as Christ Himself now dwells in us, He excites, kindles, increases, and preserves in us through the Spirit the remembrance of Himself through the power of His body and blood, lest that forgetfulness of which Scripture speaks (2 Peter 1:9) come upon us by stealth, or, if it has come, that it be shaken off.

Moreover, as Augustine says, Christ in His Supper consecrated the mystery of our peace and unity, and through this food and drink He wanted to have understood the union of His body and of its members, which is the unity of the church.

Chrysostom says: "One table has been set before all; the same food is spread before all, and this is done openly, in order that we may acknowledge that we are one body and that we may embrace one another in mutual love." "For this sacrament is," as Augustine says, "prepared of things which are, from being many, brought together into one, namely, of kernels of grain and of many grapes or clusters, in order that we may be reminded by partaking of this sacrament that we also may be one, when we love one another and hold one faith, one hope, and undivided love." It is as Cyprian says: "Those who have one bread are also one body, and all have one heart and one soul that clings to the one Christ."

4 I wanted to restate these things briefly from the sayings of the fathers in order that I might show the reader that the point of controversy concerning which the papalists are here contending with us is not that they think and speak more highly concerning the purpose, fruit, power, and efficacy which come from receiving the Eucharist, or that we speak of the forgiveness of sins in such a way that we deny and detract from the other effects of the Eucharist. I added our confession to the statements of the ancients, which are taken from and built up from the Word of God, in order that it might become plainly evident before the whole church that we take away nothing whatsoever from the honor, power, and efficacy of the Eucharist. It is strange that the papalists wanted to shift the point that

is in dispute in this deceitful manner, seeing that otherwise they are accustomed to be angry and indignant that we, on the basis of the Word of God, praise and extol the honor and power of the Eucharist more highly than is either fitting or proper for their Mass, satisfactions, indulgences, and similar traffickings in pardons.

5 Since, therefore, the things here enumerated are taught more diligently in our churches than among the papalists, is there agreement in this part of the doctrine, so that they have nothing which they may condemn in our doctrine? Surely, they do not bring out their anathemas without cause in the fifth canon. What this cause is they indicate indirectly when they condemn "if anyone says that the foremost fruit of the most holy Eucharist is the remission of sins."

But you say: "Perhaps they mean those who dispute about the remission of sins in the reception of the Eucharist in such a way that they completely deny and take away all its other effects." Then let them name these; we, who hold that when the Eucharist is used all the benefits of Christ the Mediator are applied and sealed to believers, have nothing in common with such an opinion. But it is something else about which the good fathers are contending; this they unfold in the second chapter, namely, that the Eucharist is a remedy by which we are absolved from daily faults, that is, from venial sins; however, from mortal sins we are not absolved by the remedy of the Eucharist, but are only preserved from them.

This is what the Jesuits of Cologne set forth more clearly from the scholastics, when they say that the Eucharist indeed wipes out light and smaller sins, and sometimes even certain weighty ones, namely, those which have slipped from our memory when we go to confession, for then the power of the sacrament supplies what was lost through ignorance. Mortal sins, however, (they say) are not wiped out through the true use of the Eucharist. This, therefore, is the chief point which they criticize and condemn in our teaching, namely, that we teach that in the Eucharist, when He gives His body and blood as a most sure and extraordinary pledge and seal, the Son of God bears witness that He communicates, applies, and seals to everyone who uses this sacrament in faith His benefits, which He earned for the church through the offering up of His body and the shedding of His blood. We say that among these benefits the chief and highest place is held by the forgiveness of sins, reconciliation with God, reception into grace, and acceptance to salvation and eternal life. We say this, not as though we excluded the other benefits from the effect of the Eucharist but because these are, as it were, the bases for all the other benefits of Christ which are to be conferred on us. We do not do this on the basis of our own thinking or from rashness, but the Son of God Himself calls the Eucharist the New Testament; and Jeremiah declares that this covenant is contained in the New Testament: "I will forgive their iniquity, and I will remember their sins no more." And indeed, in the institution itself Christ expressly mentions the forgiveness of sins.

6 Let the reader consider what it means to restrict with the Jesuits the forgiveness in the New Testament, concerning which the words of the Supper speak, to light and lesser sins only, as though the blood of Christ, received in the Eucharist, did not have power to destroy mortal and weightier sins but that this merit and power were to be ascribed to our satisfactions, indulgences, the sacrifice of the Mass, and to the remaining wholesale traffic in pardons. It is worth the effort to consider why the papalists fight so stubbornly against this chief point of our teaching. Such consideration will recall many things to our minds and will show the weightiest reasons why their teaching must be contradicted.

Now they teach, in the first place, that forgiveness of weightier and of mortal sins, which have been committed after Baptism, must be sought and procured by our contrition, confession, satisfactions, by the sacrifice of the Mass, and in other ways. They see, however, that this whole structure of pardons will collapse if this forgiveness and reconciliation is sought in the body and blood of Christ. But in order that they may not ascribe nothing at all to the Eucharist, they speak about venial sins, that is (as the Jesuits explain it) about lighter and more insignificant sins. In order, therefore, that they may retain their satisfactions and the rest of the trafficking in pardons, they contend sharply that in the true use of the Eucharist no application of the forgiveness of sins is made.

Second, in order that they may retain the dogma about doubting the forgiveness of sins, they condemn also the sealing of the forgiveness of sins in the Eucharist. For the Jesuits at Cologne show clearly that they disapprove of the teaching that believers who use this sacrament in faith are strengthened by receiving it and are made sure of reconciliation with God, of forgiveness of sins, etc. They give as the reason, that this militates against the papalist teaching of doubt. Therefore, because they see that the true and salutary use of the Eucharist breaks down, by frontal attack as it were, the papalist dogma of doubt, in order that they may not leave to conscience any sure and firm consolation about confidence and certainty of the forgiveness of sins, they contend that in the use of the sacrament neither application nor sealing of reconciliation or of forgiveness of sins is made to individuals who use this sacrament in faith.

In the third place, they teach that there are indeed many excellent and extraordinary effects of the Eucharist, but that in the use of the

Eucharist these happen only to those who are free beforehand from all weightier sins, unstained, pure, and holy; that those who are situated otherwise eat judgment to themselves and commit the gravest offense against God because they do not come to the most holy mystery because of their worthiness. Also Andrada speaks approximately in this way. On the other hand, they teach that the Mass is an atoning sacrifice to blot out all manner of mortal and very weighty sins, and that *ex opere operato*, without any labor or peril to the sinner. They have discovered that by this means and in this way men are deterred from more frequent use of the Eucharist and rendered more desirous of the daily trafficking in Masses. This insidious trick they are not willing to lose; therefore they have made this separation, that they ascribe to the sacrifice of the Mass the forgiveness of all sins, but teach that in the use of the Eucharist only the lighter and smaller transgressions are blotted out and that even this is not done without great peril unless a person is free beforehand from all weightier sins, pure and holy. This reflection constitutes a true examination of the second chapter and of the fifth canon.

7 Is it then our opinion that in the true use of the Eucharist also those receive forgiveness of sins who are conscious of having committed the weightiest crimes, even if they do not desist from them but continue in their purpose to do evil, if they do not bring the fear of God or repentance and faith but knowingly persevere in sins against their conscience? This we by no means teach. For with us those people who do not repent but persevere in sins against their consciences are earnestly warned that they are eating and drinking judgment to themselves in that they sin against the body and blood of the Lord. For the offense against God is increased through the fact that they take the Eucharist in impenitence and treat the body and blood of the Lord with contempt. Therefore it is necessary that in those who are to be helped by this eating there be penitence and fear of God, which is terrified by the contemplation of sin and of the wrath of God against sins and puts off the purpose to do evil. Faith also is necessary, that seeks and accepts the remission of sins in the promise.

8 From this Andrada weaves an argument which he considers to be irrefutable. Anyone who repents and believes the Gospel receives and has the forgiveness of sins. But in order to approach Communion in a salutary manner he must bring repentance and faith. Therefore he has forgiveness of sins before Communion. But no one either seeks or receives what he already has beforehand. Therefore remission of sins is neither sought nor received in the use of the Eucharist.

But this whole fancy arises from ignorance of the teaching about the true and salutary use of the sacraments. For there is only one ground of reconciliation with God and of the remission of sins—Christ the Mediator with His obedience and merit. Him the Father has set before our faith, to be laid hold of and received for the remission of sins in both the Word and the sacraments. For reconciliation with God and forgiveness of sins is not like color or some quality which inheres immovably, indivisibly, and inseparably in a subject, so that once it has been accepted there is no longer any need to give it thought. But the perpetual action and daily exercise of faith in this life is to lay hold of Christ more and more, and ever more firmly to abide and continue in Him, lest the remission of sins be lost—but that it may be retained more firmly and surely. Indeed, in the present corruption of our flesh, in the midst of so many kinds of stratagems of the devil and offenses of the world, there is never a moment when it is not necessary for us to seek, lay hold of, and embrace the grace of God, reconciliation, and the remission of sins.

Moreover, in temptations the mind is troubled chiefly about this question, whether, in view of the fact that the promise is spoken in general, I also, who believe, have forgiveness of sins; whether I have it truly, surely, and firmly. Also, a pious mind is concerned lest it be snatched away or wrested from it. For this use therefore God, who is rich in mercy, which He pours out abundantly on the believers, instituted beside the Word also the use of the sacraments. However, we leave and ascribe both to the Word and to each sacrament what belongs to each in particular. Through Baptism we are reborn in Christ; having been reborn, we are nourished with the Word and the Eucharist; if we have fallen, we return through repentance and faith to the promise of grace, and by faith in the promise we are again reconciled to God through the Mediator. Nevertheless the Eucharist, which contains the basis for the remission of sins, namely the body and blood of Christ, is not excluded from also this use. For the Son of God testifies in the Eucharist by a most extraordinary and sure pledge, namely by exhibiting His body and blood, that He surely communicates, applies, and seals to each and everyone who uses this sacrament in faith, forgiveness of sins, reconciliation with God, and all the other benefits which He obtained for the church by the offering up of His body and the shedding of His blood that they might be offered in the Word and sacraments and be accepted by faith. And so faith has in the use of the Eucharist a firm anchor of consolation, trust, and certainty concerning the forgiveness of sins. It also has an effectual remedy for raising up and supporting a feeble faith in the midst of sorrow and trials, against want of confidence, doubt, faintheartedness, and despair. Moreover, the Son of God testifies that in the true use of the Eucharist He grafts the believers into Himself as members that He may bear, sustain, guide, and quicken them, in order that they may be united with Him more and more and may be enabled to continue more firmly in Him and hold fast the benefits they have received. This sweet, useful, and necessary comfort and strengthening of the faith the papalists endeavor to take away from the church, when they remove the application and sealing of the forgiveness of sins from the fruits and effects of the Eucharist.

9 This our teaching introduces nothing new. There are prayers in all the liturgies of the ancients that the receiving of the body and blood of Christ may result in the remission of all sins. Therefore the matter concerning which there is controversy in the second chapter and the fifth canon is of the utmost importance on account of the comfort of consciences. For they teach that also the other effects of the Eucharist which they enumerate come only to those who have rendered themselves free and exempt from weightier sins, pure and holy. But these things will need to be explained more fully in the seventh chapter, "Concerning Preparation."

SECTION III

Concerning the Superiority of the Eucharist over the Other Sacraments, That Is, Whether the Rule Is True That the Sacraments, Apart from Their Divinely Instituted Use, Do Not Have the Nature of a Sacrament

Chapter III

The most holy Eucharist indeed has this in common with the other sacraments, that it is a sign of a sacred thing, and a visible form of an invisible grace. Indeed, there is found in it this excellent and peculiar thing, that the other sacraments have power to sanctify only when someone uses them but in the Eucharist the Author of holiness is present before its use. For the apostles had not yet received the Eucharist from the hand of the Lord when He nevertheless Himself affirmed that that which He presented to them was His body. And this belief has always been in the Church of God, that immediately after the consecration the true body of our Lord and His true blood, together with His soul and divinity, are there under the form [12] of bread and wine; the body under the form of bread, and the blood under the form of wine, through the power of the words; however, the body also under the form of wine, and the blood under the form of bread, and the soul under both, by the power of that natural connection and concomitance by which the parts of Christ the Lord, who has now risen from the dead to die no more, are mutually joined together; furthermore, the divinity on account of its wonderful personal union with His body and soul. Therefore it is most true that as much is contained under one form as under both, for the whole and undivided Christ is under the form of bread and under any part whatsoever of that form; likewise the whole Christ under the form of the wine and under its parts.

CANON III

If anyone denies that in the venerable sacrament of the Eucharist the whole Christ is contained under each form and, when a separation is made, under every part of each form, let him be anathema.

---

[12] The Latin word translated here and in the following with "form" is *species*. The word means "outward appearance or form." Roman Catholic theologians have often simply used the English word "species" to translate the Latin *species*. On account of the common present-day use of the term "species" in biological science we preferred to translate it with "form."

If anyone says that, when the consecration has been performed, there is not in the wonderful sacrament of the Eucharist the body and blood of our Lord Jesus Christ, but only in its use, when it is received, not however before or after, and that in the wafers or consecrated particles which are reserved or remain over after Communion the true body of the Lord does not remain, let him be anathema.

Examination

1 The heading promises an explanation of the superiority of the Eucharist over the other sacraments. And, certainly, there is no need to argue that the Eucharist has greater dignity and excellence than matrimony and the other things the papalists count as sacraments. For between things which are not of the same genus a comparison cannot even be made. In view of the fact that for the distribution, application, and sealing of the benefits of Christ the Mediator these instruments or means have been divinely instituted and ordained, namely, the preaching of the Gospel and the use of the sacraments, such as Baptism and the Lord's Supper; in view of the further fact that the treasure which is offered and set before us in the preaching of the Gospel, in Baptism, and in the Eucharist is to be accepted by faith in Christ the Mediator with all His benefits, it would be useful to explain what difference there is or what degrees there are between these instruments or means. But the Tridentine fathers are not concerned about these useful explanations. Rather, they fight sharply to strengthen and uphold the traditions of the scholastics.

2 These teach that the Eucharist excels the other sacraments: I. In the power to signify; II. In what it does signify; III. In what it contains. This they explain as follows: that in the other sacraments there is only accidental and created grace, whereas in the Eucharist there is Christ Himself, the Author, Sanctification, and Fount of all grace. IV. In the manner in which it contains. They teach that the other sacraments are not sacraments except when they are being used, and that they have power to sanctify only when they are used. But the Eucharist, they hold, is a sacrament and contains the body and blood of Christ in a lasting manner and permanently also apart from its use.

About the first three degrees the men of Trent do not dispute at all, perhaps because they are aware how absurd it is to outlaw Christ Himself, the Fount and Author of all grace and sanctification, from Baptism and to substitute a created grace that inheres in the water, although Scripture clearly testifies that Christ Himself cleanses the church with the washing of water in the Word (Eph. 5:25-26). And Paul declares (Gal. 3:27): "As many of you as were baptized have put on Christ."

3 In defending the opinion that the Eucharist is a sacrament and contains Christ also apart from the use for which it was divinely instituted they are fighting, as it were, for what is most dear to them. The reader needs to be reminded what reasons they have to wage this battle. In the papalist kingdom they have now already for years transformed the Lord's Supper into acts which are clearly at variance with the use for which Christ instituted it. For in the Mass, when the words of consecration (as they call them) have been spoken over the bread and wine, the sacrament is not distributed to those gathered about it, is not received by the people, is not eaten nor drunk, but they pretend with certain gestures and brief prayers of the sacrificing priest that it is being offered to God the Father to blot out the sins of the living and the dead. The bread over which these words have been spoken is not distributed in order that it may be eaten, but kept, reserved, shut in, carried about, and men are persuaded that by means of lighted candles, genuflections, and other rites and acts of veneration and adoration they are there offering a special and most excellent worship to Christ, indeed a more excellent one than if the blessed bread were received and eaten according to the institution. The exhibition of the Eucharist is used against tempests, conflagrations, sicknesses, and any number of perils, likewise to procure every kind of blessing. That these last-mentioned uses are not prescribed or commanded by Christ in the words of institution the papalists themselves are not able to deny.

That also the first has no basis in the words of institution we shall demonstrate later, when we discuss the Mass. All these and similar things are refuted and overthrown by this one rule, which is both wholly true and wholly firm, that sacraments apart from their divinely instituted use are not sacraments. Therefore they are so hostile to this rule. To condemn it they set down Chapter III and Canon IV. For they see that all the things they have without grounds added to the Eucharist, outside of its divinely instituted use, cannot be held, defended, and established unless that most true rule is condemned and the teaching of the scholastics is foisted on the church as an article of faith, namely, that once the words of institution have been spoken over the bread, then, even if the use which Christ instituted is neither present nor comes to it, one must nevertheless believe that in that bread, no matter how it is treated, Christ, God and man, is present, contained, and remains by an enduring union no less and in no other way than in the divinely instituted distribution and eating. Once this opinion has been set down, human cogitation quickly adds on other uses and institutes functions of the Eucharist other than Christ prescribed in the words of institution. And then they judge that not only can these be done with a good conscience but that they should by all means be done, since indeed they teach that also apart from the use instituted in the

Word, Christ is there present with His body and blood, no less and not otherwise than in the [divinely instituted] use itself. Therefore the papalists have sufficiently great and weighty reasons why, for the strengthening of their kingdom, they have decided to fight strenuously for this dogma as their dearest possession. For if this pillar were taken away, a large part of their kingdom would collapse of its own accord.

4 However, they are aware that in this matter they are hard pressed and squeezed by the similarity of the remaining sacraments. For they themselves are compelled to confess that if the words of institution of Baptism are pronounced over the water and the act of baptizing does not take place, and no one is present who is to be baptized, it is not the sacrament of Baptism. Neither dare one say that if the water is reserved, carried about, or displayed, Christ, the Father, and the Holy Spirit are there present in the same way as the whole Trinity is present in the act of Baptism. This also the papalists themselves confess. However, lest they be compelled to concede the same thing in the sacrament of the Eucharist, with irreparable harm to their kingdom, they feign that this is the excellence of the Eucharist over the other sacraments, that also apart from its use Christ, God and man, is there present and contained in exactly the same manner as in its [divinely ordained] use. This is indeed their common and constant assertion.

5 And whereas we have until now heard only repetitions of scholastic theology, amplified and fortified only by the addition of anathemas, they are now attempting (may their gods prosper the attempt) not only to repeat that axiom in words but also to prove it, and that from the words of institution. Therefore let the reader prick up his ears in order that men may not forever say that the Council of Trent is operating without grounds and proofs but solely with vehement assertions and anathemas.

This is what they say: The apostles had not yet received the Eucharist from the hand of the Lord when He nevertheless declared that what He was offering them was His body. We indeed accept the condition that this whole controversy should be decided on the basis of the words of institution. The papalists themselves show us the way in which this decision should be made, when they prove from the words of Baptism that the water of Baptism outside of its divinely instituted use is not a sacrament. For Baptism is called a "washing of regeneration and renewal in the Holy Spirit" (Titus 3:5). Scripture says that Christ Himself with the power of His death and resurrection is there present (Gal. 3:27; Eph. 5:26; Rom. 6:3-4; 1 Peter 3:21). But because the institution employs a word signifying an action, "baptize them"; likewise, "as many of you as were baptized"

(Gal. 3:27); "be baptized" (Acts 2:38), therefore outside of this use and apart from this action it is not the sacrament of Baptism, even if the words of institution, no matter with what intention, are pronounced a thousand times over the water. Neither dare it be said that Christ is present in that water in the way He is present in Baptism.

Now someone may perhaps object: As the waters of warm springs have and retain their peculiar power even if no one bathes there (for warm springs do not receive their power from the act of washing but have it beforehand), so also the washing of water in the Word is a washing of regeneration and renewal of the Holy Spirit even if there is no one who is baptized, since it receives and has its power from the Word, not from the persons who are baptized. We answer rightly from the institution, that Baptism indeed does not obtain its power from the use which those who are baptized make of it but from the efficacy of the divine Word, that it is nevertheless an ordinance of God revealed thus in the institution, that Baptism is to be an action, and that in this action or in this use it is such a sacrament as the divine command and promise in the institution describe it.

Outside of this use, or if Baptism is transformed into another action, differing from that which is prescribed in the institution, it will not be Baptism. For the institution says: "Baptize them." But if, apart from this use, the words of institution are pronounced over water, they do not make a sacrament. Rather, it is a profanation of the divine name if the water which has been consecrated with the words of institution is not put to the use which the institution prescribes, or if it is transferred to another action than the one prescribed in the institution. As these things concerning Baptism are certain, so they are, I think, not denied by the papalists.

6 We shall apply this criterion, taken from the words of institution of the sacraments, also to this controversy concerning the Eucharist, in order that it may become evident whether it is true, as the papalists contend, that the Eucharist has this characteristic and peculiarity that it is a sacrament apart from that use and action which is prescribed and commanded by the institution, no less than in the true use itself. Now if, in the institution, there were found only these words: "He took bread, gave thanks, and said, 'This is My body,' " then the papalists might be saying something. But the institution says: He broke it, that is, divided it, gave it to His disciples, and commanded that they should receive, eat and drink it. Surely, without any controversy, these words signify an action, and indeed He expressly uses a word that signifies doing, for He says, "This do," namely, what was done in this My first Supper.

If, therefore, we are to judge according to the words of institution, the sacrament of the Eucharist will be a certain action and will consist in a use, no less than Baptism. Yes, let the reader consider this! In the institution of Baptism there is only this one word signifying an action, "Baptize them." Yet it has already been shown how mightily it demonstrates and convinces that Baptism, outside of the divinely instituted use, is not a sacrament. In the institution of the Eucharist, however, there is not just one such word, but a number of words are placed there in an order which most clearly signifies an action: He took; He gave thanks; He broke; He gave to His disciples; He said, Take, eat, drink, this do.

Now we ask, if these words are pronounced over the bread and wine, "This is My body; this is My blood," but no distribution is made, it is given to no one, and there is no one to receive, eat and drink—we ask, I say, whether the institution of Christ is being observed there. It is clear that it is not. We ask secondly, whether the genuine sacrament of the Eucharist is there where the institution of Christ is not being observed. Surely, because the sacraments of the New Testament are consecrated by the institution, it is evident and certain that there is no sacrament where the institution is not being observed.

7 However, the reader already knows what we have noted above, why the papalists argue so anxiously that not the total institution but only the little part, "This is My body; this is My blood," belongs to the consecration of the Eucharist. For in this way they hope to be able to maintain that apart from the divinely instituted use the bread is and remains the body of Christ. But when Christ says, "Do this," He understands the whole institution, not merely some small part of it.

Also Paul, when he had made mention of the blessing of the Eucharist (1 Cor. 10:16), soon afterward, in the 11th chapter (1 Cor. 11:23-25), when he is about to show how one may celebrate not a common or private but the Lord's Supper, recites and describes the whole institution of the Supper.

Also the ancients, in consecrating the Eucharist, employed not some small part but the whole institution. They judged that this is the Word which, coming to the element, makes it a sacrament. Therefore when the words of institution are spoken over the bread and wine but there is neither present nor added that use or action which is not only prescribed but commanded in the institution, loyalty to the truth compels us to think and say that Christ is not present there with His body and blood in the way He is present in the true use of the Supper according to His Word. Therefore that difference between Baptism and the Eucharist over which the papalists labor, namely, that Baptism is a sacrament when it is used but the Eucharist also apart from its use, can neither be shown nor proved from the Word of God. For as there are words in the institution of Baptism which signify use and action, so there are such words also in the institution of the Eucharist. What is more, because there are more such words in the institution of the Eucharist, the arguments conclude much more powerfully and firmly concerning the Eucharist than concerning Baptism that apart from the divinely instituted use they are not true sacraments.

8 The Lord's Supper is therefore a certain action, and has a certain use prescribed in the institution, and to this action, which the Son of God exercises through the ministry, there is joined that promise concerning which the words of institution speak. When, however, apart from this use, it is transformed into an action different and diverse from that prescribed and commanded in the institution, even though the words are spoken over the bread and wine, it will no more be a sacrament than as has been said about Baptism above; yes, it is a profanation of the Word and name of God to speak the words of institution over the bread and wine and meanwhile to remove the use of which the institution speaks, namely, that it be distributed, eaten, and drunk. This amounts to removing the very meaning of the institution or turning it into something of another kind.

9 Surely, these things are quite clear. The reader will, however, observe that the men of Trent do not dare to say (though they think and understand it) that the Eucharist apart from its divinely instituted use is a sacrament, in which the body and blood of the Lord is present, but they say, "before and after its use." Because these things seem to be somewhat ambiguous they judged that under these coverings they could establish, defend, and retain all the things which have crept into the handling of the most holy Eucharist outside of its divinely instituted use. But what, say they, if Christ did not pronounce these words, "This is My body," before He had carefully noted that every single one of the apostles was already seizing the offered and accepted bread with his teeth and eating it? Or if He said concerning that bread over which He had given thanks, at the moment when He offered it, before the apostles ate it, "This is My body," were these words false until the apostles began to eat it, so that the eating of the apostles first imparted truth to His words? In a notation in the margin at Luke 22:19 they say that the apostles had not yet received the Eucharist from the hand of the Lord when He truly affirmed that what He was handing them was His body. For Luke does not add the words, "Take, eat and drink," but: He gave them the bread and said, "This is My body."

To this last argument I shall answer first of all that the institution of the Lord's Supper is to be determined by a comparison of the descriptions which are found in four places in Scripture. Therefore those act incorrectly who want to deduce from the description in Luke that Christ gave the bread to the disciples in such a way that they either might not use it at all or use it in any manner they chose, but that nevertheless the truth would be added and remain, "This is My body." For Matthew, Mark, and Paul relate that Christ first of all commanded in express words that they should use that bread which He was giving, and that He prescribed the manner in which they should use it, namely, "Take and eat," and that then He added the words, "This is My body." Mark says in the description of the second part: "And they all drank of that cup," and He said to them, "This is My blood." Nevertheless the meaning is not that the blessed bread which is divided, which is offered, and which the apostles received from the hand of Christ was not the body of Christ but becomes the body of Christ when the eating of it is begun. For the whole action of the institution hangs together, and the words, "This is My body," belong to the entire action. Therefore it is concerning that bread which is blessed, which is broken or divided, which is offered, received, and eaten—I say, it is concerning that bread that Christ says, "This is My body." And Paul says of this broken bread that it is "a participation in the body of Christ" (1 Cor. 10:16). Moreover, he says in the words of institution, "This is My body, which is broken[13] for you," that is, what is divided in the Supper is the body of Christ. Therefore Christ, God and man, is present in the total action of the Supper instituted by Him, and offers to those who eat it His body and blood. For it is He Himself who through the ministry blesses, who divides, who offers, who says, "Take, eat; this is My body." As Chrysostom says on Matt. 26:26-28: "These are not works of human power which He performed at that time in that Supper. He works also now; He does it. We have the order of ministers, but it is He who consecrates these things; it is He who transmutes them." These things are simple, true, and clear from the words of institution. For the word "use" in this debate is most correctly defined as the total or entire action which is prescribed and commanded in the words of institution. When therefore the bread is taken, blessed, divided, offered, and received according to the institution, this action is not rightly said to be either before or apart from the use of the Supper, which has its bounds in the entire action of the institution.

---

[13] Chemnitz is here following an old Greek manuscript which has the word *kloomenon*, broken. Textual criticism has removed this word as not being found in the most ancient manuscripts.

10 But the men of Trent speak only of the eating, and because, before that eating, Christ, God and man, is present in the action of the Supper when the bread is blessed, divided, offered, and received, giving to those who eat, together with the bread and wine, His body and blood, the men of Trent attempt to construct from this that Christ, God and man, is present in the Eucharist in such a way with His body and blood, also before its use, that once the words of institution have been spoken over the bread and wine, even if the remaining action which is prescribed and commanded in the institution, namely, that it be divided, offered, received, and eaten, does not follow for a number of days, yes, for some months or even years, Christ is nevertheless compelled meanwhile to remain in the bread and wine with His body and blood in an enduring union, and this in such a way that it can meanwhile be handled in the sacrifice of the Mass, reserved, carried about, displayed, adored, and whatever is connected with these things.

11 These are the things which are not in harmony with the institution, yes, which militate against it. For the institution of the Supper prescribes the action thus: To take bread and wine, bless, divide, offer, receive, eat, and add this word of Christ: "This is My body; this is My blood," and to do all this in remembrance of Him. However, He neither commanded nor permitted us to rend asunder or separate this action into a number either of days or months or years, but commanded us to do what He prescribed to us by both word and example. He did not bless the bread in such a way as to promise that, if it were first distributed and eaten after some months or years, His body would nevertheless meanwhile be perpetually joined to the bread, but He took bread, blessed, broke, gave it to His disciples, and said, "Take, eat; this is My body," etc. He showed by His example that the dividing, offering, taking, and eating should not be spread out over a number of days, months, or years. For the account of the institution relates that the offering, taking, and eating took place at once.

12 These things are so clear and certain that there is no escape from them by any trickery, if only we hold firmly to this basic principle, that the institution is the norm and rule from which and according to which all such questions and disputes are to be decided. Therefore both of these things are clearly demonstrated from this basic principle:

1. That the blessing of the Eucharist and the promise of the presence of the body and blood of Christ ought not to be torn apart and forcibly separated from the use which is prescribed and commanded in the institution. For it is of the blessed bread, which is distributed, received, and eaten, that Christ asserts, "This is My body."

2. That under no pretext whatsoever should there be instituted, added, or amplified any use of the Eucharist other than the one which has been prescribed and commanded in the institution. For Christ delivered both to His apostles at the Last Supper, and to Paul after His ascension, in what manner He wanted His church to use the Eucharist until the end of the world. And what He delivered and repeated we have in writing. Now not even to the testament of a man is anything added (Gal. 3:15). Much less, therefore, should this be done to the testament of the Son of God. These very simple and clear basic principles shatter, demolish, and overturn two not unimportant pillars of the papalist kingdom, namely, that when the words of institution have been spoken over the bread, then, also apart from the use divinely ordained and commanded in the institution, Christ, God and man, by an enduring union is and remains in the bread in no other way than He is present in the true use, and that, over and above and apart from this use, which has the testimony and commandment of the institution, it is permissible to handle the Eucharist in another way and for a different use, namely, through sacrifice, reservation, carrying it about, displaying it, and all that is connected with these things.

13 Ambrose, on 1 Cor. 11:27, says that those are understood by Paul to be unworthy who either celebrate this sacrament differently than it was instituted by Christ or receive it differently from the way He taught. Therefore, though antiquity did not judge that it was necessary that in every gathering the whole community or all present should communicate together, it nevertheless did judge that a Mass was not lawful or complete unless some were present who would communicate with the priest. This means that the sacrament of the Eucharist should not be handled apart from the use of distribution and reception. *De consecratione,* dist. 2, ch. *Peracta; Canon apostolorum,* 10; John of Antioch, 2; Chrysostom, *Ad Ephesos,* ch. 1, Sermo 3.

Durandus, *Rationale,* Bk. 4, ch. 1, says: "That is a legitimate Mass in which there are a priest and one who gives the response and a communicant, as the composition of the prayers clearly shows."

Gabriel Biel, *In canonem lectu.,* 26, says: "After Christ consecrated His body He did not stop in the consecration, neither did He give it to His disciples that they should honorably reserve it, but gave it for its use, saying: 'Take and eat.'" And in *Lect.,* 38, he says that the fathers for this reason added these words to the form of the consecration: "Take and eat." Cassander quotes from Humbertus the bishop that it is neither a perfect Mass nor a commemoration of Christ such as He delivered to His disciples unless the blessed bread is soon broken and at once distributed.

What is reported by Justin, that when Communion has been held at an assembly of the church the deacon carries some portions to those who are absent and to the sick, likewise that, as Eusebius says, the Eucharist is sent to visiting bishops—this gives no support to the papalists. For there the sacrament remains in use; for it is carried away and sent in order that it may be distributed, offered, received, and eaten. But that some are said not to have at once eaten the Eucharist, which was distributed, offered, and received, but to have reserved it in little chests or in napkins, etc., and to have ascribed I know not what all to the reserved bread, should in no way move us. For the question is not (to borrow words from Cyprian) what someone before us has done but what He who is before all both did before and commanded us to do. For also the custom of privately reserving the Eucharist apart from its use was afterward abrogated and prohibited by public orders of councils.

14 However, the fourth canon adds that also after its use the body and blood of the Lord is in the Eucharist, i.e., in the bread and wine. We need to weigh what this means. Christ instituted that in the Lord's Supper bread and wine should be means or instruments through which He wishes to offer and communicate His body and blood to those who eat, in order that He might be and remain in the believers not only through faith and Spirit but, as the ancients speak, also by natural or substantial participation and might thereafter be united with them more and more. Therefore after the use of the blessed bread and wine in the Lord's Supper one ought not to dispute about the union of the bread and the body of Christ but there ought to be taught from the Word of God the sweetest consolation about the union of Christ, God and man, not with the bread which has just been eaten but with the soul and body of the believers, that He may bear, preserve, give life to, and rule us who have been inserted and as it were grafted into Him.

But this most useful teaching having been suppressed and buried, the gloss, *De consecratione,* dist. 2, *Olim,* teaches: "As quickly as the form[14] is ground by the teeth, so quickly is the body of Christ snatched up into heaven," namely, lest any consolation should remain from it for believers. The Tridentine fathers indeed do not now repeat the pleasant old song of the gloss, yet say nothing about the union of Christ, God and man, with believers after the use of the Supper, but argue that the body of Christ is in the bread also after the use. Perhaps they have looked back upon those shameful papalist precautions which institute an examination

---

[14] "Form," meaning the consecrated bread after it has been, according to Roman Catholic teaching, transubstantiated.

even into excrements. For if they can there distinguish the form in some way, they rave that the body of Christ is attached and clings there. Now I should think that by the words "after use" they would understand that which follows in Canon IV, namely, that the body of Christ remains in the consecrated particles which are left over after the Communion and reserved. But how can "after use" be said about those particles to which use has not yet come, that is, which have not been distributed, received, and eaten? For the very conjunction which they use in the fourth canon indicates that two distinct and different things are understood by them when they say: 1. that the body of Christ is in the Eucharist also after use; 2. that in the particles that are left after Communion the body of Christ remains. However, this latter dispute belongs to Chapter VI and to Canon VII.

Furthermore, in this third chapter and in the third canon there is treated also the question of concomitance, by which the total and complete Christ is under either form, so that just as much is contained in and received under the one form as under both. But these things belong to the debate concerning Communion under one form, which must be explained later in a special place. Therefore we shall relegate this part to that place.

SECTION IV
Concerning Transubstantiation

Chapter IV

However, because Christ our Redeemer said that what He was offering under the appearance of bread was truly His body, therefore there has been at all times in the Church of God the conviction—and this sacred synod now declares this anew—that through the consecration of the bread and wine a conversion is made of the whole substance of the bread into the substance of the body of Christ our Lord, and of the whole substance of the wine into the substance of His blood. This conversion has been fitly and properly called transubstantiation by the holy Catholic Church.

CANON II

If anyone says that in the most holy sacrament of the Eucharist the substance of bread and wine remain, together with the body and blood of our Lord Jesus Christ, and denies the wonderful and unique conversion of the total substance of the bread into the body and of the total substance of the wine into the blood, so that only the appearances of bread and wine remain, which conversion the Catholic Church very fittingly calls transubstantiation, let him be anathema.

Examination

1 Transubstantiation is also one of the pillars that support the papalist kingdom. Among the first things the reader should consider is why they labor so greatly to support and establish it. The reason is not that the true and substantial presence, offering, and receiving of the body of Christ in the Lord's Supper could not otherwise be taught, retained, believed, and confessionally expressed. For they themselves confess in the second canon that this can be done. Rather, it is that they may retain and establish the sacrifice of the Mass, reservation, carrying about, adoration of the bread, and all the things which, outside of the divinely instituted use, have been joined to these things—for this reason they fight so persistently about transubstantiation.

Among the other reasons for transubstantiation they expressly mention these: in order that no other substance save that of Christ be either adored or offered to God the Father, and that the presence of the body of Christ in the Eucharist may be lasting, also apart from its use.

2 But even as the very word "transubstantiation" sufficiently shows both the newness and the foreign nature of the dogma, so it is useful to observe when the idea of transubstantiation, which is now being thrust upon the church as an article of faith under threat of the anathema, chiefly began to be debated. The ancients make mention simply of mutation and conversion of the elements in the Lord's Supper. This they understand and explain in this way, that after consecration it is no longer common bread and ordinary wine but is the Eucharist, which is made up of two things, an earthly and a heavenly, a visible and an invisible, as Irenaeus and Augustine speak. Afterward John of Damascus, Theophylact, and others began to preach in more exaggerated language about the transformation of the elements in the Lord's Supper.

But it was only in the time of Peter Lombard, with the advent of scholastic theology, that they began to dispute in France concerning the manner of this conversion, whether it pertains to the form, or to the substance, or is of another kind. Lombard, Bk. 4, dist. 11, 12, relates that there were varying and diverse opinions about this question at that time. And Lombard clearly indicates that at that time nothing had been defined and determined in the church about this question, when he says: "I am not sufficient to define it." He describes the varying opinions of his time thus: To some it seems; some admit; others say; others teach. What the opinion of many before his time was he describes thus: Some thought that the substance of bread and wine remained there, and that the body and blood of Christ was in the same place.

3 When the seeds had been scattered in this way, since all the schools were boiling with this dispute, Innocent III, about the year of our Lord 1200, at the Lateran Council, first determined the mode of the conversion, which had not been defined in the church before, and in a new dogma also introduced and applied a new title: that in the Sacrament of the Altar the body and blood of Christ are truly contained under the appearances of bread and wine, these having been transubstantiated by divine power, the bread into the body and the wine into the blood, for these are the words of the Decrees of the Lateran Council, Bk. 1, ch. *Firmiter*.

This opinion Innocent repeats, *De celebratione Missarum,* ch. *Cum Marthae.* In the book *De officio altaris* he explains it more fully: that the bread becomes flesh in such a way that it ceases to be bread because the substance of bread and wine is changed into the substance of flesh and blood, not that the flesh and blood is formed materially out of the bread and wine, nor that anything is added to the body of Christ, but that the bread is transubstantiated into the body.

In the same place Innocent says: "There were some who taught that even as after the consecration the unessential marks of the bread remained, so would also the true substance of the bread; because just as a thing cannot exist without unessential marks, so unessential marks cannot exist without the thing, because to be unessential is nothing other than to be in the thing. Thus, while the substance of bread and wine remain, the body and blood of Christ truly begin to be under them, to prove the truth of the words, in such a way that under the same unessential marks each is received, bread and flesh, wine and blood; the one of these our senses prove, the other faith believes." In these words Innocent states the understanding which many had before his Lateran Council. For he says: "There were some," etc. And although he both thinks and formulates differently, namely, that while the substance passes away the unessential marks remain, but are without the thing itself, nevertheless he does not do as do the men of Trent—condemn that other understanding with the anathema. Let the reader diligently observe this. The same man also says: "Whether the whole passes over into the whole, or totally, He knows who does it." However, the Tridentine fathers simply hurl anathemas at those who think otherwise. Therefore these Tridentine anathemas are so recent that they were not even considered appropriate at the time of Innocent.

4 After the Lateran Council the scholastics eagerly seized this material as suitable for sharpening and exercising their prickly intellects. For they dispute whether the unessential marks, which remain in the same number after the substance of the bread and wine have been annihilated, are attached to the body of Christ, or to the air that surrounds it; or whether they stand independently, inhering in no subject, so that they cohere without a subject. Some argued that when the form of the bread is changed, the matter remains, as the matter of food is under the form of him who has been nourished. Others argued that when the matter is changed, the form of bread remains. But in common they held that the whole substance of the bread passes over into the body of Christ. It was also asked whether the matter of the bread is converted into the matter of the body of Christ, and its form into His form; whether indeed, according to the chaos of Anexagoras, anything you please may be converted into anything you please. Likewise whether the substance of the bread is dissolved into the matter it was before, or whether it is reduced to nothing. Innocent asks whether the water which is mixed with the wine is transubstantiated with the wine, or whether it remains and surrounds the body of Christ. Long and broad are the arguments over how these unessential marks, which have no substance, are able to act and to suffer, to

nourish and to be destroyed, and how anything can be created from them. Likewise whether the substance of the bread, once it has been annihilated, can return in the same quantity; what a mouse which gnaws the bread is eating. It is very certain that these and similar revolting disputes, which are the sinews and the fruits of the dogma of transubstantiation, were wholly unknown to the ancient church. Yet now they are set forth as articles of faith under threat of the anathema.

5 Scotus of Cambray[15] and others expressly confess that we can be driven to the dogma of transubstantiation neither by the words of Scripture, nor by the symbols of the faith, nor by statements of the ancients, and that the true presence and efficacy of the body and blood of Christ in the Eucharist can be taught, retained, and believed without transubstantiation; and also that the teaching concerning the Eucharist would be held without absurd questions if we taught that the substance of bread and wine remain without transubstantiation, together with the body and blood of Christ, if the Lateran Council had not decreed otherwise. Therefore they place the first and foremost grounds for the dogma of transubstantiation solely in the decree of the Lateran Council. Later, however, to embellish this decree of the council, they search for something in Scripture and the fathers with which to rouge it over.

Durandus does not want the opinion disapproved or condemned that even while the substance of the bread remains, the body of Christ is truly and substantially present in the Eucharist. However, now the framers of new articles of faith at Trent are not afraid to decree: "If anyone says that in the Eucharist the substance of bread and wine remain together with the body and blood of Christ, let him be anathema."

6 It is useful to observe these things about the beginnings and progress of the decree about transubstantiation. But let us come to the matter itself. Our papalists at the present time, when the light of the Gospel is shining so brightly, do not dare to say what Scotus of Cambray and indeed other scholastics said clearly, that transubstantiation rests most of all on the authority of the Lateran Council. But they set down two highly specious proofs. First, they say that the words of institution both establish and positively call for the transubstantiation of the bread and wine. Then they assert that the conviction has always been in the church of God that such a transubstantiation takes place. And indeed if they would rightly, clearly, and firmly prove these two things which they af-

---

[15] Scotus of Cambray, called by Chemnitz Scotus Camaracensis, and by Nigrinus Scotus von Camerich. Cambray, the ancient Cameracum, comprised a large area in northern France. This Scotus, to be distinguished from Duns Scotus, was a ninth-century Irish theologian who lived in Cambray. Therefore he wrote about 300 years before the Lateran Council, at which transubstantiation became a dogma of the Roman Catholic Church.

firm with great vehemence, it would be fair and just and altogether necessary that we should agree with them and give up our opinion. We shall therefore see first how they prove their transubstantiation from Scripture; thereafter we shall also speak about the consensus of the ancient church.

7 There are three chief arguments which they join together in order to prove transubstantiation from the words of Scripture. My Andrada weaves the following argument: Scripture affirms that with God nothing is impossible. Therefore transubstantiation is to be believed, even though it far transcends the powers and manner of nature and human comprehension. For the saying of Augustine is both beautiful and true: "When God does something which we are not able to search out, the reason for the deed is the power of the Doer." However, the answer to this argument is plain. We ought not, just because God is almighty, attribute to Him whatever seems good to us, without the testimony of His Word. Tertullian says: "God could have made man able to fly; but He did not, just because He was able, also do it." Scripture teaches this rule: "He does whatever He pleases" (Ps. 115:3). In matters of faith, however, the will of God must be learned and judged from His Word. And when there is certainty about the will of God from His Word, then the argument from His omnipotence is valid. It is therefore significant what the angel says when he affirms that no word,[16] that is, whatever He has revealed in His Word, is impossible with God. Therefore transubstantiation must first be clearly proved and demonstrated from the words of Christ, and then we shall, with the help of the Holy Spirit, gladly take our intellect captive under the obedience of Christ.

But this proof they are unable to furnish, as we shall now show. In vain, therefore, do they harangue us about the omnipotence of God.

8 Secondly, others get closer to the matter itself and argue thus: What Christ took when He wanted to institute His Supper was ordinary bread and common wine. But after the blessing He says of that bread and wine: "This is My body; this is My blood." These things cannot be said, nor ought they to be believed, about ordinary bread and common wine. Therefore some change must have come about through the blessing, and indeed such a change that it can be truthfully proclaimed about the bread that it is His body, and about the wine that it is His blood. Therefore it is necessary to assert transubstantiation.

I answer: We grant, with Irenaeus, that after the blessing in the

---

16 The text, following the Latin of the Vulgate, which has: *Quia non erit impossibile apud Deum omne verbum,* uses *verbum* to translate the Greek *rheema,* which sometimes means "thing," sometimes "word."

Eucharist the bread is no longer common bread but the Eucharist of the body of Christ, which now consists of two things—the earthly, that is, bread and wine, and the heavenly, that is, the body and blood of Christ. This is certainly a great, miraculous, and truly divine change, since before it was simply only ordinary bread and common wine. What now, after the blessing, is truly and substantially present, offered, and received is truly and substantially the body and blood of Christ. Therefore we grant that a certain change takes place, so that it can truly be said of the bread that it is the body of Christ. But we deny that it follows from this that we must therefore assert the kind of transubstantiation which the papalists teach. For one cannot, as they say in the schools, draw a valid conclusion from what is not distributed about what is distributed: Some kind of change takes place in the Eucharistic bread; therefore transubstantiation takes place. For only such a change is necessary that the Eucharist consists, according to the saying of Irenaeus, of two things—an earthly one and a heavenly one. This can come about without transubstantiation. For what Christ had in mind in the institution of His Supper, namely, the presence, offering, and receiving of His body and blood, can be taught, believed, and held even if the monstrosity of transubstantiation is not foisted upon the churches without the testimony of Scripture and without the consensus of antiquity, which also the fourth [17] canon, which we are treating, admits in a not obscure manner. Neither is it for us to prescribe to Christ a certain mode of the presence of His body in the Supper which He Himself has not revealed expressly, certainly, and clearly in His Word; but it is sufficient to believe that here the body and blood of Christ is present, offered, and received. Let us commit the mode of His presence to His wisdom and almighty power.

9 The third argument is this—and they themselves confess that if transubstantiation is not proved certainly and clearly by this, it cannot be proved from Scripture. It runs as follows: If in the Eucharist the substance of bread and wine remained together with the body and blood of Christ, He would have said: This is bread; this is wine; and with them, in them, or under them My body and blood. What He does say, however, is: "This is My body; this is My blood." And if the demonstrative pronoun [this] denotes the substance of the bread and wine (because bread and the body of Christ, and wine and blood, are two different things), the one cannot be predicated of the other. Therefore, in order that the declaration: "This

---

[17] Chemnitz may well have been a bit confused here. He was really treating not Canon IV but Canon II. However, also Canon IV admits in a not obscure manner that the real presence can be taught without transubstantiation when it speaks of someone saying that the body and blood of Christ are present "only during use."

is My body; this is My blood," may be true, there must be posited in these words an identical proposition, which is the term one uses when subject and predicate speak about one and the same thing, so that the demonstrative pronoun [this] denotes, not the substance of bread but the substance of the body of Christ only. But such a positing cannot stand unless the substance of the bread which Christ took into His hands has ceased to exist, having been annihilated through the benediction, and has been transubstantiated, so that nothing else is meant and indicated here by the little word "this" than the substance of the body of Christ only. Therefore the pronouncement: "This is My body," altogether establishes and calls for transubstantiation.

This is the whole long web of this argument, which seems to have a certain outward appearance for establishing transubstantiation. But we shall successfully dissolve or rather destroy this web with the sword of the Spirit.

To begin with, it must be noted that they dispute concerning the proposition: "This is My body," according to the rules of praiseworthy men in no other way than as if the Eucharist were something physical, which would go according to the common course and mode of nature. But because the sacrament is something supernatural, heavenly, and divine, therefore it is not right that faith in it is measured by the papalists in this debate according to the rule of Aristotle, *Metaphysics,* VI, concerning the place in the sentence of the last member of the affirmative proposition, which they interpret of an identical proposition.[18] For they invent the annihilation or transubstantiation of the bread in order that the proposition: "This is My body," might square with the aforementioned rule of Aristotle. What kind of proof this is in so great a controversy is self-evident. For in Scripture, when two things or substances are by divine decree joined together in a particular manner, and especially when a heavenly and invisible substance is present and offered together with one that is earthly and visible, then, I say, it is customary in Scripture that the one is predicated of the other. And for the truth of such a predication no annihilation or transubstantiation of the other substance is necessary, but only the union and presence of both those things which are denoted by the subject and predicate is signified. Thus when Scripture wishes to unfold

---

[18] The passage in Aristotle reads: "But since that which is in the sense of being true, or is not in the sense of being false, depends on combination and separation, and truth and falsity together depend on the allocation of a pair of contradictory judgments (for the true judgment affirms where the subject and predicate are really combined, and denies where they are separated, while the false judgment has the opposite in this allocation)." Quoted from *The Works of Aristotle,* I, 550, in *Great Books of the Western World,* Robert Maynard Hutchins, ed.

the union of the divine and the human nature in the person of Christ, it does not say, "In this man is God," but, "God is man" and "The Son of man is the Son of the living God." Neither is it necessary that one of the natures, either the human or the divine, because they are disparate, be annihilated or changed in substance in order that the truth of the proposition may stand, which otherwise does not agree with the rules of praiseworthy men, but there only the union of the two natures is significant.

This is not, however, the common way of speaking, but is unusual, because the union itself is not according to some natural manner of this world but is supernatural, heavenly, and divine. We do not, of course, assert a personal union of bread and the body, or such a one as that of the divine and the human nature in Christ, but we explain this proposition, which is in controversy here, by means of the analogy which all of antiquity has used concerning the Eucharist. And this example clearly shows that the third argument of the papalists, based on the words of institution, by no means proves or establishes transubstantiation sufficiently certainly, clearly, and firmly. Otherwise, by the same reasoning, we would also have to assert a transubstantiation of one of the natures of Christ. Thus in John 20:22 Christ, breathing on the disciples says: "Receive the Holy Spirit." Do we conclude that, because He does not say, "Receive the Holy Spirit with or under this breath," a bodily transubstantiation of the breath must be posited? Rather, together with that breath the Holy Spirit was present, was given by Christ, and received by the apostles. Neither was it necessary that the dove should be transubstantiated in order that the proposition should be true when the Baptizer affirms that he saw the Holy Spirit descend on Christ. Although there was debate among the ancients about the visible forms by which either the divine majesty itself or angels manifested their presence, nevertheless nobody dared to make an article of faith to the effect that these forms are only accidents[19] which exist and cohere without substance or external reality. When the ark of the covenant advanced, Moses said, "Arise, O Lord" (Num. 10:35); nevertheless there was no need for a transubstantiation of the wood or gold in the ark. Rather, Scripture speaks thus because these men were certain of a particular mode of the divine presence from His Word and promise.

Indeed, such ways of speaking are customary in ordinary speech. For

---

[19] The term "accidents" is here used in the sense in which logicians use it to denote any feature, element, or accompaniment of an object not essential to the conception of that object.

when we speak about a jar of wine, about a pouch and money, about swaddling clothes and a child, we say, "This is wine which a friend sends to you; take the money which I owe you; bring the child of my womb." And no one is so foolish that he imagines either an annihilation or a transubstantiation of the jar, pouch, swaddling clothes, and of similar things. But when we want to indicate that two things which are joined together are present, offered, and received at the same time, then we speak in this way also in ordinary speech.

Therefore it is clear that the long web of this third argument by no means proves, establishes, or demands that transubstantiation about which the papalists contend; rather, that argument is not able to stand up even according to their own prescriptions. For if they want the demonstrative pronoun "this" to mean the body only in such a way that the meaning is by no means, "With this or under this is My body," they will also not be able to say that the body of Christ is under the appearance of the bread. Or, if the proposition, "This is My body," can tolerate this their interpretation, that the body of Christ is contained under the appearances of bread, then the argument that for this reason transubstantiation must be asserted demonstrates nothing, because Christ did not say, "Under this is My body," for by the same reasoning there would have to be posited also a transaccidentation, as Luther says, lest it be said, "under the appearance of bread." I shall press my adversaries yet more strongly. For they teach that through the words, "This is My body," a transubstantiation comes about, so that the moment this proposition has been spoken (I am using their own words) the substance of the bread is annihilated and ceases, and the body of Christ begins to be there. Therefore when the priest says, "This," the bread is not yet transubstantiated, and the body of Christ is not yet present. This makes it false, according to the papalists' own teaching, that the pronoun "this" denotes only the substance of the body of Christ so that when the word "this" is spoken the substance of the bread has ceased to be, having been already annihilated.

Bonaventura, *Sententiae*, Bk. 4, dist. 8, quest. 1, asks what the pronoun "this" indicates. He reports that some have said these words are to be taken in a material sense and therefore one ought not to ask what they signify. Others said: "This," that is, "what is signified by this, which is to be converted into My body, is My body." However Bonaventura himself says: "Because the Word comes to the element, therefore the pronoun 'this' does not designate the body of Christ but the substance of the bread under its accidents; it is an extraordinary way of speaking, which does not signify sameness but a creative conversion: 'This is My body,' that is, as the words are being pronounced it is changed into the body."

Richard of St. Victor says that it is a mixed description: "This, that is, that into which it will be transubstantiated, that is My body," as if I were to say of food which I was about to eat: "This, that is, that into which this food is to be transmuted, is my body." Such monstrous interpretations does the dogma of transubstantiation beget. So clearly and certainly is it proved from the words of institution that these interpretations cannot even be adapted to the words of institution unless they are tortured and crucified in strange ways.

10 But even the papalists themselves notice that transubstantiation is not sufficiently established, defended, and safe with these arguments taken from the words of Scripture. Andrada, for instance, after a slight skirmish places transubstantiation among the things which are not openly defined and explained by any testimony of sacred Scripture. Therefore we rightly apply to this whole dispute the most true axiom: Nothing is to be proposed to the church as an article of faith which cannot be plainly shown and proved from clear, sure, and strong testimonies of Scripture.

11 Over and above the fact that transubstantiation cannot be clearly and surely proved and shown from the Word of God, we also have a simple and clear statement of Scripture concerning this question. For Jesus took bread, blessed it, broke it, and gave it to His disciples. And concerning that which He took, which He blessed, which He broke, which He gave to the disciples—it was concerning that, I say, that He said: "Take, eat, this is My body."

And lest there be any doubt whether the demonstrative pronoun denotes that which Jesus had taken, namely bread and the cup, Luke and Paul, in describing the second part, state this expressly by the clear addition: "He took the cup, blessed it, and gave it to them," and add: *touto to poteerion*, "this cup." And as Paul says concerning the second part (1 Cor. 10:16): "The cup which we bless is the imparting of the blood of Christ," so also he says concerning the first part: "The bread which we break is the imparting of the body of Christ." Therefore he declares and expresses clearly what the little word "this" denotes in each of the two parts, namely bread and the cup. And since we have these explanations of Scripture, why do we not adhere to the simple truth? Why should we take pleasure in disturbing it with the labyrinthine arguments about transubstantiation?

Moreover, after the blessing or consecration, in the very use [of the sacrament] Paul calls it bread, and that not once, lest you should think that the expression had slipped out inadvertently, but four or five times. 1 Cor. 10:16-17: "The bread which we break." "We all partake of the one bread." 1 Cor. 11:26-27: "As often as you eat this bread." "Whoever eats the bread . . . in an unworthy manner." V. 28: "Let a man examine himself and so eat of the bread."

12 These arguments are clear, firm, and very cogent. Therefore the papalists attempt in a variety of ways to show an example of the trick of a certain sophist, about whom antiquity once coined the proverb: "He is down; he isn't down," that is, although he was already lying prostrate on the ground, he nevertheless tried to persuade the bystanders that he was not down but was bravely standing upright. Thus, although Paul in the very use, and after the consecration, five times calls it bread, they nevertheless attempt to impose on the church the fiction of transubstantiation, that the substance of bread does not remain nor is present there. But they say that there are examples in Scripture where, although the substances have been changed and turned into something else, the earlier name is nevertheless retained, designating not what they now are but what they were before they were changed. Thus in Ex. 7:12 the rod of Aaron, having been turned into a serpent, is called a rod also after the change. Man is called earth, because he was formed out of earth. The woman is called bone of the bones of the man. Concerning the water which had been turned into wine the evangelist says: "When he had tasted the water which had become wine." In this way, therefore, also the Eucharistic bread could be called bread, although it had been transubstantiated, not because it was but because it had been bread.

The answer is, however, simple and plain. In the examples which are adduced, of the rod, earth, bone, water, Scripture openly testifies in express words that these things have been changed and turned into something else, so that neither the substance nor the prior form remain, but that they bear the appearance of those things into which Scripture says they were changed. Thus in John 2:9 it is not simply water which is named, but water which has now become wine. If the same thing could be so clearly shown and proved concerning the transubstantiation of the bread in the Eucharist, we would willingly concede the figure of speech which the matter itself would demand. However, since no clear, certain, and firm proof of transubstantiation is found in Scripture, it would be a great act of madness to depart from the proper meaning of the words. What madness also, to believe in a specter or deceptive image of bread, accidents adhering to each other without substance, whereas Paul names bread five times, and although we ascribe to Baptism without transubstantiation of the water those things which Scripture teaches concerning it.

13 Eck understands by the term "bread" in Paul not the substance of bread but the accidents without substance, that is, not bread but an empty specter of bread. But this specter does not satisfy even the papalists themselves; therefore they seek some other chink by which they may escape from the clarity of Paul's words. For because *lechem*[20] signifies every kind of food, they say that Paul calls the Eucharist bread not because the substance of bread remains there together with the body of Christ but because the body of Christ is the spiritual food of the inner man. All these things would be in place here if the transubstantiation of the bread had already been clearly, certainly, and firmly demonstrated, for then we would rightly have recourse to a metaphor, as in John 6, where Christ says expressly that He is not speaking of external or material bread and yet calls Himself bread. The institution, on the contrary, expressly describes material bread before the blessing. And since Paul, without an open attesting of transubstantiation, retains the term "bread" also after the consecration, we justly retain this word in one and the same meaning, namely the proper and genuine one. For if it were permitted, in the description of the Lord's Supper, to play with figures of speech in such a way that we would in the same speech interpret the bread, now in its normal sense, now according to our whim metaphorically, why should we not also grant the same license to the sacramentarians with respect to the words "body" and "blood"? Or, according to the same reasoning, when it is written that Christ took bread, we shall say, because He did this after the ordinary supper had been finished, that He did not take material bread but spiritual food, that is, Himself, and thus we shall remove bread entirely from the total action of the Supper. Therefore it is safest to retain the proper meaning of the word "bread" both before and after the consecration, since no clear reason of Scripture either demands or confirms a metaphor in this place.

14 All the other things they advance are weak and uncertain, which also Lanfranc confesses. For discussing why it is called bread also after the blessing, he indeed advances the usual reasons: either because it is brought about from bread, and retains the accidental marks of bread, or because it satiates the soul. Realizing, however, that these things are weak and uncertain, he adds, "or in some other way which can be understood by the learned, but not by us."

---

[20] The Hebrew word for bread.

How much simpler is the following: Scripture calls it bread also after the blessing. Why it is called "bread" the fathers explain by analogy from the resemblance of the sacrament, namely, because it satiates, nourishes, sustains, strengthens—all of which are characteristics not of the accidents but of the substance of bread. Likewise because it is a mass made out of many grains, so we are made one body because we partake of the one bread (1 Cor. 10:17) and are made one mass with Christ. So Chrysostom says. These things certainly do not fit the accidents, but the substance of the bread.

15 But someone may say: Why do we contend so over the question whether the substance of the bread either remains or does not remain in the Eucharist, although the treasure of the Eucharist is not material bread or common wine but the true and substantial presence, distribution, and receiving of the body and blood of Christ? For the Eucharist is not celebrated under the name of a testament in order that we may there receive a little bit of bread and a swallow of wine, for these things we could receive more conveniently and abundantly in our homes (1 Cor. 11:22), but because in the Eucharist there is the imparting of the body and blood of Christ. Why, then, are we troubled over whether the substance of the bread remains or whether it has ceased to exist?

I answer: We by no means judge that the bread and the body of Christ are of equal importance. Also Luther always said that in this whole dispute he paid more regard to the presence of the body and blood of Christ in the Supper than to the presence of bread and wine. But because transubstantiation is set forth as an article of faith under penalty of the anathema, it must of necessity be contradicted. For concerning the separate items which belong to the nature of the sacraments one ought not to teach and believe otherwise than the Word of God prescribes to us. Neither is anything to be accepted as an article of faith which cannot be shown and proved by certain, clear, and firm testimonies of Scripture. Furthermore, because the Son of God has instituted and ordained certain external means through which He wills to communicate Himself and His benefits to believers, we are in duty bound to acknowledge, hold fast, and so use them as they were instituted by the Son of God. For so and in no other way does God normally want to deal with us. And since He ordained that in the Eucharist bread and wine should be the means through which He wills to communicate to us His body and blood in the Supper, and with them all the benefits of the New Testament, these means are not to be cast out from the use of the Lord's Supper, for He did not want to communicate His body and blood to us in the Supper without means. Moreover, the opinion of transubstantiation agitates the simplicity of the faith with unnatural and unnecessary labyrinths of questions, and men are led astray from that which is most important in the Lord's Supper in order that they may cling in meditation and admiration to transubstantiation.

16 Therefore the church is not persuaded clearly, certainly, and firmly by a single passage of Scripture, or compelled to assert and believe transubstantiation, but it agrees better with the simplicity of the Word of God that in the Eucharist the substance of bread and wine remain together with the body and blood of Christ.

17 In this simplicity many unprofitable and monstrous questions are avoided. In this way also there is preserved in the Eucharist that which belongs to the substance of all sacraments, namely, that they consist of two things, the matter and the form, an earthly thing and a heavenly. For when the Word comes to the element, it does not annihilate the element, but makes it a sacrament. And if in the Eucharist we are deceived in the thing which is external and visible, so that although we see, touch, and taste bread, yes, what Scripture asserts to be bread, we nevertheless receive not bread but only the accidents without the subject, that is, a specter and a deceptive image of bread, where will our faith find confirmation that we receive the body and blood of Christ according to the Word just as surely in an invisible and heavenly manner as we receive the bread and wine?

Furthermore, through transubstantiation there is destroyed the analogy of the sign and the thing signified in the sacrament, as Augustine says: "If the sacraments did not have a resemblance to the things of which they are sacraments, they would not be sacraments." Thus in Baptism, as water cleanses outwardly, so Christ cleanses the church by the washing of water with the Word. In the Eucharist, as material bread nourishes, sustains, strengthens, so the body of Christ is spiritual nourishment of the new or inner man. As bread is a substance compounded out of many kernels, so those who partake of that one bread of the Eucharist become one body. All these meanings fall to the ground if the substance of bread is annihilated in the Eucharist and in its place there are substituted the deceptive images of the accidents, hanging together without the subject itself. So much about the statements of Scripture.

18 Moreover, the papalists boast very proudly that they have for their opinion about transubstantiation the consensus of all antiquity and the testimony of the church of all ages. For the assembly at Trent asserts in the fourth chapter that this was always the conviction in the church of God. Indeed, Andrada declaims in a tragic manner that this is the consensus of the whole church, of all times, of all nations and peoples who ever professed the name of Christ, so that nothing different was ever the judgment of the church. Truly, this is quite a boastful and daring assertion, which they surely would not use if they had not laid aside all sense of shame or taken us all for blockheads and wooden posts, or (as they themselves are accustomed to say) as beasts who are entirely ignorant of the whole history of antiquity. Therefore something must be said about the opinion of the ancient church which pertains to the question of transubstantiation, in order that this shameless impudence may be laid bare.

19 They pile up many statements of the ancients in which they say that the bread is called, believed to be, and is the body of Christ, that the body of Christ is made of bread, that the bread is changed, wholly altered or transmuted into the body of Christ, or that it becomes and is the body of Christ, that created things are converted into the substance of the body and blood of Christ, that bread and wine are transformed into a divine substance. And to each of these statements they add their own exclamation that the church at all times without ambiguity always taught and believed the transubstantiation of the bread and wine as this is taught by the papalists.

20 But we shall answer in an entirely fair manner that the ancients themselves are the best and surest interpreters of their own words. The ancients say that in the Eucharist a change or conversion of bread and wine takes place. The papalists interpret this of the annihilation and transubstantiation of the elements. We understand a sacramental change, that, although before it was only common bread and ordinary wine, when the Word of Christ comes to it, it is not merely bread and wine but at the same time also the body and blood of Christ, which is present, offered, and received here in the Eucharist. But let neither our interpretation nor that of the papalists be the authentic one! Let us rather hear the ancients themselves, how they interpret these words of theirs and of the ancient church, and how they want them understood. We shall show, however, by a number of arguments that although the ancients speak of change and conversion, they nevertheless did not mean the kind of transubstantiation for which the papalists contend.

21 First of all, Lombard expressly states, Bk. 4, dist. 11, that even in his time[21] it had not been defined in the church what kind of change or conversion this might be about which the ancients speak, whether it is of form or of substance, or indeed of another kind. Therefore it is false— Lombard himself being witness—what the papalists assert, that it is a

---

[21] Peter Lombard died A.D. 1164.

catholic dogma that the bread of the Eucharist is changed and converted through annihilation and transubstantiation.

22 In the second place, we have a testimony which ought to be so great that even the papalists themselves cannot take exception to it. For Gelasius, a Roman pope some 500 years after the birth of Christ, in a book on the two natures in Christ, says against Eutyches and Nestorius that the bread and wine are changed into a divine substance through the working of the Holy Spirit, namely, into the body and blood of Christ.

These words certainly seem to speak powerfully for establishing transubstantiation, for what has been changed into another substance, and that through the operation of the Holy Spirit, surely does not seem to remain in its former substance. But Gelasius himself expressly and clearly explains his own opinion and that of the ancient church as to how they want the mutation or conversion of bread and wine in the Eucharist understood, and that in three ways:

1. They are so changed into the body and blood of Christ that nevertheless the substance or nature of bread and wine does not cease to exist;

2. They are changed into a divine substance, with bread and wine nevertheless continuing in their own peculiar nature;

3. Even as in Christ the two natures of which He is composed individually persist;

4. They are truly said to be changed into a divine substance because through them we are made partakers of the divine nature, the body and blood of Christ having been communicated to us.

This is how Gelasius interprets the way in which the ancient church understood that the bread and wine in the Eucharist are changed or converted into the body and blood of Christ. At the Colloquy of Ratisbon, in the year 1541, Contarini was struck with amazement when he saw what is clearer than the light of noon, that the papalist transubstantiation is refuted with so manifest and clear a testimony from the statement of a Roman pope. And still they are not afraid now to boast about the perpetual consensus of the church of all times so far as the dogma of transubstantiation is concerned.

Ambrose says, *De sacramentis,* Bk. 4, that through the consecration the body of Christ comes into being from the bread and out of the bread. But he immediately explains that he does not mean the annihilation or transubstantiation of the bread, for he says: "If there is such great power in the words of Christ that things which were not, now begin to be, how much more powerful are they, that they should be what they were and yet be converted into something else?" Lanfranc was unable to escape this testimony in any other way than by saying that these words are not found in the books of Ambrose. But because this is not so, Pedro de Soto says that the meaning of Ambrose is that they remain, but changed into something else, as if water changed into wine is said to remain. But Ambrose distinctly says two things: That they should be what they were, and that they should be changed into something else. He is therefore his own interpreter, that he understands such a conversion of bread and wine in which they are what they were before the conversion, and there is added this grace that there is present there at the same time the body and blood of Christ, as Theodoret and Hesychius speak.

Theodoret, who was present at the Synod of Ephesus and was praised at the Council of Chalcedon, in his first dialog, entitled *Atreptos*, takes these principles, which were at that time confessed in the church both by Catholics and by Eutychians. He says that Christ calls the bread His body for this reason, that those who partake of the sacrament may not give their attention to the nature of the things which are visible but may believe the transformation which has come about by grace. You hear Theodoret say that one should not direct his attention to the nature of the visible things but should believe the transformation, for he calls it *metabolee*.[22] But lest someone should interpret this transformation as transubstantiation, he immediately explains clearly what kind of transformation he means. For he says: "Christ honored the visible signs with the designation of His body and blood, *ou teen physin metaboloon, alla teen charin tee physei prostetheikoos*," that is, not transforming the nature of the signs but adding grace to the nature of the signs, namely, that they are at the same time also the body and blood of Christ. Here you have the explanation of what antiquity in the Greek church understood by the transformation of the bread and wine in the Eucharist, namely, not that the nature of the bread and wine is changed but that grace is added to it.

In the second dialog, entitled *Asygchytos*, he explains the understanding of the ancient church still more clearly. For a Eutychian argues thus: As bread and wine are one thing before consecration, but after the consecration are transformed and have become something else, so also the body of Christ, after His ascension, has been transformed into the divine essence. To this an orthodox person responds: You are caught in your own net. For after the mystical signs have been consecrated, *ou tees oikeias existatai physeoos*, that is, they are not changed in such a way that

---

[22] *Metabolee:* a change or changing.

they lose their own nature. For things which do not keep their nature but are transformed, corrupted, destroyed, and degenerate into something else are called by the very meaningful word *existamena*.[23] Thus spoiled wine is called *oinos exesteekoos*. Theodoret adds besides: *Menei gar epi tees proteras ousias, kai tou scheematos, kai tou eidous*, that is, after the consecration these signs remain in their former substance, form, and appearance, so much so that they are both seen and felt, just as before; nevertheless we understand, believe, and adore what they have become.

We have therefore a sure and clear interpretation of how the ancients explain their understanding and that of all antiquity, what they want understood when they speak of transformation and conversion of the bread and wine in the Eucharist, namely, that the substance and nature of the bread and wine is neither changed nor ceases, but there remains in the Eucharist not only the form and appearance of bread and wine but the former substance and peculiar nature itself. For these are the words of the ancients. By the transformation they understand that, although before it was only common bread and ordinary wine, now at the same time there is present, distributed, and received the body and blood of Christ. Therefore, when the papalists heap up statements of the ancients about transformation and conversion, let this interpretation of the ancients, which was the understanding of both the Eastern and of the Western church, be opposed to them.

And, seeing that they are not ignorant of this understanding, let the reader consider how nobly they conduct themselves when they twist the language of the ancients against the intention of the ancients to the fabrication of their substantiation. The Council of Trent declares that the dogma of papalist transubstantiation was always the understanding in the church of God. But we have already shown with the clearest testimonies of the Latin and Greek church that this is totally false.

23 Thirdly, antiquity knows and confesses two things of diverse kinds in the Eucharist. Thus Irenaeus says that after the broken bread and the mixed cup has received the call of God, it is no longer common bread but the Eucharist of the body and blood of Christ. Does he mean it in this way, that the substance of the bread, having been annihilated, has utterly ceased to be? We shall not use conjectures but shall hear how Irenaeus himself explains himself. For he at once adds that the Eucharist consists of two things, an earthly, namely bread and wine, and a heavenly, namely the body and blood of Christ. That the bread in the Eucharist is not

---

[23] *Existamena:* degenerate, changed.

common bread Irenaeus interprets thus: "While before it was only one thing, namely an earthly, it is now the Eucharist, consisting of two things, bread and the body of Christ, wine and the blood of Christ."

This interpretation of Irenaeus shows in what way the church understood what Augustine said later, *De verbis Domini, sermo* 28: "Before the words of Christ that which is offered is said to be bread; but when the words of Christ have been brought forth, it is no longer said to be bread but is called the body of Christ." But in order that there may be even less doubt, let us hear Augustine himself interpreting his words. He says in the book of sentences of Prosper, *De consecratione,* 2: "This is what we say, what we strive to prove in all ways, that the sacrifice of the church is made with two things, consists in two things, the visible form of the elements and the invisible body and blood of Christ." Let the reader observe that the papalists set the term *species*[24] in opposition to the nature, substance, and reality of the elements of bread and wine. And whenever they read in the ancients about the *species* of bread and wine, they at once affix their transubstantiation. However, Augustine will explain to us what the church has understood when it speaks of the *species* of bread and wine. For when he had named the *species* of the elements and the body of Christ in that statement, he adds: "As the person of Christ consists of God and man, since He is true God and true man, because everything contains in itself the nature and reality of those things of which it is made up, the sacrifice of the church is made up of two things, the sacrament and that which the sacrament gives, that is, the body of Christ." It is clear that Augustine acknowledges two things in the Eucharist. And by the *species* he does not understand the accidents without the substance, but the nature and reality of the things, that is, of the elements out of which the sacrament is made up. For these are his own words. However, antiquity was pleased with the term *species,* because the Baptizer is said (Luke 3:22) to have seen the Spirit descend on Christ "in bodily form,[25] as a dove." Let the reader diligently observe this interpretation of *species* from Augustine in this topic.

Hesychius also acknowledges two substances at the same time in the Eucharist, which he defines as being at the same time bread and body, wine and blood. For he says, *In Leviticum,* Bk. 20, ch. 8: "He commands to eat flesh with bread, in order that we might understand that that is called a mystery, because it is at the same time bread and flesh."

24 In the fourth place, the writers of antiquity commonly use the

---

[24] See footnote 12, above.
[25] The Vulgate has *species* here.

analogy by which they compare the Eucharist, which consists of two things, and the unity of the two natures in the person of Christ. In the struggle against Apollinaris and Eutyches, Chrysostom, Theodoret, and Gelasius prove by means of the sacrament of the Eucharist that the human nature in Christ is not absorbed by or transformed into the divine, but that there are two true, distinct, and entire natures in Christ, just as the Eucharist consists of two things and is brought about by two. That argument would have greatly strengthened rather than refuted Eutyches, if the dogma of transubstantiation had at that time been known and accepted in the church. Surely, this argument alone could strongly prove that transubstantiation was unknown to the true and purer antiquity; neither do I see what the papalists can devise in order to escape the clarity of this argument. Therefore also Justin, in the description of the Lord's Supper, speaks of *metabolee*,[26] but at once adds the analogy of the two natures in the person of Christ.

The papalists are accustomed to flaunt boastfully the saying of Cyprian from the discourse on the Lord's Supper. It is not, however, certainly established that it is by Cyprian. The statement is as follows: "The bread which the Lord offered to His disciples was changed, not with respect to appearance but with respect to its nature; by the omnipotent Word it was made flesh." Immediately the papalists demand that no one should doubt that Cyprian held to transubstantiation. He is, however, the best interpreter of his own words. For presently he adds how he wants that transubstantiation understood, when he says: "As in the person of Christ the humanity was seen, and the divinity hidden, so the divine substance infuses itself in an inexpressible manner into the visible sacrament, in order that men may devote themselves to the fear of God around the sacraments." Therefore, as the two natures in Christ are and remain whole, so the transformation of the bread of which Cyprian speaks does not destroy the substance of the bread.

25 In the fifth place: Irenaeus, Eusebius of Emesa, and Ambrose compare the transformation of the bread in the Eucharist with the renewal of the regenerate and with the transformation of those who believe in Christ, so that they become one mass[27] with Him. But yet the renewal does not bring about the annihilation or transubstantiation of the nature of man, neither is our substance swallowed up when Christ says, in a work of Augustine: "But you will be transformed into Me."

Thus Ambrose, *De sacramentis*, Bk. 4, ch. 4, after he had discussed

---

[26] See footnote 22, above.

[27] Chemnitz uses the term *massa*, which seems best rendered "mass." It also means "lump," "dough." Nigrinus strangely renders it *"ein Kirche."*

the transformation of the bread at length, adds: "You were yourself, but you were an old creature; after you have been consecrated, you have begun to be a new creature."

Eusebius of Emesa, *De consecratione,* dist. 2, ch. *Quia corpus,* explains this analogy more clearly. For when he had said that Christ converts visible created things into the substance of His body and blood by His Word, the papalists at once exclaim that this is transubstantiation pure and simple. However, Eusebius of Emesa interprets himself. For when he wishes to show that it is not a new or impossible thing that earthly and perishable things are converted into the substance of Christ, he says: "Ask yourself, you who have been regenerated in Christ. At one time you were a foreigner to life, a stranger to mercy; inwardly dead, you were banished; suddenly initiated into the saving mysteries, you leaped over into the body of the church, not by seeing but by believing, and from a son of perdition you became an adopted son of God." Do these things happen through transubstantiation? Hear what Eusebius of Emesa adds: "Although you are the same, and yourself, you have come forth a very different man through the advance which faith brings. On the outside nothing has been added, and within everything has been changed." Therefore as the believers enter into the body of Christ and become one mass with Him without transubstantiation, so the ancients also understood the transformation of the bread and wine in the Lord's Supper; thus there is no need for transubstantiation.

Irenaeus says: "Just as the Eucharist consists of two things, so our bodies, when they take the Eucharist, are not corruptible, having hope of immortality." Nevertheless the glorification of our body has not yet taken place (Phil. 3:21), but we have hope. Therefore the transformation of the bread is not proved by this.

26 In the sixth place: Not even at the time of the Council of Florence, a little over a hundred years ago, had the dogma of transubstantiation been approved and received with the consent of the universal church and of all nations and peoples. For when, during the fourth session, they listed the articles in which the Greek church dissented from the Roman, they listed as the fourth item, "Concerning the Divine Transubstantiation of the Bread in the Eucharist." And when a document of union was to be prepared, there was excepted clearly and in so many words, with the assent also of the Roman pontiff, this article of the transformation of the bread in the Eucharist, which the Latins at that time taught. Therefore the boasting about a universal consensus of the church of all times and peoples is false so far as the dogma of transubstantiation is concerned. For even a hundred years ago, as this account shows, those who did not accept or approve the opinion of transubstantiation were not yet subjected to the anathema. Therefore the anathema of the second canon of this third session is clearly something new and recent. And thus it has, as I think, been shown sufficiently clearly that the ancient and purer church in no way supports the papalist dogma of transubstantiation.

27 Concerning more recent writers, at whose time a great alteration of the doctrine had already begun, such as John of Damascus, Theophylact, Richard, Hugo, Lombard, and similar men, we shall not argue when the question is about the opinion of antiquity. Therefore this example shows how empty is the boast of the papalists when in all their disputations they puff out their cheeks and then proclaim that the universal consensus of the whole church of all times and of all nations and peoples stands on their side.

28 There is no need to examine each and every statement of the ancients, for we know from their own interpretations how they want their words about this matter understood.

Ambrose, *De sacramentis*, Bk. 4, ch. 5, says that we should believe that after the consecration there is nothing other than the flesh and blood of Christ. This is not ill said. For because faith has to do with things which are not apparent and seen, there is no need for faith in order to understand that bread, which the eyes see, is present there. But that the body of Christ is present there, that faith alone learns from the Word. This division, since there are two things in the Eucharist, one to be apprehended by the senses, the other by faith, the statement of Augustine clearly teaches. He says: "What you see on the altar is bread and the cup, which also your eyes tell you; however, what faith demands to be taught is: This bread is the body; this cup is the blood."

29 Often the ancients also look to the fact that the Lord's Supper is not an earthly action but a heavenly, having to do with the kingdom of heaven, concerning which the Gospel tells, in which we seek not food which perishes but the spiritual nourishment of the new man. Therefore they often speak in exalted terms of the second part only, namely, concerning the body and blood of Christ. And they want our hearts to be lifted up on high; they do not want us to give our attention to the earthly elements of bread and wine but to Christ, God and man, who is present in the Supper and gives to those who eat His body and blood; even as, on the other hand, when they argue about the elements in the Eucharist, they often speak of signs, figures, and symbols. However, even as the sacramentarians do not act rightly, who on account of the last-mentioned statements of the ancients cast out the substance of the body and blood of

Christ from the Supper, so also the papalists do not act rightly when they twist the earlier statements to annihilation and transubstantiation of the elements. For in other places the ancients speak distinctly about the two things which make the Eucharist, as Origen says on Matt. 15, when he argues that the bread of the Lord does not have this power to sanctify from its own nature: "What is of a material nature in the bread of the Lord enters into the belly and is cast out into the privy; however, that which is through public prayer and the Word of the Lord benefits the soul according to the measure of faith. Therefore it is not the material thing which is useful, but the Word which comes to it profits the soul." Thus Origen.

30 Chrysostom, looking to the fact that the Lord's Supper is a supernatural, heavenly, and divine mystery, says: "Is it bread that you behold? Does it go into the privy? Perish the thought!" Likewise: "You receive the body of Christ not from the hand of man but from the seraphim." As with these words Chrysostom does not want to cast off the external ministry, so also not the elements from the action of the Lord's Supper; rather, he wants us to cling neither to the hand of the minister nor to the elements of bread and wine, but to lift up our minds to those things of which the Word speaks. As therefore it does not follow from this statement of Chrysostom that the outward ministry of the priest who distributes the Eucharist should be done away with and the coming of seraphim awaited, so also transubstantiation cannot be concluded from it. For that bread and wine are seen in the Eucharist both our senses and all antiquity testify.

SECTION V

Concerning the Cult and Veneration
To Be Shown This Most Holy Sacrament

Chapter V

There is therefore no room left for doubt that[28] all the faithful of Christ, after the custom always received in the Catholic Church, should render the cult of *latria*,[29] which is owed to the true God, in veneration to this most holy sacrament. For it is not to be any less adored because it was instituted by God in order that it might be received. For we believe that the same God is present in it of whom the eternal Father says, when He introduces Him into the world: "And let all God's angels worship Him"; whom the Magi, prostrating themselves, adored; of whom finally Scripture testifies that He was adored by the apostles in Galilee.

The holy synod declares further that this custom was introduced very piously and religiously into the Church of God, that every year, on a certain festival day, this exalted and venerable sacrament is celebrated with special veneration and solemnity, and that it should be borne about reverently and with honor in processions through the streets and public places. For it is most just that there should be some set holy days on which all Christians may testify with a special and universal demonstration that their minds are grateful and mindful to their common Lord and Redeemer for so inexpressible and truly divine a benefit, by which the victory and triumph of His death is represented. And so indeed it was proper that truth victorious should celebrate a triumph over falsehood and heresy, in order that her adversaries, in view of so great splendor and placed in the midst of such great joy of the whole church, should either pine away, weakened and broken, or, moved by shame and confusion, at length recover their senses.

CANON VI

If anyone says that in the holy sacrament of the Eucharist Christ, the only-begotten Son of God, is not to be adored with the cult of *latria* also in external worship, and that it is therefore not to be venerated with a special festive celebration,[30] nor solemnly carried about in processions according to the laudable and universal rite and custom of holy Church, or that it should not be publicly set

---

[28] Chemnitz here has *cum,* while the official Roman Catholic version has *quin,* which our translation follows.

[29] *Latria:* the worship due only to God, as distinguished from *dulia,* the homage due the saints, and from *hyperdulia,* due the Virgin Mary.

[30] The editions of the *Examen* have omitted this whole clause from the canon. We have added, according to the official Roman Catholic version: *atque ideo non festiva peculiari celebritate veneranda.*

276

before the people in order that it may be adored, and that those who adore it are idolaters, let him be anathema.

Examination

1 First of all we must show what it is that has been placed into controversy in this fifth chapter and sixth canon. For a number of things are not in controversy; these I willingly concede. That Christ, God and man, is to be worshiped no one but an Arian denies. And that also His human nature, because of its union with the divinity, is to be worshiped no one but a Nestorian calls into question. For when the eternal Father is about to introduce His Only-begotten into the world, He says: "And let all the angels worship Him." So also Matthew clearly testifies (28:17) that the apostles worshiped Christ in Galilee.

It is certain also that the worship of God is not restricted to either time or place (John 4:21; 1 Tim. 2:8). Therefore Christ is to be worshiped always and everywhere. Therefore if we believe that Christ, God and man, is present with a peculiar mode of presence and grace in the action of His Supper, so that there He truly and substantially imparts His body and blood to those who eat, by which He wants to unite Himself with us in such a way that with this most precious pledge He applies and seals the gifts of the New Testament to everyone who eats in faith, gifts He gained for the church by the offering of His body and the shedding of His blood; if, I say, we truly and from the heart believe these things, it neither can nor should happen that faith would fail to venerate and worship Christ, who is present in this action. Thus Jacob (Gen. 28:16-22), Moses (Ex. 34:8-9), and Elijah (1 Kings 19:4 ff.) doubtless did not have a special commandment that they should worship God in these places; but because they had a general commandment that they should worship God everywhere, and were sure that God is truly present under these external and visible signs and that He there reveals Himself by a peculiar mode of grace, they certainly worshiped that God whom they believed present there; neither would it have been true faith if invocation and worship, that is, the honor owed to God, had not followed. When the servant of Abraham (Gen. 24:24-27) understood from Rebekah's response that God was present with him in that mission with His grace and blessing, he "bowed his head and worshiped the Lord." In Ex. 4:31, when the children of Israel heard that God had looked on the affliction of the people and had now determined a gracious visitation, "they bowed their heads and worshiped." In Ex. 12:12-27, when they had heard of the passing of the angel of death and of the institution of the Passover, the people bowed and worshiped. 1 Cor. 14:24-25: "If all prophesy, and an unbeliever or outsider enters, he is convicted by all, he is called to account by all . . . and so, falling on his face, he will worship God and declare that God is really among you." These did not worship God as being far removed from themselves and absent in distant heaven; they worshiped Him as truly present, and indeed present in a particularly gracious manner.

2 Therefore Augustine rightly says in a discussion of Ps. 98:5:[31] "Since the earth is the Lord's footstool, as the psalm says: 'Worship His footstool,[32] for it is holy,' I turn to Christ, because here I seek Him and find Him. How can the earth, the footstool of the Lord, be worshiped without impiety? He took onto Himself earth from earth, because flesh is from the earth; and from the flesh of Mary He took on flesh. And because He walked here in this flesh and gave this to us to eat for salvation, no one eats this flesh unless he has first worshiped. There has been found a way in which such a footstool of the Lord may be worshiped; and not only do we not sin in worshiping, but we sin when we do not worship."

Thus Ambrose says on the same verse of this Psalm: "By His footstool let the earth be understood; by the earth, however, the flesh of Christ, which today also we worship in the mysteries, which also the apostles worshiped in the Lord Jesus."

Gregory of Nazianzus says in the epitaph for his sister: *ton epi thysiasteerioo timoomenon anakaloumenee,* that is : "She called upon Christ, who is honored upon the altar, namely, when the sacrament of the Supper is celebrated." And a statement of Eusebius of Emesa says: "When you go up to the awe-inspiring altar, desiring to be sated with spiritual food, look in faith on the holy body and blood of your God, honor them, marvel at them, touch them with your mind, take them with the hand of the heart, and most of all, take them with a deep draught of the inner man."

Luther also, writing against the theologians of Louvain, in Art. 16 calls the Eucharist a venerable and adorable sacrament. And on Gen. 47 he writes: "Not only when we pray, but also when we baptize, absolve, and receive absolution, and when we approach the holy Supper, yes, also when the promise or the text of the Gospel is recited, we ought to bow our knees or at least stand as a sign of adoration or of reverence and thankfulness. And even if in the Lord's Supper nothing else were offered except bread and wine, as the sacramentarians blaspheme, nevertheless

---

[31] Ps. 99:5 in modern English Bibles.

[32] Augustine is following the text of the Vulgate, which in turn is following the text of the Septuagint, which has "Worship His footstool." The RSV translates accurately from the Hebrew, "Worship at His footstool."

in the Supper the promise is there, and the divine voice, and the Holy Spirit through the Word. Therefore it is fitting that we should approach it reverently. But how much more fitting it is that this be done when we believe that the true body and the true blood is there with the Word." Thus Luther.

3 No one, therefore, denies that Christ, God and man, truly and substantially present in His divine and human nature in the action of the Lord's Supper, should be worshiped in spirit and in truth, except someone who, with the sacramentarians, either denies or harbors doubt concerning the presence of Christ in the Supper. Neither can the *anamneesis*[33] and proclamation of the death of Christ in the Supper be rightly done without that worship which is done in spirit and in truth. These things needed to be said lest someone should suspect that we called into doubt whether Christ, God and man, who is present in the action of the Supper, should be worshiped.

4 But you say: If these things are conceded in this question about the cult and veneration of the Eucharist, then what is there in controversy between us and the papalists? I answer: There are chiefly three points to this controversy.

First, they say that the sacrament of the Eucharist itself, or the whole of that which was instituted by Christ that it might be received, should be adored with the cult of *latria*. But now the Eucharist, according to the dictum of Irenaeus, consists of two things, an earthly and a heavenly. Therefore also the earthly elements of bread and wine in the Eucharist would have to be adored with the cult of *latria*. This could in no way be excused or defended against the open charge of idolatry or bread worship. Therefore they invent their transubstantiation, lest the substance of the bread be at the same time worshiped. But because the opinion of transubstantiation is uncertain—Paul asserts that it is bread also after the blessing, Theodoret says that the nature of the elements is not changed in the Eucharist, Gelasius teaches that they keep the property of their own nature—therefore when it is taught that the whole of that which is present in the Eucharist and is distributed and received should be adored with the cult of *latria*, there are included at the same time also the elements of bread and wine, which neither can be worshiped without idolatry nor should be worshiped. It does not follow that if Christ is to be worshiped also those creatures in which He is present should at the same time be worshiped. Therefore, to beware of idolatry, a clear distinction must be made: Christ, God and man, present in His divine and human nature in

---

[33] *Anamneesis:* remembrance. Cf. 1 Cor. 11:24-25.

the action of the Supper, should be worshiped; however, the substance or form of the elements of bread and wine should not be worshiped lest, beside the Creator, we worship also the creature (Rom. 1:25). Therefore the sacrament of the Eucharist is not to be worshiped in the same way in which, because of the personal union, we worship and venerate the humanity and the divinity in the person of Christ with one worship, for the union of the bread and of the body of Christ in the Supper is not personal; but because the Eucharist consists of two things, an earthly and a heavenly, worship and veneration is not to be directed to the earthly elements, bread and wine, but to Christ, God and man, who in this action decreed and promised His presence in a particularly gracious manner. So the Israelites worshiped, not the wood, not the gold, not the cherubim of the ark of the covenant, but God Himself only, who had promised His presence there. Neither is the worship of Christ to be tied or affixed to the elements of bread and wine, for He is not contained in them as being locally shut in. We eat the bread of the Supper reverently, but in our worship we look upon Christ Himself, supernaturally present in heavenly majesty in the Supper.

Second, when the papalists dispute about cult, worship, and veneration, they do not regard chiefly this, that in the action of the Lord's Supper, or in its divinely instituted use, Christ, God and man, be worshiped in spirit and in truth, but strive, as Canon VI clearly shows, to establish and confirm the worship of the bread apart from its use, or apart from that action which Christ ordained and commanded when He instituted it; namely, when the bread is carried about in processions or reserved in a repository, that then it should be set before the people to be adored.

We have shown above that the words: "This is My body; this is My blood," are by divine institution, command, and promise bound to the action which is prescribed in the words of institution; that is, when the bread is taken, blessed, distributed, received, and eaten. For when the words are indeed spoken over the bread but the action which is prescribed and commanded in the institution is either not observed or is changed into another use, then we do not have the promise of the presence of the body and blood of Christ there, as it is present in His Supper. Let us diligently ponder in the fear of God what and what manner of act it is to set this bread, apart from its proper use, before the people to be adored, although we have no word of God concerning it that it is the body of Christ! For surely the dangers of idolatry must be diligently avoided, lest we transfer the honor which is due to God alone to some other object. It does not follow that if in the true use of the Lord's Supper Christ is rightly worshiped then a particular cult or worship of the bread should be instituted apart from this use, as when it is carried about or reserved. For without faith no one is able to worship rightly; however, without the Word there is no faith. And there is no word of God about the bread of the Eucharist being reserved or carried about in processions; in fact, it conflicts with the words of institution when the bread which has been blessed is not distributed, not received, not eaten. What other judgment can we render, therefore, according to the norm of the Word of God, than that such worship is not Christ worship but bread worship?

Third, there is controversy between the papalists and us about the cult and veneration of Christ in the Eucharist over the question as to what it is or in what it consists. For the men of Trent show in a not obscure manner in the sixth canon that they are troubled and concerned chiefly about the external worship of the Eucharist—that it should be honored with splendid housing, extravagant processions, gold, silver, silk, bowing, genuflection, prostration of the body, elevation of the hands, smiting of the breast,[34] candles, musical instruments, the noise of firearms, and similar outward pomp. And to this external cult they ascribe I know not what merits, without true repentance and faith. In order that we may say nothing more severe about the things which are done in the Eucharist outside of the divinely instituted use—Scripture gives two rules which will show on what basis to decide about the definition of worship or cult.

The first is that the assumed outward appearance of worship, without the inner spiritual impulses, does not please God, as He says: "This people honors Me with their lips, but their heart is far from Me." But true worshipers will worship in spirit and in truth. The second rule is that ways of worship either instituted or chosen by men are not pleasing to God, for He says: "In vain do they worship Me teaching as doctrines the precepts of men." And in Col. 2:23 Paul expressly condemns *ethelothreeskeia*.[35] God wants to be worshiped in the manner He Himself has prescribed in His Word. Otherwise He says: "Who has asked these things of your hands?" (Is. 1:11-15)

Therefore men must first of all be taught from the Word of God how they ought to worship Christ, God and man, in the true use of the Eucharist with a true, inner, and spiritual worship. Thereafter the true external indications of inward reverence finally and rightly follow. For

---

[34] The text of 1574 has *tonsione,* shearing. Ed. Preuss has corrected this to *tunsione,* smiting or striking.

[35] The King James version translates "will-worship"; the RSV "rigor of devotion"; the NEB, "forced piety"; Phillips, "self-inspired efforts at worship."

God takes no pleasure in any outward gestures of reverence whatsoever which are without true, inner worship of the heart; rather, He hates and abominates them as hypocrisy. Therefore instruction about veneration and worship of Christ in the Lord's Supper must not be begun with outward gestures. For many worship Christ in this way who do not worship or venerate Him aright, as Augustine says about such acts of worship in Letter No. 120, on Ps. 21:30:[36] "All the fat of the earth have eaten; also the rich have indeed been led to the table of Christ and have received of His body and blood; but they merely worshiped, they were not also satisfied, because they do not imitate [Him]." Likewise: "These also come to the table and eat and worship; but they are not satisfied, because they do not hunger and thirst for righteousness." Therefore one must first begin with the inner and spiritual worship. However, the true inner and spiritual veneration and worship is comprehended in these words of the institution: "Do this in remembrance of Me." Likewise: "You proclaim the Lord's death."

When do you do this? When, in the first place, the heart believes and thinks rightly, piously, and reverently about the essence and use of this sacrament, according to the Word. Second, when with a thankful mind we faithfully ponder and consider, and with the heart and mouth praise these immeasurable benefits of the Son of God, the Mediator, that coming down from heaven for us men and for our salvation He assumed a body[37] of our substance, and offered it to the Father on the cross for our redemption, and poured out His blood in a most bitter death; and that in addition He communicates this His holy body to us that it may be eaten, and this blood that it may be drunk in this His Supper, in order that in this way He might apply and seal the benefits of the New Testament to the believers with a most sure and precious pledge, that He might unite Himself by means of the firmest covenant with this our poor and defiled substance, and that He might transform and prepare our soul for health and our body for immortality, etc. Third, when, having considered our uncleanness and wretchedness, we call in ardent prayer upon Christ, God and man, whom we believe to be truly and substantially present in that action, that He would be our Mediator, Propitiator, Advocate, Intercessor, Justifier, and Savior, that we may, because of His death, be received and preserved in the covenant of the New Testament, by which the Father wills, because of His Son, to be reconciled to the believers; likewise, when faith in prayer interposes the sacrifice of Christ the Mediator be-

---

36 Ps. 22:29 in English Bibles.
37 Chemnitz has the word *massa,* lump, dough.

tween our sins and the wrath of the Father, as Anselm speaks. When we consider the greatness of the mystery and our own unworthiness, we pray that we may not by unworthy eating become guilty of profaning the body and blood of Christ but that, ingrafted by this eating into the body and blood of Christ, we may draw life from it as branches from the vine and that this eating may benefit us for strengthening of faith, increase in love, mortification of the flesh, etc. Therefore we pray that the gifts of repentance, faith, and love may be bestowed on us, preserved, confirmed, and increased in us.

5 This is the true inner and spiritual veneration and worship of Christ in the use of the Lord's Supper. For worship embraces these three things: 1. That we rightly know God, on whom we call, think rightly concerning Him, and that we seek to move Him in the way He revealed His essence and will in His Word; 2. That we ask of Him the things which He has promised to give; 3. That we give thanks for benefits bestowed. However, in what way these things ought to be done in the use of the Lord's Supper, that is, how we should seek to move Him, what we ought to ask, and for what to give thanks, that the words of institution, the other statements of Scripture about the Eucharist, and particularly the following words teach and show: "This do in remembrance of Me," and "You proclaim the Lord's death." This is the true[38] and sure rule for the true adoration of Christ in the use of the Eucharist.

6 This kind of worship is certainly observed in the liturgies of the ancients, in praying and giving of thanks. Justin calls the bread and wine *eucharisthenta,* which the translator of Irenaeus rendered: "The bread over which thanks has been given." And the *communio* of Dionysius begins with prayer and ends with the sacred act of thanksgiving. The liturgy of Chrysostom and Basil praises the whole economy of our redemption and prays for worthy reception. For when this true, inner, and spiritual worship has been excited and is present in the heart, then the outward manifestations of reverence and veneration toward this sacrament follow of their own accord, and rightly. For it belongs to a genuine confession that we also bear witness publicly both with the voice and with outward signs to the faith, devotion, and praise of which we have just spoken. By these we show what we think about the substance and fruit of this Supper, with what reverence and devotion of mind we come to it, what food we believe we receive there. With such external confession we separate ourselves from the sacramentarians and from the Epicurean

---

[38] The edition of 1574 has *vita,* which yields no acceptable sense. Nigrinus read *via,* and translated: *Diss ist der Weg.* Ed. Preuss has changed the *vita* to *vera.*

despisers of these mysteries; we incite others to true reverence, lest occasion be given, either to the simple for profane thinking, or to swine, to trample on these mysteries. For outward irreverence is a sign of a profane mind, as Paul says of the Corinthians, that they do not discern the body of Christ, because they did not in the Lord's Supper treat it with greater reverence than ordinary eating together.

The simplest and safest rule with respect to these external marks of reverence is that they are testimonials to the inner faith concerning the Eucharist, according to the Word, and that they correspond to that faith. Let us not, on the basis of human judgment, establish other, self-related external acts of worship, but let us think that honor is most pleasing to the One who is being honored which His Word tells us He desires.

7 This, then, is the true worship and veneration of Christ in the use of the Lord's Supper. About this the papalists are not greatly contending; they are concerned only about outward acts of worship, instituted by men, apart from the true use of the Eucharist. These they nevertheless apply in common to the whole Eucharist, that is, both to Christ and to the elements. What we miss in this teaching of the papalists, and what we find objectionable, and for what reasons, has been shown briefly but, I think, with sufficient clarity.

SECTION VI

Concerning the Corpus Christi Festival

1 For once, finally, they do right, namely when they confess that this festival has no witness either of Scripture or of apostolic tradition or of the true antiquity in the ancient and purer church. But they say that this custom was introduced into the church of God. They understand, however, that Urban IV first invented this festival about A.D. 1260 because (as he himself says in a bull) it had been revealed to certain persons that this festival should be both instituted and generally celebrated. Now there was a certain woman, a recluse, [39] from whom Urban, when he still held a lesser position, is said to have received this revelation. As soon as Urban had become pope he at once instituted this new festival on the basis of the revelation of the woman[40] and ordered by a strict command that it should be everywhere celebrated. But as the gloss says, *De reliquiis et veneratione sanctorum,* this order of Urban about the new festival was not accepted by all. However, 50 years later, in the year 1311, at the Council of Vienna, Clement V commanded that this order should be observed by all. Yet the Greek churches, even today, do not observe the solemn processions and customs of this feast. Whence then does so new a festival have such great authority that it now hurls the lightning of anathemas in the assembly at Trent, seeing that otherwise they are accustomed to rattle only apostolic traditions and the catholic consensus of the church of all ages, nations, and peoples, all of which are lacking to this festival?

In order that they may not always hide themselves under the cover of antiquity, it is useful to observe in the progression of history and of the times, how after the better times of antiquity, slowly, little by little, they arrived, after a longer tendency to change, at these spectacles of the papalist kingdom.

According to Eusebius, Bk. 5, ch. 24, the Roman bishops simply sent the Eucharist to visitors. For Irenaeus has the word *epempon* [sent]. In

---

[39] Chemnitz calls her "a certain Eve." The woman in question was Juliana of Liege. She is described as a *reclusa,* i.e., a nun who led an even more secluded life than nuns generally did, the better to follow the contemplative life.

[40] Chemnitz uses the term *muliercula,* which appears to be somewhat derogatory.

285

the sixth book of Eusebius, ch. 34, the presbyter gives the Eucharist to a boy to take it to Serapion. Exuperius carries the body and blood of the Lord in a basket of wicker work and a glass. In Tertullian and Cyprian the Eucharist was given to women to carry home. There are no testimonies or examples in the history of the true antiquity of lights carried before it, of bells, and of the rest of the pomp which is customary with the papalists. It is worthy of note also that no such thing is found in the decree of Gratian.

But at the time of the Lateran Council, about A. D. 1200, Innocent began to decree that the Eucharist should be reserved in safe custody, under lock and key, *De custodia Eucharistiae,* ch. *Statuimus.* Soon thereafter, around the year of our Lord 1220, Honorius III commanded in a strict order that the Eucharist should be devotedly and faithfully reserved by the priests, being always honorably placed in a special, clean, designated place; that the priest should frequently teach his people that they should bow reverently when in the celebration of Masses the host is elevated; that they should do this also when the priest carries it to a sick person; that he should be becomingly dressed as he carries it, going and coming, a clean cloth placed over the host, which is to be held before his breast, with all reverence and fear; that a light should always go before, since it is the radiance of the eternal light—all this in order that from it faith and devotion may be increased in all.

Now these things are recent, for in the genuine histories of the true antiquity such things are nowhere read. Nevertheless, until now these things were ordered with some regard to use, namely, when the bread is consecrated and when it is carried to the sick in order that it may be offered and eaten.

Afterward, however, when the Corpus Christi festival was instituted by Urban and confirmed by Clement, little by little they departed further from the use of the Eucharist which was instituted by Christ. And I would wish that the reader might diligently consider the bull by which this was instituted. It is found in the Clementine writings, Bk. 3, title 6. For no mention at all is made in this bull of carrying the sacrament about and displaying it; neither is there so much as one syllable there about shutting up the consecrated bread for eight days in a monstrance,[41] carrying it about, and displaying it. Neither is mention made there of such a spectacle, procession, and external adoration of the bread as it is carried about and displayed. The purpose for which this festival was instituted is

---

[41] Monstrance: a transparent receptacle in which the consecrated host is shown to the multitude.

there explained as follows: "That they may strive to prepare themselves in such a way that they may be worthy to be partakers of this most precious sacrament on that day, and may be able to receive it reverently and by its power receive an increase of graces." These are the words of the bull, in which it is clearly said that this festival was instituted primarily in the interest of a more solemn use, participation, or Communion, and that in this use, in which due reverence and devotion is required, thanks is to be given to Christ for this immeasurable benefit, that He gives us His body as food and His blood as drink.

Also this must be diligently noted, that the things which are today customarily done at the Corpus Christi festival in the pope's kingdom were not even known at the time of Urban and Clement, things such as confinement, carrying about, exhibition, beholding, and adoration of the bread, apart from the use by distribution and eating. These things were therefore invented and introduced long after A.D. 1311. So new is the spectacle of this feast, as it is observed under the papacy; yet the men of Trent labor with so great an effort for its retention that they do not scruple to employ a flood of anathemas. Therefore they give heed neither to Scripture nor to the traditions of the apostles nor yet to the judgments of antiquity; but they have set themselves this one purpose, that the power of the papalist kingdom may remain and be made firm by any and all means.

Also the very name of the feast has been mutilated. Both Urban and Clement call it the festival of the body and blood of Christ. And in the responses of that festival they sing: "We all who partake of the one bread and of the one cup." Today, however, it is called the feast of the body of Christ.

2 Pomerius says that the indulgences of this feast were increased by Martin V and by Eugenius, who followed him. Therefore these recent innovations seem to have been greatly multiplied around the time of the Council of Constance, because a new law had been brought in about the mutilation of the Eucharist. Once carrying the bread about, displaying and adoring it apart from its use had been permitted to come in on that feast, there was no stopping. For in the greater metropolitan churches they bring the reserved host forward with lights for adoration, not only during the eight days of the feast but daily; they bring it out for extinguishing conflagrations and to avert similar misfortunes. And, as it generally happens, when one has once turned aside from the royal road, unless he returns to the true way, there is no end or measure to the straying. Thus the carrying of the Eucharist in procession, apart from the use instituted by Christ, finally was carried to the point where the most holy sacrament of the Eucharist is now compelled to serve the pomp of the Roman pontiff, a truly pontifical or rather heathenish pomp, greater certainly than that of king or emperor. For at Rome, in the pontifical processions, the bread of the Eucharist is handled in no other way than as in the parade of the Persian kings they formerly carried their sacred fire, which they called Ahura Mazda, on a horse before the king. For in the middle of the papal procession, a short distance in front of the pope, there is led a white horse, tame and richly ornamented, carrying the sacrament enclosed in a repository, on a beautiful pillow which the sacristan has placed upon it. On its neck the horse has a bell with a beautiful sound. Over it is carried a baldachin with the pope's coat of arms. Preceding the horse are 12 servants of the pope on foot, garbed in red, carrying 12 torches before the sacrament; after them two servants, sacristans, mounted, also garbed in red, carrying lighted lanterns of silver before the sacrament.

There are extant three books of the ceremonies of the Roman church, ascribed to Leo X, in which this description is repeated a number of times. Bk. 1, section 2, "Concerning the Procession of the Crowned Pontiff to the Lateran"; section 5, "Concerning the Procession of the Pontiff and the Crowned Emperor Through the City"; section 12, "Concerning the Order in Which the Pope in the City Rides from Place to Place in Solemn Procession or in Papal Vestments." And in Bk. 3, "Of the Office of the Sacristan."These recent prodigies are unknown not only to the ancient but also to the more recent antiquity.

3 I have instituted this recitation chiefly for two reasons: 1. that I might set forth for consideration what, of what kind, and how great are the things they wrap up in Chapter V and Canon VI about the festival they call Corpus Christi; 2. that I might show to what extent and how far they have now, in this feast, departed from the manner of the old church even of the Middle Ages; likewise, how recent, late, and new are the things that are now being practiced in the papalist kingdom on this festival and in other processions.

4 Now that the beginning and the progress of this festival have been shown, let us say some few things also about the thing itself. For the sake of order the whole year is divided into certain festivals which are profitably observed among us for the edification of the people, namely, in order that the chief articles of faith may annually be set before the people in some kind of order, repeated, and held fast against any and all corruptions; in order, also, that the believers may be reminded and incited to consider the benefits of God, concerning which these articles tell, and that great thanksgiving may be rendered to God in the church for these benefits. Thus no godly person would disapprove if over and above what ought to be done always, every day, the church would, for the sake of order, come together at a certain time of the year and if in that meeting the doctrine concerning the Lord's Supper were set forth simply and plainly with a suitable treatment and all falsifications which contaminate the purity of this doctrine were refuted; if men were reminded how great a treasure Christ bequeathed to the church in His testament; if great thanksgiving were rendered in the church to Christ the Savior for these benefits, which the Lord's Supper offers and confers; if negligence were censured and men were invited to more frequent use of the Eucharist throughout the whole year, etc.

5 In this way the church could, as victor over falsehood and heresy, conduct, as it were, a public triumph. And if this were the reason for this feast, it would be a piece of impudence to attack its celebration in a hateful manner. But it is a very different thing for which the papalists fight in connection with this festival. Neither did we, on our side, abrogate this festival as being enemies of and opposed to all good order. The reasons behind the controversy over this festival are far other. I shall only briefly recite them, because they are clear from the historical reminder above.

1. The celebration of this festival, such as it is under the papacy, sets forth, strengthens, and establishes the mutilation of the Eucharist; for only the one form is set forth, contrary to the institution. Also, this festival was marred with new additions at the very time when this mutilation was everywhere foisted on the churches, and men were not lacking who contradicted, as Alexander of Hales testifies concerning the monks.

2. The celebration of this festival changes the sacrament from its divinely instituted use into another action and to a different use, which does not have the testimony of the Word of God; for it is not distributed, nor received, nor eaten, but carried about and displayed. It is for the purpose of retaining the chief power of the papalist kingdom, namely, that the Eucharist has the true nature of a sacrament also apart from its divinely instituted use, even if it is changed into another action and to a different use—it is for this that they fight so earnestly to retain this feast.

3. Men are persuaded that Christ is not less and not otherwise present in the bread when it is carried about than in the true, divinely instituted use of the Supper. And indeed they want Christ to be worshiped there, although there is no word of God to the effect that Christ wants to be present with His body and blood in such a use of the bread, as He promised He would be in the use of the Supper.

4. The pretext they advance about recalling to mind and celebrating the memory of Christ in the Eucharist is nothing but an opinion which militates against the institution. For in the Eucharist Christ instituted a memorial of Himself which is not to be celebrated as one pleases, but in a definite way. That way is not that the bread be carried about, placed before the people, and displayed; rather, He took bread, blessed, broke, and gave it to His disciples, saying: "Take, eat; this is My body; do this in memory of Me." And when Paul explains this commemoration he says expressly: "As often as you eat and drink," etc. However in this feast the very things Christ instituted and commanded, namely, the distribution and eating, are overlooked, and another use, recently instituted by men, or rather advanced by women, is substituted. And no matter what good intention of honoring the Eucharist is used as a pretext, we ought always to think: "They worship Me in vain with the commandments of men."

An outstanding example, most fitting to this debate, is described in 1 Sam. 4:3-11, where the ark of the Lord is brought into the camp without instruction and command of the Word, with an intention that was not evil, and a highly probable result, in order that it might be an aid against the attack of the enemies. This example, rightly considered, overthrows the whole pretext of a good intention outside the Word in the matter of carrying the bread about.

5. The celebration of this festival proposes that Christ should be worshiped in the Eucharist in another way and in other modes than He Himself prescribed in His Word, and that apart from the divinely instituted use. And men are persuaded that this worship, invented by men, is much superior and more pleasing to God than if the Eucharist were distributed, taken, eaten, and drunk in memory of Christ.

6. Through this festival men are led away from the more frequent and true use of the Lord's Supper, for they are persuaded that the eating is connected with great danger but that the worship of this festival is without danger and much more meritorious.

7. Christ instituted the Eucharist for this purpose, that He might offer, give, apply, and seal to us the benefits and merits of His death. Of this festival, however, Urban says in his bull, that it is observed for the forgiveness of sins. Pomerius explains this as follows in his sermons: "When a contrite man is present at this feast at Mass and at the procession, and shows solemn reverence to the sacrament as it is carried about, then by this worship and work he merits and obtains very many good things, namely, acceptance by God, blessing, turning from sin, defense against all perils and evils, fruitfulness in merits, and the hearing of

prayer, for prayer is hearkened to more when the sacrament is present and carried about, as in conflagrations." And he quotes from Richard: "But if also someone is in mortal sin, although he does not receive forgiveness of sins, he nevertheless acts prudently if on that festival he does what is prescribed in the form of indulgence, because good deeds done while in mortal sin dispose to penitence *de congruo*[42] and, through its mediation, to remission of sins."

8. The popes promise and dispense many, varied, and copious indulgences to those who at this festival show solemn reverence, such as they themselves describe, to the bread of the Eucharist apart from its use. Urban prescribed a definite number of these indulgences in his bull concerning this feast. Afterward the measure of these indulgences was multiplied and increased by Martin V and Eugenius, in order that it might be pressed down and shaken together.[43] Pomerius brings the total together thus: "Those who are present on this festival for the first or second vespers, or for Mass, or for matins, receive for each attendance indulgence for 400 days." The total for one feast day therefore rises to 1,600[44] indulgences. Farther down in the octave[45] 400 in all for each separate day. The sum total for the feast and its whole octave will be indulgences for 4,400 days.[46]

On those who commune on that day[47] indulgences of 400 days are bestowed. Let the reader note that just as much indulgence is promised to the spectator as to the person who communes, namely 400 days. But if the whole sum is added together, the veneration of the sacrament apart from its use prescribed by Christ will exceed the Communion, that is, the divinely instituted use, by four times. Pomerius adds that anyone who wishes to attain these indulgences ought to be firm in faith, namely, that he believes that the church is so powerful that it can give so many and such indulgences; for heretics, who deny the power of indulgences, do not attain them. The gloss *De reliquiis et veneratione sanctorum* says concerning these indulgences: "To want to explain these remissions, in which few share, is neither seemly nor useful."

6 These are the things which the Corpus Christi festival in the papalist church embraces and which cause the controversy over this feast. If

---

[42] *De congruo*, i.e., to a degree suitable to such good deeds.

[43] Cf. Luke 6:38.

[44] The Latin text has 16,000, an obvious mistake. The correct figure is 1,600.

[45] *Octava:* the eighth day from a feast day, beginning with the feast day as one; also, the lengthening of a festival so as to include a period of eight days.

[46] The Latin text has 44,000 days. Nigrinus has corrected this, and we follow his figure.

[47] I.e., the day of the Corpus Christi festival, the first day of the octave.

these are compared with the institution of the Lord's Supper, the reader will see that this festival is in truth nothing else than a public and solemn protestation against the institution of the Son of God. This festival was instituted once upon a time to obscure, push into the background, and bury the things which are prescribed and commanded in the institution, and in order that other and different uses, concerning which nothing is either prescribed or commanded in the institution, might be put in their place and that the people might be persuaded that this is a more excellent worship. For this purpose this feast was instituted once upon a time, and for this it is retained and celebrated today, as is clear from the things we have noted.

SECTION VII

Concerning Reserving the Sacrament of the Eucharist And Carrying It to the Sick

Chapter VI

The custom of reserving the holy Eucharist in a sacred place is so ancient that even the age of the Council of Nicaea knew it. Moreover, carrying the holy Eucharist to the sick and reserving it in the churches for this use is not only entirely fair and reasonable but is also found taught in numerous councils and is observed by a very ancient custom of the Catholic Church. Therefore this holy synod ordains that this salutary and necessary custom is by all means to be retained.

CANON VII

If anyone says that it is not permitted to reserve the holy Eucharist in a sacred place, but that it must of necessity be distributed immediately after the consecration to those who are present, or that it is not permitted that it be carried to the sick in an honorable manner, let him be anathema.

Examination

1 The principal question here is whether the bread of the Eucharist, when it has been blessed, hallowed, or consecrated by the recitation of the words of institution, should be at once distributed, taken, and eaten in commemoration of Christ, or whether, after it has been blessed, the distribution, taking, and eating may be omitted and the bread put away, inclosed, reserved, carried about, displayed, and put to other uses, so that finally, after a number of days, weeks, months, or years the taking and eating may follow.

The Tridentine decree which sanctions and establishes such reservation confesses that it was brought into the church, though it is prescribed neither by the Word of God nor by the tradition or example of the apostles. Instead, it says that it is an old custom and a most ancient practice.

With respect to custom, no matter how ancient, Gratian furnishes us an answer from the sayings of the fathers, dist. 8: "Cyprian says that custom without truth is the antiquity of error." And Gregory quotes from Cyprian: "The Lord says in the Gospel, 'I am the truth.' He does not say, 'I am the custom.' Therefore all custom, no matter how universal, must always be esteemed less than the truth. And any custom which is contrary to the truth must be abolished.''

Augustine says: "This clearly is true, that reason and truth are to be placed above custom; but if the truth supports a custom, then nothing should be held more firmly." And the judgment of Cyprian, where he argues about the Eucharist, is: "If Christ alone is to be heard, we need not heed what someone else before us thought should be done, but what Christ did first, because He is before all others; for we ought not to follow the custom of man but the truth of God."

2 Since, therefore, in this debate about the reservation of the Eucharist the men of Trent bring forward an old usage and ancient custom, we must see above all else whether the truth of the divine Word supports this custom, that is, what Christ, who is before all, did before. The matter is very clear in the account of the institution. For Jesus took bread and gave thanks or blessed it. He did not, however, after the blessing put it away to be reserved, but broke it and gave it to His disciples. Neither did He command that they should put away this bread, reserve it, carry it about, or display it to others, but said: "Take, eat." Nor was there interposed a delay or interval of some hours, days, weeks, months, or years between blessing, distribution, taking, and eating. But when He had blessed, He at once distributed. And that the disciples at once took what had been distributed, and that they did not put to some other use what they had taken, but ate and drank as they had been commanded—this Mark shows in the description of the second part, when in the midst of the description he interposes these words: "And all drank of it."

Also the fact that the time is noted down shows that no such delay was interposed as could lend any support to the reservation of the consecrated Eucharist, apart from its use. For Christ ate the Passover in the course of the two vespers, according to the Law, namely, between sunset and nightfall. After He had distributed this, and the common supper had been finished, then only did He institute the Eucharist, and after that institution He held the lengthy discourse written down in John. From there He went out into the garden, prayed there in agony, was arrested, and led first to Annas, afterward to Caiaphas, in whose palace many things were transacted before the first denial by Peter. Then came the time of the first cock's crow. This computation shows plainly that there was no long delay in the action of the first Lord's Supper.

However, when Christ says: "Do this," He commands that as often as we do it we should follow and do what was done at the first Lord's Supper. There is not a trace to be found in the history of the apostles to indicate that they did something else or different, such as separating or tearing apart the distribution and reception from the blessing; neither can any apostolic example of reserving the Eucharist be produced. Therefore the truth of the divine Word lends no support whatever to the custom of reserving the Eucharist. But if, following the judgment of Cyprian, we ought not, in the action of the Lord's Supper, heed what others before us thought ought to be done, but what He who is before all did first and commanded to be done until He comes to judgment, we will not put away the bread and wine which have been blessed with the words of the Supper, shut them in, reserve them, carry them about, and use them for display, but will distribute, receive, eat and drink them, and proclaim the death of the Lord. Thus the obedience of our faith will do what Christ did before and commanded to be done.

3 If we follow this rule, we will not turn aside either to the right or to the left. It is the sad and deplorable inquisitiveness or wantonness of human nature which leaves the simple, clear, and even way of the teaching, instruction, and command of Christ and of apostolic example and dares with its own impudence, under the pretext of custom, either to change something in the testament of the Son of God or to place something above it, namely, to omit the distribution and reception which have the command of Christ and to invent in their place reservation, putting aside, shutting in, carrying about, displaying, etc., of the blessed bread. These things are not supported by even so much as one syllable or letter in the words of Christ.

4 But they say that the practice of reserving the Eucharist is old and was observed by the custom of the most ancient catholic church; therefore the reservation which is customary in the papalist church cannot be criticized and condemned without at the same time also condemning the universal church of Christ. Therefore the Synod of Trent decrees that this custom must by all means be retained as being salutary and necessary.

I answer, however, that not all ancient churches are at once condemned when the papalist reservation, shutting in, display, carrying about, etc., is reproached. For first of all we say what Cyprian says, Bk. 2, Letter No. 3: "If someone of those who were before us either from ignorance or in his simplicity did not observe what the Lord taught us by His example and instruction to do, forgiveness may be granted to his simplicity from the gentleness of the Lord; in our case, however, this cannot be pardoned, who have now been admonished and instructed by the Lord, in order that the evangelical law and the tradition of the Lord may be everywhere observed and that there may be no departing from what Christ both taught and did." He adds the statement which he quotes in dist. 8:

"He who errs in simplicity may be forgiven; but after inspiration and revelation of the truth has taken place, whoever consciously and knowingly perseveres in his previous error no longer sins under the pardon of ignorance, for he relies on presumption and on a certain obstinacy, although he is vanquished by reason."

5 Secondly, we shall consider and mentally weigh whether the testimonies of antiquity which they advance concerning that old custom and ancient practice prove that the custom of reserving the sacrament of the Eucharist is necessary, as the Tridentine decree maintains; likewise, whether the testimonies of antiquity prove and establish the reservation, shutting in, display, and carrying about of the consecrated bread, as these are observed and practiced in the papalist church. But before we come to the explanation of the examples itself, we shall briefly examine whether the custom of reservation can or should be said to be necessary and catholic, as the Tridentine decree affirms.

6 Now whatever is declared to be necessary in the church of Christ must be prescribed and commanded by the Word of God and have examples in Scripture. We have, however, shown above that Christ neither by instruction nor by His example (to use the words of Cyprian) either prescribed or commanded the reservation of the Eucharist. Therefore no other examples can impose on consciences a necessity of observing this custom. To assert that the custom of reserving the Eucharist is necessary is a tyranny which tries to rule over the faith of the church and militates against Christian liberty, since neither a prescription nor a command nor any example of it can be shown in the Word of God.

Vincent of Lerins has rightly defined that that is catholic which has always, everywhere, and by all alike been observed. Therefore whatever is declared to be catholic [universal] for the whole church of Christ, and therefore necessary, must absolutely have either a word or an example of Christ and the apostles. When we speak about the catholic or universal church of Christ, we ought not to cut off the Head from the members, that is, Christ from the church, nor the foremost members, that is, the apostles with their teaching and examples, from the rest of the body of the church. But that is truly catholic for the universal church which can be shown and proved to have been taught or commanded by Christ the Head[48] and observed by the apostles. But when this basis is lacking, not even the consensus of the whole world is sufficient to prove that something is catholic for the church of Christ. But it is manifest, as we have shown, that

---

[48] The text has *a capite Christi,* which does not yield good sense. We understand with Nigrinus that the text should read: *a capite Christo.*

the institution of Christ prescribes or commands the reservation of the Eucharist outside of its use in distribution and reception neither by teaching nor by example (as Cyprian has it). Neither can any example of the apostles be shown; nor is it enough to teach that it is an apostolic tradition, without proof and documentation. It is therefore false to say that the reservation of the Eucharist apart from distribution and reception is a catholic custom of the universal church and must be retained. For that which is the chief thing in whatever ought to be catholic and necessary is lacking to this custom. Perhaps it was for this reason that the Tridentine decree did not want to call it a catholic custom, but a "custom of the Catholic Church." The Creed, however, defines that church as catholic which is apostolic, on which Christ placed this inscription: "Teaching them to observe all that I have commanded you" (Matt. 28:20); likewise: "My sheep hear My voice." (John 10:27)

7 But they will argue that they mean the custom and usage of the whole church after the time of the apostles. Let us therefore examine also this, whether the reservation of the Eucharist was received, approved, and observed as a catholic and necessary dogma always, everywhere, and by all in the whole church of all ages and of all nations and peoples. Canon law itself, *De consecratione,* dist. 2, ch. *Tribus gradibus,* copies the statement from Clement, a Roman pontiff, prescribing how a presbyter, deacon, and minister ought to care for the leftover fragments of the body of the Lord. He does not by this care understand reservation, but adds a clear explanation in the words: "Let as many wafers[49] be offered on the altar as ought to suffice for the people. But if any are left over, let them not be reserved until the next day, but let them be eaten with fear and trembling by the attentive clergy." Lest this be understood of the offerings of the people, he adds at once: "These clerics eat the remnants of the body of Christ which are left in the sacristy." A gloss attempts to evade this, as though only reservation for the work of those who perform the consecration were prohibited there. But the text speaks expressly of the Communion of the people.

There is a book which contains an interpretation of Leviticus, which some ascribe to Origen, others to Cyril. There, in the explanation of ch. 7 (v. 15), about the flesh of the sacrifice being eaten on the same day so that nothing of it may be left over until the morning, is read a description of the churchly custom, taken from the words of institution of the Supper. "For also the Lord said to the disciples with respect to the bread which He

---

[49] *Holocausta:* literally, whole burnt offerings, but evidently referring to Communion wafers.

gave to them: 'Take, eat.' He did not delay, nor command them to reserve it till the next day.''

Hesychius, a disciple of Gregory of Nazianzus, explaining Lev. 8:32: "What remains of the flesh and of the loaves shall be consumed by fire," indicates that the custom in his time was that if anything remained after all had communed, it should be burned with fire.

Nicephorus, Bk. 17, ch. 25, writing the story of the servant of a certain Jewish worker in glass at the time of Justinian, about A.D. 250, says that for a long time there had been a custom in the church at Constantinople that when after the Communion a somewhat larger amount of the parts of the immaculate and divine body was left, it was not reserved, but certain boys were sent for from the elementary school who were to eat these remnants. This custom can be understood from Clement, who says that the remnants should be eaten by the clergy on the same day; but when a larger amount of remnants was left over, so that the clergy could not eat it all, also scholars were summoned in the church at Constantinople.

8 A little later this custom was altered somewhat. For the Second Council of Matiscona[50] says that the remnants which are left over after the Communion has been completed are to be received by these boys on the fourth or the sixth day. Afterward, indeed, they began to reserve them for almost a whole year.

Among the Greeks (not among the most ancient) there is a liturgy *proeegiasmenoon,* that is, of previously consecrated elements. For during the 40 days of Lent no consecration takes place during five days of each week, only on Saturday and on the Lord's day, but distribution and reception is only of preconsecrated elements, that is, of elements consecrated on the Lord's day.

But Humbert, bishop of Sylva Candida, writing against the booklet of the monk Nicetas, as quoted by George Cassander, criticizes this rite of the Greeks sharply on the basis of the words of institution, and says among other things: "We read that the Lord did not teach His disciples an imperfect but a perfect commemoration, blessing the bread and at once breaking and distributing it. For He did not just bless it and then reserve it to be broken the next day, neither did He only break it and then lay it away; but having broken it, He immediately distributed it. Therefore Alexander, the martyr and fifth pope from Peter, when he introduces the passion of the Lord into the canon of the Mass, says: ' "As often as you do this," that is, bless, break, and distribute, "you do it in memory of Me." ' "

---

[50] The Second Council of Matiscona (the modern St. Macon in France) was held A.D. 585.

For whatever of these three is done without the rest, namely, either blessing without breaking and distribution, or breaking without blessing and distribution, does not display a perfect memory of Christ, even as distribution without blessing and breaking." Thus says Humbert.

Gabriel Biel, in the 26th lecture on the canon, adduces a statement from Paschasius and says: "Christ, desiring that His disciples might become partakers of the fruit of this sacrament, did not, after He had consecrated His body, stop with the consecration; neither did He give it to the disciples in order that they might preserve it in an honorable manner, but gave it for its use, saying: 'Take, eat'; and because in the course of use what is eaten is spent and consumed, He gave them the power to consecrate as often as they would, when He adds: 'This do in memory of Me.' " Therefore reservation of the consecrated Eucharist without distribution and reception has not been received, approved, and observed either always, or everywhere, or by all as a catholic dogma and necessary custom. Rather, there were those who not only did not observe this custom but strongly condemned it on the basis of the words of institution.

9 Thus we have now shown three things:

1. That Christ neither by instruction nor by example taught reservation, rather that it is not in harmony with the words of Christ's institution;

2. That neither a tradition nor an example of reservation can be shown from the apostles;

3. That reservation was neither approved nor used everywhere and by all in the ancient church, but rather there was no lack of persons who condemned the custom of reservation, and that on the basis of God's Word.

Since this is how matters stand, it is truly a piece of papalist impudence and a tyranny of Antichrist, what Chapter VI decrees about reservation: "The synod ordains that this salutary and necessary custom is by all means to be maintained." For no one attempts to impose a necessity on consciences without a testimony of the Word of God except he who, sitting in the temple of God, proclaims himself to be God and exalts himself above all that is called God. (2 Thess. 2:4)

This also is clear from what has been shown until now, that our churches are being unjustly accused and condemned because they do not observe reservation of the Eucharist.

10 But the papalists also have certain examples of a reserved Eucharist. Therefore we shall give an answer concerning these in an orderly fashion and clearly.

First of all, it is worth the effort to hear from what sure, firm, and authentic testimonies the Tridentine lawgivers prove the custom of reserving the Eucharist. For they say that it is so old that even the age of the Council of Nicaea knew it. The authority of the Nicene Synod is indeed very great, because it decided and terminated controversies about the faith according to the norm and rule of Scripture. But that was around A.D. 300. Therefore the age of the Nicene Synod is not the most ancient time of the church of Christ.

11 But let us hear with what testimony of the Nicene Synod they prove reservation! They cite from a certain canon of the Nicene Council concerning deacons, that these are to receive Communion from the bishop or presbyter. But if neither bishop nor presbyter is present, then the deacons themselves may bring it forward and eat it. However, the same canon says that the deacons do not have authority to offer the sacrifice. Therefore it was necessary for the Eucharist to have been consecrated beforehand, either by the bishop or a presbyter, so that it could be brought forward by a deacon and eaten in their absence. This is the testimony they advance from the Nicene age. And indeed, there is no doubt that the fathers at the Nicene Council did, over and above the exposition of the faith, also lay down certain rules. But on the question what and how many these canons are, the opinions are very uncertain. Gratian, dist. 16, counts 70 canons, of which only 20 were later left in the Roman church. There is added to the Lateran Council a little book in three parts. In the third part, ch. 10, the author says: "The ancient councils, and also later ones, are difficult to discover." He adds: "It is strange that the Roman church neglected this in this way." So great is the uncertainty of the canons which bear the title of the Nicene Council.

But in the case of the canon from which they attempt to prove reservation, the matter is not only doubtful but altogether suspect. For the later sentence, which alludes to reservation, namely, that the deacons themselves may bring it forward and eat, is not read in that canon in Greek, neither in the decrees, dist. 93, ch. *Pervenit,* nor in the first edition of the councils. But the second edition, even as it makes canon 14 canon 18, so it also patches on the statement about which we are now disputing. In Rufinus, Bk. 1, ch. 6, there is read some such addition, but not in the way it reads in the books of the councils. For he has nothing about bringing forward, as if it had been reserved, but says simply: "Let the deacons not distribute the Eucharist when presbyters are present; but if no presbyter is present, then it is permitted also to them to distribute it." Since therefore matters stand thus in the statement of the Nicene canon which alludes to reservation, and since at the Sixth Synod of Carthage the Romans were convicted of having falsified the Nicene canons, it is clear what manner of proof that is in the Tridentine chapter which attempts to defend and establish the papalist reservation, carrying about, and displaying from this patched-on and doubtful Nicene canon, although also this addition does not speak of carrying about and display for worship and adoration but says: "They may bring forward and eat, or distribute." If therefore the men of Trent were earnestly attempting to show sure, firm, and solid grounds to consciences in the articles which are in controversy at this time, they would certainly not base reservation on this doubtful statement of the Nicene canon. But because in the name of the pontiff they apply the opinion of the canonists also to themselves, that the pope may take his will as his reason in matters which he wills; likewise, that he can do all things above the law and outside of the law—therefore they only say a thing, whatever it may, be *pro forma* and at once add their usual dictum: "We decree that it is altogether necessary," or: "Let him be anathema."

12 Second: They have, however, from the history of antiquity certain other, surer testimonies, by means of which they think they can prove their reservation. The most proper way to explain these is to remember that our dispute with the papalists is about their reserving, shutting in, carrying about, and displaying the consecrated bread for worship and adoration, apart from distribution and reception. I say that the testimonies of antiquity have nothing in common with such papalist reservation. This can be clearly demonstrated and shown by a comparison of the examples of antiquity with papalist reservation. According to Justin the deacons give the bread and wine which have been consecrated by means of thanksgiving to all who are present, and the same elements are given to deacons to be carried to those who are absent. You hear that the Eucharist is given to deacons not that they may lay it away, shut it in, and reserve it for a number of days or months without distribution and reception; but from the assembly of the church they carry it to those who are absent in order that they may commune. Thus there is preserved the total divinely instituted action, namely, blessing, distribution, and reception.

But you say: If at the time of Justin the Eucharist was carried by the deacons to those who were absent, then the papalist carrying about and display is proved from this. I deny this. The papalist carrying about does not have joined in that act distribution and reception; neither is it carried about in order that it may be distributed and taken, but that it may be displayed, viewed, and thus a peculiar worship by means of outward adoration may be instituted. All of this is totally unknown to the whole true antiquity.

Irenaeus, as quoted by Eusebius, Bk. 5, ch. 24, in the epistle to

Victor relates that all Roman bishops before Victor, although they disagreed with the Asiatics in the observation of Easter, nevertheless cultivated peace with them. And because fellowship at the Lord's table is a testimony of consensus, harmony, and unity in doctrine and faith, as Paul says: "We who are many are one body, for we all partake of the one bread" (1 Cor. 10:17), therefore Irenaeus says that it was the custom that when bishops or presbyters either of Asiatic or of other churches came to Rome the Roman bishops would send the Eucharist to them as a witness of harmony and peace.

In order that the papalists may be able more easily to twist this example to their reservation and carrying about, they misuse the version of Rufinus, who says that the Eucharist was solemnly transmitted to them. It is worthwhile to observe the trickery of Andrada, who feigns on the basis of this history that formerly the Eucharist was carried to places over great distances, namely, all the way from Rome to Asia. But when Eusebius quotes the words of Irenaeus, he simply has *epempon,* "they sent," and expressly says that these guests had come to Rome from Asia. Therefore the Eucharist was not at that time put away and reserved for a number of days, months, or years, that it might be borne about from Europe all the way to Asia in order to be transmitted to the guests as they advanced on their journey, with bells, lights, and all the rest of the pomp customary to the papalists; but because Communion was then commonly celebrated daily in the churches, as is well known from the histories of antiquity, alike according to Irenaeus and Justin, when the Communion of those present had been completed, the Eucharist was sent and carried from the assembly of the congregation to those who were absent, that they might participate in it.

That the Eucharist was not reserved or laid back for strangers, but was celebrated for arriving strangers on the same day on which they were to commune, Ambrose indicates most clearly when he writes, on 2 Tim. 2: "It is to be offered every week, even though not every day for strangers; nevertheless at least twice a week for the local people."

13 Therefore examples about the Communion of strangers, as they call it, neither prove nor establish papalist reservation and the theatrical carrying about of the eucharistic bread, apart from distribution and reception. For in order to bear witness to unity the ancients admitted believing strangers, whose faith was known, to the fellowship of the Eucharist, communicating the Eucharist to them either in the assembled congregation or sending the Eucharist to them from the assembled congregation.

14 Irenaeus also tells of another example in the above-mentioned epistle, namely, that Anicetus and Polycarp communed each other even though they differed on the Easter question, and that at Rome Anicetus granted Polycarp the Eucharist out of respect. This must not be understood so simply, as if Anicetus had offered or held out the Eucharist to Polycarp, but that he permitted Polycarp to celebrate and administer the Eucharist in the church at Rome. For Irenaeus uses these words: *parechooreese too Polykarpoo teen eucharistian.*"[51]

In all these examples there is still observed the use or action instituted by Christ. For once the Eucharist had been blessed, it was immediately carried from the assembled congregation, not to be carried about, displayed, and adored apart from its use, but to be distributed and received. Moreover, it was not carried away in the ancient church with the kind of theatrical display used in the papacy. For it was given to boys to be carried away; according to Dionysius of Alexandria, to women; according to Cyprian, in little baskets; according to Satyrus, in a napkin. Jerome praises Exuperius, bishop of Toulouse, because, when he dispensed the treasures of the church to the poor, he carried the body of the Lord in a wicker basket, and the blood in a glass. He did not, however, carry it in order that it might be borne about, neither for display, but he carried the Eucharist about in the assembled congregation for the purpose of communing (as was done in the age of Cyprian) or, when the Communion had been completed, he carried the Eucharist for distribution and reception on behalf of the absent, according to the custom of Justin.

15 But the papalists hope to be able to prove both the reservation of the Eucharist and their little tabernacles or houses for the sacrament from the first epistle of Chrysostom to Innocent. But this also is in vain. For Chrysostom says that the soldiers entered the *sacrarium.*[52] Therefore the *sacrarium* of the ancients was not such a little tabernacle for reserving the sacrament; but the place in which the consecration, though not the distribution, of the Eucharist was celebrated was called the *sacrarium.* But, say they, the account of Chrysostom relates that the soldiers, toward the evening of the day, entered into the *sacrarium* and that in the disturbance the blood of Christ was poured out on the clothing of the soldiers. But it was not then the time for Communion, for it was the evening of the day; and the blood of Christ was nevertheless in the *sacrarium.* Therefore [say they] the Eucharist must have been put away and reserved, apart from use or the action of distribution and reception.

I answer: This conclusion is by no means necessary, but is falsely

---

[51] Literally: "He yielded the Eucharist to Polycarp."

[52] *Sacrarium:* used for both the sacristy, a room where the sacred vessels were kept and were prepared by the clergy, and, in another use, for the small tabernacles in which the consecrated elements were later reserved in the Roman Catholic Church for the purpose of processions, display, and adoration.

added to this account of Chrysostom, as the circumstances clearly show. For Chrysostom relates that this happened at the time of the great sabbath, when the women had already divested themselves in order that they might be baptized. For it was customary in all antiquity, when adults were baptized, that they were led immediately from Baptism to the assembly in order to partake of the sacrament of the Eucharist. And therefore Chrysostom relates that he, together with all the clergy, was then present in the *sacrarium*, namely, in order to administer the Eucharist to those who had been baptized. This is not contradicted by the fact that the account says that it was the evening of the day, as if it had not then been the time for Communion. For after Baptism had been administered there followed in ancient times the administration of the Eucharist. Cassander proves by many testimonies of the ancients that Masses were customarily celebrated not only in the forenoon but also about the ninth hour, sometimes also in the evening, especially on the sabbaths of Easter and Pentecost. Therefore papalist shutting in, carrying about, and display is also not proved from this account of Chrysostom. For when the soldiers entered the sacrarium, they saw the sacred elements. Therefore they were not shut in, and the particular action which the Son of God prescribed in the institution was observed. For while the women were being baptized, the bishop together with his clergy meanwhile prepares the Eucharist, in order that, according to the then-prevailing custom, it might be distributed to those who had been baptized and be received by them.

16 Let the opposite papalist assertion be compared with this explanation of the examples of the ancient church, and it will be evident that we have two very different things:

1. For the sake of their reservation the papalists mutilate the sacrament in the matter of the second element. Indeed, they want to prove from examples of reservation on the part of the ancients that Communion under one form only was customary in the ancient church, because they judge with respect to the wine that it could not be reserved without peril. However, the history of Exuperius and Chrysostom clearly shows that this is false.

2. The papalists put back and shut in the consecrated bread, reserve it for a number of days, weeks, and months, and then set it forth for a specific worship. The examples show that the ancients did not practice this.

3. Among the papalists the person who had consecrated the bread which has been carried about does not in the end distribute it to others, but takes it himself. No example of this can be shown in the true antiquity.

4. With the papalists the bread is carried about, not that it may be distributed and received but that it may be displayed and set forth for adoration, apart from the use instituted by Christ. It is carried about and displayed without distribution and reception in order to avert conflagrations and other disasters. Concerning papalist pomp, or rather concerning the Persian Ahura Mazda, when the bread is placed upon a horse before the pope in order to be carried about, we have spoken above.

These are the things concerning which the papalists contend. With these the examples of antiquity clearly have nothing in common. It is sufficient for an answer to have demonstrated from the antithesis the difference between the papalist reservation, carrying about, and displaying and the examples of antiquity.

17 Third: Nevertheless it cannot be denied that in some places and by some persons the Eucharist was reserved for the Communion of the sick, as the example of Serapion, found in Eusebius, Bk. 6, ch. 14, shows.

I answer: Also that reservation is not universal nor perpetual, for we have shown earlier that formerly such reservation was neither observed nor used in some places and by many persons; also, there was no need for it, since in those times Communion was celebrated daily at the third and ninth hour, toward evening, and even at night, because necessity dictated this, as Cassander proves from the ancients. And when diverse customs are appealed to, one must always consider what most simply, rightly, and closely agrees with the divine institution and is most consonant with it, and what, because of the circumstances, serves most for edification. The church has followed this norm or rule in the matter of the reservation of the Eucharist. For the custom of private Communion, or Communion at home is most ancient and was very widespread—when Communion was celebrated in the assembly of the congregation, then, after the bread of the Eucharist had been divided, a part of it was either given into the hands of those who were communing or, as Clement of Alexandria says, every one of the people was permitted to take part of it, which they either ate in the church or carried home with them, reserving it either in a basket (as Cyprian has it) or in a linen napkin (as Augustine says, Sermon 252, *De tempore*) and consumed it at home, either before a meal, or in dangers, or when they were about to undertake something. And so (as Ruardus Tapper, dean at Louvain, concludes from the sermon of Cyprian about the lapsed) the cup of the Lord was offered in the church to those who were present, from which the communicants drank; however, the bread of the Lord was given into the hands of the communicants in order that they might consume it at once or might take it home with them and eat it there, so that, with intervals of time intervening, they first drank of the cup in the church but ate the body of the Lord afterward at home. Thus Ruardus.

However Gorgonia, the sister of Gregory of Nazianzus, carried the antitype of the body and blood of the Lord home with her from the assembly of the congregation. Witnesses to this custom of private reservation of the Eucharist are Tertullian, Bk. 2, *Ad uxorem;* Cyprian, Treatise 5, *De lapsis;* Ambrose, on the death of his brother Satyrus; Jerome in the *Apologia* in behalf of his books against Jovinian. Basil writes *Ad Caesariam patriciam*[53] that the hermits, who did not have access to a priest in the desert, were accustomed to carry the Eucharist with them from the assembly of the church to the desert, and to reserve it at home in order to commune themselves when there was need; and he adds that in Alexandria and Egypt this was done very much by the people. It is known also how greatly some of the ancients praised this private reservation, e.g., Gregory of Nazianzus in the epitaph for his sister, and Ambrose on the death of his brother Satyrus.

18 Surely, if the antiquity of a widespread and long-taught custom could either impose necessity or prescribe to the truth, this private reservation ought not for any reason to have been changed or abrogated. Yet later this custom, regardless of its age, was changed, abrogated, and severely forbidden. The First Council of Toledo, ch. 14, says: "If anyone does not eat the Eucharist which he has received from the priest, let him be cast out as a sacrilegious person." Caesar Augustanus,[54] ch. 3, says: "With respect to the Eucharist, if anyone is proved not to have consumed it in the church, let him be anathema forever."

Without doubt they had reasons for the abrogation:

1. Because such a reservation is neither instituted nor commanded by Christ;

2. This tearing apart of eating and drinking in the Lord's Supper does not agree sufficiently with the words of institution—first comes the drinking from the cup, and after some intervals of time the bread, which was received long before, is finally eaten;

3. This private reservation spawned many abuses and various superstitions, and therefore it was prohibited under threat of perpetual anath-

---

[53] The text here has *ad Caesarem Patriciam,* which means literally: "To the Emperor Patricias." Nigrinus translates: *"An Patriciam, den Kaiser."* History, however, knows no emperor Patricias. The text of Basil's letter, as found in Migne, op. cit., XXXII, col. 48, has *Ad Caesariam patriciam,* which might be translated: "To a noble lady of Caesar's household."

[54] The text seems to be defective here. The translator has not succeeded in clearing up the difficulty.

ema and the whole matter was recalled to the prescription of the institution;

4. When the reasons for which this reservation had been begun had ceased to exist, the custom was freely changed. The strongest reason seems to have been that in a time of persecution they could not come together to celebrate the Lord's Supper as often as they wished. When therefore they could not everywhere or always have access to Communion, they reserved at home some particles they had received in the assembly of the church, lest when some danger befell them they should be wholly deprived of Communion. But later it was judged that it would be most right to observe and follow the prescription of the institution of Christ.

19 I have spelled out these things in order that it might become evident that also in this matter the church has always judged that custom, be it ever so ancient, cannot impose the necessity to observe it nor to prescribe to the truth in such a way that, because something either builds up or destroys, one ought not to follow the prescription of the institution of Christ rather than custom. This reminder will show what one ought to judge concerning the examples of the Eucharist reserved by the priests for the Communion of the sick. And indeed, that after the Communion of those who were present the Eucharist was carried from the assembly of the congregation to those who on account of illness or for other weighty reasons were absent, the account of Justinian shows, and the example of Exuperius teaches the same thing.

However, of a Eucharist reserved, if there were need of it for the Communion of the sick, there is in the true and ancient antiquity only the lone example of Serapion (so far as I know and have seen adduced). For the account in Eusebius, Bk. 6, ch. 34, relates that it was night when the presbyter, lying sick in his house, gave the Eucharist to a young man to take to Serapion. This therefore is the one and only example of such reservation in the true antiquity (for we are not now speaking of more recent examples). And indeed, it also is not from the most ancient time, for it took place during the time of the Novatian schism. And because Dionysius of Alexandria[55] confesses in that epistle that he had issued this instruction to the presbyters, therefore it is neither an apostolic tradition nor a universal and very ancient custom, for its author and time are named.

Now then, since the private reservation of which we are speaking is both older and has more examples from antiquity, because it was more

---

[55] Died A.D. 265.

widely practiced, and was nevertheless not judged to be necessary but was freely changed and abrogated, by what authority do the men of Trent judge the other kind of reservation, of which we are now treating, which is not so ancient, neither has so many examples from the true antiquity, to be a necessary custom which must by all means be retained?

20 We do not condemn those ancient men who observed this custom, because they had weighty reasons on account of the nature of the times. Reflection on this will show what the difference is. For they did not introduce and observe this custom as necessary, as though they had not dared to do otherwise, but the nature of the times furnished them the occasion for this custom. For the Novatians were contending that the lapsed, and particularly those whose lapse had occurred under persecution, were not to be again received and admitted to the fellowship of the church, even if they repented. However the church did not refuse reconciliation and fellowship to those who repented; nevertheless, in order that the lapsed might serve as an example to deter others from a like sin, and in order that she might explore whether their repentance was genuine, she used a rather severe discipline. For she did not at once admit penitents to Communion, but their penitence was first tested by a certain discipline over a certain interval of time.

However, lest any of the penitents should die while the time fixed by canon law had not yet expired, it was decreed that in peril of death they should be reconciled by private absolution and Communion, and received into the fellowship of the church, and that such reception and Communion, even though it had taken place privately and not before the whole church, should nevertheless be a testimony of public reception and admission to the fellowship of the whole true church. For they judged that a particle of the very bread which had been blessed in the assembly of the congregation, of which the other believers had partaken, should be given, so that the lapsed might have no doubt that they were received into the communion of the mystical body of Christ. "Because there is one bread, we who are many are one body, for we all partake of the one bread" (1 Cor. 10:17). And since (as Cyprian complains, Treatise III, par. 14) some priests absolved and communed the lapsed privately without the consent of the bishop and of the church, this custom pleased all the more, that for the Communion of penitents in danger of death those particles should be used of which the assembled church had previously communed, that in this way, even though it was in a private place and by a presbyter alone, a sick person might nevertheless be judged to have been received, as it were publicly, by common testimony, into the fellowship of the whole church.

Moreover, because heresies and schisms were disturbing the church in various ways, with the result that the heretics gathered their own assemblies where they were celebrating their Communion, as the *Historia Tripartita*, Bk. 3, ch. 11, shows, they chose to offer Communion to the sick from the very same bread and wine of which the church had partaken in the public assembly, lest the sick be defiled by the heretical Communion, and that the dying might separate themselves from all heretics and might testify that they were and desired to remain in the fellowship of the true church. And in order that on days and at hours when the service of the Eucharist was not publicly celebrated in the church they might be able to come to the aid of those who were living in danger of death, they determined to reserve something from one day of the public celebration to the next following one. Now a public worship service was held either every day, or on Sundays, Wednesdays, and Fridays. The reservation in this case was free from any superstition and without any special worship apart from use. It is also worth noting that Innocent, as quoted by Cassander, says concerning the divine offices, that the priest customarily divides the Lord's consecrated body into three parts, one of which he casts into the cup, the second a deacon may distribute, the third he may reserve in the paten for the *viaticum*[56] if there is need, until the end of the Mass. However, if there is no need, the priest or one of the servants receives it in Communion. Let the reader observe that, when there were no sick persons to be communed, nothing was reserved or put back.

21 This, so far as I am able to gather from the narratives of those times, was the cause and reason for the kind of reservation of which mention is made in the story of Serapion. Nevertheless that custom was neither before those times, nor during those times, nor after those times observed everywhere and by all, as we have shown above by contrary testimonies of the ancients. For the reasons for such reservation, which we said they had, as they are not to be condemned outright, so also they are not necessary; neither were they judged necessary during those times. For there is also another way to satisfy the institution of Christ and to come to the aid of the dying. For all believers in the most diverse places in the whole world are one body and partake of one bread (1 Cor. 10:17); not as though one mass of wheaten bread were stretched through all places in the world, but because the same body of Christ in the bread is received in all places where the institution is celebrated. In later times, when a change in the doctrine and rites took place, when they no longer

---

[56] *Viaticum:* literally, food for a journey. The Eucharist is viewed as the Christian's food for the journey to eternity.

had those causes and reasons, such reservation was retained and observed as a peculiar worship and something necessary.

22 It is useful to consider the antithesis:

I. The papalists in their reservation for the sick do not have the causes which we say the ancients had.

II. The example of Serapion speaks of Communion in danger of death; the papalists commune all the sick from the reserved elements.

III. The reservation of the ancients was only for those days and hours when the Eucharist was not publicly celebrated in the church; however, although they celebrate the Mass daily, the papalists nevertheless reserve parts from the Easter or some other solemn Communion for the sick for nearly a whole year.

IV. The reservation of the ancients was used simply, without superstition, and without a peculiar worship apart from use. For the presbyter, as Eusebius says, lying sick, has the Eucharist with him at home and gives it to a young man to carry it to the sick man.

With the papalists it was Innocent III who first commanded that the Eucharist should be reserved in the church, under guard and under lock and key. A little later Honorius III decreed that whenever the reserved Eucharist is carried to a sick person the people should bow reverently. He also wanted lights to be carried before it at all times. Later popes added a certain number of indulgences, namely, 200 days in return for reverence when it was carried to a sick person with lights, 100 when it was carried without lights. These things are unknown to all of antiquity.

V. Various and strange questions and disputes, calculated rather to tear down faith than to build it up, were occasioned and spread about these reserved particles. Thus a legend about Basil invents the fiction that he divided the consecrated bread into three parts. With one he communed, another he placed in a golden dove suspended above the altar, and the third he reserved that it might be buried with him. This truly would be an extraordinary profanation of the Lord's Supper. That such a thing arose out of reservation is gathered from the fact that afterward it was forbidden to give the Eucharist to the dead.

VI. Now it is decreed that this custom [reservation] is necessary.

VII. Under the papacy only the species of bread is reserved, although examples concerning both species are extant, both in the history of Serapion and in that of Exuperius.

VIII. The opinion is invented and defended that blessing with the words of Christ is not effective and that it is not a true sacrament even though the Word of Christ comes to the elements of bread and wine, unless the consecration takes place in a church or at an altar which has been pontifically consecrated. Thus the genuineness of the Eucharist is judged to depend not so much on the words of Christ as on the place.

IX. There is added also this, that the Eucharist is not rightly consecrated for Communion apart from the act of the papalist sacrifice of the Mass.

X. Because the papalist carrying about and displaying of the bread apart from its use has no testimony of the true antiquity, therefore they fight about the reservation of the Eucharist for use in communing the sick in order that they may be able to bring forward some show of right for their reservation for the purpose of carrying about.

23 Because the ancient church did not judge the custom of reservation as it practiced it to be necessary, and we no longer have the causes which gave the ancients some occasion for reservation, and since the church under the papacy has departed far from the example of antiquity in the matter of reservation, and many abuses, various superstitions, and false and dangerous opinions have become attached to it, it is simplest, most correct, and safest that this whole matter should be examined according to the norm of the institution of Christ and that we should consider what comes closest to what is prescribed in the institution, agrees best with it, and serves for edification of the church. For that is done according to the example of the ancient church, which did this very thing in the dispute about private reservation, or reservation at home.

24 The matter is not obscure if we set before ourselves as norm and rule the description of the institution. For Christ first of all used His words, which He wanted to have come to the element in order that it might become a sacrament; He used them in the place and at the time where and when He was about to distribute Communion, and in the presence of those to whom He wanted to communicate His body and blood. Therefore it agrees better with the description of the institution and the example of Christ to recite the words of institution and by means of them to bless the Eucharist at the place and time of Communion, in the presence of those who are to be communed, rather than at another place and time in the absence of those to whom it is to be offered.

Second: The words of the Supper: "He said, 'Take, eat; do this,' " etc., are directed not to the elements but to those who were about to commune. Therefore it is not in accord with the institution to direct these words only to the bread and wine, and that in the absence of those who are to be communed.

Third: Christ did not want Communion to be a silent action, as a physician gives and applies a medicine prepared at another place and time, but when He gave the bread He had broken and the cup He had blessed to His disciples, He spoke. And indeed He added the command: "Do this in remembrance of Me." Paul interprets this as proclaiming the Lord's death. Indeed, he says that this proclamation ought to be made not only in blessing the elements, as though when they are eaten the action should be silent, but "As often as you eat this bread and drink of this cup, you proclaim the Lord's death." And He did not want this done only at the time of the apostles, but until the Lord comes to judgment. These things are certainly very clear.

Fourth: Comfort concerning the use and benefit of the Eucharist is necessary most of all for the sick. There is no doubt that this is included and taught in the words of Christ by means of which this sacrament is effected. Faith also seeks and apprehends it in the Word, as Paul says of Baptism: "Cleansing the church by the washing of water with the Word" (Eph. 5:26). Therefore it is right and beneficial that the words of the Supper, with which the bread and wine of the Eucharist are blessed, are recited in the presence and in the hearing of the sick person.

Fifth: In this way many questions and arguments about the particles of the elements reserved apart from use, which disturb the simplicity of the doctrine and faith concerning the Eucharist, are obviated and cut off.

Finally, because they make the custom of reservation absolutely necessary, Christian liberty must be expressed by an example, principally lest the genuineness of the Eucharist be thought to depend on the place where it is blessed, or as though the action of the papistical[57] sacrifice were necessary for the genuineness of the Eucharist.

25 For these reasons our men, in the Communion of the sick, recite the words of the Supper, which are in fact the consecration, in the presence of the sick person. Neither has anyone the right to reprove or to condemn us on account of this custom; for we are following both the prescription and the example of Christ, concerning whom the Father called out from heaven: "Hear Him." It is manifest that this custom agrees with the institution of Christ. And, according to Augustine, what decides in matters of faith is not: "This I say; that you say; that he says," but: "Thus says the Lord." And, speaking of the Supper, Cyprian says: "We ought not to give heed to what someone before us thought should be done, but to what He, who is before all, did first." This truly is the most ancient custom, with which the ancient church is not in conflict, in which

---

[57] One of the rare instances in which Chemnitz uses the pejorative term "papistical."

the custom of reservation was neither universal nor held to be necessary.

Although they had churches or parishes in which lawful and orderly assemblies were held, in which also the regular administration of the sacraments was celebrated, nevertheless they did not want the consecration of the Eucharist bound to these places. For also the canon *Sicut non alii, De consecratione,* dist. 1, makes an exception of a case of necessity, and adds, "Because necessity knows no law." And what follows, namely, that the Eucharist should not be celebrated in homes, the gloss explains: "Unless necessity compels." And the Council of Agatha, 1. Canon 21: "If anyone wishes to have a prayer chapel in the country outside the parishes in which there is a lawful and regular worship service, for other festival occasions, in order to hold Masses there, we permit it, except on major festivals." And the Canon of Orleans says: "It is permitted to every believer to have a prayer chapel in his house. It is not, however, permitted to celebrate Masses there." But the Canon of the Sixth Synod, *De consecratione,* dist. 1, ch. *Clericos,* says that with the permission of the bishop this can be done. Yes, in a rural house where there was no special prayer chapel a presbyter celebrates the Eucharist, as reported by Augustine, *De civitate Dei,* Bk. 22, ch. 8.

But what need is there of anxiously searching for such testimonies and examples to see whether a peculiar quality of place is necessary for a true Eucharist, when the examples of Christ and of the apostles are sufficient for all and ought to satisfy all? For it was on an ordinary table in the home of a host that Christ celebrated His first Lord's Supper. Neither did the apostles have special church buildings, but even as they "devoted themselves to the apostles' teaching and . . . prayer" when they gathered in private houses, so also they broke the bread in the homes. For the sake of order it is useful to have set and public places for the administration of the sacraments, but to tie it to these special and public places in such a way that they pretend that the sacraments are not true sacraments if, in case of urgent necessity and with Christ's institution observed, they are celebrated and administered in some ordinary or private place, as if the truth and efficacy of the sacraments depended not on the words of Christ but on the quality of places, is certainly totally false. This is clear with respect to the administration of Baptism in common or private places if the case and necessity occasions it. For even as the circumstance of time, so also the circumstance of place is not required for the essence of the sacraments.

SECTION VIII

Concerning the Preparation
Which Is to Be Exercised in Order That One
May Receive the Holy Eucharist Worthily

Chapter VII

If it is not seemly that a person should approach any sacred function at all except in a holy manner, then surely, the more a Christian man is informed with respect to the holiness and divine quality of this sacrament, the more he should diligently take heed not to approach this sacrament without great reverence and holiness, particularly since we read with the apostle these words full of awe: "Whoever eats and drinks unworthily, eats and drinks judgment to himself, not discerning the Lord's body."

Therefore he who would communicate is to be reminded of the precept: "Let a man examine himself." The custom of the Church declares that this examination is necessary so that no one who is conscious of having committed a mortal sin, no matter how contrite he may seem to himself, ought to approach the holy Eucharist without prior sacramental confession. This holy synod has decreed that this should be observed in perpetuity by all Christians, also by the priests on whom it is incumbent by virtue of their office to celebrate, provided there is no lack of a confessor. But if, in case of urgent necessity, he celebrates without prior confession, let him confess as soon as possible.

CANON XI

If anyone says that faith alone is sufficient preparation for receiving the most holy sacrament of the Eucharist, let him be anathema. And lest so great a sacrament be received unworthily, and therefore for death and condemnation, this holy synod decrees and declares that, in the case of those whose conscience is burdened with mortal sin, sacramental confession must of necessity go before, no matter how contrite they consider themselves, provided a confessor can be had. But if anyone shall presume to teach, preach, or stubbornly assert, or even in a public disputation to defend the contrary, he is by that very act excommunicated.

Examination

1 I shall explain first of all in a few words what is the teaching and understanding of our churches concerning this preparation on the basis of the Word of God. After that it will not be obscure what it is that the

314

papalists want to condemn in this our teaching. The antithesis will also show the errors in the papalist teaching concerning this preparation.

2 First of all, so far as the question whether there is such a preparation is concerned, there is no doubt or controversy. For Paul clearly asserts that not all receive the Eucharist worthily, but many unworthily. Neither does he want unworthy reception to be something about which one does not trouble oneself, as if it either did not matter or were some infirmity which clearly did not harm one's salvation, even if one did eat and drink unworthily at the Lord's Supper. Rather, he thunders with great vehemence against such levity and security, and affirms that those who eat unworthily eat judgment to themselves, so that they become guilty of violating the body and blood of Christ. And indeed he adds that God often shows this judgment on those who eat unworthily already in this life with external punishments. Therefore he demands that whoever is about to approach this table should first examine himself, and so eat of that bread and drink of that cup. Therefore Paul does not preach concerning this examination and preparation in a casual or cold manner, but earnestly and with true apostolic fervor, lest someone partake of the Eucharist unworthily.

There is also no doubt that it is incumbent on all ministers of the church that they diligently and earnestly admonish their parishioners, and indeed set before them the very grave threats of guilt and divine judgment, lest they approach the Lord's Supper without making the prior examination or preparation of which Paul speaks. And if those sin who from ignorance or thoughtlessness eat unworthily, the sin of those will be much more grievous who, although they owe it from the nature of their office, yet do not instruct them by reproving, admonishing, exhorting, and teaching that and in what way they should examine themselves, or what preparation they should make, lest they eat and drink unworthily to their judgment, but may worthily receive the Eucharist together with its fruits and effects. These things are diligently and earnestly taught and transmitted among us. This I wanted to show briefly, lest someone should suspect that there is a controversy over this matter, as if we held and taught that no examination or preparation at all should be made in order that a person may receive the Eucharist worthily.

3 But this must chiefly be asked, what and what manner of preparation is to be made, or what the Pauline examination is and in what it consists, in order that we may be able to eat and drink worthily in the Lord's Supper, so that we may be partakers of all the good things or benefits which are offered in the Supper. This is truly a difficult question, and of the greatest importance. Therefore it is not to be explained either by our own private thoughts, or by the opinions of other men, no matter who they may be, but it must be explained according to the teaching of the Word of God. Moreover, we must here understand worthiness, not merit, nor yet a comparison or analogy of excellence in the recipient with the excellence of the food, namely, the body and blood of Christ. For so the ancients piously used the words of the centurion: "Lord, I am not worthy to have You come under my roof," and what Jacob says: "I am not worthy of the least of all the steadfast love and all the faithfulness which Thou hast shown to Thy servant." David also says: "Who am I, and what is my father's house?" Likewise: "What is man, that Thou art mindful of him?"

But to eat worthily is to use the Eucharist in the manner and for the purpose for which it was instituted by the Son of God Himself. For so Ambrose correctly understands and explains this worthiness. Paul indeed embraces this whole teaching in the one word *dokimazein,* which means to think about, consider, and investigate whatever we are examining. Thus Rom. 12:2: The godly, commanded to institute the new obedience, ought to prove what is the good will of God. Eph. 5:17: They understand what pleases God. 1 John 4:1: We are commanded to "test the spirits to see whether they are of God." 1 Thess. 5:21: "Test everything; hold fast what is good." And Rom. 1:28: A *nous adokimos,* "base mind," is one which orders life in such a way that it neither considers nor cares, even though the things it does are condemned by God and man and by its own conscience.

Therefore that man may be said to examine himself in preparation for the Lord's Supper who in a certain way and according to a certain rule looks attentively at himself and examines and investigates whether he approaches the sacrament with the kind of heart and disposition of mind which the institution of the Lord's Supper prescribes and requires. For St. Paul says thus (2 Cor. 13:5): "Examine yourselves, to see whether you are holding to your faith," and he immediately explains the word "examine," namely, "that you may know that Christ is in you." Therefore the interpretation of the word *dokimazein* shows that he who is about to approach the Lord's table ought to regard attentively, explore, and examine his mind, heart, conscience, and his whole self, whether he is able to use the Lord's Supper, not to judgment but worthily and with profit.

Now there needs to be some sure norm and rule for this consideration, examination, and exploration, so that anyone who disagrees with it and fights against it is judged to eat unworthily. If, however, the mind is informed and disposed according to this rule, then we may be certain that we are not eating and drinking unworthily to judgment in the Lord's

Supper, but worthily and with profit. However, the simplest, surest, and safest norm and rule is the institution of the Lord's Supper itself. For also Paul shows (1 Cor. 11:23-34) from the rule of the institution that some among the Corinthians were eating unworthily. And when he wants to show how they could eat the Lord's Supper worthily and with profit, he sets before them the institution itself as he had received it from the Lord.

4 For the sake of teaching, this instruction about the eating of the unworthy and the examination or preparation of the worthy can be divided into three parts:

I. That the mind, from the words of institution, understands, believes with firm assent, and in the use of the Lord's Supper reverently ponders what this sacrament is, what its use is, and what the nature of this whole action is—that here the Son of God, God and man, is Himself present, offering and imparting through the ministry to those who eat, together with the bread and wine, His body and blood, in order that by means of this most precious testimony and pledge He may unite Himself with us and apply, seal, and confirm to us the New Testament covenant of grace. And this faith, resting on the words of institution, excites and shapes reverence and devotion of mind as this sacrament is used.

Even as the institution itself shows that this is necessary and required for worthy eating, it is seen also from Paul, who says that those among the Corinthians were eating unworthily who thought no more reverently of the Lord's Supper than about some ordinary supping together, came to it with no greater reverence and devotion, and thus did not discern the body of the Lord, that is, they did not consider how immeasurably more precious and worthy is the food of the Lord's Supper than in other, ordinary suppers, where the gifts of God are also present. Therefore those persons eat unworthily who approach the Lord's Supper filled with perverse, wicked, or worldly opinions concerning this sacrament; likewise those who approach either with stupid or with studied ignorance, or with irreligious thoughtlessness with respect to the teaching and faith of the Eucharist, so that they plainly either do not understand or do not at all consider what manner of action is there instituted by the Son of God Himself, and so they bring no devotion of mind or reverence toward this action of the Son of God. Ambrose calls it receiving the body of the Lord thoughtlessly and negligently. Here also belong those who either pervert the action of the institution or invent other uses and purposes for it, outside of or against the institution.

II. Those eat unworthily who come without repentance, that is, those who do not consider their sins in such a way that they may grieve over them. These are not greatly terrified by a consideration of the wrath of God, but persevere in transgressions against conscience, yield to evil lusts, and do not lay aside the purpose to do evil. For Christ says: "Do this in remembrance of Me." Paul interprets this as referring to proclaiming the death of Christ. Now consideration of the death of Christ is at the same time also a forcible reminder of the abominable nature of sin, and of the fierce wrath of God against our sins. Since the virtues or merits neither of any men or angels were able to placate this wrath, it was necessary that it should be placated by the death of the Son Himself.

Now the Son of God did not institute His Supper in order that we might learn to think lightly of sin, and by its use be strengthened in the purpose to sin, as though we received there the privilege of being base, without the fear of God, without contrition and conversion, and could securely persevere and continue in sins against conscience or return to them. Therefore anyone who approaches the Lord's Supper with such a purpose and with this mind, by this very fact treats the body of Christ with contempt and heaps up new sins on top of his prior sins by this even sadder offense.

Therefore he who would eat worthily at the Lord's Supper ought to examine himself that he may bring to it repentance or the fear of God. Now repentance embraces at the same time also a good purpose. Thus Paul says that those Corinthians were eating unworthily who came together not for better but for worse, who nourished dissension, shamed the poor, and despised the church of God at the very celebration of the Lord's Supper.

III. To worthy or salutary eating at the Lord's Supper faith is above all things necessary. For in the action of the Lord's Supper the Son of God, by the imparting of His body and blood, offers, applies, and seals the remission of sins and the whole benefit of the New Testament. Now this promise calls for faith; not merely that you say in a general way that these things are true which God promises about His grace on account of the merit of the Mediator, but that in the Supper the Son of God by a special action testifies that He wants to receive into the fellowship of His body and blood everyone who eats, that by the impartation of His body and blood He wants to communicate, give, apply, and seal to each one the benefits of the New Testament. Therefore faith is called for, seeking and accepting with thanksgiving the blessings there offered and given, so that all may confess that this promise pertains also to them, that it is communicated, applied, and sealed to them, and that this is done by the imparting of a most precious pledge—the body and blood of Christ. Yes, it is for this reason that we come to the Lord's Supper, that this faith may be kindled and strengthened in us. For this is the true remembrance of Christ. And in the words of institution Christ says to everyone who eats: "Take, this is My body, which is given for you; take, this is the New Testament in My blood, which is shed for you for the remission of sins."

Ambrose testifies that in former times the Eucharist was given with these words. To these words all who ate added the confession of their faith by answering, "Amen." This formula pleases me exceedingly, because it applies the very words of institution to everyone who eats, in harmony with the true nature of the sacrament. Therefore those do not do rightly who, though they are truly penitent over former sins, flee the use of the sacrament because they are conscious of sins and are weak in faith. For this glorious pledge is offered to us in order that, reconciled to God, we may be restored to the covenant of grace of the New Testament from which we had fallen and be confirmed in it, and that, by means of its use, faith may be kindled and strengthened.

5 The antithesis will show who those are who eat unworthily, because they do not bring true faith to it, namely, those who imagine that the eating profits *ex opere operato,* without a good impulse in the user, who as they eat rely for its salutary use on their own worthiness and purity, as though they were worthy of this heavenly food, or who imagine that by the act of eating they merit remission of sins. For in His Supper Christ does not want to distribute the merits and rewards of our works, but even as He offers His merits gratis there, so He wants them accepted by faith. Likewise, those who teach that men neither should nor can assert that in the use of the Supper the benefits of the New Testament are certainly given and applied to them, but should always be carried to and fro in uncertain doubting, even though the sealing is made by the offering of the body and blood of Christ—surely these make the Son of God Himself a liar in the institution of the Supper.

Also those eat unworthily who come without faith in this sense, that they give no thought to what they seek and receive there; likewise those who come with an Epicurean persuasion, as though the privilege of turpitude were given there, so that they might be able further to persevere freely and with impunity in crimes, continue in them or return to them. For true faith does not ask and seek that sins may remain and be increased; it asks and seeks remission of sins and liberation from sins. And this faith is afterward the mother of the good intention to avoid sins in the future and to obey God according to His commandments.

6 There is no doubt that this is the true examination or preparation, for it agrees with the norm or rule of the institution of the Lord's Supper.

Moreover there is preserved in our churches the godly practice that all who are about to partake of the Supper are first examined, to ascertain what they understand concerning the sacrament. They are admonished to examine themselves, as has been said, lest they eat unworthily; the more unlearned are instructed how they should and can examine themselves.

Moreover, because the Lord's Supper was instituted so that by its use faith in the reconciliation with God may be confirmed and sealed, a godly person will not neglect but will with thanksgiving use all those means by which God has proposed to faith that it should seek and receive grace or reconciliation, such as the proclamation and hearing of the Gospel promise, either in public preaching or in private absolution. Afterward there follows the confirmation and sealing of this application in participation in the Lord's Supper. For these reasons and in this manner the practice of confession before Communion is devoutly observed in our churches.

7 This examination and preparation is not, however, prescribed and demanded in such a way that it is wholly perfect, without any infirmity and weakness, so that it lacks nothing. For Christ instituted His Supper for this purpose, that repentance may be kindled and increased in us by the remembrance of His death, in order that faith may be strengthened and invigorated by the giving and sealing of the New Testament in the use of the Supper. He knows our frame, that we are flesh; therefore He joins Himself to us by the bestowal of His most holy body and blood, that the body of sin may be mortified, the old leaven more and more purged out, and the newness which has been begun may grow and increase. Therefore the preparation is not required that we may, by our own worthiness and purity, render ourselves worthy of this food so that it may be salutary for us because we are worthy of it on account of our own cleanness. For this persuasion truly makes men unworthy. But Paul demands an examination in order that we may become hungry and thirsty for this food and drink, which is set before us for our salvation in this Supper, and that, knowing our weakness, we may know that we have need of the medicine and remedy of this physician, who provides this Supper for us, and in what way it must be received and used in a salutary manner for our healing.

8 This is the simple and true teaching, drawn from and constructed on the basis of the words of institution, about the examination or preparation which a person should employ in order that he may receive the sacrament worthily. For it is on this basis that Paul preaches to the Corinthians about the eating of the unworthy.

So also the ancients speak about the preparation. Hesychius says that that person receives the Eucharist unworthily, through ignorance, who does not know its power and greatness. Augustine says: "This sacrament looks for the hunger of the inner man"; therefore whoever does not feel his sin and infirmity is not fit to partake of this sacrament. The judgment of Chrysostom is: "Because those who are well do not need a physician, but those who are ill, therefore that person is shut out from the power of this sacrament who, proud of himself, approaches resolutely but with disgust." The same man says: "Let no one commune unless he is a disciple of Christ; otherwise he eats and drinks judgment to himself." Augustine frequently argues thus: "Whoever believes in Christ eats Him in order that He may both remain in Christ and also have Christ remaining in him. But whoever comes to the Eucharist devoid of this faith indeed eats outwardly but not inwardly. He lays hold with his teeth but does not grasp with his mind." It is as Gregory says: "He receives the body and blood of Christ according to its substance but not according to its saving power. He receives the sacrament, but the life of Christ he does not receive." Very beautiful is the statement of Augustine in which he says of his mother Monica that she bound her soul with the chain of faith to that sacrifice which is dispensed in the Lord's Supper so that neither lion nor dragon could tear it away.

9 Now that these things have been thus set forth, the manner of our examination of the seventh chapter and the 11th canon will be neither difficult nor unclear.

I. They say they condemn those who hold that faith alone is sufficient preparation for taking the Eucharist. The words are, however, put in such a way that they seem to ascribe to us this opinion: Even if a person perseveres in crimes without repentance and holds fast to the purpose to do evil, so long only as he holds the historical faith concerning the essence of the sacrament, or holds the Epicurean persuasion that impenitence is not punishable, he is sufficiently prepared for worthy eating of the Lord's Supper. But that this is falsely attributed to our churches is clear from what we have said concerning the true examination.

II. Let us consider why they use this trick. The reader will discover that in this whole chapter, where they specifically undertook an explanation of the teaching about preparation for taking the Eucharist, no mention is made by so much as even one syllable of faith, which seeks, apprehends, and accepts the promise of the New Testament, which the Son of God offers, communicates, and seals by the giving of His body and blood in the use of the sacrament to each and every one who eats. For this faith, applying as it does the forgiveness of sins to individuals, since indeed it is sealed and strengthened by partaking of Christ's body and blood, is diametrically opposed to the teaching of the papalists concerning uncertainty. It is for this reason that they are unwilling to concede any place to this faith in the preparation for the salutary reception of the Eucharist. Nevertheless they have not dared to banish faith simply and clearly from this preparation. Therefore they set faith alone in opposition to repentance or contrition, and condemn anyone who says that faith alone is sufficient preparation. If this is understood of the opinion of ungodly persons, who imagine that they can continue without repentance in the purpose to do evil, I willingly grant this. But it is a far different thing, as I will now show, which they have undertaken to condemn in this canon.

III. We must observe in what sense Luther, in *De captivitate Babylonica,* says that worthy preparation is nothing else than faith that trusts the divine promise set forth and offered in the Lord's Supper. For it is from there that the men of Trent picked something in the 11th canon. Luther does not, however, exclude the acknowledging of our sins, and contrition or repentance, but is fighting against the papalists, who themselves have and teach others many and varied preparatory works. They think that when they have performed these they are sufficiently worthily prepared to attend or hear Mass, and also for the Communion itself, with the result that they are not concerned about faith, which asks, seeks, apprehends, and accepts the promise of the New Testament in the Supper. They also demand penitence in order that they may ascribe worthy preparation to its works and merit, so that salutary eating may rest on our preparatory works by virtue of our worthiness and purity.

Against these opinions Luther teaches that the Lord's Supper was instituted by Christ not that we may there confer something on God and thus procure salvation for ourselves in the Lord's Supper by our works; but what the Son of God earned by offering up His body and shedding His blood, that, His gratuitous mercy coming before any merit on our part, He offers to us in the promise of the Gospel, to which He adds as pledge and seal the gift of His body and blood under the bread and wine. Now the gratuitous promise of the Gospel is apprehended and accepted, not by our works and merits but by faith (Rom. 4 and 11). And this is the task solely of faith, without which the promise is of no use to us, as we have shown in the first part of the *Examination* about faith.

In addition the contrast between our unworthiness and the divine excellence of the food and drink in the Eucharist disturbs and terrifies the conscience. From this temptation we cannot escape if we place our confidence in our contrition, confession, satisfaction, preparatory works, and our own worthiness, purity, and capability. Therefore we must look at the promise of the New Testament which is set before us in the Lord's Supper and freely offers to us the body and blood of Christ, and with them all the benefits of the New Testament. For their acceptance it does not demand our merits and worthiness but only that we acknowledge our poverty, weakness, and unworthiness, and hunger and thirst for this grace and so accept by faith the things which, because of the merit of Christ, are offered to us in the Lord's Supper. Surely these things, flowing as they do from the nature of the gratuitous promise of the Gospel and from the mutual relation between the promise and faith, are most certain and true. It is in this sense that Luther says that faith alone is the true and sufficient preparation for receiving the Eucharist. He specifically states: "Upon this faith there will follow at once of its own accord the sweetest mood of the heart, that is, love." He also teaches that this faith is manifest in repentance.

This is the teaching which Canon XI condemns in order that it may uphold the contrary dogma about trust in our contrition, confession, satisfaction, worthiness, and purity through preparatory works, in order that they may teach that salutary eating in the Lord's Supper depends on these. But in this way the enjoyment of the Lord's Supper is rendered either useless or hollow to us, or certainly doubtful and uncertain. For the scholastics teach that there is a certain preparation which is sufficient and true. Bonaventura says that this consists in the expulsion of all sin, in reverence and love. Those who come so prepared, they say, attain the benefit of the Eucharist. They say that another preparation is that of probability, when a person does what he can, and believes in the judgment of his own conscience that he is prepared. But this preparation is often not truly sufficient. Here they agree that whoever comes thus does not receive the effects of this sacrament. They argue, however, over whether such a one eats unworthily and involves himself in a new mortal sin by communing thus. And since it is uncertain when we have a truly sufficient preparation, and when of probability only, the conscience will always remain uncertain whether one eats worthily or unworthily. Thus the necessary consolation which is set before us by Christ in the use of the Lord's Supper will always be wrenched away. This truly is, briefly put, the way by which they scare people away from more frequent use of the Lord's Supper, in order that they may the more avidly follow and embrace the trafficking in private Masses, which is said to be meritorious without peril to wipe out any and all mortal sins. The reader should know that all these things are wrapped up in this 11th canon, which are not easily noticed at first glance, unless the debates from which this canon was plucked are looked into and considered.

IV. This also must be carefully weighed, that Chapter VII says that one should not go to the Eucharist without great holiness, lest we eat judgment. Now the apostles quite commonly use the phrase which calls believers or disciples of Christ saints, to whom also God Himself says: "You shall be holy, because I am holy." However, even as this word *qadosh* signifies what has been separated from common and worldly use for sacred use, and is applied to either divine service or cult, so people are called saints not because they are so perfectly pure and clean and cleansed of all filth that they either can or should stand before God relying on their own purity; but those are called saints both by way of imputation and by way of a beginning who have turned from sin by repentance and have by faith been implanted in Christ, who is our sanctification, and have begun to be renewed by the Holy Spirit, even though they confess with Paul (Rom. 7:7-25) and with Isaiah (64:6) that they are still contaminated with much wrongdoing and uncleanness. They are called saints in Christ Jesus. Thus therefore the ancient church rightly cried out before the Communion: "Holy things for the saints." For Communion is given to none but the baptized, whom Christ has sanctified, cleansing them by the washing of water with the Word (Eph. 5:26). And certainly, as has been said, those who would come to Communion worthily ought to bring repentance, which according to the Hebrew way of speaking is sanctification, that is, a turning from sin or uncleanness. They ought also to bring faith in the promise of the Gospel. Truly, the Word is the truth in which those who believe are sanctified (John 17:17), for by faith the hearts are purified. (Acts 15:9)

We do not deny that one must come to the Eucharist with this kind of holiness, lest we eat judgment to ourselves. For whoever perseveres in sin without repentance, and holds fast to the purpose of doing evil, is truly unclean and unworthy. In this sense Augustine says, *In Johannem homilia*, 88: "He who comes ought to be filled with holiness, and spotless." Thus also Hesychius, Bk. 6, ch. 22, *Levitici*, says that the defiled are not to be admitted, nor the pure to be kept away. And he adds the explanation: "If a person who examines himself is conscious of sin in himself and feels that his soul is polluted, he is undoubtedly penitent, and after repentance is able to eat of the bread and to drink of the holy and unstained cup." Also he says, Bk. 7, ch. 26, that this is proof that with a pure heart and conscience, intent upon repentance for those things in which he once sinned, he participates with the saints for ablution of their sins. This is the intent also of the saying of Augustine: "Let him who wishes to receive life change his life. For if he does not change his life, he will receive life to judgment and will be corrupted by it rather than healed, killed rather than made alive." *De ecclesiasticis dogmatibus,* ch. 53. "I say that whoever still has the will to sin is burdened even more, rather than purified, by reception of the sacrament."

This is also the purpose of the custom of the ancient church, which dismissed from the assembly the catechumens, and those on whom public penitence had been imposed on account of known crimes, when the time had come to partake of the sacrament. Then the priest, about to offer the Eucharist to the people, said with a loud voice: "Holy things for the saints," in order that everyone might examine himself. If what Chapter VII says is understood in this sense, that one must come to the Eucharist with great reverence and holiness, I do not oppose it, for we also teach the same thing. But I see that the papalists interpret holiness to mean that we should by our own works and satisfactions, before communing, acquire for ourselves the highest purity and innocence of soul (for so Andrada says), so that it is not necessary in receiving the sacrament to seek and receive either the application or the sealing of the remission of sins but that our purity is already worthy that Christ should join and communicate Himself to it with His body and all His benefits. For with this one argument Andrada proves that remission of sins is not received in the use of the Lord's Supper. This audacity conflicts with the very institution of the Lord's Supper and either makes proud Pharisees or frightens terrified consciences away from the use of the Lord's Supper.

V. They say that this examination is necessary in order that sacramental confession may of necessity precede Communion. I have indicated above in a few words for what use confession is preserved in our churches as useful for a true examination. But the men of Trent place the preparation in the work of confession itself, in the enumeration of all transgressions, and especially in the works of satisfaction which are imposed at confession. This examination they want to set down as necessary. But we shall have to speak of sacramental confession later, under the topic of penitence. For the present I only wanted to show what kind of preparation the papalists dispute about after they have buried faith.

SECTION IX

Concerning the Use of This Admirable Sacrament

Chapter VIII

So far as the use is concerned, our fathers rightly and wisely distinguished three ways of receiving this holy sacrament. They taught that some take it sacramentally only, as sinners do; others only spiritually, namely, those who, eating in desire the heavenly bread set before them, experience its fruit and usefulness through a living faith which works by love; the third kind take it both sacramentally and spiritually; these are the ones who previously so examine and prepare themselves that they come to this divine table clothed in the wedding garment.

It has, however, always been the custom in the Church of God, when the sacrament was received, that the lay people received the Communion from the priests, while the celebrating priests communicated themselves; this custom, coming down as it were from apostolic tradition, ought rightfully and deservedly to be retained, etc.

CANON VIII

If anyone says that Christ, offered in the Eucharist, is eaten only spiritually, and not also sacramentally and in reality, let him be anathema.

CANON X[58]

If anyone says that it is not lawful for the celebrating priest to communicate himself, let him be anathema.

Examination

1 This distinction of the ancients, that the body and blood of Christ is eaten and drunk in three ways, I approve as true, fitting, and useful.

First, it is received spiritually only, by those who also apart from the use of the Lord's Supper apprehend and apply to themselves the merit of the offered body and the shed blood of Christ by true faith in the promise of the Gospel. Of this eating Christ preaches particularly in John 6.

Second, sacramentally only, by those who eat unworthily of that bread of which Christ declares: "This is My body."

Third, both sacramentally and spiritually, by those who, in the use of

---

58 Later editions incorrectly have "Canon IX."

the Lord's Supper, receive the body and blood of Christ orally together with the bread and wine. Thus at one and the same time faith, according to the promise, holds that in this eating Christ applies and seals to it His benefits, which He earned by offering up His body and shedding His blood, and with thankful mind and joyful confidence embraces and accepts these benefits.

I do not approve of the opinion of those who hold otherwise than the words of institution teach, namely, that in the use of the Lord's Supper the body and blood of Christ are eaten only spiritually, by faith, so that our mouth receives only the elements of bread and wine, not however also at the same time the body and blood of Christ, though in a supernatural and heavenly manner. For of that which is offered to us in the Lord's Supper, which our mouth receives, the Son of God declares: "This is My body; this is My blood." But because I have, in a small book, explained the grounds for this conviction more fully, I shall add nothing here.

2 Now I would not search further into this eighth chapter if I had not in earlier chapters a number of times noticed snares, where at first glance one would not have suspected them. Two things, so far as I can see, have been stated treacherously in this chapter. These, I judge, must be examined.

3 The first is that they do not say that the body and blood of Christ are eaten and drunk by true believers also outside of the action and use of the Lord's Supper, but say that the sacrament of the Eucharist is eaten only spiritually by some who do not receive with their mouth what is offered in the Lord's Supper. And indeed because they say that the Eucharist is eaten in desire, one could understand this of those who are unable to have the full sacramental Communion, or of those in the assembly of the church who, also when they do not commune sacramentally, nevertheless, because they cling to Christ in true faith, eat His flesh and drink His blood spiritually. But this, I think, is not what the men of Trent want. But because in their private Masses, on account of the circumstances, the sacrament is offered to no one, there is no one who receives, eats, and drinks. Nevertheless, lest they seem manifestly and intentionally to violate the institution of Christ, they teach that the command of Christ, where He describes the use of the Lord's Supper in the words: He gave it to them saying, "Take, eat, drink; do this in remembrance of Me," is satisfied even if the Mass is celebrated in such a way that the sacrament is distributed to no one and no one receives and eats, so long only as a few eat the flesh of Christ spiritually, by a living faith.

Now, in John 6 Christ describes one mode of eating His flesh, apart from the action and use of His Supper. However, He instituted and described another mode, which is to take place in the action and use of His Supper, namely, that together with the bread and wine His body and blood be offered, taken with the mouth, eaten and drunk, and that in remembrance of Him, that is, that to the sacramental eating there come the spiritual. Therefore the action of the Lord's Supper is not satisfied by spiritual eating alone, namely, if the sacrament is offered to no one and no one receives it, eats and drinks.

4 The other point which I judge should be examined is when they argue concerning the custom according to which the celebrating priest communicates himself. I do not, indeed, judge that it militates against the essence of the institution of the Lord's Supper if the minister who communicates others also himself eats of that bread and drinks of that cup, particularly since examples of the ancient church bear witness to it. This is done simply, without superstition, in our churches. But it is not possible to prove that that custom, as having come down from apostolic tradition, must necessarily always be observed. Things which do not have a commandment of God in Scripture must not be laid on conscience as necessary. Nicholas of Cusa says to the Bohemian clergy that the celebrating priest customarily receives the cup from the hand of a deacon.

5 There is, however, something else still for which Canon X treacherously works, namely, that it is a true Communion, in harmony with the institution of Christ, even if the priest alone, in a private Mass, communicates only himself. This does not agree with the description of Paul (1 Cor 11:20-21), for he says that the Lord's Supper cannot be celebrated if everyone goes ahead with his own private or special supper, which he does not share with anyone else. Christ gave it to others also, to whom He said: "Take, eat." Although it is therefore not unlawful if the celebrating priest communicates himself along with others, it is nevertheless not a true Communion of the Lord's Supper if the priest in a private Mass holds a private supper which he shares with no one.

These are the things in this chapter which I judge to have been stated treacherously and which are in need of some reflection.

SECTION X
Concerning the Frequency of the Eucharist

CANON IX[59]

If anyone denies that each and all believers in Christ of either sex, when they have reached the age of discretion, are held to commune every year, at least at Easter, according to the precept of Holy Mother Church, let him be anathema.

Examination

1 Among other complaints about the collapse of doctrine and discipline in the church, this is not the least, that the papalists have hindered people from more frequent use of the Eucharist, in part by persuading them to observe private Masses, in part frightening them away through their teaching about preparation. Thus the common people were persuaded that it was enough and more than enough if they communed once a year, and that this was a more excellent work if it was done at a set time, namely at Easter, not from proper devotion, on account of the commandment of Christ, but on account of a precept of the church. I would have thought that if the Synod of Trent would make some statement about this matter, even if they wanted to retain the custom of Communion at Easter, they would nevertheless exhort people to more frequent and diligent Communion throughout the year and not drive them to Communion at Easter through the necessity of a command or law. But even as in this entire synod it was their purpose not to correct even the least bit of the things which are accepted and customary under the papacy according to the norm of the Word, or at least to mitigate it, but simply to repeat, confirm, and strengthen each and every thing, whatever it may be, so throughout this whole session they were not willing to say one word about more frequent use of the Eucharist, but in the end repeat the chapter: everyone of either sex; concerning one Communion a year; and this at a stated time; and because of the precept of the church.

Nevertheless, just in passing, and very lightly, there is added the little word *saltem* [at least], lest they seem to have prohibited entirely if

---

[59] Later editions incorrectly have "Canon X."

someone wished to commune more frequently. Meanwhile the conviction remains that it is enough if a person uses Communion once a year. But if someone uses it more frequently, there is at once attached to it the idea of merit, of a work of supererogation, because it is not done on the basis of a commandment. We shall therefore note down a few things concerning the time of Communion.

2 Now indeed Christ exercised diligent care in the institution lest someone should think that Communion is bound to a certain time, because He instituted His Supper at the time when the Jews, according to the Law, ate the Passover. For there was a set day in a certain month, appointed beforehand, for eating the Passover. For He says: "This do, as often as you eat and drink, in remembrance of Me." This phrase, omitted by the other evangelists, Paul repeats twice with special care. The words "as often as" are to teach us two things: first, that we should not think that the celebration or reception of the Lord's Supper is like the Passover of the Jews, bound to a certain fixed time; second, that we should not think that that of which Christ says, "Do this" should be done only once a year, as it was sufficient under the Law to eat the Passover only once a year. In fact, it was not lawful to eat it either oftener or at another time of the year than had been predetermined in the Law, whether for the clean or for the unclean. It is very significant that Paul says, by way of what may be done, "as often as you eat and drink." It is therefore wholly certain and clear from the institution of Christ that, as partaking of the Lord's Supper is not bound to a certain or fixed time of the year, so also it is not to be used only once a year. For Christ sets the words "as often as you drink," etc., over against the Jewish Passover, which was celebrated only once a year, and at a fixed time of the year.

Nevertheless, He did not want to permit believers to use Communion arbitrarily, so that it would make no difference whether they used it occasionally or not at all or when they pleased, as one does in matters indifferent. For He does not say: "When it pleases you," as in indifferent matters, but says: "As often as you do this." It is not the same as with Baptism; we are baptized only once, but it is not sufficient to use the Lord's Supper only once. For He says: "As often as," in order that we may eat of that bread and drink of that cup as often as we recognize and feel that that medicine and remedy which our Good Samaritan pours into our wounds is useful and necessary to us, so long only as we examine ourselves lest we receive it to judgment. For the rule about when and how often one should go to Communion must be taken: I. From the teaching about the fruit and power of the Eucharist, namely, when and as often as we recognize that we have need of this power; II. From the teaching about self-examination, lest we receive it unworthily.

On this basis people are to be taught, admonished, and exhorted to more diligent and frequent use of the Eucharist. For because Christ says: "As often as you do this," it is wholly His will that those who are His disciples should do this frequently. Therefore those are not true and faithful ministers of Christ who in any manner whatever lead or frighten people away from more frequent use and reception of the Eucharist.

3 There are beautiful examples of frequent use of the Eucharist from the true antiquity. Some had the custom of receiving the Eucharist daily, some twice a week, some on the Lord's day, Wednesday, Friday, and Saturday, some only on the Lord's Day. Testimonies to this are found with Jerome, in the epistle to Lucinius; with Ambrose, on 1 Tim. 2; with Augustine, Letter No. 118; *De fide ad Petrum,* ch. 19; *De ecclesiasticis dogmatibus,* ch. 53; with Socrates, Bk. 5, ch. 22.

There was a custom in the ancient church which pertains most particularly to the explanation of this canon, namely, that at the more solemn festivals the whole multitude came together at the larger churches and there a solemn Communion was celebrated, so that everyone might show by a public profession that he was a member of the church. Thus the First Council of Agde,[60] Canon 21, permits the use of Communion in private prayer chapels, but wants all to come together on the major festivals to their parish churches, where the lawful assembly is ordinarily held. And in *De consecratione,* dist. 2, ch. *Saeculares,* the Lord's birthday, Easter, and Pentecost are named. Chrysostom indicates that such a solemn Communion had been celebrated in his church at Easter, Homily 11, *Ad populum Antiochenum.* But writing on Heb. 10 he mentions one reception a year. On this account Leo writes to Dioscurus of Alexandria: "If a more solemn festival should bring together a more numerous assembly of people, so that one church could not receive them all at one time, the offering of the sacrifice should undoubtedly be repeated," etc. After this custom had broken down, a number of Masses remained on one day in the same church, apart from the first and true use.

Rhenanus thinks this vestige remains from the more frequent assemblies for the solemn Communion, after this custom had fallen away, that the market days in the more populous cities of Germany are still called masses. This solemn Communion was not at first instituted with bad

---

[60] This council, called *Agathense* in the ancient records, was held A.D. 506 in what is now the town of Agde on the Mediterranean coast of France. The canons of this council are found in Mansi, *Collectio,* VIII, 319 f.

intent, but that all might show by a public profession that they are members of the true church, that as there is one bread the many might be reminded that they are one body, that they might show they are different from all heretics, and that in this way unity and consensus in doctrine and faith might be preserved. Thus the canon of the Synod of Agde says: "The lay people who do not commune on the Lord's birthday, Easter, and Pentecost are not to be reckoned among the catholics." But this custom, though not in itself evil, soon degenerated into abuse. For many thought it was sufficient if they communed only at these more solemn times; at other times they neither cared about nor sought Communion, particularly since they saw that hermits came forth only once a year or even after two years from the desert to the churches for Communion, as Chrysostom indicates, on Heb. 10.

The fathers severely rebuked this evil opinion and most earnestly exhorted the people to more frequent use of Communion. Chrysostom says, on Eph. 1: "In vain is the daily sacrifice held; in vain we stand at the altar; there is no one who partakes." And, on Heb. 10, he says: "In saying this I do not forbid you one reception in the year, but I want you to come always." Ambrose says, *De sacramentis,* Bk. 6, ch. 4: "If this is daily food, why do you take it only after a year has passed, as the Greeks in the East are wont to do?" And Chrysostom, Homily 11, upbraids the people of Antioch because they quarreled during the 40-day fast and nevertheless at Easter came to the solemn Communion from mere custom, without a true examination. And, on Eph. 1: "At other times you often do not come, even though you are clean, but at Easter, even if you have committed some rash act, you nevertheless come. What a custom! What presumption!"

4 Let the reader here diligently observe these very harsh reproofs. I have recounted them that I might show that the ancient solemn Communion at Easter is something far other than what is now observed among the papalists. For the former, by means of teaching, admonition, exhortation, and argument, urged more frequent use of Communion; the papalists, however, judge that no one is obligated by the commandment to more than one Communion a year, so long as meanwhile he liberally purchases the spectacle of private Masses. Surely these things are far removed from the manner of the ancient church. The ninth Apostolic Canon concerning the Communion of those who are present at the assembly states clearly: "It is necessary to separate all those believers who come in and hear the Scripture, but will not remain for the prayer and the Holy Communion, as makers of disorder in the church." This opinion is repeated also in the second canon of the Council of Antioch.

Although daily Communion on the part of the people later ceased, the religious or clergy nevertheless came together daily for Communion, as Cassander quotes from the *Micrologus*. Of this Communion they want us to note what the Canon of Anacletus says, *De consecratione,* dist. 2: "When the consecration has been completed, let all who do not want to be without the light[61] of the church commune." Thus they wanted no Mass to be without communicants. On the Lord's days and on other festivals the people came together for Communion. Afterward, when also this was neglected, it was decreed that all should commune three times a year, if not oftener, *De consecratione,* dist. 2, ch. *Et si non frequentius.* Finally the Lateran Council indicated that it was enough for the laity to go to Communion once a year. Also the daily Communion of the clergy gradually ceased. And thus, after the collapse of the more frequent use of the Communion, private Masses without either clergy or lay communicants throughout the year took over; to this came the persuasion that beholding the Mass and going to Communion were of equal value, or rather, that beholding the Mass was fraught with less peril and produced greater fruit than Communion itself. Thus the people were finally directly led away from more frequent Communion, and the Lord's Supper began to be transformed into a show, so that whereas Christ says: "Take; eat; drink," the papalists are not afraid to substitute: "Come and behold; it will be the same as if you ate and drank."

5 And now that these perverse opinions have already had a foothold in the church for a number of years with very sad detriment to souls, what remedy, I ask, do the Tridentine fathers bring forward? Do they attempt to restore more frequent use of Communion according to the command of Christ? Do they want people exhorted to it? Indeed, not even one word can be found in this whole session which would even lightly indicate this, but they simply say that all believers are held, by command, to communicate at least once a year. However, they add the phrase "at least," lest they seem to forbid people, although they should have been earnestly and strongly exhorted to more frequent use of Communion. I have therefore shown that this custom and persuasion of the papalist church agrees neither with Scripture nor with the examples of the ancient church. Surely it is an extraordinary piece of shamelessness that they do not mention more frequent Communion with so much as one word but only repeat their customary song about one Communion a year. The *Antididagma* of Cologne proceeds somewhat more modestly because, while it defends

---

[61] Nigrinus apparently read *liminibus* (threshold) instead of the text's *luminibus* (lights). His reading would give the meaning "outside the pale of the church."

this custom, it nevertheless adds that people are to be diligently admonished to prepare themselves more frequently to receive the Eucharist. But it was judged that not even such a token of modesty was becoming to those who were standing in the place of the Roman pontiff at the Council of Trent.

Fifth Topic

CONCERNING COMMUNION
UNDER BOTH KINDS

*From the 21st Session
of the Council of Trent*

SECTION I

[Concerning Communion Under Both Kinds]

THE TEACHING CONCERNING COMMUNION UNDER BOTH KINDS, AND OF LITTLE CHILDREN

*Published in the Fifth[1] Session of the
Ecumenical Council of Trent Under Our Holy Master[2]
Pius IV, Sovereign Pontiff,
on the 16th Day of July, A.D. 1562*

Preface

The sacred ecumenical and general Synod of Trent, lawfully assembled in the Holy Spirit, the same legates of the Apostolic See presiding, seeing that various monstrous errors are being carried about in diverse places concerning the tremendous and most holy sacrament of the Eucharist by the crafts of the evil spirit, on account of which in not a few territories many appear to have departed from the faith and obedience of the Catholic Church, judged that whatever pertains to Communion under both kinds and of little children should be set forth here. Therefore it forbids all believers in Christ to presume hereafter either to believe or to teach or preach otherwise than is explained and defined in these decrees.

Chapter I

THAT LAYMEN AND CLERGY, WHEN THEY ARE NOT CELEBRANTS, ARE NOT BOUND BY DIVINE RIGHT TO COMMUNE UNDER BOTH KINDS

Therefore this holy synod, taught by the Holy Spirit (who is the Spirit of wisdom and understanding, the Spirit of counsel and godliness) and following the judgment and custom of the Church, declares and teaches that lay people, and clergy who are not celebrating, are not obliged by any divine command to receive the sacrament of the Eucharist under both kinds, and that it can in no way be doubted without injury to faith that Communion under either kind is sufficient to them for salvation. For although Christ the Lord at His last supper instituted this sacrament with the form of bread and wine, and gave it to the apostles, nevertheless that institution and tradition do not aim at this, that all believers in Christ are

---

[1] Not the fifth session of the council, but the fifth under Pius IV, the third pope during the Council of Trent. It was the 21st session of the council.

[2] The words "our holy master" applied to the pope are not found in the editions of the *Canons and Decrees of the Council of Trent* available to the translator. All give the heading as follows: *Sessio Vigesimaprima, quae est Quinta sub Pio IV Pont. Max. Celebrata.* The translator has been unable to find the source of the additional words in the *Examen.*

bound by the commandment of the Lord to receive both kinds. Neither is it rightly concluded from the discourse in John 6—no matter how it be understood according to various interpretations of the holy fathers and teachers—that Communion under both kinds is commanded by the Lord. For He who said: "Unless you eat the flesh of the Son of man and drink His blood you have no life in you," also said: "He who eats this bread will live forever"; and He who said: "He who eats My flesh and drinks My blood has eternal life," also said: "The bread which I shall give for the life of the world is My flesh." And finally, He who said: "He who eats My flesh and drinks My blood abides in Me and I in him," nevertheless says: "He who eats this bread will live forever."

Chapter II

THE POWER OF THE CHURCH WITH RESPECT TO THE ADMINISTRATION OF THE SACRAMENT OF THE EUCHARIST

It [the synod] further declares that this power has always been in the Church, that in the dispensation of the sacraments, provided their essence is preserved, she may order or change whatever she judges, according to varying circumstances, times, and places, to be most useful to those who use them or to reverence for the sacraments themselves. This the apostle appears to intimate in a not obscure manner when he says: "This is how one should regard us, as servants of Christ and stewards of the mysteries of God." That he himself also made use of this authority, as in many other things so also in this sacrament, is quite certain; when he had ordered a number of matters about its use, he says: "About the other things I will give directions when I come." Therefore Holy Mother Church, aware of this her authority with respect to the administration of the sacraments, although she had from the beginning of the Christian religion not infrequently used both kinds, nevertheless as time went on, and this custom was widely changed, persuaded by weighty and just reasons, approved this custom of communicating under one kind and decreed that it should be considered a law which it is not permitted to condemn or to change at will without the authority of the Church.

Chapter III

THAT THE WHOLE CHRIST AND THE TRUE SACRAMENT ARE RECEIVED UNDER EITHER KIND

It [the Synod] further declares that although our Redeemer, as was said before, at that last supper instituted and delivered this sacrament to the apostles in two kinds, it is nevertheless to be acknowledged that also under one kind the whole and entire Christ and the true sacrament are received, and therefore, so far as its fruit is concerned, those who receive only one kind are not defrauded of any grace necessary for salvation.

CANON I

If anyone says that by God's command, or because it is necessary for salvation, each and every believer in Christ ought to receive both kinds of the sacrament of the Holy Eucharist, let him be anathema.

CANON II

If anyone says that the Holy Catholic Church was not moved by just causes and reasons to commune the laity, and also clergy who are not consecrating, under the kind of the bread only, or that she erred in this, let him be anathema.

CANON III

If anyone denies that the whole and entire Christ, the Fount and Author of all graces, is received under the one kind of bread, because (as some falsely assert) it is not taken according to the institution of Christ under both kinds, let him be anathema.

Examination

The reader will, I think, not be disturbed by the fact that at this point in our examination we are not proceeding according to the order of the sessions of the council, in which they broke off the treatment of the Eucharist and interposed the teaching about penitence and extreme unction. For I judged that it was most fitting that those questions which are in controversy between us and our opponents with respect to the sacrament of the Eucharist should be examined and explained in an orderly and uninterrupted treatment.

The Synod of Trent finally gets to the famous and generally discussed controversy about Communion under both kinds. Concerning this not only silent groans, not obscure sighs, nor only private disputations, but universal complaints and public demands of the whole Christian world have now for many years filled all churches and, without doubt, also heaven itself with resounding voice. Certainly, these have all but deafened the ears of the papalists, thick as they are. Neither has it been the men on our side only who, advancing the clearest and strongest proofs and reasons from the Word of God, strenuously and with great zeal, both orally and in writings, pursued this; indeed, also among those who still adhere to the papalist side the evidence in the matter has brought it about that throughout various nations and realms the restoration of the Lord's cup has been sought and demanded by public petitions and urgent daily demands, and this repeatedly also in solemn assemblies of kingdoms and nations. These demands did not come from the common, ignorant crowd, but there are extant also complaints, petitions, judgments, and advice concerning this matter from most eminent men who under the rule of the pope are celebrated for learning and dignity; yes, this among other things frequently was solemnly demanded both on other occasions but most of all by public legations of kings and princes at the assembly of the Synod of Trent, also on the part of such as are not totally alienated from the papalist doctrine, that the unjust denial of the use of the Lord's cup should be done away and the cup restored to the church of God, according to the institution of Christ and the custom of the primitive church.

These common and public demands did not proceed from some blind impulse, not from some kind of levity or impudence, not from foolish striving for novelty or stubborn desire to disagree; indeed, they have the weightiest, strongest, and clearest reasons. It will not be alien to the plan of our undertaking to enumerate these here after I have brought them together and summarized them under a few heads, in order that we may proceed the more conveniently with the examination of the Tridentine decrees. For when the reasons of both sides are set over against each other, much light will be shed on the explanation of this controversy.

ARTICLE I

Arguments from Scripture for Communion Under Both Kinds

1 The first argument is taken from the institution of the Eucharist itself. For because one must judge concerning the sacraments on the basis of their institution, no godly person will be able to doubt, nor should doubt, that the one and only way of administering, dispensing, and using the sacraments—so far as their essence is concerned, the best, most correct, and safest way—is the one which was taught by the Son of God Himself in the institution. For sacraments are not created by nature or formed by human ingenuity, but the institution of the Son of God, coming to the elements ordained by Him, makes sacraments. If, however, the institution of the Son of God is either taken away or adulterated or mutilated and changed, then we can in no way make or have true sacraments. This axiom cannot be shaken even by the gates of hell. Now it is beyond controversy that Christ instituted His Supper on the night in which He was betrayed. He took bread, gave thanks, broke it, and gave it to His disciples, saying: "Take, eat; this is My body, which is given for you." He also took the cup, and when He had given thanks He gave it to them saying: "Drink of it, all of you, etc." And Luke (as should be diligently noted) shows that Christ willed that both parts should be equal in the way they were distributed and used. For when the description of the first part was completed, he adds: "In the same manner He took and gave also the cup."

Matthew reports that it is the intention of the institution that all should drink of the Eucharistic cup who partake of the bread. For He said to those who had already received the bread which had been blessed: "Drink of it, all of you." Therefore as the institution teaches that the bread which had been blessed should be distributed, so also it teaches that the cup should be distributed, and indeed to the same persons, yes, to all those to whom the body of Christ is offered to receive and eat.

This reason cannot but violently move pious minds when they see a departure made from the very institution of the Son of God, see that mutilated, changed, and rent apart of which the Word of God asserts that Christ instituted it similarly, in the same way, and jointly; for the foundation stands immovable that the institution must be preserved in order that we may be certain that we have the true sacrament. There is, however, no other institution of the Eucharist than this, which teaches that the distribution and use of both parts alike was instituted.

2 The second reason is taken from the command of Christ. For not only has the institution of the Lord's Supper been handed down as a dogma, but there are used in it a number of words which expressly signify a precept and command of Christ: "Take; eat; drink of it, all of you; do this." However, just as He did not institute His Supper for only the 12 apostles who were then present, so also the words of command are not meant for only the time and action of that first Supper, but there is added the perpetual and universal command, that that which was done at that first Supper should in future be done in the church even to the end of the world. For He says: "This (namely what has now been done in the first Lord's Supper) do in remembrance of Me." There is no obscurity with respect to what was done at the first Lord's Supper. Christ took the bread and the cup, blessed them by giving thanks, distributed and gave them to His disciples, and said, etc. The disciples took, ate, and drank.

Moreover, the commemoration of Christ, that is, the proclamation of His death, is added to both parts. Therefore the command: "Do this," embraces both parts, both what the ministers of the church ought to do when they administer and dispense the Eucharist, and what the faithful people ought to do in taking or using it, namely, what we read in the description of the institution as having been done at the first Lord's Supper. That description tells us that both the bread and the cup of the Lord, separately, were dispensed and taken. In order that everything might be very clear, Paul reports that he had received from the Lord Jesus, who was already sitting in His glory, that this command: "Do this," pertains not only to one but to both parts of the Eucharist. For he asserts that there was added clearly and separately both to the bread and to the cup of the Lord the command of Christ: "Do this." And lest anyone think that this command of Christ is satisfied if only one is done, Paul, in speaking of the cup, uses the words, "in the same way,"[3] in order to show that this command applies also in the same way and with equal reason to the cup, no less than to the bread. For when Paul wants to indicate that the deacons no less than the bishops should be irreproachable, the same little word[4] is used. The little words: "Do this," pertain not only to those to whom the duty of administering and dispensing the Eucharist was entrusted by Christ. For in describing the cup Paul quotes the words of Christ in such a way that he clearly shows that this command pertains also to those to whom the Eucharist is dispensed, given, and offered. For he says: "Do this as often as you drink." Therefore the commandment of Christ, that He wants His Supper to be administered, dispensed, received, and used until the day of judgment by eating and drinking the bread and the cup of blessing, is certain and clear.

It is not surprising that this argument strongly moves the conscience of the godly. For it is a universal judgment, repeated a number of times in Scripture, that nothing is to be added to the commandments of God, nothing taken away from them, that men are not to depart from them either to the right hand or to the left. Very beautiful is the saying of Cyprian, Bk. 2, Letter No. 3: "If not even one of the least of the commandments of the Law should be dissolved, much less is it permissible to infringe upon one of these great commandments which pertain to the sacrament of our Lord's passion and of our redemption, or to change it by human tradition." And Ambrose, on 1 Cor. 11, disputing about those who handle this sacrament in an unworthy manner, so that they get judgment for themselves, says: "That person acts unbecomingly toward the Lord, who celebrates this mystery in a manner other than that taught by Him. For he cannot be faithful who dares to do otherwise than it was given by the author."

3 The third reason is taken from the law concerning testaments. The saying of Paul (Gal. 3:15) is well known, that it is not permitted without falling into the crime of sacrilege either to abrogate or to appoint anything additional even in a man's testament when it has been confirmed. Now the whole Lord's Supper is the particular sacrament of the New Testament. Indeed, Christ says in particular and specifically concerning the cup: "This cup is the New Testament in My blood." This testament the Son of God, the Mediator, established the same night in which He was betrayed; this testament He sealed with the shedding of His most precious blood. In this testament He bequeathed to His church not earthly

---

[3] The Greek word is *hoosautoos,* which the RSV in 1 Cor. 11:25 translates "in the same way."

[4] In 1 Tim. 3:8 *hoosautoos* is translated "likewise."

and transitory but heavenly and eternal goods. And since He commanded that the cup of this New Testament should be dispensed to and drunk by all for whom He shed His blood, it is surely a dreadful piece of presumption to take away and forbid the use of this testamentary cup from the greater part of the church. Who but the Antichrist would be displeased that the church, the bride, should petition and implore that the testament of her bridegroom should be restored to her inviolate and whole?

4 The fourth reason is taken from the example of the apostles. For although the apostles saw that, when He offered them the cup, the blood had not yet been separated from the body of Christ nor shed, they nevertheless did not judge that for this reason the use of the cup depended on their will or that it might simply be omitted since they were receiving the not bloodless but living and whole body of Christ already in the bread; but as they were commanded: "Drink of it, all of you," so they complied in simple obedience with this command, without inquiring into the reason and without the pretext that it was dangerous. For Mark says: "And they all drank of it." Thus the apostles have instructed us by their example that in the mystery of the Supper we should adhere with simple obedience to the institution and command of the Son of God and that no reasons or arguments should be admitted against the express words of institution.

5 The fifth reason is taken from the apostolic tradition, which is found in writing and is not subject to doubt. The papalists argue that the command in the institution about the cup does not pertain to all the faithful but only to the apostles and to those who followed them in the ministry. But how Christ wanted this command to be understood and in what sense the apostles taught it to the church is most surely understood from Paul. For he testifies most clearly (1 Cor. 11:23 ff.) that he taught the church of the Corinthians the distribution and use of both kinds, as we commonly say now. For in that one chapter he speaks at least six times of the body and blood of Christ, of eating and drinking, both singly and jointly, and that in such a way that he asserts that he had received what he taught to the Corinthians from the Lord, who was already sitting at the right hand of the Father. He taught them the distribution and use of both kinds. This, without any controversy, is certain and manifest. Did he teach this only to the priests among the Corinthians? Surely, the address of the epistle reads: "To the church of God which is at Corinth, to those sanctified in Christ Jesus, called to be saints." Nor did he address this epistle to the Corinthians only, but adds: "Together with all those who in every place call on the name of our Lord Jesus Christ, both their Lord and ours." This is a very clear testimony. For the papalists argue that, because

Christ at the first Supper summoned only the 12 apostles to the table, the command of the institution about the use of both kinds pertains only to the apostles and to those who succeeded them in the ministry, so that the lay people are not obligated by the divine command to take the Eucharist under both kinds but that Communion under one kind only is sufficient for them. But Paul testifies clearly that in the Corinthian church he taught all who are called and sanctified in Christ the use of both kinds, and asserts that he had received what he taught the Corinthians from the Lord Himself. Thus he applies the commandment of Christ about the use of both kinds to the whole church. For it is false what some imagine, that Paul here only tells the bare story of the institution of the Lord's Supper, and indeed only as a historical description, although the whole context cries out[5] that Paul repeats and adduces the words of institution in order that, on the basis of this norm and rule, he may correct the errors and abuses which had crept into the Corinthian church with respect to the administration and use of this sacrament and that he might show them the true way to administer and use the Lord's Supper from the source and basis of the institution. The application to the Corinthian church is clear in these words: "As often as you eat this bread and drink the cup. . . . Let a man examine himself, and so eat of the bread and drink of the cup," etc.

This teaching and this command about eating the bread and drinking the cup of the Lord he takes and constructs from the words of institution. Thus he applies the command of Christ about the cup to the whole church and assures us that he had received both the words of institution and their application, as he taught it to the church of the Corinthians, from the Lord. Thus he overthrows the false conclusion of the Jesuits, who say that Paul indeed taught the use of the cup of the Lord to all the sanctified in the church of the Corinthians but that he did not command it, because teaching is not the same thing as commanding; for he does not say: "I commanded you," but: "I delivered to you." But I see that Paul studiously spoke thus, in order that he might take away the power of commanding and forbidding anything in essentials of the Lord's Supper from each and every human authority and assign it to Christ alone. Therefore, though he was a distinguished apostle, he nevertheless neither wished nor dared to take this onto himself, that in the administration and use of this sacrament, which is called a testament, he would either command or forbid anything on his own authority, but adduces the precept and command of

---

[5] The Latin text here has a *non*, which would turn the meaning into the opposite of what the context calls for. We have disregarded the *non* in the translation.

the Lord: "Take, eat; drink." By his application, which he received from the Lord, he shows that this pertains not only to the 12 apostles, nor only to the priests, but to all who are called and sanctified in Christ Jesus, not only in the Corinthian church but in every place. Therefore when Paul says, not: "I command you," but: "The precept and command which I received from the Lord Himself, that I have by His order delivered to you, the called and sanctified in Christ," he obligates much more strongly than if he had said: "I command you." This can be beautifully understood and illustrated from what he says in 1 Cor. 7:10: "I give charge, not I but the Lord." Therefore when Paul says (1 Cor. 11:23): "I delivered to you," it is the same as if he said: "So far as the administration and use of the Lord's Supper is concerned, I do not give advice but have a precept of the Lord." This beautiful argument I would not have noticed in the words of Paul if the sophistry of the Jesuits, that Paul did not command but delivered to the Corinthians the use of both kinds, had not led me to notice it. For it is false when they say that Paul was merely reporting the words of institution for the sake of the history, without application to the called and sanctified in Christ in every place. For he recites the history of the institution in this way so that he may presently apply it to the Corinthians and to all to whom he has addressed the epistle. And indeed Paul, as he had received it from the Lord, applies the command of the Lord concerning Communion under both kinds, given to the apostles at the first Supper, to every person called and sanctified in Christ Jesus, when he says: "As often as you eat and drink," etc. And lest someone should think that Paul leaves this to man's will, he quickly repeats in the imperative mood, in the form of a command: "Let a man examine himself, and so eat of the bread and drink of the cup."

It is worth the labor to consider how Andrada and Horst of Cologne try to escape this very clear statement of Paul. They say that this command of Paul pertains only to the examination, not however also to the eating and drinking in the Lord's Supper, so that the meaning is (says Horst): "So long only as a man is approved, it is all the same whether he takes one or both kinds." But this sophistical, or rather deceitful, attempt amounts not so much to an escape from as rather a distortion of a very clear statement. It is true that Paul teaches that a man about to use the Lord's Supper should first examine himself. But Paul asserts that when a man has examined himself it is the commandment of God, and indeed a connected commandment, that the man who was examined should eat of that bread and drink of that cup. For the words: "Let him eat and drink," are imperatives, no less than: "Let him examine himself," formed in the same way and connected with "and." Paul indeed did not teach the use of both kinds on account of the circumstances of place and condition of the Corinthian church, as though it were not a universal but a particular tradition. For the title of the epistle shows that what is there taught pertains not only to the Corinthians but to all who call on the name of the Lord in every place. Moreover, in treating of the Lord's Supper he uses a general term: "Let a man examine himself, and so let him eat and drink." Therefore the Pauline application of the command of Christ about eating the bread and drinking the cup of the Supper is universal, to all men, called and sanctified, in every place.

That this was observed in the practice of the apostolic church is certain. For even as he says (1 Cor. 10:17): "We are one body, for we all partake of one bread," so he also says (1 Cor. 12:13): "All were made to drink of one Spirit."6 Surely Paul did not ordain these things thus for a time only, as though the tradition were temporary, as the sophists imagine that when Paul said: "About the other things I will give directions when I come," he wanted afterward to abrogate the use of both kinds, since he is not speaking about the things he had received from the Lord but says, "the other things." We have the very clear words of Paul. He taught that the death of the Lord is to be proclaimed when we eat of the bread of the Lord and drink of His cup in the Supper until Christ returns to judgment, that is, the commandment of the Lord about eating and drinking in the Lord's Supper ought to endure until the end of the world and the last judgment. Nor does he say that only the priests should eat and drink in the Lord's Supper. Therefore Paul does not speak in the first person: "We eat and drink," but, directing his speech according to the inscription of the epistle: "To the called and sanctified in Christ, all who call upon the Lord in every place," he says: "As often as you eat this bread and drink the cup you proclaim the Lord's death until He comes." The Corinthians were not, however, to remain in this life to the end of the world. Therefore Paul delivers the teaching about the use of both kinds of the Eucharist as applying "to all who call upon the name of the Lord in every place," not only at the time of the apostles but also in future times. This apostolic tradition, received from the Lord Himself, ought to endure until the end of the world, until the Lord returns to judgment.

These things are so clear that we rightly use the saying of Augustine: "When a thing is clear it is able to prove itself."

The teaching and tradition of the other apostles was no different. For concerning other traditions he says (1 Cor. 15:11): "Whether then it was I or the other apostles, so we teach and so you have believed." And 1 Cor.

---

6 Chemnitz has 1 Cor. 10. The correct reference is 1 Cor. 12:13.

14: "Thus I teach in all churches."[7] Because Eck does not have sufficient confidence in the other arguments, he finally goes so far as to imagine that there is an unspoken tradition of the apostles about Communion under one kind. Therefore I have rightly and truly said against the Jesuits, although this has angered Andrada, that the papalists will freely depart from the things concerning which it is clearly established from the writings of the apostles that they taught them, make them dependent on the will of men, yes, forbid them, as is manifest in the matter of the use of the cup. The fictions they foist upon the church under the pretext of unspoken traditions, as Eck imagines in the matter of Communion under one kind, without even a spurious testimony of antiquity, they make so necessary that because of them they persecute the godly with fire and sword. We, however, rightly oppose to them what Paul says in Gal. 1:8-9: "If anyone is preaching to you a gospel contrary to that which you received, let him be accursed, even if he should be an apostle or an angel from heaven." However, the church received the use of both kinds from the tradition of the apostles. Therefore let whoever teaches otherwise be anathema!

6 The sixth reason is taken from the resulting comfort which the words of Christ, added to the Communion of the cup, offer. True, application of the benefits of Christ is made in believers also apart from the use of the Lord's Supper, through the hearing of the Gospel. Still, in the Supper Christ, by imparting His body, gives, applies, and seals to believers the benefits He earned by offering up His body; nevertheless, the power and efficacy of the sacraments must be appraised from the Word which by a voice from God is joined to each sacrament as being proper and peculiar to it. It is a very sweet promise which is joined to the Communion of the cup by the voice of the Son of God: "Drink of this, all of you; this cup is the New Testament in My blood, which is shed for you for the remission of sins." The New Testament includes the grace of God, reconciliation, forgiveness of sins, adoption, etc., according to the statement of Jeremiah. (Ch. 31:31-34).

A pious mind is greatly troubled about the question: "Does the covenant of the grace of God in Christ pertain also to me in particular?" I wish and sigh that I may truly and certainly be received into this covenant of the New Testament, that I may be, be found, and ever remain in this covenant, that it may be for me forever firm and unalterable. Now the Son of God added to the Communion of the cup the most delightful words, by which He testified that He instituted the cup of His Supper that

---

[7] The reference appears to be to 1 Cor. 4:17.

it may be a means or instrument by which He wants to apply, seal, and confirm this New Testament personally and effectively to everyone who receives it in faith. In order that our faith may be certain that we truly and certainly are received, are found, and are confirmed in this covenant, that it may be unalterable and firm to us, He asserts that He offers and imparts to us in this cup that very blood of His by the shedding of which the New Testament has been earned, established, and confirmed. Of the enjoyment of the sweet and needed consolation with which the Son of God mildly looked upon His church, pious consciences are not willing to be deprived, but use this testament of the Son of God with true gratitude of mind for the strengthening of their faith.

No matter what is set against this understanding of the message of the Gospel and of the Communion of the body of Christ, it is certain that it is not in vain or from want of any other occupation that the Son of God instituted for His church beside the preaching of the Gospel and the Communion of His body also the cup of His blood, adding indeed glorious words concerning the application, sealing, and confirming of the New Testament to everyone who takes it in faith. For even as God is rich in mercy, offering, applying, and sealing His grace to us by various means instituted by Him, so we have need of various modes of healing and strengthening. Such means, therefore, concerning which it is certain that they were instituted by the Son of God, we use reverently, and we do not grant audience to profane arguments, as if we were defrauded of no necessary grace even if we receive only one kind, although Christ instituted both. For we are not treating chiefly about either the appearance or the substance of the wine, but about the comforting words which the Son of God in His own voice wanted to have joined to the Communion of the cup. We are treating of the necessary consolation and strengthening of faith which is contained in those words, and of the most precious sealing of this promise through the imparting of the blood shed for the remission of our sins. For Christ wanted these words specifically connected not to the bread but to the cup: "Drink of this, all of you; this cup is the New Testament," etc.

Those who deprive the church of the use of the cup and forbid it take away this treasure from her. It is not sufficient that they say that when we eat the body of Christ we at the same time receive also His blood. For the Son of God ordained that the imparting of His blood and the sealing of the promise: "This is the New Testament in My blood," should be made specifically through the Communion of the cup. Neither has any creature the right to tear these words away from the cup and to transfer them elsewhere. For the power and efficacy of the sacrament is judged from the word of Christ which, by His own voice, He wanted joined to each.

ARTICLE II

Testimonies of Antiquity Concerning Communion Under Both Kinds

1 Finally, many outstanding reasons are taken from the testimonies and examples of the first, true, and purer church. For from these we rightly gather against all recent sophistries that the primitive church understood the words of institution of the Supper concerning Communion of the cup from apostolic tradition to pertain not to the priests only but to the whole church. There are testimonies and examples noted down by many, according to the sequence of times, from all ancient writers, to the effect that in a lawful and solemn celebration of the Lord's Supper, when the church assembled, the sacrament of the Eucharist was administered and dispensed in no other way than under both kinds, namely bread and wine. Indeed, in the Eastern church this is done to this day; in the Western church it was done continuously for a thousand years and longer.

Passing over this noting down of examples, which is public and well known, I judge that this argument from the testimonies of antiquity can be usefully elucidated if the examples are not merely noted down, but if in particular the reasons are observed for which the true and purer church of antiquity judged that the use of Communion under both kinds should be steadfastly observed. For so we shall have testimonies of antiquity not only about the fact but, a thing which confirms the godly even more, the right of Communion under both kinds. For it is not the examples alone which are to be noted in the history of antiquity, but one must take account especially of the teachings and of the grounds they had for the teachings. Such observation will show at the same time that solutions and refutations of the false reasoning with which the papalists attempt to defend the mutilation of the Lord's Supper, contrary to the clear words of institution, can be taken from this history of antiquity.

2 The first observation about the reasons of the ancients is that they not only in fact dispensed both kinds to the whole church but that it was the teaching in the ancient and purer church that the words of the Supper concerning Communion of the cup, on the basis of the institution and command of Christ, pertain not to the priests only but to the whole church.

Chrysostom, Homily 18, on 2 Corinthians, says: "There is a place where a priest is no different from a subject, for instance, when the sacrament is to be received. For we are all alike considered worthy to receive it. It is not as it was in the time of the Old Testament, where the priest ate certain things, the lay people other things, and it was not lawful that the people should partake of the things the priests ate, but (namely now, in the time of the New Testament) one body is set before all, and one cup."

Ignatius, writing to the whole church at Philadelphia, makes mention of the bishop, priest, presbyter, deacons, and people. He says: "I exhort you to use one faith, one proclamation, and one Eucharist. For the flesh of the Lord Jesus is one, and His blood is one, shed for us; also, one bread is broken for all, one cup distributed to all."

Theophylact, on 1 Cor. 11, says that the awe-inspiring cup of the Lord is given to all on the same condition.

The author of a discourse on the Lord's Supper, attributed to Cyprian, says: "The Law forbids the eating of blood; the Gospel prescribes that it be drunk. Now we drink of the blood of Christ at His command, as partakers of eternal life with Him and through Him. And we confess that through tasting sin we should have been deprived of bliss and damned if the mercy of Christ had not brought us back to the fellowship of eternal life by His blood. To us therefore, for whom the blood of Christ was offered on the cross, whom this sacrifice reconciled to God, Christ Himself, as cup-bearer, presents this cup."

Jerome, on 1 Cor. 11, writes: "The Lord's Supper ought to belong to all, because He delivered the sacraments equally to all His disciples who were present."

Augustine says in *Quaestiones super Leviticum*, ch. 57: "What does this mean, that the people are totally forbidden the blood of the sacrifices which were being offered for sins, if by these sacrifices this one sacrifice was foreshadowed in which there is true remission of sins? For from the blood of this sacrifice, taken as nourishment, not only is no one barred, but rather, all who want to have life are exhorted to drink of it."

Paschasius, in collecting the explanations of the fathers about the Lord's Supper, says, ch. 15: "It is Christ who breaks this bread and distributes it to the believers through the hands of His ministers. In the same manner also He offers them the cup, saying: 'Take and drink of it, all of you, the ministers as well as the other believers.' "

Nicephorus, Bk. 1, ch. 28, having quoted the institution of the Supper about both kinds, added that Christ had personally taught that this should be done in the same way to the faithful thereafter in times to come for a pure and clear memorial.

The distinction between ministers and people, so the ancients note, is that through them there is dispensed to the people the same thing which is taken by them, namely, the bread and cup of the Lord.

So John of Damascus says, *De orthodoxa fide,* Bk. 4, ch. 14: "Christ distributed the New Testament to His holy disciples, and through them to others who believed in Him."

In the liturgy of Basil and Chrysostom the priest prays: "Be pleased, O Lord, to give us Your body and blood, and through us to the people."

And in the hymn for the Corpus Christi festival the papalists themselves chant: "He gave to the frail the food of His body, and to the downcast the cup of salvation, saying: 'Take the vessel which I give; drink of it, all of you.' " Thus He instituted this sacrifice, the charge of which He wanted to commit to the priests alone, whom it therefore behooves to take it and to give it to the others.

3 Second, when in administering the Communion cup to the people something else was tried than the words of institution indicate, the fathers opposed the weightiest reasons from the example, instruction, precept, and command of the Lord. These reasons are found set forth in Cyprian, Bk. 2, Letter No. 3. For when at that time, under the pretext of sobriety, they used only water without wine in administering the cup of the Lord to the people, Cyprian opposed arguments from the institution of the Supper which speak not only to that particular case but are general and universal, and expressly treat this question: What must be done in consecrating the cup of the Lord and administering it to the people? Therefore these things are rightly applied to this our controversy, which is about administering the cup of the Lord to the people.

Now these are the chief arguments of Cyprian: In consecrating the cup of the Lord and administering it to the people the manner of evangelical truth and of the tradition of the Lord must be held fast; there is to be no departing through a human and new institution from what Christ, the teacher, both commanded and did. He declares that those err who, in consecrating the cup of the Lord and administering it to the people, do not do what Christ, the author and teacher of this sacrament, did and taught. He says that when men have fallen into this error, they must return to the guide and origin of the Dominical tradition so that nothing other is done by us than what the Lord did for us first. Likewise: "But if it was taught by the Lord, and the same thing was confirmed and handed down by the apostle, that as often as we drink in commemoration of the Lord we should do what also the Lord did, then, unless we do the same thing the Lord did, we shall be found failing to do what is commanded."

Likewise: "The Father bears witness from heaven that Christ only ought to be heard, when He says: 'Hear Him.' But if Christ alone is to be heard, we ought to give no heed to what someone before us thought ought to be done, but to what Christ, who is before all, did first. For we ought not to follow the custom of men but the truth of God, since God says through Isaiah: 'In vain they do worship Me, teaching commandments and doctrines of men.' " Likewise: "If in the sacrifice, which is Christ, no one but Christ is to be followed, then surely that priest who imitates what Christ did discharges his duty in the stead of Christ." And: "Therefore if one of our predecessors, either from ignorance or from simplicity, did not observe and keep what the Lord by His example and teaching taught us to do, forgiveness may be granted his simplicity by the indulgence of the Lord, but it cannot be ignored in our case, who have now been admonished and instructed by the Lord." Finally he concludes this disputation thus: "We must also direct letters to our colleagues that the evangelical law and tradition may be everywhere observed and that there may be no departure from what Christ taught and did."

These are solid arguments, and indeed in the weightiest words, as if they had been diligently drawn up for this present controversy and opposed to the sophistic arguments of the papalists. I know, however, that Cyprian is disputing in this epistle against those who served only water at the Lord's Supper, not against Communion under one kind, which was unknown to the church at that time. But the arguments are general and tell expressly what must be done in consecrating the cup of the Lord and administering it to the people in order that the tradition of the Lord may be preserved. Arguing from the lesser to the greater, these arguments of Cyprian are rightly applied to the present controversy. For if he battles so sharply with the weightiest arguments against the water-dispensers, who left the cup itself and the words about the cup to the people, and only changed something in the element, how much more sharply, do you think, he would have risen up on the same basis if someone at that time had wanted to take away and forbid the whole cup of the Lord, and the words concerning the cup, to the faithful people?

So, when about the year of our Lord 340 some men offered the Eucharist to the people by means of a wafer dipped in the cup in place of full Communion, Julius pronounces this to be contrary to the teaching of the Gospel and of the apostles. He says that this is proved from the fountain of truth itself, from which the ordained mysteries of the sacraments came forth. And soon afterward he says that the proof for this is the testimony of the Gospel, where mention of the charge concerning the bread and the cup is made separately for each. Therefore Pope Julius proves from the institution of the Supper described in the Gospel that the cup is to be offered to the people separately, and disapproves the intinction of the Eucharist, because it is not in agreement with the institution.

4 The third reason of the ancients was that Christ, in the institution of the sacrament of the Eucharist, offered two kinds, namely bread and wine, and added the command to each one: "This do" (1 Cor. 11:24-25). On this basis the fathers taught that the use of both kinds is necessary for the integrity, wholeness, and consummation of this sacred Communion. Indeed, they call the use of the cup the completion of Communion and the consummation of the mysteries. Thus when Paschasius and Algerus discuss why Christ instituted the Eucharist under two kinds, separately and divided (for this is how the ancients speak), they adduce this saying of Augustine: "Neither the flesh without the blood, nor the blood without the flesh is lawfully communicated."

Gelasius judged thus concerning those who abstained from the cup of the consecrated blood, *De consecratione,* dist. 2, ch. *Comperimus:* "Let them either receive the sacraments entire or be excluded from the entire sacraments, for a division of one and the same sacrament cannot be made without great sacrilege."

Julius, dist. 2, ch. *Cum omne,* calls this the completion of Communion, because in the witness of the Gospel the charge of the cup is related separately.

In Ambrose, Bk. 1, *Officiorum,* ch. 41, the deacon Laurentius says that the distribution of the blood of the Lord had been entrusted to him by Bishop Sixtus, and he calls this a participation in those things which must be done in completing the sacraments. Therefore the dispensation of the cup is the completion of the sacraments.

Cassander quotes from the Roman order concerning the celebration of Masses that the dispensation of the cup is called the confirming of the Communion. These are the words: "The archdeacon, having received the cup from the hand of the bishop, confirms with the blood of the Lord all whom the bishop had communicated with the body of the Lord."

Leo I, Sermon 4, *Quadragesimali,* says of the Manichaeans: "They receive the body of Christ with an unworthy mouth; the blood of our redemption they entirely refuse to drink." Therefore the fabrication of the sophists that those who receive the body of the Lord under one kind at the same time drink His blood in the bread, even if they abstain from the cup of the consecrated blood, was unknown to Leo.

5 The fourth reason of the ancients was that they understood from the words of institution which were added to the Communion of the cup by the voice of the Son of God that the use of the cup has a special benefit, power, and efficacy, brought about by this word which is added to the cup.

Ambrose says, *De sacramentis,* Bk. 4, ch. 6: "If every time the blood is poured out it is poured out for the remission of sins, I ought to receive it always, that my sins may always be forgiven me; because I constantly sin, I constantly need to have the remedy." Bk. 5, ch. 3: "As often as you drink, you receive remission of sins and become drunk in the Spirit."

Cyprian, Bk. 1, Letter No. 2: "Let us not leave those whom we exhort to go into battle unarmed and naked, but let us fortify them with the protection of the blood and body of Christ. For how shall we summon them to shed their blood in confession if we deny them the blood of Christ when they are about to wage war? Or how shall we render them fit for the cup of the martyr if we do not suffer them, by the right of communicating, to drink the cup of the Lord beforehand?" Let the reader observe that Cyprian says that the people are to be admitted to the cup of the Lord in the church according to the right of communicating.

Hilary, Bk. 8, *De Trinitate,* speaking of the body and blood of Christ, says: "When these have been taken and drunk, they will cause you to be in Christ, and Christ in you."

Remigius, as quoted by Cassander, caused these lines, composed by himself, to be engraved on the chalice:

Out of this let the people drink life from the sacred blood
Which the eternal Christ shed from the wound inflicted on Him.

6 Fifth, because Paul says: "As often as you eat this bread and drink the cup, you proclaim the Lord's death until He comes," therefore the ancients felt that just as the passion or death of Christ consists in the offering of His body and the shedding of His blood, so also the commemoration of the death of Christ must be shown and celebrated in the Supper by the eating of the sacramental bread and the drinking of the consecrated cup, and that not only by consecration and reception on the part of the priest but also by distribution to and participation on the part of the faithful people.

Thus Augustine says, *Contra Faustum,* Bk. 20, ch. 18: "Christians celebrate the commemoration of this accomplished sacrifice by the most holy offering of and participation in the body and blood of the Lord."

Ambrose says, on 1 Cor. 11: "Because we have been set free by the death of the Lord, we signify, as we call this to mind in eating and drinking the body and blood which were offered for us, that in these we have received the New Testament."

In the aphorisms of Prosper, Augustine says: "When the host is broken, while blood is being poured from the chalice into the mouths of the faithful, what else is represented than the offering of the body of the Lord on the cross and the shedding of His blood from His side?"

7 Sixth, Lombard asks why we receive under two kinds although the whole Christ is present under either. He takes his answer from Ambrose: "In order that the acceptance of the soul and of the flesh in Christ, and the liberation of both in you, may be signified. For that which we receive is able to guard body and soul, because the flesh of Christ is conveyed to us for the salvation of our body, but the blood for our soul. But if it were taken in one kind only, it would mean that it could guard only one, that is, either the body or the soul, but not both equally."

Hugo of St. Victor: "It is taken under both kinds to signify that the effect of this sacrament is twofold. For it is the redemption of the body and of the soul. This would not be signified if it were taken under one kind only." Likewise: "Reception under both kinds signifies at one and the same time the redemption of the body and of the soul of the person receiving it."

Augustine uses this argument: "Just as in this life complete and perfect refreshment and nourishment consists of food and drink, so also in the Eucharist there is placed before us the body of Christ in the bread for eating, and the blood in the cup for drinking." *In Evangelium Johannis tractatus*, 26: "With food and drink men seek this, that they may not hunger nor thirst; nothing fulfills this except this food and drink, which makes those by whom it is taken immortal and imperishable." Thus Paschasius quotes from Augustine: "Neither is the flesh without the blood nor the blood without the flesh lawfully communicated. For the whole man, consisting of two substances, is set free; therefore he is nourished simultaneously by the flesh and the blood."

8 Seventh, the fathers say that the figures of the Old Testament about manna, water from a rock, likewise of the Passover lamb and of its blood are fulfilled in the New Testament in this, that generally the sacramental bread is placed before the whole people of Christ to be eaten, and the cup of the Lord to be drunk.

Thus Chrysostom, Homily 23, on 1 Corinthians: "In the same way as you eat the body of Christ, so also they ate the manna, and as you drink the blood, so also they drank the water from the rock." Likewise: "To them He gave manna and water, to you the body and the blood."

Ambrose, *De his qui initiantur mysteriis*, ch. 9: "To them water from the rock; to you blood from Christ. Them He satisfied for an hour with water; you His blood washes forever."

Augustine, *In Evangelium Johannis tractatus*, 26: "All drank the same spiritual drink; they one kind, we another, but under a visible form, which is nevertheless the same in spiritual power."

Thus the Passover lamb was eaten; its blood, however, was put on both doorposts. Gregory explains this mystery thus: "What the blood of the lamb is you have learned not by hearing but by drinking. This blood is placed upon both doorposts when it is drunk not only with the mouth of the body but with the mouth of the heart."

9 The occasion to consider the reasons of the ancients for Communion under both kinds more attentively was given me by a booklet of Cassander, and it helped me more than a little. This observing of the reasons of antiquity is more useful and clearer than a lengthy and bare heaping together of examples. For in this way the bases of the matter are shown, namely, how and from what bases and reasons the dogma about Communion under both kinds was treated, established, and explained. Such observation shows clearly that most of the false arguments of the adversaries were exploded and refuted by the ancients before they were even born, as we shall show later.

10 Therefore the testimonies and examples of antiquity furnish many very strong arguments against the papalist mutilation of the Lord's Supper. For in the first place there is not found in all antiquity this opinion of the papalists that the institution of the cup does not pertain to the laity but only to the priests. On the contrary, this opinion is clearly rejected by the ancients.

Second, the papalist argument that, since Christ is present whole and entire under either kind, Communion is not necessarily under both kinds, but is sufficient under either kind, is unknown to the true antiquity. In fact, the opposite is found in Hugo and Lombard.

Third, also the remaining arguments of the papalists in defense of Communion under one kind are totally unknown to antiquity, or rather, most of them have been refuted by the ancients.

Fourth, in all of the true antiquity this teaching is not found debated and treated dogmatically, that in a legitimate and ordinary assembly of the church the Lord's Supper either should or could be administered in such a way that only one part of it is dispensed to the people.

Fifth, although the attempt was repeatedly made to take the cup away from the sacred Communion of the faithful people, the purer antiquity resisted sharply and defended the use of the sacramental bread and of the consecrated cup in the Communion of the church from the Word of God. These examples must be explained later.

11 These reasons and these grounds from Scripture and from the testimonies of the true antiquity, seeing they are certain, firm, manifest, and clear in their truth and weight, have not only persuaded the people on our side in favor of the use of both kinds but have also persuaded the minds of those who are still held in the Babylonian captivity of the papal kingdom, so that they judge that the withholding and prohibition of the cup is not right, but ask and earnestly entreat that the ancient right of the primitive Communion be restored to the church according to the intent of Scripture and the testimonies of antiquity.

12 However, the stubbornness of the papalists in this matter is surprising and indeed shocking, that until now they have not been moved in the least by the clear light of the truth nor by the justest complaints and demands of the whole Christian world but have obstinately and persistently defended this unjust prohibition and ungodly mutilation, not so much with arguments as with sword, fire, and banishment of godly persons, according to the clause of the decree of Constance about invoking the secular arm. And now, at the Council of Trent, when after many varied and long delays something finally had to be decided about this controversy, when the matter itself shows that the earnest petitions of men can no longer be put off but that something must be yielded in this matter, they nevertheless use this trickery, that they condemn the wholly just pleas for the restitution of the cup and justify the papalist mutilation before they attack the question of whether, what, how much, and in what way there should be a yielding.

Someone may, however, wonder why, although they pretend not to begrudge the blood of Christ to the Christian people, because, as they say, they give it to them with the body in the bread, and although they imagine that only the accidents[8] without the substance are in the cup—why, in view of this, they fight so stubbornly that the use of the cup should not be restored to the church of God in accord with the intent of Scripture and the testimonies of antiquity. But there is no doubt that underneath there are strong reasons why they judge that this restitution, as demanded, cannot be made without cost and loss to the papalist kingdom. It is useful to think about these reasons, for in this way it will be possible to understand the plan, mind, goal, purpose, and the whole craftiness of the Tridentine decrees.

13 Although they pretend far other things, they strenuously hide the true causes. These are not, however, so hidden and obscure that they cannot be understood from what they say and do, so there is no need of

---

[8] On the term "accidents" see Fourth Topic, footnote 19. The term is here used of the appearance of bread and wine, which, according to Tridentine teaching, remains although the essence of the elements has been changed into the body and blood of Christ.

forensic conjectures or mathematical divinations. And because this consideration can furnish some light to the examination of the decrees, we shall briefly note down the principal reasons the papalists seem to have for defending the mutilation of the Lord's Supper so stubbornly and pertinaciously with whatever arguments they can collect against the clearest light of truth.

Now the first reason is, as they themselves write, that they are afraid that if the prohibition of so many years is removed, and the use of the cup is restored to the church as this is sought in accord with the intent of the Scriptures and the testimonies of antiquity, it will come to pass that many other things in the rest of the close-knit structure of the papalist kingdom may be shaken and fall down. For because the mutilation of the Lord's Supper, decreed by a number of councils, namely that of Constance and that of Basel, has been confirmed by many popes and been approved by protectors of the papal kingdom now for many years as godly, just, and by all means to be retained, and has until now been upheld, not so much by arguments as by the exile and martyrdom of many godly persons, they have a presentiment that, if now a change and correction according to Scripture is permitted, it will come to pass that they may not be able any longer to restrain men from either demanding or making a change also in other matters which in the papalist kingdom have been decreed contrary to the intent of Scripture and have become established through long use. Thus the restitution of the Dominical cup would be, as it were, a confession of error and would gradually furnish an opening, little by little, for the ruin of the whole papacy; for it would come to pass that men might no longer tolerate it that they are given words under titles of councils, church, custom, etc., in matters which are received and customary under the papacy against Scripture, if weakening in any one thing is permitted. For they are acquainted with the simile of Philo about the embassy to Caius: "As in buildings, when one stone is removed, even though the rest seem firm, they are nevertheless weakened and settle, and little by little incline to ruin." Osius clearly explains this reason, for these are his words: "The error of those who say, 'If the cup is granted to the laity, and wives to the priests, agreement will easily be reached between the papists and the Lutherans,' is as broad as heaven itself, as the saying is. A fine concord, by which not the faults of the papacy, which can be borne, but the papacy itself is wholly overthrown." These are the words of Osius.

The second reason is that until now the pope has arrogated to himself and his the authority and power of imposing whatever he pleases on consciences, even if it cannot be shown and proved from Scripture, and again of changing, mutilating, and abrogating even those things which have the institution and testimony of Scripture.

This has spawned the strange sayings of the canonists that the pope can do all things against the law, above the law, and outside of the law, and that he can grant dispensations against the four councils, yes, against the words of the Gospel, although not against its intention. With respect to the epistles of Paul they say that the pope is not only able to dispense from them but to decree against them. They foresee, however, that a dangerous and destructive prejudice will be generated against this papalist tyranny if the use of the cup is restored to the church according to the command of Scripture. Therefore they judge that nothing dare be yielded in the matter of the petition about the restoration of the cup, or that the concession should be so qualified that the absolute papalist rule in the church may remain whole, in good repair, and safe. This reason the Tridentine fathers themselves indicate obscurely in the second chapter of this session.

The third reason concerns the hearths and altars of the papalists. For after they had taken the use of the Dominical cup away from the laity, they transferred the words of promise about the application of the New Testament and of the remission of sins to the sacrifice of the Mass and began to preach grandly about propitiation, atonement, and many other divine benefits, how these are acquired through the sacrifice of the Mass and applied by the priest to whomever he wills. But with respect to the mutilated Communion they greatly exaggerated the danger of eating to judgment, and that without the necessary explanation of the true preparation. Thus people were frightened away from Communion and ran together in crowds to purchase Masses, for which they offered and heaped together almost all the treasures of the world. For all wanted to be included under the cup of the Lord on account of the comforting promise connected with it, as an old German saying shows. Many thought they were preparing for themselves propitiation and atonement for sins more adequately through the *opus operatum* of the priests when they gave the priests money for Masses than when they underwent the danger of judgment in Communion, because worthy preparation was placed in our purity, and even so it was added that remission of sins is not received in Communion even by those who eat worthily. This conviction increased the wealth and power of the papalist kingdom immeasurably. Therefore they fear for this profitable trafficking in Masses, lest it suffer some loss if the use of the Dominical cup together with the teaching of the application[9] and sealing of the New Testament should be restored to the church. This argument looms very large in the papalist kingdom. They also explain it in words that are not obscure when they say that among the reasons for the prohibition of the cup this is not the least, that there may be a distinction between the Communion of the priests and of the laity.

I judge that the fourth reason is the dogma that we must doubt our reconciliation and the forgiveness of our sins. For the Son of God testifies that in the use of the cup He applies the benefits of the New Testament, which He has purchased with His blood, and seals them to everyone who receives the cup in faith, by imparting to each the most excellent pledge of His precious blood. The dogma of doubt cannot stand together with this teaching. Once the opinion of doubt has been removed, vows, pilgrimages, purchasing of Masses, brotherhoods, indulgences, and whatever else belongs to the revenue system of the papalist kingdom will collapse. Hence these tears.

14 This consideration of reasons will show, among other things, also with what intention and what trickery the Tridentine fathers place the justification of the denial of the cup at the head in this fifth session, although there are on all sides requests for the restoration of the use of the Dominical cup; namely, in order that, no matter what happens afterward by way of concession in the matter of the cup, it may not be upright, that is, in accord with the intent of Scripture and the testimonies of antiquity, but that even this may be used to serve to confirm and strengthen the tyranny of Antichrist, as we shall demonstrate later at the proper place.

15 But let us now, with the gracious help of God, come to the examination of the decrees and canons of this fifth session. The sum and substance of it is that Communion under both kinds is not commanded by the ordinance of Christ to faithful lay people and to clerics who are not officiating, and that therefore it is not necessary for them, but that Communion under one kind is sufficient for them for salvation, for they are not cheated out of any grace necessary for salvation even if they receive only one kind while the other is neglected. The purpose of these decrees is to show that the papalist church has not erred in the prohibition and denial of the cup, but that when she did this she was moved by weighty and just causes and reasons. All this is aimed at taking slight notice of and flouting the petitions of kings and princes which were laid before the council in behalf of restoration of the cup. For if the Commu-

---

[9] The text of the *Examen* has *appellatione*, while Nigrinus, who translates *Zueignung*, evidently read *applicatione*, which seems to be demanded by the context.

nion of the cup has been taken away and prohibited for weighty and just reasons, then the petition for its restoration is unjust and not without levity.

Now, however, we shall have the antithesis, that is, we shall hear the causes and arguments for the changed and mutilated Communion, which they assert are weighty and just and which they set against what we have noted down on the basis of Scripture and the testimonies of antiquity in behalf of preserving Communion in its entirety as it was instituted by the Son of God and handed down and confirmed by Paul. It will not be unpleasant to collect them and to consider with what unequal weight sophistic darkness and human suppositions battle against the clear light of the Word of God. However, not all causes and arguments with which papalists have heretofore defended their mutilation are repeated in the Tridentine decrees, but all of them, no matter what they are, are in the second chapter and the second canon pronounced weighty and just.

In order therefore that the antithesis may be more complete, we shall note down as briefly as can be done the chief reasons which have hitherto been argued with great effort by papalists in defense and justification of the mutilation of the Lord's Supper, showing only the sources and grounds for their refutation, in order that it may become apparent what are the causes and reasons which are judged to be so weighty and just in the papalist kingdom that on their account what the Son of God instituted and commanded in His testament must be abrogated and prohibited. Afterward we shall examine the arguments of the Council of Trent more fully and carefully.

ARTICLE III

Arguments Urged at the Time of the Council of Constance for Communion Under One Kind

1 Now the Council of Constance, in prohibiting and forbidding Communion under the form of both bread and wine to lay people and to clerics who are not officiating, under threat of excommunication and even with calling to aid the secular arm, gives these reasons for its prohibition:

1. Even though Christ administered this venerable sacrament to His disciples under the form of both bread and wine, nevertheless, in spite of this, the custom of Communion under one kind only must now be held as law.

The reader sees that a different custom is set against the institution of

Christ, and set against it in such a way that a testamentary institution, not of man or of any creature, but of the Son of God Himself, is compelled to yield to a custom. Indeed, it must be compelled to yield in such a way that if anyone prefers to follow the testamentary institution of the Son of God rather than the differing custom of men, he is punished as a heretic by excommunication, even with invocation of the help of the secular arm.

However, there is no need for a lengthy and elaborate refutation, for the antithesis itself sufficiently shows to pious minds what manner of argument this is which ascribes greater weight to a recent custom of men than to the testamentary ordinance of the Son of God. The little clause, "even though Christ instituted under both kinds, nevertheless, in spite of this," etc., is so infamous that even the papalists themselves are now ashamed of it. For now they formulate this argument differently, as we shall show later.

Therefore I shall add only this, that in Cyprian, Bk. 2, Letter No. 3, there is found a clear refutation of this argument which is, as it were, expressly opposed to this decree. For disputing about the consecration of the cup and its administration to the people he says: "If only Christ, concerning whom the Father testifies from heaven, 'Hear Him,' is to be heard, we ought not to consider what someone before us thought ought to be done but what Christ, who is before all, did first. For one ought not to follow the custom of man but the truth of God, because God says through Isaiah: 'They worship Me in vain, teaching commandments and doctrines of men.' " Known are also the statements of ancients which Gratian cites, dist. 8, about the antithesis of custom and truth.

The reader will, however, observe that at the Council of Constance that argument which now is judged among the papalists to be the chief one was not yet known, namely, that the words of Christ about the institution of the cup do not pertain to the laity but only to the priests. Otherwise there would have been no need in the reasoning of the Council of Constance to oppose only custom to the institution of Christ. We shall put this observation to use later.

2. Granted, that in the primitive church the sacrament was received by the faithful under both kinds, nevertheless, in spite of this, the custom which was introduced, etc.

The reader must again be admonished to observe how the papalists afterward changed the grounds for this mutilation. For now they contend that the custom of communicating the laity under one kind only has always been there, also in the primitive church, even as far back as the time of the apostles. But the Council of Constance confesses simply and clearly what the facts are, namely, that Communion under one kind only was unknown to the primitive church.

However, the argument of the Council of Constance sets two customs in opposition to each other, of which the one, namely, that the Eucharist is received by the faithful under both kinds, agrees with the institution of Christ, that is, with the truth, and is the oldest, the custom of the ancient and purer church; the other, about one kind, was introduced into the church when it was growing old, during the most recent times, when in many things there had already been a departure from the purity of the primitive church. Now the question is: Which custom should give way to the other? Augustine adduces a most fitting saying from Cyprian: "If truth supports a custom, nothing ought to be held more firmly; in other cases, however, truth ought to be set above custom." Pope Julius, *De consecratione*, dist. 2, refutes the custom of presenting the Eucharist dipped in the cup from the earlier custom of the church, which agrees with the teaching of the gospels and of the apostles, where the command regarding the bread and that concerning the cup are reported separately.

But the Council of Constance decrees that the most ancient custom of the primitive church, which accords with the institution of Christ, should yield to a different, more recent, and later custom, which is in opposition to the institution and command of Christ. And the chief point in this argument, the *maxima,* as the dialecticians call it, is the clause, "in spite of this."[10] What this argument is worth the naked antithesis alone sufficiently shows.

3. Christ gave His apostles the Eucharist during the Supper, after the food, or after they had eaten. Nevertheless the authority of the sacred canons and the laudable custom of the church has retained and still retains that now it is offered to those who have fasted. Therefore, by the same reasoning, even though Christ gave His disciples both kinds, the custom can nevertheless be introduced that the lay people are communicated under one kind only.

I answer: There is a vast difference between the things that pertain to the substance of the sacraments, which have the institution, precept, and command of God, and the external circumstances, which do not have the precept and command of God but are freely observed for the sake of edification. Such a circumstance is whether this sacrament is to be re-

---

[10] The Latin is *hoc non obstante,* which might also be rendered, "this notwithstanding."

ceived after eating or, indeed, by those who have fasted. For Christ, who wanted at that time to put an end to the figures of the Old Testament and to institute in their place the sacrament of the New Testament, for this reason first ate the Passover with His disciples and afterward instituted the Eucharist. He did not, indeed, command us that before Communion we should kill and eat the Passover; rather, the ancient Passover was at the time of this action abrogated. And Paul plainly declares that we are not obligated to that circumstance of the time so that we cannot celebrate the Lord's Supper save at that time, that month, day, and hour, for he says: "As often as," etc. However, the Communion of the cup belongs to the very substance of the Eucharist. For it is beyond debate that the substance of the sacraments consists in matter and form, that is, in the Word of God and the external element divinely instituted for this purpose. Thus Irenaeus says that the Eucharist consists of two things, an earthly and a heavenly. Now Christ ordained as the element of the Eucharist two distinct kinds, apart or separately (as the ancients speak) to be consecrated, dispensed, and received, namely, bread and wine, and He adds to them separately the command: "Eat; drink; do this." And Paul adds that this ordinance of the Son of God should continue even to the end of the world. Therefore the deduction of Constance is by no means valid: Christ gave the Eucharist to men who had supped; we, however, give it to those who have fasted; therefore the church is able to abrogate, forbid, and prohibit the Communion of the cup.

There are those who are not afraid to ascribe this argumentation and deduction to Augustine himself, of whom they continue to assert that in Letter No. 118 he ascribes so much to the custom of the church that on account of it one should depart from the institution of Christ. But they do Augustine a manifest and very great wrong. For as he is about to discuss church rites, he at once, in the very first part of the epistle, excepts the celebration of the sacraments which is recommended in the canonical Scriptures. And afterward, when he wants to explain this question, whether the Eucharist should be received by those who have fasted, or after they have eaten other food, he uses a threefold distinction: 1. If the authority of the divine Scriptures prescribes which of these should be done, we are not to doubt that we should do according to what we read; 2. If any of those things, namely, rites which the authority of the divine Scriptures does not prescribe, is frequently done by the whole church throughout the world, then it is an act of the most insolent madness to argue that it should not be done; 3. However, customs which vary in different localities and regions are under the law of liberty.

Now our question about the Communion of the cup clearly belongs to the things which divine authority prescribes, as we have shown above from the evangelists and from Paul. And Augustine himself, in the beginning of his epistle, expressly refers the communication of the body and blood of Christ to this first class. Therefore that applies which Augustine declares in this place, that we are not to doubt that we should do as we read.

The other question, namely, whether you should commune after fasting or after eating, Augustine refers to the third class, concerning which there is liberty. He proves this as follows: The reason why Christ instituted the Eucharist after His last supper was that He wanted to impress this last one on the hearts and memory of the disciples. However, He gave no instruction in what order (that is, of time) it should be received thereafter. And Augustine adds: "For if Christ had instructed them that it should always be received after eating other food, I believe no one would have changed this custom." Indeed, from Paul he shows a different custom. For Paul reproves and corrects those who were mixing the Lord's Supper with their own meals and eating. There is therefore a vast difference between these two: to give the Eucharist not after other foods but to those who have fasted, and utterly to take away the cup from the faithful lay people.

4. The basis for the decree of Constance is: The custom that the Eucharist should be received by lay people only under the form of bread has been introduced in accord with reason in order to avoid certain dangers and offenses.

The danger they understand to be that some of the content of the cup might be spilled. From this, they judge, such great offenses of profanation of holy things (as they call it) would spring that, for the sake of avoiding these dangers and offenses, they forbid the use of the cup entirely to the lay people.

But we answer: If these dangers and offenses are so great and are so necessarily and absolutely connected with the Communion of the cup that provision against them can be made by no other precaution than that the use of the Dominical cup is entirely taken away from the faithful laity and forbidden and prohibited to them, then the whole primitive and ancient church must be charged with sacrilege. And this reproach will fall upon the Author of the sacrament Himself, who instituted such a thing which cannot be observed in the church without the danger of offense and sacrilege. But if these dangers are not absolutely and of necessity connected with the Communion of the cup, then it will be possible to meet these dangers in another way and with other precautions, so that it will not be necessary on their account simply to do away with the use of the cup. Augustine testifies, quest. 1, ch. 1, *Interrogo,* that it is possible also for the consecrated bread to fall to the ground. Should therefore also the other kind, and thus the whole sacrament, be taken away from the laity? Certainly, this preposterous solicitude and prudence, that for this reason the cup is entirely forbidden, was unknown to the ancient church, where such dangers were much more to be feared than now. For every day, or certainly every Lord's Day, the whole fellowship communicated, and indeed often in so great a multitude that the largest churches were not able to contain them all at one time, so that it was often necessary to repeat the celebration of the Lord's Supper on the same day, as Pope Leo shows, Letter No. 81.

In some places the Eucharist was also given to small children; yes, sometimes communicants carried the blood of Christ home with them, as Gregory of Nazianzus relates about his sister Gorgonia. The Eucharist, poured out, was given to the youthful servant of Serapion to be carried to a sick man. And indeed, according to Canon 76 of the Fourth Council of Carthage and Canon 11 of the Council of Toledo, the blood of Christ was given also to sick men who had difficulty swallowing.

It is therefore a mere pretext and not a genuine reason what the papalists allege about danger. Yes, such things happened fairly frequently in the ancient church. For according to Cyprian, Treatise 3, *De lapsis,* in the case of a very young girl who resisted and pinched her mouth shut with her lips, the deacon poured in something from the cup, which, however, as we read, burst forth from her polluted inwards shortly thereafter. We read in Chrysostom that the blood of Christ was spilled on the garments of some soldiers who broke into the sanctuary.

The fathers were greatly troubled when something like this happened, as Augustine testifies, ch. *Interrogo vos,* yet they did not consider it so monstrous a sacrilege that on account of it the use of the cup should be entirely abolished; but they were careful, and used precautions as much as they could, that such a thing should not happen through negligence. Now, however, in this sluggish old age of the church, when the prosperous times of the church have passed, we want to be more prudent in this matter than the fathers, martyrs, confessors, and even the apostles themselves; yes, the wisdom of God is justified by her children.

What therefore the pretext, or rather, that shamming of danger can avail against such outstanding, solid, and compelling arguments from Scripture and testimonies of antiquity those also do not deny who are not totally estranged from the papalist side.

5. Since it is to be firmly believed that the whole Christ, body and blood, is as truly present under the form of the bread as under the form of

the wine, therefore the Eucharist is to be received by the laity only under the form of the bread.

This argument is repeated in the third Tridentine chapter; therefore we shall defer its explanation until we get to that chapter.

6. This custom has been observed for a long time; therefore it must be regarded as a law.

We shall take it as an acknowledged fact that during all of 1,400 years after the birth of Christ there had been no law in the church, no conciliar or dogmatic constitution to the effect that the sacrament of the Eucharist is to be received by the laity only under the form of the bread, but that such a custom, even as many other things, was little by little brought into the church during these latter times. What kind of argument this is when they say that this custom has long been observed we shall explain in connection with the second Tridentine chapter. So far as the argument is concerned, I know that it has force in civil matters. But in the church no custom either should or can prescribe to or pass sentence upon the Word, institution, instruction, and command of God. In this matter, namely, about consecrating the Dominical cup and administering it to the common people, Cyprian clearly overthrows this argument. For when the Aquarii[11] adduced in their own behalf a custom of certain men who had been before Cyprian, Cyprian is by no means willing to grant that this custom is to be considered a law, but sets against this custom the law of the gospels about consecrating the Dominical cup and administering it to the people; for he says that the law of the gospels and the tradition of the Lord are to be observed everywhere, that there may be no departure from what Christ taught and did.

These are the arguments and the grounds for the decree of Constance, on which the law which abolishes, takes away, prohibits, and forbids the Dominical cup was first built up. These arguments I wanted to recount in an orderly way, in bare form, that it may become apparent how weighty and just they are, as the Tridentine chapter calls them, and that, when a comparison has been made of the arguments which followed about the same matter after the council, we may consider how afterward other grounds were sought and how, when the arguments proved weak, the papalists later caused new remedies to be applied so that they might be able to set it forth in a more plausible form and manner.

2 To a fuller clarification of the decree of Constance there belongs the treatise of Gerson on the Communion of the laity. It is worthy of note that after the interdict of the cup had been promulgated, when the elders

---

[11] The Aquarii used water instead of wine at the Lord's Supper.

of the Council of Constance noticed that many were not satisfied with the reasons on which the Council, as on a foundation, built its prohibition, they requested of John Gerson that he should search for other, more weighty and solid reasons, more persuasive arguments and proofs, by which those could be overcome who found it hard to bear that Communion under both kinds as instituted by Christ, confirmed by the apostle, and observed by the primitive church, should be snatched away from them with such feeble and trifling reasons as are laid down in the decree of Constance. This was done in the two-year period after the decree was promulgated. For the promulgation was made A.D. 1415, on the 15th day of June. Gerson published his treatise at Constance in the year 1417, on the 20th day of August. It is worthy of perpetual memory to all posterity that we have from this writing of Gerson the opinions which were expressed by the theologians at the Council of Constance when they deliberated about the reasons for the prohibition and removal of the cup.

Gerson says the following: "There are present in this council theologians from the most famous universities who are eminent both in numbers and in merit; many of those who were gathered together to consider this matter say that the custom of not communicating the laity under both kinds was introduced rightfully and for good reason, especially after the faithful had become numerous, and that it was done for the avoidance of manifold danger, irreverence, and offense in connection with the reception of this blessed sacrament. They enumerate these dangers thus:

"1. In spilling. 2. In carrying from place to place. 3. In polluting of the vessels, which ought to be kept sacred, not handled and touched indiscriminately by lay people. 4. In the long beards of the men. 5. In preservation for the sick, for vinegar could develop in the vessel; and in summer midges or flies might be generated, and at times it might even grow putrid. 6. It might, as it were, become unappetizing for many to drink, when many others had drunk before. 7. In what kind of vessel would the consecration of such an amount of wine be made as would be required at Easter for several thousand persons? 8. There would be loss on account of the expense for the wine, for in some places wine can scarcely be found and in others it is expensive to buy. 9. There would be danger of freezing. 10. There is danger that a false belief would be brought in, as if the dignity of the laity in receiving the body of Christ were as great as that of the priests. 11. People would think that the Communion of the cup had always been, and that it is necessary. Thus all the clergy, doctors, and prelates would have sinned who had not opposed a different custom both orally and in writing. 12. It would be thought that the power and efficacy of the sacrament was more in the receiving than in the consecration. 13. It would follow that the Roman church does not hold rightly concerning the sacraments and that it is not to be followed in this. 14. It would follow that the Council of Constance had erred with respect to faith and good practice. 15. It would be an occasion for schisms in Christendom."

3 We learn from Gerson that these were the reasons of the theologians at the Council of Constance. There is no need to add specific refutations to each of them, since for the most part they are such that the papalists themselves are now ashamed of them. We have spoken above about the danger of spilling. About the danger in carrying the sacrament about, reserving it, likewise about the handling of the vessels, the answer is easy. For Christ, as Origen rightly says, did not command that the consecrated bread and the cup of blessing should be reserved for tomorrow, but said: "Take; eat and drink." These are therefore human traditions. And because for the sake of preserving these traditions the use of the cup, which has the institution and command of Christ, is forbidden and taken away from the laity, the answer of Christ in Mark 7:8-9: "You leave the commandment of God and hold fast the tradition of men," likewise: "You make the commandment of God of no effect in order to keep your tradition," is rightly applied here. And a wise antiquity, which carried both the bread and the consecrated cup to the sick and the absent, and for this use in some places and at some times reserved them for a short time, was not so worried about these dangers that it abolished the use of the cup on their account. Therefore this prudence of the papalists is new and only lately learned, sprung up finally after 1,400 years. None of these dangers would need to be feared if the traditions of men had been abandoned, if the cup of blessing had not been reserved but immediately dispensed according to the institution of Christ.

Among the ancients the question about the size of the vessels did not even arise, although there was at times such a multitude of communicants that not even the largest churches could hold them, as Leo shows, *Ad Dioscorum,* Letter No. 81. Furthermore, how ridiculous is the reason about the long beards of men! Surely in the primitive church not all the faithful were beardless. And among the apostles themselves (if the description of Nicephorus is true) Peter had a thick, curly beard. But if it were wholly necessary that one of two things should be done, should not rather the long beards of the men have been cut back than that the use of the Dominical cup should be prohibited? What indeed do they invent about beards in females, since they deny the cup of the Lord to them also? This, I suppose, is one of those just and weighty causes which the Council of Trent praises! Of the same weightiness and justice is the argument about the great expense of the wine, and that it is abhorrent if many drink out of one cup. It is evident, therefore, that the church has now become quite dainty, seeing that antiquity often reiterates that the sign and token of the church's unity is that one cup is offered to all, as Chrysostom says. The other reason, where they say that the use of the cup was taken away from the laity in order that in the reception of the Lord's body the dignity of the priests might be greater than that of the lay people is not only without weight and ridiculous but downright false, for Paul teaches that in Christ Jesus the believers are all one (Gal. 3:28). This argument was already expressly exploded, as it were, by Chrysostom, Homily 18, on 2 Corinthians.

In the final reasons the theologians of the Council of Constance openly confess what is the foremost and principal reason why they contend so stubbornly about the prohibition of the cup, namely, that the clergy, doctors, prelates, the Roman church, and the Council of Constance may not seem to have erred. The reader should mark this reason well.

Surely, if Gerson were not a capable witness, scarcely anyone would believe that such trivial, feeble, worthless, and ridiculous arguments had been advanced in so grave and serious a matter by theologians gathered from the foremost universities of the whole world.

Therefore, when the papalists in this dispute bring forward the name of an ecumenical council as if it were the head of the Gorgon, let there be opposed to them the naked shame of the arguments and grounds on the basis of which this decree of the prohibition of Constance is reared. And indeed Gerson himself did not sufficiently trust these arguments, which are not worthy to be called theological; therefore he searched for others when this was requested of him by the elders of the council. Of what kind these can be in such a cause I shall set forth in a table, as it were, so they can be viewed nakedly, chiefly with this purpose in mind that the reader may consider on the basis of the collation what the men of Trent have borrowed from the school of Gerson and how they put forward these very reasons under another form, more cautiously and with more expert skill. This collation will be of some use later.

Now Gerson's first reason is this: With respect to the institution and administration of the sacraments certain things are of necessity in a sacrament, and of divine right, namely, that the consecration be carried out with such and such a form of words and with such and such an element, e.g., bread. Certain things, however, are necessary only on account of a command of the church, and by human right or appointment, such as that the consecration be performed with unleavened bread, in a church or on an altar which has been consecrated, with such and such vestments, with light, with Epistle and Gospel, likewise with an empty stomach. Such things are variable and can be changed by the church. Among these things he places also the use of the cup; that is, he places the use of the cup, which has the Word, instruction, precept, and command of the Son of God, in the same place and on the same level with papalist vestments of priests at Mass, with lighted candles, with stones[12] enchanted by means of certain rites, etc.

The second reason: Reception of the Eucharist under both kinds by the laity never was a command of divine right, even though it was done well when it was done on the basis of the teaching or persuasion or counsel of the church. Now, however, when the opposite custom has grown up on account of a sure reason praised and commanded by the church, such reception is rash, presumptuous, offensive, seditious, and consequently leads to eternal damnation.

It will be a pleasure, afterward, to see how these same arguments are put forward by the men of Trent, not in so open and crass a form, but refined with more subtle skill.

Third: Christ says in John 6:52 ff.: "Unless you eat the flesh of the Son of man and drink His blood, you have no life in you." But in the same place He says soon afterward: "He who eats this bread will live forever." Therefore Communion under both kinds is not necessary, but it is sufficient if it is received under the form of the bread only. The same argument is repeated in the first Tridentine chapter.

Fourth: Spiritual eating and drinking is always necessary. In little children and in a case of necessity total sacramental Communion is not necessary for salvation. Therefore a part of it, namely, the use of the cup, can even apart from necessity be forbidden to and withheld from the laity. The first Tridentine chapter covertly takes note of this argument when it says, *ex necessitate salutis* ["because it is necessary for salvation"].

Fifth: Gerson knows very well how bad it sounds to pious ears that the decree of Constance, although it concedes that the institution of Christ prescribes the use of both kinds, sets up against this only the brief phrase, *hoc non obstante* ["this not withstanding," or: "in spite of this"]. Therefore he searches for other remedies that he, as a prudent man, may bring to this weak argument some remedy, according to a saying of Euripides. It all comes to this, that Holy Scripture is not to be received on its own and completely, regardless of other traditions of men, but to have a true understanding one ought frequently and humbly use human laws,

---

[12] The text of 1574 has *lapidibus*, stones. This has been emended by Ed. Preuss to *lampadibus*, torches.

canons, and decrees, and the glosses of the doctors. In fact, the exposition of Scripture handed down by the ancients ought to receive the interpretation of more recent expositions. He finally concludes that Scripture, in its interpretation, is dissolved into the authority and custom of the universal church.

This opinion of Gerson is later explained more fully and at greater length by Nicolaus of Cusa in his second letter to the Bohemians. He says that the Scriptures are adjusted to the times and understood in various ways, so that at one time they are explained according to what is then the current universal usage; when this usage is changed, the meaning may also be changed.

The papalists retain the sinews of this argument, but now that the light of the Gospel is shining, they do not dare to set it forth in such a form but elude the institution of Christ with other stratagems, as we shall show later.

Sixth: Gerson sees that this also is rather awkward, that the decree of Constance simply grants that in the primitive church, when the congregations met, the common and universal practice was Communion under both kinds. And although Gerson is unable to deny this and to teach the contrary either with testimonies or with examples, he nevertheless adds that it seems more probable that this observance never was common with all since the time of the doctors. This reminder of Gerson stirred up the papalist agents of our time to make a search for some examples by which they try to prove this in particular, in order that they may no longer have need of that abominable phrase: *hoc non obstante* ["this notwithstanding"].

Seventh: Gerson says that when the testimonies and examples of antiquity witness that the faithful people ought to drink the blood of Christ, these should be explained of the priests, who celebrate for all the people, so that the people are said to drink the blood of Christ because the ministers drink it for them, namely because (as Gabriel Biel says) the priest is the mouth of the church. This reason is of such a nature that no one of the papalists dares to use it openly and in this form.

Eighth: Although Augustine repeatedly speaks of the Communion of the laity under both kinds as being necessary, he is also found to have said: "Believe, and you have eaten." And in the same way he could say: "Believe, and you have drunk." Therefore Communion of a lay person under the form of wine is not necessary, but prohibition of the use of the cup can be made a law so that the Eucharist is received by the laity only under the form of bread. But there is much more in this conclusion than in the premises. For Augustine did not in this pronouncement so much as dream anything about mutilating and changing the testamentary institution of the Son of God.

But Gerson argues that Christ in the sermon in John 6 is not speaking of Capernaitic butchery of His body but of spiritual eating which is done through faith, for He says: "Why do you prepare teeth and belly? Believe, and you have eaten." This saying is rightly applied to salutary reception of the Eucharist, which one ought to approach in faith. It is also used in a case of necessity, namely, when frequent sacramental Communion cannot be had, for then the saying of Augustine is valid: "Believe, and you have eaten." However, the conclusion of Constance in no way follows from this. But if some such thing should follow from it, it would not be the use of the Dominical cup but the use of the Eucharistic bread which would have to be abrogated and prohibited, and that not to the laity only, but universally to all, for Augustine speaks generally: "Believe, and you have eaten."

Gerson's foremost and the final reason is this: Since the determination of the council has already passed to the stage of a matter decided, the aid of the secular arm should be called for rather than dealing through reasoned arguments. Likewise, in overcoming those who think otherwise, it would seem advantageous if the emperor would undertake to prosecute and terminate this matter even with the power of the secular arm. Thus says Gerson.

Let it be noted that this is the foremost and the final proof of Constance, because it seems to be a much shorter way. Gerson also declares expressly against whom he is disputing. For he says that those who say that reception of the Eucharist is lawful and useful to the laity err just as much as those who say that it is necessary—necessary because of the divine precept and of a law from which there is no dispensation.

These are the reasons which were debated and put forward at the time of the Council of Constance, when that unjust and wicked law was first born which forbids and takes away the use of the Dominical cup from the laity, contrary to the institution of Christ, contrary to the tradition of the apostles and the observance of the primitive church.

ARTICLE IV

Arguments of the Council of Basel

1 Soon, however, namely almost 20 years later, at the Council of Basel, the same prohibition was repeated and confirmed. It is worth the trouble to observe how already then certain reasons of the Council of

Constance began to be put forward in another form, because they had been set forth too openly and grossly.

1. Because they sensed that pious ears were not without reason offended by the clause of Constance: "Even though Christ instituted it under both kinds, this notwithstanding, the custom," etc., they now put forth the reason slightly changed, thus: "Lay persons and clergy who are not celebrating are not bound by the precept of the Lord to receive both kinds." This amendment they have taken from Gerson's reminder, which also the Council of Trent imitates, as we shall explain at the proper place.

2 2. The following formulation of the argument of Constance did not please the men of Basel either: "Even though in the primitive church the Eucharist was received by the faithful under both kinds, this notwithstanding," etc. Therefore the Council of Basel formulates the argument thus: "It is the church's business to order how this sacrament is to be administered in a manner which it sees as advantageous for reverence toward the sacrament itself and for the salvation of the faithful." We shall see later how this argument is repeated in the second Tridentine chapter.

3 3. So long as they communicate according to the ordinance and observance of the church, whether under one kind or under both, it is profitable for salvation to worthy communicants. Why not rather according to the ordinance of Christ and the tradition of the apostles, which the primitive church religiously followed? Now let this be considered, I beg, what it means to promise salvation to those who, forsaking the commandment of God, hold to the traditions of men, yes, who abrogate the commandment of God on account of their traditions (Mark 10).[13] Surely, faith is altogether necessary for communing worthily. But faith comes by hearing, namely, through hearing of the Word of God. Therefore where there is a departing from the Word of God there can be no true faith. When Cyprian was disputing about consecrating the cup of the Lord and administering it to the people, he applied the word of Isaiah to those who by a human institution depart from what Christ the Master did, taught, and commanded: "In vain they worship Me, teaching doctrines and commandments of men." It is worth remembering how Jacob Ziegler amplified and clarified this argument of Basel against the Waldensians. These are his precise words about Communion under one kind: "We eat this bread in obedience to the Roman church, certain that on account of this obedience of faith we shall live eternally."

---

[13] The reference should be Mark 7:1-23.

4 4. The whole Christ is contained under one kind; therefore the other can be either omitted or abrogated and prohibited.

5 5. The men of Basel judge that the not very ancient custom of communing under one kind should be considered a law for these reasons: 1. Because it was introduced for good reasons. The reasons are of the kind we have recounted above from Gerson's description. 2. Because it has been very long observed. We shall show in the explanation of the second Tridentine chapter that this is false. 3. Because it has been recommended by the doctors. However, these are understood to be not the doctors of the ancient and purer church but those who were at this time ruling in the schools. How weighty their recommendations were we have already shown from Gerson's writing.

ARTICLE V

Arguments in Behalf of the Mutilation of Communion Debated in Our Time

1 Let us now come to the debates of our own times, in which, when the light of God's Word was by God's special favor again kindled, necessity was imposed upon the papalists to seek for some pretext from Scripture for this mutilation. And because they saw that in this light of God's Word there was no longer any place for the phrase, "this notwithstanding," arguments had to be fashioned with new and more subtle skill. We shall not, however, unravel these arguments in their entirety, but shall only show by a comparison how afterward other and new grounds were sought, because the earlier ones did not satisfy even the papalists themselves, and how the old arguments, refined with new skill, were afterward reshaped in another form.

This is a clear indication that the cause which the papalist agents uphold in this dispute is evil, doubtful, weak, feeble, and in ruins. For the new grounds that are now mixed in are not the ones out of which this decree of mutilation was first constructed, but hired rhetoricians thought out such things with sophistic skill after the fact, in order that they might bountifully serve and somehow satisfy the side to which they had hired out their service. Therefore we shall briefly note down only those things which in our time, either new or renewed, have been put forward in this dispute by the agents of the papalist kingdom.

2 First of all let this be observed! Because there is in Scripture a clear and sure description of the testamentary institution of the Son of God, they saw that this light cannot, at this time, be torn away from the minds of men if it is said with the Council of Constance: "this notwithstanding," or if one feigns with the Council of Basel without proof that not all the faithful are bound by this commandment of Christ. Therefore they had to search for a pretext from certain distorted statements of Scripture if by chance they could with this trick becloud the vision of the more simple, or certainly that they might accomplish what Augustine says, *Contra litteras Petiliani:* "Ambiguous and strange testimonies sustain a bad cause at least by creating delays."

3 And indeed, although at the time of the councils of Constance and Basel they were not able to find any arguments in Scripture except in John 6, the more recent patrons of papalist shame find so great a supply of arguments that they are able (if it please the gods) to prove also from the Old Testament that the use of the Dominical cup should be taken away from the believing laity. For Hosius argues thus in the Confession of Piotrkow:[14] "As in the Old Testament there was this distinction between the priests and the laity, that the people ate together with the priests of the sacrifices which were composed of solid matter, but of the libations, which consisted of liquids, only the priests were permitted to drink, not the people (Lev. 4, 6, 16), therefore in the New Testament the use of the cup must be prohibited to the laity, that there may be the same distinction between the priests and the laity which obtained in the Old Testament."

But in the Old Testament it was not the priests who ordained this to defend and glorify the honor of their order, but it was ordained by God. However, in the New Testament the Son of God instituted the Supper to be shared by all the faithful, that is, His disciples, in which the cup of the Lord was given to all on an equal basis, as Theophylact says. And Paul says concerning the whole church: "We have all drunk into one Spirit." Therefore it does not follow: In the Old Testament there was by the command of God a distinction between priest and people in participation in the sacrifices; therefore even though Christ instituted the Communion of the Eucharist under both kinds, and the apostles handed it down and the primitive church preserved it thus, nevertheless, in order that this distinction of the Old Testament may remain in the same way also in the New Testament, the testamentary institution of the Son of God should rather be changed and mutilated by men, as if indeed there ought to be no difference between the times of the Old Testament and of the New.

What, then, is the abrogation of the Old Testament, if the institution

---

[14] Stanislaus Hosius, a Polish bishop and leader in the Counterreformation, was requested at the Synod of Piotrkow by the assembled bishops to draw up a confession of the Catholic faith. This confession was subscribed to by the bishops and published.

of Christ is to be changed in order that there may be no distinction between the Old and the New Testament? And what need is there for a long refutation, since that argument in this form has been clearly and, as it were, specifically rejected and exploded in the true and purer antiquity, particularly by Chrysostom, Homily 18, on 2 Corinthians, whose words we have cited above. The ancients also proved from the use of manna, and from waters out of the rock, that the use of both kinds belongs to all the faithful in the New Testament.

4 It is a marvelous feat that Eck, in his *Loci communes,* justifies the sacrilege of the denial of the cup from this, that the Lord foretold concerning the descendants of Eli that whoever comes to the priest will say to him: "Put me, I pray you, in one of the priest's places, that I may eat a morsel of bread." A fine deduction, by Hercules, to draw the curse and punishment which God threatens to the descendants of Eli on account of atrocious crimes to the whole faithful people in the church, and that in such a way that on their account the benefit and privilege of the Dominical cup granted by Christ and handed down by the apostles should be forbidden and taken away from the faithful laity! Truly, this argument of Eck is worthy to be placed among the arguments of the theologians of the Council of Constance which have been recited above. For as the cause is which they defend, so are also their arguments.

5 But let us hear further what arguments they bring forward from the New Testament, by which they attempt to escape the clear words of institution. Among other arguments Eck adduces the statement of Paul (1 Cor. 5:7): "Christ, our paschal lamb, has been sacrificed. Let us therefore celebrate the festival . . . with the unleavened bread of sincerity and truth." Because mention is there made of eating[15] and not of drinking, likewise of unleavened bread and not of wine, he pretends that he has proved that Paul taught the Corinthians the use of only one kind in the Communion of the Eucharist. I interpret it as a special judgment of God that the godless mutilation of the Lord's Supper has received such patrons and such arguments. Surely, if it were not otherwise evident, the quality of the reasons and arguments could show what manner of cause this is which the papalists defend. For it is clearly evident that Paul taught the Corinthians the use of both kinds (1 Cor. 11:23-29). Nevertheless the agents of the papalist kingdom are so totally devoid of shame that they are not afraid to pretend the contrary of Paul, and that with a statement which clearly has nothing to do with the matter. Let us grant to Eck that

---

[15] The word in the Vulgate is *epulor,* to feast or banquet, then also simply "to eat." The RSV translates: "celebrate the festival." The papalists fastened on the meaning "to eat."

he may translate the word *heortazein* according to his custom as "getting intoxicated."[16] But surely, Paul says nothing in this statement about taking the Lord's Supper either under one or under both kinds. Rather, he explains himself clearly that he does not speak about unleavened bread of wheat, or material bread, for he says "with the unleavened bread of sincerity and truth." In fact, he calls the believers "unleavened." Why, then, does Eck not on the basis of this passage take away also the consecrated bread from the Lord's Supper in order that the Christians may devour themselves, seeing they are unleavened? Yet on account of such arguments they want us to cast aside the clear words of the institution of the Supper!

6 Equally felicitous is also this argument of Eck's: "We pray daily, 'Give us this day our daily bread.' " Perhaps the reader may wonder by what trick this petition of the Lord's Prayer can be applied in defense of the mutilation of the Lord's Supper. I will tell you. A certain inquisitor of heretical perverseness wrote against the Waldensians. He frames the argument thus: "The ancients testify that the apostles at the celebration of the Lord's Supper added the recitation of the Lord's Prayer. But in it there is mention only of bread, not also of wine. Therefore it is apostolic to forbid and take away the use of the cup from the laity." Consequently, even though Christ instituted His Supper under the forms of bread and wine, the church nevertheless from the times of the apostles on aimed the Lord's Prayer against this institution of Christ, seeking abrogation and prohibition of the Dominical cup in order that Communion might be under one kind only. For she prays for bread only. This prayer of the church God did not grant until the Council of Constance, for the space of 1,400 years. Thus Christ in the Lord's Prayer taught to pray against Communion under both kinds, and indeed two years before He instituted the Lord's Supper. How then does the Roman pontiff grant the use of both kinds to certain nations if this militates against the Lord's Prayer, in which we ask for bread only? Has the Lord's Prayer by chance been prescribed only for the laity? What if the priests, when they celebrate, also pray: "Give us this day our daily bread?" Is therefore the use of the cup to be taken away from them also?

7 Although these things are so absurd, yet the Council of Trent is not afraid to whitewash all these arguments out of one and the same pot and to declare that they are weighty and just, although it is as certain as can be that this petition of the Lord's Prayer is not speaking of the Lord's

---

[16] The word in Latin is *crapulatio,* which is not a true translation of the Greek word, which simply means "to feast." *Crapulatio* means getting intoxicated. Ed. Preuss has substituted *epulatione* (feasting) for *crapulatione.*

Supper. Granted that some of the ancients constructed an allegory from it, the rule is nevertheless well known that dogmas not grounded in other sure and clear passages of Scripture dare not be made on the basis of allegories. Much less, therefore, may an allegorical proof be accepted contrary to the clear words of a testamentary institution of the Son of God. Moreover this allegory, if it is stubbornly pressed, simply does away with both kinds in the Eucharist. For even as it makes no mention of wine, so the allegory wants this petition to be understood neither of the substance nor of the form of material bread. The ancients who used this allegory never thought of prohibiting, abrogating, or taking away the use of the Dominical cup. And in the ancient church not even the slugabeds ever dreamed of anything like this argument from the Lord's Prayer against the words of institution.

But the papalists move in closer, desiring to prove from Scripture that Communion under one kind was used and approved by Paul and the other apostles, yes, by Christ Himself.

This is the trick, wholly unknown to the councils of Constance and Basel.

8 The Jesuits of Cologne argue as follows from Paul (1 Cor. 10:16-17): Where mention is made of breaking of bread and of blessing the cup, there both kinds are indicated. Soon thereafter, however, where he comes to participation or receiving, he says: "We all partake of the one bread." Therefore the priests who are consecrating ought to receive both kinds, but for the lay people one kind only suffices. This was, however, unknown to the church at the time of the ancient translator, who has: "We all partake of one loaf and of one cup."[17] And the Tridentine decree declares that this ancient and common edition must be accepted as the authentic one, which no one should dare or presume to reject under any pretext whatsoever.

Who decides that in this passage the ancient edition is not held as authentic by the papalists, but is rejected on the pretext that the Greek here does not make mention of the cup? Let the reader understand that the intention of the decree is this: When the ancient edition seems to support the errors and abuses of the papalist kingdom, then it is to be held authentic; however, when it is judged to oppose them, then it can be freely rejected.

But let us respond to the matter itself. In describing the manner of Communion in the Corinthian church . . . Paul makes mention of the

---

[17] Chemnitz is here following the reading in the Vulgate current in his time. In modern editions of the Vulgate the words *et de uno calice* have been placed among the variant readings, as have the corresponding words in the Greek New Testament.

bread and of the cup of the Lord. For when he wants to construct an argument from the Communion of the Eucharist which he might apply to the debate about things sacrificed to idols, it is enough to have taken this from one part. It is not as though it had been customary with the Corinthians to take only one part, for immediately he says to those whom he is urging to abstain from things offered to idols: "You cannot drink the cup of the Lord and the cup of demons," etc. Now this argument of Paul about things offered to idols does not pertain to the ministers of the church only. He also says (1 Cor. 12:13): "We all were made to drink of one Spirit."

In ch. 11 it is clearly written that Paul taught the Corinthians the use of both kinds. Therefore that statement of Paul, as it is read in Greek, in no way supports the mutilation of the papalists.

9 Some fashion an argument against the use of both kinds from the distinctive word ["or"] that Paul uses in 1 Cor. 11:27. For Paul says: "Whoever eats the bread *or* drinks the cup of the Lord in an unworthy manner." But in things that are separated [they say] it is sufficient to consider one part only. Therefore they pretend that Paul leaves it free whether the Eucharist be taken under one or under both kinds. The answer is, however, easy and clear. If Scripture had used the separating word ["or"] in the words of institution and in the passages where the form of the Lord's Supper is set down and described, the argument would certainly have considerable force. But now, as Paul recites the institution of Christ, he uses the connecting word ["also"], for he says: "In the same way also the cup," etc. Second, as Paul repeats his teaching, how he applied the institution of Christ to the whole church and how he prescribed the manner of celebrating the Lord's Supper, he repeatedly uses the connecting word. Third, when he describes the Communion custom in the Corinthian church he also uses the connecting word. These things are so clear that that argument about the separating word ["or"] in the other statement is approved by very few among the papalists themselves. For Paul does not in this statement prescribe, set down, or teach about the manner of Communion as he does in other statements through the connecting word ["and"] but, speaking of worthy and unworthy reception, he uses the separating word ["or"] in order to show that equal reverence is owed to each part and that, in receiving the Eucharist, guilt can be incurred in a number of ways, for whoever offers an insult to either part will be guilty.

This argument is therefore rightly turned back against the adversaries themselves. This is so because, according to the statement of Ambrose, that person insults the Lord who celebrates this sacrament differently than the Lord instituted it. Therefore those who in one part observe the institution of Christ but in the other violate, change, and mutilate it are not helped by any pretext. For the separating word ["or"] shows that those who act outside of or contrary to the institution either in the use of the bread or of the cup incur guilt. Therefore the separating word in Paul does not prove or confirm the papalist mutilation but sharply reproaches and condemns it. It also shows the grounds for the refutation of the foremost papalist argument: that it satisfies the institution of Christ if one kind is received in a worthy manner since the whole and entire Christ is present also under the one form. Paul declares that guilt is incurred when anything is done contrary to the institution, either in regard to the bread or to the cup of the Lord.

10 But no matter how things stand with respect to the teaching of Paul and the custom of the Pauline churches, they say that Communion under one kind was both taught and practiced by other apostles. But by what documents, I ask, do they prove this? John Fisher quotes from the apocryphal Gospel to the Hebrews that Christ, after His resurrection, gave the Eucharist to James the Just under the form of bread only. And from the *Legenda* he quotes that Christ administered this sacrament to Dionysius under one form only, and that Communion under one kind has its origin from this. But because we desire neither the falsehoods of the Apocrypha nor the fictions of fables but demand the Scriptures, therefore a different pretext had to be sought. Therefore Hosius declares that no matter what Paul either taught or did in the matter of both kinds, James certainly both taught and practiced Communion under one kind in the church at Jerusalem, because in Acts 2:42, in the description of the practices of the Jerusalem church, the breaking of bread only is reported and no mention is made there of wine. But because Hosius notices how awkward it is if Paul and the other apostles are said to have taught contrary things, since also James was among those who had given to Paul the right hand of fellowship (Gal. 2:9), before the Epistle to the Corinthians was written, therefore he supposes that this was done in the Jerusalem church not because he wanted to act contrary to Paul but in order to show that the church is free to communicate either under both kinds or under one only.

But let us consider whether the strength of this argument is sufficient to enable the papalists to mutilate the institution of the Supper. For because the words of the institution of Christ and of the Pauline teaching are very clear, it is necessary, if they want to move us away from them, that the arguments by which they want to bring this about should be much clearer, more certain, and stronger than the institution itself. However, the description in Acts 2:42 does not show sufficiently clearly, certainly, and strongly whether this passage is to be understood of common feasts, or indeed of the Lord's Supper. For Chrysostom does not interpret the breaking of bread (Acts 2:42, 46; 20:7) of the administration of the Lord's Supper, but of common and daily food. And Oecumenius, in bringing together the interpretations of the Greeks, interprets the passages of common eating, namely, that cheap and easily procured food, without fancy dishes, is meant when Luke says that "breaking bread, they partook of food." And indeed, the Greek text shows clearly that it is speaking of the kind of breaking of bread which pertains to food or nourishment. For it says that the believers were day by day gathered in the temple to hear the Word, and that afterward they broke bread in their homes for nourishment. For it says: "Breaking bread, they partook of food."

Now who that is of a sound mind will let himself be moved from the clear light of the words of Christ and of Paul on account of a passage that is ambiguous and unclear? Surely, if at the time of the councils of Constance and Basel they had judged that the use of only one kind could be proved with some show of right from this passage, this argument would not have been neglected and there would have been no need either for the other feeble arguments or for the infamous phrase: "this notwithstanding." There is therefore no firm and clear certainty in the argument which is taken from Acts 2 against Communion under both kinds.

I am, however, not ignorant of the fact that some of the ancients understand Acts 2 of the celebration of the Eucharist. I do not reject this interpretation, chiefly because of Acts 20:7, which says that on Sunday, when Paul was going to preach, the church came together to break bread, which Bede, following Augustine, interprets of the celebration of the sacrament. But not even in this way will this breaking of bread support the papalist mutilation, as I shall prove with three very strong arguments.

1. Not one of all the ancients interprets that breaking of bread in such a way that the apostles dispensed to the faithful in the church only one kind in the Eucharist while they omitted or abrogated the other. Much less did they construct from this a dogma that the words of institution about the cup do not pertain to the laity but that the use of the Dominical cup either could or should be forbidden, prohibited, and taken away from them. I am certain that nothing like this can be produced from all the true antiquity. Therefore the question here is not properly whether any ancients understood the breaking of bread in Acts 2 of the celebration of the Eucharist, but whether they taught that the apostles offered only one part of the Eucharist to the laity and abrogated and took away the other;

indeed, also whether they constructed from this the dogma of the papalists about mutilating the institution.

2. It is an axiom of the papalists that it is a sacrilege if the celebrating priest does not consecrate both kinds, but only the bread. If therefore in Acts 2 the cup of the Lord is simply to be excluded because only the bread is mentioned, it will follow that the apostles celebrated the Lord's Supper with the consecration of the bread only, and not also of the cup. This the papalists cannot admit. If therefore they will say, as otherwise they are not able to say, that through a synecdoche[18] the words about the consecration of the other kind must be supplied from the institution, even though this is not expressly said, they are already clearly admitting a synecdoche and are conceding that this brief account of the history must be understood and interpreted according to the description of the institution of the Lord's Supper. Neither will this way of escape be open to them: to say that Luke does not describe what the apostles either consecrated or what they themselves took, but what they dispensed to the people. For in Acts 20:11 it is written that the apostle Paul broke bread and himself ate. They cannot say, according to their own axioms, that Paul there took only one kind, for he was then "effecting"[19] (as the papalists speak), because he broke the bread. Therefore whether they want to or not, they are compelled in these passages to concede and admit a synecdoche, where the missing part cannot be supplied from anywhere except from the words of institution. Therefore also we rightly say that in the breaking of bread the apostles dispensed the Eucharist not apart from or contrary to but according to the institution of Christ, who distributed both the bread and the cup. For the instruction to the apostles is: "Teach them to observe what I have commanded you."

3. This breaking of bread is reported not only of the other apostles but also of Paul (Acts 20:11). That Paul taught the celebration, dispensation, and use of the Lord's Supper under both kinds not to the Corinthians only but to all who call upon the Lord in every place, he himself testifies (1 Cor. 11:17-32). But Luke the historian employs the phrase "breaking of bread," which was common usage among the Hebrews. When they wanted to describe a social feast, a supper, or a refreshment, they simply called it breaking or eating of bread. A man would be out of his mind if, when he reads histories and comes across the expression "to eat bread," he wanted to contend that these people lived without drink.

---

[18] Synecdoche: a figure of speech in which a part is mentioned for the whole.

[19] The word is *efficiens*, which together with the related word *conficiens* was used by the papalists for bringing about the transubstantiation of the elements in the Eucharist by means of consecration.

Moreover we are not disputing about synecdoche on the basis of this phrase alone. Paul clearly shows that this synecdoche was used, and used in this sense by the apostles. For in 1 Cor. 11, where he expressly teaches the use of both kinds, he nevertheless says thus: "It is not the Lord's Supper that you eat." Likewise: "When you come together to eat." In the same passage he says: "Not discerning the Lord's body," where nevertheless in the same sentence he twice connects eating and drinking with the connecting word ["and"].

11 Furthermore, I shall in passing also throw in this, that John Fisher and after him the Jesuits of Cologne attempt to prove from an incomplete work on Matthew which is ascribed, but falsely, to Chrysostom that Paul on the ship (Acts 27:33-38) dispensed the Eucharist under one form only to Luke and the rest of the disciples. If the sophists would play games like this in worldly matters, as for instance in praising the ague which occurs every fourth day, or the despotic rule of Busiris,[20] and similar things, it could somehow be borne. But in a serious matter which concerns the consciences of the godly to make sport in this way with statements of Holy Scripture, and indeed for the purpose of overturning the clear words of a testamentary institution of the Son of God, is surely wicked and infamous. For Luke declares in Acts 27:33-38, not briefly, not obscurely or ambiguously, but expressly in the clearest manner with many repetitions, that in this account he is not treating of the celebration of the Lord's Supper but of the eating of ordinary food after much and long fasting.

Now to interpret this account of the Eucharist, if it is done without harm or perversion of the institution of Christ, is indeed a misuse, not by any means to be approved or imitated, for it misses the true meaning of the account, yet it can in a measure be tolerated. For the author of the incomplete work does not establish anything from it which disagrees with the institution of Christ. But to twist this account to the mutation, violation, and mutilation of the Lord's Supper, although absolutely nothing is there indicated about the dispensation of the Eucharist, is certainly wicked and infamous.

12 Surely it is possible to judge from this with what kind of conscience the hired agents of the papalist kingdom prosecute this cause. For when Eck sees that in all these arguments wrenched out of the writings of the apostles there is not enough help, he finally says that the Communion of the laity under one kind is one of the things which come from the secret tradition of the apostles. And he cannot name even one writer who places

---

[20] A legendary Egyptian king who every year sacrificed a foreigner to Zeus.

this dogma among the apostolic traditions. But the papalist church has an axiom which Pedro de Soto explains in these words: "Whatever the Roman church believes and observes which cannot be proved from Scripture should simply be believed to come from a tradition of the apostles."

13 Indeed, they brand this blot not on the apostles alone, as though they had departed from the testamentary institution of Christ, but they imagine that the Son of God Himself after His resurrection tore down by His example and deed what at the Last Supper He had built up by His institution and precept. For they maintain that Christ after His resurrection offered the Eucharist to the two disciples at Emmaus [Luke 24:13-35] under the single form of bread only and that thus He Himself, as His own most dependable interpreter, showed by His own action how He wants the institution of the Supper understood, namely, that the commandment about reception under both kinds pertains not to the laity but only to the priests and that for the lay people Communion of one kind is sufficient.

This argument would have considerable force if it could be demonstrated with certainty, clearly, and firmly that Christ had taught by deed and example that the whole institution does not pertain to the laity, but only a part of it, namely, that about the form of the bread. But because the words of institution are plain, and Paul's testimony is most clear, that the institution of the Supper pertains to the whole church, a matter which he testifies he received from the Lord, it will be absolutely necessary that a testimony which teaches something different should be far clearer, more certain, and more firm in order to move us by the strength of the evidence and certainty from the words of institution and from the teaching of Paul, which he had received from the Lord.

The question is therefore whether these three points can be demonstrated clearly, with certainty, and firmly from this account:

1. That Christ gave the Eucharist to those two disciples at Emmaus;

2. That He gave it to them under one kind only; and

3. That He did it in such a way that by this action He wanted to teach that one kind only should be given to the laity, the manner of the institution not being adhered to.

Many arguments convince us and demonstrate that these three points cannot be shown with certainty, clearly, and firmly in this account. That the breaking of bread at Emmaus was the dispensation of the Eucharist is neither clear nor certain from Luke's description. For also ordinary supping together or refreshments are called "breaking of bread" in Scripture (Is. 58:7; Lam. 4:4; Matt. 14:19). Neither do the words: "He took the bread and blessed, and broke it and gave it to them" [Luke 24:30], show convincingly that it was the dispensation of the Eucharist. For also in Matt. 14:19 and 15:36, in the matter of the loaves and fishes in the desert, the same words are used, where nobody would dare even to imagine that it was a dispensation of the Eucharist. For we do not read in that account that the formal words, which must come to the element in order that it may become a sacrament: "Take, eat; this is My body," were added by Christ to the breaking of the bread. Neither is the opening of their eyes ascribed to the power of that bread, but the account simply relates that while Christ broke the bread and distributed it their eyes were opened, even as they told the apostles afterward that Christ was recognized by them during the breaking of the bread, not through the strength and power of the bread. Therefore it cannot be proved clearly and with certainty that that breaking of bread was a dispensation of the Eucharist. In fact, the context clearly speaks about an ordinary meal. For it was suppertime, and they were reclining in their lodging at the table of their host, which was spread for the meal. According to a custom which is even now in use among the Jews, Christ blessed the bread and distributed it after breaking it. And because the disciples were familiar with Christ's ways, they recognized Him from them during the blessing and breaking of the bread. Indeed, it is so far from certain that this account speaks of the dispensation of the Eucharist, that neither the councils of Constance and Basel in former times nor now the Council of Trent has dared to quote this testimony for the defense of one kind, although this would be a very strong argument if it were certainly and clearly established with respect to the things which the papalist agents boldly impute to this account.

Nicolaus de Lyra, who wrote almost a hundred years before the Council of Constance, interprets this account not of the Eucharist but of common breaking of bread. And William Wideford, who wrote against the articles of Wyclif, expressly said in the year 1396 that it cannot be proved either from the text or from a gloss or from the ancient doctors that the breaking of bread (Luke 24:30) was of consecrated bread. And Alphonse de Castro concludes in Bk. 6 of his work against heresies, after he had disputed long and much about this account, that he did not want to decide anything definite in the matter.

Since therefore it is not certain that the account in Luke 24:30 refers to the dispensation of the Eucharist, we would certainly be foolish if we would allow ourselves to be drawn away from the clear, sure, and firm teaching and command of the institution by means of a doubtful, uncertain, and ambiguous testimony. Here that is rightly applied which Augustine says in *Contra litteras Petiliani*, ch. 16: "Let them not gather together and recount the things which were said obscurely or ambiguously or figuratively, which everyone interprets as he wills, according to his own understanding. For such things cannot be rightly understood and explained unless the things which are said plainly are first held in firm faith. But produce something which does not need an interpreter and about which you are not convicted that it was spoken of another matter and that you are attempting to bend it to your understanding." Thus Augustine.

We have, indeed, a very clear testimony not only about how Christ at His last supper instituted the Eucharist but also about how after His ascension He delivered to Paul that He wants the institution about the two kinds applied to the whole church, as we have shown above.

One ought not to imagine that Christ wanted, by what He did at Emmaus, to weaken and overthrow what He instituted at the last Supper and confirmed by the tradition repeated to Paul after His ascension, since Paul says about that eating and drinking, "until He comes to judgment."

No matter, therefore, what may be argued about this account, this much is certain, that the manner of celebrating and administering the Eucharist is not prescribed to the church in it. For no command is added that this action of Christ be imitated. Such a command and prescribed manner for the administration of the Lord's Supper is, however, added in the words of institution and in the Pauline tradition. If we hold fast to this foundation, we cannot go astray. For in other matters we are not bound to imitate all the actions of Christ without a sure word pertaining to us. Neither are the papalists, who interpret this act as referring to the consecration, administration, and dispensation of the Eucharist, able to adhere to it in so naked and simple a fashion that they are not compelled to add and supply from Christ's words of institution many things of which no explicit mention is made in this account. I shall prove this in such a way that there will be no room for evasion for the papalists.

I ask whether it is lawful for a priest to celebrate the sacrament of the Eucharist with the consecrated bread only, with the cup wholly left out. Surely they teach that this would be a great sacrilege. Yet that follows from this account if the institution may be set aside and only those things need to be done in the celebration of the Eucharist of which Luke writes in so many words that they were done in the breaking of bread at Emmaus.

I ask also whether the Eucharist either can or ought to be confected without these fixed words: "Take, eat; this is My body," etc. This will, however, of necessity follow if the Lord's Supper is to be celebrated not according to what is prescribed in the institution but only according to what is described as having been done in the breaking of bread at Emmaus.

These two points the papalists cannot allow and yield. No matter, therefore, in which direction they turn, they are compelled on these two points to return to the form of the institution if they contend that the Emmaus account is to be interpreted as referring to the administration of the Eucharist. It suffices us that, whether they want to or not, the papalists must necessarily admit that the manner of celebrating the Eucharist cannot be simply and in its entirety taken from the Emmaus account but must be taken from the prescription of the institution. Thus the sinew of this argument has been cut. We have weighty reasons why we prefer to interpret the Emmaus account, if it is at all to be understood of the Eucharist, from the words of institution rather than to change and mutilate the prescription and commandment of the institution because of this obscure account, that is, that we prefer to take the manner of celebrating and administering the Eucharist from the institution rather than from this account. For this we have weighty reasons. For to each part of what Christ did at the institution there is added: "This do!" Paul asserts that this should continue until the end of the world. Concerning what was done at Emmaus, however, there is no command of God that it should be imitated.

However, the papalists base what they argue about the Emmaus account not so much on the context of Luke as on certain statements of the fathers, who through an allegory apply this breaking of bread to the doctrine of the Eucharist. Much could be answered to these statements. For not all the passages which the fathers apply to it speak of the celebration of the Eucharist, as is clear from John 6:32-59 and Acts 27:33-38. But no matter how things stand with these allegorical interpretations of the fathers, it is certain that with respect to the point of this controversy there is found with the fathers not only no dogma but not even an argument to the effect that Christ by that action at Emmaus wanted to show that not the whole institution of the Supper but only half of it pertains to the laity and that one ought, or at least is permitted, to dispense only one kind in the Eucharist and omit and take away the other from the laity. With respect to these things it can be shown in the writings of the fathers that they not only did not dogmatize but that they did not even argue about them. Rather, the Greeks not only retained the use of both kinds for the whole church but taught and often repeated the dogma that, because of the institution of Christ, the use of both kinds pertains to the whole church, both priests and laity, as has been shown above from their testimonies.

There is a very clear passage in Augustine, *In canonicam Johannem tractatus,* 2, where in this allegory about the breaking of the bread at Emmaus he clearly and in so many words makes mention of eating and drinking in the Eucharist, saying of the whole church (for these are his words): "The disciples did not recognize Him except in the breaking of the bread. And truly, he who does not eat and drink judgment to himself recognizes Christ in the breaking of the bread." This statement shows very clearly that the allegory of Augustine and of the other fathers about that breaking of the bread offers no protection to the mutilation of the Lord's Supper which has been brought into the church by the papalists.

14 These are about all the statements of Scripture which the papalist agents in the disputations of our times twist to justify the mutilation of the Lord's Supper. The additional arguments they weave from John 6:32-59, with which they argue that the prescription and commandment of the institution does not pertain to the whole church but to the priests only — these will have their place in the explanation of the first Tridentine chapter.

15 This is one kind of argument which the papalists use in this matter, namely, from testimonies of Scripture. The other kind of argument, on which they rely greatly and principally, they take from the authority and power of the church. It is, however, worth the effort to observe how among the papalists some apply the teaching of the authority and power of the church to defend the mutilation of the testamentary institution of Christ more openly, others more guardedly; some in more subtle and circumspect fashion, others more crassly and shamelessly. Pighius, in disputing about Communion under one kind, simply says that it was said by Christ to the Roman pontiff, the vicar of Peter, whatever he would in his whole kingdom here on earth fix, unfix, bind, or loose, the same would be held before God in heaven to be fixed, unfixed, bound, and loosed. He also applies the statement of Deut. 17:9-13 (however with omission of the limiting clauses: "They shall there indicate to you the true judgment," and: "You shall do whatever they shall teach you according to the law of the Lord"[21]) to the decree of Constance, as to the authority of councils by and large, without any limitation or exception, as follows:

---

[21] Chemnitz is following the text of the Vulgate. The Hebrew text makes no mention of the law of the Lord.

"You shall do whatever those who are over the church tell you; you shall follow their decision; you shall not depart either to the right hand or to the left. Anyone who is proud, not willing to obey the rule of the priest, that man shall die at the decree of the priest, and all the people shall fear."

Hosius applies to this law of Constance the statement of Plato, *De legibus*, 1: "One law certainly will be most excellent for you, which commands that none of the young men shall dare to question whether the laws are right or wrong, but prescribes that it must be admitted with one mouth and one voice by all that they are rightly stated, as though by the gods themselves, and that the young must by no means be allowed to think anything else."

Latomus, writing to Bucer, says: "Since the first church was as yet inexperienced, it held religiously to the custom received from Christ until, taught by the fathers, she understood that both kinds were befitting to the priests but that the laity could be content with the bread only." This crude pronouncement is not approved even by the papalists themselves, because it shows that he attributes a kind of ignorance to the primitive church such as Ovid describes when he says:

A raw, unordered mass.

16 These statements frankly and openly explain what is the opinion of the papalists on the subject of the authority and power of the church. Others indeed set forth this same opinion, but a bit more covertly and subtly. For they say that the Gospel grants the church liberty in outward rites or ceremonies, so that it can vary and change them for the purpose of edification. And here they loudly declaim that the churches are not to be disturbed nor their unity disrupted on account of outward rites. They adduce also the example of Urbicus, whom Augustine sharply rebukes, Letter No. 86, because he was disturbing and condemning whole churches on account of fasting on the Sabbath. But this argument, no matter with what show of right it may be enlarged upon, is easily taken away from them and struck down. For in rites that are adiaphora the church has power, not for tearing down but for building up. It does not, however, have liberty and power to teach or establish anything against the commandments of God, or of abrogating and prohibiting any part of a divine commandment which pertains to the church, to the ministry, and to the New Testament. For the statements of the ancients are known to the papalists: "In no way does a good servant change what the master commands." And, 25, quest. 1: "It is most necessary to know that the pontiff is able to lay down new laws in matters about which the evangelists have said something, and the prophets nothing. But where the Lord or

His apostles and the holy fathers who followed them have defined something in the form of axioms, there the Roman pontiff ought not to give a new law, but should rather stand on what has been proclaimed even to the giving of his life and the shedding of his blood. For if he should attempt to tear down what the prophets and apostles have taught (which God forbid), he would stand convicted that he had not rendered a judgment but rather that he erred."

But what need is there to search out more statements of the ancients when we have the clear statement of Paul: "If anyone should preach a gospel to you contrary to that which you have received, even if he were an apostle or an angel from heaven, let him be anathema" [Gal. 1:8-9]? Now what the churches received from Paul about the administration of the Lord's Supper is certain and clear. (1 Cor. 11:23-26)

17 But, coming closer, they say that in the celebration of the Lord's Supper as it was used by the Lord many things have been varied, changed, and abrogated in which no one is able to condemn the church as if it committed a wrong against the command of Christ. For Christ gave the Eucharist in the evening, after supper, after first washing their feet, and after eating of the Passover lamb. These things the church does not observe, nor does anyone demand as necessary that only 12, and indeed reclining at table, as was done at the first Supper, should be admitted to Communion.

But this argument is easily dissolved through the familiar rule: "You cannot make the same judgment about things which are dissimilar." For in the institution of the Lord's Supper some things pertain to the essence of the Lord's Supper. These have the command of Christ: "Do this"; namely, to take bread, bless, break, distribute, eat. Likewise also to take the cup, bless, distribute, drink—and to do this in remembrance of Christ. With respect to other circumstances which Christ observed by reason of the time, He gives neither prescription nor command. For He says: "Do this." However, He does not add that this should be done at such and such a time with observance of other circumstances that are not commanded. Most discreet is the statement of Augustine, Letter No. 118: "If the Lord had not prescribed it, but had only admonished that the Eucharist should always be dispensed and received after supper, I believe that no one would have changed that custom." Therefore it is not valid to draw conclusions from circumstances that are free, and not commanded, about the substantive things of the Lord's Supper, which have a divine prescription and command which Paul says should continue until the glorious advent of Christ. (1 Cor. 11:26)

18 The *Antididagma* of Cologne finally goes to the heart of the matter. For it seeks to prove that also in the very essentials of the sacraments, in the matter and form, which have a divine prescription and command, the church even at the time of the apostles showed its freedom and power of changing, varying, and abrogating some things—and that in the very sacrament of Baptism, the need for which is even greater, since it is written: "Unless one is born of water and the Spirit, he cannot enter the kingdom of God."

The instances which prove this are: Christ commanded to baptize in the name of Father, Son, and Holy Spirit. This is the form of Baptism instituted, prescribed, and commanded by the Son of God Himself. But the apostles changed, varied, and for a time abrogated this form. For we read that they baptized only in the name of Christ (Acts 2:38; 19:5). This argument can plausibly be applied to the present controversy. Although Christ in the form of Baptism expressly and clearly mentions the name of Father, Son, and Holy Spirit, nevertheless the apostles judged that this was not utterly necessary but could be changed because, on account of the unity in essence, the name of the Father and of the Holy Spirit is comprehended in the name of Christ. Therefore in the same manner, although Christ instituted both kinds in the Eucharist individually and separately (as the fathers speak), nevertheless because the whole and entire Christ, with body, blood, soul, and spirit, is present also in the one kind, therefore the church rightly judged that both kinds are not necessary for the laity but that one only could be sufficient for them. For as the apostles, on the basis of the argument from the unity in essence, changed the institution of Baptism, so the church, on the basis of the argument of concomitance, was rightly able to change the institution of the Supper in the matter of the two kinds.

But I answer: Scripture does not say that the apostles baptized in the name of Christ in such a way that the form of Baptism prescribed and commanded by the Son of God was changed and abrogated, the name of the Father and of the Holy Spirit utterly neglected, omitted, and excluded in the action and administration of Baptism; that is, that in Baptism no express and separate mention was made by the apostles of the name of the Father and Holy Spirit, but only of the name of Christ. I remember that a certain monk quoted Acts 8:16 in opposition: "They had only been baptized in the name of the Lord Jesus," although the text there simply says that the Samaritans had not yet received the visible gifts of the Spirit, but had only been baptized in the name of Jesus, as this is clear in the Greek text. Therefore Peter, who says (Acts 2:38): "Be baptized . . . in the name of Christ," expressly names God the Father when he says (1

Peter 3:21): "Baptism is an appeal to God for a clear conscience through the resurrection of Christ, who . . . is at the right hand of the Father." And in Acts 2:38-39, where he names baptism in the name of Christ, he says clearly and in so many words: "You shall receive the gift of the Holy Spirit." Likewise: "The promise is to you and to your children and to all that are far off, whom the Lord your God will call to Himself." Thus the same Paul who says (Rom. 9:3): "We have been baptized into Christ," and (Eph. 5:26) that Christ cleanses the church by the washing of water with the Word, in his teaching concerning Baptism (Titus 3:5-6) clearly and expressly makes mention of the name of the Father, Son, and Holy Spirit. For he says: "God saved us . . . by the washing of regeneration and renewal of the Holy Spirit . . . through Jesus Christ our Savior." Yes, in Acts 19:1-6 Paul declares that those who did not know that there is a Holy Spirit had been baptized neither rightly nor in the name of Christ. In disputing about this passage, Ambrose says, Bk. 1, *De Spiritu Sancto,* ch. 31, that it is not a full baptism unless it is performed in the name and with the confession of Father, Son, and Holy Spirit.

It is plain, therefore, that the apostles by no means changed or altered the form of Baptism which was handed down and prescribed by Christ, so that they baptized only in the name of Christ without mention and name of the Father and the Holy Spirit. For they knew that this clause is added to the institution of Baptism (Matt. 28:20): "Teaching them to observe all that I have commanded you." But because it was not the purpose of the account of Luke to describe in what manner and with what formula the apostles baptized, for this was well known from the institution, and because he wanted in a brief account to take note of and name the baptism of the New Testament instituted by Christ, he had no need always to repeat the whole institution about the matter, form, use, and benefit of Baptism. But in order that he might by a particular appellation distinguish this baptism from the baptism of John and from the ceremonial washings of the Jews, he called it baptism in the name of Christ. He took this appellation: 1. From its effect, for in Baptism the Father, Son, and Holy Spirit dispense, apply, and seal participation in the merits, death, and resurrection of Christ, as Scripture teaches (Rom. 6:3-4; Gal. 3:27; Titus 3:5-7; 1 Peter 3:21). 2. The appellation is taken from the Author who instituted Baptism, so that baptizing in the name of Christ is the same thing as baptizing at the order and command and under the direction of Christ. Now in what way He Himself commanded to baptize is clear from the institution. Baptism in the name of Christ is therefore not rightly administered unless it is done according to the institution, in the name of the Father and of the Son and of the Holy Spirit. Therefore it is not true that the apostles changed, mutilated, and abrogated the form of Baptism prescribed by Christ.

19 The other argument of the *Antididagma* is: Christ taught to baptize with immersion of the whole body in water; for they assert that this is what the word *baptizein* means. But the church declares that this is not necessary, that it is sufficient if the baptizing is done either through pouring or through sprinkling water on the person. And yet this belongs to the essentials of Baptism.

I answer: If it were true that *baptizein* signified only to immerse the whole body in water, no one either could or should have changed the custom of immersion. But Paul, a very dependable interpreter, says that to baptize is to cleanse or purge through the washing of water in the Word. Whether therefore the application of water be by washing (Eph. 5:26; Titus 3:5; Acts 2:41), or whether it be done by immersion, dipping, pouring, or sprinkling, it is Baptism, for it is a purging or cleansing through the washing of water. Immersion under the water is not necessarily required for washing. Also the washing of hands, couches,[22] brazen vessels, and cups, which is done by applying water, whether it be done by immersion, or dipping, or pouring, is called a baptism. (Mark 7:4)

In the baptism of Christ no such scouring of the body with water is necessary as is required when the body is to be cleansed of filth (1 Peter 3:21). Therefore the commandment of Christ is that in Baptism there be a purification or cleansing by a washing with water. Christ does not prescribe in what way this cleansing should be done, whether by immersion, dipping, pouring, or sprinkling. There is therefore in this no change in the essentials of Baptism.

They also argue about threefold dipping, which has been changed. But it is certain that Christ did not prescribe or command either single or double or triple dipping and that He did not forbid that it be done a number of times in the one Baptism. The institution is satisfied when there is washing through the application of water.

However, when they say that Christ prescribed and taught that infants should not be baptized before they can be taught and that the church has changed this on its own authority, contrary to the prescription and commandment of Christ, this is Anabaptistical and false, as we showed in the topic concerning Baptism. Therefore it is by no means true (for it cannot be proved) that the church has the authority to change, alter,

---

[22] By including "couches" Chemnitz is following the reading in the Vulgate, which is also found in some Greek manuscripts of Mark's gospel.

mutilate, abrogate, and prohibit any of the things which have been handed down, prescribed, and commanded by the Son of God with respect to the essentials of the sacraments. For the true church does not lord it over the faith (2 Cor. 1:24) but, sitting at the feet of the One Teacher, Christ, she reverently and obediently listens to His Word (Matt. 21; Luke 19),[23] for she is "built upon the foundation of the apostles and prophets" (Eph. 2:20), always holding this before her eyes: "Teach them to observe all that I have commanded you" (Matt. 28:20). Augustine says, *Contra litteras Petiliani:* "If, therefore, we are sheep of Christ, let us hear the voice of our Shepherd." This is the second kind of argument, about the freedom, authority, and power of the church.

20 The third kind of argument is that they attempt to prove by testimonies of antiquity that the use of both kinds was observed neither always nor everywhere in the ancient church, but that Communion of the laity under one kind only was always in use also in the primitive church. But there will be a more suitable place for these things in the explanation of the second Tridentine chapter. For I see that this material has grown more voluminous than I had expected and intended. I judge, however, that this account will not be found useless, for it shows what kind of grounds the papalists have for their cause. Also, a collation showing how subsequently either new grounds were thought up, or old ones reshaped with new colorings, will not be without its use. For from this collation of arguments it will be possible to understand many things which are touched more briefly and correctly in the Tridentine decrees.

ARTICLE VI

Arguments of the Tridentine Synod About Communion Under One Kind

1 Let us now finally come to an examination of the decrees of the fifth session. To begin with, the reader will observe that the Tridentine assembly did not want to make all the arguments which were urged by papalist writers in this dispute up to this time its own by repeating them. They passed over very many, as if they had made a selection, without doubt because most of them seemed uncertain, weak, inept, and absurd. But they retained and culled out a certain few, without doubt those which out of that whole pile were judged to be the best and strongest. However, lest it seem that they simply disapproved and condemned the zeal and

---

[23] Luke 10:38-42 would seem to fit the context best.

labor of the agents of their kingdom, they decree in Chapter II and in Canon II that all such reasons and causes are weighty and just.

2 I see that there are five reasons which the Council of Trent leads forward into the battle line in this contest, as being the foremost and strongest of all its troops, to defend the papalist mutilation of the Lord's Supper. These we shall therefore examine one by one.

3 The first reason is this: Although Christ instituted this sacrament and handed it down to the apostles under the forms of bread and wine, the lay people, and clergy who are not confecting, are bound by no divine precept to receive both kinds. Therefore Communion under one kind is sufficient to them for salvation.

In this argument they, by their conclusion, beg the question around which the controversy revolves. For in every argumentation there is required the cause, that is, the reason why when certain things are asserted and granted the conclusion follows from this by true and necessary reasoning and is proved to be certainly so. Now in the antecedent premise of this argument it is stated and conceded that Christ instituted the use of both kinds. How, I ask, does one conclude and prove from this that the commandment of Christ about receiving both kinds does not pertain to the laity? Unless perhaps it is taken from that ancient dialectics[24] whose stratagem is described in Gen. 3:1-5: Although God commanded that you should not eat of every tree, you can nevertheless do it!

Surely, the dispute here is about a great and lofty matter, namely, about the testamentary institution of the Son of God. This institution is neither ambiguous nor obscure, but its light is so great that it rushes into the eyes of all, also when they have conceived the audacity to depart from the words of institution. Therefore the Tridentine fathers judged that they should above all things give diligence in whatever way they could to tear down the massive structure of the institution, by which they felt they were hard pressed.

The Council of Constance wanted to give some reason for the mutilation, no matter how crass and violent. For it decreed that, the Dominical institution notwithstanding, recent custom must be considered as law. But our times, illuminated by the light of the Word, will not tolerate this principle. Therefore the men of Trent borrow another stratagem, from the Council of Basel, namely that, although absolutely no reason has been shown, brought forward, and explained, they nevertheless declare and proclaim nakedly and simply, as a command and with more than

---

[24] The word in Latin is *topica,* a word borrowed from the Greek language. A work of Aristotle which bears the title *Topika* deals with the method of drawing conclusions in a matter which is only probable.

praetorian authority, that although Christ instituted the use of both kinds, lay people are nevertheless obligated by no divine precept to receive both kinds. But it is precisely this which, drawn into controversy, needed to be proved and established by clear and cogent evidence. For in the institution we read words which order, prescribe, command, and teach, not only for one but for both parts: "Take; eat; drink." And to both parts alike there is added the command: "Do this." It is seen, therefore, that to whomever the first part refers, to them also the second part must be referred. But while the Tridentine fathers decree that the words of command in the first part pertain to all the faithful of Christ, priests and laity, they decree that in the second part the words of instruction obligate only the priests, not the laity.

For this separation and division they show no reason whatever in the institution, although the second part is joined to the first not only by the copulative "and" but also by the word "likewise"[25] and although in the second part the generalizing word ["all"] is expressly used, which is not found in the first: "Drink of it, all of you," and there is added: "Do this."

4 I have carefully weighed every word in the first Tridentine chapter. However, I have not been able to discover that they give so much as the tiniest reason from the Word of God by which they might attempt to instruct and quiet the consciences of the lay people so that they could state with certainty that, although there are words of command in both parts, also the lay people are obligated by those in the first part but the precepts in the second part do not pertain to the laity at all.

However, I find two other reasons set forth in this first chapter, but in such a way that they do not want to show cause or give reasons for this decree of theirs through them, but to protest that, as a matter of principle, no other reason dare be required of them except: "He said it." For according to the canonists, even as the pope so also a council has its will as the reason in the matters it wants. And the men of Paris say against Luther that the law for defining in the papalist church is this, that they explain briefly what they think, but do not commit to writing any reasons why they define in this way.

5 Now the first reason is this: "The Tridentine Synod, instructed by the Holy Spirit, declares and teaches: 'Although Christ instituted,' " etc. But where was the synod instructed by the Holy Spirit with respect to this declaration? Was it from some passage of Scripture? For it is the custom of Scripture, as Jerome rightly says, that what is said more briefly and

---

[25] Or "in the same way." (1 Cor. 11:25)

obscurely in one place, it explains and clarifies in another place. They certainly do not indicate any passage of Scripture from which they have taken this declaration, but set the Holy Spirit in opposition to Christ. Thus, as Christ did indeed once upon a time in the Lord's Supper institute both kinds as a prescription, the Holy Spirit now, at the Synod of Trent, inspired a different declaration in the fathers.

This is truly a noteworthy reason why, although they put forward this declaration without any testimony from the Word of God, yes, against the clear words of Christ, it is nevertheless to be embraced as the most certain article of faith, namely, because the Holy Spirit is the Spirit of wisdom and understanding, the Spirit of counsel and godliness. The conclusion they draw is as valid as when you reason from a stick to an angle.[26]

6 The second reason is: "The Tridentine Synod, following the judgment and custom of the church, declares and teaches," etc. But of which church? Not of the apostolic nor of the primitive, for we have shown above what has been their judgment, but of that church which about the time of the Council of Constance brought in this custom contrary to Scripture and the custom of the primitive church and which afterward at the Council of Constance indicated that this custom was to be considered a law.

Truly excellent reasons! Everywhere, also in the Babylonian kingdom of the papalist captivity, pious consciences bitterly complain that they are moved by the brilliant light of the words of institution, which have been handed down and committed to the church in the form of a testament by the Son of God Himself, not by way of advice but in the form of a precept and command. But the Council of Trent simply repeats and bolsters the old song that the precept of the institution about receiving both kinds does not obligate the laity. But while they seek reasons by which a pious mind may be taught, strengthened, and made certain, they are offered dead coals[27] instead of treasure, namely: "The Synod of Trent so teaches and declares"; and: "The church at the Council of Trent so judged"; therefore: "Although Christ instituted," etc.

7 Up to this time the papalist agents have been striving to show in some way and with some semblance of right from the words of institution that the command about drinking from the cup does not pertain to the laity, in order that they might not seem to have taken away the use of the

---

[26] A Latin proverbial saying, *a baculo ad angulam.* It was used to characterize a ridiculously illogical argument.

[27] *Carbones:* literally, "dead coals," often used for something worthless or of little value.

Dominical cup from the people out of pure tyranny, entirely without any reason. But the Tridentine Synod does not want its troops to be led into this narrow strait, where this declaration would be no more certain and firm than it can certainly and firmly be proved to be from the words of institution. Therefore the decree is set forth without a reason. Nevertheless one can see, although very obscurely, that they are alluding to these debates.

For instance, the first canon says that not all believers are bound, for the sake of their salvation, to receive both kinds. The argument to which this canon alludes is this: In a case of necessity believers are saved, even if they simply cannot have full sacramental Communion; therefore the use of one part can be abrogated, also apart from a case of necessity, without loss of salvation. For whatever is right for the whole is right also with respect to the parts. So far as the antecedent is concerned, we have explained above, about the sacraments in general, in the fourth canon, in what way the sacraments are necessary for salvation. For with respect to cases of necessity the statement of Augustine, which also Lombard quotes, is true: "It is not to be doubted that each and every believer is a partaker of the body and blood of Christ the moment he becomes a member of the body of Christ in Baptism, and that he is not shut out from participation in this bread and cup nor deprived of participation in, and of the benefit of, this sacrament even though, while established in the unity of the body of Christ, he leaves this world before he has eaten that bread and drunk of that cup." In a case of necessity, therefore, where full sacramental Communion is not obtainable, these rules are valid: God has not tied the salvation of believers to the sacraments. Likewise: Believe, and you have eaten.

But let us consider what kind of conclusion this is: In a case of necessity believers are saved without sacramental Communion. Therefore, apart from a case of necessity, it is lawful to change and mutilate the testamentary institution of the Son of God. Surely, if we must argue from a case of necessity to abrogation and prohibition apart from a case of necessity, it will follow that not only the second part but also the whole Communion of the Eucharist can be abrogated, prohibited, and taken away from the church. For the thief on the cross is saved although he received neither kind of the Eucharist. However, we have noted down more things that belong to the explanation of this argument about a case of necessity from Augustine in the explanation of the fourth canon under "Concerning the Sacraments in General."

8 This, however, seemed exceedingly strange to me that, although all papalist writers of our time have labored and sweated with great efforts to make it possible to demonstrate with some show of right from the account of the Lord's Supper itself that the commandment and precept about receiving the cup obligates not the laity but only the priests (for they see that with this one argument, if it could be shown and proved, it would be possible wholly to answer all arguments which are opposed to the papalist mutilation from the institution)—I say, I wondered exceedingly at first why the Synod of Trent was not willing to base its decree clearly and in so many words on these arguments of the papalists. But later on I noticed that this was done from a weighty consideration, namely, because they sensed how very far from strong is this not so much a twisting as rather a mockery of the testamentary institution of the Son of God. This is also the reason why this argument is repeated neither by the Council of Constance nor by that of Basel, in spite of the fact that many and varied arguments were there devised. Nevertheless the Tridentine fathers allude obscurely to this fabrication when they say: "Although Christ handed down the Eucharist to His apostles under both kinds, nevertheless all Christians are not therefore bound by a law of the Lord to reception of both kinds." The only possible conclusion from this kind of argumentation is that what Christ said to the apostles in the institution of the Supper does not pertain to the whole church for the simple reason that these things were said only to the apostles. Therefore, because the men of Trent obscurely allude to this argumentation, which they are not willing to make their own by openly repeating it, we must see what manner of new fabrication that is which at the time of the councils of Constance and Basel was still unknown. For thus it will become clear that the brilliant light of the institution cannot be obscured by sophistic darkness. For the more sharply it is attacked, the more clearly the truth shines forth.

9 Now Pighius and Andrada, above others, push this fable with great effort. I shall note down their arguments briefly. For it is useful, for the sake of a reminder, to set forth such examples which show how boldly and shamelessly, how wretchedly and wickedly the papalists play with, corrupt, twist, and torture the most holy words of the testamentary institution of the Son of God in order to protect their mutilation. Pighius takes the words of institution as they are recorded by Luke and Paul, and totally disregards the accounts of Matthew and Mark. With this artifice he makes sport of the testamentary institution of Christ. In the first part of the institution, he says, Christ commands the apostles two things: I. "Take, eat"; II. "Do this (namely, what you have already seen Me do) in remembrance of Me," that is, He commands that in future they shall take bread, give thanks or bless it, and distribute it to be received and eaten by others, with these words added: "This is My body," etc. But in the second part of the institution, about the cup, the account of Luke and Paul does not say that Christ gave the apostles the cup, nor that He said by way of precept or command: "Drink of it, all of you." Therefore when He adds: "Do this," He is not teaching that the apostles and priests should dispense the cup of blessing to be drunk. For He taught them to do in future only what they had seen Christ do in the first Supper. Now Christ, according to the account of Luke and Paul, did not dispense the cup at the first Supper, even to the apostles, with the added precept: "Drink of it, all of you." For Luke and Paul do not have these words: "Drink of it, all of you." But when Christ says in the account of Paul: "Do this, as often as you drink it," He wanted to indicate that the priests should drink of the cup of the Lord only when they perform, that is, when they sacrifice, and that also the priests, when they are not performing, that is, sacrificing, have no command to drink of the cup of the Lord.

This is the Pighian design, which simply asserts that Christ, at the institution, did not give the consecrated cup to the apostles, nor commanded them: "Drink of it, all of you." Will that therefore be false, and a lie, which Matthew and Mark write, that Christ at the institution of the Supper gave the cup of blessing to the disciples and said: "Drink of it, all of you"? Pighius answers that Christ, after His ascension, revealed the words of institution more fully to Paul. Did He do this in such a way as to charge what is written by Matthew and Mark with falsity and lying? It is well worth the trouble to hear how he eludes the account of Matthew, which speaks of the cup as a command, and that with a term which has universal significance. For he says one could without inconsistency understand that what Matthew writes about the cup does not pertain to a fixed rule for celebrating this mystery in the future but that it pertained only to that action with the apostles. But why so? Namely, because in the account of Matthew the command: "Do this," is not added. Thus Pighius.

But because this rending asunder of the institution is too crass and violent, so that no collation at all of the descriptions of the institution as it is found in the four places in Scripture is allowed, and it is not permitted to supply what is passed over in the account of the one from the repetitions of others, so that when the account of Matthew is being pressed we may simply say that Christ did not say: "Do this in remembrance of Me," that if the account of Luke and Paul is being treated we may simply deny that Christ at the institution gave the cup to the disciples and deny that He said: "Drink of it, all of you," because the account of Luke and Paul does not have these words—because these things are entirely too shamefully wicked, they are not approved by all papalists. For it is one and the same institution which is described in the four passages; and the holy writers handed down their works in such a way that what the earlier Matthew and Mark omitted, the later Luke and Paul supplied. As to the things which had been explained sufficiently well in the accounts of the earlier ones, the later ones did not judge that these should all be repeated, since they wanted all the accounts to be considered together.

I wanted to record this Pighian stratagem in order that there might be available a clear example showing to what shameless and cross mockery of Scripture human intellects are carried away once they have undertaken the defense of the papalist mutilation.

10 Andrada, the new craftsman, concedes that the institution contains a command about receiving the cup. But he follows a different road than Pighius when he wants to prove that the words of institution about the cup do not pertain to the laity but only to the priests. The reader will observe that the papalists are not laboring about taking away only the form of the wine from the laity, but are fighting for this, that the lay people clearly have no right to the very comforting words of Christ which are joined to the participation of the cup, because these words pertain to the priests only.

I have chosen to consider most of all the words of Andrada. For because the men of Trent do not explain fully what the thinking of the council in the first argument was, I believe we shall understand this most correctly from Andrada, who was both present at the council and wrote during the council. He says: "Granted that the precept about drinking the cup, with a word which indicates that it is for all, was taught by Christ in the institution, it still does not follow that all believers in Christ are included under this sign of universality and are obligated by this precept."

You hear the same words and the same meaning as you read in the first Tridentine chapter. But the cause and reason for this pronouncement, which the council studiously concealed, is made known to us by Andrada, the interpreter of the council; namely, that when Christ handed down this precept with the note of universality ("Drink of it, all of you") He was addressing no one outside of the apostles who were present; for although not a few of the 70 disciples and of the pious women were present at Jerusalem at the time, the evangelists nevertheless expressly mention that Christ summoned only the 12 apostles to that table. And Mark, intending to explain whom Christ wanted to be understood by the word "all," says that all whom He had then summoned when He said: "Drink of it, all of you," at once drank of the cup at that first Supper. These certainly were none other than the 12 apostles, who were then present at the Supper. This is Andrada's first onslaught.

But I ask whether Christ wanted what He ordered at that time to be done once only, namely, at that first Supper. This Andrada will deny. For Christ adds the command: "Do this"; that is, what had been done at the first Supper should be done afterward or in future until the end of the world (as Paul explains). If this command had not been handed down by Christ, no man would have dared or ought to have imitated what was done at the first Supper.

The other question is whether only those 12 persons should later have done this at the command of Christ, so that apart from and after those 12 what is prescribed and commanded in the institution pertains to no other believers at all. Andrada denies also this, for he makes all these things common also to other priests. Therefore he himself confesses and shows in what follows that what he had contended for first is false, that when Christ says: "Drink of it, all of you," He does not by the word "all" want any others to be understood except those 12 who were then present.

The third question finally is: Who are those in the church, besides and after the apostles, to whom Christ wanted the commandments of the institution to apply? This is the crucial point in a very difficult and weighty question. In defining this we dare not use bare but vehement assertions, but sure arguments, strong proofs, and the clearest examples. Andrada, as he perhaps learned at the council, boldly asserts that the commandments of the whole institution of the Supper pertain only to the priests. Let us hear how he proves this. He says: "Three things are commanded in the institution: 'Eat; drink; this do.' And these are joined in such a way by connecting words that to whomever the command: 'This do,' pertains, to them pertain also the commands which go before. But for the future Christ instituted the power of consecrating, celebrating, administering, and dispensing the Eucharist when He said: 'This do.' But this power is not equally appropriate to all the faithful, but to the ministers of the church. Therefore also the foregoing commands: 'Eat; drink,' pertain only to the priests." This not, however, in such a way that both kinds are dispensed to the priests when they are not confecting, for he denies also this, but only that the priests should take both kinds when they celebrate. Surely, this Lusitanian[28] argument goes entirely too far. By it not only the lay people but also the priests who are not confecting are altogether excluded from the right to the entire Communion of the Eucharist. For he says that both commands: "Eat," and "Drink," pertain solely to the priests to whom the command: "This do," pertains.

---

[28] Lusitania: ancient Latin name for Portugal. Andrada was a native of Portugal.

However, when he is about to answer the objection, by what right one kind will be dispensed to the laity if the whole institution pertains solely to the priests, he is stuck like a mouse in pitch. He wants to say that the apostles received one kind while they were still laymen, namely, before they were consecrated priests by the words: "This do." But a little earlier he had said that, because of the connecting word, the commands: "Eat," and "This do," referred to the same persons. Therefore he thinks that on the basis of John 6 the laity is admitted to Communion under one kind, or certainly on the basis of the general nature of the sacraments. Finally he says that Christ had indeed ordered in general that believers should use the Eucharist, but that it had been left to the judgment of the church which of the two kinds it would be best to offer to the common people. But where, my good man, is this written? I do not read the commandment of Christ about receiving both parts of the Eucharist generally, but specifically. But what do you think is the reason why they argue that not even one kind is given to the laity by the command of Christ? Without doubt it is this, that the lay people may put up with receiving their Communion from the liberality and authority of the pope rather than from the institution and command of Christ.

11 But this argument of Andrada must be pondered a little while. The whole force of the argument is in the command: "This do." Concerning this we must say clearly to what extent it pertains to the ministers of the church and to what extent it pertains to the rest of the church. We shall make clear that, no matter to whom the command of Christ: "This do," is referred, whether to the priests or to the rest of the church, our judgment is confirmed and established, namely, that Communion under both kinds is by divine right and command. Christ commanded that what He did at the last Supper should in future also be done in the church, namely, to take bread and the cup, to bless them with thanksgiving, and to distribute what has been consecrated, which properly pertains to the ministers. Therefore we do not deny that the commandment of Christ: "This do," pertains to this extent to the ministers of the church. But because the whole of what was done in the first Supper not only by Christ, by way of blessing and distribution, but also by the disciples, by way of taking, eating, and drinking, is included in the command: "This do," for it refers to the whole preceding action—therefore the command: "This do," according to sound reasoning, pertains not only to the priests who are celebrating the Eucharist but also to those to whom the Eucharist is dispensed that they may eat and drink, as we shall afterward clearly demonstrate from Paul. For the whole of what was done in the institution

of the Supper, and not merely some small part of it, is included in the command: "This do."

First we shall see in the light of the institution itself what these words: "This do," intend and can do and accomplish if they are referred to the priests or ministers of the church. For without doubt when Christ said: "This do," He prescribed to the ministers of the church, commanded, and taught how in . . . future they should celebrate, administer, and dispense the Lord's Supper until the end of the world, namely, that they should do what Christ did at the first Supper. Now if Christ had blessed the bread and the cup, had consumed them only Himself, and had added the command: "This do," then perhaps what the papalists want would follow, namely, that only the celebrating priest would take both kinds. However, I do not read that Christ Himself ate the blessed bread and drank the blessed cup of the Eucharist, although Chrysostom asserts this without a sure and clear testimony of Scripture. I do, however, read most plainly that Christ distributed the blessed bread and cup to others and added the command: "Eat; drink." Insofar, therefore, as the command of Christ: "This do," includes only the ministers of the church to whom the administration of the Eucharist belongs, it requires not only that they consecrate the Eucharist and receive it themselves, but requires on the basis of the divine precept and command that they dispense and distribute the consecrated Eucharist to others. For this is what Christ did at the first Supper, and earnestly commanded that what He there did should be done in future, when He said: "This (namely, what you have seen Me do) do." It is clear from the institution what it is that the priests should distribute and dispense in the administration of the Eucharist, namely, what Christ distributed and dispensed. For He says: "Do what you have seen Me do." Now Christ distributed the blessed bread, saying: "Take, eat," etc. And to this part of the action He adds the command: "This do." Similarly also He distributed the cup of blessing, saying: "Drink," etc.

Also to this part of the action, just as to the first, Christ adds the command: "This do." Therefore if a priest celebrates the Eucharist and is the only one who eats it, dispensing it to no one else, he does not do what Christ did. But if he dispenses one part only, he is again not doing what Christ did. For even as He consecrated both kinds, so also He distributed both kinds. And what He did then, He commanded to be done in future when He said: "This do." Therefore the demonstration is very clear, clearer than the light of noon, that the command of Christ: "This do," insofar as it pertains to the priests alone, by no means takes away Communion under both kinds from the rest of the church. For this command does not intend that the priest who celebrates the Eucharist should alone take it, but it enjoins and imposes upon the celebrating priest with a divine precept that he should dispense and distribute the Eucharist, and that in the way Christ dispensed it. For He dispensed both the bread and the cup which He had blessed, and to each part expressly and distinctly added the command: "Do this," namely, what I have just done, from now on, until the end of the world.

12 There remains, then, the final question: Who are those to whom the celebrating priest is held, on the basis of the divine precept, to dispense and distribute the Eucharist? Christ dispensed it to the apostles, who, the papalists say, stood in the place of priests. But the apostles were not at that time confecting, as the papalists express it. Therefore both kinds of the Eucharist would have to be dispensed at least to the priests who are not confecting, even if it did pertain to the priests only. For Christ gave both kinds to the apostles, who were not then confecting. And what He then did He commanded by a precept to be done in future. Yet the papalist church does not dispense both kinds to priests when they are not confecting. This difficulty[29] I had earlier proposed to the Jesuits. But Andrada, their advocate, was not willing to touch it. For it is impossible that it should be rightly refuted by any argument. But passing over these illogicalities, we must look for a safe interpreter of Christ's command, that is, to whom the Eucharist is to be dispensed in the same way in which Christ dispensed it to His disciples, namely, under the form of bread and wine.

This interpreter will be Paul, who received his Gospel not from man but through a revelation of the Son of God (Gal. 1:11-12). He says that he handed on the doctrine concerning the Lord's Supper just as he had received it from the Lord [1 Cor. 11:23-29]. However, he did not hand it down as a bare account without explaining, adapting, and applying it to the practice (to use this expression) of the church. But he set forth the institution in such a way that it should be a rule and norm for administering, dispensing, and receiving the Eucharist. Having recited the words and commands of the institution of Christ, he at once adds an application about the dispensation and use of both kinds. Does what Paul there writes about Communion under both kinds pertain only to the priests? Surely, the inscription of the epistle addresses the whole "church of God which is at Corinth." Yes, he adds that it is written to "all who call on the name of the Lord," and that "in every place."

---

[29] The edition of 1574 has *modum,* which does not yield good sense in the present context. We have followed the emendation of Ed. Preuss, who has substituted *nodum,* i.e., knot, difficulty. Nigrinus has *diesen Knoten.*

Therefore just as we know from the words of institution that in the celebration of the Lord's Supper a dispensation or distribution of both kinds—of bread and of the cup of the Lord—must by divine precept be made, for this Christ did, and commanded that the same should be done afterward, so we know from Paul's interpretation that this dispensation of bread and of the cup of the Lord should, by divine precept, be made to every man who examines himself, yes, to all who call on the name of the Lord. For that is what Paul says.

Thus we have briefly but certainly and clearly demonstrated that the priests or ministers of the church are bound and obligated by divine precept, when they celebrate and administer the Lord's Supper, not only to consecrate and themselves take the Eucharist but to dispense and distribute what has been consecrated, not half but whole, namely, the bread and the cup of the Lord, just as Christ did, and to dispense and distribute both kinds, not to the priests only but to every man who examines himself and to "all who in every place call on the name of the Lord."

Perhaps it was not without particular cunning that the Tridentine decree was not willing to speak about the precept to dispense but rather about the precept to take. But although the latter is already clear from the former, from the nature of mutually related things, nevertheless it can also be shown clearly from Scripture, that is, from the command to take. For at the first Supper not only was this done, that Christ blessed and dispensed the bread and the cup, but also this was there done, that the apostles received the bread and the cup of the Lord, ate and drank, and that not as something they might do or leave undone but by the precept and command of the Lord. For He had said: "Take; eat; drink." To the whole action of the Lord's Supper Christ added the command that this should in future be done until the end of the world, when He said: "This," namely, what has been done at this first Supper, "do." Therefore just as in the first Supper the apostles by divine precept took, ate, and drank both kinds, so the instruction and command of Christ is that the same be done in future in the celebration of the Lord's Supper, until the end of the world.

Paul is a reliable witness that Christ Himself, in the institution, applied the command: "Do this," not only to the consecration and dispensation but expressly also to the reception, and indeed in the second part in so many words with respect to the cup. For he quotes the words of Christ thus: "Do this, as often as you drink it." And Paul himself, at once supplying the interpretation of the words of Christ: "Do this in remembrance of Me," says: "For as often as you eat this bread and drink the cup, you proclaim the Lord's death until He comes." Therefore Paul applies the command of Christ: "Eat; drink; do this," to those who receive. And just as the taking of the consecrated bread is by divine right and precept, so also the taking of the Dominical cup is by divine right and precept. Moreover, Paul writes these things to "all who in every place call on the name of the Lord."

13 Whether therefore the command of Christ: "Do this," is referred to the priests or to those who receive, it has become clear that Communion under both kinds is by divine right, precept, and command—and that for a twofold reason: I. Because the ministers of the church are obligated and bound by a precept of the Lord in the administration of the Lord's Supper to dispense the Eucharist in the same way Christ dispensed it at the first Supper, namely, under the form of bread and wine, and that not only to priests but to all who call on the name of the Lord in every place. II. Those who receive the Eucharist have the command of Christ that, when they receive it, they are to do what Scripture says was done in the first Supper, namely, eat the bread which has been blessed and drink the cup of the Lord. They are obligated and bound to do this by the bond of a double command. I. Because Paul shows by his interpretation that the command: "Eat; drink," pertains to all who take. II. Because Christ adds to each part the particular command: "Do this," that not only in the dispensation but also in the taking that may be done which was done in the first Supper.

14 By this right of the divine institution, prescription, command, and precept the primitive church dispensed the Eucharist under both kinds both to the priests and to the laity in the legitimate and customary assemblies of the church. She also taught expressly that in the use of and participation in these mysteries there is no distinction between a priest and a lay person, as has been demonstrated above. The ancient church never either felt or taught that Communion under both kinds was an arbitrary matter. But because both Christ and Paul speak by way of precept or command about reception under both kinds, the ancients also likewise taught that this is by divine right and precept. Cyprian says concerning the Lord's Supper: "The Law forbids the eating of blood; the Gospel teaches that it should be drunk. However, we drink the blood of Christ at His command—we, for whom that blood was shed." And in Bk. 2, Letter No. 3, where he discusses the consecrating of the cup of the Lord and its administration to the people, he calls attention repeatedly to the divine precept, as when he says that we must not, on account of a human institution, depart from what Christ our Master both taught and did. Likewise: "It is taught by the Lord and confirmed by the apostle that as often as we drink in remembrance of the Lord we should do what the Lord did." And finally he calls the institution of Christ an evangelical law.

Bernard, Sermon 3, *De ramis palmarum*, says that on that day the food of the body and blood of Christ was first offered, on that day commended and commanded, and thereafter received frequently. Cyprian, Bk. 1, Letter No. 2: "How shall we render them fit for the cup of martyrdom if we do not first admit them by the right of Communion to drink the cup of the Lord in the church?" And when Justin, a very ancient writer, had described the rite of Communion under both kinds in the church in his time, he at once added that the apostles taught in the Gospel that Christ had commanded them thus. Therefore we have shown, from the institution of Christ, the interpretation of Paul, and the tradition of the ancient church, that the dispensation and reception of the Eucharist under both kinds is by divine right and precept.

15 The second argument against the words of institution is fabricated by the Synod of Trent out of the discourse recorded in John 6. This is customarily set forth by papalist writers in twofold form:

I. Christ, speaking in John 6 of the taking and partaking of His body and blood, sometimes speaks of eating His flesh and drinking His blood; sometimes, however, He reduces this to eating only, as: "He who eats Me will live because of Me." Therefore Communion under both kinds is not prescribed as though it were necessary, but eating alone can suffice.

II. In the Polish Confession Hosius fashions the argument thus: When Christ in John 6 speaks of eating His flesh and drinking His blood, He makes no mention of the wine, but only of bread. Therefore the use of the Dominical cup can be abrogated and forbidden.

However, the answer is easy and plain: The evangelists testify and Paul clearly asserts that Christ instituted the Lord's Supper in the night in which He was betrayed. However, the discourse in John 6 was spoken by Christ a whole year and more before the institution of the Supper. Yet the Tridentine fathers are such honorable men that they are not ashamed, under a pretext taken from John 6, to reform, change, and mutilate the testamentary institution of the Son of God. In the same manner someone could frame an argument from the discourse in John 4, to the effect that one should only drink in the Lord's Supper, and indeed that not wine but water should be employed in the cup, because Christ there says: "Whoever drinks of the water that I shall give him will never thirst."

Furthermore, it is evident that Christ in John 6 is not treating of eating and drinking which is done with the physical mouth, nor of material bread. For when the Jews were pressing the sign, "Our fathers ate the manna in the wilderness," Christ replies: Indeed, My heavenly Father sent you, not bodily food but another bread, namely, His incarnate Son. "I," says He, "am that bread of life." So, when the crowds who had eaten of the five loaves returned to Him to be satisfied once more with bodily eating, Christ opposes to material bread and bodily eating another food, a spiritual, and spiritual eating, which takes place by faith, even as He repeats a number of times: "Whoever believes in Me has eternal life." If, therefore, one had to judge from the sixth chapter of John about the essence of the Lord's Supper against the words of institution, it would follow that also the element of bread ought not to be used in the Eucharist and that it is not necessary that something be received with the bodily mouth in the Lord's Supper; yes, it could be concluded from there that the use of both bread and the Dominical cup, as the institution of the Supper speaks of them, could simply be abrogated and forbidden. So excellent is the argument taken from the discourse in John 6 and opposed to the institution of the Supper by the papalists! And yet this single argument was the chief one which was opposed on the basis of Scripture to the use of both kinds at the time of the Council of Constance.

In explaining the sixth chapter the ancients are indeed generally accustomed to treat the doctrine of the Lord's Supper—not as though it had been instituted there, or as though one had to learn from John 6 what the material and what the form is, that is, what the element and what the Word in the sacrament of the Eucharist is, but because sacramental eating is not enough for salutary use of the Lord's Supper unless spiritual eating is added, and what that is and ought to be is described in John 6. To this extent and in this manner the ancients rightly adapted the sixth chapter of John to the teaching about the Eucharist. It cannot, however, be shown in any of the ancients that they even argued on the basis of John 6 that the use of the cup could be either abrogated or prohibited in a lawful and ordinary celebration of the Lord's Supper. Therefore the teaching about the material and form, about the element and Word of the Eucharist, about the rule for the administration and dispensation of the Lord's Supper, and about the mode of sacramental Communion has its seat, not in John 6, for at that time the Eucharist had not yet been instituted, but in the words of institution, in which it is plain that the dispensation and Communion of both kinds has been instituted as a precept. This the papalists simply overthrow. From this one should judge what kind of cause it is that rests on such arguments and foundations.

16 The third argument of the Synod of Trent is taken from the authority and power of the church.

Let the point at issue in the dispute be considered! The words of institution about both kinds are plain and certain. From them the papalist church has departed. Now, when you ask what reasons they have for this departure, they oppose to you the authority and power of the church. Therefore it will be necessary that the church have some power and authority against the express words of God, and indeed for refuting the testamentary institution of the Son of God, to which He wanted the church to be bound by a twofold command in the separate parts of the Eucharist until the end of the age, until He returns to judgment: "Eat; do this; drink; do this." Surely, the statement of Augustine, *Contra Cresconium*, Bk. 2, ch. 21, is both beautiful and true: "Paul says, 'The church is subject to Christ.' Therefore the church ought not to put itself above Christ, since He always judges in accord with truth, while ecclesiastical judges, being men, often err." But most things pertaining to this argument have already been explained earlier; therefore we shall examine only the words of the second Tridentine chapter.

They play deceitfully with the ambiguity of the word "dispensation." For also Gerson argues that there is indeed an instruction about drinking the cup, but it is the kind that can be dispensed from by the authority of the church. Now they define dispensation as a relaxation of the common law, after a cause has been examined by the one who has the right and power to dispense, so that there is license either to change something in the law or to do something against the law. Therefore the Tridentine chapter declares that the church has power in the dispensation of the sacraments and that by virtue of this power, even though Christ instituted both kinds as a precept, the church was nevertheless able to abrogate and forbid the Communion of the cup. Hear how they prove this from Scripture! "For Paul says: 'We are stewards[30] of the mysteries of God.' " The mysteries are the sacraments, and to dispense is to relax the common law. Those things, therefore, which Christ instituted in the dispensation and use of the Eucharist the church is able to abrogate; what He enjoined she can forbid, namely, the use of the cup of the Lord for the laity.

Indeed, the opinion of the canonists is that the pope is able to dispense against the first four councils, likewise against the words of the Gospel, although not against their intent. But if anyone had been able at that time, when barbarism and ignorance of language reigned, to prove this papal power of dispensing from the saying of Paul: "We are stewards *(dispensatores)* of the mysteries of God," this proof would truly have been held to be the work of a master. But now that the light shines so brightly, I would think no sane man would dare to play with words in so

---

[30] The Vulgate has *dispensatores*.

serious a matter. But the shameless front of the Babylonian harlot dares to do this, and indeed according to her own right. From this let us judge with what kind of conscience they pursue this cause and how much faith should be accorded them.

Paul here understands by mysteries the revelation of the whole evangelical doctrine and calls the apostles ministers,[31] intimating this very contrast, that they are not masters of these mysteries, who have power to change and abrogate, but they are only overseers, in whom this faithfulness is required, that they dispense according to the institution, prescription, and command of the Master the things committed to them. In this sense the ancient translator used the word "dispensation."

The ambiguity of the word seemed just right to the Tridentine fathers for justifying the mutilation of the Lord's Supper. Therefore it was not without reason that they made the ancient version authentic by their decree, so that no one should dare to reject it in disputations on any pretext whatsoever, even though, as in this passage, *oikonomia* does not signify the power of changing and of establishing something against that which the Lord prescribed by an express command. But it seems that the men of Trent themselves do not sufficiently trust this "dispensation." For they tone down the wording in such a way as if they wanted to say: In the dispensation, that is, in the administration of the sacraments, the church can, in external circumstances, establish and ordain whatever serves edification—in arrangements of this kind, if they are made in circumstances about which there is no command of God, to this end, that those things which are prescribed and commanded in the administration of the sacraments instituted by the Lord may be observed the more rightly and diligently for edification.

We do not deny, I say, that with respect to such arrangements the church has power, namely, that all things may be done in orderly fashion, decently, and for edification. However, the papalists stretch this power beyond its proper bounds, as if the church could, by a similar power, change, mutilate, prohibit, and take away also those things which the Son of God instituted, ordained, prescribed, commanded, and taught in the institution of the Supper. This we deny, because it cannot be proved. Let it be observed how the Tridentine argumentation moves from dispensation in circumstances that are adiaphora to abrogation, mutilation, and prohibition of things which have a word and command of God. Truly, it is false when they say that Paul uses such power when he writes to the Corinthians: "About the other things I will give directions when I come."

---

[31] *Oikonomous:* stewards, managers.

For he clearly places first those things which have the institution, ordination, prescription, and command of Christ. From these he afterward separates the things he promises to set in order when he comes. Therefore he means those things which have no prescription and command of Christ.

Indeed, the council itself also is not able simply to deny this distinction; therefore they add that dispensation can be made "provided the essence of the sacraments is preserved." This is very strange, that the Eucharist can be mutilated in its one part and its essence nevertheless be preserved. Lombard and the scholastics certainly assert that the essential things in the sacraments are the matter and the form, that is, the divinely instituted element and the word connected with the element by the divine voice. Now Christ instituted as the elements in His Supper not the use of bread only but also of the cup. How, then, does the essence of the Lord's Supper remain unharmed if one of its parts is abrogated, mutilated, and forbidden? But perhaps they want the essence of the Eucharist to be spiritual participation in the body and blood of Christ. Since this is done also under one kind, where the whole and entire Christ is present, they judge that the essence of the Eucharist remains unharmed also if the cup of the Lord is taken away from it. But because spiritual participation in the flesh and the blood of Christ can also take place without bread and wine, in the Word of the Gospel, by faith alone (John 6); therefore, by the same kind of reasoning, the essence of the Eucharist will remain unharmed even if both kinds, bread and wine, are removed from it. But what belongs to and is necessary for the essence of the Lord's Supper must be learned and determined not from human argumentations but from the testamentary institution of the Son of God.

17 The fourth argument of the Synod of Trent is taken from the examples of the ancient church, namely, that the use of both kinds, though indeed not infrequent in the ancient church, was nevertheless not universal, but Communion under one kind only was always in use at the same time. To this freedom of communicating either under both kinds or under only one there afterward succeeded a change of custom from Communion under both kinds. This was finally followed by the law about one kind only.

The reader will observe that the papalists learned much from experience in this matter which in the beginning was not sufficiently considered. For when the Council of Constance first introduced the law about the mutilation of the Lord's Supper, it simply conceded that it had been the custom of the primitive church that the Eucharist should be received under both kinds by the faithful. But then, two years later, Gerson noticed how much damage this confession was causing. And although he could not prove and show the contrary, he nevertheless said that it seemed more probable that this was not generally observed by all. From this remark the Tridentine Synod has this stratagem, that it does not say that in the beginning of the Christian religion the use of both kinds was universal, yes, it does not even say that it was frequent, but according to the figure called miosis[32] it says that it was not infrequent. They are, however, looking back upon the disputations of the papalists by which they attempt to prove that also in the primitive and ancient church, where Communion under both kinds was customary, Communion under one kind only was nevertheless also always in use. Therefore some things must be noted down about these disputations as briefly as it can be done. For these notations will also show that, when the papalists lack genuine testimonies both of Scripture and of antiquity, they corrupt the testimonies of the ancients just as they play with statements of Scripture.

Now, when the argument is about testimonies and examples of the ancient church, one does not ask about cases of necessity and exceptions but about the lawful, ordinary public and solemn celebration, administration, and dispensation of the Eucharist. However, it has been shown from many sources, from ancient forms of liturgies, from descriptions of celebrations of the Lord's Supper which are found with the ancients, particularly with Justin and Chrysostom, and from many other testimonies and examples of the ancients, that in the ancient church, in the lawful and ordinary administration of the Lord's Supper, Communion under both kinds according to the institution of Christ was always and everywhere customary with all. Neither can any example be brought forward from antiquity where in a lawful and solemn administration of the Lord's Supper only one kind was dispensed to the faithful people while the other was withheld. Since these things are so, it is worth the effort to see with what ingenuity the papalists corrupt also the testimonies of antiquity, which are very numerous and quite clear.

ARTICLE VII

How the Papalists Attempt to Prove Their Mutilation with Testimonies from Antiquity

1 I. Eck and many others attach great importance to this testimony, that in the writings of the ancients and in ancient canons mention is made

---

[32] Miosis: a figure of speech by which a thing is understated or a statement belittled.

of lay Communion, to which those were directed who had been cast out of the clerical order. "Therefore," say they, "there was in the ancient church one kind of Communion for the clergy, under both kinds, and another of the laity, under one kind." But now even papalists like Vicelius, Tapper, Lindanus, and others perceive and confess that this is false. For it is crystal clear that during those times where mention is made of lay Communion both kinds were given to the laity. And Chrysostom expressly says that in participation in the sacraments there is no distinction between the priests and the believing people. It was called lay Communion by the ancients when a clergyman was either suspended from the duty of the ministry or entirely removed from it on account of some offense, for then he did not himself administer the Eucharist but only received it, and that not among the clergy but after the clergy, with the lay people and in the place where the lay people were communicated. Therefore the papalists themselves acknowledge and confess that lay Communion among the ancients is not to be understood of another kind of Communion but of the station, order, and place of Communion.

2 II. Some, whom also Hosius in the Polish confession follows, imagine that it was decreed at the Synod at Ephesus that only one kind be given to the laity in the Eucharist, because Nestorius taught that under the bread there was a bloodless carcass. But this is a mere figment of the imagination. For no one among the ancients ascribes this opinion to Nestorius. Also in the history and in the records of the Ephesine council there is found not even a trace of such a discussion or decree. But such a cause is worthy of such proofs.

3 III. This also is one of the papalist stratagems, that where mention is made of the Eucharist in ancient writers, they understand it of one kind only, as when in Eusebius, Bk. 5, ch. 24, the Eucharist is sent to bishops of the same communion when they arrive from a journey; the papalists contend that this must simply be understood of the species of bread only. But the term "Eucharist" embraces both kinds. For when Justin describes the rite of Communion under both kinds, he says: "This food is called Eucharist with us." Irenaeus, Bk. 5: "When the Word of God is added to the cup which has been mixed and the bread which has been broken, it becomes the Eucharist of the body and blood of Christ." Cyprian, Bk. 1, Letter No. 2: "We fortify them with the protection of the body and blood of Christ, because the Eucharist is made for this, that it may be a protection to believers." In the third treatise, *On the Lapsed,* where mention is made expressly only of the cup, Cyprian calls it "Eucharist."

4 IV. From the fact that the Eucharist was carried to the sick they

attempt to prove the use of one kind only, because, as they say, wine could not be carried without danger. But Justin, in the second Apology, and Jerome, *Ad Rusticum monachum, de Exuperio,* expressly testify that it was customary in the ancient church to carry both kinds to the absent and the sick. In the story of Serapion, found in Eusebius, Bk. 5, ch. 44, Andrada labors mightily to refer this to one kind, because the word *apobrechein,* to besprinkle or to moisten, agrees only with the species of bread. But I ask Andrada to say to which kind it refers when the account says *epistaxai* and *egcheai,* to pour or instil into the mouth. Here, say the Jesuits, was unconsecrated wine, in which the youth was commanded to moisten the bread. This, however, Eusebius does not say. Rather, Nicephorus asserts, Bk. 6, ch. 6, that it was the Eucharist which the young man trickled into the mouth of the old man. For he says: "He instilled the Eucharist into him." Now it is known from the histories of the ancients that it was customary in a case of necessity to give the sick the bread of the Eucharist dipped into the consecrated wine, as we shall show later.

5 V. They endeavor to prove the use of one kind only from the reservation of the Eucharist, of which mention is made somewhere among the ancients. But this also is futile. For according to Chrysostom, Letter No. 1, to Innocent, also the blood of Christ is reserved in the sacristy. And Gorgonia, the sister of Gregory of Nazianzus, had reserved the antitype of the body and blood of the Lord, as Gregory of Nazianzus testifies.

6 VI. Where in writings of the ancients mention is expressly made only of the body of Christ or of eating, there the papalists immediately attach their preconceived opinion about one kind only. But I shall demonstrate by a number of very clear examples that they sophistically pervert the meaning of the ancients. Eck quotes from the epistle of Ignatius to the Ephesians: "Breaking one bread, which is the medicine of immortality," etc. And because Ignatius does not there expressly mention the other kind, therefore Eck vociferates that the custom of Communion under one kind was handed down by the apostles themselves and preserved by their disciples. But Ignatius protests that a great wrong is being done him. For in his epistle to the Philadelphians he says: "There is one bread, broken for all, and one cup, distributed to all."

Cyprian, Treatise 3, *De lapsis,* tells of certain miraculous things which happened in one kind, namely, the consecrated bread. From this, Horst of Cologne attempts to prove against the very learned Hamelmann that at the time of Cyprian Communion under one kind only was in use in the church, and adds that this Communion was at that time approved by God with miracles. But this is a shameless fiction. For Cyprian by no means says that those miracles were done to approve Communion under one kind only, but relates far other causes for these miracles. It does not, however, follow: A miracle took place in the species of bread; therefore the cup of the Lord was at that time not distributed in the church. For in that very same discourse, as he describes the rite of Communion during his times, Cyprian says: "When the ceremonies have been completed, the deacon would offer the cup to those present."

With great to-do they bring also the Council of Nicaea onto the stage and are not ashamed to assert that there Communion under one kind only, if not decreed, was nevertheless approved and confirmed, namely, because Canon 14 says: "If the bishop or presbyter are not present, then let the deacons themselves bring it forward and eat." But this canon does not read thus, neither in Greek nor in the Decrees nor in Rufinus. And even though only the body of Christ is expressly named there, nevertheless Communion under one kind only is not rightly concluded from this. For in the Council of Neocaesaraea, ch. 15, and dist. 95, ch. *Presbyteri,* where clearly the same matter is repeated about the deacons, it speaks expressly about giving the bread and offering the cup. Therefore antiquity explains itself very clearly, that it often speaks by way of synecdoche. For also Paul himself, writing to the Corinthians, where he most expressly treats of Communion under both kinds, nevertheless designates it several times by means of a synecdoche, as when he says: "to eat the Lord's Supper," "you come together to eat," "discerning the Lord's body." Likewise: "All were made to drink of one Spirit." Now if someone wanted to conclude from this that Paul had taught and observed Communion under one kind only, he would be acting wickedly against the clear meaning of Paul. Thus also Augustine, *De symbolo,* Bk. 3, ch. 5, likewise *De feria,* 4, ch. 4, likewise Jerome, *Ad Eustachium,* make mention expressly only of the blood of Christ. Could one rightly infer from this that in the times of Augustine and Jerome not bread but only the cup of the Lord was dispensed to the laity in the administration of the sacrament?

7 VII. With great pomp they bring forward examples of Communion in homes in behalf of the mutilation of the Lord's Supper, namely, when they carried the Eucharist which they had received in the church home with them. For Tertullian, Bk. 2, *Ad uxorem,* makes mention only of bread. And Jerome, *Apologia pro libris adversus Jovinianum,* makes mention only of the body. Although this domestic or private Communion was something out of the common order, it is nevertheless not difficult to answer. For because they received the Eucharist in the church, the question is not what they took at home but what had been dispensed to them in

the church. And lest I go far afield, I shall bring forward the explanation of Ruard Tapper, the dean of Louvain, who is a man of the highest authority among the papalists. This man, in treating the example of Satyrus the brother of Ambrose, says: "It is evident from Treatise 3, *De lapsis,* in Cyprian that in those times all drank the blood of the Lord from the cup and that the body of the Lord was given into their hands in order that they might either eat it at once or carry it home with them and eat it there, so that there would be intervals of time between the drinking of the cup of the Lord and the eating of the body of the Lord." So says this man. Because this rending asunder of the parts of the Lord's Supper does not accord with the institution, this domestic or private Communion was later abrogated and strictly forbidden in the councils of Toledo and Caesar Augusta.[33] By no means, therefore, can it be proved from that domestic Communion that the dispensation of only one kind in the Eucharist was at that time customary in the church.

Also Tertullian, in the same book where, speaking of domestic Communion, he makes mention in one place only of bread, soon thereafter in another place speaks also of partaking of the cup; and finally he mentions both together, food and cup of the Lord. Gregory of Nazianzus, moreover, writes of his sister Gorgonia that she had preserved the antitypes of both the body and blood of the Lord, which she had brought home with her from the assembly of the church. And Ambrose, describing the reception of the Supper in the story of his brother Satyrus, mentions drinking and pouring into the inwards. Therefore dispensation and reception of the Eucharist under one kind only cannot be proved with sufficient certainty and clarity from this story either.

Even if, in examples of this domestic Communion, something were shown that is opposed to the institution of Christ and the established custom of the primitive church (which, however, I do not yet see done), what would be accomplished by this, since these are private and extraordinary examples and indeed such as were afterward for weighty reasons abrogated? Our question is not what one or the other did privately, but what was the public, lawful, ordinary, and established custom of the ancient church in the administration of the Lord's Supper. This is the issue in this controversy, about which we demand testimonies and examples of antiquity. And I do not yet see any such sure and clear testimony or example from the true antiquity brought forward by the papalists. For the rest of what they bring forward, from uncertain authors, as for in-

---

[33] Caesar Augusta: ancient name for Saragossa in Spain. This council was held A.D. 380. Only 12 bishops were present. All voted to anathematize anyone who received the Eucharist in church and did not consume it there. (Mansi, *Collectio,* III, 634)

stance from the life of Jerome and Ambrose, where there is doubt about the authors, and from the legends of the saints, is not worthy to be refuted.

These are the chief points in the proofs by which they try to cloak and establish the papalist mutilation with examples from antiquity; surely, these prove nothing about the matter which is in controversy, namely, about the public, lawful, ordinary, and established custom of the ancient church in the administration and dispensation of the Lord's Supper. Most of them, indeed, are pure fictions or manifest corruptions of the meaning of the ancients, as we have clearly shown. Nevertheless the Council of Trent is not ashamed fondly to kiss and approve all these things as if they were oracles, not of Apollo but of the Holy Spirit Himself, as though it were already certain and demonstrated that although Communion under both kinds was not infrequent in the primitive church it was nevertheless not catholic or universal, but that Communion under one kind only was also always in use.

ARTICLE VIII

A Historical Exhibit: How Often and in How Many Ways This Mutilation Was Tried Until It Was Finally Introduced

1 Moreover, because the Tridentine chapter wants to justify the papalist mutilation from the change of the custom of communicating under both kinds and from the introduction of the contrary custom, I judge that it will be useful to note down certain things concerning the introduction of this custom. They assert publicly that this custom is so old that its beginning cannot even be shown in the histories. But we shall show from the true histories how in the ancient church the attempt was made repeatedly and in a number of ways to change Communion under both kinds, and how sharply the overseers of the churches resisted this change during the better and purer times of the church until finally in later times, namely 1,200 years after Christ, together with other errors and abuses this change in particular, although not without contradictions, was brought into certain churches—then, having spread more widely, finally was confirmed by a law of the Council of Constance.

A certain change of Communion under both kinds according to the teaching of Christ was first attempted by those who drank of the cup of the Lord in the church but carried the consecrated bread home with them, which they ate afterward, sometimes after a fairly long interval of time, as Basil writes concerning the hermits. But this custom was abrogated and prohibited at the First Council of Toledo, around the year 390, and afterward around the year 500 at the Council of Caesar Augusta.[34] Communion was restored to the form of the institution—that the Eucharist should be consumed in church, where at that time both kinds were distributed.

Second, at the time of Leo I, around A.D. 440, the Manichaeans attempted to introduce the taking of one kind only, because they detested wine as something abominable and taught that the body of Christ, being something imaginary, had no real blood. But Pope Leo, Sermon 40, 4, calls it a sacrilege if anyone refuses to drink the cup of the blood of our redemption. Here he applies the word of Paul in Rom. 16:17: "Take note of those who create dissensions and difficulties, in opposition to the doctrine which you have been taught."

Lindanus imagines that prior to Leo Communion under one kind was in use in the church but that Leo at that time again commanded Communion under both kinds for a time in order that the Manichaeans could in this way be caught. But Andrada says rightly that this is an extraordinary dream. For Communion under both kinds was at that time used to such an extent that Leo could catch the Manichaeans by these signs. Therefore Leo declares around A.D. 449 that it is a sacrilege, a division and offense against the doctrine received from the apostles, to take the body of the Lord with the mouth but to refuse to drink the cup of our redemption.

Third, at the time of Gelasius, around A.D. 490, a change from Communion under both kinds was again attempted, not by heretics, as in the time of Leo, but by superstitious men. But, as Gelasius tells, that superstition was sharply repulsed and driven out of the church, as the canon *Comperimus, De Consecratione,* dist. 2, testifies: "We have learned that some, having received only a portion of the sacred body, abstain from the cup of the consecrated blood. These, because they are bound by I know not what superstition, should either receive the sacraments whole or be excluded from the entire sacraments, because a division of one and the same sacrament cannot be made without great sacrilege." You hear that one kind is not a complete sacrament but that both kinds belong to one and the same sacrament; also, that it is a great sacrilege if only one kind is received.

Also the word "superstition" is to be noted in this canon. For from it one can gather under what pretext certain people at the time of Gelasius

---

[34] Chemnitz appears to be in error here. According to Mansi, op. cit., there were three councils of Caesar Augusta. The canon referred to was approved at the first of these, A.D. 380.

wanted to introduce the custom of communicating under one kind only. For superstition, according to the scholastics, is to want to worship God, however in a way in which it ought not to be done, that is, in a way different from and against the one which He Himself prescribed and commanded. Therefore those who at the time of Gelasius abstained from the Dominical cup, beside and contrary to the form of Communion taught and prescribed by Christ, had and held out a pretext of religion and divine worship and of reverence toward the sacrament. And because the words of the canon read: "They are taught by a superstition to be bound," this could even be understood to mean that there were at that time some who taught thus. Let this be noted well! For no matter what pretense is made of religion and reverence for the sacrament in Communion under one kind, it is superstition, because it is done differently from and contrary to what Christ instituted. Indeed, Gelasius declares that those are to be kept from Communion, that is, excommunicated, who out of superstition abstain from partaking of the Dominical cup.

That Gratian, together with the writers of glosses, restricts this canon only to the priests who are confecting conflicts with the ecclesiastical history of those times and with the text itself. For it speaks about those who are either admitted to receiving the sacraments or are shut out from them. This fiction of Gratian is now rejected by papalists themselves, such as Lindanus and others.

Fourth, on account of the fear of the danger of spilling, some already early considered a departure from the form of the institution of Christ; however, lest they should take away and abrogate Communion under both kinds altogether, they gave the communicants consecrated bread dipped into the cup of blessing for a full Communion; that is, they judged that it would not be a full Communion if the Eucharist were given under the species of bread only, without the consecrated wine.

It is worth observing from where this crept into the church. For since we read that among the ancients in a case of necessity, in Communion of little children and of the sick, a dipped and infused sacrament was sometimes given, as is seen from the story of Serapion; from Cyprian, Treatise 3, *De lapsis;* and from Prosper, *De promissionibus,* ch. 6 and ch. 26, quest. 6, ch. 15, in *Decreta,*[35] some afterward wanted to bring the custom of a dipped sacrament from these extraordinary cases into the lawful and ordinary Communion of the church, contrary to the institution of Christ and the custom of the ancient church, and that under the pretext of the danger of spilling, and of reverence toward the Eucharist. But Pope

---

[35] We follow the reading of Nigrinus. The Latin is *Is in decretis,* which may well be an error of the typesetter.

Julius, about A.D. 340, sharply rebukes this custom in an epistle to the bishops of Egypt (and this is quoted in *De consecratione,* dist. 2, ch. *Cum omne).*

It is worth the effort to consider on what grounds he refutes it. He says that it is contrary to the divine order, contrary to the apostolic institutions, likewise that it is contrary to the evangelical and apostolic teaching and ecclesiastical custom. He also shows (and this must be especially noted) from where the proofs in this matter must be sought and taken. For he says: "It will not be difficult to prove this from the fountain of truth itself, from which the ordained mysteries of the sacraments have come forth." The reader notices that the Roman church at that time used far different bases in controversies about the Communion of the Lord's Supper than are used now. For the divine order, the apostolic institutions, the evangelical and apostolic teaching, and ancient ecclesiastical custom are named. To these bases also we are now appealing. But opposed to us are the power of the church, later custom, and arguments from reason. Julius finally concludes: "When they give a dipped Eucharist to the people for a full Communion, they have not received this as a proved testimony from the Gospel, where He commended His body to the apostles, and also His blood; for the commendation of the bread is mentioned separately and that of the cup also separately." In this way the custom of a dipped Eucharist was at that time suppressed.

Later, however, it spread again, about A.D. 580. For on this account the decree of Julius was repeated at the Third Council of Braga.[36] So frequently have human intellects meditated upon a departure from the form of Communion prescribed by the Son of God Himself. But in the better times of the church there were men who retained and sharply defended the testamentary institution of the Son of God against all customs and pretexts.

Fifth, when afterward, around A.D. 920, a greater departure from the purity of the ancient church in the matter of doctrine and rites occurred, the order of Cluny again instituted intinction, but against the custom and usage of the other churches. For Cassander quotes from the regulations of the monks of Cluny, Bk. 2, ch. 35, as follows: "In the case of all to whom the priest gives the body, he dips in the blood for each one, although this is against the usage of the other churches, because some, most of all our novices, are so clumsy that if they received the blood thus separately, they might commit some act of carelessness." You see that

---

[36] This council is called Bracarense, after the Latin name of the modern city of Braga in Portugal. According to Mansi, op. cit., XI, 155, it was not Bracarense III but IV where part of Julius' decree is repeated verbatim, however without mention of the source.

although they disputed at that time about fear of the danger of spilling and lack of reverence, they nevertheless did not dare to judge that therefore the use of the cup should be omitted and abrogated.

Afterward, at the Council of Tours, the use of a dipped Eucharist for the sick was granted for use also in other churches. And the reason is added: "The wafer should be dipped in the blood of Christ in order that the presbyter may be able to say truly: 'May the body and blood of our Lord Jesus Christ benefit you for the forgiveness of sins and eternal life.' " The reader will note that although there was then a slight departure from the form of the institution of Christ, they nevertheless considered both kinds so necessary that they preferred to counsel the giving of a dipped Eucharist. But most of all let it be noted that it cannot be truthfully said that the body and blood of Christ is given and received under the species of bread only.

Finally, in the time of Ivo,[37] around A.D. 1120, permission was granted to communicate the people with dipped bread elsewhere also, and that not with an appeal to authority but on account of extreme necessity caused by fear of spilling the blood of Christ. For thus Cassander quotes Ivo, *De divinis officiis.* I relate these things in order to show that although disputes were raised and magnified about fear of the danger of spilling and irreverence, it was nevertheless not judged that for this reason one kind either could or should be entirely taken away and omitted from Communion; but rather, they used intinction so that nevertheless both kinds might be given. Nevertheless the custom of a dipped Eucharist was not universal at the time of Ivo, for elsewhere both kinds were then given separately, as is gathered from those who lived around those times, notably from Bernard and Lombard.

Sixth, after Lombard, in the time of the scholastic writers, about A.D. 1250, mention first began to be made openly of a particular custom, brought in somewhere, of communicating the people under one kind, on account of fear and the danger of spilling. And yet in the history of those times many disputations pertaining to this can be noted. For that custom had not then been accepted by all churches, neither did all permit the use of the Dominical cup to be taken away from them. For Thomas, in the third part of the *Summa,* quest. 80, art. 12, says that in some churches it is carefully observed that the blood of Christ is not given to the people. And in *Sententiae,* 4, dist. 11, art. 2, quest. 1, he says: "In some places participating in the blood is customarily given to the clergy, that is, those who minister at the altar, of whom it is assumed that they are more careful."

---

[37] Ivo of Chartres (1040-1116), bishop of Chartres and an influential churchman in his own time and beyond.

Richard Middleton and Peter of Tarentaise, later called Innocent IV, testify that in their time the Eucharist under both kinds was given not only to those who ministered at the altar but also to the more highly esteemed among the people, in whose case these dangers were not feared. Peter of La Palu [c. 1277—1342] writes in *Sententiae,* 4, dist. 11, quest. 1, that in his time the custom in some churches was to communicate generally under both kinds, but with such caution that nothing would be spilled. Cassander cites from William of Mont Lauzun [d. 1343]: "By receiving the body of Christ he receives His whole truth, but not the whole sacrament. And therefore in many places Communion is with bread and wine, that is, with the whole sacrament."

Durandus, around A.D. 1280, in *Rationale divinorum,* Bk. 4, ch. 42, tells that in his time there was a custom in some places that, after the priest's Communion, something of the blood was reserved in the cup and pure wine poured over it, in order that from this the communicants might be able to receive something of the blood of Christ. Earlier he gives the reason, from Innocent III: "Although under the species of the bread the blood is taken together with the body, nevertheless the blood is not drunk under the species of bread." Therefore the custom of Communion under one kind had at that time been brought into certain churches in particular.

Furthermore, scrutiny of the histories of that period shows also this, that the recent custom of Communion under one kind was contradicted by many at that time. For Alexander of Hales [1185—1245] relates that certain monks bore it with difficulty that the cup of the Lord was taken from them and demanded restoration of Communion under both kinds. But he says that their petition was suppressed with a contrived miracle— that blood flowed out of a sacred wafer. And although the scholastic writers yield to the custom recently received by some for one reason only, the danger of spilling, they nevertheless argue in many words and publicly that Communion under both kinds is more fitting, more consistent, more perfect, more complete, and of greater efficacy. Among these the very oldest, Alexander of Hales, says, quest. 32, memb. 1, art. 2: "When this sacrament is received worthily under both kinds, there is greater effect of the one mystical body with the Head than when it is received under one kind." Quest. 53: "Although reception under one kind suffices, nevertheless reception under both is of greater merit, in part by reason of increase of devotion, in part by reason of the actual enlarging of faith, in part by reason of more complete reception." Likewise: "Reception under both kinds, which manner of reception the Lord taught, is of greater efficacy and fulness." At quest. 31 he says that he who receives the sacrament under the species of bread does not receive the complete sacrament so far as sacramental reception is concerned.

Closest after Alexander of Hales follows Albertus Magnus [1193—1280], who says, *Sententiae,* 4, dist. 8, art. 13, that there is a twofold completeness in this sacrament—that of Christ Himself and that of the sacrament, depending on the way it comes into the use of the faithful. According to the first mode, he says, it is true that Christ is complete under each species, but according to the second mode it seems to him false, because the use of the faithful and the unity of the mystical body is not perfectly signified and brought about except by the twofold sign, and therefore, for the perfection of the sacrament, it ought to have both.

After him Thomas says, *Summae,* 3, quest. 66, art. 2: "Although the whole Christ is under each species, it is not in vain. For in the first place it serves to represent the suffering of Christ, in which His blood was separated from the body. Secondly, it fits the use of the sacrament that the body of Christ should be offered to the faithful separately in the food, and the blood in the drink." Likewise he says, *Contra gentiles,* Bk. 4, ch. 61: "Because the fulness of our salvation was brought through the passion and death of Christ, through which His blood was separated from His flesh, the sacrament of His body is given us separately under the bread, and His blood under the species of wine, that in this way we might, in the sacrament of the passion of the Lord, have a memorial and a representation, and that in this way the word which the Lord spoke might be fulfilled: 'My flesh is food indeed, and My blood is drink indeed.' "

These testimonies cannot be referred to as the eating of the priests only, for he speaks expressly of the offering and giving of the sacrament which is made to the faithful. Peter of La Palu, dist. 11, art. 1, says: "The material of this sacrament must be twofold, namely, the material of food and drink. The effect of the sacrament must be perfectly represented by the material, for the sacraments effect what they represent. Now the effect of this sacrament is complete refreshment of the soul; therefore the material which represents this should be something which completely refreshes the body, which can be done only through food and drink." Bonaventura, dist. 8, quest. 2, teaches: "In this sacrament one complete sacrament results from two signs, whose wholeness results in an orderly way from nature; for bread by itself does not fully refresh, neither does wine, but from both together comes full refreshment. Its fulfillment comes from the divine institution. This institution ordained these two signs, in order to signify one perfect refreshing."

2 George Cassander, who is very learned with respect to antiquity, gathered these testimonies from the scholastic writers.

Durandus, *Rationale*, Bk. 4, ch. 54, says: "Whoever receives only the host does not receive the whole sacrament sacramentally. For although the blood of Christ is in the consecrated host, it is nevertheless not there sacramentally, because the bread is the sign of the body, not of the blood, and the wine is the sign of the blood, and not of the body. Therefore, so far as its being a sacrament is concerned, there is no complete sacrament under one kind only." Granted that Durandus is here speaking chiefly of the receiving on the part of the presbyter, the reason is nevertheless general.

This historical display is exceedingly useful, for it shows that, when the custom of Communion under one kind first began to invade the churches, which happened after A.D. 1200, it was not accepted by all churches but that many spoke against it—and indeed, that the teaching of the ancient church about sacramental Communion was not at once changed and bent to this custom but that the scholastics, even though they yielded to this custom, nevertheless opposed to it the teaching from the institution of Christ, namely, that Communion under both kinds, because it was instituted by Christ, is more fitting, more harmonious, more complete, more perfect, of greater efficacy, and gives a clearer representation. Also, the total material of this controversy was not, even at the time of the scholastics, argued in the way it is now treated by the papalists.

Later, when this custom gained more and more strength, a greater change also followed in the doctrine, although Lyra acknowledges, writing on 1 Cor. 11, that Christ instituted the sacrament in two kinds. And, writing on Prov. 9, he testifies that in the primitive church the faithful received this sacrament in both kinds. He adds, however, that on account of the danger of spilling it was ordered that it should be given to the laity under one kind.

And yet, before the Council of Constance, Communion under both kinds had not simply been taken away from all lay people everywhere. For Thomas Waldensis,[38] who about the time of the Council of Constance wrote against Wycliffe, although he defends Communion under one kind, nevertheless testifies, Bk. 2, chs. 88 and 94, that to presbyters, deacons, ministers of the altar, the chief men among the people, rulers of important places and monasteries, and to others of outstanding dignity, to believers strong in faith and discreet, for instance, doctors, kings, and others who were judged worthy of so great a thing, it was granted that they were admitted to the sacrifice and its drink offering, namely, to be communicated in both kinds.

---

[38] Thomas Waldensis Netter (c. 1380-1430).

Yes, the very petition of the agents of the Council of Constance testifies that Communion of the laity under both kinds was then still practiced in many places. For two causes are cited in the acts of the Council of Constance for which the cup was forbidden. The first is explained in the petition of the agents of the council in these words: "Because in some parts of the world the priests do not cease to communicate the laity under both kinds, namely bread and wine, against the custom of the Roman church, we, the agents of the council, petition that it may be provided as salutary for the church, " etc. The second cause is explained by the decree itself, namely, because in some parts of the world certain men were teaching that the Christian people should be communicated under both kinds and that the people ought to receive the sacrament of the Eucharist under both kinds. This Aeneas Sylvius explains thus in the history of Bohemia, that a certain Jacobellus of Meissen, an exhorter[39] of the church of Prague, having been admonished by a certain Peter, a schoolteacher from Dresden, searched the ancient codices of the holy doctors, especially of Dionysius and Cyprian, and found Communion of the cup lauded. He began to exhort the people that they should thereafter not neglect Communion of the cup for any reason whatsoever. Therefore the true reason for the forging of the papalist law about the mutilation of the Lord's Supper was that nothing differing from the custom of the Roman church should either be done or taught in any church. This could not, however, be obtained unless a wicked law was forged on the basis of a bad custom. However, the Greek church never accepted that law.

On the basis of this historical reminder one can most correctly examine and judge how much trust and authority should be given to the things that are said at the end of the second Tridentine chapter about the very wide custom of Communion under one kind only, which the papalists later decreed should, for weighty and just reasons, be held as law.

3 The final argument of the Synod of Trent was also the principal one at the councils of Constance and of Basel—that the cause, purpose, effect, and fruit of Eucharistic Communion is partaking of the body and blood, yes, of the whole Christ, and that this is accomplished also under one kind. For the whole and entire Christ is under each species, because the blood is no longer separated from the body in Christ. Therefore those who receive one kind only are not defrauded of any grace necessary for salvation. And truly, if the Lord's Supper were a natural work, or if we were permitted to justify the wisdom of the Son of God with our reason,

---

[39] The Latin *concionator*, derived from *concieo*, to urge, incite, stir up.

this argument would have some force. For it is commonly said that it is a sin to apply much force when a thing could be done with less. But on whom will this sin fall except on the Son of God Himself, who instituted His Supper under the two kinds of bread and wine at a time when His blood had not yet been separated from His body and when He knew that there would not be any separation after His resurrection? Surely, if it were once permitted to use such argumentation against the clear institution of Christ, the Lord's Supper could be abrogated entirely, for we are made partakers of Christ by faith in the Word (Heb. 3:14). "Christ dwells in your hearts through faith" (Eph. 3:17). Moreover, in Baptism we have put on Christ (Gal. 3:27). To what end, therefore, will there be need of the Communion of the Lord's Supper? Likewise: Why do the priests take the blood of Christ twice, once under the species of bread, and again under the species of wine? If the answer is that it was not in vain that Christ instituted it thus, that is also our opinion. For we have shown above that Christ instituted His Supper not for the priests only but for the whole church. Therefore I answer: Because this sacrament is not a work of nature nor an action of reason and the senses but a mystery of faith which is conceived from the Word of God and rests upon it, therefore its institution, taught by a sure and clear word of God, is not to be reformed, changed, or mutilated on the basis of arguments of reason about natural concomitance, but it belongs to the obedience of faith that it clings to the Word of God and follows what it prescribes simply and without questioning. In this sacrament, therefore, let us believe what Christ has said and do what He commanded. For reason must be taken captive to obey Christ. (2 Cor. 10:5)

But if we want to be wiser than Christ, that will happen to us which is written in Rom. 1:21-22: "They became futile in their thinking. . . . Claiming to be wise, they became fools." But they say: "What is greater in this sacrament, Christ or the species of the wine? Since, therefore, we receive Christ whole and entire under the species of the bread, why do we quarrel about the element of the wine? Or why are we so concerned about the accidents which hang together without the substance?" I answer: We are not fighting about the substance or the accidents of the wine insofar as the quality of the substance is concerned but because we know that Christ wants to communicate Himself and His benefits to us not without means but through specific means divinely instituted for this. But if these means are spurned and rejected, we neither can nor should promise ourselves partaking of Christ, as the enthusiasts do; but these means must be used, and that in the way they were instituted, prescribed, and ordained by God. For this reason it is right that we fight in this controversy, lest the means for partaking of the blood of Christ and of the New Testament in His blood that was divinely ordained by the Son of God Himself in a testamentary institution be taken away from us by human presumption. For the efficacy of the sacraments hangs from the Word of Christ. It was not, however, of the bread but of the cup that He said: "This is the New Testament in My blood." And when I take the cup of the Lord in true faith, then I am sure from the Word that the New Testament in the blood of Christ is given, applied, and sealed to me. The papalists say that the same thing is accomplished in the taking of the bread. But we know that the efficacy of the sacraments must be judged from the Word.

The following consideration also is useful. It was known to the ancients that, wherever Christ is present, He is present whole and entire, that His body is not present without blood, nor His blood apart from His body. Nevertheless, no one in the ancient church so much as even argued that for this reason the testamentary institution of Christ about the dispensation and reception of both kinds could be changed and mutilated. Lombard, Bk. 4, dist. 11, indeed sets forth this argument, but he does not forge a dogma from it about the abrogation of one kind, but he repeats from Ambrose the reason why Christ wanted this sacrament to be received under two kinds although He is whole under either. In the same way this argument is both set forth and resolved by Hugo[40] and Haymon.[41] Yes, the scholastics themselves, at whose time the custom of communicating under one kind had already begun to invade the churches, did not judge that this argument was sufficient to establish reception under one kind only. For they answer that Christ is indeed perfect, entire, and whole also under one kind, but that nevertheless the sacrament is not complete, perfect, entire, and whole if it is taken under one kind only. The opinions of Lombard, Hugo, Haymon, and the scholastics have been given in the foregoing. Durandus quotes from Innocent III: "Granted that under the bread there is not a bloodless body, nor under the wine blood separated from the body, nevertheless the blood of Christ is not drunk under the bread, nor Christ's body eaten under the wine." Therefore this invention of the papalists is of recent date, that because the entire and whole Christ is also under the species of the bread, the cup of the Lord can be abrogated, prohibited, and taken away from the laity.

I judge that this also should be mentioned in passing, that whereas the decree of Constance and of Basel says that the entire Christ is truly

---

[40] Either Hugo of St. Victor (c. 1096-1141) or Hugo a Sancto Caro (c. 1200-63).

[41] Haymon of Faversham, English Franciscan and scholastic (died c. 1243). He was very influential in the revision of the liturgy of the Roman Catholic Church of his time.

present and contained under the species of the bread, the men of Trent here say that He is taken whole. And although they do not dare to say, against the scholastics, that the complete sacrament is taken under one kind, they nevertheless say that the true sacrament is taken if only one kind is received, that is, in spite of the fact that the institution of Christ is not being observed. But these things can easily be judged in the bright light of the Word of God.

Of the innumerable arguments which were anxiously brought together with singular skill during the 150 years since the Council of Constance, these are the five the Synod of Trent selected, indicating that they were such that it seemed that with them, in these times where the light of the Word of God shines so brightly, the papalist changing, mutilation, abrogation, and prohibition of the testamentary institution of the Son of God could be justified and defended. What kind they are, what they can accomplish, what they are worth has been sufficiently shown to the extent that it could be done in this brief treatment.

SECTION II

[Concerning the Granting of the Cup]

DECREE ABOUT THE PETITION FOR GRANTING OF THE CUP

Published in Session VI[42]

Moreover, since the same holy synod had reserved for another time, when it should have opportunity, the examination of and decision with respect to two articles which had been proposed on another occasion and had not yet been discussed, namely, whether the reasons by which the holy Catholic Church had been moved to communicate lay people and also noncelebrating priests under only the one species of bread are to be adhered to in such a way that the use of the cup is under no circumstances to be permitted to anyone, and whether, if it seemed that for reasons that are honorable and agreeable to Christian charity the use of the cup ought to be granted to someone, either a nation or kingdom, under some conditions, and what these conditions are,[43] this same holy synod, wanting what is best for the salvation of those in whose behalf these petitions were presented, decrees that this entire matter should be referred to our holy master as in the present decree it does refer it. In his singular wisdom he will do what he shall judge to be for the good of the Christian commonwealth and salutary for those who plead for the use of the cup.

Examination

1 Among the requests of kings and rulers laid before the Council of Trent was also this petition, that the use of the Dominical cup, which had been taken away by the unjust prohibition of it, should be restored to the church according to the institution of Christ and the custom of the primitive church. But before the fathers of the council deliberate about this, they approve, confirm, and establish the wicked law which abrogates and prohibits the Dominical cup, as though a repetition, confirmation, and ratification of the decree of Constance had been requested of them. These things are arranged in this way by the council:

1. That they may indirectly knock out and condemn this petition of kings and rulers, as though they were asking for what does not belong to

---

[42] Session XXII of the council, but the fifth under Pius IV.

[43] From here on there is a discrepancy between Chemnitz' text and the Waterworth and Schroeder editions of the *Canons and Decrees of the Council of Trent*. The Schroeder text has only (p. 135): "the same holy council reserves for examination to another time, at the earliest opportunity that shall present itself."

the laity either by right or by divine precept and what the church, moved by weighty and just reasons, not only abrogated once upon a time but strictly prohibited as rash presumption, yes, as heresy, under the penalty of excommunication, for that is how the decree of Constance speaks;

2. That whatever concession may be made in future will be made without detriment to the papalist kingdom and without diminution of the power of the Roman church, yes, that this very concession, if one should be made in future, would be a confirmation, and obtaining the request would be a recognition of this immense privilege which, according to Pighius, has been granted to the Roman see, that whatever it fixes, re-fixes, binds, or looses here on earth in matters of faith should be considered fixed, refixed, bound, and loosed, and should so remain;

3. That those who, on the basis of a concession either of a synod or of the Roman pontiff, would use Communion under both kinds should nevertheless be deprived of its benefit. For according to the decree of the fifth session of the Council of Trent they would be taking the cup, which really does not belong to them, not on account of the institution, teaching, law, and precept of Christ but by the mercy, kindness, and liberality of the Roman pontiff. Therefore the lay people would apply the words added to the cup in vain to themselves, since they pertain only to the priests; neither would they receive any grace necessary for salvation from such Communion, for these are the words of the third chapter.

2 Fortified thus, they nevertheless flung the petition that the cup be granted from one session to another, until it was finally simply thrown from the Synod to the papal see. It would be very useful to know what kind of considerations entered into these deliberations, that the Synod itself was unwilling to decide anything about this petition but referred the whole matter to the Roman pontiff. But because these things are perhaps reserved among the secret mysteries of the council, I shall only note down a brief remark which came forth from the very bosom of the papalists, from which remark much can be learned.

In the year 1564 at Cologne an inquiry was published, *De communione Christiani populi sub utraque specie* [*Of Communion of Christian People Under Both Kinds*], truly learned, inasmuch as it had Cassander as author. In its preface we are told in the person of the publisher that the Synod of Trent had been occupied throughout the summer of the year 1564 with arguments over the petition for the granting of the cup. What the outcome of these arguments was is described in these words: "While the greater part of the more learned and therefore more powerful bishops was proceeding unitedly in the direction of judging that the cup should be granted the laity, others heatedly resisted this. Lest the great heat of the

discussions should bring harm to what had been begun by way of reformation of morals and beliefs, they left this controversy to be settled by the
judgment of Pope Pius IV." This is what is written there. From it the
reader can gather much that is pertinent here.

3 This matter was thrown back to the Roman pontiff, however with
certain conditions noted, under which it seemed that the cup could be
granted. These were indeed published, but were not inserted into the
published decree. I shall therefore add them and shall add nothing else
besides, except that the reader may learn from these conditions how
dearly the Roman pontiff sells the concession of the cup. Up to now
Germany has complained about the plunderings, because Rome was selling her indulgences and dispensations for too much money. But now the
pontiff sells the granting of the cup, not for gold or silver but for what is
much more precious, for denial of the true doctrine, for approval of all
the abominations of the papalist kingdom, and for defection from Christ,
the Head, to the man of sin and the son of perdition (2 Thess. 2:3).
Therefore let pious consciences be on guard lest they buy so dearly what
Christ commanded to be accepted freely, freely to be given to the church.
When these conditions have been thoroughly examined, the reader will
more rightly understand why Luther said that when the pope, as pope,
would out of the plenitude of his power grant Communion under both
kinds, then he would not use it. This saying of Luther has repeatedly been
attacked in a hateful way by papalist writers. But the matter itself and
experience under these conditions now bring the true interpretation. Let
us therefore hear what the council suggests to the pontiff by way of
conditions for the granting of the cup.

Conditions Under Which It Seems the Use of the Cup Could Be Granted

First: That those who want to communicate under both kinds agree with the
heart and with the confession of their mouth in all other matters both insofar as
this sacrament and also insofar as the other sacraments are concerned, also in
every other matter so far as faith, doctrine, and rite are concerned with all the
things that have been accepted by the holy Roman Church, also with all decrees of
this holy synod, both those that have been promulgated and those yet to be
promulgated.

Second: That the pastors of the said nations and the preachers believe and
teach that the custom approved by the church and long observed, namely, of
communicating under one kind only, is not foreign to divine law but rather laudable and to be observed as law unless the church establishes otherwise, and that
those who hold otherwise are to be judged heretics, and that they do not give this
Communion under both kinds to others but only to those who believe this truth
and have confessed it.

Third: That they owe it to show all reverence with a faithful and sincere mind to our most holy master, the pope, as the lawful bishop and pastor of the whole church.

Fourth: That they likewise render due obedience and reverence to their archbishops, bishops, and other prelates.

Fifth: That this use of the cup be granted only to those who have confessed and are contrite, according to the custom of the Catholic Church, likewise that the ordinaries provide as diligently as possible for all cautions lest in the administration of the blood some sacrilege or profanation be allowed to happen, over all of which things mentioned their conscience may be burdened.

SECTION III

[Concerning the Communion of Little Children]

Session V

Chapter IV

THAT LITTLE CHILDREN ARE NOT OBLIGATED TO SACRAMENTAL COMMUNION

Finally, the same holy synod teaches that little children, who lack the use of reason, are not obligated by any necessity to the sacramental Communion of the Eucharist, since, regenerated by the washing of Baptism and incorporated into Christ, they are not able at that age to lose the grace of children of God, which they have obtained. Nevertheless, antiquity is not therefore to be condemned if at some time it observed this custom in certain places. For even as those holy fathers had a believable cause for what they did, by reason of their time, so it is to be certainly and without controversy believed that they did not do this from any necessity for salvation.

CANON IV

If anyone says that Eucharistic Communion is necessary for little children before they have arrived at the years of discretion, let him be anathema.

[Examination]

There is no controversy between us and the papalists about this question. Therefore I judge that it is not necessary to unravel this whole dispute, since this discussion was instituted chiefly for the sake of the things which are in controversy.

Sixth Topic

CONCERNING THE MASS

From the 22nd Session
of the Council of Trent

SECTION I

[Concerning the Sacrifice of the Mass]

Sixth Session

THE TRUE CATHOLIC TEACHING THAT IN THE MASS A TRUE SACRIFICE
AND ATONEMENT IS OFFERED

Preface

The most holy synod, etc., in order that the ancient, absolute, and in every part perfect faith and teaching of the great mystery of the Eucharist may be retained in the holy Catholic Church and preserved in its purity (all errors and heresies having been driven out), having been instructed by the enlightenment of the Holy Spirit concerning it, since it is a true and singular sacrifice, teaches, declares, and decrees that what now follows should be preached to the faithful.

Chapter I

Because under the former Testament, as the apostle Paul testifies, there was no perfection on account of the weakness of the Levitical priesthood, it was necessary (God, the Father of mercies, so ordaining) that another priest should arise after the order of Melchizedek, our Lord Jesus Christ, who would be able to perfect, and to lead to what is perfect, all who are to be sanctified. He therefore, our Lord and God, although He was about to offer Himself once on the altar of the cross to God the Father through His intervening death in order that He might there work out an everlasting redemption, nevertheless, because His priesthood was not to be ended through His death, in order to leave to His beloved bride, the Church, in His last supper, which He gave in the night in which He was betrayed, a visible sacrifice (such as human nature requires) by which that bloody sacrifice once to be performed on the cross might be represented, its memory remain to the end of the world, and its salutary power applied for the remission of the sins we daily commit, declaring Himself constituted a priest forever after the order of Melchizedek, offered up His body and blood under the species of bread and wine to God the Father. Under the signs of these same elements He gave it to the apostles (whom at that time He constituted priests of the New Testament), that they should receive it, and instructed them and their successors in the priesthood that they should offer it, through these words: "Do this in remembrance of Me," as the Catholic Church has always understood and taught. For when He had celebrated the old Passover (which the multitude of the children of Israel sacrificed in remembrance of the exodus from Egypt), He instituted a new Passover, Himself, to be sacrificed by the church through the priests, under visible signs, in remembrance of His passing out of this world to the Father, when through the shedding of His blood He redeemed us and rescued us from the power of darkness and translated us into His kingdom. This indeed is that pure offering which cannot be defiled by any unworthiness or wickedness of those who offer it. The Lord also foretold through Malachi that it would be offered pure in every place in His name, which would be great among the nations. The apostle Paul indicates this in a not obscure manner when, writing to the Corinthians, he says that those who have been polluted by participation in the table of demons cannot be partakers of the Lord's table, understanding by tables in both places the altar. This, finally, is that sacrifice which was prefigured by various similitudes in the sacrifices during the time of nature and of the Law, inasmuch as it is that sacrifice which embraces all the good things signified through them, or is the summing up of them all.

Chapter II

And since in this divine sacrifice, which is accomplished in the Mass, that same Christ is contained and bloodlessly sacrificed who once, on the altar of the cross, offered Himself a bloody sacrifice, the holy synod teaches that this sacrifice is truly propitiatory and that through it it comes to pass that, if we approach God with a true heart and right faith, with fear and reverence, contrite and penitent, we obtain mercy and find grace in timely help. Placated by this One's sacrifice, the Lord, granting grace and the gift of penitence, forgives offenses and sins, even enormous ones. For the sacrificial Victim is one and the same, the same now offering through the ministry of the priests who then offered Himself on the cross, the manner of offering alone being different. The fruits of this offering (I speak of the bloody one) are exceedingly abundantly received through this unbloody one. There is no chance at all that anything would be detracted from the former by the latter. For this reason it is rightly offered, according to the tradition of the apostles, not only for the sins, punishments, satisfactions, and other necessities of the faithful who are living but also for those who have died in Christ and have not yet been fully purified.

CANON I

If anyone says that in the Mass there is not offered to God a true and proper sacrifice, or that to be offered is nothing but that Christ is given to us to eat, let him be anathema.

CANON II

If anyone says that with these words: "Do this in remembrance of Me," Christ did not constitute the apostles priests, or did not ordain that they and other priests should offer His body and blood, let him be anathema.

CANON III

If anyone says that the Mass is merely a sacrifice of praise and thanksgiving, or a bare commemoration of the sacrifice performed on the cross, not however a propitiatory sacrifice, or that it benefits him only who eats and that it ought not to be offered for the living and the dead for sins, punishments, satisfactions, and other necessities, let him be anathema.

If anyone says that through the sacrifice of the Mass a blasphemy is imposed on the most holy sacrifice of Christ accomplished on the cross, or that the former takes something away from the latter, let him be anathema.

Examination

1 We come now to the papalist sacrifice of the Mass, which Daniel 11:38 calls the god *Ma'uzim*,[1] because it is the citadel, bulwark, strength, stay, and stronghold of the reign of Antichrist, of which the papalists themselves have repeatedly testified at public meetings of the diet that they could suffer anything rather than allow the sacrifice of the Mass to be taken away from them.

2 We shall not follow up at length every single thing that pertains to this dispute, for this has been discharged in an outstanding manner by others, in complete and adequate discussions. I see also that this writing is growing beyond what I intended and thought. But we shall note down as briefly as possible those things which will seem to belong to an examination and explanation of the decrees of the Council of Trent.

3 Before all else the point at issue in the dispute about the sacrifice of the Mass must be established. For the word "sacrifice" has many meanings, and the action of the Mass has many and varied parts. Therefore it is altogether necessary that we establish, by means of a division, what it is in the action of the Mass about which specifically and principally the papalists contend that it is a sacrifice for the living and the dead, and what kind of sacrifice it is, since there are many kinds of sacrifices. This diligence is necessary because I see that this whole dispute is thrown into disorder, obscured, and made difficult most of all by this stratagem, that the point of the controversy is not clearly established. Therefore, since both Scripture and statements of the ancients speak about various kinds of sacrifices, papalist writers twist all these statements in which mention is made of sacrifice to prove and establish the sacrifice of the Mass, and, after they have heaped up many statements of this kind, they boast before the inexperienced and incautious that the propitiatory sacrifice of their Mass has the witness of the prophets, of Christ, of the apostles, and of the church of all times.

4 Thus Vicelius, with the intention of defending the papalist Mass, gathers many statements of the ancients in which the term "sacrifice" is applied to the administration or celebration of the Lord's Supper. Like-

---

[1] *Ma'oz:* Hebrew for a fortified place or fortress.

wise, he proves laboriously that in the meetings of the ancient church it was always customary that something was read from the prophetic writings (particularly from the psalms), the gospels, and the apostolic writings, that joint prayers and giving of thanks were customary, that praises of God were chanted, etc. And because certain vestiges of these observances remain in the Mass of the papalists (even if, as Vicelius himself says, in most of them scarcely a shadow of antiquity is left), he immediately adds on the conclusion, which is wider by many miles than the proof which went before, that the propitiatory sacrifice of the papalist Mass for the living and the dead has the testimonies and votes of the first and ancient apostolic church and of the whole purer antiquity.

Tricks of this kind are quite easily detected once the point of the controversy has been shown. When this has been established, the explanation of the arguments which are adduced for the defense of the papalist Mass will be easier. Also the contrary arguments by which the abomination of the papalist Mass is shown will be all the clearer. Also, many things from the Tridentine chapters and canons will be more correctly understood if the point at issue in the dispute about the Mass is first established.

ARTICLE I

Concerning the Term "Sacrifice"

1 We shall therefore speak first of all about the term "sacrifice," what all it covers; thereafter we shall apply it to the individual parts of the Mass, in order that we may finally be able to find and establish the true issue in this controversy about the sacrifice of the papalist Mass.

2 Also in the Old Testament there certainly were external ceremonies and visible sacrifices. Of these there were various kinds. The difference came first from the material cause. For sacrifices were brought either of animals of a certain kind, which sacrifices were fitly called victims; or they were of a dry earthly material, such as bread, fine flour, grain, incense, salt, etc., properly called immolations;[2] or they were made of liquid material, such as wine and olive oil, properly called libations.

In the second place, the difference among the ancient sacrifices is taken from the mode and cause of the offering. Thus some were whole burnt offerings, either daily or on the sabbath; some were propitiatory sacrifices for sin; some were peace offerings for benefits either to be

---

[2] From *immolare*, which originally meant "to sprinkle a sacrificial victim with meal."

granted or already granted; others were sacrifices of profession, as the tithe, the firstfruits, etc. Augustine rightly says that these external ceremonial sacrifices signified two things: 1. The sacrifice of Christ on the cross; 2. The true, inner, invisible, and spiritual sacrifices of believers, *De civitate Dei,* Bk. 10, ch. 5.

From this it came about that, when the ceremonial sacrifices were out of date, the apostles in the New Testament nevertheless retained the term "sacrifice." For so they called in the first place the suffering of Christ (Eph. 5:2 and in Hebrews); second, the ministry of the Gospel (Rom. 15:16); third, the conversion of the Gentiles and the faith of those who embrace the Gospel (Rom. 15:16; Phil. 2:17); fourth, prayers (Heb. 5:7; Rev. 5:8; 8:3); fifth, sacrifices of praise or thanksgiving (Heb. 13:15); sixth, deeds of kindness toward the poor and for the support of the ministry (Heb. 13:16; Phil. 4:18); seventh, mortification of the old man, or rather, the whole man when he is consecrated and devoted to God, that he may die to the world and live to God, they call a sacrifice (Rom. 12:1); eighth, Peter calls the whole worship of Christians in proclaiming the benefits of God, in abstaining from sin, and in diligence in the new obedience spiritual sacrifice.

So also statements in the Old Testament speak of spiritual sacrifices. Ps. 4:5: The sacrifice of righteousness is to hope in the Lord; Ps. 50:14-15: "Offer to God thanksgiving . . . and call upon Me"; Ps. 51:17: "The sacrifice of God is a broken spirit, a contrite and humbled heart"; Ps. 141:2: "The lifting up of my hands as an evening sacrifice"; Hos. 14:2: "So will we render the calves of our lips"; Micah 6:6-8: Not burnt offerings, not calves, not rams, etc., "but to do justice, to love mercy, and to walk carefully with God."

On account of this very wide meaning of the term "sacrifice," Augustine gives a general definition, *De civitate Dei,* Bk. 10, chs. 5 and 6: "A true sacrifice is every work which is done in order that we may through holy fellowship inhere in God, and to the same end have regard for our neighbor." And in ch. 5 he says that these true sacrifices consist in love of God and the neighbor.

ARTICLE II

In What Sense the Action of the Liturgy May, According to Scripture, Rightly Be Called a Sacrifice

Now that we have established these things about the term "sacrifice," we shall apply them in an orderly way to the individual parts of the

Mass. For when the things about which there is no dispute have been removed and set aside, the true point of the controversy will finally become clear. Afterward we shall explain for what reason the ancients applied the term "sacrifice" to the celebration of the Lord's Supper. Under the fifth chapter [Section IV] we shall have to note how the papalists have perverted each and every part of the Mass. Now we shall only, by way of a division, investigate the point at issue.

1. Because in the Communion service the prophetic and apostolic writings are read, the death of Christ is announced there, and the causes and benefits of the suffering Christ are set forth for consideration from the Word of God, the Mass could for this reason be called a sacrifice according to Scripture (Rom. 15:16; Phil. 2:17; and 1 Peter 2:5-9). But this is not the sacrifice about which the papalists are contending. For such things are carried out among them either by secret murmuring or inarticulate bellowing or in a foreign tongue.

2. In the administration of the Lord's Supper the praises of God are repeated, told, and sung. Now the sacrifice of praise has the testimony of Scripture (Heb. 13:15; Ps. 50:14-15). But that this also is not the sacrifice about which the papalists are contending in their Mass the third canon of Trent clearly explains.

3. On account of public prayers and common thanksgivings the term "sacrifice" could, according to the meaning of Scripture, be given to the Mass. But that is not what the Council of Trent wants in the third canon.

4. Because a contribution of alms for the poor was always customary at the celebration of the Lord's Supper, the term "sacrifice" could for this reason, according to Scripture, be applied to the total action. But this also is not that sacrifice concerning which there is controversy in the papalist Mass.

5. In the Communion service the whole man consecrates himself to God, and this is done in order that we may by this holy union inhere in God. Here, in the true use of the Lord's Supper, there is an exercise of repentance and faith; here love of God and of the neighbor is kindled. If anyone would call the Mass a sacrifice for this reason, and would apply the things themselves rightly, he would be doing nothing foreign to Scripture, as has been shown. But neither is this the sacrifice about which the papalists are contending in the Mass.

6. Because the blessing or consecration of the Eucharist is an act of the Gospel ministry, it could to this extent and with the addition of this declaration admit and bear the name "sacrifice," as Paul (Rom. 15:16) calls the total ministry of the Gospel a sacrifice. But the papalists distin-

guish the consecration from the offering, for they say that what has been consecrated is being offered.

7. Because the dispensation and participation or Communion of the Eucharist is done in commemoration of the one and only sacrifice of Christ, and because the sacrificial victim, who was once offered on the cross for our sins, is dispensed and taken there, it could for this reason, and with this explanation added, be called a sacrifice, even though Scripture does not so call it. But the papalists expressly distinguish their sacrifice from the dispensation and partaking of the Eucharist. And Gropper got a bad reception in the council because he asserted that Communion belonged to the essence of the sacrifice of the Mass.

ARTICLE III

What, in the Mass, the Papalists Understand as a Sacrifice in the Proper Sense

1 Now that we have removed and set aside these things, it will become clear what it is in the action of the Mass about which the papalists particularly and principally contend that it is the sacrifice of the Mass. Eck explains and sets this forth most clearly of all in *De missa,* Bk. 1, ch. 10. There he says that the very celebration, dispensation, and taking of the Eucharist could be called a sacrifice, because it is a certain likeness, representative of the passion of Christ, which was a true immolation, as Augustine says: "The likenesses are customarily called by the names of the things whose likenesses they are." But because it would follow from this that the Mass is not truly and properly a sacrifice, just as a man in a picture is not the real man, and also the Mass would not be a sacrifice in any other way than the figures of the Old Testament, therefore Eck says that the Mass is a sacrifice in another, special way, namely, because the church not only uses the Eucharist for a remembrance of the passion but because in the Mass she represents the sacrifice of the suffering of Christ by the total action of gestures, words, ceremonies, and vestments, and by means of this representation offers Christ Himself anew for a sweet-smelling savor to God the Father.

2 Eck explains this opinion with this analogy: If the triumph of some king were engraved on a coin, pictured on a wall or on a pillar, it would indeed please the king (so is also the celebration of the Eucharist). But if there were enacted before him the whole course of that history, and it were thus presented to him again through its various parts as if it were presenting to him the actual triumph itself, how much more pleasure do you think the king would find in that representation than in the other which is pictured or sculpted? Such a vivid and solemn representation of the passion of Christ, says he, is the sacrifice of the Mass in the eyes of God in the action of the gestures, words, ceremonies, vestments, etc. For the Mass, according to Innocent and Durandus, consists of these four: persons, works, words, and things. The persons are the celebrants, ministers, and bystanders. The works are gestures, acts, and motions. The words are prayers, songs, and readings. The things are ornaments, vessels, and the elements.

Therefore the sacrifice of the Mass about which the papalists contend consists of this, that the priest uses (together with certain ornaments and vessels) various gestures, motions, and actions over the bread and wine of the Eucharist, such as genuflecting repeatedly, now bowing, now stretching out clenched hands, now drawing the arms back, now turning around, now being loud, now murmuring something very quietly, looking up high, then hanging forward, not standing still in one place, but moving, now to the right side, now to the left of the altar, pointing with the fingers, breathing on the bread and the cup, now elevating them, afterward putting them down, breaking the bread, casting it into the cup, smiting the breast with the fist, sighing, closing his eyes, representing sleep, waking up, showing the gilded patella to the people with outstretched arm, but with his back turned, moving it to his forehead and breast, kissing now the altar, now the little image inclosed in metal, etc. Thus Sleidanus has described the whole drama of the sacrifice of the Mass in an elegant sketch. They imagine that by means of these actions, motions, gestures, and ceremonies, with certain words added about sacrifice, oblation, and victim, they are sacrificing and offering the body and blood of Christ, yes, Christ, the Son of God Himself, anew to God the Father through such a theatrical representation (which is either a comedy or a tragedy) of Christ's passion.

ARTICLE IV

What Kind of Sacrifice the Papalists Understand the Mass to Be

1 Now that we have shown what, in the service of the Mass, is held to be that sacrifice for which the papalists fight as though it were their altars and homes, we must see for what kind of sacrifice they are selling it, for so we shall have the whole issue of this controversy. It is strange and worth noting in what way certain of the papalists in our time have begun to paint this sacrifice in new colors. So Gropper, in the *Institutio* and in the *Antididagma* of Cologne cries out that an extraordinary wrong is done the papists[3] by our side, as though they taught that the Mass is a propitiatory sacrifice for sins. For, convinced by the clear light of the Word of God, he knows and confesses that there is only one true propitiatory sacrifice for sins, namely, the one the Son of God Himself once offered to the Father for a sweet savor by offering up His body and shedding His blood on the altar of the cross, but that the sacrifice of the Mass is a representative, commemorative, and applicatory sacrifice. This stratagem Vicelius, Sidonius, and the architects of the formula of the *Interim*[4] imitated. They explain it thus: Because in the Mass the sum of the whole Gospel, particularly of the passion of Christ is set forth and, as it were, pressed in upon the senses by words, signs, ceremonies, gestures, ornaments, vessels, vestments, etc., therefore the Mass is a visible representation of the sacrifice of Christ through which the remembrance of the suffering of Christ is renewed to the faithful, that they may be aroused to faith, devotion, thanksgiving, fear of God, love, etc. For so Vicelius defines the Mass, that it is a commemorative sacrifice, likewise a sacrifice of praise and thanksgiving. And in the examination of those who are being ordained he says: "The Mass is a recollection of the passion of Christ in a public gathering of Christians, where thanks is given by many for the price of our redemption." Gropper says that this sacrifice is offered in this way, and placed before the Father, when faith, distrustful of our merits, apprehends the price of our redemption, the body of Christ, given for us, and His blood, shed for us, and sets it before God, that is, places it between His wrath and our sins, in order to obtain the forgiveness of sins which Christ merited and procured on the cross.

Gropper explains the applicatory sacrifice of the Mass thus, that in the Mass nearly the sum of the whole Gospel, especially the passion of Christ, is set forth in such a way that everyone may apply it to himself by means of his own faith and become a partaker of the remission of sins earned in the bloody sacrifice of Christ. And because in the Mass also the sacrifice of prayer is offered, that God may make all men partakers of the redemption of Christ, that therefore the Mass is rightly applied also to the absent and to those who are not communing. Yea, by Jupiter, a wise

---

[3] This is one of the few times Chemnitz uses the pejorative term *Papistae*. Generally he uses the neutral term *Pontificii*, which we have consistently translated "papalists."

[4] The *Interim:* a document meant to provide a temporary agreement according to which Lutherans and Catholics might get along until such a time when a diet or council should make a more permanent arrangement. Many sincere Lutherans rejected the *Interim* as compromising the truth restored by the Lutheran Reformation.

medicine! For they have perceived what crass abominations are inherent in the sacrifice of the papalist Mass. Nevertheless, because they do not dare to censure and condemn them openly, they have brought the Mass forward onto the stage painted in new colors, such as neither the learned nor the common people knew heretofore. Many things could be said about these colors, but I have recited only these, in order that we may arrive the more conveniently at establishing the point at issue. For these encrusters of the papalist Mass, of whom we have just now spoken, wanted to indicate obliquely and indirectly that there are a number of things in the papalist doctrine of the Mass concerning which there is desire that they should be reformed according to the Word of God, and they show a possible way.

2 Now what of the Synod of Trent, which in the sixth session spoke in the preface about casting out errors and heresies? Does it take counsel that at least something of the crass abominations of the sacrifice of the Mass should be cut off? Certainly, there is nothing they desire less! But the articles about the sacrifice of the Mass which were put before the theologians for examination were written in such a way that they seemed, as it were, expressly opposed to any and all mitigations. For the first article was: Whether the Mass is only a commemoration of the sacrifice accomplished on the cross, not however a true sacrifice. The 13th Article: Whether the Mass is only a sacrifice of praise and thanksgiving, not also a propitiatory sacrifice for the living and the dead. The Synod itself afterward decreed, Chapter 2, that the sacrifice of the Mass is truly propitiatory. And Canon 3 says: "If anyone says that the sacrifice of the Mass is merely an action of praise and thanksgiving, or a bare commemoration of the sacrifice performed on the cross, not however a propitiatory sacrifice to be offered for the sins both of the living and the dead, let him be anathema." From what we have said earlier it is clear what and whose opinions are being condemned in that chapter and canon.

In the *Antididagma* of Cologne Gropper had said that the Mass could perhaps be called a propitiatory sacrifice, not because it really is that, but because it is a representation of the one and only propitiatory sacrifice, once offered on the cross, just as certain sacrifices of the Old Testament were called propitiatory because they prefigured the one and only true propitiatory sacrifice of Christ, which was to come. But to this mitigation the Tridentine chapter opposes the decree that the sacrifice of the Mass is truly propitiatory. So tender and delicate is the papalist Mass, that it cannot bear it if one either lightly touches or ever so gently mitigates even its crassest abominations.

3 Moreover the Synod does not ascribe to the Mass only the naked

title of a propitiatory sacrifice, but adds a lengthy explanation to the effect that the action of the Mass, which handles the bread and wine of the Eucharist with the words, rites, and gestures we have described above, is the kind of propitiatory sacrifice which is offered for the sins, punishments, satisfactions, and other necessities not only of living believers, but also for the dead. Likewise, that through this propitiatory sacrifice of the Mass it is accomplished that, if we approach God with true faith, we receive mercy and find grace in timely help; likewise that the Lord, appeased by the offering of the sacrifice of the Mass, granting grace and the gift of penitence, forgives even enormous transgressions and sins.

The first chapter says that by the sacrifice of the Mass the bloody sacrifice of Christ once accomplished on the cross is represented. However, it understands the kind of representation Eck describes. A little later the first chapter says that the saving power of the sacrifice on the cross is applied through the propitiatory sacrifice of the Mass for the forgiveness of the sins daily committed by us. And the second chapter says that the fruits of the bloody offering of Christ are most abundantly received through the propitiatory sacrifice of the Mass. Therefore the intention of the Synod of Trent was not either to mitigate even the least thing in the received abominations of the Mass or to reform them according to the Word of God. But, having condemned the opinions of those who in the very bosom of the papalists indicated even in the gentlest way that something in the prevalent opinion about the sacrifice of the Mass was displeasing to them, they simply repeat, confirm, and strengthen everything which has ever been written and taught by papalists about the sacrifice of the Mass.

4 In order that the Tridentine decree about the Mass may be more fully understood, and the point of the controversy clearly established, we shall note down certain traditions of the papalists about the sacrifice of the Mass. For otherwise they will cry out that many things are ascribed to them which they themselves do not acknowledge. Now the canon[5] says: "We offer Thee this sacrifice for the redemption of souls, for the hope of salvation and safety. Be pleased to receive this offering, dispose our days in Thy peace, and order us to be delivered from eternal damnation and numbered with the flock of Thine elect." The canon concludes: "May this sacrifice which I have offered be acceptable to Thee, and may it according to Thy compassion be a means of propitiation for me and for all for whom I have offered it."

---

[5] The term "canon" here denotes the canon of the Mass, to be distinguished from the canons of the Council of Trent.

Cricius Polonus highly approves this secret prayer: "Receive, O Holy Trinity, this offering, and grant that it may mount up acceptable in Thy sight and work my eternal salvation and that of all believers, through the same Christ, our Lord." In explaining these words of the canon: "For the redemption of the soul, for the hope of salvation and safety," Innocent, *De officio missae,* says that the sacrifice of the Mass is offered: (1) for such bodily blessings as safety from harm; (2) for spiritual blessings, such as the redemption of the soul, which he interprets as the remission of sins; (3) for eternal blessings, such as salvation.

The offering of the Mass, which in the canon is called "credited, approved, and acceptable," Innocent interprets thus: "Credited, through which God adds us in writing to the elect; approved, through which the promise of our salvation is approved; acceptable, through which God makes us acceptable to Himself." However, the point of the controversy must always be recalled to mind, that these things are not ascribed to Communion but to the sacrifice of the Mass, as we have earlier copied this from Eck.

The same Innocent, disputing about the threefold washing of the priest in the Mass, says that the sacrifice of the Mass is offered for the purging and cleansing of original, criminal, and venial sin, likewise of sin in thought, word, and deed, or of sins stemming from ignorance, negligence, or obstinacy. And in explaining the words: *Ite, missa est,*[6] he says: "This sacrifice is called *missa,* as though the victim were sent from us to the Father to intercede for us with Him. For this is the only sufficient and fit mission or embassy for doing away with the enmities and offenses between the Lord and men."

In a little work about the venerable sacrament of the altar Thomas says: "The second reason for the institution is the sacrifice of the altar against the daily ravages of our transgressions, in order that, as the body of Christ was once offered on the cross for the original debt, so it may now be offered continually upon the altar for our daily transgressions, and that the church may have in it a service for reconciling God to herself, more precious and acceptable than all the sacrifices of the Law."

Gabriel Biel says that the sacrifice of the Mass differs from the sacrifice of Christ on the cross only in that it is offered in an unbloody manner, but that it is the same as regards its substance and has the same operative effects, or that the purpose of the sacrifice of Christ on the cross and on the altar are one and the same, namely, propitiation for the offense to the

---

[6] The words with which the priest dismisses the congregation after Mass, where this is conducted in Latin. The precise origin of the formula is disputed.

Father, and the obtaining of eternal salvation. He adds: "Whatever our Savior, when He offered Himself on the cross, merited for all in general, both in removing evil and in collecting good for those who are still on their pilgrimage, for those in purgatory, and for those who are in bliss, that is applied to individuals in particular in the sacrifice of the Mass." He teaches also that the priest is able, through the Mass, to apply the power of the passion of Christ to whomever he wills, most generally to the catholic church, most specifically to the priest, and especially to the founder in whose name the Mass is performed. In the *Epitome* he says that the priest represents our cause before Christ, the supreme judge, as mediator between the Bridegroom and the bride, that is, between Christ and the church, and that he procures for the church many bodily, spiritual, and eternal gifts by his prayer and sacrifice.

Eck says, *De missa,* Bk. 1, Ch. 10: "In the Mass we offer the Eucharist to God the Father not only as a memorial gift of the Lord's passion but also as a service most acceptable to God, by which we are able both to placate God for our offenses and obtain His grace together with spiritual goods." Likewise: "Through the sacrifice of the Mass the faithful of the church become partakers of the manifold fruits of the Lord's passion. For as the graces and merits of the Savior are applied to the believers through the application of the sacraments, so the merits and fruits of the Dominical oblation are applied to the faithful through such an action of representation in the sacrifice of the Mass." Likewise: "Through the sacrifice of the Mass the effects of the passion of Christ flow toward, reach, and descend into the faithful." And at the end of the third book he says: "Through the sacrifice of the Mass aid is given to the living and the dead in their varied needs."

A certain doctor at the Sorbonne recently published a long fabrication about the Mass in which, in the beginning, he shapes the issue of the dispute in this way, that in the Mass one must sacrifice to God not only by an inward but also by an outward act, not only with a Eucharistic but also with a propitiatory sacrifice. And he sets down this definition: "A propitiatory or atoning sacrifice is an offering made to God for an atonement for sins and for obtaining the grace of God or the remission of sins."

In the *Panoplia,* Bk. 4, ch. 46, Lindanus says that the Mass is properly called a sacrifice not only of thanksgiving or commemoration but also of propitiation, and this for blotting out the sins of the dead as well as of the living, yes, for any and every need of Christian people. And in ch. 50 he says that the Mass is a propitiatory and true sacrifice for sins, for the dead as well as for the living, and finally for obtaining every kind of benefit from God, bodily as well as spiritual.

In ch. 51 he says that the sacrifice of the Mass is the application of the blood shed on the cross, and that this application through the sacrifice of the Mass makes us partakers of the redemption of Christ.

Ch. 52: "Through the daily sacrifice of the Mass the church draws from the fountain of the Lord's passion the merits of Christ and finally the propitiation itself." In ch. 5 he explains it thus: "Namely, if a person with his own faith wishes, desires, and brings it about that the sacrifice of the Mass is celebrated for him."

This then is the point at issue in the controversy about the sacrifice of the Mass, which I have set forth not in my own words but in the words of the papalists themselves, lest someone think that these things are invented by us to press our adversaries and to exaggerate things by means of hateful words.

5 Now that the issue of the dispute has been established and explained, the manner of the examination will be much easier, namely, of what kind the arguments are which are customarily brought forward by the papalists for constructing, confirming, and establishing the sacrifice of the Mass, what they are worth, and what they can accomplish. Since these arguments are many and varied, it is worth the effort to observe how the Council of Trent, having made, as it were, a choice among its military troops, rejected most of them and retained a certain few which had been judged the strongest and most solid; so it may seem that this business of the Mass has gotten down to a last stand.[7] Because this collection of arguments is of no little usefulness, I shall, before we come to the Tridentine arguments, briefly note down how weak, inept, and strange most of the arguments are by which papalist writers have until now held together the sacrifice of the Mass, as if they were the strongest foundations and supports. The Council of Trent, by choosing among them, does not disguise this fact. But for the sake of brevity we shall not explain these arguments at length but shall only set them down in order.

ARTICLE V

Arguments of Papalist Writers
in Behalf of the Mass

1. Schatzgyer, that is, a man eager for treasure, expressing by his

---

[7] The Latin has *ad Triarios rediisse*. The *triarii* were a class of Roman soldiers who formed the third rank from the front. When you were down to the *triarii*, the first two ranks had been beaten.

fatal name the character of the patrons of the papalist Mass, used this argument: In Is. 53:7 it is said of Christ: "He was offered because He Himself wanted it." This cannot be understood of the Jews who crucified Christ, for their intention was not to offer Him but to destroy Him. Neither can it be understood of Christ Himself, offering Himself on the altar of the cross, for it is said by Isaiah: "He was offered," namely, not by Himself, but by others. Therefore the statement, which at the same time says that Christ wanted such a sacrifice, must be understood of the sacrifice of the Mass, where Christ is offered to the Father by the priest, for he says: "He was offered because He wanted it."

But this argument is rejected even by Eck himself. For Heb. 9:28 also speaks in the passive voice of the offering of Christ on the cross: "Christ, having been offered once." And in his own language Isaiah clearly does not have the statement: "He was offered because He wanted it," but says: "He was oppressed, and He was afflicted." Perhaps it was by an act of fate that this passage in Isaiah was applied to the sacrifice of the Mass, in order that it might be shown that, so far as the priests are concerned, the papalist Mass is an oppression and affliction of Christ.

2. Not the least among the reasons in this controversy was also this argument, based on Heb. 10:26: For those who sin willfully "there no longer remains a sacrifice for sins." Therefore there does remain for our daily transgressions still, that is, after the sacrifice on the cross, a sacrifice for sin. This can be none other than the sacrifice of the Mass.

This argument also is the kind repudiated by Eck himself.

3. A monk at Augsburg proves the sacrifice of the Mass from Dan. 7:13: "Angels in the clouds of heaven offered the Son of Man before the Ancient of Days." Therefore, when Christ is sacrificed in the Mass by the priest, then He also at the same time is sacrificed in the clouds of heaven by the angels themselves. Therefore the canon says: "Command that these things be brought before the face of Thy Majesty by the hand of a holy angel."

Because this is a manifest perversion of the statement of Daniel, not even the papalists themselves approve this argument. For Daniel is there telling how the Father gave all things into the hand of the Son, the Mediator (John 3:35), gave Him a name above every name (Phil. 2:9-10), has given Him authority to exercise judgment (John 5:27), has given Him the kingdom of David (Luke 1:32), etc. The verb which Daniel uses there is indeed sometimes used of sacrifices, but very often it means "to approach, to convey to, to lead to." And the meaning of sacrificing simply does not fit in that passage in Daniel.

4. Eck uses, among others, also this argument: Jerome translates Ps.

72:16:[8] "There will be abundance of wheat in the land; on the top of the mountains it will be elevated!" Rabbi Solomon explains this verse of the psalm of a kind of cakes in the days of the Messiah. Therefore David is there prophesying about the sacrifice of the papalist Mass, where the unleavened bread is elevated above the shaven crowns of the priests.

Keep a straight face, my friends, when you see that the papalist Mass is shown to rest on such labored foundations!

5. The apostle says (Heb. 13:10) that we in the New Testament have an altar, which he calls *thysiasteerion,* from "sacrifices," as you might say, "a place for sacrifice." Therefore there must be, in the New Testament, some external and ceremonial sacrifice. And nothing else can be found except the sacrifice of the Mass. Eck lays very great stress on this argument.

But by the same kind of reasoning the same sacrifice would also have to be instituted in heaven. For the Apocalypse tells us in numerous places that there is an altar also in heaven (6:9; 8:3, 5; 9:13; 11:1; 14:18; 16:7, etc.). In Heb. 13:10 ff. the text itself afterward explains clearly what sacrifices it understands, namely of praise, thanksgiving, and beneficence. And with respect to the altar it explains that through Christ we offer such sacrifices as are pleasing to God. What a trick it is, therefore, to fashion a strange and false meaning for the words of the apostle, against the clear explanation of the text itself!

6. Dan. 11:31 says of the Antichrist that he "shall take away the continual burnt offering." This cannot be understood of prayers and other spiritual sacrifices, which cannot be taken away from the godly by external force. Rather, prayers are more ardent during persecution. Therefore what the Antichrist will effect in the New Testament must be understood of the sacrifice of the Mass. And those who abrogate the Mass, them Daniel pronounces to be ministers of Antichrist.

This is certainly a broad, generous, sweeping deduction. It is certain that Daniel is there speaking specifically about the wicked, criminal tyranny of Antiochus. In his second oration against the Jews, Chrysostom refers this prophecy to the times of Antiochus and quotes Josephus as a witness for this. Antiochus indeed not only took away the continual sacrifice, described in Ex. 29:38-42 and Num. 28:1-8, but changed the whole Levitical worship into heathenish superstitions, as the history of the Maccabees shows. All this Daniel embraces through the synecdoche of the continual sacrifice. Therefore, when that passage in Daniel is explained of the Antichrist, this is done through an allegory. And it is

---

[8] Chemnitz, following the Vulgate, has Ps. 71 instead of 72.

known that dogmas which do not have certain, firm, and clear testimonies in other passages of Scripture must not be made on the basis of allegories. Therefore nothing else can be made of this passage in Daniel except this, that there will be, in the New Testament, a sacrifice which the Antichrist will take away. We have shown above that Scripture expressly enumerates several kinds of sacrifices of the New Testament. But what audacity it is to pass over the sacrifices of the New Testament which Scripture clearly portrays and to expound the passage in Daniel, which speaks of sacrifice in general, of the Mass, which Scripture neither lays down nor portrays when it enumerates the sacrifices of the New Testament.

A much surer explanation of these sacrifices and of how the Antichrist will take them away can be taken from the Scripture of the New Testament itself (2 Thess. 2:3-12; 1 Tim. 4:1-5; 1 John 2:18-23; and the Apocalypse). For through false teaching, through strange, self-chosen, and wicked ceremonies he will obscure, corrupt, and take away the purity of the ministry of the Word, of the sacraments, and of the divine worship. These things have been accurately fulfilled through the Antichrist of the Roman see, as has been clearly shown by many. For us it is sufficient at this point to have shown that this passage in Daniel gives no aid whatever to the sacrifice of the papalist Mass. For in the first place it speaks properly of Antiochus and is applied to the Antichrist through an allegory; (2) it speaks about sacrifice in general and is therefore rightly understood of sacrifices which are expressly mentioned in the New Testament; (3) and lest any doubt remain, the Scripture of the New Testament itself explains what sacrifices the Antichrist will take away in the church and how he will do it. For this reason the Council of Trent was not willing to use help from this passage in Daniel. Neither does the fact that in Dan. 12:11 the taking away of the continual sacrifice is connected with the setting up of the abomination of desolation do anything for the sacrifice of the Mass. For it is understood of the abrogation of the Levitical worship.

7. Eck, wishing to display his knowledge of the Hebrew language, philosophizes about the affinity between the word "Mass" and *minchah*.[9] Wherever the word *minchah* is mentioned in the Old Testament, he imagines that it establishes the sacrifice of the papalist Mass. And where Lev. 21:6 and Num. 28:2 speak of the sacrifice of the bread of God, Eck translates *lechem* [bread] as "flesh of God." He brings in many testimonies from the rabbis about the sacrifice of bread and wine at the time of the Messiah.

---

[9] *Minchah:* a bloodless offering of food, generally translated "meat offering" in the King James Version but "cereal offering" in the RSV.

These things are not only laughed at by those who are expert in Hebrew, but the papalists themselves are ashamed to use these arguments.

8. In the disputes of the theologians at the Council of Trent, some of which I have seen noted down in writing, this argument was frequently repeated by many: In the institution of the Supper Christ puts words which, as no one will deny, speak about sacrifice, not in the future tense, "It will be given; it will be shed," but in the present, "It is given and shed for you." Therefore Christ sacrificed His body and blood, not only on the cross, but also in the Lord's Supper.

At first many were favorably impressed by this argument. For it seemed that the sacrifice of the Mass could be proved not from strange statements of Scripture but from the institution of the Supper itself, as the true seat of the doctrine, for what Christ did in that Supper He commanded to be done thereafter. But when this argument was examined somewhat more diligently, it was finally realized that this not only could not support or establish the papalist Mass, which had been shattered and cast down by the sword of the Spirit, but that it could not even stand by itself, and that for many reasons.

First because, if these were essential words of the sacrifice of the Mass, a great crime would be pinned on the canon of the Mass, which in the first part of the institution entirely omits the words, "which is given for you." In the second part the canon has, not the present tense but the future, "which will be shed." Therefore the sinew of this argument, to which some attached great weight, has not only been cut into but wholly cut out by the very canon of the Mass.

Second, how can the sacrifice of the Mass be called unbloody if, when it was offered at the first Supper, the shedding of the blood was made in the present?

Third, when and where the body of Christ was given for our redemption, and His blood shed for the remission of sins, is not unknown to the Christian faith. For Scripture declares in very many statements that this was done in the passion and death of Christ.

Fourth, the use of the present tense does not accomplish what they are after. For there is used and well known in Scripture an exchange of tenses, not only of the present but also of the past for the future, to express certainty: "To us a child is born" [Is. 9:6]; "The Lamb was slain from the foundation of the world" [Rev. 13:8 KJV]; "Behold, the Lamb of God, who takes away the sins of the world!" [John 1:29]; "I lay down My life for My sheep" [John 10:15]. Also in the Lord's Supper Christ spoke in the present tense, for He was then in the very act of His passion, which was afterward consummated on the cross. Thus He says on Palm Sunday (John 12:27, 31): "I have come to this hour. . . . Now is the judgment of this world." After the Supper He says (John 14:30-31): "The ruler of this world is coming. . . . I do as the Father has commanded Me." John 17:11, 13, 19: "Now I am no more in the world. . . . I am coming to Thee. . . . For their sake I consecrate Myself."

9. The monk of Augsburg says: In the Supper Christ took the bread in His hands, lifted up His eyes to His Father in heaven, and gave thanks; therefore He there sacrificed His body and blood to the Father. He draws this conclusion because *therumah*[10] in the Law is the term for a sacrifice which was lifted on high as it was being offered.

But nowhere do we read that Christ elevated the bread and cup which He had taken. Yes, and of His eyes lifted up to heaven neither the evangelists nor Paul mention anything, but this is an addition of the canon. And even if this were granted, one could not at once construct a sacrifice from this. For also when Christ blessed the five loaves and two fishes He looked up to heaven. He did this also at the resurrection of Lazarus and when He healed the deaf and dumb man. Why then do we not make sacrifices also of these things if so much can be deduced from His lifting up His eyes to heaven?

ARTICLE VI

Arguments of the Synod of Trent in Behalf of the Mass

Such things were seriously and with great effort argued by many for the defense of the sacrifice of the papalist Mass, received with extraordinary applause by the papalist church, held up against us, and put forward hitherto for the more uneducated as undoubted and immovable grounds. But the Council of Trent, recognizing them, though reluctantly, for what they are, does not mention them with even one word. Having thrown them, as it were, among the camp followers and servants, they commit the defense of the Mass to the *triarii*,[11] placing in the front line of the battle certain selected arguments which they judged to be without any doubt the strongest and firmest.

Therefore we shall first unfold those arguments which the Council of Trent puts forward to prove, confirm, and establish the sacrifice of the

[10] *Therumah:* commonly used in the O.T. to designate various kinds of offerings. Some authorities hold that the basic meaning is "elevation" or "lifting up."

[11] See footnote 7, above.

Mass; for often, according to a trick of orators, they embrace the whole argument in one or two words. Then, when we have unfolded them, we shall examine them for effectiveness and soundness. The manner of the unfolding will be short, simple, and most sure if all arguments are referred to and measured against the point at issue in the controversy. For what the individual argument certainly ought to prove and effect firmly and clearly is this: (1) that the body and blood of Christ in the Lord's Supper are to be handled by means of this theatrical representation in words, ceremonies, gestures, and actions, as the papalist Mass does; (2) that such a representation is a sacrifice, instituted by Christ and most pleasing to God the Father; (3) that it is a propitiatory sacrifice for expiating and destroying sins, for receiving remission of sins, and for securing benefits of every kind from God—and finally for sins, punishments, satisfactions, and other necessities of the living and the dead; (4) that through this sacrifice the merits of Christ's Passion are applied to anyone who causes a Mass to be celebrated for him, yes, for all, whether present or absent, living or dead—to whomever the priest wants to communicate it by applying it to him. This ought to be the conclusion from every argument by good, sure, firm, and clear reasoning. But if this is not done by each and every one of the arguments, it will be easy to judge what should be thought and stated about the Tridentine thinking concerning the papalist Mass. We shall therefore survey the arguments one by one.

I. The priesthood requires a sacrifice. However, the priesthood of Christ was not to be abolished by His death, but is everlasting (Ps. 110:4). Therefore it was necessary not only that He should offer Himself once on the cross but that He should institute the sacrifice of the Mass, where He is offered repeatedly and daily to God the Father for the living and the dead, in order that He may in this way be a priest forever.

I answer: If we had to judge by way of deductions without the light of Scripture, purely according to our reason, this argument might have some validity and might accomplish something. But Scripture gives us, as it were expressly, the clear explanation of this argument in the Epistle to the Hebrews. It tells us what the sacrifice of the priesthood of Christ is, how, when, how often, and by whom it was offered, and indeed it diligently and clearly describes the perpetuity of the priesthood of Christ— and that both negatively and affirmatively. For it says clearly that Christ is not therefore a priest forever that He should offer Himself repeatedly, for as our High Priest He entered once, and with a one-time offering, into the Holy Place (Heb. 9:12). Heb. 7:26-27: "It was fitting that we should have such a high priest . . . who had no need . . . to offer daily . . . for the sins of the people; for He did this once for all when He offered up

Himself." And the reason is set down there, namely, that the offering of Christ cannot be repeated, unless one denies that what was once done was perfect and complete, because the repetition of a sacrifice is a sign of weakness—of the priest, of the priesthood, and of the sacrifice.

But how can the priesthood of Christ be eternal if He once only, by a unique offering, as High Priest perfected and completed the sacrifice of His priesthood? This the Epistle to the Hebrews explains very clearly, showing many reasons, as in 7:24: "He holds His priesthood permanently, because He continues forever," because the Son is eternally perfect.

But what are the priestly functions He performs after He has completed the unique sacrifice on the cross? Does He perhaps offer Himself repeatedly and even daily for the sins of the people? "By no means," says the text, "but because He is able to save eternally those who come to God through Him, He lives forever for this, that He may intercede for us" [Heb. 7:25]. And Heb. 9:11-12: "Christ, a high priest of good things to come . . . through His own blood entered once into the Holy Place . . . having procured an eternal redemption." "He entered . . . into heaven itself, now to appear in the presence of God on our behalf" [Heb. 9:24], not that He may offer Himself repeatedly. Heb. 10:11-14, 19-22: The Levitical priest offers the same sacrifices repeatedly and without ceasing, but Christ, having offered one sacrifice for sins, sits forever at the right hand of God, "then to wait until His enemies shall be made a stool for His feet. For by a single offering He has perfected for all time those who are sanctified." "Therefore . . . since we have a great High Priest over the house of God, let us draw near with a true heart in full assurance of faith, with our hearts sprinkled," etc.

These things are clear, so that there is no need of a fuller explanation or refutation of this first argument. Neither does it follow from the fact that the sacrifice of Christ is eternal that Christ should be repeatedly and daily sacrificed to the Father for the living and the dead. For the Holy Spirit teaches that the priesthood of Christ is eternal for far other reasons, namely: (1) that the priest may live forever; (2) that the power of His one offering may endure and be efficacious forever; (3) that He may live forever in order that He may appear before the face of God and intercede for us; (4) that through Him as our High Priest we may have access to the Father; (5) because He is able to save eternally, and does save, those who come to God through Him. Therefore it has been shown clearly from Scripture that there is neither rhyme nor reason to the conclusion in this first Tridentine argument; yes, if it is held against the point at issue in the controversy about the propitiatory sacrifice, it will be clear that the conclusion of the argument, namely, that Christ is offered daily in the Mass for the sins of the living and the dead, is in diametrical opposition to the express and oft-repeated statement of the Word of God in Heb. 7 and 10. This is perhaps the reason why this argument is not set forth in its entire form but only briefly touched upon and covered over by heaping up other reasons with sophistic trickery.

II. Human nature demands a visible sacrifice. Therefore Christ instituted this theatrical representation of His passion in the Mass. Other papalist writers fashion and set forth this argument more clearly in this way: It is prescribed to all peoples by nature that they should use some visible sacrifice in their religions to secure and merit the grace of God for the gifts of this earthly life and for eternal salvation; therefore Christ, taught by the law of nature, instituted the sacrifice of the Mass.

However, the refutation of this argument is quite easy. For in matters of religion and faith one must not judge or establish anything from what nature, blinded and perverted by sin, prescribes. For here is the fount and source of all superstitions and all idolatrous worship. But, "Thy Word is a lamp to my feet" (Ps. 119:105). And the canon and rule for faith is not a pronouncement of corrupted nature but the voice of the apostles (Ps. 19:4). Indeed, reason must be taken captive into obedience to the Word (2 Cor. 10:5). But if the Tridentine chapter says that it means only that the weakness of our nature cannot be raised up to God in any other way than by having some visible sacrifice, I answer very simply: What is useful and necessary for raising up and restoring our weak and corrupt nature must be judged from nowhere but the prescription and ordinance of our Physician.

III. It is certain that in the Last Supper Christ instituted a memorial of His bloody sacrifice which should remain until the end of the world. Likewise, it is not doubtful that Christ instituted His Supper in order that the power of His passion should be applied to believers for the remission of sins. Now the papalists say that the sacrifice of their Mass is representative and applicatory. Therefore Christ in the Last Supper instituted the sacrifice of the papalist Mass.

I answer: This argument must be referred to the point at issue in the controversy, namely, whether Christ in the Last Supper ordered that the remembrance of His passion in the church should be made by means of this theatrical representation of ceremonies, gestures, and actions in the papalist Mass; likewise, whether Christ ordained and promised that if anyone arranged that such a papalist representation be made for him or her, then and through this work the power of the passion of Christ would be applied to that person for the remission of sins. Certainly, nothing of this can be shown or detected in the institution of the Dominical Supper; rather, Christ in His Supper not only in general instituted a remembrance and application of His passion, in such a way that He entrusted to human regulations how and in what way this commemoration should be made, but He expressed and prescribed that the memory of His passion should be celebrated in the Lord's Supper by giving of thanks, distribution, eating and drinking of His body and blood, and by proclamation of His death. Thus He also defined and prescribed the manner of application in the Supper, namely, that in His Supper Christ Himself, through the ministry, wants to apply the power of His passion to believers by means of the Word and the distribution of His body and blood under bread and wine, in order that the faithful may apply the merits and benefits of His passion to themselves in true faith as they use the Supper by taking the body and blood of Christ.

Now, because the institution of the Lord's Supper says nothing about the representation and application of the papalist Mass in the manner described when we established the point at issue in this controversy, but rather defines and prescribes a different, sure mode of both commemoration and application, therefore the third Tridentine argument accomplishes absolutely nothing for establishing the sacrifice of the papalist Mass. Rather, because that institution of Christ was given in the form of a testament (and it is a crime to add something even to the testament of a man), therefore it is clear that the conclusion of this third argument does violence to the very testamentary institution of the Son of God, because it fashions and institutes a commemoration and application that is different from the one handed down and prescribed by Christ in the words of institution.

IV. The fourth argument is one on which the whole papalist Mass hinges to such an extent that, unless it is proved and established by this argument, it is all over and done for, namely: whether Christ in the last Supper not only gave His body and blood to the disciples but also sacrificed it to God the Father under the species of bread and wine. For they realize that if Christ did not sacrifice His body and blood to God the Father in the Supper, the sacrifice of the papalist Mass cannot be anything but a fiction and an abomination. But if it could be demonstrated that Christ in the Supper sacrificed Himself to the Father, then it would follow further from the commandment of Christ that this should be done in the church until the end of the world.

They tried by various stratagems to prove this, for instance by Christ lifting up His eyes to heaven, or from the present tense, "It is given and shed," or from the word "do," because Vergil says:

When I "do"[12] a heifer.

But the Council of Trent perceives that these proofs cannot certainly, clearly, and firmly demonstrate what is being argued, namely, that Christ in the Last Supper sacrificed His body and blood to God the Father. Therefore they run to their last defense and put forward the one demonstration of the question to which they ascribe so much that they repeat it twice. Therefore if this Tridentine demonstration does not prove sufficiently clearly, certainly, and firmly that Christ in the Supper sacrificed Himself to the Father, the whole sacrifice of the papalist Mass will reel, sway, and collapse. But that is how things stand with the Tridentine demonstration: It was necessary that the figure of Melchizedek should be fulfilled in truth in the priesthood of Christ, for He is a priest after the order of Melchizedek. But Melchizedek offered bread and wine to God the Father. Therefore it was necessary that also Christ should offer to God the Father, not bread and wine only but, in order that truth might fulfill the figure, His body and blood under the species of bread and wine. This could, however, be done nowhere but in the Supper.

It is a difficult question, and it concerns an important matter. For the things we read that Christ did in the Supper in no way, shape, or form indicate the nature of a sacrifice. He took bread, gave thanks, broke it, gave it to His disciples, commanded them to take and eat, and said: "This is My body." Likewise He took the cup, gave it to them, commanded that they should drink, and said: "This is My blood." And this He commanded to be done in remembrance of Him. We neither read nor hear anything to the effect that Christ in the Last Supper sacrificed His body and blood to God the Father for the living and the dead. Therefore it will take a powerful demonstration to persuade us that Christ did that in His Supper of which no trace appears in the description of the Lord's Supper in the New Testament.

But you say: Is it not more certain than any demonstration that Christ is a priest after the order of Melchizedek? It is indeed, for Scripture affirms it (Ps. 110:4; Heb. 6:20; 7:11, 15, 17). But the controversy is not about this proposition itself, but about the things that are added to it: (1) whether Melchizedek sacrificed bread and wine to God the Father in the account written in Gen. 14:18-20; (2) whether the priesthood of Christ after the order of Melchizedek consists in this, that in the Supper He

---

[12] Among the many meanings of *facio,* "to make" or "do," is also the meaning, "to offer sacrifice."

sacrificed His body and blood to the Father under the species of bread and wine.

The old translation indeed has: "Melchizedek offered bread and wine, for he was a priest of the Most High." But Moses did not write thus. For he does not use a verb that denotes sacrifice, but says *hotsi"*, which means simply "to fetch, bring forward." Thus the sword is drawn forth (Ezek. 21:3);[13] the winds are brought forth (Ps. 135:7); lice are brought forth (Ex. 8:18); water is brought out of the rock (Num. 20:8); meal which has been brought forth out of Egypt is cooked, etc. Add to this that neither the Chaldaean paraphrase nor the Greek translator render this statement by means of a word meaning sacrifice, but by a simple word meaning "to bring forward." Josephus interprets that Melchizedek brought forward bread and wine to refresh the army of Abraham. Chrysostom explains the passage of bread and wine brought forward, not sacrificed. Also the old Latin fathers do not read in the text of this passage *obtulit* [he sacrificed] but *protulit* [he brought forward] bread and wine, as is clear from Cyprian. Also Moses does not say: "He was a priest; therefore he offered bread and wine." But he twice repeats the word "and": "And he was a priest, and he blessed." The Greek translators do not have the word *gar* [for], but *de* ["however"]: "However he was a priest, and he blessed," so that the thought is divided as follows: Because he was a king, therefore he brought forward bread and wine; because he was a priest, therefore he blessed.

Now let us consider the Tridentine argument. They want to prove what the New Testament Scripture do not say, namely, that Christ sacrificed Himself to God the Father in the Supper. But how do they prove this? Because, they say, Melchizedek sacrificed bread and wine to God. However, Scripture does not say this, as has been shown. What kind of argumentation is this in so important and serious a matter? But they say: Even though the words of Moses do not expressly say this, it could still be that he sacrificed bread and wine. For the ancients generally did not go to solemn banquets unless they had first sacrificed. Vicelius says: "Because Moses does not expressly say for whom Melchizedek brought forward bread and wine, therefore it can be understood that he brought it forward not for the refreshment of Abraham but to bring a sacrifice to God."

We are not, however, arguing about how either this man or that man either wants to or can interpret this passage in Moses, or what he wants to or can conjecture or imagine about its meaning. The question is what Moses writes, what Scripture says. For that is what counts everywhere,

---

13 In the Hebrew, Ezek. 21:8.

both in all of Scripture and in particular in the story of Melchizedek, seeing that he is a type of Christ. For who, seeing Moses is silent on this, would not conclude that Melchizedek, because he is neither God nor angel but a man, had a father, a mother, a beginning of days, and an end of life? But Scripture shows that in the story of Melchizedek, insofar as he is a type of the priesthood of Christ, we must follow that only which is expressly said in Scripture; so it declares that in the type of the priesthood of Christ Melchizedek was without father, mother, beginning of days, and end of life. For this reason Moses does not say these things expressly, but omits them in order that this very omission might serve the type of the priesthood of Christ after the order of Melchizedek. These things stand firm against all sophistries.

Furthermore, even if it were granted that Melchizedek sacrificed bread and wine, we nevertheless know that dogmas are not to be fabricated from figures, without a sure and clear Scriptural explanation. Therefore Ps. 110:4 declares that Christ is a priest after the order of Melchizedek. But it does not say how and wherein the priesthood of Christ and of Melchizedek agree. However, the Epistle to the Hebrews undertakes to explain this expressly in a lengthy and adequate explanation. But although it enumerates and explains many parts of the comparison of the priesthood of Melchizedek and of Christ, it makes no mention at all of sacrificing bread and wine or that Christ fulfilled this in the Supper by offering His body and blood to the Father. Nor is there any force to what Hosius says, namely, that the apostle omitted that part of the comparison because he was unwilling to open up the mystery of the sacraments to the unlearned and not yet initiated, to whom he wrote this epistle. For he says (6:1): "Let us leave the elementary doctrine of Christ and go on to maturity."

Lastly, the type of the priesthood of Melchizedek consists in the things which it does not have in common with the Aaronic priesthood, but in which Melchizedek and Aaron are set apart. However, the sacrifice of bread and wine was offered daily in the Aaronic priesthood (Ex. 29:38-42; Num. 28:4-8). But how could the conclusion stand that the priesthood of Christ is not after the order of Aaron but after that of Melchizedek if the sacrifice of bread and wine were the most important and even the whole thing in the priesthood of Christ?

Therefore it has been demonstrated with certainty, firmly, and clearly, that the figure of Melchizedek, insofar as it has been set down and explained in Scripture, by no means effects or proves that Christ in the Supper offered His body and blood to the Father. Although the fathers sometimes make use of such an allegory, we know that the fathers neither should nor can establish articles of faith either by their allegories or by their interpretations without[14] testimonies of Scripture. No matter how the fathers speak of the sacrifice of bread and wine, they do not have in mind the kind of sacrifice the papalists have in the Mass, as described when we established the point at issue in this controversy. But of the fathers we shall speak later. For the present it is sufficient to have shown that it cannot be proved either from the Old or the New Testament that Christ offered Himself to the Father in the Supper. And if He did not do it, nobody ought to do it. For what He Himself did in the Supper, that He commanded the apostles to do thereafter.

V. Christ said: "Do this." Therefore He commanded that the priests should offer the body and blood of Christ in the Eucharist. The men of Trent teach that the reasoning leads to this conclusion: In the first Lord's Supper Christ Himself offered His body and blood to the Father, as did Melchizedek.

We have already shown that this assertion is false. Consequently the conclusion the papalists invent does not follow from it.

But they state by way of rejoinder that the verb *'asah* ["to do"] is often used for "to sacrifice," e.g., Ex. 29:39: "One lamb you shall offer" [Heb. *'asah*]; Judg. 6:19:[15] "Gideon . . . prepared [*'asah*] a kid"; Ps. 66:15: "I will make an offering [*'asah*] of bulls and goats"; Num. 6:11:[16] "The priest shall offer [*'asah*] one for . . . a burnt offering."

I answer: As with the Latins the word *facere* ["to do"] acquires various meanings according to the context, so for the Hebrews *'asah* does not always mean "to sacrifice", but only where the text clearly speaks of sacrifice.

Let us therefore consider the words of the Supper: "Do this." They contend that the word "this" refers not to the whole account but only to the foregoing words "body" and "blood," so that the sense is:"Do My body and blood," i.e., "sacrifice them." But even if this were granted, it would first have to be demonstrated with certainty that a sacrifice was performed in the first Supper. Now Paul is the most reliable interpreter that the pronoun "this" in the command of Christ: "Do this," is to be referred to the whole preceding action: "This (namely, what was done at the first Supper) you are to do hereafter." Therefore the command of Christ: "Do this," means nothing other than that the ministers of the

---

[14] The edition of 1574 as well as the Preuss edition of 1861 have *sive Scripturae testimoniis*. The translator assumes that *sive* is a misprint for *sine*, which is called for by the context.

[15] The text has Judith 6, an evident misprint.

[16] The text has Num. 16, an evident misprint.

church in the administration of the Lord's Supper ought to do that of which it is established and certain that Christ did it at the institution of the Supper. We do not, however, read there that He sacrificed or offered His body and blood to the Father. Therefore the priests ought not to do this either, unless they want to be accused of being faithless ambassadors by Christ the judge. But behold the character of the Babylonian harlot! What is known for sure to have been done by Christ in His Supper, that the papalists either neglect or prohibit, such as the public proclamation of the death of the Lord and the distribution of both kinds. The papalists fight only about doing things of which we do not read that Christ did them in His Supper. Yet it is a testamentary institution, and it is a crime to change or add anything in a testament.

VI. Christ made the apostles priests of the New Testament; therefore He taught them that they should offer His body and blood. This argument is amplified with many reasons by papalist writers: because, they say, Scripture prophesies that the priesthood of the New Testament will follow the abrogation of the Levitical priesthood, so that the ancient priesthood was a type of the new (Is. 66:20-23; Jer. 33:17-22; Mal. 3:2-3). But the definition of a priest is given as follows (Heb. 5:1): "Every high priest chosen from among men is appointed to act on behalf of men in relation to God, to offer gifts and sacrifices for sins." Therefore it is the duty of priests to offer the body and blood of Christ to God the Father in the Mass for the sins of the living and the dead, because only the presbyters are priests of the New Testament.

This argument embraces many parts, which must be briefly explained in their order. For thus it will become crystal clear what a crass fallacy there is in this argument.

To speak first about the statement in Heb. 5:1: It is certain that the text is not there speaking in general about what is the task of the ministers of Word and sacrament in the New Testament, but about the priesthood of the Old Testament, and that it speaks expressly and solely about the high priest, who was a type of Christ. Later on it teaches that this type was fulfilled in the priesthood and sacrifice of Christ, not in such a way that in the New Testament this same sacrifice should be often and daily repeated and offered by many priests who should succeed one another, for this the apostle denies in express words (Heb. 7:23-28;9:6-14; 10:1-18). But this type was fulfilled in the one sacrifice of Christ once made upon the cross (Heb. 9 and 10), and that indeed in such a way that when in the New Testament an everlasting redemption had been devised, and full remission of sins gained through the one offering once made on the cross, there should be no further offering for sin. But if there is posited in the New

Testament another offering for sin beside the one once offered on the cross, or a repetition of the same, it will follow that the sacrifice of Christ on the cross has not been finished and has not merited remission of sins and eternal redemption, for those are the words and this is the meaning of the Epistle to the Hebrews. Therefore the statement in Heb. 5:1 is most falsely distorted to strengthen the sacrifice of the papalist Mass for the sins of the living and the dead. Furthermore, nobody doubts that the Levitical priesthood was a type of the priesthood of the New Testament. But what this priesthood of the New Testament is, which follows when the old is abrogated, we cannot establish more correctly and surely than from the explanation of the New Testament itself.

Now, first of all, the Epistle to the Hebrews in chs. 5 to 10 explains at great length that the Levitical priesthood prefigured the priesthood of Christ and that this type was fulfilled by the one sacrifice of Christ made once on the cross for sin and that thus, through this fulfillment, the Levitical priesthood has become obsolete and has been abrogated. The Scriptures of the New Testament mention besides this also a royal and holy priesthood (1 Peter 2:5,9; Rev. 1:6; 5:10; 20:6). "Christ has made us kings and priests." In only these four passages is any mention made in the New Testament of a royal priesthood beside the unique priesthood of Christ. However, these passages do not speak only of the presbyters but about all believers in general, with whom the papalists certainly will by no means consent to share the right to perform Masses. Moreover, Scripture clearly says that the sacrifices offered in the New Testament priesthood are spiritual, and enumerates them expressly and by name to show of what kind they are, as we have noted down these testimonies of Scripture in the beginning of this discussion (Rom. 12:1-2; 15:16; Phil. 2:17; 4:18; Heb. 5:7; 12:28; 1 Peter 2:5,9). However, no mention is made there of the sacrifice of the Mass. You see, therefore, how illogical, yes, how sophistical it is in the conclusion to restrict the priesthood to the Mass-priests only, when in the promises Scripture speaks either of the unique priesthood of Christ or of the spiritual priesthood of the New Testament which all the faithful have in common. And although the Scriptures of the New Testament enumerate the sacrifices of the New Testament priesthood expressly and by name, the conclusion of this argument omits these things and invents the propitiatory sacrifice of the papalist Mass, of which Scripture makes no mention in the description of the New Testament priesthood, yes, which, as the Epistle to the Hebrews shows, is opposed to the one offering of Christ once made for sin.

But they take exception: Do you then make and observe no distinction between the ministers of the church and the rest of the faithful? We most certainly make and observe a distinction so far as the ministry is concerned. But it does not follow from this that what Scripture tells us about the priests of the New Testament pertains only to the ministers of the church. For it is worthy of note that although the Scriptures of the New Testament apply various terms to the ministry, yet in no passage of the New Testament are the ministers of the Word and the sacraments called priests. Nevertheless it is wholly true that, by reason of their ministry, certain things belong to the ministers of the church which the rest of the faithful are not commanded to perform. But the question is which and of what kind these are. It is not sufficient if one says that in the Old Testament the act of sacrificing made the distinction between priests and laity; therefore it should be the same also in the New Testament. For, first of all, the teaching about the abrogation of the Levitical priesthood of the Old Testament must be noted. Second, the term "priest" is nowhere in the New Testament applied to the ministers of the Word and of the sacraments. Third, in the Old Testament the priests did not sketch out for themselves on their own authority what they wanted to have belong to their ministry, but they had a prescribed Word and command of God which they followed in the actions of their ministry. Let us not fight about the question whether the term "priest" may be applied to the ministers of the New Testament. However, this foundation is firm and immovable, that we must judge and decide about the duties of the ministers of the New Testament on the basis of the Word, prescription, and command which has been handed down about the ministry in the New Testament Scriptures. These passages are found in Matt. 10:1-15; 26:13; 28:19-20; Mark 16:15; Acts 1:8,22; 6:2; 1 Cor. 4:1; 12:27-31; 14:6, 26-33; 2 Cor. 5:18-21; Eph. 4:11-16; Acts 20:28; 1 Tim. 3:1 ff; Titus 1:5 ff. In all these passages there is found no discourse, no word, no syllable, nor even a letter to the effect that the ministers of the New Testament should by a theatrical representation in the Mass offer the body and blood of Christ to God the Father as a propitiatory sacrifice for the sins of the living and the dead; yes, this is in conflict with the statement of the Word of God in the Epistle to the Hebrews. Therefore it is manifest how effective and how valid is the argument in the sixth Tridentine session [17] [under Pius IV]: Christ constituted His apostles priests of the New Testament; therefore He commanded them and their successors in the priesthood that they should sacrifice in the Mass, etc.

VII. The Passover lamb was a type of Christ. But the Passover in the Old Testament was not only eaten but at the same time also sacrificed.

---

[17] The text has "chapter."

Therefore the Eucharist is not only to be distributed and taken but also offered in the Mass as a propitiatory sacrifice for the sins of the living and the dead.

The reader notices that in a controversy about a great and burning issue the papalists operate not with sure and clear testimonies of Scripture but with shadows and types, whereas in this debate we should have regard most of all for what Augustine says in *Contra epistolam Petiliani*, ch. 16: "Let them not collect and quote what has been spoken obscurely, ambiguously, and figuratively, which everyone may interpret as he wills, according to his own understanding, for such things cannot be correctly understood and expounded unless what has been very clearly set down is first held with firm faith. But bring forward something which does not need an interpreter, neither something about which you may become convinced that it was spoken about something else and which you may try to twist to your divergent meaning." And in ch. 19 he says: "These things are mystical, secret, figurative; we demand something clear, which does not need an interpreter." Likewise: "What if things are stated ambiguously and can be interpreted both for us and for you? Surely, they do not help your cause at all, but it is plain that such things sustain a bad cause only by causing delays." Thus says Augustine.

Moreover, many things can be construed from the type of the Passover lamb which are not even tolerable for the papalist Mass. For as the Passover lamb was not simply offered but slaughtered, so the Mass ought to be an exceedingly bloody sacrifice, for the word *shachat* signifies to slaughter with the shedding of blood. Neither was the Passover lamb sacrificed by priests but by the multitude, and that not as a propitiatory sacrifice for sin but as a commemoration of the liberation from Egypt. The papalists will certainly not allow these things to be applied to their Mass. Therefore we could turn aside this whole argument about shadow and type in this way; but we shall respond about the thing itself.

We do not deny that the slaughtering of the paschal lamb was a type of the sacrifice of Christ. For Paul says: "Christ, our paschal lamb, has been sacrificed." However, the question is where and when this figure of the slaughtering of the paschal lamb was fulfilled by Christ. The papalists say that this was not done on the cross but in the Supper. However, the Scriptures of the New Testament assert the contrary. For in John 1:29 the Baptizer calls Christ "the Lamb of God, who takes away the sin of the world." Peter clearly asserts that Christ "bore our sins in His body on the tree" (1 Peter 2:24). Rev. 5:9, 12:"Worthy is the Lamb who was slain and has redeemed us to God by His blood," etc. 1 Peter 1:18-19: "You were ransomed . . . not with perishable things . . . but with the precious blood of

Christ, like that of a lamb without blemish." And the clearest testimony of all is written in so many words in John 19:36, that the figure of the sacrificed paschal lamb was fulfilled in Christ on the cross: "Not a bone of Him shall be broken." And so the church sings: "When Christ our Passover was sacrificed, for He is the true Lamb, who has taken away the sins of the world, who in dying destroyed our death," etc. Therefore it is certain that in Christ both the sacrificing and the eating of the Passover lamb have been fulfilled. How, when, and where this was done must be learned not from our allegories but from the explanation of the New Testament Scriptures, which assert that Christ, our Passover, was once sacrificed on the cross, that He is given to be eaten in the Supper as often as we do what Christ did in the first Supper, in accord with the institution. In 1 Cor. 5:6-8 Paul, by way of an allegory, uses the eating of unleavened bread as a picture of the newness of life; but the sacrifice, says he, was fulfilled nowhere else but in the slaying of Christ.

VIII. Malachi prophesies (1:10-11): "In every place . . . there is sacrificed and offered to My name a pure offering; for My name is great among the nations." That sacrifice cannot be understood of the Levitical sacrifices, for he is there speaking of their abrogation: "I will not accept an offering from your hand." Neither can it be understood of the sacrifice on the cross, which was made at Jerusalem, for he says: "It is offered in every place." Now can it be understood of the inner and spiritual sacrifices of the faithful, for these were present also in the time of the Old Testament. The prophet is there prophesying about what is clearly a new sacrifice which was not in existence before. Likewise, Isaiah says about the righteous acts of the faithful that of themselves they are before God like the cloth of a menstruating woman. This offering, however, he calls "pure." It remains, therefore, that it be understood of the sacrifice of the papalist Mass, for there the offering, namely Christ, is of itself pure, and no unworthiness or malice on the part of those who offer it is able to pollute it.

I answer: Let the point at issue in this controversy be recalled to mind, namely, whether Malachi says that the priest should, in the Mass, represent the Passion of His Son to the Father with bread and wine, accompanied by particular mimicking gestures, ceremonies, and actions, as is done among the papalists, and that this action of representation is a sacrifice pleasing to God and, indeed, propitiatory for expiating and blotting out the sins of the living and the dead and for whatever else we have shown above to be ascribed to the papalist Mass. Of these things Malachi certainly says nothing with so much as even one word. How much this prophecy of Malachi contributes to proving and establishing the sacrifice of the papalist Mass is therefore clear from the mere comparison of the point of the controversy with the statement of the prophet.

But they say: Nevertheless he prophesies about an offering which is sacrificed and offered among the nations in every place, that is, in the time of the New Testament.

I do, indeed, read this in the words of the prophet, but generally stated, without an explanation of what this sacrifice will be. But in the New Testament Scriptures I find the explanation which shows what the sacrifices of the faithful in the New Testament are, namely spiritual sacrifices, as shown by the Scripture passages noted above. Neither is it true what the papalists say, that the prophet is foretelling a new sacrifice which was not in use at all among the faithful in the time of the Old Testament. For he is not speaking of a new but of a pure sacrifice, and he makes a contrast, not between the spiritual sacrifices of the ancients and the pure offering among the nations, but names the Levitical sacrifices, which were offered in one place only in Judaea, and he is vexed because they were offered improperly; to these he opposes the pure offering among the nations. Moreover, he explains in a not obscure manner what he wants understood by it, for he says: "My name is great among the nations." Therefore, because the public praise of the divine name, which hitherto had been limited by the narrow confines of Palestine, was to be extended among the nations, so that in every place the name of God would be magnified by preaching, believing, invoking, giving of thanks, praising, etc., he calls this magnifying of the name of God an offering and a sacrifice, as the prophets were accustomed to describe the worship of the New Testament in terms of the ceremonies of the Old Testament, as for instance, "to ascend into the hill of the Lord," "to lay calves on the altar," etc. Thus the same prophet says (3:3): "They shall present right offerings," and Ps. 4:5[18] says that trusting in the Lord is a right sacrifice.

We have, therefore, the interpretation of the prophet himself; to this comes that the New Testament (1 Peter 2:9) lists among the spiritual sacrifices to "declare the wonderful deeds of Him who called you out of darkness into His marvelous light"; Rom. 15:16: to sacrifice the Gospel; Phil. 2:17: "the sacrificial offering of your faith"; Heb. 13:15[19] "The

---

[18] The text has Ps. 3.
[19] The text has Heb. 12.

calves[20] of the lips are to acknowledge the name of the Lord; likewise: the sacrifice of invocation and thanksgiving.

The comparison makes plain that Scripture by the use of these terms shows what is the true meaning of the passage in Malachi. It is certain that the prophet is there speaking of the conversion of the Gentiles. Of it also Paul speaks in Rom. 15:16 and Phil. 2:17. Malachi calls it a sacrifice and an offering. And Paul describes the calling of the Gentiles in plainly the same words (Rom. 15:16). In Phil. 2:17 he calls it "the sacrificial offering of your faith." In Ps. 141:2,[21] where David calls the lifting up of hands a sacrifice, he uses exactly the same word which is found in the statement in Malachi. In 1 Tim. 2:8 Paul speaks of "lifting holy hands." Therefore Scripture indicates in no obscure fashion what the pure sacrifice in Malachi is. And when we have such an interpretation taken from Scripture itself, we cannot go wrong. But of the papalist sacrifice of the Mass for the living and the dead the Scriptures of neither the Old nor the New Testament say anything; in fact, they are diametrically opposed to it, as the Epistle to the Hebrews shows. What madness it is, therefore, to depart from the simple meaning which has sure and clear testimonies of Scripture and to fabricate a foreign explanation about the sacrifice of the Mass which rests upon no testimonies of Scripture, yes, which conflicts squarely with Scripture!

That Malachi calls it a pure offering in spite of the fact that the righteous acts or the godly in this life are like the cloth of a menstruating woman does not prove that this passage is not rightly understood of the spiritual sacrifices of the church. For Peter says: "Offering spiritual sacrifices acceptable to God through Jesus Christ" [1 Peter 2:5]. On this account it is said that in prayer the faithful "lift up holy hands" (1 Tim. 2:8), for "to the pure all things are pure." (Titus 1:15)

Also the ancient writers of the church understand and interpret Malachi's statement as referring to the spiritual sacrifices of the New Testament. Thus Tertullian says in his book *Contra Judaeos:* "Malachi undoubtedly prophesies thus because he knew that the preaching of the apostles would go out into every land. For with respect to the fact that one must sacrifice to God not with earthly sacrifices but with spiritual, we read: 'The sacrifice of God is a crushed heart.' And of the spiritual sacrifices he adds: 'In every place a pure offering shall be sacrificed in My name.' " Thus he writes in that place. And in *Contra Marcionem,* Bk. 3,

---

[20] The expression "calves of our lips" is taken from Hos. 14:2 (see the King James version), to which Heb. 13:15 is alluding. The passage in Hebrews interprets the Old Testament passage: "A sacrifice of praise to God, that is, the fruit of lips," etc.

[21] The text has Ps. 142.

he takes this prophecy as referring to making known His glory, blessing, laud, and the singing of His praise. In Bk. 4 he understands it of simple prayer, flowing from a pure conscience.

Chrysostom, *Oratio 2 adversus Judaeos,* explains it of spiritual worship. So also Jerome in his commentaries explains it of prayer and spiritual worship.

Eusebius, *De demonstratione evangelica,* Bk. 1, ch. 6, says that Malachi means nothing but that neither at Jerusalem only, nor at any other place, but in every region the nations would offer to God most high the incense and sacrifice of prayer, which is called a pure offering, not through the shedding of blood but through godly acts.

Justin, in *Trypho,* does indeed interpret this passage in Malachi of the bread and wine in the Eucharist, not as though he thought that the body and blood of Christ are offered to God in the Supper for the living and the dead, but he explains himself in these words: "He commanded to make the bread into the Eucharist for a remembrance of His passion, in order that we may give thanks both that He created the world and all things for man's sake and that He freed us from sins and destroyed the evil powers through His passion." It is therefore on account of spiritual sacrifices that he applies the passage in Malachi to the action of the Lord's Supper.

Also Irenaeus, in Bk. 4, interprets that statement of Malachi of the celebration of the Eucharist, not however in such a way that there, by means of a theatrical representation, the body and blood of Christ is offered to the Father for the living and the dead but (as he himself explains) because at that time it was customary at the celebration of the Eucharist to offer to God, who gives us our food, the firstfruits of His gifts or of His creation, not as though He needed this but to give thanks for His gifts, as Solomon says: "He who is kind to the poor lends to the Lord" [Prov. 19:17]. Likewise: "I was hungry, and you gave Me food" [Matt. 25:35]. These are the words of Irenaeus, from which it is clear that he is thinking of giving alms to the poor, which was done in connection with the action of the Eucharist. He calls this a sacrifice because (as he himself says) through a gift honor and love is shown toward a king; likewise, because we ought in all simplicity and innocence, with pure intention, faith devoid of hypocrisy, in firm hope, in fervent love, with giving of thanks, to offer the firstfruits of His creatures for that use which Scripture indicates when it says: "He who is kind to the poor . . . ." Likewise: "I was hungry, and you gave Me," etc.

Therefore Irenaeus interprets the passage in Malachi not about the papalist sacrifice but about spiritual sacrifices, which, although they should always be brought also on other occasions, should be made especially in the administration and use of the Eucharist. And at the end of ch. 33 he adds: "The altar is in heaven; thither our prayers and offerings are directed."

Thus Augustine, *Contra adversarium legis,* Bk. 1, ch. 20, interprets this prophecy of Malachi as referring to sacrifice after the order of Melchizedek and makes mention of the Eucharist. He does not, however, speak of the farcical representation of the papalists but says: "He offers to God in the body of Christ a sacrifice of praise" (Ps. 50:14). He adds: "John explains that the incense of which Malachi speaks is the prayers of the saints." (Rev. 5:8)

These passages in Justin, Irenaeus, and Augustine should be heeded, in order that the trick of the papalists may be understood. For because these ancients apply the passage in Malachi to the action of the Eucharist, although they clearly explain how they want this understood, the papalists nevertheless ignore all this, and whenever they hear the Eucharist mentioned, they immediately claim the ancients as proponents of their Mass. Therefore neither Scripture nor the interpretations of the ancients permit one to understand the passage in Malachi as referring to the theatrical sacrifice of the papalist Mass.

IX. In 1 Cor. 10:21 Paul compares the Lord's table with the table of demons, and by a table he in both instances understands an altar. Therefore, as the Gentiles had altars on which they sacrificed and afterward ate of what had been sacrificed, so also there ought to be an altar in the Mass, where the body and blood of Christ are first sacrificed and afterward partaken of.

To begin with, let the reader consider what kind of testimonies and defenses the papalist Mass has. From the shadows and figures of the Old Testament they anxiously gather up whatever they can and bend it to the Mass. But since they do not trust these things sufficiently, they are not ashamed to summon support for the lamented Mass from the sacrifices of the heathen, which they offer to their demons for a reason not unlike that of the man in Vergil who says:

> Befriend me, departed spirits,
> since the will of the gods is against me!

But as far as that comparison of Paul is concerned—if the matter itself, of which Paul speaks, is considered, to see how it stands, it will be apparent how falsely that passage of Paul is being twisted to establish the sacrifice of the papalist Mass. It was a custom among the Jews, after the sacrifice had been completed on the altar, to spread a sacrificial meal or a solemn banquet from the parts left over from the sacrifice, as the examples in 1 Sam. 1:3-5 and 16:2-5 show. So also the heathen, after they had performed their sacrifices on their altars, spread tables or solemn banquets, to which they invited their friends, as, according to the eighth book of the *Aeneid*, Evander, after the sacrifice to Hercules, invites Aeneas to the feast.

However, with the Corinthians the dispute was not over the question whether it was permitted to Christians to be present at the altars of the Gentiles at their sacrifices and sacrifice together with them to demons, for it is manifest that this is not permitted, because it is clearly idolatry. But the question was whether, when the heathen had performed the sacrifices in their temples and on their altars, and afterward spread tables or banquets at home of what had been sacrificed, and invited to these meals friends and neighbors, also such as had already become Christians—I say, the question was whether Christians could with a good conscience be present at these meals or banquets; that is, the question was not about the altars where the sacrifice took place but about the meals where the things which had been sacrificed were eaten.

From this the Tridentine deception is exposed, namely, that by table the altar for sacrificing is to be understood, since neither the Jews nor the heathen ate at altars but at tables what had been sacrificed.

Therefore Paul answers the question which has been proposed as follows (1 Cor. 8:4 ff.): Because both the idol itself and what is offered to the idol are nothing, therefore, if one understands his Christian liberty correctly, it is possible, without harm to his conscience, to eat and also to buy meats offered to idols, unless this gives offense; consideration must, however, be given to the weak. Then (10:23 ff.) he adds this admonition: Although it is free, nevertheless it is not fitting that a person should be at one and the same time a partaker of the Lord's table and of the table of demons. And he adds the reason: Because, says he, those Israelites who eat the sacrificial victims become, by that eating, partakers of the altars, that is, of the sacrifice which has been offered on the altar. And because the Gentiles offer to demons the things they offer, therefore partaking of a meal of things sacrificed to idols shows that the table companions desire to become partakers of the idolatrous sacrifice, yes, of the grace and help of demons, for the sake of which that sacrifice has been offered to the demons. At the Lord's table Christians become partakers of that sacrifice which was offered by Christ on the cross. Therefore it is not becoming that they should be at the same time partakers of the table of demons.

This is the simple, true, and genuine meaning of the Pauline comparison between the Lord's table and the table of the Israelites and also of demons. This comparison most beautifully illustrates the teaching concerning the Lord's Supper. For just as the Israelites were made partakers of the sacrifice offered on the altar by partaking not of other food but of that very thing which had been offered in the sacrifice, so the Son of God makes us partakers of His sacrifice performed on the cross, not by eating a small piece of bread but by the dispensation and eating of that body which was delivered up for us on the cross. And as Moses (Ex. 24:6-8), when he was about to apply and seal the Old Covenant to the people, does this not by sprinkling the blood of another victim but of the very one that had been sacrificed for the confirmation of the covenant, so Christ in the Supper gives us to drink of that very same blood by the shedding of which the New Testament has been confirmed. This comparison both confirms the doctrine of the true and substantial presence of the body and blood of the Lord in the Supper and shows the sweetest consolation from its use.

Now that all this has been explained, it will be easy to see whether the sacrifice of the papalist Mass is confirmed and established from this Pauline comparison. The comparison fits to this extent: As Jews and Gentiles ate what had been sacrificed at the tables of which we have just spoken, so also the things we eat at the Lord's table must first have been sacrificed. But where and when? Was it perhaps necessary that at these meals their banquet should be made a sacrifice? By no means! For in that case Paul would not have said that Christians could be present at the tables or banquets of the heathen. Neither was it necessary, if the meal was held one or two days after the sacrifice, that the action of the sacrifice be repeated at the table, but it was sufficient that what was eaten at that banquet had been sacrificed on the altar earlier. Thus, since Christ by one offering once offered up His body and blood to the Father on the cross for our sins, it is not necessary that they should be sacrificed again at the Lord's table as often as we go to receive them, but it is sufficient that we take the things that were sacrificed earlier, namely on the cross. Although there was freedom to repeat the Levitical sacrifices and those of the heathen, Scripture certainly expressly and repeatedly witnesses that the sacrifice of Christ neither can nor should be repeated (Heb. 9:24-28; 10:10-18). Therefore Paul's comparison between the Lord's table, the table of the Jews, and the table of demons gives no support whatsoever to the sacrifice of the papalist Mass.

X. The types of the Old Testament must be fulfilled in the New. Therefore the sacrifice of the Mass, prefigured in various similitudes in the sacrifices of the Old Testament, must be observed in the New Testament.

I answer: The first part of the syllogism we grant; but we say that what is inferred from it is utterly false and cannot be proved. For just because it is true that the New Testament contains the fulfillment of the types of the Old Testament, it is not therefore left to our own allegories and deductions to imagine how and in what things each individual wants these things to be fulfilled, but the Scriptures of the New Testament teach and explain how that fulfillment was accomplished and in what things it is found; neither must other things, which cannot be demonstrated from Scripture, be invented outside of this explanation. Now the New Testament Scriptures teach that the types of the Old Testament sacrifices have been fulfilled in a twofold manner: (1) in the one propitiatory sacrifice of Christ on the cross; (2) in the spiritual sacrifices of the faithful, which are enumerated by name and explained in the New Testament.

In this way also Augustine teaches and explains the meaning and fulfillment of the Old Testament sacrifices, *De civitate Dei*, Bk. 10, chs. 5 and 6. However, no mention is made in the New Testament Scriptures of the theatrical representation and propitiatory sacrifice of the papalist Mass. Therefore it is false that the papalist sacrifice of the theatrical Mass must be instituted and observed for the sake of the fulfillment of Old Testament types.

XI. There is no doubt that the body and blood of Christ is a propitiatory sacrifice for sins. But in the Lord's Supper Christ is present with His body and blood. Therefore the Mass is truly a propitiatory sacrifice, of the same power as the sacrifice on the cross, for the sacrificial Victim is the same in both.

I answer: There is a labyrinth of deceit in this argument. Once this has been uncovered, the unraveling will be easy. For the body and blood of Christ to be a propitiatory sacrifice it is not sufficient that their substance exist and be present, for it was present in the womb of His mother, in the manger, in the swaddling cloths, etc. Was it therefore a sacrifice for sins that Mary went into the hill country, that she wrapped her firstborn in swaddling cloths and laid Him in a manger? He sits at the right hand of God, dwells in the believers. Is therefore His session and indwelling that propitiatory sacrifice for sins of which Scripture speaks? A sheep in a stable and in a pasture certainly was a sheep; nevertheless it was not at once a sacrifice. For it is required for a sacrifice not only that the substance for the sacrifice exist and be present, but there is required some certain action by which that substance is offered. Does just any and every action make a sacrifice? By no means! For if a sheep is shorn, it is not therefore, by that action, sacrificed. To a true and God-pleasing sacrifice there is required: (1) the substance of the sacrifice; (2) a certain action of offering, not thought out by men but prescribed by God Himself; (3) that this action be performed by a person designated and ordained for this by God; (4) that this be done with the intention and for the purpose which has been prescribed by God in His Word. For the distinction between the Levitical sacrifices which is taken from their ultimate purpose, namely, that some are sacrifices for sin, either for this or for that, while others are peace offerings, depends entirely on the prescription of the Word of God.

When these reasons, which are simple, plain, and solid, are set alongside the argument which is before us, the explanation will be easy. For the body and blood of Christ are a propitiatory sacrifice for sins not simply for the reason that they exist but because the Son of God, as our true High Priest, designated for this by the Father, offered Himself to God the Father and did so according to the command He had received from the Father (John 14:31), namely by delivering up His body and shedding His blood. God Himself has proclaimed the power, greatness, and efficacy of this sacrifice in His Word. If the first proposition of the argument is stated in this way, it will be clear what a patched-on thing the second proposition is. For in the Lord's Supper there is present, according to the Word of Christ, His body and blood, but the things which, as we have just said, are required for the nature of a true sacrifice are lacking. For the action of the Lord's Supper, as it was instituted and commanded by Christ, is not the action of a sacrifice but of a sacrament. Christ is there present not in order that He may be sacrificed but that He may be distributed and taken.

But the papalists object that they have the intention, by the action of their representation, of offering the body and blood of Christ to God—to the end that it may be a propitiatory sacrifice for the living and the dead. I am not ignorant of the fact that the papalists do this. But the question in this argument is: (1) whether God instituted, prescribed, and commanded such a representation by means of such ceremonies, gestures, and actions as is done in the papalist Mass; (2) whether He has declared His will that He wants to accept such a representation as a well-pleasing sacrifice; (3) whether we have a divine promise that such an action of representation is a propitiatory sacrifice for sins.

Because these things cannot be demonstrated from the Word of God, therefore this argument does not prove that the Mass is such a sacrifice and that it has the same power as the sacrifice on the cross, even if it is conceded that the body and blood of Christ are present there. For Ambrose judges rightly that those who handle and celebrate the Eucharist in a manner different from that which is taught by the Lord are subject to the statement of Paul about the judgment of God. Yes, because Christ is offered by many priests in the Mass as an offering for sin, contrary to the statement of the Word of God in the Epistle to the Hebrews, therefore it is a horrible abomination.

XII. The catholic church has always understood and taught thus; therefore such a rite has always been present in the church from the time of the apostles, also such a doctrine of the sacrifice of the Mass as it is now in the papalist church.

Mention is made of this argument in the middle of the first Tridentine chapter, but for the sake of order I have divided my answer in such a way that after what is being adduced from Scripture had first been explained the testimonies of the fathers might have the last place. It is well known, however, that pious minds are greatly moved by the consensus and the testimonies of antiquity, particularly of the antiquity during the purer, best, and most flourishing times of the church. Therefore the papalists have in this dispute placed the greater part of their defense in heaping up many statements of the fathers, in order to deceive the more simple, as if the rites and the teaching about the sacrifice of the Mass for the living and the dead, as it is now used and taught by the papalists, were of the most ancient tradition of all the writers of all antiquity and universally observed in the church of all times, as far back as the times of the apostles.

But also this fog is dispelled without difficulty if the whole dispute about the testimonies of the ancients is brought side by side with the point at issue. Therefore, when many and varied statements of the ancients are heaped up, one must watch whether what has come into controversy is certainly, clearly, and firmly proved from them, namely, that all the ancients have, by a consensus of testimonies, always taught these dogmas as catholic and defended them from the Word of God:

1. That it was instituted by Christ, taught by the apostles, and observed in the primitive church that the body and blood of Christ should, in the Supper, be presented and offered to God the Father with the kind of words, ceremonies, gestures, actions, and trappings, by a theatrical representation, as it is now done in the papalist Mass;

2. That this action and representation of the body and blood of Christ on the part of the priest is a propitiatory sacrifice for expiating and blotting out sins, for stilling the wrath of God, for obtaining the grace of God, remission of sins, and all other benefits from God;

3. That the priest, through this representation, applies all the fruits and merits of the Lord's passion to the onlookers who are not commu-

nicating but have only made provision that such action of representation should be made either for themselves or for others, yes, for the absent and the dead, and for whomever he wills;

4. That we must approach God through this action of representation if we want to find grace and help. What else is ascribed to the papalist Mass we have shown above.

These are the things the advocates of the papalist Mass ought to have demonstrated clearly in the true and catholic consensus of the purer antiquity and from writings which are not spurious. For that with the passing of time certain of the ancients began to turn aside to strange opinions does not make a catholic consensus of all antiquity. But certain and clear reasons show that these things cannot be proved in this way from antiquity.

First of all, there are the descriptions of the rites of the ancient church in the celebration of the Lord's Supper in Justin, *Apologia,* 2; in Dionysius, *Ecclesiastica hierarchia;* in Augustine, Letter No. 59; in Chrysostom, Homily 18, on 2 Cor. But nothing is discovered there about the theatrical representation of the papalist Mass by means of ceremonies, gestures, acts, words, etc.

Second, the papalist writers themselves bear witness that the full armor of words, ceremonies, gestures, acts, trappings, and vestments, which are the sinews and therefore the very substance of the papalist Mass, did not exist at the time of the apostles, for they say that the apostles consecrated simply with the words of the Lord, to which they added only the Lord's Prayer. So Gregory, in *Registrum,* Bk. 7, ch. 65; Platina, in *Vita Sixti,* 1; Rupert, in *De divinis officiis,* Bk. 2, ch. 21; Walafrid Strabo, in *De rebus ecclesiasticis,* ch. 22; Durandus, Bk. 4, ch. 1; and others. And, indeed, they note clearly at what time after Christ and the apostles, and by what authors, the individual parts of the theatrical representation were invented and instituted, so that it was only after nearly 600 years from the birth of Christ that this whole drama of representation was somewhere nearly complete as it is now customary in the papalist church.

Now because that which, according to Eck's description, is properly the Mass was really not yet present in the most ancient church, for the papalist writers themselves bear witness that it was first instituted at a later date, therefore also the opinions which are now falsely imputed to the Mass could not have been present in the primitive church.

Third, the most ancient writers give the designation "expiatory, propitiatory, atoning sacrifice for sins," according to Scripture, only to the one offering of Christ, made on the cross, but all declare with one voice that the sacrifices of the faithful in the New Testament are spiritual. And Lactantius even says expressly in *Epitome divinarum institutionum* that the sacrifices made with hands or made outside of man are not true sacrifices. Also, the argument that in the New Testament another ceremonial sacrifice beside the sacrifice of Christ on the cross came in after the abrogation of the Levitical sacrifices was unknown to the ancients.

Fourth, what the papalists now claim for their sacrifice of the Mass, that the ancients ascribe to the dispensation and reception of the body and blood of the Lord in the Supper. But our adversaries are suave and, indeed, accomplished rhetoricians. Although they ought to bring forward testimonies from the most ancient writers about the matter itself, in the way described above about the point at issue, because they see that this cannot be done with profit to their Mass, they pounce on certain terms in the writings of the ancients, and when they have pointed them out in a number of statements, they suppose that the papalist Mass has been sufficiently proved and fortified by the testimonies and consent of antiquity. Now there are two such terms, namely, "Mass" and "sacrifice." And wherever these terms are found with the ancients, the remark is at once added: This is a witness for the Mass. And when the more inexperienced hear such things alleged: "The Mass was in use at the time of Ignatius and of the other most ancient teachers"; "all antiquity held and taught that the Mass is a sacrifice," they think of and understand nothing else than such a Mass and such a sacrifice as is now in use with the papalists.

Some few things must therefore be said about these two terms, which make up the whole collection of statements which the papalists rake together in behalf of their Mass. For once these two terms have been correctly explained, the fog which they spread before the inexperienced will be dissipated by the roar of the testimonies from the ancients. We shall do this as briefly as possible, for these things have been abundantly demonstrated and explained by others.

ARTICLE VII

Concerning the Term "Mass"

When the papalist Mass had begun to be attacked from the Word of God, its first defenders, such as Eck and others after him, anxiously examined the term "Mass," and wherever they found it in the translators of Greek writers they immediately exclaimed: The papalist Mass is so old that Masses were celebrated at the time of Ignatius, of Dionysius, and of the rest of the most ancient fathers. For Ignatius says to the Smyrnians: "to celebrate the Mass." Also Dionysius calls it "Mass," *Ecclesiae hierarchia,* ch. 3. In the *Historia tripartita*[22] we are often told that the ancient fathers of the church celebrated Masses, Bk. 3, ch. 11, that they made Masses, Bk. 4, ch. 13, that they celebrated the solemn rites of Masses, Bk. 7, ch. 31, Bk. 9, ch. 9, that the people assembled for Masses. They rejoice in earnest over these testimonies. But it is wholly certain that the term "Mass" is not contained in a single one of the Greek authors, but that these are the words of the translators. Thus the translator of Dionysius renders *hierourgian* now "Mass," and again "the offering of the sacrifice of salvation," although the word signifies the administration of a sacred action. Where Ignatius wrote *docheen epitelein,* that is, to celebrate the Lord's meal, the translator renders it: "to celebrate Masses." Thus, where Sozomen has *ekkleesiazein,* and Socrates *synagein,* words which signify public meetings and the solemn gatherings of the church, Epiphanius Scholasticus[23] rendered: "to make Masses; to celebrate Masses." And although that is how matters stand, this has nevertheless been the chief proof for the antiquity of the papalist Mass, although not even the term "Mass" was known to the ancient Greek church. But the question is not how the translator rendered it but what the authors wrote.

The term "Mass" is indeed found with Latin writers, like Ambrose, Bk. 5, Letter No. 33, and Leo in the Letter to Dioscurus of Alexandria— not, however, with the most ancient ones. But these men call that Masses, which Hilary, on Psalm 65, calls "the ceremonies of the divine sacraments," namely, when in gatherings of the church either the sacraments were administered, dispensed, and partaken of, as is clear from the epistle of Leo, or when they came together for prayer. Thus we read in Cassian, Bk. 2, *De modo psalmorum,* ch. 13, that after the nightly Mass they were not to sleep. Ch. 15: "After the prayer-Mass let everyone return to his cell." Bk. 2, ch. 8: "After the Mass of the nightly vigil let sleep be permitted until daylight." Cassander shows from the rule of

---

[22] *Historia tripartita:* About the middle of the sixth century Cassiodorus, a Christian writer and scholar, caused the works of three Christian historians who had written in Greek, Socrates (c. 380-c. 450), Sozomen (c. 400-450), and Theodoret (c. 393-c. 466), to be translated into Latin. These works were then amalgamated into one complete narrative under the title *Historia tripartita.* The text of this work is found in Migne, *Patrologia Latina,* Vol. LXIX.

[23] Epiphanius, surnamed Scholasticus, in the middle of the sixth century prepared the *Historia tripartita,* on which see the previous footnote.

Benedict and from Honorius that the prayers which are commonly called collects are called the customary Masses.

From the term "Mass," therefore, whether it be read in the translators of the Greek writers or in Latin writers, no encouragement or help whatsoever comes for the papalist representation. Those who now want to be the more learned in the papalist kingdom notice and sense this; therefore they judge it to be more satisfactory to refrain entirely from using this argument based on the term "Mass," which in the beginning of this controversy was looked upon as the firmest support. So sure and immovable are the foundations of the papalist Mass.

ARTICLE VIII

In What Sense the Ancients Called the Liturgy a Sacrifice

1 The testimonies taken from the term "sacrifice" appear much more plausible. For it cannot be denied that when the ancients speak about the celebration of the Lord's Supper they use the terms "sacrifice, immolation, offering, host, victim," likewise that they use the verbs "offer, sacrifice, immolate." Is it not therefore the universal consensus of all antiquity that the Mass is a sacrifice? I answer very simply: If the strife were only about terms or names, we should in no way be able to escape but would be compelled to grant that the ancients frequently applied the terms for sacrifice to the celebration of the Lord's Supper. But because the controversy is about the matter itself, I answer: We have shown above, when we established the point at issue, that it does not follow that if the ancients called the Lord's Supper a sacrifice they therefore taught and felt it is the kind of sacrifice the papalists imagine it to be. For the word "sacrifice" is a very broad term and, according to the custom of Scripture and of the ancients, is applied to a variety of things, exercises, and actions, as we have made plain above by examples both from Scripture and from antiquity.

2 Therefore a simple, short way of explaining the testimonies of the ancients which are adduced by our adversaries about the sacrifice of the Mass is that the point at issue in this controversy be set before our eyes, namely, what kind of sacrifice the papalists understand when they dispute about the Mass, as was explained above in their own words, and that it be shown by contrast that when the ancients call the celebration of the Lord's Supper a sacrifice they do not understand that about which the papalists fight, but that they apply that term to many and varied other exercises of true piety which come together in the action of the Lord's Supper and were customary with the ancients. For in this way it will become clear that it is a great falsehood when wherever in the writings of the ancients the term "sacrifice" is applied to the celebration of the Lord's Supper the papalists at once attach to it the fiction of the sacrifice of their Mass.

3 We shall therefore note down in order, as briefly as possible, the kinds of sacrifices the ancients wanted to indicate and have understood when they used the term "sacrifice" in the action of the Lord's Supper.

First: It was customary in the ancient church that, whenever the Lord's Supper was to be celebrated, bread and wine and other gifts were offered on the Lord's table or on the altar for the maintenance of the ministry and of the poor. Of these offered gifts of bread and wine parts were taken and consecrated for the Eucharist. This custom seems to have been taken from 1 Cor. 11:20-22, 33-34. Mention of this custom is made by Pontius Paulinus, *De Gazophylacio,* by Irenaeus, Bk. 4, by Justin, *Apologia* 2, and in *Decreta de consecratione,* dist. 1, ch. *Omnis Christianus,* also quest. 12, ch. 2, *Vulturanae,* and the following. Now because in Scripture the giving of alms is called a sacrifice (Phil. 4:18; Heb. 13:16), therefore the ancients called this exercise of piety in the Lord's Supper a sacrifice and offerings. Cyprian says, in the treatise *De eleemosyna:* "You, a rich matron, come into the house of the Lord without a sacrifice and take a part of the sacrifice which a poor man brought." Irenaeus says, Bk. 4, ch. 32: "We offer to God the firstfruits of His creatures with thanksgiving." And he says that this is done according to the statements of Scripture: "He who is kind to the poor lends to the Lord"; "I was hungry and you gave Me," etc. And he shows that what was consecrated to be the body and blood of Christ was taken from these firstfruits of God's creation. Among other reasons it is also on this account that he calls the total action an offering. In Letter No. 122 Augustine says that the women offer sacrifices at the altar of the Lord in order that they may be offered to God by the priest. For the names of those who offered something were repeated aloud at the altar and commended to God in prayer, as the canon of Gregory testifies. And many collects bear witness to the same thing, as the one spoken on the fifth, sixth, and seventh Sunday after Pentecost shows.

Second: The common and appointed public prayers, the form of which is prescribed in 1 Tim. 2:1-8, were customarily made among the ancients at the action of the Lord's Supper, as Augustine testifies, Letter

No. 59 to Paulinus. And because the prayers of the faithful are called sacrifices in Scripture (Ps. 141:2; Heb. 5:7; Rev. 5:8; 8:3), therefore Irenaeus, speaking of the offerings of the New Testament in the action of the Eucharist, says among other things, Bk. 4, ch. 33: "He wants us also to offer a gift without ceasing at the altar. The altar is in heaven, for thither our prayers and offerings are directed." Chrysostom says, Homily 18, on 2 Corinthians, that one might see the people offer in their prayers at one and the same time for those possessed of the devil and also for penitents, for they pray jointly and all say the same prayer. Tertullian says, *Ad Scapulam:* "We sacrifice to God for the safety of the emperor, but in the way He Himself commanded, with pure prayer." And in *Apologeticus,* ch. 30: "I offer to God the fat sacrifice which He has commanded me, namely prayer."

Third: The Lord's Supper is called Eucharist by the most ancient fathers, Ignatius, Justin, Irenaeus, etc. They do this, as Chrysostom explains, Homily 16, on Matthew, because in its celebration there is placed before us the contemplation of many and varied blessings of God, chiefly, however, of the foremost work of God's love toward us, that He sent His Son, who by delivering up His body and shedding His blood redeemed us lost ones, that in this way we might be challenged to thanksgiving. The sacrifice of praise and thanksgiving is frequently lauded in Scripture (Ps. 50:23; 69:30-31; Sirach 35:1-2; Heb. 13:15). The fathers apply the term "sacrifice" also to hymns, praises, and giving of thanks, e.g., Augustine, Letter No. 120; Eusebius, *Demonstratio,* Bk. 1, ch. 10; Tertullian, *Contra Marcionem,* Bk. 4. And the Greek canon expressly mentions hymn, glorification, etc.

Fourth: Because Paul interprets the commemoration of Christ as proclaiming the death of the Lord in the Supper, therefore public preaching and the solemn proclamation of the passion, death, resurrection, and ascension of Christ was always observed among the ancients. Cyril says in the synodical epistle to Nestorius: "Proclaiming the death, resurrection, and ascension of the only-begotten Son of God according to the flesh, we celebrate the unbloody sacrifice or an unbloody divine worship." For Paul calls the whole ministry of the Gospel a sacrifice. (Rom. 15:16)

Fifth: Many exercises of true piety come together in the celebration and use of the Lord's Supper, which are called spiritual sacrifices (1 Peter 2:5), such as repentance, faith, hope, patience, love, a good intention, etc. Faith, which has its object chiefly in the use of the Lord's Supper, is called a sacrifice (Phil. 2:17). Thus Irenaeus, Bk. 4, ch. 32, disputing about the sacrifice of the New Testament in the celebration of the Eucharist, enumerates: a pure understanding, faith devoid of hypocrisy, firm hope, fervent love, mercy, obedience and justice, good works with thanksgiving.

Sixth: In the true use of the Eucharist the church and the individual believers solemnly vow, consecrate, and dedicate themselves wholly with body and soul to the Lord and, on account of the Lord, to their neighbor. Likewise, by its prayers the church is offered, that is, commended to the Lord. Paul says (Rom. 12:1) that our bodies are "presented to God as a living sacrifice, holy and acceptable to God, which is your spiritual service." Therefore Augustine writes, *De civitate Dei,* Bk. 10, ch. 6: "This is the sacrifice of Christians that we, being many, are one body in Christ. The church frequently makes use of the sacrament of the altar, which is known to believers, where it is demonstrated to her that in the offering which she offers she is herself offered." And Letter No. 59: "All things which are offered are consecrated to God, most of all the offering of the sacred altar. By this sacrament our greatest vow is proclaimed, in which we vow that we will remain in Christ and in union with the body of Christ. This is what the sacrament is about, that we, being many, are one bread and one body." Likewise: "When the blessing is pronounced on the people and intercessions are made, then the priests or counselors offer those in their charge to the merciful and all-powerful God."

4 You see to what varied actions and exercises of piety which were customary with the ancients at the celebration of the Lord's Supper the term "sacrifice" or "offering" was applied. As a result the whole action received this name among the ancients. Since these things are not unknown to the papalists, let the reader judge what kind of trick it is that they indiscriminately bend all statements of the ancients about sacrifice to the theatrical sacrifice of the papalist Mass, although the ancients are speaking of far other things, actions, and exercises when they call the celebration of the Lord's Supper a sacrifice.

5 But they object: Not only those exercises of piety which according to the custom of the ancients were used in the action of the Lord's Supper are called sacrifices by the fathers, but the action of the Lord's Supper itself and the body and blood of Christ themselves in the Lord's Supper are by the ancients called sacrifice, offering, host, sacrificial victim, etc.

This I do not deny. For it is certain that the ancients transferred the designation "sacrifice, offering, victim, host," etc., to the very action of the Lord's Supper, in fact, to the very body and blood of Christ in the Supper.

But this I do deny, that the ancients by the term "sacrifice" understood the theatrical representation by which the papalists define the sacrament of their Mass, and that the histrionic action of the priest, handling the body and blood of Christ with certain gestures and acts, is a propitiatory sacrifice for expiating and blotting out sins, for placating the wrath of God, and for obtaining any and all benefits from God. For we have the explanations of the ancients, how they want it understood that they call both the action of the Lord's Supper and the body of Christ in the Supper a sacrifice and a sacrificial victim.

6 As we have shown earlier in what way the fathers applied the term "sacrifice" to the exercises of piety performed in connection with the celebration of the Lord's Supper, so we shall also clearly note down in what sense the ancients applied the term "sacrifice" to the very action of the Lord's Supper and to the body and blood of Christ in the Supper. Moreover, these things must at the same time be set side by side with the point at issue in this controversy, namely, whether the fathers understood such a sacrifice as the papalists devise in their Mass, according to the explanation set forth above in their own words.

First: The fathers call the very administration or celebration of the Lord's Supper, such as its hallowing, consecration, and dispensation, a sacrifice. Dionysius calls it a *hierourgia* [24] because it is a sacred action, or the administration of a sacred action. And he says that the priest sacrifices when he does what Christ did at the first Supper. And lest there be any doubt about what he means by *hierourgia,* when the priest prays that he may be rendered fit for this *hierourgia* he enumerates all the parts it embraces: (1) to confect, hallow, or consecrate these divine gifts for the imitation of Christ; (2) to distribute in a holy manner what has been hallowed; (3) that those who are about to commune may partake of this sacrament in a holy manner. And to explain at once how the priest performs this most holy sacrifice, he says: "He divides the undivided bread and distributes the one cup to all." Therefore the *hierourgia* of Dionysius is not the theatrical representation of the papalists; it is nothing other than the preparation, hallowing, consecration, dispensation, and distribution of the Eucharist, which he calls a *theomimeeton hierourgian,* the administration of a sacred action which is done in imitation of what Christ, our God, did.

This *hierourgia,* that is, this sacred action, which belongs to the ministry of the Gospel, the Latins call a sacrifice, and *hierourgein* they translate "to sacrifice or offer." For also Paul (Rom. 15:16) describes the actions which belong to the ministry of the Gospel, not the smallest part of which is the administration of the sacraments, by means of the terms

---

[24] *Hierourgia:* a sacrifice or religious service.

"sacrifice" and "offering." Thus Augustine, Letter No. 5, to *Paulinus,* 9, calls it the offering of the holy altar, which is offered to God, namely, "when that which is on the Lord's table is blessed, sanctified, and broken and prepared for distribution." For these are his words.

Cyprian, Bk. 7, Letter No. 1, 3, where at the start he sets down the argument of the entire epistle about consecrating the cup of the Lord and administering it to the people, afterward repeats the terms "sacrifice" and "offering," and that Christ took the cup, not of water only but of wine and water mixed, blessed it, and distributed it to the disciples. Cyprian sets this forth thus: "Christ offered to God the Father not water only but wine mixed with water in the cup." This the proponents of transubstantiation cannot admit with respect to their offering. Nor is it offensive, if it is correctly understood, that He says it is offered to God the Father. For in Acts 13:2, which treats of the ministry of the Gospel, which Chrysostom interprets as referring to preaching, Luke says: "While they were worshiping the Lord." And elsewhere the fathers explain themselves very clearly when they say that in the Supper Christ is brought as an offering [immolation] to the people. Augustine, Letter No. 23, uses the expression: "to be offered *(immolari)* to us." Augustine, on Ps. 79: "to be offered to the faithful." Jerome to Damasus: "Thus Paul in 2 Cor. 2:15-16 says of the preaching of the Gospel: 'We are the aroma of Christ to God for life to those who are being saved.' " In his letter to Nestorius Cyril calls it an unbloody sacrifice or worship, "when we call what has been confected the body and blood of Christ, when we draw near the mystical blessings and are sanctified, being made partakers of the body and blood of Christ, the Redeemer of all."

Second: The action of the Lord's Supper is called a sacrifice, offering, immolation, etc., by the ancients because the Lord's Supper is celebrated and used for a memorial or commemoration of the one sacrifice of Christ, once performed on the cross. Thus Augustine says, *In lib. sententiarum Prosperi:* "When the wafer is broken, while the blood is being poured from the cup into the mouths of the faithful, what else does it signify but the immolation of the Lord's body on the cross and the shedding of His blood from His side?" In *De fide ad Petrum,* ch. 18 and *Contra Faustum,* Bk. 20, ch. 18, he makes a comparison among these three: the Levitical sacrifice, the sacrifice of Christ on the cross, and the offering of Christ's body in the Supper. Then he shows this difference among them: On the cross the sacrifice of the body and blood of Christ was rendered in truth; in the sacrifices of the ancients there were figures and types which promised the sacrifice of Christ that would come; in the Lord's Supper, through the sacrament of remembrance, there is celebrated remembrance or commemoration and thanksgiving for the completed and consummated sacrifice of Christ on the cross. And in Letter No. 23, to Boniface, likewise Letter No. 120, to Honoratus, he treats examples showing that a thing which is a memorial of something receives the name of the thing of which it is a memorial, on account of the resemblance. Thus, when Easter draws near, we say: Tomorrow or the day after is the passion of Christ, although in fact He suffered once only, many years ago. And on the Lord's day we say: Today Christ rose from the dead, for on account of the similarity the day is said to be something which it really is not. And afterward he adds: "Was not Christ offered once? Yet He is offered for the people daily in the sacrament. He who says that Christ is offered is not lying. For if the sacraments did not have a likeness to the things of which they are sacraments, they would in no way be sacraments, but from the likeness they often take their names." By the same analogy, as Easter day is called the resurrection of the Lord because it is a memorial of the resurrection of the Lord, Ambrose explains in a comment on the Epistle to the Hebrews what kind of sacrament the Lord's Supper is. He says: "What we do is a remembrance of the sacrifice." Thus Chrysostom, Homily 17 on Hebrews, as he discusses the daily offering of the Lord's Supper, finally says: "What we do is done as a commemoration of that which was done once, on the cross; we do not make a different sacrifice, but always the very same one. But even more, we bring about a remembrance of the sacrifice, because He Himself says: 'Do this in remembrance of Me.' " Cyprian says: "The passion of Christ is the sacrifice we offer." Theophylact says, on Heb. 10: "Someone will ask: 'Do we also offer without blood?' Yes indeed! But then we remember the death of Christ: We offer the same always, or rather, we make a remembrance of that sacrifice, just as if He were being sacrificed at the present time." Augustine says, on Ps. 79: "Behold, Christ has made us new, has forgiven us all our sins, and we are converted. If we forget what has been given us, and by whom it has been given, we forget the gift of our Savior. However, when we do not forget the gift of our Savior, is not Christ offered for us daily? Christ was offered for us once; when we came to faith, then we reflected; now, however, it is the leftovers of reflection by which we remember who it was that came to us and what He has given us out of these remnants of reflection, that is, through this remembrance He is daily offered for us, as though He who renewed us through His first grace now renewed us daily."

The reader should observe that Augustine says that Christ is offered for us when we are converted through the preaching of the Gospel, when we are renewed by the grace of God, namely in Baptism. For also Origen says, on Rom. 2, speaking of circumcision: "To offer the blood of circumcision." Yes, Augustine says that Christ is offered for us when we remember the benefits of Christ, that is, as he says elsewhere: "Then is Christ slain to every man, when he believes that He has been slain."

These explanations of the ancients should be pondered. They say expressly that Christ was in fact, or in truth, offered only once—on the cross—and that the action of the Lord's Supper is called a sacrifice, offering, immolation on account of the similarity, not because a sacrifice of Christ is really made there but because it was instituted and is used in remembrance or commemoration of the sacrifice of Christ, made once on the cross. And lest this commemoration be bent to the fictitious representation of the papalists, the ancients themselves explain their meaning, namely, that they call that the immolation of Christ, when the wafer is broken, while the blood of the Lord is poured from the cup into the mouths[25] of the faithful, *De consecratione,* dist. 2, ch. *Cum frangitur.* And in *De Trinitate* Augustine says: "We who have been set free by the death of Christ signify the remembrance of this by eating and drinking what has been sacrificed." Likewise: "We call that the body of Christ which, taken from the fruits of the earth and consecrated by sacramental prayer, we receive in memory of the Lord's passion."

Lombard says, Bk. 4, dist. 12: "Men ask whether what the priest exhibits may properly be called a sacrifice or immolation, and whether Christ is offered daily, or whether He was offered only once. To this one can answer briefly: That which is offered and consecrated by the priest is called a sacrifice and offering because it is a memorial and representation of the true sacrifice and of the holy offering made on the altar of the cross. And Christ died once on the cross; there He was sacrificed in His own person; He is, however, sacrificed daily in the sacrament because in the sacrament a remembrance is made of that which was done once."

The reader will, however, observe that this statement of Lombard, which he proves and confirms with testimonies of the fathers, namely, that the sacrifice on the cross is a true sacrifice while the action of the priest is not properly a sacrifice, is directly opposed by the first Tridentine canon: "If anyone says that in the Mass there is not offered to God a true and proper sacrifice, let him be anathema." You see that the papalist Mass cannot stand unless the explanations of antiquity, which the church still used even at the time of Lombard, are condemned with the anath-

---

[25] The text has *ara,* altar, a manifest misprint for *ora,* mouths. Both Nigrinus and Ed. Preuss have so corrected it.

ema. For also Augustine says, *De civitate Dei,* Bk. 10: "What is called a sacrifice by men is a sign of the true sacrifice."

Third: The fathers call the body and blood of the Lord which are present in the Supper a saving sacrifice, a pure host, our ransom, the purchase price of our redemption, the ransom for the sins of the world, a propitiatory sacrifice and a propitiation, not because the body and blood of Christ are offered in the Mass by the action of the priest in order that they may become the ransom and propitiation for the sins of the whole world, but because that sacrifice which was once offered on the cross for our redemption and for the sins of the whole world—the body and blood of the Lord—is present, is dispensed, offered, and taken in the Lord's Supper, so that the power and efficacy of this offering, once made on the cross, is applied and sealed individually to all who receive it in faith. Thus Cyprian says of the Lord's Supper: "This life-giving bread and the cup of blessing, hallowed by the solemn benediction, benefits the life of the total man, being at the same time a medicine and an offering, to heal our infirmities and to purge our iniquities." He at once adds an explanation about Communion, that the cup, which the Lord offers to us, has such power.

There is also a very beautiful statement in Augustine, Bk. 9, ch. 13, about his mother Monica: "She desired only that she be remembered at Your altar, from which she knew the holy sacrifice to be dispensed, by which the handwriting is erased which was against us, by which the foe is triumphed over, who counts up our transgressions and seeks something to bring up against us, and finds nothing in Him in whom we conquer. To the sacrament of this our ransom she bound her soul as a handmaiden with the bond of faith. No one can tear her away from Your protection. No one shall come between, neither by power, nor by deceit, neither lion, nor dragon," etc. For faith, having accepted the things Christ offers in the sacrament, sets them between our sins and the wrath of God as satisfaction and propitiation. Thus Bernard says, Treatise 22, *In Cantica:* "When my power fails, I am not confounded; I do not despair. I shall know what to do; I shall take the cup of the Lord." And Treatise 1, *De Epiphania:* "All I am able to give is this poor body. And if this is not enough, I shall add also His body. For it is of mine, and is mine; for to us a Child is born, and a Son is given to me. From You, Lord, I supply what I lack in myself. O sweetest reconciliation and most delightful satisfaction!"

Eusebius of Emesa says, *De consecratione,* 2, ch. *Quia corpus:* "He consecrated for us the sacrament of His body and blood in order that He might be worshiped continually through the mystery which He once offered as the purchase price, in order that, because redemption was running daily and unwearied for the salvation of all, there might be a perpetual offering of redemption and that the sacrificial Victim might live forever in memory and be always present in grace — a true, unique, and perfect sacrifice. Therefore when you go up to the awe-inspiring altar, to be satiated with spiritual food, look upon the holy body and blood of your God in faith, grasp it with the hand of your heart, put on the inner man," etc. What Eusebius of Emesa calls a perpetual offering has this meaning, as Cyprian says of the baptism of Christ: "The offering of Christ, made on the cross, is no less efficacious in the sight of God today than it was on the day on which blood and water flowed from His wounded side. For the afflictions which remain in the body always call for the price of man's salvation and require the gift of obedience."

7 These statements of the ancients about the sacrifice of the body and blood of Christ, even as they are in harmony with the faith, so give no support to the theatrical sacrifice of the papalists. Nevertheless this also should be observed when we read the ancients, how with the passing of time those expressions about sacrificing and offering the body and blood of Christ in the Supper began little by little to obscure the true use of the Lord's Supper and to introduce strange opinions about the merit of the priest's action. On anniversary days gifts or alms were offered in memory of departed believers for a confession of the faith in which they had fallen asleep. Afterward, however, these were turned into propitiations for sins, even for those of the dead. Traces of this are found in some of the ancients; this we freely confess. For it is not all kinds of sayings of the ancients but the canonical Scriptures which are the rule and norm of faith and of judgment in this controversy.

8 This consideration about the blemishes of certain of the ancients shows why we prefer that the Lord's Supper should be called a sacrament rather than a sacrifice. For first, Scripture, which is able to give things the most correct and fitting names of all, nowhere calls the Lord's Supper a sacrifice. Second, the name "sacrifice" obscures the true doctrine and use of the Lord's Supper more than a little. For a sacrifice is an action by which we give or offer something to God. However, Christ instituted the Lord's Supper that in it (as is the nature of sacraments) He might deal with us—giving, offering, applying, and sealing with the pledge of His body and blood the merits of His passion. And it is His will that we should accept in faith what He there offers and gives us. The term "sacrifice," however, leads us away from these things to what we, in the action of the Lord's Supper, offer and give to God. Therefore it is more correctly and fittingly called a sacrament rather than a sacrifice. Third, the theatrical

sacrifice of the papalist Mass, which has been constructed on the basis of these not skillfully understood expressions, shows sufficiently what trouble the improper terms denoting sacrifice cause when they are applied to the Lord's Supper.

9 These are the arguments which the Council of Trent sends into the battle line for retaining, confirming, and establishing the sacrifice of the papalist Mass. They are refuted without difficulty by a simple explanation, if only a comparison is made between these arguments and the point at issue in this controversy, which we have for this reason set forth at length in the beginning. For this comparison shows clearly that no true, firm, and solid aid or support comes to the papalist Mass from these arguments.

ARTICLE IX

Arguments Showing the Abomination
of the Papalist Mass

That it lacks true, firm, and solid grounds in Scripture is, however, not the only thing we criticize in the papalist Mass; what we complain about most of all is that it is an abomination, conflicting with the doctrine of the Word, the sacraments, and faith— yes, that it is full of abuse against the unique sacrifice of Christ and against His perpetual priesthood, as this has been demonstrated at length by the men on our side in fair and honest writings. Therefore, lest I depart too far from the plan of this examination, I shall draw together only the chief arguments against the papalist Mass under a few general heads and briefly note them down.

I. To institute a form of worship beside and without the Word of God, and indeed one to which is ascribed propitiation for sins, appeasement of the wrath of God, and the procuring of grace and other benefits from God, is a vain thing; it cannot please God; yes, it is idolatry. For "in vain they worship Me with doctrines and commandments of men." Likewise: "Without faith it is impossible that a thing should please God." Faith, however, "comes by hearing, and hearing by the revealed Word of God." Yes, the prophets proclaim that all sacrifices, not only of the Gentiles but also of the Jews, which were instituted outside of the Word, and without a commandment of God in groves, on high places, etc., are idolatry.

But the theatrical representation through words, ornaments, ceremonies, gestures, acts, etc., as is done in the papalist Mass, has no testimony of the Word. For Christ, in the institution of the Lord's Supper, does not mention it even in one syllable. True, some say that the papalist Mass has James as its author. But papalist writers themselves acknowledge that these things were unknown to the apostles, and write of them that they used only the Lord's Prayer in addition to the words of the Supper in the celebration of the Lord's Supper; we have noted down the passages in the authors a little earlier. And indeed, papalist writers themselves note down which Roman pontiffs invented and instituted the individual acts and scenes of the drama of the Mass and at what time they did it. From these things that whole representation was afterward put together. Because therefore the papalist Mass is a human invention, without the Word of God, without a tradition and example of the apostles, it is a vain thing which cannot please God; yes, it is an abomination and idolatry to ascribe to a human fabrication propitiation for sins, etc.

II. To transfer sacraments outside of the use instituted by Christ into another action of a wholly different kind is a great crime. For Ambrose, in treating the doctrine of the Lord's Supper, placed among the unworthy those who celebrate this mystery in a manner other than was instituted by the Lord. However, Christ prescribed and commanded the action of a sacrament, not that of a sacrifice, in the words of institution. This is manifest. Moreover, the papalists themselves teach that the action of a sacrament and that of a sacrifice are different from each other. Therefore the papalist Mass is an affront to the Lord's Supper.

III. When Christ was about to die, He instituted the administration and use of the Lord's Supper in the form of a testament. Now it is a great crime to add anything to even a human testament when it has been ratified and confirmed. It is manifest, therefore, what the papalist Mass is, which adds to the testament of the Son of God something which is not contained in it, is not instituted, is not prescribed.

IV. The papalist Mass, as we have described it in the beginning, militates against the one propitiatory sacrifice of Christ in many ways and is an affront to it. For there is only one propitiatory sacrifice that expiates and renders satisfaction for sins—the offering of Christ made on the cross (Heb. 7:27; 9:12, 26; 10:12). He offered Himself once for sins, for taking away the sins of many, "having found an eternal redemption." "For with one offering He has forever perfected those who are sanctified." Therefore it is a detestable affront against the sacrifice of Christ to invent another propitiatory sacrifice for sins. Neither does it relieve the situation for the papalists that they say they do not offer another but the same sacrifice which was offered on the cross, repeated more frequently, and indeed daily, for sins. For the Epistle to the Hebrews says clearly and expressly and repeats a number of times that Christ offered Himself once for sins in such a way that He might not have need to offer daily for sins, and that He would not offer Himself repeatedly, as the Levitical priest entered into the holy place every year.

Pighius says that Christ indeed does not offer Himself repeatedly, but that this does not hinder His being offered repeatedly by the priests. But Heb. 9:12, 28 not only says that Christ offered Himself once only, and not oftener, but in the same place it is also written: "Christ was offered once to take away the sins of many." Likewise Heb. 10:18 says in general: "Where there is forgiveness of sins, there is no longer any offering for sin." Yes, the apostle declares that it is a testimony to infirmity, weakness, and imperfection when the same sacrifice is offered for sins repeatedly and by many priests. And he sets down this contrast between the Levitical priesthood and that of Christ: In the former there were many priests and frequent repetitions of one and the same sacrifice, which was a sign that sins were not taken away by those sacrifices. However, Christ is the one and only eternal priest of the New Testament, who with one sacrifice offered for sins procured an eternal redemption and complete remission of sins. Scripture, by means of the same statement a number of times repeated, clearly shows what an abomination the papalist Mass is and how it insults the sacrifice of Christ.

But they say: Granted, that Christ by one offering perfectly earned redemption and remission of sins; nevertheless, in order that we may be saved through it, it is necessary that it be applied and accepted. This I grant; but Scripture does not say that the application of the one offering of Christ is accomplished through a new and repeated offering for sins, but shows other means, instituted by the Son of God Himself, namely, that it is applied through the Word and the sacraments and accepted by faith. Many attempt to escape the clarity of the testimonies of the Epistle to the Hebrews by means of this distinction, that Christ by one bloody sacrifice offered Himself once, and that He neither can nor should be offered more often in this manner; but that by an unbloody sacrifice He must indeed be offered for sins repeatedly and daily by the priests. But the Epistle to the Hebrews speaks generally without any distinction or exception whatever: "He was offered once for sins." "He has no need to be offered daily for sins." "Where there is forgiveness of sins, there is no further offering for sin." And the text in Heb. 9 clearly sets down these three things about offering for sins: 1. Without the shedding of blood there is no remission; 2. If Christ were offered repeatedly, it would be necessary for Him to suffer repeatedly; 3. Death had to intervene in order that those who are called may receive the promise of the eternal inheritance through the offering for sins.

Therefore Scripture does not grant that Christ is to be offered repeatedly for sins, whether it be done by a bloody or an unbloody offering. Indeed, when the fathers speak of an unbloody sacrifice, they understand spiritual sacrifices. Now let these statements be applied to the papalist Mass! The offering of Christ for sin does not take place without the shedding of blood; but it is necessary that He should suffer, death intervening, when He is made an offering for sin (Heb. 9). Therefore the papalists, who imagine that in the Mass Christ is again offered for sins, crucify and kill Him again, so far as they are concerned. "Christ being raised from the dead will never die again; death no longer has dominion over Him" (Rom. 6:9). But there are those who "crucify the Son of God on their own account and hold Him up to contempt" (Heb. 6:6). Such and so dreadful is the abomination of the papalist Mass.

V. The papalist Mass militates against the eternal priesthood of Christ. For no one is able to offer Christ for sins save only Christ Himself. Heb. 5:4: "No one takes this honor upon himself," etc. Heb. 9:14: "Through the Holy Spirit He offered Himself to God." Moreover, the apostle declares that the sacrifice for sins in the New Testament belongs to the one and only priesthood of Christ, and that not in such a way that it is repeatedly offered by many priests who succeed one another, but because He Himself offered Himself once to God.

However, the papalist Mass militates against the eternal priesthood of Christ also for another reason. For Christ is our High Priest and Savior not only by reason of His merit but also by virtue of His power. In Heb. 7:25 His eternal priesthood is described thus: "He is able for all time to save those who draw near to God through Him, since He always lives to make intercession for us." Heb. 9:24: He "entered . . . into heaven itself, now to appear in the presence of God on our behalf." Likewise [Heb. 9:15]: "He is the Mediator of a new covenant, so that those who are called may receive the promised inheritance, since a death has occurred." Heb. 10:14: "By a single offering He has perfected for all time those who are sanctified." Likewise [Heb. 10:21-22]: "Since we have a great priest over the house of God, let us have complete confidence to draw near with a true heart," etc. Heb. 4:14, 16: "Since then we have a great high priest who has passed through the heavens . . . let us . . . with confidence draw near to the throne of grace, that we may obtain mercy and find grace to help," etc.

Let these things, which according to the testimony of Scripture belong to the eternal priesthood of Christ, be brought together under one head; then, by way of contrast, let it be considered that the papalist Mass takes all these things away from the priesthood of Christ and transfers them to itself. For that Christ may appear in the presence of God for us, that coming to God through Him we may be saved, that we may be sanctified, that we may receive the promise of the inheritance, that we may have access to God, that we may receive mercy and find grace — for all this the papalists say the priest interposes himself as mediator between God and us with his theatrical representation, and that through it Christ is made to stand in the presence of the Father in order that we may, through this action of the priest, approach God, find grace, and receive mercy.

Scripture, however, teaches that these things must be sought by faith in the eternal priesthood of Christ, at the right hand of God, through the means of the Word and the sacraments, which have been instituted for this by the Son Himself. It is manifest, therefore, that the papalist Mass drives Christ out of His eternal priesthood and puts in His place the most unreliable priests, in order that we may trust that through their representation we will receive the things which belong solely to the priesthood of Christ.

VI. The papalist Mass obscures and overturns the means which the Son of God Himself instituted and ordained in order that through them the merit, power, and efficacy of His death and passion might be applied and accepted for the remission of sins and eternal salvation. For just as a sure and sufficient merit of salvation has been ordained by God, namely, the sacrifice of Christ, so, because an application of His merit must be made, the Son of God instituted and ordained certain means for this purpose, namely, the means of Word and sacrament. And He ordained them in this way because through them He Himself in His ministry as eternal priest wants to be efficacious, to set before us, offer, convey, give, apply, and seal His merits for life and eternal salvation. Moreover, He wants these things to be accepted by us by faith, which faith He works in us through His power and confirms through Word and sacrament, that in this way the praise and glory for our reconciliation and salvation may be wholly given to Christ, our only high priest.

But the papalist Mass takes away this glory from Christ and transfers it to the action of the priest, who, as they imagine, is able to apply the merits of the passion of Christ to whomever he wills. Thus, while Christ wants His merits, which are offered and conveyed to us in Word and sacrament, to be accepted by us in faith as free gifts, the papalist Mass makes a sacrifice of the sacrament, that is, it changes the action of God into our work, and of gratuitous acceptance it makes a meritorious and achievable work. For a sacrifice, according to Augustine, *Contra adversarium legis et prophetarum,* Bk. 1, and *De civitate Dei,* Bk. 10, is a work which we offer, render, and dedicate to God in order that we may dwell in Him in holy fellowship. A sacrament, however, is a holy sign through which God freely offers, conveys, applies, and seals His gratuitous benefits to us. It is therefore an extraordinary perversion of the Lord's Supper to make a sacrifice out of a sacrament, in the way the papalists speak of the sacrifice of their Mass, namely, that the representatory action of the priest procures for us the application of the benefits of Christ and that anyone who causes a Mass to be celebrated in his behalf by this work procures grace and whatever other things are ascribed to the Mass. Paul says, Rom. 3: "The Father put forward His Son (namely, in the Word and the sacraments) as an expiation by His blood, to be received by faith." Heb. 9:24: "Christ has placed Himself . . . into the presence of God in our behalf." All these things the papalist Mass transfers to the work of the priest.

In addition there is this perversion, that whereas Christ instituted the use of His Supper for all who receive it, who take, eat, and drink, the papalist Mass transfers the use and benefit of the celebration of the Lord's Supper in our time to the onlookers, who do not communicate, yes, to those who are absent, and even to the dead.

I merely note down the chief arguments which have been explained more at length by others. From them one can judge how horrendous is the abomination and idol-mania of the papalist Mass.

SECTION II

Concerning Masses in Honor of the Saints

Chapter III

And although the Church has at times been accustomed to celebrate some Masses in honor and in memory of the saints, it nevertheless does not teach that a sacrifice is being offered to them, but to God alone, who has crowned them. Therefore the priest does not say: "I offer a sacrifice to you, Peter or Paul," but, giving thanks to God for their victories, he implores their aid, that they, whose memory we observe on earth, should deign to intercede for us in heaven.

CANON V

If anyone says that it is a fraud to celebrate Masses in honor of saints and to obtain their intercession with God, as the Church intends, let him be anathema!

Examination

1 The examination of this chapter and canon is neither difficult nor dark. For the 10th article, dealing with the Mass, which was laid before the theologians at the Council of Trent for their examination, asks: Is it a misuse to bestow certain Masses on certain saints? And the third chapter says that Masses are celebrated in honor of the saints in order in this way to implore their protection. The canon of the Mass interprets this to the effect that God grants to the merits and prayers of the saints that we are defended in all things by the aid of divine protection. The question is therefore whether the most holy Lord's Supper was instituted for this, that by its celebration, administration, and use the pleas of the saints should be implored and procured, so that in all things in which we have need of the help of divine protection God grants it on account of the merits and prayers of the saints.

2 Surely, this wicked profanation of the Lord's Supper militates directly against its institution, and that not only visibly but even palpably. For Christ says: Do this, not in remembrance of the saints, but of Me. And in the use of the Lord's Supper He gives us His body and blood in order that, when we approach the throne of grace, we may obtain mercy and find grace in timely help, may lay hold of and in faith set before God

the merits of the one offering of Christ, and His intercession, because He appears before the face of God in our behalf, forever living that He may make intercession for us, that He may save eternally those who through Him come to God. (Heb. 4; 7; 9)

On these merits and this intercession we should rely; on account of these merits and this intercession we can entreat and believe that we will be defended in all things by the aid of divine protection. And in order that we may be certain that our prayers are heard and granted, the Son of God Himself unites Himself to us in the use of the Supper by communicating to us His body and blood. Surely, these things are very clear from the teaching of the Word of God about the use of the Lord's Supper, and full of sweet and needed comfort.

3 The papalists, however, not only use and defend the invocation of the saints apart from the Mass, but compel also the most holy Supper of the Lord to serve this wickedness, namely, that by means of the very action of the Lord's Supper this is sought, that the saints should interpose their merits and prayers between our unworthiness[26] and God in such a way that the fact that we are in all things shielded by the help of divine protection is credited to their merits and prayers. And to those Masses about the saints, which they call votive Masses, they ascribe extraordinary effects and much greater privileges than to other, plain Masses. Surely, this not only joins other mediators to Christ, through whose merits and prayers we come to God in order to find mercy and grace for help, but it simply amounts to thrusting Christ out from the right hand of God. For Scripture declares that He sits there forever, in order to appear before the face of God in our behalf and plead for us with His merits and intercession, that we may approach God through His merit and intercession, obtain mercy, find grace for timely help, and be saved. These things the papalists ascribe to the saints in such a way that they imagine that they therefore celebrate Masses in honor of the saints that by the action of the Lord's Supper the protection of the saints may be implored and obtained, so that on account of their merits and intercessions God grants that we obtain mercy and find grace for help. Surely, this is a wicked and dreadful profanation of the Lord's Supper.

4 Who would not have thought that at the Council of Trent this palpable wickedness would, if not entirely corrected, at least have been somehow mitigated? Some patrons of the papalist kingdom tried to do this. The *Antididagma* of Cologne tries to escape from the statement of

---

[26] The text of 1574 has *dignitatem.* Ed. Preuss has corrected this to *indignitatem,* for which the context clearly calls.

Augustine, *De civitate Dei,* Bk. 22, ch. 10, where he says that in the administration of the Lord's Supper the saints are indeed named but that they are by no means invoked, in this way, that it is permitted to invoke the saints apart from the Mass but not in the very action of the Lord's Supper. But the Council of Trent, pondering what is written in Rev. 17:4-5, that the Babylonian harlot, clothed (namely, in the Mass) with purple and scarlet, gold and pearls, should bear on her forehead the inscription that she is the mother of fornications and abominations on earth, therefore brazenly professes without dissimulation that Masses about the saints are celebrated for this, that through the very action of the Lord's Supper the protection of the saints might be implored. And Canon 5 says that Masses are celebrated in honor of the saints in order to obtain their intercession with God, namely, in the manner to which the canon of the Mass and the collects concerning the saints bear witness.

5 By no show of right can anything be brought forward from the teaching of Scripture about the Lord's Supper in defense of this godless profanation. They try to excuse and defend this wickedness only by the examples of certain of the ancients. But they do a great and serious injustice to the genuine and purer antiquity, as we shall show briefly.

6 It is clear from the histories of antiquity that, when in the great persecutions of the primitive church many daily became martyrs because they confessed the Christian faith, the church solemnly celebrated the memories of these martyrs annually; indeed, in those places where the bodies of the martyrs were buried, they customarily held public assemblies of the church; there the Word of God was discussed; there the administration of the Supper was celebrated, as Paul says (1 Cor. 15:29) that the administration of Baptism was celebrated over[27] the dead. And indeed, at the assembly of the congregation, before the consecration of the bread and wine, the names and struggles of the martyrs were publicly recited according to order and place. As time went on, the bodies of martyrs were even placed under the tables or altars on which the Lord's Supper was celebrated. This was done most of all during the time of Ambrose and Augustine, as Ambrose testifies, Bk. 10, Letter No. 85. These things we know for sure from the history of antiquity. Now, indeed, the papalists falsely add: Therefore antiquity celebrated Masses about the saints in order that, by the action of the Lord's Supper, they might implore the protection of the saints, so that, on account of their merits and prayers, they might obtain mercy and find grace and help.

---

[27] Chemnitz evidently understands this passage as referring to Baptisms performed at the graves of martyrs.

7 But the ancients themselves not only explain expressly how, why, to what end, and with what understanding and intention they were doing this, but also, when the things done in memory of the martyrs were wrongly understood by many, they clearly rejected the very things the papalists now ascribe to Masses about the saints. In Eusebius, Bk. 4, ch. 15, there is a letter of the church at Smyrna which tells that at the place where the bones of Polycarp were buried the godly were accustomed to gather, that is, to hold public meetings of the church, most of all on the day of his suffering. But hear how the enemies interpreted what was then customary in the church! For the letter from Smyrna reports that the Jews advised the governor not to deliver the body of Polycarp to the Christians for burial, for it would come to pass that they would forsake the Crucified One and begin to worship the martyr. But how do the Christians worship the crucified Christ? Surely, they do it in the way the Epistle to the Hebrews describes the eternal priesthood of Christ, namely that, having been crucified for our sins, He now appears in the presence of God in our behalf, through the merit of His one offering, and through His intercession pleads for us with God, in order that, coming to God through Him, we may obtain mercy, find grace for help, and be saved. (Heb. 7:23-27; 9:11-14, 24-28)

The Jews thought that when the Christians held their assemblies for the Lord's Supper on the graves, they were showing honor and worship to the martyrs with this intention and to this end. But the Christians answer: "The poor men do not know that we can never forsake Christ, who underwent death for the salvation of the whole world, nor worship any other." But with what intention and to what end did they hold their assemblies for the Lord's Supper on the tombs of the martyrs? The letter from Smyrna answers: "For a remembrance of those who in former time contended for Christ, *kai eis toon mellontoon askeesin kai hetoimasian,* which Rufinus translated not unfittingly: "That the minds of those who come after may be encouraged by notable examples to follow the way of those who went before."

Mention was, however, made of the martyrs also in the prayers of the church. But hear how the church at Smyrna explains also this: "We love the martyrs," it says, "on account of their unconquerable friendship for their King and Teacher, as disciples and imitators of the Lord, and we desire to become their partners." This [last clause] is expressed very meaningfully in Greek: *hoon genoito kai heemas sygkoinoonous genesthai.* For Paul says in the same way that the Philippians are his partners in grace. Rufinus interprets the relative pronoun *hoon* as referring to the faith, charity, and perseverance of the martyrs. Therefore the church prayed that it might finally become a partner and companion of the martyrs in eternal life and, having received similar powers from the bounty of God, might become a partaker of those moral perfections which it was celebrating in the martyrs.

This testimony of the ancient church about the remembrance of the martyrs about the year 160 should be diligently noted. For it shows both an explanation of the true meaning and a refutation of those things which were falsely ascribed to them with respect to the cult of the martyrs. In Dionysius the names of those who had fallen asleep in Christ are read out from tablets. But Dionysius states as the reason, that this was not done either to implore their protection, or on account of purgatory, but in order that those present might be called on to imitate them; that it might be proclaimed that they are now truly alive, having already been translated from death into a life truly divine; and that it might thus be signified that the dead in Christ are inscribed in the memory of God.

Julian[28] accused the Christians, according to Cyril, Bk. 6: "You reverence wretched men who have followed a hard and harsh law." Cyril answers: "We neither say that the martyrs are gods, nor are we accustomed to worship them, but we praise them with the highest honors because they have contended for the truth and have preserved purity of faith." And later he says that what they do is similar to what the very ancient Greeks did. Those who had fallen at Marathon were annually crowned with praises when people gathered at their graves. Let the reader note whence the custom of the annual remembrance of the martyrs, which has not the semblance of either an express testimony or example in Scripture, drew its origin!

The Manichaean Faustus accused Augustine, Bk. 20, ch. 21: "You have replaced the idols with the martyrs, whom you worship with similar votive offerings; you placate the shades of the dead with wine and sacrificial feasts." However, it is not unknown what the votive offerings of the Gentiles to their idols were. For Augustine describes these beliefs as follows, *De civitate Dei,* Bk. 8, ch. 20: That the demons[29] act as mediators between the gods and men, that as mediators with the gods they are necessary to men, ch. 23, and that they are treated to gifts, flattered with honors, accorded religious worship, ch. 17, in order that they may bring the prayers of men before the gods and bring back from there and deliver to men the concessions and requests they asked for, ch. 18. Those who could not be persuaded that the demons are gods were persuaded that

---

28 Julian the Apostate: Roman emperor 361-63.

29 In Greek mythology the demons were deities of lesser rank than the chief gods. They were not considered devils in the Christian sense.

they are go-betweens between the gods and men and that they procure benefits and are therefore not altogether unworthy of divine honor.

I have copied these things from Augustine in order that the discussion which I am undertaking may be the more correctly understood and that this fabrication of Apuleius[30] may the more easily be held side by side with the fictions of the papalists about the protection of the saints.

The question, therefore, is whether Augustine acknowledges, in the memorial feasts of the martyrs, the things Faustus throws up to him, namely, that the martyrs were worshiped by the Christians with devotions like those with which idols are worshiped by the Gentiles. Nothing could be farther from the truth. For in *De civitate Dei,* Bk. 8, ch. 27, he says: "We do not establish temples, priesthoods, sacred rites, and sacrifices for the martyrs." This, however, has been done and is still defended under the papacy. But why, with what intention, and to what end did the ancients celebrate the action of the Lord's Supper in connection with the memorial feasts of the martyrs? Augustine answers: "In order that we may by this celebration both give thanks to the true God for their victories and that we may incite ourselves by the renewal of their remembrance to imitate such crowns and victories." But were the saints invoked in order to obtain these? By no means, says Augustine, but the same God was called upon for help who made them both men and martyrs and joined them in heavenly honor with saints and angels. Nevertheless the names of the martyrs were recited at the Eucharistic assembly; was there therefore an invocation of them? Augustine answers, Bk. 22, ch. 10: "At the sacrifice of the Supper the names of the martyrs are named according to their place and order as men of God who overcame the world in their confession of Him; they are not, however, invoked by the priest who sacrifices." *Contra Faustum,* Bk. 20, ch. 21: "We offer to God at the memorial feasts of the martyrs in order that from the admonition of their locations a greater disposition of mind may arise to incite to love both toward those whom we can imitate and toward Him by whose help we are able to do it."

Up to this point Augustine correctly reports the judgment of antiquity in harmony with Scripture. But I do not deny that, as time went on, particularly in the age of Augustine, strange and corrupt opinions began to be attached to the memorial feasts of the martyrs. For because certain miracles occurred at the feasts of the martyrs, which without doubt God Himself performed for no other purpose than the one testified to in 2 Kings 13:20-21—that the doctrine in the confession of which the martyrs had sacrificed their life was true and divine, and that by these miracles

[30] Apuleius: pagan writer of the second century A.D.

men might be invited and strengthened to embrace and confess that doctrine—people who did not consider this began to dispute about special intercessions of the martyrs in behalf of those who worshiped them, and about the merits and works of the martyrs, as it is written in *De civitate Dei,* Bk. 8, ch. 27. Some carried banquets to the monuments of the martyrs and believed they would there be made holy through the merits of the martyrs. But Augustine says that this was not done by the better Christians and was tolerated in the weaker ones.

8 A beginning was also made at the time of Augustine to argue about the prayers, merits, works, and aid of the deceased martyrs on account of the miracles which occurred at the memorial feasts of the martyrs. But these things were left undecided at the time, as an opinion neither ancient nor certain. As he says, *De civitate Dei,* Bk. 22, ch. 10: "The martyrs do these things, or rather God does them while they plead or work together with Him, in order that faith may be strengthened by which we believe that they are not our gods but that they together with us have one God." And ch. 19:[31] "Whether God works these things Himself in His own person, or through His servants; whether He does some things also through the spirits of the martyrs, or whether He does all these things through angels, so that what is said to be done by the martyrs is only done by them through praying and pleading, not however worked by them; whether some things are done in one way, others in other ways—which can in no way be understood by mortals," etc. The same says about concern for the dead, ch. 16: "Whether the martyrs themselves are present whenever miracles are done at their memorial services; whether God Himself assists through the ministry of angels and hears the martyrs, who generally are praying — these things are beyond the reach of my understanding, and too abstruse for me to fathom." Thus Origen says, on Rom. 2: "Whether the saints who are with Christ do and perform anything for us like the angels, who perform services in the interest of our salvation, should be counted among the secret things of God, nor should mysteries be committed to paper." In this way these opinions first began to be discussed without vehement assertions.

9 In his dispute against Vigilantius, Jerome indeed asserted something more boldly concerning this question, but without genuine testimonies from Scripture and antiquity. Basil and Gregory of Nazianzus in their rhetorical speeches yielded more than a little. Augustine also began to ascribe something to these opinions, even though he left them in doubt. For instance, he says, *De civitate Dei,* Bk. 22, ch. 9, that the

---

[31] The reference should be to ch. 9, not 19.

martyrs are able to obtain such things from the Lord and that they have power in return for their patience. Likewise, *Contra Faustum,* Bk. 20, ch. 21: "The Christian people celebrate the memory of the martyrs with religious festivals both in order to incite to imitation and that they may share in their merits and be helped by their prayers." What he says about imitation he says in accord with the judgment of the ancients. The other, about sharing in their merits, is not the same thing which the papalists teach, that the merits of the saints are applied to others; but the fathers apply the term "merits" to the good works and moral perfections of the saints, to which God gives rewards. That therefore we may become companions of the saints in like moral perfections and in the crowns of these perfections — for this he says the celebration of the struggles and victories of the martyrs is useful, but only when the true God, who made them martyrs, is called to help and does help. For these are the words of Augustine.

What kind of association he has in mind can be gathered from his statement in *De civitate Dei,* 8, that God joined the martyrs with the angels in celestial honor. There he also says that we are to be joined to the merits of the martyrs, that is, to their moral perfections. The expression about being joined or associated clearly has the same meaning as the statement in the letter from the church at Smyrna, namely, that we should wish to become companions and associates of the martyrs.

The last thing in Augustine, about aid through prayers, arises from that opinion which Augustine left in doubt, as was stated above.

10 In most recent times the matter of the protection, merits, intercessions, help, aid, and benefits of the saints was forged into an article of faith. If anyone doubts it but the least bit, he is at once subjected to the anathema, as Canon V shows. And indeed (this is dreadful) the very action of the Lord's Supper is bent to support it. But it cannot be shown from Scripture that the Lord's Supper was instituted by Christ for this use; yes, it is a profanation, warring against the institution of the Supper, as has been shown above.

With respect to the examples and testimonies of antiquity we have shown above what the understanding of the most ancient and purer antiquity was and how afterward, with the passing of time, other opinions crept in, which were left undecided, or rather, in doubt, until finally, established under papalist rule, they developed into that profanation of the Lord's Supper which is now deplored by the complaints of all godly people. And although it would only be fair that these things should be brought back to their first sources, according to the counsel of Cyprian, and a channel brought from there to our times, as Augustine says, the

Tridentine fathers simply cut off all hope of emendation, establish Masses about the saints, binding them with the cords of superstitions, all under threat of the anathema.

However, there will be a special section about the invocation of the saints later. For the present it was necessary to note down a few things about the memorial feasts of the martyrs, showing for what reason the ancient church celebrated them. This third chapter alludes to these examples in a not obscure manner, although the papalist memorial feasts of the saints have nothing in common with the memorial feasts of the ancients. For these set forth and celebrated the struggles and victories of the martyrs by public preaching for imitation. The papalists, however, more truly dream with silent murmuring rather than celebrate the memory of the saints. And yet they ascribe to this sleepy viewing those things of which we have spoken above. These things were totally unknown to antiquity.

SECTION III
Concerning the Canon of the Mass

Chapter IV

Now since it is fitting that holy things should be administered in a holy manner, and since this sacrifice is of all things the most holy, the Catholic Church, in order that it may be worthily and reverently offered and received, many centuries ago instituted the sacred canon, so pure from every error that nothing is contained in it which is not in the highest degree redolent of a certain sanctity and piety and lifts up to God the minds of those who offer. For it is composed on the one hand from the very words of the Lord and on the other from the traditions of the apostles, as well as from the pious institutions of holy pontiffs.

CANON VI

If anyone says that the canon of the Mass contains errors and should therefore be abrogated, let him be anathema.

Examination

1 The power, yes, the substance and as it were the soul of the papalist sacrifice is the canon of the Mass. Therefore they labor much more for its retention than about the canon of Scripture itself, which they are not afraid to corrupt by mixing in other, noncanonical books. In order that the authority of this canon might be the greater with everybody, the opinion was spread abroad by the papalists that it is a tradition of Christ and of the apostles, even though this cannot be shown from Scripture. That is how Innocent answers, *De celebratione missarum*, ch. *Cum Marthae*. Eck cites from Isidor that the order of the Mass as it is now celebrated in the papalist church was first constituted in this way by St. Peter. The decree *De consecratione*, dist. 1, teaches that James, the brother of the Lord, first published the celebration of the Mass as it is now customary among the papalists. And this persuasion so bewitched certain among the scholastic writers that they argued that the words of institution should be read as they are set down in the canon of the Mass rather than as they are found written in the evangelists and in Paul.

2 At the time of Bessarion[32] there was a sharp dispute over the

---

[32] Bessarion, 1395-1472, patriarch of Constantinople.

statement: "For the consecration of the Eucharist the words of the canon are of equal necessity with the words of institution." And although there are many things in the canon over which many writers labored fruitlessly for a suitable interpretation, Critius[33] Polonus says that all explanations of the canon are improper; that no interpretation of the canon should be sought; but because it is a mystery handed down by Christ and the apostles, therefore it is not to be understood but adored. But first of all it is impossible by any reason or appearance of a reason to teach on the basis of Scripture that the canonical prayer which is customary for papalists was either used by Christ or handed down by the apostles. Moreover the papalist writers themselves, as we have shown above, teach openly that the apostles consecrated the wafer for the offering without the canon, by means of the words of institution, with only the Lord's Prayer.

3 There are available many testimonies of writers to the effect that this canon was put together bit by bit, or a part at a time, by Roman pontiffs and that it was scarcely finished in the first 600 years after the birth of Christ. Therefore the fourth Tridentine chapter does not dare simply to assert that the canon of the Mass was composed by Christ and the apostles, but says that the catholic church instituted it. However, lest it be thought to be only a human tradition, they at once add that the canon is established from the very words of the Lord, from the traditions of the apostles, and from the institutions of pontiffs. Therefore we shall separate out those things in the canon which come from Christ and the apostles, in order that it may be possible to know which those are which were instituted by pontiffs.

4 Now the words of institution of the Supper are the words of Christ. And, according to Gregory, it is apostolic tradition to recite the Lord's Prayer at the celebration of the Supper. Therefore with the exception of the words of institution and the Lord's Prayer, all the rest of the canon of the Mass is a human invention and a human composition, or, as the men of Trent say, the canon of the Mass is an institution of the Roman pontiffs.

5 But they add that this canon was instituted by the church many centuries ago; they do not, however, enumerate these so many centuries. It is however a fact, as we shall show later, that the composition of the canon which is now customary with the papalists did not exist in the church for 500 years and more after Christ.

6 Also about the author, or rather the patcher-together, there is not sufficient certainty. Some ascribe the composition of the canon to Dam-

---

asus, about A.D. 370, others to Leo, around A.D. 450, many to Gelasius, around the year 490, in order that a certain amount of authority may be borrowed from the Roman see. But Gregory, speaking of the composition of the canon, Bk. 7, Letter No. 63, would undoubtedly not have disregarded it if it had been some Roman pontiff but says: "Scholasticus composed that prayer." But neither Eusebius nor Jerome nor Sophronius make mention of this Scholasticus, yes, not even Gennadius,[34] who around the year 500 put together a catalog of ecclesiastical writers.

Therefore the patcher-together of the canon lived at the time of Gregory, around A.D. 590 or a little before. For at the time of Gregory the term "Scholasticus" was a proper name for many, as the philologists say. Thus a certain judge in Campania, Bk. 2, Letter No. 54, and a defender of the church, Bk. 9, Letter No. 14, have the name Scholasticus. And yet not even the composition of Scholasticus is wholly preserved in the papalist church. For it is known from the histories that Gregory later added certain clauses which are now read in the canon.

Therefore Innocent, disputing about the author, naming now Gelasius, now Scholasticus, finally says that the canon was composed neither by one author nor at one time, but piecemeal, by many authors and at various times. Thus the miserable body of the papalist canon, like a patchwork quilt, was sewed together by many authors and at various times. Alexander I , around A.D. 110, added in the canon: "Who on the day before He suffered." Siricius, about A.D. 380, ordained in the canon: "Those who communicate and venerate the memory." Leo I, around A.D. 450, instituted the part of the canon: "This offering therefore." Gregory the Great, around the year 590 added: "Our days in peace," etc., likewise: "Which offering," etc.

7 Therefore it is fog and nonsense what the Tridentine fathers say about the antiquity of the institution and composition of the canon. But they say by way of opposition that they are not primarily seeking by what author and at what time the canonical prayer was joined together in the form which is now common and customary, since it can be shown that it is taken and collected from Justin, Dionysius, Basil, Chrysostom, Augustine, and Ambrose, among whom both sentences and words of the canon can be read. But also this boast is vain and false. And it is useful to know the history of antiquity with respect to the prayers which were customary in the liturgies or in the celebration of the Lord's Supper. For from this many things can be judged when we compare on the one hand the papalist

---

[34] The text of 1574 has Gimodius. Nigrinus has Gennadius, a reading followed also by Ed. Preuss.

canon and on the other the freedom with which prayers of this kind have been rightly used in our churches according to the analogy of faith.

Justin says, *Apologia,* 2, that after the reading and interpretation of Scripture all rise for prayer and that, when the prayers are ended, bread and wine are brought to the overseer in order that he may begin the action of the Lord's Supper. And in this action he makes mention of praise and glorification through prayers, and of thanksgiving. When these are ended, the people assent, saying "Amen." "After the Communion," he says, "we admonish one another to love and fraternal union; we also give alms by which the needy are aided. And over that which is so offered we bless the Father, the Maker of all things, through the Son and the Holy Spirit."

In Irenaeus, Bk. 4, these offerings for the poor with thanksgiving for the gift precede the action of the Lord's Supper, "for from these gifts from the firstfruits of the fruits of the earth there is taken that which through the words of Christ receives the call to be the body and blood of Christ."

According to Dionysius, prayers and readings of the sacred books are made, and then the catechumens, the possessed, and the penitent are commanded to go out. After that the bread and the cup are brought forward and the sacred prayer is made. After this there follows the sacred Communion, which ends with the giving of thanks.

Augustine, Letter No. 59, to Paulinus, as he explains the words of Paul in 1 Tim. 2:1 about "supplications, prayers, intercessions, and giving of thanks," says that in the celebration of the sacraments prayers are made before that which is on the table of the Lord begins to be blest; thereafter prayers are made while it is blest, consecrated, and broken and prepared for distribution; that an interruption is made when the people are blessed before Communion; and after Communion, he says, everything is concluded with the giving of thanks.

Chrysostom says, Homily 18, on 2 Corinthians: "First, common prayers are made by the priest and the people. Second, when those have been excluded who cannot be present at the mysteries, another prayer is made. Third, peace is pronounced on those who are to be communed. Fourth, it all ends with the giving of thanks.

8 Therefore in the liturgies of the ancients: 1. Prayers were made before they began to bless what was on the table of the Lord; 2. They had certain prayers during the blessing, consecration, and preparation of the bread and cup of the Lord; 3. After the consecration but before Communion a blessing or peace was given to the people who were to communicate; 4. After Communion the whole action was concluded with the giving of thanks.

9 But now the question is what the subject and the substance of these prayers was, for this observation properly pertains to this controversy. This can be gathered quite clearly from the writings of the ancients.

10 The subject of the prayers which were made after the interpretation of Scripture, but before the blessing of the Eucharist, is explained very well by Chrysostom, on 1 Tim. 2, where he says that in the daily service of the offering of the sacraments supplications and giving of thanks are made by the church, not only for the faithful but also for the unbelievers, for kings and for all who are placed in high positions, that, defended by their protection, we may lead a quiet life in godliness and purity and that this would cause them to come to the knowledge of the truth. Likewise: "We give thanks to God for everything that turns out well—that He makes His sun to rise, that He sends rain on the just and on the unjust." Likewise: "We give thanks especially for those who are joined to us and for the benefits which have fallen and daily fall to us and to them, whether secretly or openly, whether happy or sad." The same, Homily 26, on Matthew: "The priest who assists at the altar commands us to give thanks to God for the whole world, for those who are absent, for those who are present, for those who have been before us, and for those who will be after us." Homily 18, on 2 Corinthians: "In the prayers one may see the people offering together with the priest for the possessed and for the penitents." Tertullian confirms this same thing in the *Apologeticus:* "We pray for the emperors, for their ministers, for the state of the world, for a quiet state of affairs, for the delay of the end," etc. Thus Ambrose writes, *De consecratione,* 2, ch. *Panis est:* "Through all the rest that is said in what goes before the consecration, praise is rendered to God, entreaty is made by prayer for the people, for kings, for all others." And the statement of Augustine, ch. *Utrum,* says: "Everything else the priest says before the consecration is nothing but praise and thanksgiving, or certainly the supplications and petitions of the faithful.

This, then, was the subject matter and the substance of the prayers before the consecration of the Eucharist. Here belong also the prayers with which the Father is blessed through the Son and the Holy Spirit for the gifts offered by the faithful, as Justin says, and they pray that God would be pleased to accept these gifts of His people, sanctify and bless them, as many so-called secret prayers testify.

11 Justin describes the subject matter of the sacred prayer, as Dionysius calls it, in the blessing and preparation of the Eucharist as follows:

"As he receives the bread and wine, the leader give praise and glory to the Father in the name of the Son and the Holy Spirit and offers a long thanksgiving for the fact that Christ judged and made us worthy to institute these mysteries for us." For this is the meaning of Justin's words: *hyper tou kateexioosthai toutoon par' autou* ["for deeming us worthy of these things from Him"].

Dionysius describes the contents of the sacred prayer in the consecration of the sacrament thus: "Standing at the altar, the priest proclaims the divine works of Jesus for the salvation of the human race, which He accomplished according to Scripture by the good pleasure of the Father in the Holy Spirit. After that he goes on to the administration of the sacrament. First he excuses himself by an apology for daring to approach the sacred administration of these things, and cries out: 'You have said, Do this in remembrance of Me!' Then he asks that he may be made fit to perform this sacred administration by which he must imitate Christ, who is God. For he calls this a service in imitation of God, that he is able to distribute in a holy manner and that those who will partake will partake in a manner becoming to saints." There the fathers preached much about the use and benefit of communing at the Lord's Supper, because there the sacrifice which is the satisfaction for our sins and the price of our redemption is dispensed to those who take it.

Cyril says that the incarnation, death, resurrection, and ascension of Christ is proclaimed. A beautiful formula of this is found in the liturgy of Basil. And what kind of thanksgiving was rendered there about the mystery of redemption Chrysostom shows, Homily 16, on Matthew. In this sacred prayer the chief thing was the recitation of the words of institution, as Ambrose testifies, *De sacramentis,* Bk. 4. And this prayer, Augustine says, to Paulinus, practically the whole church concludes with the Lord's Prayer.

Moreover, in that sacred prayer there was also offered to God our solemn promise in which we vow to God that we will remain in Christ and in union with the body of Christ; for we, being many, are one body in Christ. And so, to signify the communion of saints, the names of the patriarchs, prophets, apostles, martyrs, saints, and of those who had fallen asleep in Jesus were recited, as we have explained in the preceding chapter.

To this prayer belong also the blessing and the peace given to those who are about to communicate, namely, in order that they may be fit for the sacred mysteries of Christ and be able to communicate worthily. Augustine says: "The priests, then, as advocates, present those whom they have received to the most merciful Supreme Monarch."

It is certain from the descriptions found among the ancients that this was the content and the subject matter of the sacred prayer when what was on the Lord's table was blessed, consecrated, and prepared and broken for distribution. That these prayers were common to the people and the priest Chrysostom testifies, Homily 18, on 2 Corinthians. "When these things had been done, and this great sacrament had been partaken of," says Augustine, "the thanksgiving concluded the whole." The content of this was, as Thomas noted, that the people rejoiced over receiving the sacrament, and the priest offered thanks to God through the prayer. This had its origin in the fact that Christ also sang a hymn after He had given Communion to the disciples, as Chrysostom writes, Homily 83, on Matthew.

12 Until now we have shown what was the order, what the content, and what the subject matter of the sacred prayers in the liturgies of the ancients. This observation will be useful later, when we examine the papalist canon. However, one certain form for these prayers, with fixed words, to which all churches were bound under peril of mortal sin was not prescribed, but there was freedom to use any form so long as it agreed with the faith. Thus at the time of Augustine, in the African Council, ch. 70, and in the Council of Mileve, ch. 22, it is stated about the prayers or discourses at the Mass that they should first be referred to the more prudent ones and that nothing should be said except the things treated by the more prudent or approved at a synod, lest by chance something should be composed against the faith. Thus the Greeks had one form for such prayers in the church of Dionysius, another in the church of Basil, and yet another in the church of Chrysostom. Among the Latins Ambrose had one form, Isidor another, Gregory still another. And yet, when Augustine[35] wanted to lay a question before Gregory, because one custom at Mass was held in the Roman church, another in the Gallican churches, Gregory did not want all churches bound to his form of prayers but answered: "In whatsoever church you find what is able to please God more, choose it diligently." Therefore that they want to compel the churches to recite the papalist canon as something necessary, as though the consecration and Communion of the Eucharist could not be done without this canon, is done outside of and contrary to the opinion of antiquity. And our churches are unjustly condemned because in the celebration of the Lord's Supper they, as did the ancients, freely use prayer formulas which are in harmony with the faith and because they accord

---

[35] Not the great African church father, but the British monk Augustine, d. 604. He was a contemporary of Pope Gregory the Great, who also died in 604.

with the nature of our times and make for the edification of the church, in which nevertheless the essential things are comprehended which were customary in the prayers of the ancients.

13 But to return to the canon of the papalists. It is false what they say, that its words and meaning are found in Justin, Dionysius, and in Augustine, to Paulinus. But they say: Many things in the Latin canon are found in the Mass of Basil and of Chrysostom. But even as I do not deny that Basil and Chrysostom composed some form of such prayers for their churches, so I nevertheless assert that it cannot be proved that those Masses which are now circulated under the names of Basil and Chrysostom were written by these authors in the way we now have them, for there is a great and very dissimilar variety of examples. Thus in the Mass of Basil the ancient translation agrees neither with the Greek copy nor with the new version; and the liturgy which the Syrians use under the name of Basil agrees with neither the ancient nor the new translation. So also in the Mass of Chrysostom there is a great difference among the copies of Leo the Tuscan, Erasmus, and Pelargus, who says that his copy does not agree in everything with the copy of the Tuscan nor with that of Erasmus, and adds that he had seen another copy in the Rota at Rome which differed from all these. Therefore not all things which we now read under the names of Basil and Chrysostom in their liturgies are genuine, pure, and certain, but many things in them have been varied, changed, and patched on, which can very easily be gathered from the fact that there, in the commemoration of the saints, also the names of Basil and Chrysostom are read, which without doubt was not written thus by the authors themselves. Therefore the great matter about which we are treating in this controversy neither can nor should be decided on the basis of what is itself doubtful and uncertain. Ambrose, on 1 Tim. 2, calls it a churchly rule, which he says our priests use, that they make supplication for all. What kind of supplication this was we have shown from Augustine and Chrysostom. In the book *De sacramentis*, 4, chs. 5 and 6, some words are found which we now read in the Latin canon. But it is not certain that these books are by Ambrose, and the words are there used in another sense, which the papalist canon applies to its propitiatory sacrifice, as we shall presently show.

I have mentioned these things in order to show that it is a vain boast which they make about the antiquity, authority, and certainty of the papalist canon. For it does not follow: The ancients were accustomed to using certain specific prayers in their liturgies; therefore this was the same form of prayers which is now found in the papalist canon. Or: Certain words of the canon are found among the ancients; therefore the whole papalist canon, as it is now found, has the most ancient fathers as authors. What need is there to say more? The papalist writers themselves note, not which sentences of the canon were taken from which fathers, but by which Roman pontiffs they were invented and instituted. Moreover, the Tridentine chapter says that, with the exception of the words of institution and the Lord's Prayer, the canon consists of arrangements of pontiffs. I judge that this was put into the Tridentine decree in order to show that they do not approve of the arguments which contend that the canon of the Mass was not written and put together by Roman pontiffs but from the writings of the fathers.

14 But let us grant this, that certain small parts of the papalist canon have kinship with the canon of either Basil or Chrysostom or Ambrose or Augustine. One cannot at once conclude from this that the whole system of the papalist canon is for that reason godly and salutary. For many other things have been patched on which, although they have affinity with the prayers of the ancients, have been transformed into what is clearly a different sense and use, as we shall presently show, so that the miserable composition of the papalist canon has been patched together out of what is entirely corrupt, and of many things which have been corrupted. Therefore when you hear some papalist vociferate: "Why should not our whole canon be godly and salutary, when certain of its sentences are read almost word for word in certain of the fathers?" let there be opposed to him the elegant simile of Irenaeus, which he uses, Bk. 1, ch. 1, against those who picked out certain statements of Scripture and fitted them to their fabrications, lest they should seem to be without any witness. For he says it is the same as if someone took apart the picture of a king constructed of precious gems by a skillful workman and put the materials together in a different way, so that it became the picture of a dog or fox, and would afterward boast that it was a beautiful picture of the king because the material was the same; or, if those who sew together a patchwork of various verses of Homer wanted to boast that it was a divine poem of Homer.

Now, because the Tridentine chapter judges that the canon of the Mass is so completely free from any error that they pronounce the anathema on anyone who says it contains errors, we shall not indeed undertake a long treatment but shall briefly and in an orderly way recount the chief points and set forth in a table as it were the errors and corruptions the papalist canon contains, showing by contrast how the things which were used in a godly manner in the prayers of the ancients are now transformed in an ungodly manner in the canon into a repeated sacrifice of Christ for sins.

I. In old time the following prayer was spoken over the gifts of the faithful which they offered at the altar for the poor, as we have shown above: "We offer our supplications that You would regard as acceptable and would bless these gifts, these presents, these sacrifices." Now that this custom has fallen and been done away with, these words are applied to the theatrical sacrifice of the papalist Mass, a description of which, taken from Eck, is found above. Moreover the canon says that it is offered to God for the church even before the consecration, and promises that through this it will come to pass that God will govern His church, grant it peace, and guard it. All this they ascribe to the exhibition of mere, simple bread, because these things are said long before the consecration. So many monstrous abominations are contained in the very beginning of the canon as it is now used by the papalists.

II. With respect to what follows in the canon: "We offer to you this sacrifice of praise for the redemption of our souls, for the hope of salvation," it is plain from the words themselves that these words were in ancient time spoken of the spiritual sacrifices of praise, glorification, and thanksgiving. For as we showed earlier from Dionysius and Chrysostom, in the liturgy giving of thanks was observed for the benefit of the redemption performed for us by Christ, by which we have hope of salvation. And this observance can in harmony with Scripture rightly be called a sacrifice of praise for the salvation of souls brought about by Christ on the cross.

Having buried this sacrifice of praise through use of an alien language and through secret murmuring, the papalists accomodate these words to the theatrical representation of the priest, which they say is done for the redemption of souls, not the redemption accomplished on the cross, but one which must be brought about and obtained through this representation. Let the reader observe how wickedly the words are being perverted. The sacrifice of praise for the redemption of souls earned and effected through the cross of Christ is bent to the representation of the priest for procuring and meriting the redemption of souls.

III. Ps. 116:12-14 says that because we are not able to render God thanks for His benefits, His benefits are to be celebrated with thanksgiving—and that these are the vows which are to be paid to God in the presence of all His people.

This statement about paying our vows was formerly quite properly applied to the public and solemn celebration of the benefits of Christ which was customary in the liturgies. But now that this public celebration has ceased, the canon refers the paying of vows to votive Masses, namely, when someone pays a certain sum and causes such a theatrical representation to be celebrated for him and his, then, they say, this word of the psalm is fulfilled: "I will pay my vows to the Lord in the presence of all His people."

IV. We have shown in a previous chapter how among the ancients the memory of the martyrs was celebrated with public preaching about their struggles and victories, and for what purpose this was done. Through their silence in the canon the papalists do not celebrate the memory but venerate it, and to this silent remembrance and naming they ascribe the things which follow in the canon.

V. In the most ancient church no invocation was connected with the recitation of the names of the saints, as is evident from Dionysius and from the epistle of the church at Smyrna. Later, about the times of Augustine, men began to discuss the opinion that we are aided by the prayers of the martyrs. But these private opinions were then not yet inserted into the public prayers of the liturgy. For Augustine says, *De civitate Dei,* Bk. 22, ch. 10: "At which sacrifice the martyrs, as men of God, are named according to their place and order; they are not, however, invoked by the priest who sacrifices."

The papalist canon, however, seeking the grace of God, sets before God both the merits and the prayers of the saints in the very action of the Lord's Supper— in such a way that it gives rise to the hope that God will grant to the merits and prayers of the saints that in every situation we may be defended by the aid of divine protection. And for the sake of honor (as the saying is) there is added, "through Christ," etc., as though believers could not find help with God through Christ unless God grants this to the merits and prayers of the saints. Surely, this militates directly against the statements of Scripture (Heb. 4:16; 7:19; 10:22) where we are taught to draw near to God and to the throne of grace through Christ in order that we may receive mercy and find grace for help. Augustine also says: "The saints of God are indeed named at the altar, but they are not invoked by the priest." Therefore the papalist canon in this part conflicts both with Scripture and with the opinion of antiquity. For although that prayer of the canon is not directed to the saints but to God, it is nevertheless a very real invocation of the saints. For to pray the Father in the name of Christ, setting before Him Christ's merit and intercession, is to invoke Christ; therefore it is an invocation of the saints when I pray that God would grant to the merits and prayers of the saints that in every situation we may be defended with the aid of His protection. What a dreadful abomination it is, in the very celebration of the Lord's Supper to set before God the merits and prayers of the saints, that for their sake we may find grace for help, we have stated in the examination of the third chapter.

Let the reader observe out of what diverse patches the papalist canon has been pieced together and how, as time went on, wicked opinions were patched on to the prayers of the ancients. For in the second mention of the saints the words of the canon are very beautiful: "Deign to grant also to us sinners, Thy servants, who hope in the greatness of Thy compassion, some share and fellowship with Thy saints; we pray Thee to admit us to their company, not by appraising our merits but by granting forgiveness through Christ our Lord." This was without doubt the formula of the ancient commemoration of the saints, and it agrees beautifully with what the Smyrnian epistle relates concerning the memorial feast of the martyrs. But later a contrary fabrication was patched on: "To whose merits and prayers you will grant," etc. This recent patch was placed into the earlier part of the canon. The ancient commemoration of the saints, however, was placed after the beginning, into the last part. This consideration teaches and clarifies much.

VI. At the celebration of the Eucharist the ancient church offered prayers to God for obtaining temporal and eternal benefits through Christ. To this sacrifice of prayers these words could aptly be applied: "Graciously receive this offering, and order our days in Your peace, and command that we be saved from eternal damnation." The papalist canon, however, transfers these things to the farcical representation by the priest of the not-yet-consecrated bread and prays that God would receive it in such a way that on its account He would order our days in peace and save us from damnation.

VII. "Deign to render this offering blessed, ascribed to us, approved, reasonable, acceptable." Of this bit of the canon in particular the papalists boast, for it is found in Ambrose, *De sacramentis,* Bk. 4, ch. 5. And in *De consecratione,* dist. 2, ch. *Utrum,* it is ascribed to Augustine. But let a comparison be made to see what meaning these words have with the fathers, and the purpose to which the papalist priests bend them! Augustine says that the priest prays that by the Word of the Creator and the power of the Holy Spirit the bread and wine may become the body and blood of Christ. Moreover, he clearly interprets it of receiving, when he says: "Because we have received the likeness of the death of Christ in Baptism, let us take on also the likeness of His flesh and blood." Therefore he calls the crucified body and the shed blood of Christ, when we take it in the sacrament, a blessed sacrifice, through which we are blessed; ascribed, through which we are inscribed in heaven; approved, through which we are judged to be of the members of Christ; acceptable, as persons displeasing to ourselves but acceptable to God through this sacrifice. So understood, the ancients did not pray badly, because bread and wine cannot bring it about that they become for us the body and blood of Christ. For when we take this sacrificial victim, it is for us blessed, approved, acceptable. Also the very context of the canon seems to intend this, for it adds the interpretation: "That it may become for us the body and blood of Christ." Also the word "offering" is not there taken for the action but for the bread and wine which had been offered by the people. For the preparatory prayer, which bears the name of Ambrose, says: "May the Holy Spirit make this our offering to be the body and blood of Christ." The papalist priests, however, fit all these things to their pantomimic representation, and interpret that this is the sacrifice which is ascribed to us, through which we are inscribed in heaven; acceptable, through which we are acceptable to God; approved, through which our reconciliation with God is approved. It is clear how far these things are removed from the meaning of the ancients, and of what nature they are.

VIII. Earlier when we treated the consecration, we spoke of how the words of institution are changed in the canon. What follows after the words of institution: "Wherefore, mindful of the passion, resurrection," etc., was without doubt taken from the ancients. But mark the degeneration! Cyril says it was proclamation. Dionysius uses the word "to sing praise." But the papalist canon guards it by a law that it should be murmured in such a way that no one may hear it clearly.

IX. In ancient time a part of the gifts and presents offered by the people was taken and consecrated with the word of Christ, that it might become the Eucharist of the body and blood of the Lord, and this taking and consecration was called a sacrifice. Now, since this custom is no longer observed, the words are transferred to the representation of the priest.

X. After the consecration the priest prays over the body and blood of Christ that God would deign to deem them acceptable, like Abel's dumb sheep and Melchizedek's offering of bread and wine. That certainly is an unworthy and dreadful comparison. Therefore the expositors of the canon torment themselves that they may somehow mitigate and remove the absurdity. But the patches in the canon have been transposed. For in the liturgy of Basil, when the gifts of the people have been gathered and arranged by the presbyters, then the priest prays that God may find this unbloody offering acceptable, even as he received the gifts of Abel, the sacrifice of Noah, the burnt offering of Abraham, etc. For the collect which is read on the seventh Sunday after Pentecost prays thus: "Bless the gifts of the people with an equal blessing as the gifts of Abel." In the patchwork of the canon these words, now placed after the consecration, are prayed over the very body and blood of Christ. Nevertheless they judge that the canon contains nothing erroneous or absurd.

XI. After the consecration the priest prays over the body and blood of Christ: "Command that these things be carried by the hand of a holy angel to Thy altar on high, in view of Thy majesty." The apostle says[36] to the Hebrews that Christ entered into heaven itself, now to appear before God on our behalf. And the priest (which is dreadful) prays that He may first be carried there by the hand of an angel. What meaning these things had in ancient times we can gather from Irenaeus, who says about the gifts with which we have compassion on the poor, Bk. 4, ch. 14: "There is an altar in heaven; there our prayers and our offerings are directed." And the ministry of the angels is described in the speeches in Rev. 5 and Tobit 12. This little part, misplaced in the patchwork of the canon, gave rise to this absurd and ungodly opinion. The statement of Augustine, *De consecratione*, 2, ch. *Utrum*, shows that these words were customarily spoken before the consecration. He himself interprets them of the consecration of the bread in order that it may become the body of Christ.

XII. In various places there are found certain examples of the remembrance of the dead in Christ on the part of the ancients. But Dionysius says that this remembrance was observed in order that men might imitate them and that it might be a witness that the dead are living with God. Out of this remembrance prayers and discourses were afterward made by which the souls of the dead were commended to God. Indeed, the papalist canon teaches that the work of representation in the Mass is a propitiatory sacrifice for sin, penalties, and satisfactions, which may be applied to the dead in purgatory for their liberation. Thus the practices of the ancients gradually degenerated until finally the use of the Lord's Supper, which was instituted for the living, that they may eat, drink, and proclaim the death of the Lord, was transferred to the dead after the manner of a sacrifice. But about purgatory and what belongs with it there will be a special section later.

XIII. Formerly also these words were spoken along with other prayers over the gifts of the faithful: "Through Christ, through whom You always create all these good things for us, hallow, bless, and grant them to us; through Him be to Thee, God the Father, all honor and praise in the unity of the Holy Spirit." This agrees perfectly with what Justin says, namely, that God is blessed over the alms of the faithful in the name of the Son and of the Holy Spirit, and with what Paul says, that the

---

[36] The text of 1574 strangely says: *Non dicit.* Both Nigrinus and Ed. Preuss have removed the *non*, which the context does not tolerate.

creatures are sanctified through the Word of God and prayer. At a later time the rhapsody of the canon, which follows the consecration, transferred these words to the body of Christ, as though this were always created anew in the Lord's Supper.

XIV. At the time of Gregory, about A. D. 600, another and new invocation was patched onto the canon, namely, that because of the intercession of the saints God would graciously grant peace in our days and that we may be free from sin and safe from every disturbance. This invocation of the saints is placed in such a way in the canon that it is inserted after the words "Deliver us from evil" in the Lord's Prayer and before the singing of "O Lamb of God, who takest away the sins of the world, grant us peace," so that deliverance from evils and the granting of peace is ascribed to the intercession of the saints, lest these things be ascribed to Christ alone, as the Lord's Prayer and the invocation in the *Agnus Dei* give it, so that we may be persuaded that these things are indeed given us through Christ but not unless the saints intercede.

XV. Pope Julius declared that intinction is not in harmony with the institution of Christ, the tradition of the apostles, and churchly custom, *De consecratione,* 2, ch. *Cum omne.* Nevertheless in the canon the priest not only casts a part of the consecrated wafer into the cup but adds that this mingling will bring to those who receive it health of mind and body to eternal life. Thus the canon of the Mass agrees neither with Scripture nor with the fathers nor with the more ancient Roman pontiffs.

XVI. The conclusion of the canon does what none of the prayers of the ancients do. It sets the representation of the priest before God as a propitiatory sacrifice. And the priest pretends that he applies this to whomever he wills, for he says: "May this sacrifice which I have offered be to me and to all for whom I have offered it a propitiation." What a host of abominations that figment about the propitiatory sacrifice contains has been explained above.

XVII. When the priest in private Masses, contrary to the custom of the ancient church, alone takes, eats, and drinks, he nevertheless in mockery afterward repeats the words in the canon: "As many as have taken of this participation of the altar, may it bring salvation to all of us who have taken. Keep the bond of peace that you may be fit for the sacred mysteries of Christ. Go, we who have received with the mouth."

Although he dispenses only one kind to those who commune, he nevertheless prays: "As many of us as have taken the body and blood of Christ from this participation of the altar," etc. I did not want to amplify and heap up these things by a long speech, but wanted only to mark the chief errors by a brief notation, set them forth for consideration, and show by means of this contrast how things that were used in the prayers of the ancients in a way that was not bad are now applied and twisted in a godless manner to the papalist sacrifice of the Mass. I judge this is the simplest way to explain the canon of the Mass.

SECTION IV

Concerning the Ceremonies of the Mass

Chapter V

Because the nature of man is such that it cannot easily be raised up without outward aids to think upon divine matters, holy Mother Church has instituted certain ceremonies to be spoken in the Mass, some with lowered, other with more raised voice. She has likewise employed ceremonies, such as mystic blessings, lights, incense, vestments, and many other such things derived from apostolic teaching and tradition, in order that by them the grandeur of this great sacrifice might be commended and the minds of the faithful incited, through these visible signs of religion and piety, to contemplation of the exalted things which lie hidden in this sacrifice.

CANON VII

If anyone says that the ceremonies, vestments, and outward signs which the Catholic Church uses in the celebration of Masses are incentives to impiety rather than matters of piety, let him be anathema.

Examination

1 The ceremonies of the Mass are not all of one kind. For some have a divine command and examples of Scripture that they should be done at the celebration of the Lord's Supper, being as it were essential, e.g., to take bread and the cup in the public assembly, to bless, distribute, eat, drink, proclaim the death of the Lord. Some indeed do not have an express command of God, that they must of necessity be done thus in the celebration of the Lord's Supper, nevertheless they are in their nature good and godly if they are used rightly for edification, such as psalms, readings from Scripture, godly prayers and giving of thanks, confession of the Creed, etc. Some are *per se* superstitious and ungodly, for instance the sacrifice of the Mass for the living and the dead, invocation of the saints, satisfaction for the souls in purgatory, the private Mass, consecration of salt, blessing of water, etc. Some ceremonies indeed are adiaphora, such as vestments, vessels, ornaments, words, rites, and things which are not against the Word of God. Things which are of the first kind must of necessity be observed, for they belong to the substance of the Lord's Supper. Of the things that belong to the second and fourth kind,

many which make for the edification of people are observed in our churches without infringing on Christian liberty.

2 The third kind, however, being superstitious and godless, has deservedly, rightly, and of necessity been abrogated and done away with. But let us examine this fifth chapter!

1. The first thing we notice is that they speak without distinction of the ceremonies of the Mass and whitewash all out of one pot. For this is their sophistical custom, that they habitually magnify the things in the Mass which are in themselves godly and good, meanwhile concealing others, in order that, because some are godly and good, all the rest may be judged to be one of the same kind. Or, if someone criticizes manifestly superstitious and godless things in the Mass, they at once clamor that all salutary exercises of piety and all things that serve decency and order are overthrown and taken away. Therefore it is altogether necessary in this dispute that the distinction be applied which I set forth in the beginning.

2. They say that all the ceremonies they use in the celebration of Masses come from apostolic tradition and teaching. This is manifestly false. For the evangelists describe how Christ celebrated the Lord's Supper; St. Paul describes the apostolic Eucharistic meeting (1 Cor. 11:17-34). It is not enough that they say it appears to be true that the ceremonies were handed down and instituted by the apostles because Paul says: "About the other things I will give directions when I come." It would have to be shown by sure documents what the things were about which Paul then wanted to give directions, and that he wanted them to be of universal and necessary observation.

There is, however, no need for conjectures of this kind. For the papalist writers themselves bear abundant witness that the apostles celebrated the Lord's Supper in stark simplicity, with nothing more than the recitation of the words of institution, the Lord's Prayer, and the added commemoration of the death of Christ. Therefore they apply the words of Prudentius:

> Her face uncultured and wild,
> Her shoulders bare, her hair unshorn,
> Her arms outstretched,

to the apostolic Mass on account of its stark simplicity. These same papalist writers, moreover, note down at what time and by which popes the individual ceremonies of the Mass were instituted. Therefore it is false that the whole armor and the entire apparatus of the papalist Mass comes from apostolic tradition and teaching.

3. With what intent and to what end and use the fathers added some

such ceremonies to the celebration of the sacraments we have indicated above, in the First Topic, "Concerning the Sacraments in General," in the explanation of the 13th canon [p. 110]. In the celebration of the Lord's Supper, however, they observed such ceremonies as might aid and explain the proclamation of the Lord's death, which was made by means of the public preaching of the Word; such ceremonies, together with the Word, would usefully teach men something about the doctrine and use of the sacrament and would incite them to give heed more attentively to the doctrine of the Word and the things which belong to the substance of the Lord's Supper. Such ceremonies were observed in Christian liberty, for they were not the same and alike everywhere, nor did any force others to the observation of their ceremonies. We gladly approve and observe good and useful rites in such liberty.

But the papalists have heaped up the ceremonies of the ancients, mixing in many useless, foolish, and superstitious rites, with the result that the doctrine and true use of the Lord's Supper began, little by little, to be obscured and overwhelmed by the multitude of such rites, until finally the action of the Lord's Supper was transformed into what is clearly a thing of another kind— a sacrifice. Neither do the papalists use these ceremonies of theirs to clarify the doctrine, but either pronounce the words before the common people in a strange language or do it so secretly that no one is able to understand. Openly, meanwhile, they gesticulate with outward signs; and while the use of the Word has been buried, they ascribe to these human rites this power and efficacy, that they incite and raise up the onlookers to contemplation, meditation, and faith in divine things. However, the Word and the sacraments are the divinely instituted instruments through which the Spirit wills to be efficacious, illumine minds, arouse in them faith and godliness, nourish, strengthen, increase, and preserve them. There is therefore a very great difference both in the ceremonies and in their use between the way it was in the ancient church and as it is now in the papalist Mass.

4. They make the observance of these ceremonies so necessary that they declare that he sins mortally who neglects in them, and they scarcely believe that the Lord's Supper has been rightly celebrated if the whole apparatus of ceremonies is not employed. What must be diligently considered is what in the Lord's Supper is by divine right and command, namely, that the things which have been consecrated be dispensed to others, and that under both kinds, in order that the death of the Lord may be publicly proclaimed in a language which can be understood by the uneducated (1 Cor. 14:19). These things they freely neglect, change, and bury. But they fight with fire and sword for the retention of human rites.

Thus, forsaking the command of God, they hold to the traditions of men, or rather, they make the command of God of no effect in order that they may observe the traditions of men (Mark 7:6-8).

5. They ascribe special merits to the performed ceremonies and rites *per se.* And many ceremonies in the papalist Mass are used to lead people away from the true use of the Lord's Supper and to strengthen the superstitious and godless opinions about the *opus operatum* of the sacrifice of the Mass for the living and the dead. For this reason, and on account of this abuse, it has been rather well said about the papistical ceremonies of the Mass that they are incitements to wickedness rather than aids to godliness. We have noted down more things pertaining to this dispute under the 13th canon [p. 110, in the First Topic], "Concerning the Sacraments in General," and we will speak about the lowered voice on Chapter 8 [Section 7, p. 542].

SECTION V
Concerning Private Masses

Chapter VI

The sacred Synod would wish that at every Mass the faithful who are present would communicate, not only with spiritual desire but also with sacramental reception of the Eucharist, by which a more abundant fruit of this most holy sacrifice would accrue to them. Nevertheless it does not, if this is not always done, for this reason condemn as private and illicit those Masses in which only the priest communicates sacramentally but it approves and even commends them, since indeed also these Masses ought to be considered common, partly because in them the people communicate spiritually, and partly because they are celebrated by a public minister of the church, not for himself only but for all the faithful who belong to the body of Christ.

CANON VIII

If anyone says that Masses in which only the priest communicates sacramentally are illicit and should therefore be abolished, let him be anathema.

Examination

1 It is useful to know and rightly to consider the origin of the private Mass, where only the priest communicates, as it is now found with the papalists. For this consideration will bring light into this whole dispute. In the beginning, when the people were fervent in their devotion, which was inflamed the more by the storms of persecution, the church came together daily for the celebration and reception of the Lord's Supper, as we have shown by examples in the examination of the 13th canon[37] on the Eucharist. Later, when the ardor of the people cooled, the general gathering of the people could only be held on Sundays and on the more solemn feast days on account of occupations in worldly affairs. Then the clergy and religious nevertheless daily attended the sacred offices. It was not that they celebrated Masses without communicants, but the clergy themselves retained daily Communion in their own midst. For Cassander quotes from Walafrid as follows: "Since particularly to the clergy all days are reckoned as holidays, it seems very reasonable that we should daily be

---

[37] The reference seems to be to the 9th canon, p. 329.

occupied with sacred things and should continually desire the body and blood of the Lord, without which we cannot live."

It was then that the distinction between public and private Masses began. Gregory calls them *peculiares* [belonging particularly to one's self], Odo of St. Cambray *solitarias* [solitary]. For when the Lord's Supper was celebrated in a general and solemn assembly of the faithful people, which was done on Sundays and on the more solemn festival days in a public place of worship, it was called a public and solemn Mass. However, when on private days (for so Cassander quotes from the Book of the Beginning of the Cistercian order) only the clergy and religious gathered for Communion, they were called private, not public, Masses. Thus Gregory says to Castorius, bishop of Ariminum: "We strictly forbid that public Masses be held in cloisters, lest occasion be offered for a gathering of the people in the secret places and refuges of the servants of God." Odo of St. Cambray says on the canon: "Although originally no Masses were held without a congregation of people, afterward the custom grew in the church to celebrate solitary Masses, especially in the cloisters." Thus, when the Communion of the Lord's Supper was celebrated for the sick, or for pilgrims, or for others outside of the public and solemn gathering of the people, or when this was done in a private place, they were called private Masses. Thus Gregory says, *De consecratione,* dist. 1, ch. *Et hoc attendendum:* "Let all who are in the city or in the surrounding area, both priests and people, come together in one place for the public celebration of the Mass. But let private *(peculiares)* Masses be performed, not at the altars, nor in public, nor at the time of public gatherings, lest the people be drawn away from the public solemnities." Thus Gregory of Nazianzus celebrated the sacrament in a small oratory, *Historia Triparta,* Bk. 9, ch. 8. And Victor, *De persecutione Vandalica,* Bk. 3, tells that on account of the savagery of the Arians the godly held meetings in private homes and there lawfully used the sacraments. In *De consecratione,* 1, ch. *Clericos,* it is permitted to the priests to celebrate in oratories in private homes. These indeed were not private Masses without communicants. For Gregory says, Homily 37, *In Evang.:* "Then, being compelled, he held Masses in the oratory of the bishop and gave to all the body of the Lord and peace with his own hand."

2 Now when also this daily Communion of the clergy and religious, of which I have already spoken, was no longer attended, the priests nevertheless, on account of old custom, prepared the altars. There then in some places, when no communicants were present, prayers, lessons, and the other ceremonies which belong to the Communion service were conducted without consecration and Communion, as Socrates writes

about the church at Alexandria, Bk. 5, ch. 22. And this Mass was called *sicca* (dry). In some places the celebrating priests began to communicate alone, when they had nobody else, lest they be robbed of the offerings of the people if they celebrated only a dry Mass. In order, however, to attract the people to the offerings which brought them some profit, they began to exaggerate the mode of preparation and the danger of unworthy eating beyond the truth, and on the contrary to invent, little by little, many things about the usefulness and efficacy which would accrue from this work and action of the priest also to those who were not communicating, so long only as they brought offerings, until finally this action of the priest without communicants was turned into a propitiatory sacrifice for sins which applies all the merits of Christ and obtains all the things we ask of God.

Once these opinions had been instilled into the minds of men, sales and purchases of such private Masses were multiplied without measure. For men judged it to be possible by a very short route to obtain all these things without great preparation and without danger of unworthy eating, namely, by the performed work of the priest's private Mass, yes, to obtain far more and greater things than the Communion of the Lord's body itself offers.

3 This is the origin of the private Mass, which the Synod of Trent does not condemn but approves and even commends, and [from their standpoint] justly. For the one chief source of income for the papalist kingdom is the huckstering and selling of private Masses.

The matter itself is clear enough. The question is whether a celebration of the Lord's Supper without communicants, where the celebrant dispenses the sacrament to no one, but he alone takes it, and the rest are only spectators, is a true and lawful celebration. For when Christ instituted this sacrament, He did not take it alone while His disciples were either only looking or listening; neither did He promise the disciples from this work, if they did not communicate but just devotedly stood by, looked, and listened, that they would obtain the grace of God; in fact, we do not even read that He took the sacrament Himself, but that He dispensed it, gave it to the disciples, and commanded that they should eat and drink it in remembrance of Him. What He Himself did at the first Supper He commanded to be done in future until He comes to judgment.

It is therefore entirely certain and crystal clear against all sophistical quibbling that Christ did not institute the celebration of the Supper in such a way that he who consecrates takes it alone while the rest only look on, and that from this action of one man the fruit of the Eucharist, on account of the show, flows forth to others who do not[38] communicate. But when we want to do rightly and lawfully what was done at the first Supper, the institution of Christ requires that in the celebration of the Lord's Supper there be one who gives thanks and dispenses and that there be present also persons to whom it is given, who take, eat, and drink. For that is what was done at the first Supper and was commanded to be done in the future. Therefore when the Eucharistic service of the apostles is called the breaking of bread, it is shown sufficiently clearly that there was dispensation and distribution.

Paul describes most clearly of all what the celebration of the Lord's Supper was like in the apostolic church. For he not only repeats the words of institution but says (1 Cor. 10:16-17) that the body of Christ, together with all He merited and earned by delivering up His body, is communicated—not by watching how one person takes it, but he says: "The bread which we break," that is, dispense and distribute for eating, "is the communication of the body of Christ." The same apostle says that the faithful are partakers of the table of the Lord, not by viewing but by eating. He states: "We who are many are one body," not because we see one person eating but "because we all partake of that one bread" which is broken, that is, dispensed and distributed. Yes, in 1 Cor. 11:20-22 he sets the Lord's Supper and a private supper over against each other, and that in such a way that he asserts that where a private supper is being held, there the Lord's Supper cannot be celebrated. And he describes a private supper as one where a person eats privately what belongs to the Lord's Supper, and takes beforehand and not at the same time with the other participants. He also says that it is like when a meal is served where one is full while another is compelled to go hungry. However, he speaks in one breath about the taking of the Lord's Supper and about the joint meals which, according to the custom then in use, followed after. Surely this passage, like a bolt of lightning, overthrows the private Masses of the papalists, in which only the celebrating priest communicates sacramentally.

Very clear is the statement of Chrysostom on this passage of Paul: "They make what belongs to the Lord a private thing. For the Lord's Supper ought to belong to all. For the things that are the Lord's do not belong to this servant or to that, but are common to all. For what belongs to the Lord, the same is also common. For if it is the Lord's, you ought not to take it to yourself as if it were your own, but as something belonging to the Lord, to offer it commonly to all, since indeed it is the Lord's. But

---

[38] The edition of 1574, as also Ed. Preuss, omits the *non,* without which the text does not make sense. Nigrinus supplies it, and translates: *so nicht mit communiciren.*

now you do not allow it to be common but eat it up for yourself."

4 Moreover the ancient church, following the institution of Christ, the tradition of the apostles, and the example of the apostolic church, in the celebration of the Lord's Supper always observed the dispensation and distribution of the sacrament, as all descriptions of the liturgies which are found with the fathers testify. In the ancient and purer antiquity such a private Mass, where the priest communicates to no one what he has consecrated, but takes it alone, was wholly unknown. For the fabrication that the celebration of the Lord's Supper benefits those who do not communicate, but are only present, hear, and behold with devotion what the priest alone does, was not only unknown to antiquity but was earnestly and gravely reprehended and condemned in the earliest times of the church.

Chrysostom says, Homily 3, on Eph. 1: "In vain is the daily sacrifice held when there is no one who will partake of it." Without doubt Chrysostom communicated with his priests and deacons, as the form of his liturgy shows. However, when there was no one of the people who would partake, he does not say: What I do is beneficial for you, so long as you are present at the action with devotion, listen, and look, but he says: "In vain is the daily sacrifice held." This he soon explains more clearly: "Whoever does not partake of the mysteries is an impudent and wicked bystander." Likewise: "If someone has been invited to a feast, washed his hands, and sat down, yet tastes nothing of the food, does he not offer an insult to the host by whom he was invited? Would it not have been better that such a one had not put in his appearance at all?" You hear not words but thunderbolts against the papalist persuasion about the show of the private Masses. In Homily 18, on 2 Corinthians, he says that in the celebration of the Eucharist it is not as it was in the Old Testament, where only the priest ate something.

5 The belief about private Masses, such as it is among the papalists, was severely curbed by the canons in the earliest times of the church. Among the canons which go by the name "Apostolic," the 10th says: "Let all the faithful who come together at the church on the holy days hear the Scriptures. Those who do not continue in prayer until the Mass is performed, nor receive Holy Communion, should, as movers of disorder in the church, be denied Communion." This canon is repeated and confirmed in the second chapter of the Council of Antioch, *De consecratione*, dist. 2, ch. *Peracta*: "When the consecration has been completed, let all who do not want to be put out of the church commune. For thus the apostles decreed and the holy Roman church holds."

6 In fact, when private Masses had already crept in, many nevertheless criticized this persuasion. Humbertus says, against the monk Nicetas, that it is an incomplete Mass in which there is not at the same time consecration, breaking or distribution, and communication.

Walafrid says, *De rebus ecclesiasticis,* ch. 22: "Although one can understand that when the priests alone celebrate Masses those for whom the offices are then celebrated cooperate in the same action, also those whose person the priest mentions in certain responses, nevertheless it must be said that that is a legitimate Mass at which there are present a priest, some who respond, some who offer and communicate, as the language of the prayers clearly demonstrates."

Regino quotes from the Council of Nantes that it is laughable to whisper to the walls and foundations what concerns the people. And truly, it is a mockery that in private Masses, where the Eucharist is dispensed to no one, the priest nevertheless repeats:"May it be for salvation to all of us, as many as have partaken of this participation of the altar. The sacraments we have taken," etc.

7 It is an even more shameful mockery that in private Masses, where there is no distribution, the wafer is nevertheless broken, that is, as Augustine says, divided for distribution. And in place of the distribution instituted and commanded by Christ they imagine wonderful things about the broken particles of the private Mass, which can be read in Durandus, in *Rationale,* Bk. 4, ch. 51. "The three broken parts of the body of Christ signify: The first, His flesh and the saints; the second, those in their graves; the third, the living," etc. Or: "The first part signifies the saints in heaven; the second, the church militant on earth; the third, the dead in purgatory." Likewise: "One part is offered for those who do not live holy lives on earth but wallow in sins; the second, for the saints in heaven; the third, for the souls in purgatory." These are the fruits of the private Mass, and from such fruits of figments we know what kind of tree the private Mass is.

8 Since matters stand thus, and since it is manifest that the papalist private Mass is in conflict with the testamentary institution of the Son of God, with the written tradition of the apostles, with the example of the apostolic church, with the testimonies of the ancient church, with the ecclesiastical canons— what, I ask, has the Council of Trent decided about private Masses? Just hear! The synod would wish that at every Mass the faithful who are present would also communicate through reception of the sacrament. Why do they wish this? Without doubt because they are compelled against their will to acknowledge and confess that it is not in harmony with either Scripture or antiquity that in the private Mass only the priest communicates. But if they are in earnest about this hope,

they ought to banish the false persuasion about the power and efficacy of the show of the private Mass and urge men on a genuine basis to more frequent Communion, namely, that they can obtain the fruit of the Lord's Supper only in the manner which was instituted and commanded by Christ and in no other; and in order that they might return more easily to the rule of the institution of Christ and the model of the primitive church, private Masses ought to be abolished, so that no Mass would be celebrated if none were present to whom the sacrament would be dispensed.

However, the fathers remembered that they had assembled to see to it that the papalist state does not suffer damage, especially so far as the treasurer's chest and the office of the tax gatherers is concerned. Therefore they overturn the wish which the evident nature of the matter has squeezed out of them, for in spite of it they approve and indeed commend to the people these Masses in which the priest alone communicates sacramentally. There was therefore not even a need to wish that at every Mass there might be some who would communicate.

But let us hear their reasons. They say that these are not private but common Masses, also where only the priest alone communicates. However, they themselves have now for many hundreds of years called them private. In the record of Gregory the term "private Mass" is frequent. The explanation in *De consecratione,* dist. 1, ch. *Et hoc attendendum,* calls them private, and this term is altogether common. We thank the council that it grants and confesses that the Mass ought not to be private but common. The controversy is not about the term but about the matter itself, namely, what kind of Communion the Lord's Supper is.

This Communion is described thus in 1 Cor. 10:17: "For we all partake of the one bread." Therefore when one person snatches this to himself, and communicates to no one, it is certainly not a common but a private Mass, according to the saying of Chrysostom: "Indeed, we do not hold that the Lord's Supper should never be celebrated unless the whole church is assembled in one place, or that all the faithful are of necessity held always to communicate at every single Mass. For Christ summoned only the Twelve to the first Supper and said: 'As often as you drink it.' But this is what we are urging, that the Lord's Supper should never be celebrated unless some are present to whom the sacrament may be dispensed."

9 However, they have two arguments by which they try to persuade the world that what is private is really common. The first has to do with spiritual Communion. In order that this may be the more correctly understood, we shall bring it into proper form. The Lord's Supper requires communication of the body and blood of Christ, and when this takes place, then the demand of the institution is satisfied. But if a person hears and sees a Mass, meditates on the teaching of the passion and resurrection of Christ, and apprehends it by faith, he partakes of the body and blood of Christ spiritually (John 6). Therefore the institution of Christ is satisfied in a private Mass, even if no one of the people but only the priest communicates sacramentally.

What then if also the celebrating priest were to communicate only spiritually? Certainly, by the same reasoning, he would satisfy the institution of Christ in an outstanding fashion, even if he himself did not take the consecrated elements nor dispense them to others. This artifice for satisfying the institution of Christ was unknown to antiquity. Neither would there have been any need to set down the above-mentioned canons about sacramental Communion so sternly if what this argument attempts to bring about were true. Therefore Chrysostom, who so severely reprimanded those who stand by but do not communicate, would deservedly have been driven into exile, since, according to the papalists, those bystanders would have been able to satisfy the institution of Christ by spiritual Communion.

But we shall speak of the matter itself. It is certain that, apart from the celebration and use of the Lord's Supper, faith, which in the Word lays hold of Christ, who was crucified for us, communicates spiritually, or eats the flesh of Christ and drinks His blood (John 6). And when the use of the Lord's Supper according to the institution of Christ cannot be had, spiritual Communion is sufficient for salvation, according to the popular saying of Augustine: "Believe, and you have eaten." Neither do I deny that he who stands by and is not prepared for Communion both could and should, from hearing and pondering the Supper's words of institution and the total action, be led to meditate on the mystery of redemption and justification.

This also is certain, that in the use of the Lord's Supper spiritual Communion should take place, for without this spiritual Communion one eats judgment to oneself. But the question is what kind of communication Christ instituted, prescribed, and commanded in the Supper, for it is clear that this satisfies the institution. However, He says:"Take, eat, drink, and do this in remembrance of Me," i.e., it is Christ's commandment that in the Lord's Supper both sacramental and spiritual Communion should take place simultaneously.

Paul says that in the Supper a communication of the body and blood of Christ takes place. But how? He says it is when we partake of one bread. Therefore in the celebration of the Lord's Supper the institution is not satisfied by spiritual Communion alone, without reception of the sacrament. And it is a perversion of the testament of Christ to set up a show in place of the sacramental eating and to ascribe to that show what the Son of God in His institution ascribes to sacramental eating and drinking.

The other argument is this: The priest is a public minister of the church, and the liturgy is a public ministry. Therefore he celebrates the Lord's Supper not for himself only but for all the faithful. But how? Is it that he alone may use it and that this may profit the church for the forgiveness of sins? Surely, also the preaching of the Gospel is a public ministry, and the preacher is a public minister, preaching the Gospel not for himself only but for the whole church. Does he do it in such a way that he alone hears and believes and that this profits the church for eternal life even if she herself neither hears nor believes? Surely, the just shall live by his own faith, and whoever does not believe will be condemned. Therefore just as the public minister of the church sets the doctrine of the Gospel before the whole church in order that she may hear and accept it, so also he celebrates the Lord's Supper for the whole church, not in order that he alone may use it but that through his ministry the rest may take, eat, and drink according to the institution of Christ. The public minister celebrates the action of Baptism not for himself but for the church. Does he do it in order that he may baptize himself and that this work may profit those who are not baptized for salvation? By no means! Therefore it is plain what kind of argument this is.

But I understand very well what the most holy synod is after—that the priest by his private action makes a sacrifice that is propitiatory, applicatory, and effective for the living and the dead, as these things have been explained above. And this is that Helen about whom the Synod of Trent is contending, namely that, as Gabriel says, the priest is the mouth of the church, and what he consumes, that profits the church, which does not consume, for remission of sins and life eternal. This is the correction of abuses which many promised themselves would come about in the council!

SECTION VI

Concerning the Mixing of Water in the Chalice

Chapter VII

Moreover, the holy synod reminds the priests that they are commanded by the Church to mix water in the chalice with the wine which is to be offered; for one thing, because Christ the Lord is believed to have done so, then also because water together with blood flowed forth from His side, which sacrament is recalled to mind by this mixing, and since people are called waters in the Apocalypse of blessed John, the union of the faithful people with Christ the Head is thereby represented.

CANON IX

If anyone says that water is not to be mixed in the cup with the wine which is to be offered, because this is contrary to the institution of Christ, let him be anathema.

Examination

1 Behold, I beg you, the absurd religious belief of these men! The church, they say, prescribed to the priests that water should be mixed in the cup with the wine which is to be offered. They attach such importance to this precept that they do not scruple to condemn with the anathema those who do not observe it strictly. But the use of the cup of the Lord they wholly and completely take away, forbid, and prohibit to the laity, although we have the hortatory words of Christ concerning the cup: "Drink of it, all of you; do this as often as you drink."

Now they say that they are contending about the mixing of the cup in order that the union of the faithful people with Christ the Head may be represented. This is a new form of godliness, that they are concerned about the union of the people with Christ. But how? Christ instituted the use of the total sacrament, that these things, when eaten and drunk, may bring about that we are in Christ and Christ in us. Of the cup Paul says (1 Cor. 12:13): "We were all made to drink of one Spirit." And Christ says: "This cup is the new covenant in My blood, which is shed for many for the remission of sins." Why then do they not grant the use of the entire sacrament to the people? Why do they deny the cup of the new covenant, whose mediator is Christ, to the faithful people? Why do they forbid them to drink into one Spirit, if they are concerned about the union of the faithful with Christ?

But there is something hidden in this chapter which must not be ignored. The water mixed with the wine in the cup represents the union of the people with Christ. Therefore when the priest offers this mixed cup to God the Father as a propitiatory sacrifice, the people together with Christ are set before the Father. Thus the action of the priest is much more useful to the people than the Communion of the Dominical cup itself. For in the first place, by the mixing of water with the wine in the cup which is to be offered, the priest unites the people with Christ; in the second place, in the cup he presents both Christ and the people to God the Father. This in truth is the mystery on account of which the papalists contend about the mixed cup.

2 However, so far as the matter itself is concerned, the dispute can be settled easily and in a few words, for it does not touch any article of faith. In the regions of the Orient, where the wines are strong, it was customary that temperate and prudent people did not drink unmixed wine, but wine tempered with water. Therefore pouring out or presenting wine is called mixing wine. In Prov. 9:5 the word *masakh* ["to mix, mingle"] is found, which makes a distinction between unmixed and tempered wine. This is found also in Is. 5:22 and Prov. 23:30.

Among the Greeks the pouring out of wine is also called mixing, *kirnas aithopa oinon.*[39] Therefore also among the Latins a butler takes his name from mixing drinks.[40] Therefore it appears to be true that Christ drank not unmixed but tempered wine. And because in the primitive church, after the Communion, banquets called love-feasts were held with great sobriety with the bread and wine which had been offered at the Lord's table, they offered not unmixed but tempered wine. And lest the Gentiles should slander the Christians as though they celebrated the Lord's Supper for the sake of carousing and drunkenness, the ancients took mixed or tempered wine. Under the pretext of sobriety some even took only water. These Cyprian rightly reprehended.

3 These things about the custom of the ancient church are known from the writings of the fathers, although this custom was not universal with the ancients. For Durandus says, Bk. 4, ch. 42, that in the Greek church this was not universally done. Afterward people began little by little to argue that this was a tradition which came from Christ Himself, although it is not found in Scripture. Thus Cyprian, who is immensely

---

[39] Literally, "You mix fiery wine."

[40] The Latin for butler is *pincerna,* which is derived from the Greek *pigkernees,* one who mixes drinks.

pleased with this allegory, says that this mixing signifies and shows that in the Lord's Supper a union is brought about of the people, as members, with Christ the Head. Eusebius of Emesa later tried to prove this tradition from Scripture, namely, from the fact that blood and water flowed from the side of the crucified Christ. Out of this, Roman popes made an absolutely necessary law, as the Canon of Alexander. *De consecratione,* dist. 1, decrees, that not wine only but wine mixed with water must be offered. Julius, ch. *Cum Omne,* says that according to the precepts of the canons this must be done, so that if there were only wine in the cup, even if it were consecrated, it could not be the cup of the Lord; and if it is done otherwise he calls it an error of perverse men. He adds also that when in the cup water is mixed with the wine, then the people are united with Christ, and the common believers are linked and joined to Him in whom they believe; likewise, that if only wine is offered or consecrated, the blood of Christ is there without us.

This mixing also gave rise to various disputes, namely, whether that water is changed together with the wine into the blood of Christ, also whether the wine is changed to blood and the water into phlegm. Some argued that the water surrounding the accidents of the wine is suspended in the air without change. These disputes are described in *Extra, De celebrat. missarum,* ch. *Cum Marthae.*

4 I have reported these things in order that the guileless reader may understand what has here been placed into controversy. For if the papalists were observing and putting forth this mixing as a custom that is an adiaphoron, which is neither commanded nor prohibited by the Word of God but had a reason not out of harmony with it, there would be no controversy, because it would be an indifferent matter. Therefore the ninth canon falsely blames the men on our side as though we condemned as opposing the institution of Christ all those who use wine tempered with water in the celebration of the Lord's Supper. For then we would condemn almost all of antiquity. For the most ancient writers, Justin and Irenaeus, make mention of the mixing of the cup.

5 But because the papalists urge: (1) that it is necessary, because of a command, that in the action of the Lord's Supper this mixing take place; (2) that it cannot be the cup of the Lord if wine only is taken and blessed with the words of Christ; (3) because they ascribe the things which belong to the reception of the Eucharist to this mixing, namely, that then the people are united with Christ when in the cup wine is mixed with water— therefore, in order that these false opinions might be reproached and banished from the minds of men, those on our side rightly showed by example and deed that Christian liberty ought not to be subjected to the yoke of servitude in things which are not matters of divine right and command, particularly because such opinions as we have described have been falsely attached to this observance.

For the evangelists write expressly of the wine, or of the fruit of the vine, which was in the Dominical cup, but make no mention of water. And even if it be granted that it is probable that the wine had been tempered beforehand, nevertheless no circumstances in the institution offer the slightest evidence that Christ during the action of the Lord's Supper mixed water with the wine in the cup when He took the cup in order to bless it. For it is silly that some have wanted to prove this from the water pot of the landlord, since it lay nearer to have taken the proof from the basin out of which Christ washed the feet of disciples. Therefore wine, or the fruit of the vine, belongs to the substance of the Dominical cup so far as the external element is concerned; but whether it should be unmixed or mixed, red or white, is not essential.

This whole argument can most correctly be decided by a look at the other element. For it is certain that bread is of the essence of the Lord's Supper. Whether it should be of wheat, whether leavened or unleavened, was at one time debated with great heat, and arguments were gathered from Scripture about the grain of wheat and about the day of the Lord's Supper. But the church judged correctly that these things are free and not of necessity for the sacrament. And it clearly is all the same whether the wine is mixed or unmixed, whether it is red or white. For the chief argument does not prove conclusively but only shows that it was probably tempered or mixed wine which Christ used in His Last Supper with the disciples. Nevertheless it does not follow that Christ, in the action of the Lord's Supper, mixed water with the wine when He took the cup to bless it. For nothing like this is remarked in the evangelists.

The second argument, namely, that water and blood flowed forth from the side of Christ, does not prove that water must of necessity be mixed with the wine in the Dominical cup. For the things which belong to the substance of the Lord's Supper, and which must be done in its celebration, must be taken and shown from what Christ did when He instituted it in the night in which He was betrayed. And all the ancient fathers, when they interpret and treat the account of blood and water flowing forth from the side of the crucified Christ, apply it to the two sacraments of the church and understand by the water Baptism and by the blood the Eucharist. This interpretation does not fit badly with what is written in 1 John 5:6, about Christ coming to us through water and blood. Therefore it is clear that the necessity of mixing water with the wine in the Dominical cup is not demonstrated from this account. For some Roman pontiffs and certain later writers, such as Eusebius of Emesa, began to twist this account to the mixing of water with the wine in the Dominical cup. I could show many absurdities that follow from this interpretation, things which papalist transubstantiation cannot tolerate. But I shall content myself with having shown the basics in this matter.

The allegory that waters in the Apocalypse signify peoples is an exceedingly weak proof. It is certain that in the use of the Supper, Christ unites Himself with His members, but the mixing of water with the wine is not necessary to accomplish this. For Christ does this by bestowing His body and blood. For this bestowing He uses, according to His institution, bread and wine. What belongs to the union of the body and blood of Christ dare not be ascribed to the human ordinance of the mixing of the cup with water. But if this allegory is pressed, that many waters are many peoples, it would follow that more water would have to be used than wine. For there is one Head but the members are many, and too little water would unite far too few people with Christ. Yes, if we wanted to play with allegories, the mixing of water with wine could be explained of the adulteration of the Lord's Supper, for it is known what Isaiah understands when he says: "Your wine is mixed with water." Therefore it is simplest and safest to stick to the clear words of institution of the Supper, and to distinguish necessary and essential things from accidental and unessential ones.

SECTION VII

Concerning Sacred Things to Be Performed in a Foreign Language

Chapter VIII

Although the Mass contains much instruction for the faithful, it has nevertheless not seemed good to the fathers to grant permission that it be celebrated everywhere in the language of the common people. Wherefore, the ancient custom approved by the holy Roman Church, the mother and teacher of all churches, being retained everywhere for every church—lest the sheep of Christ suffer hunger or little children beg for bread and there be no one to break it to them, the holy synod commands the pastors and all who have the care of souls that during the celebration of Masses they frequently, either personally or through others, explain something of what they read in the Mass, and that among other things they explain something of this most holy sacrifice, especially on Sundays and on festival days.

CANON IX

If anyone says that the custom of the Roman Church, according to which a part of the canon and the words of institution are pronounced with lowered voice, is to be condemned, or that the Mass ought to be celebrated only in the language of the common people, or that water ought not to be mixed with the wine which is to be offered in the cup, because that is contrary to the institution of Christ, let him be anathema.

Examination

1 If there could have been any hope of reformation from the Council of Trent, the justice and clearness of this matter should have gained that what is transacted in church assemblies in a language which is foreign and unknown to the faithful would be corrected—in the Scripture readings, in the prayers, thanksgivings, blessings, and most of all in the administration of the sacraments. For the lessons are read in order that the people may be instructed; psalms and hymns are sung that the devotion of the people may be aroused through the Word. Public prayers and celebrations of the Eucharist ought to be held by the priest in common not only with the clergy, but with all the faithful, as Chrysostom shows in Homily 18, on 2 Corinthians, so that when the priest leads in speaking, they can answer: "Amen." Moreover, Christ expressly commanded that the Sup-

per should be celebrated in remembrance of Him, so that those who eat of the Lord's bread and drink of His cup should at the same time proclaim the death of the Lord, as Paul explains.

2 Now Christ used the particular language which was in common use at that time and could be understood by all. Also, on the day of Pentecost the gift of tongues was given to the apostles in order that they might set the doctrine of the Gospel before all peoples under heaven and administer the sacraments in a language which was known to the individual peoples and understood by all. Moreover, there is a very clear passage in Paul (1 Cor. 14) where he treats this question *ex professo* and at length from all sides—in what language the readings and explanations from Scripture, public prayers, thanksgivings, hymns or psalms, benedictions, or administration of sacraments should be set forth to the church. For where Paul calls the blessing a giving of thanks the ancients rightly understand the administration of the Lord's Supper, for the ancients called it Eucharist [giving of thanks]. Paul says (1 Cor. 10:16): "The cup of blessing which we bless."

Now Paul shows that there were some in his day who wanted to display the gift of tongues before the church, so that they would give the readings from Scripture, public prayers, psalms, giving of thanks, and the administration of the sacraments in a language that was foreign and unknown to the unlearned. The comment of Ambrose is worth noting, that those whom Paul reprimands were most of all from among the Hebrews, who in discussion or sacrifices among Greek people and others sometimes, for the sake of honor, used the Syriac language, but more often the Hebrew, namely, because it is a sacred language, which originally God Himself and also the patriarchs and prophets used. And surely, this matter of the sacred language was a splendid pretext. But Paul simply declares: Because in assemblies of the church all things ought to be done for the edification of the church, therefore that language ought to be used which can be understood also by those who occupy the place of the unlearned, for the people cannot be edified, nor rightly say: "Amen," unless they understand what is said. He proves this statement with many arguments. He faults and reproves those who think and act otherwise; he demands that things which do not edify the church but are spoken into the wind should, as being useless, be corrected. In this way he demonstrates that in the church all things are to be done in an orderly way, decorously, and for edification.

Therefore there is nothing to what the papalists bring forward, namely, that ornamentation, beauty, and majesty are secured and added to the sacraments from the use of the Latin language among those to whom it is unknown. For this could have been said more plausibly of the sacred language at the time of the apostles. But Paul declares that in the sacred assemblies a language should be used which was known to the unlearned, in order that in the church all things might be "done decently and in order," and for edification. At the end of his discussion Paul places two statements: 1. "Thus I teach in all the churches of the saints"; 2. "If anyone is spiritual, let him acknowledge that the things which I write to you are the commandments of the Lord."

We see therefore what is the opinion of the Lord about this question, what the teaching of the apostles, and what the observance of the apostolic church. And with respect to those who think otherwise Paul adds with great vehemence: "But if anyone be ignorant, let him be ignorant."[41]

3 All of antiquity observed this teaching of Paul diligently, with great unanimity, using in sacred acts in each place that language which, if it was not the popular language, was nevertheless understood by the church, as was the case with the Latin language in Africa at the time of Augustine. If any tried to do differently, they were earnestly reprehended. Thus Ambrose, writing on 1 Cor. 14, disapproves that certain persons of Latin speech at his time were accustomed to sing in Greek, delighted by the sound of the words, although neither they themselves nor others understood what they were saying. Thus the use of a foreign language in the performance of sacred acts was according to Ambrose first tried in the Hebrew language among the Greeks, and afterward among the Latins in the Greek language. But there were people at that time who criticized and checked this practice on the basis of the Word of God. Afterward, however, when there was no one who resisted on the basis of the Word, the use of the Latin language in sacred acts increased among those to whom this language is not known. This is, however, not the most ancient way. For in the *Pontifical*[42] it is said to the readers in the rite of ordination: "Strive to set forth the sacred lessons distinctly and plainly for the understanding and edification of the faithful." And around A.D. 1200 Innocent III decreed at a general council: "Because people of diverse languages live intermingled in very many places, having under one faith different rites and customs, we strictly enjoin that the bishops of such communities or dioceses provide suitable men who shall celebrate

---

[41] Chemnitz follows the reading of the Vulgate, which is also that of the King James Version, in 1 Cor. 14:38. The RSV following more ancient manuscripts, translates: "If anyone does not recognize this, he is not recognized."

[42] The *Pontifical:* in the Western church a book containing the services conducted wholly or chiefly by a bishop.

the divine offices for them in accord with the diversity of rites and languages and administer the churchly sacraments, instructing them equally by both word and example."

And of Cyril, the leader of the Moravians, who lived around the year 900, Aeneas Sylvius writes in the Bohemian history, ch. 13: "They say that when Cyril was at Rome he begged the pope that he might use the language of the Slavs in the divine services with the people of that nation whom he had baptized. While this matter was being debated in the sacred senate and not a few opposed it, a voice was heard, as though sent from heaven, saying: 'Let every spirit praise the Lord, and let every tongue confess Him,' and that as a result permission was given to Cyril," etc. Today those people who are not subject to the tyranny of the Roman pontiff observe the same thing, as the Syrians, Ethiopians, Armenians, Muscovites, etc.

4 But what does the Council of Trent decree concerning this question? It grants that the Mass contains much instruction for the faithful but says that it has nevertheless not seemed expedient to the council that it should be celebrated everywhere in the language of the common people. However, according to the dictum of Ambrose no one can teach and instruct unless he is understood. However, a language cannot be understood unless it is known. Therefore these things contradict each other: The Mass ought to serve the instruction of the people; nevertheless it is to be celebrated in a language which is foreign and unknown to the people— unless perchance they want the Mass indeed to contain instruction but do not want it to be communicated to the people but have it concealed by means of an unknown language.

But what reasons do they advance? The custom, they say, is ancient. However, a different custom, namely to use a common and known language, is older and very ancient, as we have shown. But for the papalists (as I see) a 300-year-old instruction constitutes all of antiquity, so that what was commanded by the Lord, handed down by the apostles, and observed in the church for 1,500 years[43] does not belong to antiquity.

What do they oppose to the very clear statement of Paul in 1 Cor. 14? This is indeed worth hearing. "The Roman Church," they say, "the mother and teacher of all churches, has approved the use of a language foreign and unknown to the people." Therefore the Roman church takes to itself the authority to establish something different from and to approve something contrary to those things which the Lord commanded,

---

[43] Nigrinus translates, *ueber zwoelf hundert Jahr,* correcting the Latin, which has 1,500 years.

which the apostles taught, which the apostolic and primitive churches observed—that it may fulfill what is written in 2 Thess. 2:4: "He sits in the temple of God as if he were God, exalting himself above all that is called God."

5 Still the Synod grants some freedom, namely, that at times something of what is read in the Mass may be explained. If they would understand this in this way, that when the lessons and prayers had first been recited in Latin for those who understand it there would at once be added the interpretation in the common language, so that also the people could say: "Amen," it would be some kind of reform and there would be some agreement with what Paul says in 1 Cor. 14:27: "If any speak in a tongue, let there be only two or at most three, and each in turn; and let one interpret" that thus the whole church, which consists of both learned and unlearned, may be edified. Johannes Billet says that in some churches they had this custom, that when the Gospel had been spoken in Latin it was at once explained to the people in the vulgar tongue.

6 This interchange of the Latin and the vulgar tongue is observed in our churches, in which there are well-attended schools in order that both the learned and the unlearned may be edified. But this is not the intention of the Tridentines, that the lessons, sermons, and prayers themselves should be recited in the vulgar tongue; to these they simply assign the Latin language. Otherwise they do not entirely forbid that at times something should be explained as much as pleases them; this may be done in the Latin readings, sermons, and prayers, not however in the mysteries of the canon. Paul however says: "If any speak in a tongue and there is no one to interpret, let each of them keep silence in the church and speak to himself and to God." And Ambrose says: "If you come together to edify the church, that ought to be said which the hearers understand. For what does it profit that someone speaks in a language which he alone understands? He who hears profits nothing. Therefore he ought to be silent in the church, in order that those may speak who can benefit the hearers."

Here belongs also what they mention in the fifth chapter, and what in the ninth canon they defend with the lightning of the anathema as being done rightly, namely, that part of the canon and the words of consecration are spoken with lowered voice, so that also those who could understand may not hear them. It is certain that Christ in the celebration of His Supper commanded that a remembrance of Him be made not through silence or in a silent manner but, as Paul explains, through proclamation. For Christ did not institute the sacraments that the action might indeed be visible and public but the Word, which is the chief part of the sacraments, might be hidden and buried through silence. And in 1 Cor. 14:28 Paul clearly distinguishes these two: To speak in the church, namely, about the things which belong to the public ministry, and to speak privately to oneself and to God. Therefore all of antiquity (except those who could not be in attendance at the mysteries) pronounced the prayers, thanksgivings, and especially the words of the Supper with a voice that could be heard and understood by those present, to which the people answered: "Amen."

Thus Dionysius writes in Eusebius, Bk. 7, ch. 9, about a certain man who had been baptized by heretics that, when he had heard the thanksgiving in the church, he also together with the others sang the Amen.

Bessarion says concerning the sacrament of the Eucharist that in the Oriental church the priest pronounces these words with a loud voice: "This is My body; this is My blood."

Augustine to Orosius, quest. 49: "Consider, if you can, what a shout the whole church makes when the blood of Christ is drunk and she says: 'Amen.' " In short, all descriptions of the liturgies which are found with the ancients testify to the same thing. In the liturgy which bears the name of Chrysostom it is indeed said a number of times: "The priest prays secretly, and concludes with a loud or raised voice." But that secret recitation of the prayers was not made in silence, in order that no one should be able to hear; but because there is set over against it "with a loud voice," it means that some prayers were not chanted with so loud and raised a voice. For in Homily 18, on 2 Corinthians, he says that both the prayers and the thanksgivings in the celebration of the Eucharist were shared by the people with the priest.

7 Therefore at the time of Chrysostom also those things which were not sung with a loud voice were pronounced distinctly and clearly, so that they could be heard and understood. For in these prayers the priest, according to the dictum of Paul, does not speak to himself and to God but to the church.

The following statement concerning this matter is found in the imperial decree of Justinian, where in *Novellis,* 123, we read these words: "We command that all, bishops and presbyters alike, celebrate the holy sacrifice and the prayers employed in holy Baptism not silently nor in a secret manner but with a clear voice that can be heard clearly by the people, in order that the minds of the hearers may be lifted up thereby to greater devotion in showing forth the praise of the Lord God. For so the apostle teaches (1 Cor. 14, etc.). For these reasons it is fitting that along with the other prayers also those things which are said in the holy sacrifice should be brought before God with a clear voice. The priests are to know that if they neglect any of this they will give an account about it in the fearful judgment of the great God. Neither will we, if we should know it, acquiesce and leave it unpunished." Thus Justinian.

8 The Tridentine fathers, however, in Chapter 5 decree against the opinion of all antiquity that the minds of the faithful are incited and sustained for meditating and contemplating divine matters if the words of consecration are uttered with silent voice, although Paul declares that faith comes not from silence but from hearing the Word of God. It is worth the effort to observe that the papalist writers themselves confess that this decree about secrecy is not ancient. They declare that the following is the reason for it. They say that formerly the canonical prayer was recited publicly and with raised voice. But when, through use, these words were also known by lay people, certain shepherds in the field recited them over bread and wine and suddenly found flesh and blood in front of them and so perished, struck down by God. As a result it was ordered that the canon should thereafter be spoken silently. Thus Honoratus and Billet report, as though these words were magical in nature.

Innocent assigns this reason: "Lest the sacrosanct words should become despised, if they were known also by all the lay people." This danger the Holy Spirit certainly did not foresee, since Paul interprets the commemoration of the Lord as proclamation. But God turns also this decree of the papalists to good for the elect, namely, that their ears may not be contaminated by the abomination of the canon.

9 Now, because Justinian condemns those who pronounce the words of institution and the prayers of the Eucharist with silent voice, which cannot be heard by the people, therefore the Synod of Trent murders this decree of Justinian with the anathema in Canon 9: "If anyone says that the custom of the Roman Church, according to which a part of the canon and the words of institution are pronounced with lowered voice, is to be condemned, let him be anathema." Thus they use a shortcut to extricate themselves when they see that the judgment of both Scripture and antiquity is against them.

Seventh Topic
CONCERNING PENANCE

From Session IV Under Julius III
[the 14th Session of the Council of Trent]

SECTION I
Concerning the Necessity and Institution
of the Sacrament of Penance

Chapter I

If there were in all the regenerate that gratitude toward God that they would constantly guard the justice received in baptism by His favor and grace, there would have been no need for another sacrament, different from baptism, to be instituted for the remission of sins. However, since God, rich in mercy, knows our frame, He bestowed a remedy for life also for those who afterward gave themselves up into the servitude of sin and the power of the devil, namely, the sacrament of penance, by which the benefit of Christ's death is applied to those who have fallen after baptism. Penance was indeed necessary at all times for all men who had defiled themselves with some mortal sin, for securing grace and righteousness, also for those who had asked to be washed with the sacrament of baptism, in order that, when perverseness had been cast off and eliminated, they might detest so great an offense to God with hatred of sin and with godly sorrow of mind. Therefore the prophet says: "Be converted and do penance for all your iniquities, and iniquity shall not be your ruin." The Lord also said: "Unless you do penance you shall all likewise perish." And Peter, the prince of the apostles, commending penance to sinners about to be initiated through Baptism, said: "Do penance and be baptized, every one of you." Nevertheless penance was not a sacrament before the coming of Christ, nor is it such after His coming for anyone before his baptism. However, the Lord instituted it a sacrament principally when, having been raised from the dead, He breathed on His disciples, saying: "Receive the Holy Spirit; if you forgive the sins of any, they are forgiven; if you retain the sins of any, they are retained." The consensus of all the fathers has always understood that by this extraordinary deed and by these clear words there was communicated to the apostles and their legitimate successors the power of remitting and retaining sins in order to reconcile believers who had fallen after baptism. And the Catholic Church for very good reason cast out and condemned as heretics the Novatians, who at one time stubbornly denied the power to remit sins. Therefore this holy synod, approving and receiving as wholly true this meaning of these words of the Lord, condemns the contrived interpretations of those who falsely twist these words to the power of preaching the Word of God and of proclaiming the Gospel of Christ, against the institution of this sacrament.

CANON I

If anyone says that in the Catholic Church penance is not truly and properly a sacrament instituted by Christ our Lord for reconciling the faithful to God as often as they fall into sin after baptism, let him be anathema.

CANON II[1]

If anyone says that the words of the Lord, our Savior: "Receive the Holy Spirit; if you forgive the sins of any, they are forgiven; if you retain the sins of any, they are retained," are not to be understood of the power of remitting and retaining in the sacrament of penance, as the Catholic Church has always understood them from the beginning, but twists them contrary to the institution of this sacrament to the authority for preaching the Gospel, let him be anathema.

Examination

1 The doctrine concerning repentance furnishes a clear testimony to the goodness and mercy of God toward this poor and corrupt nature of ours. For because, on account of the corruption of nature, we all fall often in many ways in this life, even the just person falls seven times in a day. For on account of the wiles of the devil and the snares of the world also those who have been reborn are sometimes overtaken by falls through the infirmity of the flesh; often also through the wickedness of the flesh they rush into dreadful crimes. Therefore God shows that He does not desire the death of the sinner but that he should turn and live, even to the point that He wants the way back into grace to be open also to those who have fallen after Baptism, provided they are converted. And indeed, He Himself instituted, ordained, and prescribed a certain mode and rationale according to which conversion should be made and repentance done after falls, so that we may be certain on the basis of a divine promise that we are again reconciled to God and have obtained remission of sins. Yes, He Himself by His Spirit through the Word begins, effects, and works in us what belongs to repentance or conversion. Therefore an explanation, on the basis of God's Word, of the true and sound teaching about saving repentance is altogether necessary in the church. This teaching, happily cleansed from the confusions and corruptions of scholastic doctrine, has been explained in adequate discussions under God's blessing by the men on our side on the basis of the prophetic and apostolic writings. And because it is not our purpose to repeat and again narrate the whole topic of repentance in an exhaustive way and by a full discussion, especially since I see that this writing grows beyond the intended bounds, I shall note down only what the plan for an examination of the Tridentine decrees seems to call for.

2 In the first chapter we must therefore show what it really is which is here placed in controversy when the question is discussed whether penance is really and properly a sacrament. Now, because the papalists are in the habit of confusing the point at issue by mixing in other questions

---

[1] This is Canon III in the *Canons and Decrees of the Council of Trent*.

which are debated by Anabaptists and other fanatics, we shall, to begin with, remove and separate these questions after we have shown the teaching of our churches, in order that we may come the more readily to what is really in controversy.

First of all: We teach specifically that if in this life the baptized commit actions against their conscience, they do not retain but cast out faith and the Holy Spirit, lose the grace of justification and life, and become subject to the wrath of God and eternal damnation, unless they are again converted and repent. What these sins are we explain from Scripture, e.g., Rom. 8:5-8; 1 Cor. 6:9-10; Gal. 1:6-9; 5:16-21; Eph. 5:3-6; Col. 3:5-9, and other passages. Therefore Art. XII of the Augsburg Confession condemns those who imagine that some attain so great a perfection in this life that they can no longer sin, or who blaspheme that those who have once been justified cannot lose the Holy Spirit, no matter how great the crimes in which they wallow.

Second: We are by no means Novatians, who either wholly denied all hope of forgiveness and reconciliation with God to those who had once been justified, if they had fallen after Baptism, or at least cast doubt on it, even if they were again converted and had repented. For we praise with deep gratitude the immeasurable blessing of the mercy of God, that He promised He would receive again to Himself into grace those who had fallen after Baptism, when and as often as they are converted.

Third: This also is not in controversy with us, that no one can be reconciled to God and obtain remission of sins unless he repents. For an impenitent man stores up for himself the wrath of God, Rom. 2:5; Luke 13:5: "Unless you repent you will all likewise perish."

Fourth: No one ought to invent for himself a special mode of repentance in order to be reconciled to God; but that mode which is taught and prescribed in the Word of God is the only and true mode of saving repentance.

Fifth: This also is with us beyond all doubt, that God in Scripture instituted and ordained certain means through which He wills to apply and seal the benefit of the death of Christ to those who have fallen after Baptism, for reconciliation and remission of sins if they are converted. Therefore the Enthusiasts and the Epicureans are condemned, who imagine that God grants reconciliation and remission of sins to the fallen without means, without the use of the ministry, without repentance and faith. The men on our side teach that the ministry of the Word and sacraments is the ordinary means or instrument through which God in this life deals with us in matters that pertain to our salvation. For by the ministry of the Law sins are condemned, and consciences terrified by the fear of divine wrath and judgment. Thereafter God offers and sets grace and remission of sins before the terrified and contrite through the ministry of the Gospel. And it is His will that through and because of Christ we may seek, lay hold of, and receive reconciliation with God by faith in Word and sacrament.

3 Therefore the dictum of Acesius, the Novatian, is deservedly rejected, who in the *Tripartita,* Bk. 1, ch. 13, says to the Emperor Constantine: "The fallen are indeed to be called to repentance, but hope of forgiveness is not to be expected from the priests but only from God, who alone has power to remit sins." For Constantine answers prudently and piously: "Therefore, O Acesius, fetch a ladder and climb up to heaven, seeing you take away the use of the ministry."

Ambrose describes the opinion of the Novatians in this way, that all hope of forgiveness should indeed not simply be cut off for those who repent after a fall, but that the priests neither could nor should announce remission of sins to them through the ministry of the Gospel or bestow absolution on them, nor with rash temerity usurp to themselves the functions of God, as they pretend. Therefore the Augsburg Confession earnestly reproves those who either seek or teach to seek reconciliation with God and remission of sins outside of and without the ministry of the Word and sacraments.

4 These things needed to be said first, in order that the point at issue concerning repentance between the papalists and the Augsburg Confession might be clearly established and shown, other questions having been removed and set aside, lest someone think and quibble, when we dispute with the papalists whether penance is truly and properly a sacrament, that we cherish and defend the fanatical opinions which I have shown to be condemned among us.

What has come into controversy here is that the papalists assert that the repentance by which the fallen are reconciled to God is a special sacrament by which the benefit of the death of Christ is applied to those who have fallen after Baptism. Now there must be added an explanation showing what is the meaning and what the cause of this dispute. Lest it seem to contend more than necessary about the language rather than about the matter itself, the Apology of the Augsburg Confession repeatedly declares expressly: Since through the proclamation and ministry of absolution there is applied to the individual believers that which properly belongs to the sacraments, namely, the general promises of God about reconciliation with God and remission of sins, it does not object when for this reason, in this respect, for this cause, and in this sense repentance is called a sacrament.

Granted, that it does not have from divine institution the kind of external and material elements found in Baptism and the Eucharist which are necessary for the full definition and genuine character of a sacrament; nevertheless, because the term sacrament is not found in Scripture, and covers a very wide range of meanings, agreement about the language could easily be established among those who do not love strife about words, if only the matter itself were sound.

5 But in this dispute the papalists do not let themselves be satisfied with this declaration. Therefore there is another reason why they maintain so stubbornly that penance is truly and properly a sacrament. This observation will show the real point at issue in this controversy; at the same time it will also show that it is not a strife about words but a fight about a far more serious matter when the papalists argue that penance is truly and properly a sacrament. For because a sacrament according to their definition is the visible form of an invisible grace; therefore, in order that it may both bear its visible form and that its purpose may stand out, they ask what is the material element in penance which, when the Word comes to the element, makes it a sacrament which not only signifies but causes (as they say) the grace of penitence, that is, reconciliation with God and forgiveness of sins.

The *Compendium theologiae* answers that here the material or element must be understood in a wide sense for everything, whether it be an external substance or a human action. And so the *Compendium* says that in the sacrament of penance the element consists of the outward actions or operations of the penitent person, namely, contrition of heart, confession of mouth, and satisfaction by work. And if the word of absolution, spoken by the priest, comes to this element, that is, to the human performances, then it thereby becomes a sacrament which effectively causes and confers grace, that is, reconciliation with God and remission of sins. Therefore when a sinner who has fallen after Baptism seeks and strives for reconciliation with God and remission of sins, the papalists lead him to human, that is, his own works through the sacrament of penance, in order that these performances may become and be a sacrament when the word of absolution comes to them, that is, the cause which effects and confers the grace of reconciliation with God and the remission of sins. Therefore the following distinction is taught in the *Compendium theologiae:* "Baptism and the Eucharist depend upon what is done to the one who is sanctified, and not on any action of his, except by way of accident, that is, these are actions of God, who offers and conveys the benefits of the Mediator. We merely receive to ourselves what God by means of His actions conveys in these sacraments. The sacrament of penance, however, consists essentially in an action of the one who is sanctified. And therefore this act of ours is the material of the sacrament. In other sacraments, such as baptism and the Eucharist, which are operative without any act on our part, an exterior element is required." Thus says the *Compendium theologiae.*

6 That it may become still more evident that the dispute is about a necessary and very grave matter when the question is debated whether penance is the kind of sacrament the papalists contend for, let us set over against the just-stated opinion of the papalists about the sacrament of penance as antithesis the way and manner of reconciliation with God for sinners after a fall which Scripture shows and sets forth both by teaching and examples. Now Scripture sets forth two kinds of teaching—Law and Gospel. The Law, in condemning sins and setting forth the gravest threats of God, is that hammer (Jer. 23:29) through which God breaks rocks, that is, crushes the spirit, renders the heart contrite and humbles it, so that truly and earnestly acknowledging the multitude and magnitude of sins and of the wrath of God over sin, the mind begins to hate and detest sin, to fear the wrath and judgment of God so that it is unwilling to perish eternally under them but sighs and struggles with groaning that it may be freed from them. There the Law indeed has and sets forth promises of life, but on condition of perfect fulfillment. But Scripture adds the explanation—because the Law is spiritual, this is the judgment of God about its fulfillment: "Whoever does not abide in all things, let him be cursed"; "Therefore no flesh is justified by the works of the Law" (Rom. 3:20); "All who rely on works of the Law are under a curse" (Gal. 3:10); "Through the Law comes knowledge of sin" (Rom. 3:20); "The law brings wrath" (Rom. 4:15); "Scripture consigned all things to sin" (Gal. 3:22).

The Gospel, however, teaches that what was impossible for the Law on account of the flesh, God provided by sending His Son (Rom. 8:3). Therefore it shows Christ, the Lamb of God, born under the Law for us, in order that He might make satisfaction to the judgment of God, revealed in the Law, by His obedience and suffering on our behalf. This Mediator the Father sets before us in the Gospel as a propitiation by faith in His blood through the remission of sins (Rom. 3:25). "For this is the will of the Father, that everyone who believes in the Son should not perish but have eternal life" (John 6:40). Thus the Gospel proclaims, offers, and sets before contrite and terrified consciences the grace of God, reconciliation and remission of sins freely on account of the merit of Christ; and it is His will that everyone should lay hold of and apply this benefit of the Mediator to himself. The ministry of private absolution applies this general promise of the Gospel to the penitent individually, in order that faith may be able to state all the more firmly that the benefits of the passion of Christ are certainly given and applied to it. Moreover, in the use of the Lord's Supper Christ offers, applies, and seals, to all who receive it in faith, the New Testament with the precious pledges of His body and blood, namely, that God wants to be gracious with respect to our sins and to remember our iniquities no more. Then it is rightly said: "Take heart, my son; your sins are forgiven." For all the prophets give[2] witness that through Christ all who believe in His name receive remission of sins. This is the manner of reconciliation with God.

In order to obscure, shake, and overthrow this, there has been set in opposition to it the debate of the papalists about the sacrament of penance in the manner we have shown, namely, that they lead the sinner who seeks reconciliation with God and forgiveness after a fall, away from faith in the obedience, suffering, and satisfaction of Christ, to confidence in his own act of contrition, confession, and satisfaction, so that when the word of absolution comes to these our works, we may have the cause which both effects and confers reconciliation and remission of sins. This is the true point at issue when the question is debated whether penance is the kind of sacrament the papalists want.

7 It is worth the effort to observe how and on what basis they prove and establish that their penance is a sacrament.

First: Before the coming of Christ into the flesh, that is, at the time of the Old Testament, it was repentance through which those who fell after their circumcision were again reconciled to God. But the Tridentine chapter denies that that repentance was a sacrament, that is, the kind they assert their penance to be. This is very strange. For in the repentance described in the Old Testament there were clear external signs of contrition, and examples are read there of public confession of sins. Chastisements were laid on the sister of Moses and on David by God after their reconciliation.

It is from these examples that the papalists attempt to prove their satisfaction. The power of remitting sin was present also in the Old Testament, for a clear example of it is found in the story of David. And this is the whole definition of the sacrament of penance, namely, contrition, confession, satisfaction, and absolution. And yet they deny that repentance at the time of the Old Testament was a sacrament, perhaps because there confession, also that which was made before the church, was not made into the ear of the priest but to God. Moreover, the chas-

---

2 The text of 1574 has *prohibent.* Ed. Preuss has corrected this to *perhibent.*

tisements after reconciliation were imposed by God Himself, not by the priest. Also, Nathan absolved David not by some judicial power of his own but through the ministry, so that God forgave the sins to David through the ministry of the prophet. It is as Peter says (Acts 10:43): The prophets taught that remission of sins is received in conversion, neither because of nor through the works of the penitent but on account of the blessed promised Seed, through faith in Him. Therefore, because the repentance of the patriarchs and prophets does not, in many respects, agree with papalist penance, therefore they are right in denying that repentance in the time of the Old Testament was such a sacrament as they argue about their penance.

We gladly accept this confession of our opponents, namely, that during 4,000 years from the foundation of the world repentance was not such a sacrament as the papalists argue about, and that during the whole time of the Old Testament there was not such a way and such a mode of reconciliation with God after a fall as the papalists prescribe in the sacrament of their penance. Indeed the apostles, both Peter (Acts 10:43) and Paul (Acts 26:20-23), declare that concerning repentance to God and the reception of the remission of sins they taught no differently from the prophets. This observation will find its use later. For when the papalists adduce testimonies and examples from the Old Testament to prove the sacrament of their penance, we can rightly answer that they prove nothing by that, because the Tridentine chapter declares that repentance in the Old Testament was not a sacrament.

8 Second: The Baptizer preached repentance for the remission of sins. Moreover, Christ's whole preaching is described thus: "Repent and believe the Gospel, for the kingdom of heaven is at hand." But the Tridentine chapter declares that before the resurrection of Christ repentance was not a sacrament and that it is not a sacrament before Baptism. But both the Baptizer and Christ taught about contrition. The hearers of the Baptizer confessed their sins (Matt. 3:6), where also he preached earnestly about the need to bring forth fruits worthy of repentance. Christ also imparted private absolution. (Matt. 9:2 and Luke 7:48)

Why then, according to the definition, is this penance not a sacrament for the papalists? I answer: Because contrition was an inward thing, and confession did not include the enumeration of individual sins. Moreover, Christ imparted absolution without a previous judicial process and imposed penalties, but freely, to those who acknowledged their sins, feared the wrath of God, and by faith sought and asked reconciliation on account of Him. In sum, because in this repentance sins were remitted freely, without works, by faith, on account of Christ, because furthermore the Baptizer as well as Christ preached that faith in the Son, the Mediator, as part of conversion, is necessary for obtaining remission— for these reasons such repentance is not a sacrament for the papalists. Let this be weighed diligently! Therefore the Council of Trent grants and confesses that the sacrament of their penance has no basis, testimony, or example in the preaching of the Baptizer and of Christ before His resurrection, just as it has none in the Old Testament.

9 Third: They show just one basis in Scripture. For the Tridentine chapter says that the sacrament of penance, as the papalists describe it, was instituted by Christ after His resurrection, when He breathed on His disciples and said: "Receive the Holy Spirit; if you forgive the sins of any," etc. Therefore we must consider whether that word of Christ accomplishes what the papalists want, that for the remission of sins there is necessary contrition, confession of mouth, and satisfaction by work, so that these outward operations of the penitent are the material element which, if the word of absolution comes to it, becomes a sacrament which both effects and confers reconciliation and remission of sins, for this is the point at issue in this controversy. Therefore we say that the Novatians are rightly condemned, who taught that reconciliation and remission of sins are to be sought and expected apart from the ministry of the Gospel. None of the men on our side denies that the power to remit and retain sins was given to the ministers of the church by Christ, if this is rightly understood. For Christ chose and sent out the apostles to preach, and gave them authority and power (Matt. 10:1 ff.; Mark 3:13 ff.; 6:7 ff.; Luke 10:1 ff.). And Paul says (2 Cor. 10:8; 13:10) that power was given him by the Lord, not for destruction but for edification.

10 Now this power of forgiving sin must not be understood to have been given to the priests in such a way that God had renounced it for Himself and had simply transferred it to the priests, with the result that in absolution it is not God Himself but the priest who remits sin. For Paul expressly distinguishes between the power and efficacy of reconciliation which belongs to God, and the ministry which was given to the apostles, so that it is God who reconciles the world to Himself (2 Cor. 5:19) and forgives sins (Is. 43:25), not however without means but in and through the ministry of Word and sacrament.

Ministers indeed are said to loose and remit sins on account of the keys, that is, because they have the ministry through which God reconciles the world to Himself and remits sins. Thus Paul says (2 Cor. 1:24) that although he has authority, he nevertheless does not lord it over their faith but is a servant and steward of the mysteries of Christ (1 Cor. 4:1), so that he who plants and he who waters is nothing, but He who gives the increase, namely God (1 Cor. 3:7). Nevertheless, he shows that the use of the ministry is useful and necessary, for, says he, we are co-workers, that is, assistants, whose labors God uses in the ministry, but where nevertheless all the efficacy belongs to Him. We are servants, says he, through whom you have believed. Likewise: "I became your father in Christ Jesus through the Gospel" (1 Cor. 4:15). Paul treats this distinction clearest of all in 2 Cor. 5:18-20. It is God who reconciles us to Himself through Christ, not counting our sins against us. To the apostles, however, He gave the ministry of reconciliation. But how so? "He entrusted to us," says Paul, "the message of reconciliation. So we are ambassadors for Christ, God making His appeal through us. We beseech you on behalf of Christ, be reconciled to God."

Thus this distinction honors God and gives Him the glory that properly belongs to Him; it also claims for the ministry the honor and authority it has according to the Word of God. For even as it is Christ who baptizes through the ministry and also imparts His body and blood, so also it is Christ who through the ministry absolves and remits sins. And here belongs the statement of Augustine, *De consecratione,* dist. 4: "It is one thing to baptize through the ministry; it is another thing to baptize through one's own power." Likewise: "Through this power, which Christ holds for Himself alone and transfers to none of the ministers, although He saw fit to baptize through ministers by virtue of this power, I say, stands the unity of the church. For if it were transferred from the Lord to the ministers, there would be as many baptisms as there are ministers." Thus says Augustine. Therefore we seek remission of sins with God and receive it from God through Christ and because of Christ, but in the ministry and through the ministry.

11 We shall presently show why this necessary distinction is passed over in the Tridentine chapter. But first we shall go through the rest, namely, how the sacred ministry of the Gospel remits sins, or rather, how God remits sins through the ministry. For herein lies the chief point of the controversy. The explanation must, however, be taken from the context, and from nowhere else. For when Christ was about to explain the remission and retention of sins, He introduced the explanation with these words: "As the Father has sent Me, even so I send you." And when He had said this, He breathed on them, etc.

How Christ had been sent, however, that He might be a minister of the circumcision, He Himself explains (Luke 4:18-19) from the prophet Isaiah (61:1-2): "He has sent me to preach the Gospel to the poor, to heal the brokenhearted, to proclaim forgiveness to the captives and freedom to prisoners, to comfort those who mourn, to preach the acceptable year and the day of vengeance for our God." Clearer, however, and to this extent more certain is this explanation, which Luke uses in describing the same event John relates in the passage: "If you forgive the sins of any," etc. Luke reports that Christ spoke about preaching repentance and remission of sins. Therefore remission and retention of sins through the ministry (John 20:23) is made through proclamation of the Word (Luke 24:47). The one is explained by the other.

But the doctrine of the Law and of sin and the doctrine of the Gospel about the remission of sins on account of Christ are not merely to be recited as history, but an accommodation or application of both the Law and the Gospel must be made to the hearers, in order that when sin and the wrath of God against sin have been shown from the Law, the wrath of God may be declared to sinners for judgment to damnation unless they are reconciled to God. However, let the Pauline exhortation: "Be reconciled to God," be formed from the Gospel, as also what is found in Ezekiel: "Why will you die, O house of Israel?" And let it be shown that it is the will of God that everyone should accept in faith and apply to himself the benefits of Christ's suffering set forth and offered in the Gospel. The Gospel declares that those who so believe are reconciled to God and receive remission of sins. In order that this proclamation may be efficacious for the remission of sins, Christ adds His Holy Spirit to the ministry by breathing on them (John 20:22). For the Gospel is the power of God to salvation for the believer (Rom. 1:16), that is, the weapons of the ministry are strong and mighty through the working of the Spirit (2 Cor. 10:4). However, those who do not believe, that is, who either from Epicurean security or from a Pharisaic opinion despise the application of reconciliation which takes place by faith on account of Christ when the message of the Gospel is accepted, to them the wrath of God and eternal damnation is proclaimed. In this way, by the public and general proclamation of repentance and remission of sins, the ministry, or rather, God Himself through the ministry and in the ministry, looses and binds, remits and retains sins.

12 Moreover, just as the doctrine which rebukes sins and proclaims the wrath of God to the impenitent is to be set forth not only in general but, as pastoral care demands (Ezek. 34:1-10), to individuals privately where necessity calls for it, and sins are to be retained and bound by annunciation of the judgment of God on the basis of the Word, so also the promise of the Gospel is efficacious not only when it is announced in general and when it is apprehended by faith in the general proclamation, but it is the duty of the shepherd, if he knows that some sheep is sick or broken, that he bind it up and heal it by applying the ministry of Word and

sacrament privately. Therefore private absolution remits the sins of the contrite who seek consolation by faith in no other way than that it privately or to individuals announces the remission of sins through the Word of the Gospel, which also Christ Himself shows by His own example (Matt. 9:2; Luke 7:48). This proclamation, whether it is called either particular, individual, special, or private, is efficacious for the forgiving of sins because it is a ministry of the Spirit, through which God strengthens faith and forgives sins. For it is the same Gospel, and its efficacy is the same, whether it is proclaimed generally to many, or privately, either to one or a few. And on account of the weakness of faith, for fuller and stronger consolation, God wants the promise of grace set forth not only in general, but to be applied also privately to individuals who seek it, not by the sacraments only but also through proclamation of the Gospel, as Christ shows in Matt. 9:2 and Luke 7:48, in order that my faith may be able to state all the more firmly that the general promise of the Gospel pertains also to me privately, that God includes also me in it, and that He gives and applies to me in particular the benefits of the suffering of Christ. Thus the statement of Christ (John 20:23) about remitting sins, whether it be understood of public or general proclamation of the Gospel, or of private absolution, says nothing else than this, that the ministry remits and retains sins by the voice or proclamation of the Word of God.

Those, however, who simply take away and condemn the use of private absolution, err. But also those err who contend that by the general proclamation of the Gospel sins are forgiven to no one, but that forgiveness takes place only in private absolution.

13 Now that the true explanation of the statement of Christ in John 20:23 has been set down, let us see how successfully the papalists build up the sacrament of their penance from it.

14 Let us consider first that the Tridentine chapter says that this statement of Christ is not to be understood of the power or authority of proclaiming the Gospel of Christ. And indeed, if they were censuring those who preach the Gospel only as history, without accommodation or application (as we have said), or who remove the use of absolution entirely from the church, they would be speaking rightly. But in the statement of Christ they understand a power of remitting sins which does not consist in the proclamation of the Gospel, whether it be done generally or privately. For Andrada, writing during the Council of Trent, says that these are very distinct and different things in the ministry of the apostles: to proclaim the Gospel, and to remit sins. But we have already shown from the words of Christ that the power of remitting sins which Christ gave to His disciples consists in the very ministry of proclaiming the Gospel.

15 Perhaps, therefore, they imagine such a power of remitting sins as Simon Magus asks (Acts 8:18-19), that power be sold to him so that anyone on whom he laid his hands would immediately be given the Holy Spirit. For also the papalists teach that the power of remitting sins has its basis not in the proclamation of the word of the Gospel but in the priestly character. The Jesuits of Cologne explain what kind of power the Council of Trent has in mind thus, that Christ by the statement in John 20:23 constituted the priests judges of the Christians, in order that, when cases have been explained and examined, they may either remit sins or retain them, and that therefore the same thing is required in the sacrament of penance which a secular court requires in a defendant, namely, that he first of all shows by external signs that he repents of his sins; second, that he confesses, one by one, the sins he wants remitted; third, that he with placid mind bears what the priest commands him, as a penalty laid on him by a judge. Then, if to these actions of the sinner and of the priest there comes the word of absolution, the sacrament is completed, by which the fallen are reconciled to God and receive forgiveness. And, say the Jesuits, Christ has promised to abide by this judgment of the priests, in John 20:23, where He says: "If you forgive the sins of any." The second Tridentine chapter says the same thing, namely, that the sacrament of penance consists in this, that penitent sinners are placed before the tribunal of the priests and through their sentence are freed from the sins they have committed. So they declare.

But Christ certainly does not say any of this in the statement in John 20:23, for not one syllable is found there about such a judicial procedure. There is found, however, in the account in Luke 24:46-47 an express statement about preaching remission of sins. No mention is made in John 20:23 of the enumeration of sins, nor of a penalty to be imposed; rather, the apostles are commanded to preach, not a payment for sins which is made through our works, but forgiveness of sins through the satisfaction rendered by Christ. Therefore the sacrament of papalist penance is not deduced and taken from the statement of Christ in John 20:23, but an alien fiction is pressed upon and thrust into this statement of Christ contrary to the plain words and the clear meaning of Christ, which can certainly be understood from the fact that the statement in John 20:23 speaks generally of the ministry of the apostles, which embraces also repentance and remission of sins before Baptism, as also Christ speaks (Luke 24:46-47) in the same narrative about preaching repentance, and expressly of remission of sins, to all nations which had not yet been baptized.

But according to the council penance before Baptism is not a sacrament, neither does it call for a judicial procedure. With what certainty can the sacrament of papalist penance therefore be proved from the statement in John 20:23? For if the power to forgive sins of necessity made the sacrament of penance, it would follow (a teaching the papalists deny) that also repentance in the Old Testament was a sacrament, for the power to remit sins was there; Nathan used it in absolving David. Therefore the sacrament of penance as taught by the papalists does not have a sure, firm, and solid basis in the statement of Christ in John 20:23.

16 Fourth: The sacrament of papalist penance can also not be proved from the teaching and examples of the apostles. For Paul, in setting forth the sum of his teaching about repentance (Acts 26:20-23), declares that he had taught nothing but what the prophets had said. Also Peter declares (Acts 10:43) that he was teaching that way of obtaining forgiveness of sins which had the witness of the prophets. But the Tridentine chapter denies that repentance in the Old Testament was a sacrament. Moreover, we never read anywhere in Scripture that the apostles demanded an enumeration of sins as necessary for forgiveness; nor do we read that they imposed a penalty on those whose sins they remitted, but they exhorted those who had been reconciled that, after they had received forgiveness, they should bring forth fruits worthy of repentance.

Without ground and false is also the claim that the apostles taught one kind of repentance, so far as the essence is concerned, by which the wicked are turned to God before Baptism, and another different repentance by which those who have fallen after Baptism return into grace with God. For they did not set a different law, another Gospel, another Christ, or another faith before those who had fallen after Baptism. But the contrition the apostles taught, whether before Baptism or in the case of those who fell after Baptism, is acknowledgment, hatred, and detestation of sin, fear of the wrath and judgment of God, terrors of conscience, coupled with the desire to escape the wrath of God. The apostles taught that reconciliation with God and remission of sins must be sought and laid hold of by faith, not in our works but in the obedience, satisfaction, and merit of Christ, the Mediator, whether it be before Baptism or in the case of sins after Baptism.

17 Moreover, in the things that are essential to repentance the apostles make no difference as to whether repentance is necessary before Baptism or for sins after Baptism, but when they teach the doctrine of repentance they speak of repentance in general. There are indeed found in the writings of the apostles examples of conversion of such as lapsed after Baptism, for example the Galatians. These Paul does not lead to another, new, and different way of reconciliation with God, but preaches most vehemently against the persuasion of justification by works, concluding all under sin. Furthermore, he teaches that they are justified before God on account of the merit of Christ alone, apprehended by faith. In essentials this repentance or conversion is the same as that by which they had first been converted from idols to God. In the case of the incestuous Corinthian, whom Paul had excommunicated, we have an example of public repentance in which certain public, external signs of sorrow and repentance are required. But Paul does not teach that these acts are the cause of the forgiveness of sins, but (2 Cor. 2:7, 10) uses the word *charizesthai* ["to be gracious to"]. Paul's judgment always is: "If it is by works, it is no longer by grace but faith has been made of no effect and the promise has been abolished."

18 Fifth: The men of Trent say that the universal consensus of the fathers and of the catholic church from the beginning understood the kind of sacrament of penance such as they themselves teach. But the following argument was unknown to all of antiquity: As there is an external element in Baptism and the Eucharist, which makes the sacrament when the Word comes to it, so also in penance there is necessary an external material or element by which the sacrament of penance comes into being when the word or absolution comes to it. It was also unknown to the ancients that the actions are the element or material.

Indeed, it is useful to observe in the history of antiquity from what beginnings, once the tendency had been started, little by little things finally progressed to the papalist arguments and opinions about the sacrament of penance. There is no doubt whatever that the first beginning resulted from the displays of public penitence which the ancient church observed with great severity in the case of open and atrocious crimes. For in it there were required external signs of contrition, acknowledgement or confession of the crime, and before they were again received into communion with the church certain external punishments were imposed—for one thing, to provide an example for others, then also for the sake of exploring whether the repentance was genuine. We read that two reminders were added by the ancients: 1. That these ceremonies were not universally necessary for all who acknowledged sins and lapses after Baptism and desired to be reconciled with God through repentance and obtain grace and forgiveness of sins. For there was a difference between public and private repentance. 2. The ancients also taught that these ceremonies of repentance do not merit forgiveness of sins but are only external signs and testimonies, as many statements of the ancients about repentance, dist. 1, testify. Little by little, however, superstitious opinions began to be patched on, to the effect that these ceremonies merited and procured forgiveness. Some of the fathers (Origen and others) began to urge the people to make known by confession to the priest also other sins, also such as were not notorious crimes or subject to excommunication, for the sake of counsel and remedy, namely, that the sins might be warded off in this way. Some also permitted ecclesiastical chastisements or punishments to be inflicted on themselves for hidden sins. These they called satisfactions. From this there came into being a general rule and doctrine that, besides contrition of heart and faith which embraces Christ, also confession of mouth, which must be made to a priest, and satisfaction by work belong to penance, by which those who have fallen into sins of whatever kind after Baptism might be reconciled to God.

19 There were varying debates, some asserting that confession and satisfaction belong not to obtaining forgiveness but to showing repentance; others argued the contrary, that this is done to obtain forgiveness. Gratian[3] collected these dissimilar statements of the ancients in the decree concerning penance. Later in the time of Gratian, around A.D. 1150, men disputed vigorously about the necessity of confession and satisfaction. Nevertheless Gratian concludes thus, after setting forth the diverse opinions, dist. 1, *De poenitentia, ch. Quamvis plenitudo:* "However, we leave it to the judgment of the reader to decide to which of these one should prefer to adhere. For each has wise and godly men promoting it." And the explanation, *De poenitentia,* dist. 5, says that various arguments were sought by which it might be proved that sacramental confession is by divine right, for instance, when God said to Adam: "Adam, where are you?" and to Cain: "Where is Abel your brother?" Or Joshua 7:19-21, where Achan confessed his transgression, or James 5:16: "Confess your sins to one another." But because the explanation acknowledges the weakness of these arguments, he finally concludes: "It is better to say that confession was instituted from a certain tradition of the universal church rather than from the authority of either the New or the Old Testament. And he adds: "With the Greeks confession is not necessary, because such a tradition did not become known to them."

Bonaventura also says that guilt is forgiven through inner repentance, which consists in acknowledging the crime and the need for punishment, and thereafter in recognizing divine mercy, and that the penance which consists of confession and satisfaction was instituted by the church.

Out of these discordant and uncertain arguments and opinions there

---

[3] Reference is to the *Decretum* of Gratian, composed during the first half of the 12th century. For a fuller description see the *New Catholic Encyclopedia,* VI, 706 ff.

was finally fabricated an article of faith, namely that confession and satisfaction, as though by divine right, are necessary for procuring remission of sins. This dogma the Council of Trent establishes with nothing more than the threat of the anathema. Such therefore is now the sacrament of penance, about which the papalists contend. It is useful to consider from whence and from what diverse and uncertain arguments it was begun before the times of Gratian and established after his times. For thus what they boast about the consensus of all the fathers is most rightly refuted.

SECTION II

Concerning the Difference Between the Sacrament of Penance and Baptism

Chapter II

As for the rest, this sacrament is seen to differ from Baptism in many ways. For beside the fact that they differ very greatly in matter and form, which constitute the essence of a sacrament, it is certain that the minister of baptism need not be a judge, since the Church exercises judgment over no one who has not first entered into it through the door of baptism. "For," says the apostle, "what have I to do with judging outsiders?" It is different with members of the family, whom Christ our Lord has once, by the washing of baptism, made members of His body. For He willed that these, if afterward they defiled themselves with some crime, should not be washed by a second baptism, since this is in no way permitted in the Catholic Church, but that they, as guilty ones, should be placed before this tribunal, that by the judgment of the priests they might be able to be set free, not once but as often as they should, penitent, have recourse to it from the sins they have committed. Moreover, the benefit of Baptism is one thing, that of penance another. For when we put on Christ through Baptism, we are made an entirely new creature in Him and receive full and entire remission of sins. To this newness and wholeness we can by no means come through the sacrament of penance without many tears and labors on our part, since divine justice demands this. Therefore penance has deservedly been called by the holy fathers a laborious kind of baptism. This sacrament of penance is, however, necessary for salvation for those who have fallen after baptism, just as baptism itself is necessary for those who have not yet been regenerated.

CANON II

If anyone, confounding the sacraments, says that baptism itself is the sacrament of penance, as though these two sacraments were not distinct, and that therefore penance is not rightly called a second plank after shipwreck, let him be anathema.

Examination

1 If the fathers at Trent had wanted to say only this that repentance is something else than Baptism and that those who have fallen after Baptism are not to be cleansed by a repetition of Baptism if they are converted but are to be reconciled to God through repentance, there would have been no need for so long a chapter, nor for so elaborate an

anathema. But it is a far other thing which wrung this long chapter from them. For they think and teach that through sins committed after Baptism the very power, efficacy, and grace of the covenant into which God has entered with us in Baptism is wholly lost and rendered invalid, so that faith can in no way and at no time return in true repentance to the grace of Baptism but must now look around for another plank, namely, our work in contrition, confession, and satisfaction, by the power of which we can swim out of the waves of our sins and be carried to the haven of salvation.

Now, because in this way the efficacy and use of Baptism are restricted to only the precise moment when we are baptized, and another way of reconciliation with God and of forgiveness of sins is set forth, different from that which is offered to faith in the gratuitous promise of the Gospel on account of the merit of Christ and sealed in Baptism, the men on our side have rejected this false opinion and have shown from the Word of God that we have been taken up in such a way by an everlasting covenant into participation in the promise of the Gospel, and into communion with the merit of Christ, that we either persevere in it or, if we have fallen from it through sins, may return in faith to this covenant sealed to us in Baptism. This repentance is not a new way of meriting remission of sins through our works but is only a return to the gratuitous promise of remission of sins on account of the satisfaction of Christ, the Mediator, which has been given and sealed to us in Baptism in order that we may have a return to it after every fall, "not seven times but seventy times seven." For the promise of Baptism saves us through Jesus Christ in order that, justified by His grace, we may be heirs of eternal life (Titus 3:7); it appeals for a good conscience before God through the resurrection of Christ (1 Peter 3:21). Now, indeed, in true repentance faith seeks this after every fall, that the conscience may be reconciled to God through the death and resurrection of Christ, that, justified by His grace, we may be heirs of eternal life. Therefore repentance is nothing else than a return to the promise of grace in Baptism, not that we may be baptized again but that we may in repentance through faith return to that grace from which we fell through sins.

2 This is the belief which the men of Trent wanted to condemn here. But let us observe what is the antithesis about which the papalists contend! In Baptism reconciliation and remission of sins are given as a free gift, without our works, on account of the merit and satisfaction of Christ, to those who repent and believe the Gospel. However, to those who have fallen after Baptism (as Hosius says) there is not such an easy, free, and gratuitous way open to forgiveness of sins, but (as the Tridentine chapter says) we are by no means able, through the sacrament of penance, to come to reconciliation with God without our own great tears and labors, since divine justice demands this. And indeed, it is a graver sin to grieve the Holy Spirit after Baptism and to profane His temple, for "the last state has become worse for them than the first" (2 Peter 2:20). Therefore contrition has greater pain, and the conscience has heavier grief in the case of one seeking reconciliation in lapses after Baptism. But it is something else that the Tridentine chapter is after, namely, that in Baptism remission of sins is indeed given gratis, without our works, on account of the merit of Christ, and is accepted by faith; however, in those who have fallen after Baptism, penance obtains forgiveness not gratis, by faith, and without works, but through and on account of the works of penance. And therefore, say they, absolution in penance is not the dispensation and offering of the gratuitous benefit of reconciliation on account of the merit of Christ, as in Baptism, but a judgment in which the sins are compared with the labor of penance, and over and above this a certain penalty is also imposed for satisfaction. In view of this, reconciliation with God is promised to the penitent. This is the sum and substance of this second chapter. This is the same thing they say elsewhere, namely, that there is a twofold justification, the first of which is made gratis, by faith, without works, on account of Christ, the second not gratis, but through and on account of works. But these things have been both explained and refuted in the first part of this examination under the topic of justification, and in the second part in connection with the sixth and the ninth canon concerning Baptism.

About the tribunal of penitential judgment we shall speak more fittingly when we come to confession. Therefore it is sufficient here to have shown what it is that the Council of Trent wants when it argues so laboriously about the difference between the sacrament of penance and Baptism. However, this belongs to a fuller explanation of what penance is, of which the papalists make a sacrament, a penance, namely, which seeks and obtains reconciliation and remission of sins not gratis, by faith, without the merits of our works, as is done in Baptism, but through and on account of the labors and works of our penitence. What labors and works these are the next chapter at once explains.

SECTION III

Concerning the Parts and the Fruit
of the Sacrament of Penance

Chapter III

The holy synod furthermore teaches that the form of the sacrament of penance, in which especially its power is situated, is placed in the words of the minister: "I absolve you," etc. To these words, by custom of holy Church, certain prayers are laudably joined. These, however, by no means belong to the essence of the form, neither are they necessary for the administration of the sacrament. However, the actions of the penitent person himself are, as it were, the material of this sacrament, namely, contrition, confession, and satisfaction. These, since they are required in the penitent person by the institution of God for the integrity of the sacrament and for the full and perfect remission of sins, are for this reason called the parts of penance. It is true, the thing itself and the effect of this sacrament, so far as its power and efficacy is concerned, is reconciliation with God. In pious persons and such as receive this sacrament with devotion, this is generally followed by peace and serenity of conscience, together with great consolation of spirit. In teaching these things about the parts and effects of this sacrament, the holy synod at the same time condemns the opinions of those who contend that the parts of penance are terrors struck into the conscience, and faith.

CANON IV

If anyone denies that for complete and perfect remission of sins three actions are required in the penitent person, making up as it were the material of the sacrament of penance, namely, contrition, confession, and satisfaction, which three are called the parts of penance, or says that there are only two parts of penance, namely, terrors struck into the conscience by the knowledge of sin, and faith conceived from the Gospel or from absolution, by which one believes that his sins are forgiven through Christ, let him be anathema.

Examination

1 Two things are treated in this chapter which must be examined. First, what is the material and what the form in penance by which it becomes a sacrament, the effect, power, and efficacy of which is reconciliation with God and perfect remission of sins; second, what are the parts of penance which are required in the penitent for full and perfect remission of sins.

We are here dealing with a most weighty matter, namely, in what way and from where those who have fallen may in true repentance again be reconciled with God and receive remission of sins; whence repentance has the power and efficacy to remit sins; what it is on which the conscience needs to lean in repentance so that it may not doubt that it has been received again into grace by God.

2 Now, because Lombard had first of all made a sacrament of repentance, the scholastics afterward began to inquire what is the material and what the form from which repentance could have the nature of a sacrament and could support the definition. For in order that a thing be a sacrament it is necessary that it have, by divine institution, an external element, a sign as it were, and a word joined to the element by divine ordinance, together with a promise about its power and efficacy. Irenaeus calls it an earthly and a heavenly thing; Augustine calls it an element or visible form, a word or visible grace. However, as I have said earlier, this discussion, whether there is in penance a sacramental material and form, is wholly unknown to antiquity. Augustine, *De fide ad Petrum,* calls Baptism the sacrament of faith and repentance. In a number of places he counts the laying on of hands, by which those who repented were publicly reconciled to the church, among the sacraments. However it cannot be shown that repentance itself, by which sins are remitted to a man, was called a sacrament in the true antiquity.

3 Therefore also, as in a new thing, since no statements were found with the fathers, the scholastics debated in various ways what in penance might be such a material which would become a sacrament when the Word came to it. In order to retain the peculiar nature of a material, some taught that the sins themselves are the material of this sacrament. Others said that the sinner himself, confessing, is the material. Afterward a transformation was made and they changed the element or material from the quality of a substance into the quality of an action and argued that the actions of penance could be the material of the sacrament. And they taught that for the visible species or form, which Augustine says is required in sacraments, it is sufficient if only there is something that can be perceived, whether it be by sight or by hearing, perhaps even by either taste or smell. Nevertheless they are not agreed on which action in penance is the material in the sacrament of penance, whether it is the action of the priest who pronounces absolution with certain ceremonies, or whether it is the actions of the penitent person, and, if so, which actions. Some set down contrition, confession, and satisfaction as the material of the sacrament. But because contrition is not visible, and satisfaction by work follows reception of the sacrament itself, some teach that confession alone is the material. Some teach that the words of absolution are the form of the sacrament of penance. But because the form of the words of absolution is not determined in the Word of God, as it is in Baptism and the Eucharist, therefore, lest the certainty of the efficacy of the sacrament should waver if the form were uncertain, others said that the actions of the priest who absolves take the place of the form and that it is sufficient if the action is expressed, even if it is not done in fixed and prescribed words—just as a secular judge, in handing down a sentence either of acquittal or of condemnation, is not bound to a certain form of words. Thus the act is the material in the penitent person; in the priest it is the form. Is there anything which one could not make a sacrament if one is willing to play in this way with material and form? In prayer outward gestures are often added; the preaching of the Gospel is some kind of action; why should not sacraments be made also of them?

4 But let us speak of the thing itself. It is a great and difficult matter to set up and consider something as a sacrament. For the sacraments are, as it were, divine vessels in which are deposited, as it were, by divine ordinance the merits of Christ, the grace of God, forgiveness of sins, etc., that through these instruments, as it were, God may distribute, apply, and seal these benefits to believers. Therefore it is necessary that the material in the sacraments be instituted, ordained, and prescribed by God Himself in the Word. There is need for a sure word, handed down by God Himself, which, when it comes to the material or element, makes a sacrament which has a divine promise of spiritual grace and efficacy. In the debate about penance we are treating of a great thing, namely, of reconciliation with God and remission of sins. In penance this grace, power, and efficacy is ascribed to human works or acts. But where is it taught and instituted that these acts of the penitent person are the material which, when the Word comes to it, becomes a sacrament, the effect of which is reconciliation and remission of sins? Where is there a certain word prescribed? Where does one find a promise given that, if this material and form are joined, the power and efficacy to forgive sins is present? Surely, it is presumptuous wickedness and wicked presumption to invent a sacrament of which neither the material nor the form nor the promise is contained in the Word of God.

5 But let the mystery of iniquity be considered which is hidden and concealed under this forged material of the sacrament of penance! It is the most ancient trick of Satan to lead men, when they seek reconciliation with God and remission of sins, to their own works in order that they may oppose them to the judgment of God to obtain remission of sins. This pharisaic persuasion was most sternly suppressed by the thunderbolt of Paul and driven out of the church. But the master of a thousand stratagems afterward tried in various ways to foist trust in works for righteousness before God upon the church. Sometimes he succeeded in this; often, however, he was restrained by the sword of the Spirit. Finally God punished the contempt of the truth and the ingratitude of the world (2 Thess. 2:11-12), and human works in penance were not only taught to be meritorious but, what is more, sacraments for obtaining reconciliation with God and remission of sins. Sacraments are, however, divine actions. Therefore when a sacrament is forged of the human works of contrition, confession, and satisfaction, then a certain divinity is arrogated to human works, that their throne may be exalted to the stars, as Isaiah says of the king of Babylon [Is. 14:13]. For Thomas argues, 4, dist. 16, art. 1, that in the sacrament of penance a human action stands in the place of the material, because it takes away the offense of the previous guilt through a measure of compensation.

6 Gropper notices this. Therefore he seeks to mitigate it in the *Institutio Coloniensis*. He says that penance is called a sacrament by reason of absolution, because it applies the general promise to individuals who seek it, and that the external action of the priest by which he bestows the absolution may be called the material, because it is the outward sign of how God inwardly frees the soul from the fetters of sin. But no command, no ordinance, no promise about external rites and gestures in absolution is found in the word of God. Neither is everything which can signify something spiritual at once a divine sacrament. But so far as absolution itself is concerned, the explanations of the Augsburg Confession and of the Apology are well known.

7 The Council of Trent, however, does not allow and receive even this mitigation, neither the one which was proposed in the formula of the Augsburg Interim,[4] but simply decrees that the human works of the penitent together with the word of absolution bring about the sacrament of penance, the effect, power, and efficacy of which is reconciliation with God and remission of sins. It adds, however, that this is done by institution of God. But it is false that there is any commandment of God in the Word of God about the enumeration of individual sins and about papalist satisfaction. It is also wholly unknown to antiquity that the actions of the penitent are the sacramental material. Also at the time of the scholastic doctors, yes, even at the time of Gabriel Biel, a hundred years ago, it was doubtful and uncertain what might be the true material of the sacrament of penance. What certainty, then, can there be about the effect of a sacrament when the material and form are uncertain and there is no

---

[4] A temporary agreement in religious matters made at the Diet of Augsburg in 1548, to be in force until the next general council.

promise? It is perhaps for this reason that the Tridentine chapter says that "the actions of the penitent are the material of the sacrament of penance, as it were *(vel quasi)*." Therefore also the sacrament will be "as it were." Also its effect, the remission of sins, will be "as it were."

8 This is the real reason why they contend about the sacrament of penance, that they may make reconciliation and remission of sins dubious and uncertain. It is not, however, doubtful that private absolution is efficacious, because it is the voice of the Gospel, which is "the power of God for salvation to every one who has faith." Therefore I approve the statement of Gerson that absolution should be imparted not in the optative mood, in the form of an invocation, but in such a way that the one who is absolved may hear and understand that through this ministry of announcing the Gospel God individually applies to him the merit and benefits of Christ for the forgiveness of sins. But also absolution itself is perverted in this papalist sacrament, for it is not permitted to be an evangelical absolution but is announced as a purely legal one. For it is not imparted gratis, by faith, without our works, on account of the merit of Christ, but on condition of the acts of contrition, confession, and satisfaction which the Council of Trent requires in the penitent person for perfect remission of sins as the material of the sacrament. But because no one can be sure whether he has these actions in the required degree, the conscience always remains in doubt and uncertain with respect to reconciliation. Yes, if justification, that is, remission of sins, is by works, "faith is null and the promise is void" (Rom. 4:14). "All who rely on works of the Law are under a curse" (Gal. 3:10). Therefore the sacrament of papalist penance is truly a torment of consciences.

9 The other question of this third chapter concerns the parts of repentance. In order that the inquiry may be more intelligible, we note that the Tridentine chapter says that it is speaking of the parts of penance which are required in the penitent person for obtaining full and complete remission of sins. Once again the dispute is about a great matter, embracing the salvation of us all. For it is certain that God wants to receive the fallen, but only if they repent. Therefore it is a burning question how one can repent in such a way that we may be sure we are receiving reconciliation and remission of sins. For if one does not repent rightly, then even though the sinner seeks remission of sins, he nevertheless does not attain it.

10 Here Scripture shows us the way by both testimonies and examples, setting before us two kinds of teaching—of the Law and of the Gospel. The Law indeed condemns sins, sets forth the threats of God, and thus, when sin has been recognized, strikes terrors into the conscience, so that it begins to fear the wrath of God and thus to detest sin. This is the first step of repentance; it does not, indeed, merit remission of sins, but this order has been instituted by God in order that, according to the saying of Bernard, "He may pour the oil of His mercy only into a vessel which is contrite and afflicted." The Law is truly a tutor leading to Christ. For because true repentance desires to escape the wrath of God and damnation, the Law declares that no flesh is justified before God by works. Therefore by this very fact the Law banishes from its presence the terrified sinner who seeks reconciliation with God. Then indeed the Gospel displays to us the obedience and satisfaction of Christ, the Mediator, which He has provided for us, and on account of this merit of Christ it offers to us grace and remission of sins. It does require this of us, that we accept this benefit of Christ by faith and apply it to ourselves, and declares that those who believe in Christ receive forgiveness through His name. It exhorts those who have been reconciled, who have received forgiveness of sins, that they should thereafter bear fruits worthy of repentance. Thus, according to Scripture, in order that we may obtain reconciliation there is required in the penitent person contrition, and faith, which lays hold of the merit of Christ; the fruits follow after reconciliation. This manner of repenting is clear and sure, for it is taught in Scripture and has the promise of the remission of sins.

11 But the Council of Trent shows without dissembling what kind of emendation it has been promising heretofore, when it proclaims with a loud voice that it condemns the opinion of those who argue that the parts of repentance are terrors of conscience and faith. They are unwilling to grant that terrors struck into the conscience by God through the preaching of the Law are part of repentance, because they want contrition to be sorrow over sin, voluntarily assumed—a punishment, as it were, which by this work merits the mercy of God, as the next chapter will explain.

It is worth the effort to observe why and in what sense they exclude and banish faith, which seeks remission of sins, from repentance even though the scholastics teach that faith is the root and basis from which repentance springs. Moreover, in the fourth chapter the Council of Trent says that contrition ought to be joined with trust in divine mercy. Does then the controversy perhaps consist only in this, that the papalists say that faith is the basis of repentance while the men on our side teach that it is a part? Certainly, if there were agreement on both sides that faith is necessary in repentance for obtaining remission of sins, the church should not be disturbed if one called faith the basis and another called it a part of repentance, since indeed it is something greater if a thing is the basis than a part.

But I beg, dear reader, that you pay close attention. The third chapter simply names faith as that which it excludes from the parts of repentance. The fourth canon, however, explicates and explains what kind of faith it is which the papalists are unwilling to tolerate in their repentance, namely a faith which is conceived from the Word of the Gospel or absolution, and by means of which the penitent person believes that through and on account of Christ sins are remitted and have been remitted to him. Therefore when they say that faith is the basis of repentance, they have in mind this persuasion, that if anyone undertakes and performs those actions of penance prescribed by the papalists, he secures forgiveness of sins and is reconciled to God by these actions. For they say that the actions of penance must be undertaken with this persuasion, and this is what they mean when they say that faith is the basis of repentance.

Therefore when Canon 4 condemns with the anathema those who say that the faith which is conceived through the Gospel or absolution, by which a person believes his sins are remitted through Christ, is a necessary part of repentance for obtaining remission of sins, what does it do but take the Gospel wholly out of repentance and condemn the very Word of the Gospel as taught by the prophets, Christ, and the apostles? For Peter says about the teaching of the prophets, Acts 10:43: "To Christ all the prophets bear witness that every one who believes in Him receives forgiveness through His name." Mark 1:15 explains the sum of the teaching of the ministry of Christ thus: "Repent, and believe the Gospel." And after the resurrection He commands the apostles to preach repentance and remission of sins in His name (Luke 24:47). After His ascension he charged Paul with the ambassadorship of the Gospel in the words: "That they may turn from darkness to light and . . . receive forgiveness of sins. . . through faith which is in Me" (Acts 26:18). Moreover, Paul himself (Acts 20:21), when he was threatened with imprisonment, summed up the content of his preaching among Jews and Gentiles under these points: "testifying . . . of repentance to God and of faith in our Lord Jesus Christ." But to those who had been reconciled he set forth the teaching that "they should . . . perform deeds worthy of repentance" (Acts 26:20). Everywhere you hear that faith—the faith which recieves remission of sins through the name of Christ—is connected with repentance. And, lest we heap up more testimonies, what will be left of the Gospel if you take away from it Christ, faith in Christ, and remission of sins, which is laid hold of by faith in Christ? And yet the Council of Trent is not afraid to condemn with the anathema anyone who says that faith, conceived from the Gospel, by which one believes his sins are forgiven through Christ, is a part of repentance!

I was indeed able to expect beforehand that the Council of Trent would not, in the teaching about repentance, teach rightly or clearly concerning faith that seeks and receives remission of sins through and on account of Christ in the voice of the Gospel. But I would never have allowed myself to be persuaded that it would come to pass that, with the Word of God shining so brightly, they would condemn with a public anathema anyone who says that faith, conceived from the Gospel, by which one believes that his sins are forgiven through Christ, is a part of saving repentance. But by means of these marks and tokens it is, by the judgment of God, revealed before the whole world what kind of church the papalist assembly is. Therefore let it be known to the true church of God for a perpetual remembrance of this thing, that the Council of Trent promises to penance reconciliation with God and remission of sins without faith which is conceived from the Gospel and through which one believes that sins are forgiven him through Christ. For so the fourth canon decrees with resounding voice

12 But let us hear what parts they themselves assign to penance, which they say are necessary and sufficient without faith for the remission of sins. They enumerate contrition, confession, and satisfaction. And because they also make these parts of penance the material of the sacrament, which must be external and visible or perceivable, therefore these parts must not be understood of inner contrition, nor of confession made to God, nor of the intention of inner betterment, but of the outward acts of contrition, of outward confession, which is made to one's priest through enumeration of all transgressions, and of the external works of satisfaction commanded by the confessor.

13 But Scripture nowhere teaches that outward signs of contrition are necessary for the forgiveness of sins. Special enumeration of all transgressions, to be made to the priest, is not commanded in the Word of God, nor has it any example there. The papalists themselves define the works of satisfaction as not being owed, that is, not commanded in the Word of God. Therefore they have parts of penance without Scripture, and indeed such parts as also hypocrites can imitate and present. Nevertheless they ascribe to these the forgiveness of sins, while at the same time they condemn under the anathema, in repentance, faith conceived from the Gospel, by which someone believes that his sins are forgiven through Christ. Now Judas, who lacked this faith, although he had the parts of papalist penance, namely contrition, confession, and satisfaction, went and hanged himself. For so great is the consolation in these parts of penance when faith in Christ is excluded.

The threefold enumeration of the parts of penitence, taken over from the public ceremonies of penitence, was afterward ignorantly applied to the general teaching of repentance, with the ceremonies in part abrogated, in part changed.

To this must be added the fact that the ancients speak in many statements about repentance not insofar as it seeks and receives remission of sins but insofar as it is a change and betterment of life. In those cases Augustine and Chrysostom are wont to speak thus: "Even as there are three different kinds of sins, and we offend God in three different ways, namely with heart, mouth, and works, so on the opposite side true betterment must be undertaken in mind, word, and work." The monks did not pay proper attention to these things and made of them three parts of penance, by which remission of sins may be achieved, and excluded faith which, conceived from the Gospel, believes that sins are forgiven through Christ. And where Chrysostom places the humility and Augustine the sanctity of the work, they afterward substituted satisfaction by the work. And yet they must pronounce the anathema on everyone who does not adore all these things, no matter where they originated, as if they were oracles of the Holy Spirit.

[SECTION IV]
Concerning Contrition

Chapter IV

Contrition, which has first place among the above-named actions of the penitent person, is sorrow of the mind and detestation of the sin which has been committed, together with the intent not to sin further. This impulse of contrition has been at all times necessary for obtaining pardon for sins, and in a person who has fallen after baptism it finally prepares for remission of sins if it is coupled with trust in divine mercy and with the desire to do all else that is required for receiving this sacrament in a proper manner. Therefore the sacred synod declares that this contrition is not merely a ceasing from sin and the purpose and beginning of a new life, but that it includes also hatred of the old, according to the word: "Cast away from you all the transgressions which you have committed against Me, and get yourselves a new heart and a new spirit" [Ezek. 18:31]. And surely, anyone who has considered these cries of the saints: "Against Thee, Thee only, have I sinned, and done this evil in Thy sight" [Ps. 51:4], "I am weary with my moaning; every night I flood my bed with tears" [Ps. 6:6], "I will reflect upon all my years in the bitterness of my soul" [Is. 38:15], and other expressions of this kind, will easily understand that they flowed from a certain vehement hatred of the life they have previously led and from a powerful detestation of their sins. It [the Synod] teaches furthermore, that although it may happen that this contrition sometimes is perfect through charity and reconciles a man with God before he actually receives this sacrament, reconciliation is nevertheless not to be ascribed to such contrition without desire for the sacrament, which is included in it. With respect to imperfect contrition, which is called attrition, since it is commonly conceived either from a consideration of the turpitude of sin or from the fear of hell and punishments, the synod declares that if, with the hope of pardon, it renounces the will to sin, it not only does not make a man a hypocrite but is in fact a gift of God and an impulse of the Holy Spirit, who does not, indeed, as yet dwell in him but is only moving him; by Him the penitent person is aided and prepares for himself the way to righteousness. And although this, without the sacrament of penance, cannot by itself lead the sinner through to justification, it nevertheless disposes him to obtain the grace of God in the sacrament of penance. For, profitably smitten with this fear, the Ninivites repented at the terror-filled preaching of Jonah and obtained mercy from the Lord. For this reason some falsely slander Catholic writers as though they taught that the sacrament of penance confers grace without a good impulse on the part of those who receive it. This the Church of God never taught nor thought. And they also falsely teach that contrition is extorted or forced, not free and voluntary.

If anyone says that the contrition which is acquired through examination, recollection, and detestation of sins, by which one thinks over his years in bitterness of soul, pondering the seriousness, multitude, and foulness of his sins, the loss of eternal bliss, and the incurring of eternal damnation, together with the purpose of a better life, is not a true and profitable sorrow, neither prepares for grace, but makes a man a hypocrite and even more a sinner, and that finally this is a forced sorrow and not free and voluntary, let him be anathema.

Examination

1 Contrition is altogether necessary in those who truly and earnestly repent. For there can be no true repentance in those who, persuaded of their own holiness, dream that they are without sin, or who disregard, minimize, excuse, cloak, and defend their sins, despise or ridicule the divine threats, do not care about the wrath of God, are not moved by His judgment and displeasure, and therefore persevere and continue in sins against their conscience, delight in sins, and seek and seize occasions for sinning and for whatever they intentionally heap up without the fear of God—in them, I say, there can be no true repentance; neither does he who either does not know or does not consider or does not care about the wrath and judgment of God against sin earnestly or rightly seek remission of sins.

2 Therefore we by no means teach a repentance without contrition. To contrition, however, belongs the following: 1. That the mind of the sinner understand from the judgment of the Law, acknowledge, and earnestly consider the manifold uncleanness, magnitude, and abomination of sin before God; 2. That, as his conscience understands from the teaching about the wrath, indignation, and judgment of God against sins how earnestly and fearfully God is moved to anger against sins and wants to punish them, he acknowledges that on account of his sins he is held enmeshed in the bands of the wrath and judgment of God to eternal damnation; 3. From this there arises in the conscience fear, terror, and trembling at the wrath and judgment of God against sins; 4. From this there follows sorrow of conscience, which grieves deeply that it has sinned and by its sins has offended God; therefore it begins to hate and detest sin and to reject the intent to sin; 5. This recognition, this trembling and grief, does indeed incite and urge the conscience to ponder and seek whether and how it may escape the wrath of God and the judgment of damnation, as the Baptizer says: "Who warned you to flee from the wrath to come?" 6. It is necessary that to these terrors there come the comfort, that is, the faith which holds that sins are remitted to us on account of the

Son of God and raises us up again by the knowledge of such great mercy lest, overcome by despair, we fall into eternal ruin. For unless this faith comes to it, contrition is flight from God and murmuring against God, by which man finally falls into eternal ruin. This step makes the distinction between the contrition of Peter and that of Judas.

3 True contrition is not, however, a work of free will or of human powers, but through the Word that is preached, heard, and pondered the Holy Spirit incites, begins, works, and effects it in us. Therefore let those who are about to repent set before themselves the Law, which shows them the knowledge of their sins, the wrath of God, punishments present and to come, spiritual and bodily, temporal and eternal, public and private, together with examples of punishments. And let those who have fallen after Baptism consider the surpassing benefits of God, in order that they may know with what foul and dreadful ingratitude they have offended God. There are, moreover, manifold testimonies of the goodness of God toward us in the creation and preservation of the world, in the nourishment and defense of body and soul, and in government, civil and domestic and private. But above all things let there be considered among spiritual benefits the making known of the Word, the gift of the Gospel, the sending of His Son, the giving of the Holy Spirit, the warding off of Satan, the promise of eternal life, etc.

To grieve the Holy Spirit by falling into sins and to offend God in the midst of these great benefits is surely a dreadful crime. Therefore the Holy Spirit is efficacious through the Word of God that is preached, heard, and pondered, inciting, beginning, and effecting true contrition, which indeed ought to increase in earnest exercises of repentance yet can never be sufficient and perfect in this life. For "who can discern his errors?" (Ps. 19:12). Who knows the power of the wrath of God? Who fears His fierce anger? (Ps. 90:11). To the sorrow of contrition there belongs therefore also this, to sorrow over the fact that we cannot sorrow enough over our sin. Forgiveness of sins does not, indeed, depend on the greatness, sufficiency, and merit of contrition but on the obedience and satisfaction of Christ, which is laid hold of by faith.

4 Therefore contrition is necessary; it is not, however, a merit which obtains remission of sins. For that is given only on account of Christ and is accepted by faith (Acts 10:43). Contrition indeed is nothing but this, that we acknowledge, feel, and confess that we are held fast to eternal damnation by the bands of divine judgment on account of our sins, and unless the mind escapes from these terrors and griefs by knowledge of and trust in mercy on account of Christ, the Mediator, it falls into despair and

eternal ruin. So far, therefore, is contrition from meriting remission of sins.

Why, then, is it necessary? I answer: Just as those who neither know nor feel their sickness do not care about nor seek nor apply a remedy, so no one sufficiently cares about, no one earnestly and rightly seeks and embraces the grace and mercy of God which is offered in Christ, except one who has been rendered contrite and terrified through recognition, feeling, and trembling because of his sins and the wrath of God against sins. For the Law is a custodian, urging and impelling us to seek the grace of God in Christ. The divine arrangement is that He indeed wants to have the Gospel proclaimed, but to the poor; He wants to heal, but those who are crushed; He wants to proclaim freedom, but to the captives; He wants to lead forth and set free, but those who are bound, that is, those who are held captive under sins; He wants to comfort, but those who are contrite and grieving; He wants to have regard, but to a contrite spirit; God has a gracious purpose, but toward those who fear Him and those who hope in His mercy; He wants to restore, but those who labor and are heavy laden; He wants to crown with mercy and compassion, but the head that is bowed down, not one that is inflated with pride; He wants to pour in the oil of mercy, but into those who are wounded, etc.

5 This statement on contrition, which has been drawn up by the men on our side on the basis of Scripture and explained in adequate treatises, I wanted to repeat briefly here, lest anyone should think that we simply deny contrition or take it out of repentance, and in order that the antithesis or comparison may show the more clearly what the chief points in the controversy about contrition in this third Tridentine chapter are. These we shall now examine briefly and in order.

6 First: So far as the description of contrition is concerned, no one denies that it should be taught that contrition includes not only a ceasing from sin and the intention of beginning a new life but also hatred of the old and a detestation of sin. Neither would there be strife about the definition if it were not for the fact that snares are hidden under the words. Contrition, they say, is sorrow of the mind and detestation of sin committed, together with the intent not to sin further. I would accept these words simply and forthrightly in the same sense in which I have just spoken about contrition; but, as I have already said, snares are hidden under the words. For the scholastics teach that, in order to have vigor and strength for the canceling and remission of sins, contrition ought to be so great a detestation of sin that it is undertaken and assumed voluntarily as a punishment for the sin committed. For Gabriel says that a voluntary penalty remits and cancels sin, just as in human affairs a punishment voluntarily assumed fully reconciles the one who has been offended. Thomas says: "Just as sin is committed through consent of the will, so it is wiped out and remitted through dissent." He adds that, by virtue of the merit of Christ, Baptism has the power to cancel sins, but that in contrition there is required for the remission of sins, together with the merit of Christ, also our act of being displeased with sin, which is meritorious because it falls under free will. And even as offenses are committed against God either through the external members, or through desire, or through the will, so contrition brings grief to the body, to the feelings, and to the will, to reconcile the offense which has been committed against God by the members, the desires, and the will. Thus Thomas.

From this consideration one can understand that the third Tridentine chapter does not want contrition to consist in terrors struck into the conscience by God through the preaching of the Law, for in that case contrition could not merit reconciliation and remission of sins. For in order to make contrition meritorious the scholastics define it as sorrow assumed, and voluntarily assumed, and indeed assumed for sins. And because the Council of Trent, in its definition, harks back to these arguments of the scholastics, I wanted to add this brief reminder.

7 Second: In this chapter one must particularly observe what and how much they ascribe to contrition. This impulse, they say, prepares for the remission of sins if it is joined with trust in divine mercy. These words could be understood in an acceptable sense, namely, that contrition prepares for the remission of sins because it incites and impels a person by a recognition and sensing of the wrath of God against sin, so that he despairs of his own works and merits and seeks and receives remission of sins in the Gospel, by faith, gratis, on account of the merit of Christ. But this the Tridentine assembly by no means wants. And lest we seem to attach a meaning to their words which they do not intend, let us hear how the chapter itself interprets and explains this preparation for the remission of sins through contrition. The impulse of contrition, they say, is necessary for obtaining pardon for sins. And later they say that contrition perfected by love reconciles a person to God even before absolution, provided the wish to confess and to render satisfaction is present. Therefore they clearly ascribe the obtaining of forgiveness and reconciliation with God to the act or work of our contrition, and that, indeed, before the absolution, which is the voice of the Gospel that proclaims and imparts reconciliation with God and remission of sins to faith—gratis, on account of the merit of Christ. What is this but to take away reconciliation with God and forgiveness of sins from the Gospel and from faith, yes, from the

gratuitous mercy of God and the merit of Christ, and to transfer it to the merit of our own works?

But you say: Nevertheless the Tridentine chapter links to contrition trust in divine mercy and the desire for absolution, and the scholastics add the merit of Christ. I indeed hear the words, but I see how the papalists understand them, namely, that penitence should conceive such confidence about divine mercy if from love of God the penitent voluntarily takes on sorrow over sins and has the purpose that he will enumerate all sins to the priest and obediently perform the satisfactions the priest will command—that then he will, through these impulses and actions, obtain pardon for sins and be reconciled to God. And these works of the penitent, they say, have from the merits of Christ such power, namely, to remit sins.

Such is the faith of papalist penance—in our works, not in Christ. They want a mercy of God which is not gratuitous and remits sins gratis on account of Christ's merit but which ascribes the reward, namely, reconciliation with God and the remission of sins, to our works. Because these things simply overthrow the doctrine of the Gospel, they have heretofore been wrapped up in strange subterfuges and painted in diverse colors by many papalist writers in our time. But the Council of Trent explains clearly without subterfuge and dissimulation what it wants and thinks. For it simply repeats and confirms what has been taught by the scholastic doctors about contrition—that by virtue of contrition, according to the division of Thomas, guilt is remitted and erased, punishment removed, and glory bestowed.

In order that what is decreed in this chapter about contrition may be more rightly examined and more clearly understood, I shall briefly state the doctrine of the scholastics, which the council wanted to repeat and confirm with this decree. Now Scotus says that a sinner is able, by his natural powers together with the common or general influence of God, to consider the sin he has committed as being against the law of God, as an offense against God, as bringing upon him the wrath of God and eternal punishment, and that the will can for these reasons renounce sin. This impulse they call attrition—an insufficient and a remote disposition to the remission of sins. But if the sinner would consider the most high and infinite greatness, goodness, and mercy of God, and that according to the dictates of reason He should be loved above all finite and created goods, then the will could conform to this dictum of reason and elicit, from natural powers, the act of loving God above all things. Thus he could renounce sin inasmuch as it is offensive to the highest good, which is loved by him above all things. And this disposition from natural powers, they say, is sufficient, immediate, and final for the infusion and reception of grace, which is the love of God; for God withholds His grace from no one who is sufficiently disposed. And when contrition is perfected in this way by charity, which loves God above all things, because charity is that grace by which sins are remitted, so, and in this way, they say, contrition cancels sins and obtains pardon for sins and reconciliation with God, because it either arises from charity, which loves God above all things, or charity coexists together with the impulse of contrition, stands firm with it, and accompanies it.

This is the teaching of the scholastics, for the strengthening of which this decree was made, which will be more correctly understood from this comparison of the scholastic doctrine, namely, that we should be taught that pardon for sins and reconciliation with God are obtained in repentance on account of our love, not by faith on account of the merit of Christ. The wickedness of this teaching is so manifest, both of itself and from what was noted down in the first part of the *Examination,*[5] that for a refutation it is sufficient to have shown what a mystery of iniquity is contained in this chapter.

8 Third: Also this should be observed, that this fourth chapter says that contrition obtains pardon for transgressions and reconciliation with God if it has been made perfect by love. The scholastics call it "sufficient contrition." And Scotus says that for this sufficiency and perfection there is required a certain intention to renounce sin, which is continued for a certain length of time, determined by God, at the end of which, and not before, the sin is canceled. Others argue that for the sufficiency and perfection of contrition only this is required, that it be formed by charity, as has been said above. But this charity ought to love God above all things, a perfection which none of the saints is able to arrive at in this life. Moreover, Scripture testifies concerning contrition: "Who can discern his errors?" [Ps. 19:12]. Likewise: "Who knows the power of Thy anger?" [Ps. 90:11]. Therefore sufficiency and perfection of contrition is an impossible thing. Imagining it either makes Pharisees or drives men to despair. For the conscience, which can never be certain about the sufficiency and perfection of contrition, will always remain in doubt and uncertain about the remission of sins and reconciliation with God. And that is the very purpose of the Tridentine synod, to confirm and strengthen the doctrine of doubt about the remission of sins. Its refutation has been explained in the first part of the *Examination.*[6]

---

[5] Chemnitz, *Examination of the Council of Trent,* I (St. Louis: Concordia Publishing House, 1971).

[6] Ibid., pp. 586-611.

9 Fourth: They condemn the proposition of Luther, condemned by Leo X, with a repeated anathema, namely, that attrition makes a man a hypocrite and even more a sinner, and that it is not a voluntary sorrow but a forced one. The explanation is easy and brief. Luther by no means thought that the Word of God, which rebukes sins and shows the seriousness, multitude, and foulness of sins, does not belong to nor is required for repentance. Neither did he teach that preaching, hearing, considering and meditating on this Word is not useful for repentance. For it is (as I said above) the instrument through which the Holy Spirit takes away the stony heart and gives a heart of flesh. Nor did Luther ever say that recognition and renunciation of sin, which the Holy Spirit works in man through hearing and meditating on this Word, is not true sorrow of contrition. But he justly and deservedly criticized the scholastic arguments about attrition on the basis of God's Word. For they teach that free will is able by its own natural powers, solely on the basis of the teaching of the law of nature, to begin, conceive, and take on true sorrow and hatred for sin, that is, attrition, and that this is a disposition for grace; this disposition they call "doing what one can," and say that it is *meritum congrui*.[7]

That is the teaching about attrition which Luther attacked because it ascribes repentance, of which Scripture says that it is a gift of God (Acts 5:31; 11:18; 2 Tim. 2:25), to the natural powers of corrupt nature, although Christ declares that a corrupt tree cannot bear good fruits. However, because experience bears witness that the natural man often takes on and assumes a certain sorrow and hatred for sin on account of fear of punishments, Luther answers in a manner similar to the argument of Augustine, *De spiritu et littera,* that when free will either does a certain thing or omits it without the Holy Spirit, from fear of punishment or hope of profit, it is only an external performance, but that the inward sin is increased the more. And, *Ad Bonifacium,* Bk. 3, ch. 4: "Whoever does a thing from carnal fear of punishment without doubt does it unwillingly, and therefore does not do it with his mind, for he altogether prefers not to do it if this is allowed with impunity, and therefore he is guilty inwardly, in his will, which God, who gives the commandment, regards."

Therefore Luther rightly says of attrition, as the scholastics teach it, that it is something forced, that it does not prepare for grace, and makes a person a hypocrite and even more a sinner, for a sinner who adds to his sins the pharisaic persuasion about his natural powers, works, and merits becomes even more a sinner. But look at the Tridentine stratagem! They

---

[7] See the discussion of *meritum congrui,* ibid., pp. 389 ff.; 541; 555-64.

do not dare to defend this opinion about attrition, which openly Pelagianizes; yet, in order that they may in some form support the bull of Leo, they say that contrition which is conceived from a knowledge of sin and fear of hell is conceived from an impulse of the Holy Spirit and is a gift of God if it has joined to it the hope of pardon and excludes the intent to sin—that such contrition is a road and step to conversion. But in this they fight without an adversary, for no one denies this, except that they seem to make that contrition a cause for obtaining grace.

I know, however, that great and long discussions are found with the scholastics about contrition and attrition, that is, when sorrow in repentance arises from fear of hell and when it arises from love of God. And there is no doubt that both happen in those who have fallen after Baptism. For they both become terrified through fear of the wrath and judgment of God, and grieve that they have offended so kind a Father, that they have been so ungrateful to the Mediator, who has deserved so well of us, and that they have grieved the Holy Spirit, the pledge of our inheritance. But these papalist discussions are dangerous and truly snares for consciences, because they amount to this, that a contrition which is terrified through consideration of the wrath and judgment of God, if it does not arise from love of God, even though faith comes to it, which asks and declares that sins are remitted to us because of Christ, is nevertheless not saving, but the repentance of Judas. For in the great, deep, and true terrors which are described in the psalms and with the prophets, we hear complaints about the seriousness and the multitude of sins and about the wrath and fierce anger of God. Nevertheless when faith in Christ comes to this, which raises up the conscience, the repentance is true and saving. Therefore it is more useful to avoid these questions and to define contrition according to the Word of God, which rebukes sins and reveals the wrath of God over sins, through which Word the Holy Spirit arouses contrition in the penitent, so that faith, which lays hold of the comfort which is set before us in Christ, in the preaching of the Gospel, makes a distinction between slavish and childlike fear, between the sorrow of Judas and the salutary sadness of Peter.

These are the chief points in the controversy about contrition, which are treated in this fourth Tridentine chapter. I wanted to point them out rather than to explain them, for the basis was shown in the preceding.

[SECTION V]
Concerning Confession

Chapter V

From the institution of the sacrament of penance as already explained, the universal Church has always understood that the entire confession of sins was also instituted by the Lord and that it is necessary by divine right for all who have fallen after baptism, because our Lord Jesus Christ, when He was about to ascend from earth to heaven, left behind Him priests, as His own vicars, rulers, and judges, as it were, to whom all mortal sins into which the faithful of Christ may have fallen should be referred, in order that they may, by the power of the keys, pronounce the sentence either of remission or of retention of sins. For it is clear that the priests could not have exercised this judgment if the case had been unknown, neither could they have preserved fairness in enjoining penalties if [the faithful] had declared their sins to them only in general and not specifically, one by one. From this we gather that all mortal sins of which penitents, after diligent self-examination, are conscious ought to be enumerated in confession, even if they are most secret and have been committed only against the last two commandments of the Decalog, which sometimes wound souls more gravely and are more dangerous than those committed openly. But venial sins, by which we are not excluded from the grace of God and into which we fall more frequently, although they may rightly and profitably, without all presumption, be told in confession, as the custom of pious men demonstrates, may nevertheless be passed over in silence without guilt and may be expiated by many other remedies. However, since all mortal sins, even those of thought, make men children of wrath and enemies of God, it is necessary also to seek forgiveness of them all from God with an open and modest confession. Therefore while the faithful of Christ dare to confess all the sins they remember, they without doubt lay all before divine mercy that they may be pardoned. But those who act otherwise, and knowingly hold back some sins, lay nothing before divine goodness to be remitted by the priest. For if the sick person is ashamed to uncover to the physician the wound of which he is ignorant, his medicine does not cure it. We gather further that also those circumstances which change the nature of the sin should be explained in confession, for without these the sins themselves are neither entirely laid bare by the penitent nor become known to the judges, and it becomes impossible for them to judge rightly about the seriousness of the transgressions and to impose on the penitents the proper penalty for them. Therefore it is not according to reason to teach that these circumstances have been invented by idle men, or that only one circumstance should be confessed, namely, that one has sinned against a brother. But it is also wicked to say that confession which is taught to be made in this manner is impossible, or to call it a torture of consciences. For it is certain that nothing else is required of penitents in the Church than that, after everyone has diligently examined himself, and explored all the nooks and corners of his conscience, he confesses those sins by which he remembers that he mortally offended his Lord and God. The remaining sins, however, which do not come to mind as he diligently thinks it over, are understood to be included as a whole in the same confession, for which we honestly say with the prophet: "Cleanse Thou me from hidden faults" [Ps. 19:12]. The difficulty of such a confession and the shame of revealing one's sins could indeed seem a grave matter if it were not lightened by so many and such great benefits and consolations which, through absolution, are surely bestowed on all who come to this sacrament in a worthy manner. As for the rest, so far as the manner of confessing secretly, before a priest alone, is concerned, although Christ has not forbidden that one may, for a punishment of his sins and for his own humiliation, be able to confess his faults publicly, sometimes for an example to others, sometimes for the edification of the Church which he has offended, nevertheless this is not commanded by a divine precept. Nor would it be wise to command by some human law, that faults, particularly secret ones, should be revealed by a public confession. Therefore, since secret sacramental confession, which holy Church has used from the beginning and is also now using, has always been commended by the most holy and most ancient fathers with a great and unanimous consensus, the foolish slander of those who are not afraid to teach that it knows no divine command, is a human invention, and had its beginning from the fathers assembled in the Lateran Council, is clearly disproved. For the Church did not decree through the Lateran Council that the faithful of Christ should confess—something it knew to be necessary by divine right—but that the command to confess should be fulfilled at least once every year by each and every one having arrived at the years of discretion. Therefore the salutary custom of confessing is now observed in the entire Church with the greatest benefit to the souls of the faithful at the holy and most acceptable time of Lent. This custom this holy synod wholeheartedly approves of and embraces as something to be piously and deservedly retained.

CANON VI

If anyone either denies that sacramental confession is instituted or necessary to salvation by divine right, or says that the manner of confessing secretly to the priest only, which the Catholic Church has always observed from the beginning and still observes, is foreign to the institution and command of Christ and is a human invention, let him be anathema.

CANON VII

If anyone says that in the sacrament of penance it is not necessary by divine right to confess each and every mortal sin which is remembered after due and diligent consideration, also secret sins and those which are against the last two commandments of the Decalog, together with the circumstances which change the nature of the sin, but that such confession is useful only to instruct and comfort the penitent person, and that it was formerly observed only in order that canonical satisfaction might be imposed, or says that those who strive to confess all sins want to leave nothing to divine mercy to forgive, or finally, that it is not permitted to confess venial sins, let him be anathema.

CANON VIII

If anyone says that the confession of all sins, such as the Church observes, is impossible and is a human tradition to be abolished by the godly, or that not each and every one of both sexes among the faithful of Christ is held to it once a year, according to the constitution of the great Lateran Council, and that for this reason the faithful of Christ should be persuaded not to confess during the time of Lent, let him be anathema.

Examination

1 The dispute about confession is a long one, pursued with great strife; many statements of Scripture are heaped up, and a variety of testimonies and examples from antiquity are gathered together. This is done with the artful purpose that the minds of the inexperienced may be disturbed and that they may think that precisely such a confession, and indeed with precisely the same understanding as it is now in use in the papalist church, was always present in the ancient church, commanded, as it were, and necessary by divine right. Therefore the simplest and most convenient way of explanation will be if we show by a division of the question how varied are the kinds of confession and how many the ways of confessing which are mentioned both in Scripture and in the writings of the ancients, and that then we show by contrast with each of these kinds what and what manner of confession it is for which the papalists fight— one which demands as necessary for the remission of sins that we reveal and enumerate to the priest specifically and one by one each and every transgression we want forgiven by God, together with all the circumstances, so that whatever is not enumerated to the priest is not forgiven by God.

2 In this way it will be possible to show plainly that papalist confession has no true and harmonious testimonies either from Scripture or from antiquity. We are, however, here speaking not of the confession of praise, in which sense the word "confession" is used a number of times in Scripture, but of the confession of crime, as Augustine beautifully distinguishes the twofold meaning of the word, *De verbis Evangelii,* Homily 8, that is, we are speaking about the acknowledgment and confession of sin.

3 First: There is a certain confession which is made to God alone, by which we acknowledge our sins from our heart before God, confessing and deploring with genuine sorrow of heart how manifold are our offenses against God, confess that we are worthy of wrath and eternal damnation, and beg for mercy. This confession belongs to true contrition lest we imagine we are without sin, or esteem our sins lightly, extenuate, excuse, bemantle, or defend them, but that we candidly acknowledge them before God and confess both our fault and its guilt.

Such confession is linked with hope and confidence in forgiveness, as Chrysostom says to Theodore, who had fallen: "What good will tears and confession do if confidence in forgiveness is not present?" It also is linked with the purpose of bettering one's conduct, as Hilary says on the 135th psalm: "What else is the confession of an error but the confession that we will leave off from the error?"

The people needed to be diligently informed about the necessity and benefit of this kind of confession, in order that we may inquire, heedful of our obligation, that is, according to the teaching of the Decalog, into our whole nature and life, testing and examining it according to each commandment in order that we may in a measure acknowledge (for the word of the psalm always remains: "Who can discern his errors?") the multitude, seriousness, and foulness of our sin and in how many ways we are guilty before God. For in this way true contrition is generated, faith is incited and sharpened, in order that it may earnestly seek, accept with gratitude, and hold fast with filial fear of the Lord the mercy of God and the forgiveness of sins.

In this way also the pride of human nature is shattered, lest it take on the pharisaic persuasion about righteousness, holiness, and innocence. Afterward this confession also makes us more careful to govern our behavior with greater diligence and to avoid lapses into sin.

These things needed to be set forth to the people from the Word of God and to be diligently inculcated. But the papalists fight only for their kind of confession, to which they also bend what is said either in Scripture or in the writings of the ancients about this confession; and the things which belong to this confession they transfer and ascribe to their auricular enumeration of sins. Now the following statements of Scripture speak of this confession: Ps. 32:3, 5: "When I declared not my sin, my body wasted away. . . . I acknowledged my sin to Thee. . . I said, 'I will confess my transgression to the Lord'; then Thou didst forgive the guilt of my sin." 1 John 1:9: "If we confess our sins, He is faithful and just, and will forgive our sins." V. 8: "If we say we have no sin, His Word is not in us." Prov. 28:13: "He who conceals his transgressions will not prosper, but he who confesses and forsakes them will obtain mercy."

This confession confesses sins to God either inwardly in the heart or publicly with the mouth, as is shown in Lev. 16:21; Dan. 9:3-19. Likewise it either presents the sinner in his totality as guilty before God, as the publican says: "God, be merciful to me, a sinner," or it inquires into all of life and therefore into our whole corrupt nature, as Pss. 19, 25, 51, and others show.

4 The fathers also speak of this confession. Thus Origen says, *Peri* *archoon,* Bk. 3, ch. 1: "If a person does not first know the imperfections of his own soul and bring them to light with the confession of his own mouth, he cannot be purged and absolved from them." This statement the papalists bend to their own confession. But Origen explains himself at length in the foregoing, and these are his words: "They do not know what they receive from God unless they have first come to the desire to receive the benefits; this finally happens if a person first comes to know himself, and senses what he is lacking, and understands from whom he either should or can ask what he lacks, for he who has not first understood his sickness does not know how to seek a physician, or, if he has been healed, he does not give thanks. Therefore, in order that he may not be ignorant of the fact that it is granted to him by grace, sins must be acknowledged and confessed." The same Origen says on Ps. 37, Homily 1: "It is fitting, after one has sinned, to confess the sin." This he explains with the example of the publican (Luke 18:13) and of David. He says: "All the things wherein I have failed, for which I have lusted, which I have committed, I bring before Thee and set before Thy sight in my prayers, and my sighing is not hidden from Thee."

Chrysostom says on Ps. 50: "How great are the sinners who live securely, who are not willing to understand the wrong they do nor to recognize the disaster which will come upon them, who moreover confidently do what is evil, and thus neither groan nor shed a tear, nor confess; these cannot be saved, because they neither acknowledge their misdeeds, nor have the judgment of God before their eyes."

Also Homily 3, on Matthew: "Confession of sins is testimony of a conscience that fears God, for he who fears the judgment of God is not ashamed to confess his sins; however, he who is ashamed does not fear. For where there is no belief in the punishment of judgment to come, there men regard the shame of confession. Do we not know that confession of sins is connected with shame and that this blushing with shame is itself a grave punishment? But God all the more commands to confess sins, in order that we may suffer shamefacedness instead of punishment."

The same says, on Genesis, Homily 4: "When in this present life we are able to wash away sins through confession and to obtain forgiveness from the Lord, then we shall depart from hence pure from sins and shall have great confidence." And Homily 20: "Whoever has done this, if he will hasten to confess his misdeeds and to show his sore to the Physician, who heals and does not reproach, and to receive the remedies from Him and to speak to Him alone, no one else sharing the knowledge, and diligently to tell all, will easily cleanse away his sins. For the confession of sins is the abolition of the faults." Lindanus rejoices over this passage because he thinks it literally teaches the secret confession of the papalists. But let the reader consider how craftily he deals with it. For in the homily Chrysostom says: "If Lamech does not shun confessing his sin to his wives, of what pardon will we be worthy if we are not willing to confess our sins to Him who knows all our faults?" And afterward he reiterates that this physician is our Lord.

Such statements of the ancients the papalists distort to their enumeration of sins. But Chrysostom explains himself most clearly; he says on Heb. 12, Homily 31: "I do not say to you that you should betray yourself in public, nor that you should accuse yourself before others, but I want you to obey the prophet who says: 'Reveal your way to the Lord.' Therefore confess your sins before God." On Ps. 59 he says: "Confess your sins in order that you may destroy them. If it disturbs you to tell anyone that you have sinned, confess them daily in your mind. I do not say that you should confess to your fellow servant, in order that he may reproach you; confess to God, who heals them. For God is not ignorant of them even though you do not confess them. Confess in this life that you may have rest in the life to come."

The same man says in a discourse about repentance and confession: "It is not, however, necessary to confess in the presence of witnesses; let only God see you as you confess." *De incomprehensibili Dei natura,* Homily 5: "I ask and plead that you will more frequently confess to the immortal God and that, after having enumerated your faults, you ask for pardon. I do not lead you into the theater of your fellow servants; I do not compel you to reveal your sins to men. Tell what is on your conscience before God; reveal yourself; show your wounds to the greatest Physician and ask a remedy of Him."

De Lazaro, Sermon 4: "Beware of telling your sins to a man, lest he reproach you. Neither confess to your fellow servant, lest he bring it out in public, but confess to Him who is the Lord."

There are many other outstanding statements of the ancients concerning this inward confession to be made to God. But I have set down these statements of Chrysostom here, for from them it is possible to gather how and from which incorrectly understood statements of the ancients a later generation forged the papalist enumeration and its necessity. The ancients say that sins are to be revealed in confession, to be weighed specifically, very carefully examined, explained, uncovered, enumerated, etc.; they say that sins are loosed through confession and that it is impossible to be saved without confession. But Chrysostom adds the explanation that these things are to be understood not of outward confession made before men but of inner confession made to God.

5 Second: There is fraternal confession, which is made to a neighbor, namely, when the one who has offended his neighbor, moved by repentance, confesses that he has sinned and asks that it be forgiven him. Luke 17:4: "If he sins against you seven times in the day, and turns to you seven times, and says, 'I repent,' you must forgive him." Augustine interprets the statement in James 5:16: "Confess your sins to one another, and pray for one another," of this confession, *In Evangelium Johannis tractatus*, 56, and Bede quotes the same, on Paul's Letter to the Colossians. Men need to be earnestly exhorted to this kind of confession, for Christ says (Matt. 5: 23-24) that whoever is not first reconciled to his brother cannot offer his gift at the altar, and Christ earnestly proclaims to the offended party, Matt. 6:15: "If you do not forgive men their trespasses, neither will your Father forgive your trespasses."

God promises that He will regard this fraternal reconciliation as valid in heaven (Matt. 18:18). On this passage Theophylact says: "If when you have been sinned against you hold him who sinned against you, after a threefold admonition, as a publican, he will be such also in heaven; if, however, you loose him, that is, forgive him when he confesses and asks for it, he will be acquitted also in heaven. For it is not only the sins the priest looses which are loosed, but also those will be bound or loosed whom we, when we have been wronged, either bind or loose. Under this confession there is included also this, when a brother is moved and led by fraternal reproof to acknowledge and confess some sin, even if it was not committed against us. For so, says Christ, you have gained your brother. And James says that this confession is useful on account of the prayer for one another: Pray for one another, that you may be saved!"

6 Third: Scripture speaks of a certain general confession of sins, in which a sinner confesses not only inwardly before God but also before the ministers of the Word and the sacraments, not indeed that he specifically enumerates each and every sin according to the circumstances, but either professes in general, whether verbally or by an act, that he acknowledges his sins and the wrath of God against sins, or confesses certain other transgressions which weigh on his conscience, and asks that forgiveness be granted him. It was such a confession in the Old Testament when someone brought a sacrificial animal to the priest to be offered for sin, for a crime, for ignorance, for obstinacy, etc.; he was not, however, compelled to explain that sin to the priest in detail and with all the circumstances. Such a confession was that of David before the prophet Nathan, in which he confesses the sin of adultery and murder without enumeration of the circumstances (2 Sam. 12:13). And he adds the general confession: "Behold, I was brought forth in iniquity," etc. "Blot out all my iniquities"

(Ps. 51:5, 9). It is to be noted that David did indeed make this confession before the prophet, according to the superscription of the psalm, but he nevertheless directs the confession to God. And to this general confession, which is not a total enumeration of the separate sins according to all the accompanying circumstances, Nathan imparts the absolution: "The Lord has put away your sin."

The manner of such a general confession is beautifully described in the history of Nehemiah. For in ch. 8 Ezra together with the Levites read to the people in the Book of the Law and explain what was read. As a result the people acknowledge the sins with which they had offended God, and begin to mourn and weep. In ch. 9 they separate themselves from all foreigners and confess their sins and the sins of their fathers before the Levites and the whole congregation. And the Levites repeat the confession of the people and pray for the mercy of God, which takes the place of absolution, and they pledge to amend their lives and, as it were, enter into a publicly composed covenant, something which belongs to the fruits of repentance. I have noted down this example because it shows the whole procedure (if I may speak thus) of confession. Thus the woman who was a sinner (Luke 7:37-38) confesses by signs and gestures in general, without specific enumeration, that she is guilty of many sins, particularly the one which was well known, and seeks absolution.

To this general confession Christ imparts absolution: "Your sins are forgiven. . . . Your faith has saved you; go in peace." In the same way the Son of Man exercises the power to remit sins on earth in Matt. 9:2. For knowing that the paralytic was terrified by a consideration of his sins, and seeing his faith, He said: "Take heart, My son; your sins are forgiven." The same word "forgive" is used here which is found in John 20:23. There the power to forgive sins is expressly explained. Nevertheless, the total enumeration of the separate sins is not required for absolution. However, Christ did not send out the apostles in a way different from the way He Himself had been sent (John 20:21). Therefore ministers ought not to require of those who seek absolution what Christ did not require. Thus (Matt. 3:6) those who are baptized by John confess their sins; for by the very fact that they undergo the baptism of repentance they confess that they are sinners.

From the story of the Baptizer one can learn the procedure John used: He preached repentance, as it is written in Is. 40:4 ff., where he accuses valleys, mountains, and hills of being crooked and rough. "All flesh is grass, and all its beauty is like the flower of the field. The grass withers, the flower fades, when the breath of the Lord blows upon it." Now when crowds, Pharisees and Sadducees, came to him to be baptized, he preached to them about the wrath of God and about escaping that wrath (Matt. 3:7-10). In Luke 3:16-17 he told them to believe in Him who was to come, that is, in Christ. Acts 19:4-5: Those who heard this doctrine confessed their sins, that is, confessed in general and indicated that they acknowledged their sin, feared the wrath of God, and were sorry that they had offended God, and asked for Baptism for the remission of sins. John admonishes earnestly that they should not offer a feigned repentance, but a true and earnest one, and that they should show this by worthy fruits. He does not, however, demand a specific enumeration of each transgression, but judges, in the case of those who sought instruction, that it is sufficient that they confess those sins by which in particular they feel their conscience to be burdened. Thus publicans and soldiers say: "What shall we do?"

In Acts 19:18 they come "confessing and divulging their practices." However, Luke says that "those who were now believers" did this, as Paul after his conversion confesses the sin of persecution, and as Augustine published his *Confessions*. No specific enumeration of each transgression was made or demanded there, but they acknowledged and confessed that their actions were not in accord with the norm of the Word of God. In particular, they burned the books of magic arts, and by that very act promised correction. Thus in Luke 19:8-10 Zacchaeus confesses that he had defrauded many, and promises correction. Indeed, Christ does not demand a specific enumeration of every single transgression, together with all the circumstances, but is satisfied with a general confession, when Zacchaeus says: "If I have defrauded anyone." Upon this confession He pronounces the absolution: "Today salvation has come to this house, since he also is a son of Abraham. For the Son of man came to seek and to save the lost." Also the prodigal son (Luke 15:21) is received upon a general confession and promise of correction.

7 I have noted down these things in order to show that the custom observed in our churches with respect to confession is in harmony with Scripture, which is content with a general confession and does not demand a specific enumeration. Nevertheless, it counsels to reveal those things which particularly burden the conscience, for the sake of instruction and comfort. Of this confession Basil speaks in *Questiones compendio explicatae,* 288, when he says: "It seems necessary that sins should be confessed to those to whom the dispensation of the mysteries of God has been committed, " for he adds: "Thus also those who in ancient time were penitent are found to have confessed their sins before the saints. For in the gospel it is written that the people confessed their sins to the Baptizer, and in Acts they confessed to the apostles themselves, by whom they were

afterward baptized." This observation shows plainly how rightly and skillfully the papalists twist these and similar statements to their whole enumeration.

8 Fourth: In the ancient church public confession, which they called *exomologeesin,* was greatly and frequently in use. For those who had been apprehended in public misdeeds which (as Augustine says) had been punished with excommunication, had to confess publicly; that is, when they were guilty of manifest misdeeds they were accused before the church as if at a public trial. There they had to acknowledge their fault before the pastor and the church, and had to show by outward signs that they were truly sorry they had offended God and dishonored the church. There a certain recital of the misdeeds was customary. For such persons were not received back unless they had declared publicly before the ministers and the church that they acknowledged their transgressions, were sorry about them, sought forgiveness, and promised correction. After the judgment of the church had been put forward, a public satisfaction was imposed on them, that it might be clear to all that they were truly and earnestly sorry, as Jerome says on Matt. 16. This public confession was, however, also voluntary, as when guilty persons of their own accord gave themselves away before the heads of the church, accused themselves, and made themselves known. The fathers diligently urged that they should do this. If, however, the sin had offended the whole church, and the guilty ones were nevertheless unwilling to acknowledge and confess this publicly, the church compelled them to make a public confession: 1. By a public reproof; 2. When the reproved person refused to acknowledge and confess his misdeed, he was excommunicated, and was not taken back unless he had first acknowledged his crime by a public confession; 3. When a brother refused to hear a private brotherly rebuke, his misdeeds were, by means of an announcement, brought before the church, which constrained the guilty ones to confession, either by public reproof or by excommunication. This severity was employed in the case of public misdeeds because many such misdeeds were not then punished by the magistrate, who at that time was not yet a Christian.

Therefore, lest the church be in bad repute among the Gentiles on account of certain manifest crimes, and lest these bad examples either be a cause of offense to weaker Christians or infect the whole flock by contagion, also in order that the others, admonished and frightened by these sights, might beware of similar misdeeds and in order that the mind of those who returned to the church might be investigated, whether they had come to their senses in earnest (for the church had been deceived by the levity and dissimulation of many), therefore they observed the custom of public confession and repentance with great strictness. And these things are in harmony with examples of Scripture. Thus in Luke 7:37 ff. the woman who was a sinner publicly confesses her misdeed by outward signs, acknowledges her guilt, seeks forgiveness, and promises betterment. And in 1 Cor. 5:1-5; 2 Cor. 2:5-11; 7:8-12 the man who had fallen is urged by public rebuke and excommunication to acknowledge and confess his sin. In Joshua 7:18 ff., when Achan had already been caught, Joshua nevertheless demands of him a public confession of his crime, and he confesses that he is guilty: "Of a truth I have sinned against the Lord, and have done so and so."

9 Of this public confession Irenaeus speaks, Bk. 1, ch. 9, in connection with certain women who had been seduced and corrupted by the heretic Marcus. When they were converted they made an open confession, bewailing and lamenting their seduction. Some, indeed, did not come to this confession, despairing in silence of the life of God. So says Irenaeus.

Tertullian calls confession an act of repentance, namely, when repentance is not rendered in the conscience alone but is performed by some act. Tertullian ascribes almost all those acts which public repentance embraces to confession, and says plainly that this confession is done not only to the presbyters but to all the brethren. And therefore he allows only one such confession, namely, a public one.

Therefore, as Eusebius writes, Bk. 6, ch. 25, when Philippus, the son of Gordianus, wanted to communicate with the people in the church in prayers, he was not permitted to do this by the local bishop unless he confessed. However, the bishop did not demand of him that he recount all his hidden sins secretly into the ear, but commanded that he stand among those who publicly repented, whom he calls *exetazomenous,* which word is taken from the courts, namely, when a criminal case is prosecuted and an examination is conducted, and therefore he also says: "On account of the many accusations against him," for they were public misdeeds.

In this way, according to Bk. 5, ch. 28, Natalis, who had fallen into heresy, put on a hair shirt, sprinkled himself with ashes, prostrated himself at the feet of the bishop, cast himself under the feet of clerics and lay people, and bewailed his error with many tears. Such a public confession was not imposed and undertaken for any and all sins but, as Augustine says, for those which were public or merited excommunication. And if at any time it was also done for other sins, it was nevertheless done by public confession and was done vocally and with gestures or signs, not only before the priests but before the lay people and all the brethren, as

Tertullian and Eusebius write concerning this confession. Out of this public confession there began afterward to be made a secret confession of those sins which belonged to public repentance. Finally this secret confession was bent to apply to inner repentance for any and all hidden sins. We shall show how this was done slowly, little by little, for it will be useful to observe this.

10 Now this custom of public confession progressed to the point where, if someone had purposed in his mind to commit a public crime, even if the crime afterward did not follow, many nevertheless voluntarily first indicated this to the priests and afterward subjected themselves to public confession and repentance. Thus Cyprian says, Treatise 3, *De lapsis:* "Those who have a greater faith and a more wholesome fear, although they are not fettered either by a crime of sacrifice or written accusation, since they nevertheless did consider this, confess this sorrowfully and straightforwardly before the priests of God, make a confession of what is on their conscience, lay bare the burden that is on their mind, and seek for a salutary remedy for what are really small and moderately sized wounds." You hear that it was neither a necessary precept nor a universal custom, for he says they were examples of some who were of greater faith and more wholesome fear. Therefore not all did this, neither were those condemned who confessed such things to God only. Nevertheless, such examples began to be commended to others and to be held up to them for imitation. Let the reader observe, however, that Cyprian is not here speaking of all single sins of thought and will of every kind as being necessary to confess to the priest, but he clearly explains that he has in mind those public crimes whose commission had been conceived by the will, as for instance the intention of denial under persecution. Therefore also these statements pertain to public repentance and public crimes. They are not general teachings about confessing to the priest all hidden sins of which the regenerate know themselves to be guilty before God.

11 Fifth: When unusual crimes had been admitted, however in such a way that they were not publicly known and manifest to the church, the guilty ones could not be compelled to public confession and repentance; however, the strictness of the discipline was such that many revealed their own crimes themselves by public confession. Scurrilous tongues took occasion from this to disparage the penitents, as Origen says, Homily 2 on Ps. 37: "The person who has fallen steps forward and makes his confession. Many of those who hear it either reproach or ridicule him, or speak evil of him." In order, therefore, that such public confession might be made for edification, the fathers counseled that this should first be laid before the priest, as an experienced physician, and his counsel should be sought whether it should be made known to the church by a public confession. Thus Origen says on Ps. 37: "Consider to whom you ought to confess your sin; test the physician first. If he understands and foresees that your weakness is such that it should be brought before the assembly of the whole church and healed, by which perhaps also others could be edified and you yourself easily restored to health, the counsel of this experienced physician must speedily be followed." In this way sins which belong to public repentance, when they were not manifest, were first shown privately to the priest; afterward public confession and repentance followed. From this it is clear that Origen is not, in this passage, speaking about generally confessing each and every sin to the priest. For in the first homily he speaks of offenses, lusts, and transgressions which are brought before God and laid bare in His sight with groaning. Then, in the second homily, he speaks first about the faults which formerly had to be confessed publicly. However, because disparagement of the penitent person had resulted from this, Origen counsels that such faults should first be made known to the priest in order that, as a result of his advice, public confession might either be made or omitted.

12 Sixth: When this ardor had cooled, and there were no people who either voluntarily of their own accord wanted to lay bare even their very great faults, which had not become manifest and known by public confession before the church, or to reveal them on advice of the priest in a public meeting of the church, yes, when also in the case of known crimes many, on account of the shame of public confession, rather spurned all penitence, the severity of public repentance was finally relaxed and almost entirely abolished. Confession began to be changed to something private, so that such faults were confessed privately and in secret to the priest, who, although he did not reveal the fault in the sight of the church, nevertheless laid a public penitence on the delinquent, that by that very fact he might in a general way confess and declare before the church that he had committed a grave wrong.

Leo bears witness to this in the 69th epistle, also Sozomen in the *Historia tripartita*, Bk. 9, ch. 35. Thus Augustine says, *De symbolo ad catechumenos*, Bk. 1, ch. 6: "Those whom you see doing penance have committed crimes, either adultery or other frightful acts."

It is profitable to observe when, how, and for what reason this public confession was changed to private or secret confession. A description is found in the 78th epistle of Leo, where he decrees that the custom according to which by means of books a written confession about the nature of the individual sins was publicly recited should be done away, "since it is sufficient to indicate the offenses which lie on the consciences to the priests only by means of a secret confession. For although the fullness of faith which, on account of the fear of God, is not afraid to blush with shame before men appears to be a praiseworthy thing; nevertheless, because not everyone's sins are of such a nature that they are not apprehensive about making known the things which call for repentance, the objectionable custom had to be abolished, lest many be prevented from using the remedies of repentance, since they were either ashamed or feared to relate their deeds to their enemies, for which they could be ruined by the regulations of the laws. Therefore that confession is sufficient which is first offered to God, then also to the priest, who comes as intercessor for the faults of the penitents, because then at last many could be persuaded to penitence, if the conscience of the one who confesses is not publicly exposed before the ears of the people."

I have quoted this statement of Leo because it shows plainly that the things we read among the ancients about making confession before men are not necessary commands, nor by divine right, but an external discipline which can be changed in the interest of the edification of the church. For this custom, that enormous crimes, whether committed only by intention or actually carried out, but not known to the whole church, were made known by public confession—a custom which Tertullian, Cyprian, and Origen praise and set forth for imitation—this custom Leo calls objectionable and says that it should be abolished. For he uses almost the same words with which Cyprian and Tertullian commend this kind of confession, namely, "on account of greater faith and more wholesome fear its publication should not be shunned."

13 This also should be noted in the statement of Leo, that he is not speaking of a general enumeration of all secret faults when he says that the guilt which lies on the consciences should be indicated to the priests by means of a secret confession, but shows that he is speaking about crimes for which, if they became public, they could be ruined by the regulations of the laws, that is, crimes which formerly were subject to public confession and penitence.

14 Seventh: In the Greek church this public confession was changed to secret confession long before Leo. For in the *Historia tripartita*, Bk. 9, ch. 35, Sozomen says that from the beginning of the church it had seemed good to the priests that sins should be made known in the presence of the assembled church, as if in a theater. This is said of public confession. Socrates, however, adds: "When after the persecution under Decius the Novatians had separated themselves from the church because it was receiving as penitents those who had lapsed in the persecution, which happened about A.D. 250, the bishops made the addition to the ancient churchly canon about public confession and penitence (for he calls it a supplement to the canon) that a presbyter of good conduct, wise, and able to keep a secret, as Sozomen says, should be appointed for this, that the lapsed might come to him and confess their sins to him. He should then indicate a punishment in accord with the guilt of each individual. And Sozomen says expressly that the matter of the indicated punishment was the same thing as the Roman church at the time observed in public and solemn confession and penitence. For he states the custom almost as it is described in dist. 50, ch. *Quadragesimae.* Therefore this supplement to the ancient canon about public confession was new, that sinners should no longer publish their lapses before the whole assembly of the church as in a theater but should indicate them by secret and private confession to the presbyter appointed to deal with penitents; and because he could keep silence, he did not make the confession public, except in certain cases, as in the matter of the lewdness of a deacon. Nevertheless, he imposed a punishment or public satisfaction.

15 Let the reader observe, however, that what was customary at the time of Origen, namely, that the lapses which had been indicated privately to the priests were afterward set forth at a meeting of the whole church, was changed scarcely 30 years later in the Greek church, namely, that confession should be and be kept secret, while public satisfaction should be demanded.

16 The Western, or Latin church, however, retained the strictness of public confession almost 200 years longer—until the time of Leo, about A.D. 450, as we have said above. However, Socrates indicates that some wer accustomed to confess not only public and notorious crimes to the priest appointed for the penitents, but also other faults committed after Baptism. Sozomen says: "They confessed what they had committed throughout their life." Nevertheless, one does not conclude from this that there was a command obligating all to enumerate each and every transgression. For only one presbyter was appointed to hear these confessions in the very great church at Constantinople, in which there were 60 presbyters at the time of Justinian. And Socrates says that a certain noblewoman confessed her sins in part to that presbyter, and that after this confession, which was not complete nor specific, the presbyter absolved her, laying on her this satisfaction, that she should by fasting and prayers show a work worthy of repentance—but that she then began to continue and to accuse herself of another lapse, namely, that a deacon of the church had had intercourse with her. Therefore the need for this kind of confession was not laid on all, for in that case one presbyter would not have sufficed, nor was a total enumeration of every individual sin demanded as being necessary by divine right, as it were, for forgiveness, as the confession of the woman who confessed only in part shows. But while it had been instituted chiefly for public and known lapses, it began, as we have already shown, to be used also for confession of other sins.

Now our question is whether this confession, either public or private, was at that time held in the church as necessary by divine right for the remission of sins. The fact that public confession was changed and abolished shows that it was not judged to be necessary by divine right for the remission of sins. Now this account shows that the order to hear the confessions of the fallen privately and in secret was abrogated and done away in the Constantinopolitan church by Nectarius on account of that crime of the deacon, made known in confession with great offense to the church. But how was this abrogation made by Nectarius? Gropper says that it was not secret confession itself that was abrogated, but only the custom was done away by which a public repentance was imposed, to be performed by those who confessed secretly. But the narrative simply says that the custom ceased at that time, namely, that a certain presbyter was appointed to hear the confessions of penitents.

17 Lindanus imagines that Nectarius abrogated only this, that a certain presbyter was appointed to hear the confessions—that the private or secret confession remained as altogether necessary, but that it was left free to which one of the presbyters a person wanted to confess. But the narrative shows clearly that this is a fiction. For Sozomen says that after this abrogation by Nectarius it was left to everyone's own conscience. Does this mean that he should confess to whomever he wished? This he certainly does not say, but says that everyone was permitted to partake of the mysteries according as his conscience and his conviction enabled him; that is, after this abrogation everyone was admitted to participation in the mysteries according as he knew himself and was able to judge that he could partake of the mysteries with a good conscience and not to judgment. Therefore, before this, they were not admitted to Communion unless they had first confessed their sins. But after the abrogation by Nectarius everyone was admitted according to his own conscience, which is clearly opposed to the judgment which was made in confession. And a much clearer argument that the secret confession itself was abrogated after Nectarius is the fact that Socrates complains that by the abrogation of this discipline that mutual reproof was taken away of which Paul says: "Take no part in the unfruitful works of darkness, but instead expose them," and that Sozomen says even more plainly that through this abrogation by Nectarius the ancient earnestness and severity began to degenerate into an arbitrary and more careless custom. And he adds that earlier, that is, before this abrogation, there were smaller and fewer sins on account of modesty and the shame of confessing one's own sins and because of the severity of those who had been appointed as judges for this thing. Therefore it is quite clear from this complaint what Nectarius abrogated.

But you say: Neither Socrates nor Sozomen praise this abrogation. I answer: They praise that discipline and its usefulness, which is also not disapproved by us. Nevertheless, neither of them asserts that confession is necessary by divine right for the remission of sins, nor do they maintain that its abrogation is contrary to divine law. But Sozomen, commending this ancient discipline, says: "As I judge." And Socrates says: "What the counsel of that abrogation has brought on the church God will see."

For us this judgment of the ancient church is sufficient, that confession, no matter how much the usefulness of this discipline is lauded and commended, is not of divine right, nor necessary for the forgiveness of sins. Otherwise it could and ought not to have been abrogated on account of any disturbances.

18 Let us sum up, therefore, what we can make of this narrative about Nectarius. It is wholly true what Sozomen says, that God has commanded to extend pardon to sinners—however to such as repent, and acknowledge and confess their sins. Those who refuse to confess their sins acquire for themselves an even greater burden, as though of increased usury from their sin. The question, however, is to whom sins must be confessed. At first, indeed, public confession was in use. But it has been shown by its abrogation that this is not necessary. After this, for a time, a confession was practiced which was made to the priest privately or in secret. That also this is not necessary by divine right for remission of sins, even though it is a useful discipline, the church showed at the time of Nectarius by its abrogation. Therefore only that confession of sins which is made to God is necessary for the remission of sins by divine right, as Chrysostom, the successor of Nectarius, showed at length and many times.

19 But against all this Pighius argues that what was done in the one Constantinopolitan church to counter the madness of the agitated populace does not at once pertain to the judgment and consensus of the catholic church. Nevertheless no one, also of those who did not sufficiently approve that abrogation, either dared or was able to censure or condemn it as opposed to Scripture or the Word of God. Rather, Sozomen says expressly: "Nectarius first abolished having a presbyter appointed over all the penitents. Nearly all the bishops followed his example." Socrates says that elsewhere, in heretical circles, the canon about hearing confessions remained in force, but in the church of the Homoousians[8] it was discontinued.

From Chrysostom, who very soon after this abrogation undertook the administration of the Constantinopolitan church, one can clearly gather that the church at that time judged that confession of sins to the priest is not by divine right necessary for the remission of sins.

20 From this account about Nectarius one can understand what cause moved Chrysostom and what he meant when he so often repeated those statements we have quoted above (namely, that it is not necessary to confess one's sins to a man but is sufficient to confess them to God). For at that time the abrogation by Nectarius was still fresh in memory.

21 Lindanus contends that Chrysostom is arguing only that a public confession of sins is not necessary, because he says: "I do not lead you into the theater; I do not say that you should give yourself away in public. It is not necessary to confess in the presence of witnesses," etc. But the same man also says: "I do not say that you should confess to your fellow servant. Let God alone hear you confess." Likewise: "Confess to God alone; let no one else know it." Therefore Chrysostom wants neither a public nor a private confession in a divine matter to be necessary for salvation.

22 Eighth: Let us return to an orderly consideration of the history. Until now we have shown that the custom of public confession was observed in the ancient church in the case of more serious or manifest crimes. Because this custom was judged to be objectionable, it was later discontinued and changed to secret confession. Nevertheless, it demanded a public punishment or satisfaction. But also this private confession was abrogated in the Greek church under Nectarius. The Latin church indeed retained this secret confession, but even as the public confession had earlier been changed to secret, so afterward also the strictness about imposing public penitence for more weighty crimes that had been secretly confessed became obsolete, and thus also the public punishment or satisfaction began to be changed to a private or secret one. From this there was born in later times the auricular confession of the papalists, which demands as necessary for salvation the enumeration of each and every transgression.

23 Ninth: Also those things we have until now quoted from the fathers are meant most of all for those crimes for which a person deserved to be excommunicated, as Augustine says, regardless of whether they

---

[8] The Homoousians were the orthodox Christians who, in contrast to the heretical Arians, confessed with the Nicene Creed that Christ is *homoousios,* i.e., of the same substance with the Father.

were open or secret or had been committed only by the purpose of the will. Nevertheless, it must not be concealed that there are, besides, many statements in the fathers in which they exhort the people to expose also other sins to the priest by means of confession. Thus Cyprian says, Bk. 5, Letters No. 14 and 15, that in the case of lesser sins, namely, such as were not committed against God, they should also go to confession. But one must consider for what reason, in what sense, and to what purpose they commended this confession. For they by no means thought that it was necessary by divine right for the remission of sins to enumerate all sins specifically and singly, together with all the circumstances, to the priest, so that those which were not confessed specifically to the priest could not be remitted even though a truly penitent person confessed them to God. They had other reasons why they observed and commended private confession, namely, because it is a useful discipline. First, to teach the more unlearned about the true acknowledgment, about the degrees, and about the seriousness of sins, likewise about the true and salutary way of repenting. Second, for a remedy, namely, in what way particular sins are to be cured and mortified so that they may be guarded against and avoided in the future, and what emendation of life is to be opposed to which particular sins. Third, for the sake of counsel, so that in doubtful cases the sheep may be instructed from the Word of God by the counsel of the shepherd. Fourth, for the sake of consolation, namely, when some particular sin burdened and troubled the conscience so that it could not take consolation from the general proclamation, then they counseled that this should be made known to the pastor in order that he might pronounce private absolution. Fifth, because absolution is not to be imparted except to one who repents, while an impenitent person is to be bound, therefore the priest should know, from some profession of the penitent who seeks absolution whether he ought to be absolved or, indeed, bound. That a total enumeration of all transgressions is not necessary for this judgment we shall show later.

24 Thus Chrysostom, who above others sharply contends that it is not necessary for the remission of sins to expose and reveal sins to the priest, nevertheless says, Bk. 2, *De sacerdotibus:* "There is no need for much skill in order that Christians who are heavy laden may finally convince themselves that they should submit themselves to the curative ministrations of the priests, yes, that they may be grateful to them for the ministration and medicine." This is also what Sozomen says, namely, that after Nectarius confession to the priest became an adiaphoron. Thus Origen says, on Ps. 37: "First test the physician to whom you must lay bare the causes of your weakness, to see whether you should do what he says and follow the counsel he gives." The same says, on Lev. 2, that you should make known your sin to the priest and seek a remedy, as he did who says: "I will confess my transgression against myself to God, and You forgave." In Homily 1 on Ps. 37 he says thus: "As God has prepared medicines for the body, so also for the soul, in those sayings which He scattered throughout the divine Scriptures in order that we may seek a remedy. Christ is the chief Physician; the ministers of the Word are the physicians to whom the knowledge of the healing of wounds has been committed." He applies this to the public rebukes of the bishops. In the same place he says: "If a blemish or wound arises in the body, you are concerned and inquire what cure you should use, in what way the former health may be restored to the body." In this same sense Cyprian says, Treatise 3, *De lapsis*, that sinners lay bare the weight on their mind to the priests in confessing and seek a salutary remedy, namely, for their small and trifling wounds. Basil says, *Quaestiones compendio explicatae*, 288: "Because the manner of conversion ought to be suited to the nature of the sin, and should show fruits worthy of repentance, the manner of confession suited to this is the one made to those to whom the dispensation of the mysteries of God has been committed." And in ch. 98 he says that the confession of sins is like a wound in someone's body, or a pain, which must be shown to a physician who is reputed to have a cure and remedy. Thus Jerome says, on Matt. 16: "As in the Old Testament the priests possessed the knowledge of who was leprous and who was not, so that they could discern who was clean and who unclean, so in the New Testament no priest should rashly arrogate the key of power to himself without the key of knowledge and discretion, but, on account of the variety of sins, he should know who should be bound and who absolved." On Eccl. 10: "If the serpent, the devil, has secretly bitten someone and infected him with the poison of sin without anyone knowing it, if the one who has been struck keeps silence and does not repent, neither is willing to confess his wound to a brother and teacher, the teacher who could tell him how to be cured will not be able easily to be of benefit to him. For if the sick man is ashamed to show his wound to the physician, the medicine will not cure what it does not know." Another saying of Jerome has the same intent: "A wound that is not known is healed more slowly."

Augustine describes this beautifully, Letter No. 111 to Count Julian: "If by means of some sin we transgress after Baptism, He has established repentance for us on account of our frailty. Therefore we should make our confessions truthfully and bring forth worthy fruits, that is, we should repeat our past sins, according to the command of a God-fearing priest, which priest, as a wise physician, knows first how to cure his own sins and afterward to cleanse the wounds of others, and to heal, not to publish. Let us obey, diligently search after, and enter into consultation with such concerning our salvation." Ambrose says to the penitent Theodosius, *Historia tripartita,* Bk. 9, ch. 30: "With what remedies have you cured these wounds?" The emperor replies: "It is your business both to show and to mix the medicines; it is mine to take them."

25 Nevertheless, they did not simply make this discipline necessary by divine right for the forgiveness of sins, for (according to Cassianus) Pynusius, an abbot, says about the purpose of penitence: "If shyness holds you back, and you feel ashamed to reveal your sins before men, do not cease to confess them with continued supplication to Him from whom they cannot be hid, and to say: 'Against Thee, Thee only, have I sinned,' etc., to Him who is accustomed to heal without any publication of our shame, and to forgive sins without any reproach."

Also Origen, Homily 2 on Leviticus, where he says that for the sake of the remedy sins are to be indicated to the priest, names also other modes by which one may attain forgiveness.

26 To these nine classes all the statements of the ancients can be conveniently referred. It is, however, something vastly different about which papalist confession chiefly contends, namely, that confession to the priest is necessary by divine right for the remission of sins, and indeed in such a way that no sin is remitted which has not been exposed to the priest through confession; likewise, that an enumeration of each and every sin together with the attendant circumstances, specifically and individually, is necessary for the remission of sins, and that if one is concealed, even if a person confesses it to God, the absolution is not valid.

27 These are the things which cannot be clearly demonstrated or proved either from Scripture or from the ancients. Granted, there may be found here and there with the ancients harsher statements, that lean toward the necessity of confession, nevertheless there can be set against them other, dissimilar statements of the ancients, even as Gratian has gathered statements for both sides. And the history of Nectarius and the discourse of Chrysostom show clearly what the understanding of the ancient church was about confession.

28 Since matters stand thus, the reader understands what sort of stratagem that of the papalists is, that, wherever they find the word "confession" in the writings of the ancients, they at once shout that their auricular confession is proved and established by the testimony of all antiquity. Indeed, I undertook this simple distribution about the various kinds of confession of the ancient church in order that the opinions of the ancients could be more rightly and readily understood and explained and that it might be shown that the confession of which the ancients speak does not support the auricular confession for which the papalists fight.

What they quote from certain forged writings which they ascribe to Augustine does not move us at all, as for instance *De vera et falsa poenitentia;* likewise *De visitatione infirmorum,* where it is said that it is not sufficient if we confess our sins to God only, but that the priest must be made inwardly a participant of our consciences, that the most secret hiding place of our inmost heart must be opened to him, and the innermost bars of our consciences revealed, etc. Such things were fabricated by later men under the names of ancients in order that they might be able the more easily to impose them on the unlearned under the pretext of antiquity.

This distribution is useful also in order that it may be possible to demonstrate to good men that when we criticize papalist superstitions, our churches do not reject or condemn those things about confession which in the writings of the ancients are true, useful, and in harmony with Scripture. For some examples of public repentance are observed among us, and indeed we wish we could recall into use certain additional things of this kind from the discipline of the ancient church, which in the papalist church have either fallen down entirely or have been changed into superstitions and abuses.

Private confession is observed among us in order that absolution may be sought by a general acknowledgment of sin and an indication of penitence. And since the key, whether for loosing or binding, is not to be used without judgment, our pastors explore the thinking of their hearers in that private conversation, to see whether they understand the teaching about outward and inward sin, about the wages of sin, about faith in Christ; they are then led to a consideration of their sins; they are examined, whether they are earnestly sorry for their sins, whether they fear the wrath of God and desire to escape it, whether they intend betterment; also they are interrogated if they are believed to hold fast to some certain sins. There the doctrine is taught, along with the exhortation to betterment; either counsel or consolation is sought in troubles of conscience, and upon such confession absolution is imparted. These things are certainly the essentials of that confession of which the ancients speak. Since they are retained and used among us in Christian liberty for edification, without snares to consciences, we are being unjustly accused as though we overthrew, trampled underfoot, and condemned all of antiquity.

29 Now that these things have been explained, the examination of the Tridentine decree about confession can be more easily and briefly carried out. First of all, we shall show from the words of the decree themselves what kind of confession they understand, about which they fight. This observation is useful for a true explanation of the controversy. Up to this time many papalist writers have tried, especially in Germany, to mitigate the harshness of the papalist law about confession with various remedies. But the council renews, confirms, and establishes the harshest conditions of papalist confession without pity.

30 Now this confession is called secret, hidden, concealed, private, and auricular. The council describes it in this way, that a sinner who fell after Baptism ransacks and explores every nook and corner of his conscience and then declares, enumerates, sets forth, explains, and lays bare to the priest each and every mortal sin, even if it is wholly hidden, not only in general but specifically and one by one, in a complete, open, and modest confession, explaining also the circumstances surrounding individual sins which can change the nature of the sin. These are all words of the Tridentine decree. And they want to have it believed under penalty of the anathema that this kind of confession was instituted by Christ.

31 They also declare in the seventh canon that they do not want a confession which is useful for instructing and consoling the penitent, but an enumeration which, they say, is necessary by divine right for the remission of sins, so that whoever does not confess all sins in this way—to him divine goodness remits nothing through the ministry or absolution. For they make all the benefits, comforts, efficacy, and certainty of absolution depend on this total and specific enumeration, even as in the *speculo exemplorum* they relate many stories about people who had revealed their sins to God, but had confessed them in general to the priest, also enumerating many things specifically, but because they had kept silence about some one thing, although they had repented of it, yet no remission was bestowed on them through absolution.

32 This truly is that old torture of conscience which our churches have for very many weighty reasons driven out with the sword of the Spirit, because (1) it is imposed on consciences, although it does not have either precept or example of Christ or of the apostles; (2) it has no promise in the Word of God; (3) it transforms the Gospel into Law, for it declares that forgiveness depends on enumeration; (4) it substitutes for a gift of grace the merit of enumeration and satisfaction, for the scholastics teach in so many words that confession is meritorious for the remission of guilt, the lessening of punishment, the opening of paradise, and the confidence of salvation; (5) it leads the conscience into doubt and despair by this exact enumeration, for seeing that it cannot gather together all faults, doubt never comes to rest; indeed, it extinguishes faith; (6) it demands an impossible thing, for it is certain that we neither understand nor remember very many sins, according to the word: "Who can discern his errors? Cleanse Thou me from hidden faults." They say, indeed, that only those sins are to be enumerated which, after diligent examination, we remember and are conscious of. But if it has once been granted that remission depends on enumeration, the conscience will always be in doubt about hidden sins and will always be uncertain whether it has applied enough diligence in the examination. Therefore, although we retain the discipline of private exploration, we are nevertheless unwilling to lay snares on the consciences as though an enumeration of each and every fault which we want remitted to us by God had to be made to the priest by divine right, so that any which are not enumerated to the priest are not forgiven by God.

33 It is worth the effort to consider by what arguments they prove and establish the kind of confession they describe. I see that there are particularly two arguments on which the Tridentine chapter builds this confession. The first is from antiquity and from the testimony of the universal church. For they say that the whole church has always understood that the kind of confession which they describe was instituted by Christ and is necessary by divine right for the remission of sins. But surely, this is an altogether too shameless lie. For there is found in Scripture no command, no testimony, no example of such a complete and detailed enumeration. Nor is such an enumeration known to the ancients; rather, both the example of Nectarius and the discourses of Chrysostom show that not even that confession which was in use in the ancient church was judged to be necessary or by divine right, as we have shown. And indeed, at the time of Gratian, although there was a sharp debate about the necessity of confession, it was nevertheless not yet considered an article of faith. For he concludes a lengthy recitation of diverse statements, some of which assert that confession is necessary, while others deny it, as follows: "We have publicly set forth on what authors and on what supporting reasons each opinion rests; but to which of these one should adhere is left to the judgment of the reader, for each of them has wise and godly men as proponents." Therefore it is not true what the Tridentine chapter asserts, that the universal church has always understood that confession to be necessary by divine right for the remission of sins. Four hundred years ago, at the time of Gratian, those were regarded as good and godly men who judged that confession was not necessary. Now a person must be anathema who says that papalist confession is not necessary by divine right for the remission of sins. And yet they are not afraid to boast about the testimony of all antiquity.

It is a similar piece of shamelessness that they say that the universal church has always understood that such confession was instituted by Christ, so that it is for this reason necessary by divine right for the forgiveness of sins. For beside the fact that this cannot be shown from Scripture, the gloss concerning repentance, dist. 5, after it had said that they had tried in various ways and by various arguments to show that this confession had a basis in Scripture, finally concludes: "But it is better to say that it was instituted from some tradition of the universal church rather than from the authority of the New or Old Testament. And the tradition of the church obligates, just like a command. Therefore confession is necessary with us in the case of mortal sins; among the Greeks it is not, because such a tradition did not become known to them." Thus says the gloss.

Known also are the arguments of the scholastics. Bonaventura thinks that confession was recommended by Christ, instituted by the apostles, promulgated by James. But sacraments cannot be instituted save only by Christ. Therefore Scotus says: "It would be most convenient if we could have a clear command of confession from the Gospel. And if anything in the Gospel would suffice for this it would seem to be John 20." But he notices that this is not strong enough; therefore he takes the saying of James: "Confess your sins to one another," etc. Yet he says: "Nor does it seem to me that James either gave this as a command or that he promulgated a command of Christ." Seeing, therefore, that this argument lacks true and strong testimonies of Scripture, he finally concludes that Christ promulgated the command of confession to the apostles, and to the church through the apostles, without any Scripture. But Jerome says: "Whatever has no authority from the canonical Scriptures is as easily scorned as approved."

Also Panormitanus argues that papalist confession is not by divine right but by human. Therefore it is false what the Tridentine decree asserts, namely, that the universal church has always understood that confession as it is practiced by the papalists was instituted by Christ and is necessary by divine right. For the opinions about this dispute were free even at the time of Panormitanus. Now an article of faith has been made of it so that anyone who says that this confession was not instituted by divine right must be anathema.

34 The other argument for establishing their confession they deduce from Scripture itself. Observe the variety of ways in which proofs from Scripture for papalist confession have been attempted. Some sought proofs as far back as paradise, as when God says: "Adam, where are you?" Or when He says to Cain: "Where is Abel your brother?"

From the New Testament they quote what is written in Matt. 3:5-6:

"They came and confessed their sins." Matt. 16:19: "I will give you the keys," etc. Matt. 8:4 "Go, show yourself to the priest." 1 John 1:9: "If we confess our sins," etc. James 5:16: "Confess your sins to one another." But the Council of Trent realizes that a wrong is done these statements of Scripture if they are twisted to apply to papalist confession. Therefore it appeals only to the statement of Christ in John 20:23. For Scotus taught that if anything in the Gospel were sufficient for this proof, it would be this statement of Christ.

Now we have above, in the first chapter [Section I], noted down certain things about the explanation and true meaning of this statement in John 20:23. Therefore we shall now only examine how this fifth chapter might demonstrate from these words that auricular confession was there instituted, so that it is necessary by divine right for the remission of sins. Christ, they say, by these words made the priests judges, in order that, on account of the power of the keys, they might pronounce a sentence either of remission or of retention of sins. But no judgment can be rightly rendered if the case is not understood. Therefore, when absolution is sought in confession, all sins must be individually enumerated, explained, and uncovered to the priest as judge.

This judicial act in absolution is, however, understood in two ways by the papalists. First as in a secular trial. After the case has been heard, an examination and exploration is made to see to what extent the guilty person brings a satisfaction of his own free will, and the priest deliberates on how much satisfaction should be imposed besides, in order that, when recompense has in this way been made for the fault, the guilty one may be absolved. Thus some want to make it necessary for the priest, after he has heard in confession an explanation of all sins, together with the individual circumstances, to explore what kind and what degree of contrition is present in the penitent, and that he should in addition deliberate about what kind of punishment should be demanded and imposed in accord with the gravity of the faults, so that when the sinner has paid by means of contrition and satisfaction he may rightly and deservedly be absolved as though in a trial. The Tridentine chapter alludes to this sense in a not obscure manner, for it repeats twice that this enumeration is necessary on account of imposing penalties for sins. But this statement conflicts clearly and, as it were, expressly with the statement of Christ. For He did not command to proclaim release from sin at such and such a time and in such and such a respect, namely, that they would pronounce judgment of forgiveness if they saw in the penitent a payment for sins, but He commanded remission of sins to be preached in His name (Luke 24:47), that is, not on account of our works but gratis, on account of the merit and satisfaction of Christ, to those who believe in Him. (Rom. 3:22-28; 5:1-11; Acts 10:43)

35 Others indeed construct the argument more subtly and plausibly as follows: The power of remitting and retaining sins cannot be rightly administered without an inquiry and a judgment whether sins ought to be remitted to a particular person or retained. This, however, cannot be done without an enumeration of the sins. Therefore the process of absolution must be undertaken after the manner of a court trial.

To this we rightly answer that there is a difference between a court trial and the function of the Gospel ministry. For in a court trial judgment is rendered according to the findings in the case, depending on whether it is good or bad, or according as the guilty one brings payment for his misdeed. The ministry of the Gospel, however, has the command to announce and impart the benefit of Another, namely Christ, for the remission of sins to such as labor and are heavy laden and seek to be revived. Now whoever seeks absolution sets two before himself: First, God Himself as the one from whom he seeks and asks remission of sins; therefore he pours out his whole heart before Him. Then he also sets before himself the minister, whose voice or ministry God uses as that of an ambassador or messenger or agent for imparting and sealing the absolution. Therefore when I have made known my fault to God, there is no need for a scrupulous enumeration before the minister, who is only the dispenser of Another's benefits.

36 But you say: Nevertheless the key of discernment is wholly necessary for the minister, which cannot exist without knowledge and judgment, namely, lest he remit sins to a person for whom they ought to be retained, or retained to one for whom they ought to be loosed. For the administration of the keys has not been committed to the minister to be used according to his own will, but with a certain injunction.

I answer: This we grant; but the question is how this judgment is to be practiced and exercised in the ministry. For in the general preaching of repentance and remission of sins, sins are remitted by the power of God to many who repent and accept the promise by faith, even though the minister knows nothing either of their sins or of their repentance or of their faith. But the matter stands otherwise with respect to imparting private absolution. For if I were to absolve someone concerning whom I did not know at all whether he had first been instructed from the Word of God about sin, repentance, faith in Christ, the grace of God and the forgiveness of sins, I would not be rightly administering the power of remitting sins. Likewise, if I did not know whether someone was penitent or believed, or if I knew that he was impenitent and unbelieving, and would nevertheless pronounce to him a sentence of remission, I would not be acting rightly. Therefore such judgment and knowledge is required that the minister knows that the person who seeks absolution knows the doctrine, acknowledges his sins, repents, and believes in Christ.

Now the question is whether the specific enumeration of every sin and of the circumstances surrounding it is necessary for such knowledge. The surest explanation and answer to this question is found in the example of the Baptizer, of Christ, and of the apostles. For also in Baptism sins are remitted privately to everyone who is baptized, and ministers must judge and know whom among adults they should admit and receive to Baptism, namely, those who repent and believe the Gospel. Now the Baptizer, Christ, and the apostles did not demand a complete enumeration of each and every sin, but were satisfied with a general confession of repentance and faith. And indeed, when Christ imparts private absolution (Matt. 9:2; Luke 7:48), He does not ask for an enumeration specifically and singly of all sins. Also we do not read that the apostles demanded such an enumeration when they used the power of remitting sins which they had received from Christ. Therefore that enumeration on which the papalists insist is not necessary for the judgment and knowledge which is required in absolution. For it is not subject to debate that the power of the keys is most correctly administered if it is done according to the example of the Baptizer, of Christ, and of the apostles. For it is certain that they in their ministry remitted sins, yet they did not demand a total enumeration of all sins but were satisfied with a general profession and token of repentance and faith.

37 But they say: In a general confession a sinner is able to deceive the minister. I answer: The same thing can happen, and often did happen, in the request for Baptism; yes, even if a total enumeration is demanded, it is nevertheless true what Augustine says, *Confessiones,* Bk. 10, ch. 53: "How do they know when they hear from me about myself whether I speak the truth, seeing that no man knows what goes on in a man except the spirit of the man which is in him?" Therefore those who seek absolution are to be reminded that they are here dealing not with a man but with God Himself, in whose sight these things are being done. And God, who searches the hearts and knows our thoughts, is not mocked. Ministers, however, act only as ambassadors and are dispensers of Another's benefits; they have not been commanded to search the hearts but to proclaim the remission of sins to those who indicate that they repent and believe the Gospel. Thus Leo writes to Theodorus, bishop of St. Frejus: "To those who lie in their death-struggle absolution is to be imparted even if they seek it not in words but only by signs, or if their friends testify that they asked for it earlier." As necessary, therefore, as judgment and knowledge is for the minister in absolution, this papalist enumeration is not necessary for it. Of the way those who seek absolution can, in the private conversation in confession, be profitably explored and examined, we have spoken above. Thus the chief argument which has some show of right for enumeration has been simply and clearly explained and removed.

Chrysostom argues expressly that the kind of judgment for which the papalists contend is not necessary for absolution. He says concerning confession and repentance: "It is not necessary to confess in the presence of witnesses. Let the search for faults be made in thought; let this judgment be without a witness; let God alone hear your confession, who does not reproach you but saves you from sins on account of confession." Homily 9, *De poenitentia:* "Here is the place for healing, not judgment; giving, not punishments but remission of sins," etc.

38 Furthermore, one must observe in this present chapter that they teach that only mortal sins are to be confessed, so that for the remission of venial sins absolution is not necessary but that these can be atoned for by other remedies. Here the reader will observe that the papalists, who demand an enumeration of all sins, exclude from confession and absolution a very great part of the things which are truly sins in God's sight. For in the first place they do not want included in confession the inner uncleanness and wickedness that dwells in the flesh, unless it is fulfilled by consent and act, because they teach that the evil lust which remains in the regenerate does not have the nature of sin. Then they judge that many actual sins are so trivial that absolution is not necessary for their remission.

However, absolution is nothing other than the voice of the Gospel announcing remission of sins on account of Christ's merit. Therefore the council teaches that venial sins are remitted not by absolution, that is, not on account of Christ, but that they can be atoned for by other remedies, namely, by smiting the breast and sprinkling holy water, as Thomas teaches.

39 We have also shown above that they say that public confession is not by divine right and precept. But what they add, namely, that the confession made secretly only before the priest is more ancient, cannot stand if the examples either of Scripture or of antiquity are considered. Rather, we have shown above that private or secret confession arose out of public confession. Now the daughter cannot be before or older than the mother.

40 So far as the Lateran decree of about A.D. 1200 is concerned, it is certain that before that time there was no command in the church about enumerating to the priest all faults for which anyone sought remission from God. For also at the time of Gratian, that is, 50 years before the Lateran decree, nothing had been decreed about the necessity of confession, but there were at that time many pious and godly men who held that such a confession is not necessary, as Gratian says, dist. 1, *De poenitentia,* ch. *Quamvis.*

41 It is useful to observe the gradual progression toward establishing papalist confession. In the fathers exhortations to confession can be found, for the sake of that discipline of which we have spoken earlier. At the time of Gratian and Lombard they began to argue whether confession is necessary. Gratian left it free to the judgment of the reader which view he wanted to embrace. Lombard, however, in his discussion inclines more toward necessity. Still even then they did not yet argue about the enumeration of each and every fault with all the circumstances as being necessary for forgiveness.

But 50 years later Innocent commanded by decree, under threat of excommunication, that all sins should be confessed to the priest. The later scholastics and summists added even harder conditions. The decree of Innocent says the priest should inquire into the circumstances of the sin; this inquisition was afterward imposed on the consciences of those who confessed. And to what the Lateran Council says, namely, that all sins are to be faithfully confessed, it was later added that all sins should be enumerated to the priest, not in general but specifically, one by one, according to all the circumstances, nakedly, totally, and clearly. It was also added that if anything were omitted in this enumeration, then not only those sins which were not specifically and singly enumerated would not be remitted, but not even those sins would be remitted which were enumerated, unless the confession was complete according to all the circumstances. From this the confessional halters which are found in the summists were finally knotted.

42 With respect to the time when absolution should be sought by means of confession, the men on our side teach that no certain time should be prescribed, because not all are prepared at one and the same time; neither can those who confess be heard and instructed if all run to confession at the same time. But the doctrine concerning the worth and benefit of absolution and of the Lord's Supper must be taught in such a way from the Word of God that men are invited to more frequent use. They are not, however, to be compelled by commands to use the sacraments when they are not prepared for it.

Among the ancients the discipline of confession and absolution of those who were publicly repenting was practiced chiefly during the time of Lent, dist. 50, ch. *Quadragesimae.* And Chrysostom, on Genesis, often admonishes that sins should be confessed to God at the time of fasting. And because they went to Communion more frequently during the time of fasting, that confession before the priest of which the ancients speak also preceded Communion, as Origen says on Ps. 37 and Augustine in Letter No. 111. From this the law of confessing to the priest during Lent, under threat of excommunication, was afterward made. And the Council of Trent decrees that this custom must be retained because that time is most acceptable, that is, because confession and absolution accomplishes more and is better accepted before God by reason of the time, contrary to the express teaching of Paul. (Rom. 14:5-6; Col. 2:16-17; Gal. 4:10-11)

[SECTION VI]
Concerning Absolution

Chapter VI

Now with respect to the minister of this sacrament, the holy synod declares that all doctrines are utterly false and alien to the truth of the Gospel which perniciously extend the ministry of the keys to any persons whatsoever outside of bishops and priests, thinking that these words of the Lord: "Whatever you bind on earth shall be bound in heaven, and whatever you loose on earth shall be loosed in heaven," and: "If you forgive the sins of any, they are forgiven; if you retain the sins of any, they are retained," were spoken to all the faithful of Christ indiscriminately, contrary to the institution of this sacrament, with the result that everyone has the power of remitting sins, public sins through rebuke, if the person rebuked accepts the rebuke, secret sins through voluntary confession made to any person whatsoever.

It teaches also that priests who are held by mortal sin nevertheless exercise, through the power of the Holy Spirit bestowed in ordination, the function of remitting sins as ministers of Christ and that those hold an erroneous opinion who argue that this power does not reside in wicked priests. However, although the absolution of the priest is the dispensation of Another's bounty, it is nevertheless not a mere ministry either of proclaiming the Gospel or of declaring that sins are remitted, but is in the nature of a judicial act in which a sentence is pronounced by him as though by a judge. And therefore the penitent person ought not to delude himself about his faith to the point where he thinks that even if no contrition is present[9] or the priest is not minded to act seriously and truly to absolve, he nevertheless is truly absolved before God solely on account of his faith. For neither does faith without repentance give this remission of sins, nor would he be anything but most neglectful of his salvation who knew that the priest absolved him in jest and did not diligently seek out another priest who acted in earnest.

CANON IX

If anyone says that the sacramental absolution of the priest is not a judicial act but merely the ministry of proclaiming and declaring that the sins are forgiven to the penitent person, provided only that he believes he is absolved, even if the priest absolves not in earnest but in jest; or says that the confession of the penitent is not required in order that the priest may be able to absolve him, let him be anathema.

---

[9] The text of 1574 reads: *etiam si multa illi adsit contritio.* The official text of the *Canons and Decrees of the Council of Trent* has *nulla* instead of *multa.* Our translation follows the official text.

If anyone says that priests who are in mortal sin do not have the power of binding and loosing, or that priests are not the only ministers of absolution but that it is said to each and every believer in Christ: "Whatever you bind on earth shall be bound in heaven and whatever you shall loose on earth shall be loosed in heaven" and: "If you forgive the sins of any, they are forgiven; if you retain the sins of any, they are retained," and that in virtue of these words anyone is able to absolve sins, public ones by reproof only, provided the person accepts the reproof, but secret sins through voluntary confession, let him be anathema.

Examination

1 This chapter has two parts. The first disputes about the minister of absolution, to whom the orderly ministry of the keys belongs; the second deals with the question of what absolution is. So far as the first part is concerned, the matter can be set right in a few words. For in our examination of the 10th canon on the sacraments in general [p. 98] the things which belong here have been explained. For although the keys were given to the church itself, as the ancients correctly teach, we nevertheless by no means hold that any and every Christian without distinction should or can take to himself or exercise the ministry of the Word and sacraments without a legitimate call. As however the ancients say that in case of necessity any Christian lay person can administer the sacrament of Baptism, so Luther says the same thing about absolution in case of necessity, where no priest is present. He says nothing different from what Lombard, Bk. 4, dist. 17, and Gratian, *De poenitentia,* dist. 5, say on the basis of the opinion of the ancients.

2 Earlier we have also noted the opinion of Theophylact, that whatever is either loosed or bound in fraternal reproof and reconciliation is loosed and bound in heaven itself. Moreover, there is no doubt that when the Word of the Gospel is proclaimed, God works efficaciously, no matter by whom it is proclaimed. Why then does the Tridentine chapter make such a great to-do over this question? I answer: Because they place the integrity, genuineness, and efficacy of the sacraments not simply and completely in the words of Christ, but in part also in the character they imagine is imprinted on priests in ordination. Therefore also, they want the comfort of absolution to depend not so much on the Word of the Gospel as on the person of the one who absolves. This the reader should understand when he reads the first part of this chapter. But with those who entirely take out of the church the use of private absolution which is proclaimed by the Word of the Gospel through the minister of the Word—with those our churches have nothing in common. Therefore what is said against them does not pertain to us.

Moreover, that the efficacy of the Word and the sacraments does not depend on the worthiness or sanctity of the ministers, so long as the purity of the Word and of the sacraments is there and remains—that has been explained under the 12th canon on the sacraments in general. [P. 109]

3   Therefore we will come to the second part of this chapter, in which the dispute is about a most weighty matter—what absolution is, what its effects are, what consolation is drawn from it, and how it is received; wherein the efficacy and consolation of absolution consists, and on what it rests as its basis. About these very weighty questions clear explanations have been handed down from the Word of God by the men on our side. Where formerly the necessary things have been overthrown, buried, and perverted by the disputations of the scholastics, the men on our side showed that absolution is nothing else than the proclamation of the Gospel itself, announcing the forgiveness of sins gratis because of Christ, generally, to all who repent and believe the Gospel. For the sake of firmer and surer consolation this proclamation of the Gospel is applied by means of private absolution to individuals who seek it. It must be accepted by faith, so that the individual believes the proclamation of the Gospel in absolution and considers it certain that remission of sins is given, applied, and sealed to him by God gratis because of Christ, through the ministry, and that by this faith he is truly reconciled to God. Thus fearful and terrified consciences receive consolation from absolution, so that they do not doubt that the benefits of the Mediator, which in the Gospel are promised generally to all who believe, belong also to themselves in particular and are given and applied to themselves in particular by God. For the Gospel is "the power of God for salvation to every one who has faith," regardless of whether it is proclaimed generally, to many, or privately to but few, or even to only one. There is therefore no doubt that faith is strengthened through the use of absolution. And although it is necessary that contrition be present in those who seek absolution, together with a good intention, nevertheless the efficacy and consolation of absolution does not rest on either our contrition or our obedience, for it bestows and proclaims remission of sins neither on the basis of our works nor according to our works but gratis, on account of Christ. Nor must faith in absolution be led into placing its confidence of the remission of sins on the quantity and quality of its contrition, but it should lay hold of the Word of promise which offers and bestows remission of sins gratis, because of Christ. For if the inheritance is of works, "faith is null and the promise is void." "That is why it depends on faith, in order that the promise may rest on grace and be guaranteed" (Rom. 4:14, 16). Nor should the conscience be worried about the intention of the minister, but if the Word of the

Gospel is proclaimed, faith lays hold of it and is certain that it is absolved before God, no matter what the priest's intention may be.

4 I have related these things in order that it may be possible to understand more clearly what opinion the Tridentine chapter condemns in the second part. They do not want absolution to be the ministry of proclaiming the Gospel, namely, the ministry by which, through proclamation of the Gospel privately, sins are pronounced and declared to be remitted gratis, on account of Christ, to him who believes the proclamation of the Gospel in absolution. But they want faith, which seeks remission of sins in absolution, to rest on our contrition and penitence, with the result that the sentence of absolution is pronounced, not from the Word of the Gospel, gratis, on account of Christ, but as though by a judge, namely, according to the measure of our contrition and satisfaction. And this is what they want to say. But, according to their custom, they mix in slander, as though we taught that the sinner is absolved before God on account of faith alone even if there is no contrition, even if the sinner is without repentence, even if the whole action is undertaken as a game or a jest, although they are not ignorant of what the Augsburg Confession teaches about repentance, about contrition, and about faith and absolution.

5 Now because the ninth canon condemns those who say that absolution is a mere ministry of declaring that sins have been remitted, I judge that some explanation must be added. For among the sacramentarians some contend that sins are not remitted through absolution, since men are not able to remit sins — a thing which belongs only to God. Therefore they contend that believers receive nothing in absolution, but that it is only an outward declaration of something they already had before. However, God, who alone remits sins, does not do this without means, but through the ministry of the Word and sacraments. Now private absolution proclaims the message of the Gospel through which God is without doubt efficacious and remits sins to those who by faith lay hold of the message of the Gospel in absolution. Therefore in absolution God Himself remits sins through the ministry of the Gospel to individual believers, and in this way the absolution of the minister is a testimony of divine absolution, from which the conscience has the testimony that one's sins are truly forgiven him by God.

6 It must also be noted with what intention they set down, without fuller explanation, the bare antithesis, namely, that absolution is not the ministry of proclaiming the message of the Gospel privately to those who seek absolution but that it is a judicial act by which a sentence is pronounced as though by a judge. There is no doubt that by this generalization they wanted to embrace the arguments of the scholastics about absolution. In order, therefore, that this antithesis may be more fully understood, I will briefly note down the pronouncements of the masters of sentences which the Tridentine chapter wanted comprehended in the bosom of the judicial act.

7 The scholastics who were before Scotus hold that sin is destroyed and forgiven through contrition itself, on account of the love out of which it arises. Therefore they say that the power of the keys or absolution does not extend so far as to remit guilt or the punishment of eternal damnation, neither as its principal cause nor as its essential cause nor as its instrumental cause. However, lest there be no use for absolution, they say that after the priest understands the nature of the transgressions of the guilty person and has probed his contrition through confession, along with the promise of satisfaction, and has compared the transgression with the contrition and laid a satisfaction on him, he shows, decides, and pronounces with his judgment through absolution that the sinner is loosed, namely, on account of his contrition and the satisfaction he has undertaken. And therefore some say that the remission in absolution is made not before God but in the sight of the church.

8 Thomas, and others after him argue that when there is enough contrition, then the sin is remitted through the contrition, before the absolution. However, when there is only attrition, which is an insufficient disposition, then through absolution grace is infused, that is, charity, through which attrition is disposed so that it becomes contrition, which by virtue of charity is able to destroy sin. Some think that by virtue of absolution eternal punishment is changed to temporal. Others argue that because after the guilt has been remitted, which they think is done through contrition, the obligation to a temporal punishment remains, which because of the strictness of divine justice is beyond our power to bear and unknown to our understanding, but for which satisfaction must nevertheless be made to God — that for this reason there was given to the priest the power of making a judgment with respect to this punishment and of remitting a part of it in absolution by virtue of the keys, the remaining part to be expiated through satisfactions. Thus to bind would mean to impose satisfactions, and to loose would mean to remit something of the temporal punishment. This is the judicial act the Tridentine chapter has in mind.

9 Therefore this observation shows most clearly what the papalists are seeking and pushing for when they contend that their absolution is not a ministry of proclaiming the message of the Gospel to the penitent but that it is a judicial act. And lest the reader be disturbed by the generalities which the Tridentine chapter assiduously follows, I wanted to add this explanation to this chapter in the very words of the scholastics in order that those whom God has given eyes to see may see how the benefit of absolution is spoiled, adulterated, and perverted by the papalists.

[SECTION VII]
Concerning the Reservation of Cases

Chapter VII

Therefore, since the nature and theory of the judgment require that sentence be passed only on those who are subject to the one making the judgment, it has always been the conviction in the Church of God, and this synod attests that it is most true, that that absolution should be of no weight which a priest pronounces on someone over whom he does not have either an ordinary or a delegated jurisdiction. Indeed, it seems to our most holy fathers to be of great importance for the discipline of Christian people that certain more hideous and heinous crimes should be absolved, not by any and all, but only by the highest priests. Therefore the supreme pontiffs, in virtue of the supreme power bestowed on them in the universal Church, were rightly able to reserve some more serious cases of crimes to their own special judgment. Neither ought one to doubt, since all things which are from God are well ordered, that this same thing is lawful for all bishops, each in his own diocese, over those who are subject to them—however for edification, not for destruction—in virtue of the authority given them above the other, inferior priests, in particular in respect to things to which the judgment of excommunication is attached. It is consonant with divine authority that this reservation of offenses should have force not only in outward administration but also before God. Nevertheless, lest anyone perish by reason of this, the custom has always been piously guarded in the same Church of God that there should be no reservation at the point of death and that therefore all priests are able to absolve any and all penitents of any and all sins and judgments. Since, with this one exception, priests can do nothing in cases reserved for another person, they strive to persuade the penitent to approach the higher and lawful judges to receive the benefit of absolution.

CANON XI

If anyone says that bishops do not have the right to reserve cases to themselves except as regards administration, and that therefore the reservation of cases does not prohibit a priest from truly absolving reserved cases, let him be anathema.

Examination

1 This one lone chapter can show what an unbridled lust for lording it over the consciences there is in the Roman pontiffs. In old time a rule was made that, for the sake of order and discipline, everyone should seek and receive absolution from his own pastor, because the life of his hearers is better known to the pastor than to another. For a pastor ought to know the countenance of his flock. Therefore lest wicked men, without true repentance, steal absolution from other ministers, to whom their life is not known, it was not in vain but in the interest of good order that the rule about being absolved by one's own pastor was instituted. In addition, no one ought to exercise the ministry of the Word and sacraments in any church unless he has been lawfully called to it. But the Roman pontiffs went even further and pretended that in order for absolution to be valid and efficacious neither the word of absolution nor the power of order is sufficient, that is, that the minister have a valid call, but that over and above this the power of jurisdiction over a certain group or person is required. This they describe in this way, that the whole power of jurisdiction resides fully in the pope as the highest ruler and prince in the church, from whom either through means or without means all the ecclesiastical jurisdiction of inferior rulers is derived, according to the pleasure of this highest prince, yet without detriment to his power. Therefore whoever does not have the power of jurisdiction over someone from the pope can neither loose nor bind him. That is what Gabriel says, Bk. 4, dist. 17, quest. 1. This chapter decrees that an absolution which a priest pronounces on someone over whom he does not have either ordinary or delegated jurisdiction carries no weight; that is, even if the absolution has God's Word and is pronounced by a legitimately called minister—this notwithstanding, the absolution carries no weight unless the priest has, derived from the pope, the power of jurisdiction over the one whom he absolves.

What is this but to sit in the temple of God, and to exalt himself above all that is called God (2 Thess. 2: 4)? The excellent statement of Ambrose is: "The Word of God forgives sins; the priest is the servant, performing his own office, not exercising the rights of the power of another person." The Roman pope, however, says: "Even if an absolution has the Word of God, and the minister who absolves has been sent through a legitimate vocation by the Son of God, who sits at the right hand of the Father, the absolution must nevertheless be of no weight unless it has been derived from the plenitude of power which resides in the shrine of the papal heart." And the Council of Trent is not ashamed to confirm this manifest mark of the Antichrist.

2 It is the same way with reserved cases. In the ancient church very great crimes, to which the censure of excommunication was attached, were referred to the bishops in order that from their advice a certain measure of public penitence might be laid on the guilty for their betterment and for the edification of the church. The *Constitutio* of Innocent says, ch. *Omnis utriusque*: "If the confessor has need in the case of some enormous crime, let him seek counsel from his superiors and teachers, but let him seek it cautiously without mentioning names of persons." From this there were later made the reserved cases in which the Word of God is not able to absolve the sinner who repents through any minister, no matter how legitimately called; it must be done either by the bishop or by the Roman pontiff, and that not for the sake of discipline and order but because the fullness of the power to remit sin resides in the pope, according to whose will this power flows to the lower ministers, as though the Word of God were not able to remit sins except where, to the extent that, and in those cases in which the power derived from the shrine of the pontifical heart assists it. Therefore the strength and power of the Word of God will vary according to the difference in those by whom it is administered, so that through some it is able to remit only small sins, but through the pope it can remit any and all sins, even the greatest. Cyprian says, and this is quoted in 24, quest. 1: "What Peter was, that also the other apostles were, endowed with equal participation in both honor and power." Likewise: "The episcopate is one; of it a part is held completely by the individual bishops." And Christ says equally to all the apostles: "If you remit the sins of any,"etc. The Tridentine chapter also confesses the same thing, that at the point of death every priest is able to absolve in reserved cases. Therefore it is false that these reservations have such force, not only in ecclesiastical administration but also before God, that in them no priest can truly absolve through the Word of God, but only the pope. But these things have been fabricated to strengthen the tyranny of Antichrist.

[SECTION VIII]

Concerning the Necessity and Fruit of Satisfaction [and] Concerning Works of Satisfaction[10]

Chapter VIII

Finally, with regard to satisfaction (which of all the parts of penance, as it is that which has at all times been recommended to the Christian people by our fathers, is the one which most of all in our time is attacked under the loftiest pretext of piety by those who hold the form of religion but deny the power of it) the holy synod declares that it is altogether false, and foreign to the Word of God, that guilt is never remitted by God without also the whole punishment being cancelled. For clear and outstanding examples are found in the sacred Scriptures, by which, beside the divine tradition, this error is most clearly refuted. Surely, also the nature of divine justice seems to demand that those who sinned through ignorance before Baptism should be received into grace by Him in one way but that those who had once been set free from the servitude of sin and of the devil and had received the gift of the Holy Spirit, and had not been afraid knowingly to violate the temple of God and to grieve the Holy Spirit, should be received in another way. It befits divine clemency that sins should not be pardoned to us in such a way, without any satisfaction, that, taking occasion from this, we consider the sins to be of lighter nature and with insult and outrage to the Holy Spirit fall into more grievous sins, treasuring to ourselves wrath on the day of wrath. For without doubt these satisfactions greatly hold men back from sin and restrain them as with a bridle and make penitents more cautious and watchful in the future; they also cure the remnants of sins and take away evil habits acquired by evil living, through contrary virtuous actions. Neither was there ever believed to be any surer way in the Church of God for averting a threatening punishment from the Lord than that men should with true sorrow of mind perform these works of penance. To this comes the fact that while we suffer for our sins by making satisfaction, we become conformed to Christ Jesus, who made satisfaction for our sins, from whom all our sufficiency comes, having from this the surest pledge that if we suffer with Him we shall also be glorified with Him. But this satisfaction we suffer for our sins is not our own in such a way that it is not through Jesus Christ. For we can do nothing of ourselves as of ourselves, but when He who strengthens us works together with us, we can do all things. Thus man has nothing to boast of, but all our boasting is in Christ, in whom we live, in whom we merit, in whom we make satisfaction, bringing fruits worthy of repentance which have their efficacy from Him, are offered by Him to the Father, and through Him are accepted by the

---

[10] The editor has moved "Concerning Works of Satisfaction" from before "Chapter X" on p. 630.

Father. Therefore the priests of the Lord ought, to the extent that the Spirit and prudence shall suggest, according to the nature of the crimes and the ability of the penitents, enjoin salutary and suitable satisfactions lest, if by chance they shut their eyes to sin and deal too leniently with penitents by enjoining certain very easy works for very grievous transgressions, they become partakers of other men's sins. But let them bear in mind that the satisfactions they impose should be not only for guarding the new life and for a remedy against weakness but also for the avenging and punishment of past sins. For that the keys of the priests were given not only for loosing but also for binding—this also the old fathers believe and teach. But they did not for this reason think that the sacrament of penance is a tribunal of wrath or of punishments, even as no Catholic ever thought that by our satisfactions of this kind the power of the merit and satisfactions of our Lord Jesus Christ is obscured or in any way diminished; since the innovators wish[11] to understand it so, they teach, in order to destroy the efficacy and use of satisfaction, that a new life is the best penance.

Chapter X[12]

[The holy synod] teaches further that the liberality of the divine bounty is so great that we are able, through Christ Jesus, to make satisfaction to God the Father, not only by punishments voluntarily assumed by us for the punishment of sin, or imposed at the discretion of the priest in proportion to the transgression, but even (which is a great evidence of love) by temporal scourgings inflicted by God and patiently borne by us.

CANON XII

If anyone says that the total punishment is always remitted by God at the same time as the guilt, and that the satisfaction of penitents is nothing else than the faith by which they apprehend that Christ has made satisfaction for them, let him be anathema.

CANON XIII

If anyone says that satisfaction is by no means made to God through the merits of Christ for sin, so far as temporal punishment is concerned, by punishments inflicted by Him and patiently borne, or enjoined by the priest, nor even by those willingly undertaken, as by fastings, prayers, almsgiving, or also by other works of piety, and that therefore the best penance is only a new life, let him be anathema.

CANON XIV

If anyone says that the satisfactions by which penitents, through Christ, pay for their sins are not a worship of God but human traditions which obscure the doctrine of grace, the true worship of God, and the benefit of the death of Christ, let him be anathema.

---

[11] The text in the *Examen* has *nolunt*. This, according to the official text, should be *volunt*.

[12] This is Chapter IX in the *Canons and Decrees of the Council of Trent*.

If anyone says that the keys were given to the church only for loosing and not also for binding, and that therefore priests who impose penalties on those who confess are acting contrary to the purpose of the keys and contrary to the institution of Christ, and that it is a fiction that when eternal punishment has been removed by the power of the keys there very frequently remains a temporal punishment which must be discharged, let him be anathema.

Examination

1 Truly, there is an abundant amount of doctrine which belongs to this topic, but I shall try to draw it together into a brief compass. In order that it may be possible to do this more easily, I shall first explain the true opinion, distributed under a few chief points.

2 First: It is most certain that God remits sin not from some fickleness, as if the Law had been done away and He no longer cared about sins nor were moved to wrath by them. For He Himself wrote down the Law with His own fingers; Himself, with His own voice, promulgated threats of His wrath against sins and spoke about the guilt and punishments of sins. And this sentence of the Law is so firm and unmovable that it is easier for heaven and earth to fall than that even the smallest particle of the Law should fall, so as not to be fulfilled either by obedience or by punishment (Matt. 5:18). Therefore God does not remit sins committed against His Law unless satisfaction intervenes which satisfies the Law so fully and perfectly both by obedience and by punishment that through it His wrath is stilled and the punishment due the sins is taken away. Such a propitiating and reconciling satisfaction for sins that it would merit remission of sins and do away with eternal death no sinful man could offer for himself, neither could any creature offer it for him.

Therefore, lest the whole human race perish eternally, the wonderful decree of the divine counsel about the incarnation of the Son of God was made—that He, as our Mediator, should assume our nature, yet without sin, that He should be put under the Law, should bear sin, the guilt of sin, the wrath of God, and the punishment of the sins of the whole world which has been laid on Him, and should make satisfaction for them to the Father by His most perfect obedience and by His most holy passion, and should so procure redemption, propitiation, reconciliation, remission of sins, freedom from the wrath of God, from condemnation, and from eternal death.

3 This redemption through Christ the grace of God sets before those who repent, in order that He may be our means of reconciliation through application or apprehension by faith for the remission of sins (Rom. 3:25). And this, and no other, is the one and only propitiating, reconciling satisfaction for sins, meriting forgiveness of sins and abolishing eternal death. 1 John 2:2: "He is the expiation for our sins, and not for ours only but also for the sins of the whole world." 1 Tim. 2:5-6: "There is one Mediator between God and men . . . who gave Himself as a ransom for all." Gal. 3:13: "He was made under the Law that He might redeem those who were under the Law from the curse of the Law." Heb. 7;9;10: "One sacrifice for sins, offered once, found an eternal redemption, and perfected forever those who are sanctified." 1 Cor. 15:54-57: "Through Christ He gave us the victory over death and hell." Rom. 5:18: "By one man's obedience many will be made righteous." Acts 4:12: "There is salvation in no one else, for there is no other name under heaven given among men by which we must be saved," etc.

These things must be set before men when they repent, lest they either, in epicurean laxness, play a game in the matter of reconciliation with God and the remission of sins, or through a pharisaic persuasion set their own satisfactions against the wrath of God for the propitiation and expiation of sins. In the reconciliation of the sinner with God it is therefore absolutely necessary to offer to God and to set against His wrath a satisfaction for sins. But this does not, either in whole or in part, consist in either our actions or our sufferings, but it is altogether the unique satisfaction of the obedience and the suffering of the Son of God, the Mediator, performed for us. Faith lays hold of this and sets it between the wrath of God and our sins, as Anselm says, asking, believing, and declaring that on account of this satisfaction sins are remitted, God is reconciled, and the sinner is received into grace and freed from eternal damnation. It is to this satisfaction that the minds of the penitents who sought reconciliation with God ought to have been led. But when the monks ruled in the matter of penance, when many things were being argued about satisfaction, this unique satisfaction of Christ for sins, which should be set against the wrath of God for propitiation and reconciliation, had clearly been buried.

4 Now when the Tridentine chapter had set down the title: "Concerning the Necessity and Fruit of Satisfaction," it was not able, in the face of the light of God's Word, entirely to pass over the satisfaction of Christ in silence; therefore it does make mention of it, however in such a way that it links to it our satisfactions which we ourselves pay for sins, in order that also we ourselves may suffer for sins, even as Christ suffered for sins. And Canon 12, disputing about the remission of sins, condemns with the anathema those who say that there is no other satisfaction for sins on the part of penitents than faith, by which they apprehend that Christ has made satisfaction for them. Therefore we are dealing with great and necessary matters in this controversy about satisfaction, namely what

satisfaction it is that the faith of penitents ought to bring to God and set against His wrath in order that they may not be condemned but, absolved from sins and freed from damnation, may be reconciled to God and received to eternal life.

5 Second: In the ancient church a canonical or disciplinary satisfaction was customary. For the ancient church did not lightly receive back at the first indication of repentance those who either had renounced the faith under persecution or had fallen into manifest and heinous crimes, but first explored those who had been reproved with certain ecclesiastical punishments. They stood in a certain place, separated from the fellowship and assembly of the faithful, with certain outward marks of their guilt—by food, drink, garb, gestures, groaning, weeping, and supplications confessing their guilt and publicly asking for absolution, as these ceremonies of public penitence are described in Tertullian, *De poenitentia*; in Eusebius, Bk. 5, ch. 28; Bk. 6, ch. 25; by Sozomen in *Tripartita* Bk. 9, ch. 35; by Nicephorus, Bk. 6, ch. 2, and dist. 50, ch. *Quadragesimae*. These public castigations of penitents Sozomen calls *epitimia kai timoorias* that is, fines and penalties. The Latins, after their own particular fashion, called them satisfactions. And because the term "satisfaction," on account of the disputings of the monks, now seems to convey something different to our ears than it meant for the ancients, it is profitable to consider the Greek terms to which it corresponds.

The ancient church imposed these public punishments on the fallen, not in the belief that they would be compensations to God for sins, or atoning satisfactions that would merit remission of sins and do away with the wages of sin, but they had other purposes, namely: (1) that by these rites the minds of the penitents might be explored, to see whether they were feigning repentance or were, indeed, in earnest; (2) that a satisfaction might be made to the church by such an outward declaration of repentance, seeing it had been offended by the scandals of the crimes; (3) that others, warned by sights of this kind, and deterred from frivolous sinning, might avoid lapses into sin with greater care; (4) that this discipline might be to the fallen themselves an inducement to a true consideration of sin, to earnest, unfeigned sorrow over their sins, to fear of the wrath of God, to faith which earnestly seeks the mercy of God because of Christ, to a firm and steadfast purpose to better their lives; (5) that these displays might give public testimony that the church does not teach freedom or impunity to sin, lest the Word of God be evil spoken of among the Gentiles. (Rom. 2:24)

Thus Paul says (2 Cor. 7:11) that by publicly rebuking the incestuous person the Corinthian church had shown "earnestness," "eagerness," "indignation," "alarm," "longing," "zeal," "punishment." Thus Augustine says, *Enchiridion,* ch. 65: "Very often the grief of one person is hid from another, although it is seen by Him to whom it is said, 'My sighing is not hidden from Thee.' Therefore temporal punishments have rightly been instituted by those who are in charge of the church, in order that satisfaction may also be made to the church in which the sins are forgiven." Jerome says, on Matt. 16: "It is different in the case of the repentance and satisfaction for crimes about which the church publicly interposes its judgment when she has been injured and offended, and imposes a heavier public satisfaction in order that all may know that those who with a ready mind undertake whatever the church has decreed are truly penitent." In the book *De Poenitentia* Tertullian says: "The counsel of satisfaction is that you confess." Likewise : "Satisfaction is prepared by confession; from it is born repentance, by which God is pacified."

6 Now because experience showed that often many coldly and carelessly attended to and performed the things which belong to true repentance for sins, and also that many who had been received on the basis of a feigned repentance afterward troubled the church, the ancients used great severity in enjoining canonical satisfactions. For certain ecclesiastical penalties were imposed to be discharged by a certain time, and for more grievous sins the punishments were harsher and of longer duration. Thus Eusebius says, Bk. 6, ch. 34,[13] that Dionysius of Corinth wrote to the Egyptians concerning the lapsed, laying down degrees of the transgressions. For they were received back little by little through certain steps. First they were placed among the hearers, who were permitted to be present during instruction in the Word. Then, after they had fulfilled a certain time, they were received into the ranks of the penitents, who were permitted to be present at the prayers of the church. In the third step they were admitted to Communion, but without the oblation. Finally they were, as it were, restored fully through the laying on of hands, as these things are described in the canons of Ancyra and of Nicaea.[14]

These penitential canons were afterward increased over-much in number, and made much harsher, both so far as the punishments and their duration are concerned, so that the bishops were compelled to remit through an indulgence many things in connection with the satisfactions that were imposed. Also there was invented the artifice of obviating the imposed satisfaction through commutation, so that, for instance, a fast could be bought off with alms or a prayer. Afterward indulgences from

---

[13] The reference should be to ch. 46.

[14] The Council of Ancyra (the modern Ankara) met in 314, that of Nicaea in 325.

satisfactions began to be bought off with money, until finally the canonical satisfactions disappeared entirely and became obsolete, and the monetary redemptions of indulgences were transferred to another kind of trafficking.

7 I have related these things because it is necessary, in this discussion, to show the difference between the satisfactions of which the ancients speak and those about which the papalists are now contending. Therefore the papalist satisfactions are not at once proved and established wherever, in the writings of the ancients, the term "satisfaction" occurs. There is, however, a difference both in the essence of the satisfaction and in its purpose, as the comparison will show when we come to the papalist satisfactions. It is useful to observe that the papalists, who use the statements of the ancients in fighting for their satisfactions, neither have nor care to have the ancient satisfactions, but only cast deceptions before people when they cite the testimonies of the ancients about satisfaction. One could wish that something of these rites of the ancient church could be brought back into use for the sake of discipline and example; however, without superstition and false opinions. But it is nevertheless certain that these rites are not necessary for conscience' sake for the remission of sins before God, which their mutation and obsolescence itself sufficiently shows and proves, as does also the fact that it was commanded that at the point of death peace through absolution and participation in the Eucharist be given, even when these satisfactions had not yet been completed, as an example in Eusebius, Bk. 6, ch. 34,[15] shows.

8 Third: From this public rite of satisfactions the term "satisfaction" was also transferred to the emendation of the penitents' lives and to the fruits of repentance. For in *De dogmatibus ecclesiasticis,* ch. 53, mention is made of secret satisfaction, through correction of one's life, through constant and perpetual grieving, so that the penitent does the opposite of the things for which he repents. It seems that the term "satisfaction" was transferred to the fruits of repentance because there remain in the flesh, after the remission of sins, certain slippery remnants of sin, as Chrysostom says, on Ps. 50, or a certain weakness, the tinder, as it were, for new lapses, especially when the sin has, as it were, taken root through long habit. These remnants must be purged, cured, and rooted out in repentance by contrary remedies lest they put forth new sprouts of sin out of this root. The statement of Augustine, *De poenitentia,* dist. 30, has it thus: "The satisfaction of penitence is to cut out the causes of sins and not

---

[15] The reference should be to ch. 44.

to permit an entrance to their promptings." And Chrysostom says, on Matt. 3: "How shall we be able to bring forth fruits worthy of repentance? If we do the things which are opposed to the sins. If you have taken what belonged to someone else, then begin to give your own; if you have harmed anyone, bring him words of blessing instead of censure, etc. For it is not enough for the salvation of a wounded man merely to pull the arrows out of his body, but medicine must also be applied to the wounds." Along the line of this thought Leo rightly says, *Sermo* 40: "Let a Christian soul diligently search its innermost heart; let it watch, lest anything discordant inhere in it, lest any cupidity be hid in it. Let purity drive out incontinence; let the light of truth drive away the darkness of falsehood; let pride subside, and humility be taken on; finally, let every plant which our heavenly Father has not planted be totally rooted out. For the seeds of virtues will be well nourished in us when every visible sprout is torn out of the field of our heart."

Augustine says, on Ps. 37: "Be not secure when you have confessed your sin, as being always ready to confess; and when you have committed sin, tell your iniquity in such a way that you may be concerned about your sin. What does it mean, to be concerned about sin? Always to strive, always to direct your thoughts, always to labor eagerly and diligently to heal sin." Because all these things are true, useful, and necessary, and built up on clear foundations in Scripture, we by no means deny or reject them; but we confess that they belong to the works or fruits of true repentance and to the instruction of Paul (Rom. 6:19): "Just as you once yielded your members to impurity and to greater iniquity, so now yield your members to righteousness for sanctification." It is not taught in Scripture that such works should be undertaken with the understanding that they merit remission of sins, but they follow reconciliation, according to the word of Christ: "See, you are well! Sin no more." Also Rom. 6:18: "Having been set free from sin, you have become slaves of righteousness." These are not works we do not owe, or works of supererogation, for there are commands in Scripture about mortification. Later on we shall explain how, under the name of satisfaction, men began to attach to these works the opinion that they atone for sins. At this time I wanted to recite in a special place the statements of the ancients, because the papalists cunningly mix them into their satisfactions, as though those who attack the papalist satisfactions rejected also the things which are taught and commanded in Scripture in order to hold those who have been converted back from sin as with a bridle and to control them, to make the penitent more careful and vigilant in the future, to serve as a remedy against the remnants of sin, and to remove the evil habits acquired by wicked living by means of contrary virtuous actions. This trick the reader will find also in the Tridentine decree. Therefore the things that are true and have the testimony of Scripture must be sorted out in order that it may be possible to show all the more clearly what has been placed into controversy in this dispute about satisfactions.

9 Fourth: Now that these things have been thus distinguished and explained, we shall be able to proceed to the examination of the decree about satisfactions. In order that the manner of the explanation may be the plainer, we shall first briefly explain the dispute about the temporary punishments which are sometimes laid on certain people in this life by God after they have been forgiven. Now the death of Christ is the satisfaction both for the guilt and for eternal punishment, and by faith we receive on account of Christ at one and the same time remission of the guilt and of eternal punishment. Hos. 13:14: "O death, I will be your death"; 1 Cor. 15:57: "He gave us victory over death on account of Christ"; John 3:16: "Whoever believes in Him shall not perish but have eternal life."

However, so far as temporal punishments in this life are concerned, people are in this life, after they have received forgiveness of sins, certainly subject to common disasters, perhaps even to special punishments on account of certain private sins, as was Adam (Gen. 3:17-19); David (2 Sam. 12:14; 24:10-15); likewise the people of Israel (Ex. 32:27-28, Num. 12);[16] and Miriam (Num. 12:10-16). The calamities that befall the baptized after their Baptism bear witness to the same thing. There is therefore no controversy as to whether believers after their reconciliation are in this life subject to common disasters, for both Scripture and experience bear witness to this. Examples from Scripture also show that in this life God sometimes, also after reconciliation or remission, imposes on certain persons extraordinary punishments on account of their sins, although this is not universal, because God does not always or in all cases impose extraordinary punishments in this life on those whose sins He remits, as the examples of the paralytic, Magdalene, the publican Zacchaeus, or Peter show, of whom Ambrose says: "I read of his tears; of satisfaction I read nothing."

Now the question is why, for what reasons, and to what end such punishments are in this life imposed on the reconciled by God after the remission of the guilt. Now I do not want to fight about terminology, whether these afflictions of the reconciled should be called punishments of sins or rather fatherly reproofs and corrections. For Scripture says also

---

[16] The reference seems to be to Num. 11:33.

of the reconciled (Rom. 8:10): "Your bodies are dead because of sin," and (2 Sam. 12:14): "Because by this deed," etc.

10 Nevertheless, it is wholly necessary that a distinction be made between the punishments or afflictions inflicted on the ungodly and those imposed on the reconciled. For in the ungodly they are signs of offense against God—that the particular person is under the wrath of God—and testimonies of eternal punishment to follow. This cause and reason they do not have in the reconciled, as though God were not yet sufficiently reconciled but still retained a certain amount of displeasure also after remission of sins has been given. Rather, they are imposed on them for their own correction and as an example to others. For in order that they may not, after receiving reconciliation, forget how great is the abomination of sin and how great the wrath of God against sin, and thus minimize their transgressions, ignore or defend them, and either lose grace through carnal security or cast it away through new wantonness and finally return to their vomit[17]—for these reasons they are, after their reconciliation, subjected either to common afflictions or to special punishments, in order that through this reminder there may afterward be kindled in them, and increase all the more, hatred and detestation of sin, fear of God, a faith which diligently cares that it may retain grace and remain in God's favor, and diligence to avoid sins, in order that evil inclinations may be repressed and mortified. In sum, by these exercises repentance is preserved and strengthened, which ought to be constant, also faith, obedience under the cross, hope, prayer for and hope of help, liberation, or mitigation, that we may always carry about the testimony that we would have to perish on account of our sin if we were not accepted on account of the Son; likewise that we may not claim praise for our own righteousness nor exalt ourselves over other sinners but may subject ourselves to God by a true and humble confession of our infirmity. Finally, when those who have been reconciled are either subjected to common misfortunes or are, on account of certain sins, burdened with extraordinary calamities, God wants us to see in these, as in a public display, examples which remind both us and others of His judgment against sins, that they may ponder the reminder of Peter: "If judgment begins with the house of God, what will be the end of those who do not believe the Gospel?"(1 Peter 4:17). Thus, when Moses prayed for his sister, when she had been smitten with leprosy on account of her sin and acknowledged the sin, he heard the Lord say: "If her father had but spit in her face, should she not be shamed seven days?" (Num. 12:14)

---

[17] Cf. Prov. 26:11, and 2 Peter 2:22.

11 Therefore such temporary punishments which God imposes on the reconciled in this life are by no means to be interpreted as if they either merited remission of sins or were compensations for eternal punishment; they have other most weighty causes.

12 Furthermore, also this is certain from Scripture with respect to these temporary punishments, that God, on account of His goodwill toward the reconciled, by which, on account of the Son, the Mediator, He dispenses all things in such a way that they yield good to them (Rom. 8:28), does not always, nor in the case of all the reconciled, impose extraordinary punishments for their sins in this life, and that He does not impose them equally on all, but that those that are imposed are often mitigated or removed by God, while sometimes they remain and are not removed in this life. And from this the reconciled take occasion for the most beautiful exercises of repentance, faith, prayer, humility, patience, obedience, hope, etc. They do indeed ask for mitigation and deliverance, but yet in such a way that, because they acknowledge their sin, they humbly and patiently submit to the scourging of God according to His goodwill. They ask that these may be fatherly chastenings; they acknowledge that God does not kindle His wrath totally in these punishments and that He turns them to good for us because we are reconciled. In sum, with respect to these temporary punishments they pray that God may either keep them from them or mitigate them or free them from them or, if He wants the punishments to remain, that He give patience and finally deliver them.

Thus Micah [7:9] says: "I will bear the indignation of the Lord because I have sinned against Him." And Lam. 3:27-29: "It is good for a man that he bear the yoke in his youth. Let him sit alone in silence when He has laid it on him; let him put his mouth in the dust—there may yet be hope." Likewise: "It is of the Lord's mercies that we are not consumed."[18] He does not kindle all His wrath. In wrath His mercy will be remembered. "Rebuke me not in Thy anger" [Ps. 38:1]. Jeremiah [10:24] says: "Correct me, O Lord, but in just measure; not in Thy anger, lest Thou bring me to nothing." David says: "Deliver me from bloodguiltiness, O God, Thou God of my salvation" [Ps. 51:14], etc.

13 Scripture also teaches that these temporary punishments are often either mitigated or else entirely removed for the reconciled on account of the Son, the Mediator, when they acknowledge their sin in true humility, call upon God in faith, mortify the old man, and earnestly purpose to lead a new life; that is, not in the prescribed works of human

---

[18] We follow the text of the King James version here (Lam. 3:22), because it agrees with the Vulgate used by Chemnitz.

traditions but in total repentance, which has God's command, these punishments are mitigated because of Christ. 2 Chron. 7:13-14: "When I shut up the heavens so that there is no rain, or command the locust to devour the land, or send pestilence," etc., "if My people . . . humble themselves and pray and seek My face, and turn from their wicked ways, then I will hear from heaven and will forgive their sin and heal their land." Jer. 18:7-8: "Suddenly I will say that I will destroy it. But if that nation turns from its evil, then I also will repent of the evil that I intended to do to it." Ps. 91:[19] "Call upon Me in the day of trouble; I will deliver you." Joel 2:12-13: "Return to Me with all your heart, with fasting, with weeping, and with mourning; and rend your hearts and not your garments," etc.

One must observe that temporary punishments are remitted by total repentance not because its works are compensations or merit forgiveness of sins but because by these chastisements God seeks nothing else than this, that true humility, recognition, hatred, and detestation of sins, exercise of faith, mortification of the old man, patience, hope, etc., may be preserved, kindled even more, grow, and be increased in the reconciled. Therefore, when God in the midst of these punishments sees such exercises of repentance in the reconciled, He has gained what He is accustomed to seek with these chastisements. And thus these punishments are either mitigated or wholly taken away on account of the Son, the Mediator.

This is what Paul teaches in 1 Cor. 11:31-32: "If we judged ourselves truly, we should not be judged. But when we are judged by the Lord, we are chastened so that we may not be condemned with the world." It pleased Paul in this statement to employ a play on the forensic words *krinein, diakrinein,* and *katakrinesthai.* For by the word *krinesthai* he here understands the temporary punishments, because he immediately interprets it with *paideuesthai* (to be trained, or chastened), meaning the things God sends on them on account of their sins, by which, like a disciplinarian with a rod, He reminds us of our sin and of His wrath against sins in order thus to bend, incite, and impel us to repentance and emendation. *Katakrinesthai* embraces the ultimate and eternal punishments of the damned in the afterlife. However, when he says: "If we judged ourselves," he does not use the word *krinein,* as the papalists interpret it, of self-chosen punishments, which are either voluntarily assumed as satisfactions or payments for sins or are enjoined by the confessor, but he uses the word *diakrinein,* which is often used in a forensic sense, as 1 Cor. 16,[20]

---

[19] The passage is found in Ps. 50:15.
[20] Reference appears to be to 1 Cor. 14:29.

and very often by the Greek translators, e.g., Ex. 18:16; Lev. 24:12; 1 Kings 3:9; Ps. 81:1-2,[21] namely, whenever a case is being tried. Therefore what Paul wants to say is this: If we judged ourselves, that is, if, after driving out carnal security by constant repentance, we would search into our nature and way of life, mortifying the root of sin, repressing wicked desires, etc., then there would be no need for God to remind us of them with the rod. However, when we are secure, make light of the sin that dwells in us, and little by little give in to it, then God recalls us to repentance through castigations, lest we be condemned with the world in our sins.

14 However, repentance itself together with its fruits cannot and should not prescribe to God the end or measure either of mitigation or of deliverance from these correcting punishments, but the obedience of a humble faith assigns and commends all this to the fatherly will of God toward us. Since we are certain that "in everything God works for good with those who love Him" (Rom. 8:28), therefore, when they ask God in true repentance for mitigation and deliverance from temporary punishments, they add: "Who knows whether He will not turn and repent, and leave a blessing behind Him?" (Joel 2:14). And in 2 Sam. 12:14-23, when Nathan had said, "The child shall die," David fasted and, lying all night on the ground, besought the Lord. Yet the child died, afflicted for seven days with the stroke of the Lord. David was not angry with the Lord because of this, but arose, laid aside the garb of mourning, and went into the house of the Lord, although the punishment had not been taken away, "for," said he, "I prayed: Who knows whether the Lord will be gracious to me, that the child may live?"

15 This most useful teaching, containing the most beautiful exercises of piety, has been most miserably and foully obscured and corrupted by the papalist satisfactions, as we shall presently show. However, I wanted in this place, before we would proceed to the examination of the Tridentine decree about satisfactions, to explain the true teaching of Scripture about the temporal chastisements which are laid by God on believers in this life after their reconciliation, either by common disasters or sometimes by extraordinary scourges, in order that the manner of the examination might be easier and less involved. For I see that in this dispute about satisfactions certain things are mixed in by the papalists which in themselves, when they are rightly understood, are true, such as the necessity of mortifying the remnants of sin, and the matter of temporal punishments, in order to clothe their fictions with some semblance of truth and to burden us with the suspicion as though we denied and re-

---

[21] In our English Bibles, Ps. 82:1-2.

jected also the things which are true and useful. Therefore I judged that first of all the true view concerning these questions ought to be set forth. For it will be possible, from a comparison, to consider and understand more rightly how the true and useful teaching has been obscured and corrupted by the fictions of the papalist satisfactions.

16 But once the true understanding has been explained, we must show how little by little strange and superstitious opinions began to be attached to these rites and works of satisfactions—opinions which thereafter were heaped up even more. For in order to commend these rites of satisfactions the more to people, they often spoke of these rites in a hortatory manner by way of hyperbole, according to the dictum of Chrysostom, beyond what the truth could bear, namely, that by these works of satisfactions sins and the punishments due sins are blotted out, paid, covered; that the Judge is placated and reconciled. Thus Origen calls these works the price by which sins are paid for, Homily 15, on Leviticus. Cyprian says, Bk. 1, Letter No. 3, that transgressions are paid for by satisfactions; Letter No. 8, that God is placated; in Bk. 3, Letter No. 14, he says that penitents by their works make satisfaction to God for mercy. Ambrose says to a fallen virgin that sins are atoned for by satisfaction. Augustine says, *Enchiridion,* ch. 70, that God must be propitiated by means of alms. Gregory says: "Whoever remembers that he has committed something unlawful, let him strive to abstain from lawful things to the extent that he may through this render satisfaction to his Creator." Cyprian goes so far in these excessive commendations of satisfactions that he declares that sin is not remitted unless the canonical satisfactions have first been performed and completed, and in a discourse about alms this ill-considered word escapes him: "The sins which were contracted before Baptism are cleansed by the blood and satisfaction of Christ; the filth which is contracted afterward is washed away by almsgiving." And he adds that the remedies for propitiating God for those who have lapsed after Baptism are these: to make satisfaction to God by just works, to purge the transgressions through the merits of mercy, etc. Surely, this speech goes far beyond the truth, for John says to those who sin after Baptism: "I am writing this to you so that you may not sin; but if any one does sin, we have an advocate with the Father, Jesus Christ the righteous; and He is the expiation for our sins, and not for ours only but also for the sins of the whole world." (1 John 2:1-2)

17 Later on, when these ancient rites of satisfactions, the fulfillment of which was demanded before absolution, had fallen, there arose another kind of satisfactions, that of works not owed, or of supererogation. Now these new and secret satisfactions were commanded to be fulfilled after absolution had been received. And the scholastics began to apply the grand pronouncements of the ancients, which they increased by new exaggerations, to these unowed works.

Thus Scotus defines satisfaction that makes restitution of equal value as being an outward work, laborious or punitive, voluntarily assumed for punishing the sin committed by the person in question and for placating the wrath of God, or that it is suffering or punishment willingly endured, appropriate to the sin or to the remission of the sin.

Thomas argues that satisfaction is an act of justice, because by means of satisfaction the sinner himself compensates for the offense he has committed against God, in order that the friendship of God may in this way be restored to him. To prove that man can make satisfaction to God for sin he builds his argument thus: A man is able to render satisfaction to another man; yet God is incomparably greater in mercy than any man; therefore it is much more possible for man to make satisfaction to God. Because, however, there is required in satisfaction something equivalent to the sin, Thomas says that it is an equivalence not of quantity but of proportion, and that thus it is possible for man to render satisfaction to God if man on his part does what he can, and God on His part accepts it as if it were the equivalent; likewise, that our satisfaction has a certain infinity on account of the charity by which it is shaped, and on account of the goodness of God by which it is accepted; and that in this way there comes about a correspondence of our satisfaction to the sin, which is infinite. The same says that satisfaction should be through works that afflict us, because it is a balancing of accounts with the divine wrath.

Bonaventura says that no work or suffering of the sinner is an equivalent satisfaction for sin unless it is linked by faith to the vicarious suffering of the Mediator.

Against this Thomas argues that even if the merit of Christ had not intervened, a man who has grace or charity could nevertheless render satisfaction to God for sins.

Furthermore, after it had been set down as a fact that man can and should make satisfaction to God for sins, they argued in various ways about what it is in sin for which man makes satisfaction.

Thomas says simply that the satisfaction of the penitent is rendering an equivalent for the offense against God. Bonaventura distinguishes two things in sin, aversion or enmity, thereafter a turning to improper desire. For the first [he says] no one can make satisfaction; for the second one can. Gabriel says that the guilt of sin and the offense against God are remitted either by contrition or by contrition together with absolution, but that the works of satisfaction are ordained for the remission of punishment.

Here indeed some argue that once the guilt of sin has been forgiven, eternal punishment is by the power of the keys changed into a temporal one, and that for it we are able to make satisfaction in this life. Others hold that both the sin and eternal punishment are remitted through contrition, but that there remains an obligation to some little temporal punishment and that God had promised to the rulers of the church that they may, by the power of the keys, remit a part of it and impose satisfactions for the remaining part. They define the works through which satisfaction may be made as unowed, or not commanded; these are the works of supererogation. For Richard says that God established a certain measure to which a person must necessarily be held, namely, the keeping of the commandments, in order that with the rest, that is, with the works of supererogation, he might be able to make satisfaction for sins committed.

18 This is the sum of the fiction of papalist teaching about satisfactions, which I wanted to set forth briefly here in their own words—first in order that we might consider from the contrast how foully the scholastics have adulterated and perverted the teaching we set forth a little earlier according to the meaning of Scripture; secondly, in order that it may be possible to understand the words of the Tridentine decree more correctly as to their intention and purpose.

The examination of this chapter, therefore, can now be accomplished quite briefly. For what they say about healing the remnants of sins, about taking away evil habits in order that penitents may be made more careful and diligent, lest they fall into similar or even graver sins— we have explained above how this doctrine can be rightly and profitably taught and used according to the prescription of the Word of God. This, however, is deservedly criticized, that the papalists transfer this teaching to unowed works, or works of supererogation, which have not been commanded by God; and they mean such fruits of repentance which they want to consider as belonging not only to the guarding of the new life and as a remedy against the remaining infirmities but as a payment for past sins; what kind of payment this is has been shown from the scholastics, namely, that they are a payment to the wrath of God. Likewise we have explained in the preceding what is the true understanding so far as temporal punishments are concerned to which believers are subjected in this life and even after this life.[22]

19 Let the reader observe how timidly and softly the Tridentine chapter enters in among these disputes of the scholastics—whether our satisfactions pay for the guilt of sin, or eternal punishment, or indeed only

---

[22] This is the reading in the Frankfurt edition of 1574, Ed. Preuss has the same reading. Nigrinus either had a different text or felt the need to amend the text, for he translates: *Und nicht nach diesem Leben.*

temporal punishment; or whether the temporal punishment is to be understood as that into which eternal punishment was commuted, or whether they distinguish temporal punishment from the remission of guilt and eternal punishment. Many papalist writers of our time say expressly that guilt and eternal punishment are taken away only by the satisfaction of Christ and that our satisfactions pertain only to temporal punishments. But the Council of Trent with unique skill wanted to speak with such restraint that it might not appear to criticize or condemn anything in the disputations of the scholastics.

20 The council explains its opinion thus: It says that those who transgressed before Baptism are received into grace by God without satisfactions of their own, on account of the merit and satisfaction of Christ; to those, however, who have fallen after Baptism, it says, divine clemency does not forgive sins without any satisfaction of their own which they themselves render for their sins.

Let the reader note this well, that the Council of Trent fights about satisfactions so that people should not believe that sins are forgiven solely on account of the merit and satisfaction of Christ to those who have fallen after Baptism, if they are converted. But they contend that also our satisfactions are necessary in order that the sins we have committed after Baptism be forgiven us, and that therefore we must render satisfactions for our sins. Until now many among the papalists, aware how blasphemous it is to apply our satisfactions to the remission of sins, complained loudly that this was being falsely attributed to them, as though they taught that our satisfactions pertained to the remission of sins itself, although they wanted them understood only of certain temporal punishments.

Now the Council of Trent indeed also speaks of temporal punishment. Nevertheless it says in plain words that sins after Baptism are not remitted to penitents by God without some satisfaction on their part. And they add at once that we must render satisfaction for our sins. Now the reader should understand this thus: The scholastics say that to complete remission of sins belongs remission of the guilt and of the total punishment, whether it be eternal or temporal. Therefore when the guilt and the eternal punishment have been remitted, the remission of sins is not yet complete, for there still remains the temporal punishment. And because [as they think] works of satisfaction are necessary for its remission, since they teach that eternal punishment has been commuted into temporal, they say that in this way our satisfactions belong to the remission of sins and are necessary to it. Therefore they understand that God does not let go all His wrath when He remits the guilt, but retains some part of it, which He pours out in the temporal punishment He imposes after He pardons the guilt, and that for the remission of this wrath satisfaction must be made by our works. But of the rationale behind the temporal punishments laid on people by God after their reconciliation we have spoken above. For God does not remit sins to believers in the way men are accustomed to do it, who often feign forgiveness and nevertheless meanwhile retain their anger, and pour it out when they have the chance.

21 This masterpiece is worthy of special note, yes, of perpetual memory, that the Tridentine chapter says thus about our satisfactions: "Just as Christ by His suffering made satisfaction for our sins, so also we, in making satisfaction, suffer for sins."

We, alas, hitherto believed Paul, that only Christ Jesus suffered for sins. "For One," says he, "died for all" [2 Cor. 5:14]. "By a single offering He has perfected for all time those who are sanctified" [Heb. 10:14]. There is one Mediator, who gave His life as redemption for all. Now, however, we learn from the Council of Trent that as Christ made satisfaction for sins, so also we, in making satisfaction, must suffer for sins. Therefore John does not faithfully instruct the baptized when he says: "If we have sinned, Christ is our expiation" (1 John 2:1-2), for according to the Tridentine chapter he ought to have said: "If you have sinned after Baptism, Christ is not alone the expiation for our sins, but as Christ made satisfaction for sins, so also you should suffer for your sins as you make satisfaction." And I marvel greatly, seeing that many things in these decrees are hidden and wrapped up with extraordinary skill, that so crass a piece of impudence slipped out from them in this chapter. But I do not doubt that this happened by a special judgment of God, that it might be a clear mark of Antichrist, namely, that it is not Christ alone who suffered for our sins, that not He alone made satisfaction for our sins, but that also we, in making satisfaction, suffer for our sins. Let them go now and protest that they do not in any part obscure or diminish the power of the merit and satisfaction of Christ by their satisfactions.

22 It is, however, worth the effort to hear by what arguments they would prove this; namely, because Paul says (Rom. 8:28-29) that through sufferings we become conformed to Christ. But Paul by no means asserts that that conformity consists in this, that as He suffered for our sins, so we also, in making satisfaction, should suffer for sins. Peter says: "Christ suffered for us, leaving an example for us" [1 Peter 2:21]; but he explains clearly wherein that example consists. And lest he seem to divide the suffering which makes satisfaction for sins between our sufferings and the sufferings of Christ, he adds: Christ bore our sins that we, healed by His stripes, and dead to sins, might live to righteousness. [Cf. 1 Peter 2:24]

The second argument of the Tridentine chapter is this: Paul says: "I can do all things in Him who strengthens me" [Phil. 4:13]; therefore I am able also, in making satisfaction for sins, to suffer. Is Paul therefore able to redeem the world, destroy death, and bring back life? If he can do all things, so that there is no longer any distinction between the Head and the members, then also this will no longer be true which is written in Col. 1:18, "that in everything He might be preeminent." Why then does he say (1 Cor. 1:13): "Was Paul crucified for you?" You see, I think, how the Council of Trent plays with the statements of Scripture. It is the same kind of argument when they say: "We live in Christ; therefore in Christ we earn merit and make satisfaction for sins." Why then do we not also in Christ create and govern heaven and earth? Surely, those things which belong to the office of Redeemer, Mediator, and Savior belong to Christ alone in such a way that they are communicated to no one. For there is one Mediator, and we are made perfect by one sacrifice for sins. "There is no other name . . . given among men by which we must be saved." [Acts 4:12]

23 The following is indeed a more than magisterial, and a truly pontifical demonstration: Formerly, in the case of public repentance, absolution was not given unless the satisfaction which had been imposed was first completed; now, however, the papalists command satisfactions which must be performed after absolution has been received. But hear where in Scripture this has been commanded! "The keys of the priests," they say, "were given not only for loosing but also for binding." Likewise: "The apostles are commanded not only to remit but also to retain sins."

I know all this. But I understand these words simply, the way they read. Christ commands the apostles to loose sins and to forgive those who repent and believe the Gospel; but with respect to those who are not willing to repent, or are unwilling to seek and to accept the reconciliation offered in the Gospel, He commands that their sins should be bound and retained, that is, He commands that to them should be declared: "By your hard and impenitent heart you are storing up wrath for yourself on the day of wrath" (Rom. 2:5); "He who does not believe in the Son, the wrath of God rests upon him" (John 3:36); "He who does not believe will be condemned" (Mark 16:16).[23] This declaration, Christ asserts, will be valid in heaven.

With this statement the Tridentine satisfaction makers play thus: Because the power of the keys should both loose and bind, remit and

---

[23] The Latin text gives the reference as "Matth. 16." Nigrinus has corrected this to Mark 16.

retain, therefore complete remission of sins on account of Christ is not to be announced. Rather it must be enjoined on those who are absolved that also they themselves should make satisfaction and suffer for their sins, in order that in this way in absolution sins may be at the same time both loosed and bound, remitted and retained. Indeed, to bind and to retain sins means to impose satisfactions on those who are to be absolved, by which also they themselves in some part make satisfaction for their sins; that is, sins are remitted to us in this way, if also we ourselves suffer for our sins in making satisfaction. Therefore Christ must have commanded to announce the forgiveness of sins in His name in such a way that He wanted the sins of those to whom they are remitted in His name also both bound and retained in such a way that, in making satisfaction for them, they should also themselves suffer as Christ suffered for sins. Therefore the minister will remit sins on account of Christ to believers in such a way that he retains a part of them, for which, in making satisfaction, they suffer.

And such, not so much perversions as mockeries of Scripture, are put forward at the Council of Trent itself, and indeed with the anathema!

24 When it is said that a new life is the best and most fitting repentance, the meaning is that after remission of sins on account of Christ has been accepted by faith, no other satisfaction or expiation for sins is required, since we have been made perfect in Christ, but that this is required which Scripture prescribes: "Depart from evil, and do good" [Ps. 34:14]; put off the old man, mortify his evil desires and actions, and put on the new man, that you may walk in newness of life; being dead to sin, live to righteousness; put off the works of darkness and put on the armor of light; etc. Now, indeed, to such newness of life there belong fasting, almsgiving, prayer, patience in afflictions, and other exercises of godliness prescribed by the Word of God. But the papalists do not demand these things insofar as they belong to newness of life and insofar as they have a command of God, but insofar as they are works not owed, or of supererogation, in order that they may for this reason be satisfactions for sins. However, they have in mind certain laws about fastings, a prescribed form of almsgiving, the recitation of a certain number of prayers, not as commanded by the Word of God but as undertaken of one's own accord or enjoined by the priest. For insofar as things are commanded by God, they belong to newness of life; however, insofar as they are undertaken of one's own accord or enjoined by the priest, they become satisfactions for sins. And so we will not only be able to do something more than the law of God requires, but the works which we do not owe, that is, which are not by divine command but of human traditions, will be more excellent, more worthy, of greater efficacy and merit than those which are divinely commanded. And this is why they set in opposition to each other, as though they were different things, satisfaction and newness of life, although we have shown earlier from Jerome and Augustine that they are one and the same thing.

Eighth Topic

CONCERNING EXTREME UNCTION

From the 14th Session
of the Council of Trent

Concerning Extreme Unction

Chapter I

It has seemed good to the holy synod to join to the preceding doctrine of penance what now follows about the sacrament of extreme unction, which was deemed by the fathers to bring to completion not only penance but also the whole Christian life, which ought to be a perpetual penance. First of all, therefore, it declares and teaches with respect to its institution that our most gracious Redeemer, who wanted His servants to be at all times provided with salutary remedies against all weapons of all enemies, even as in the other sacraments He prepared the greatest aids, by which Christians are able to preserve themselves whole, while they live, from every more serious evil of the spirit, so He fortified the end of life with the sacrament of extreme unction as with a very strong defense. For although our adversary seeks and seizes opportunities throughout our whole life to devour our souls in any way he can, nevertheless there is no time during which he strains every nerve of his cunning more furiously to destroy us utterly, and to drive us, if he can, also from trust in divine mercy, than when he sees that the end of our life is at hand.

Now this sacred anointing of the sick was instituted to be truly and properly a sacrament of the New Testament by Christ our Lord, alluded to indeed in the Gospel of Mark, but commended to the faithful and promulgated through James, an apostle and brother of our Lord. "Is any among you sick?" he says, "Let him call the elders of the church, and let them pray over him, anointing him with oil in the name of the Lord; and the prayer of faith will save the sick man, and the Lord will raise him up; and if he has committed sins, he will be forgiven" [James 5:14-15]. Through these words, handed down by apostolic tradition, the church has learned and teaches what the material, form, proper minister, and effect of this salutary sacrament is. Now the Church has understood that the material is oil, blessed by a bishop. For anointing represents most fittingly the grace of the Holy Spirit, by which the soul of the sick person is invisibly anointed; furthermore, that these words are the form: "Through this anointing," etc.

Moreover, the thing signified and the effect of this sacrament are explained in these words: "And the prayer of faith will save the sick man, and the Lord will raise him up; and if he has committed sins, he will be forgiven." For the thing signified is the grace of the Holy Spirit, whose anointing takes away sins, if there are any still to be expiated, also the remnants of sins, raises up and strengthens the soul of the sick person by exciting in him a great confidence in divine mercy, supported by which the sick person both bears more easily the inconveniences and troubles of sickness and more readily resists the temptations of the devil, who lies in wait for his heel, and sometimes regains the health of the body when it is expedient for the health of his soul.

Now, so far as the prescription with respect to who should receive and who should administer this sacrament is concerned, this also was taught in a not obscure manner in the aforesaid words. For there it is shown that the proper ministers of this sacrament are the presbyters of the Church, by which word there must be understood in this place not those who are called elders by reason of age, or the foremost among the people, but either the bishops or priests validly ordained by them through the laying on of hands of the priesthood. The words also declare that this anointing is to be applied to the sick, and in particular to those who are so dangerously laid low that they seem to be about to depart this life; for which reason it is also called the sacrament of the departing. But if the sick should recover after receiving this unction, they will be able to be helped again by the assistance of this sacrament if they should fall into another similar crisis in their life. Therefore those are under no circumstances to be listened to who, contrary to the open and clear meaning of the apostle James, teach either that this unction is a human figment or a rite received from the fathers which has neither a command from God nor a promise of grace; nor to those who say that it has already ceased, as though it should be referred only to the grace of healing in the primitive church; nor to those who say that the rite and use which the holy Roman Church observes in the administration of this sacrament is opposed to the understanding of the apostle James and should therefore be changed to something else; nor, finally, to those who assert that this external anointing may be spurned by the faithful without sin. For all these things militate most clearly against the plain words of this so great apostle. Nor, indeed, does the Roman Church, the mother and teacher of all other churches, observe anything other in administering this unction, so far as the things are concerned which make the substance of this sacrament, than what blessed James prescribed. Nor, indeed, can there be contempt for so great a sacrament without a heinous crime and affront against the Holy Spirit Himself.

CANON I

If anyone says that extreme unction is not truly and properly a sacrament, instituted by Christ our Lord and promulgated by the blessed apostle James, but only a rite received from the fathers, or a human fiction, let him be anathema.

CANON II

If anyone says that the sacred anointing of the sick does not confer grace nor remit sins nor relieve the sick, but that it has now ceased, as if it had formerly been only a grace of healing, let him be anathema.

CANON III

If anyone says that the rite and use of extreme unction which the holy Roman Church observes militates against the statement of the blessed apostle James and that it should therefore be changed, and that it may without sin be spurned by Christians, let him be anathema.

CANON IV

If anyone says that the elders of the Church whom blessed James urges to be brought for anointing the sick are not priests, ordained by a bishop, but the men in each community who are older in years, and that for this reason the priest is not the sole minister of extreme unction, let him be anathema.

Examination

1 There is no doubt that it is true what the Tridentine decree asserts, that our adversary, the devil, who all our life seeks and tries to seize an opportunity to devour our souls, strains every nerve of his cunning when he sees that the end of our life is at hand, to destroy us utterly and, if he can, to drive us from our trust in divine mercy. In the weakness of our flesh there come in addition terrors and trepidations in view of threatening death, when we look at our sins. From this there arises the last and hardest struggle of faith against sins, against the temptations of the flesh and of Satan, which then rush in in throngs, and more grievously than usual, and finally against death itself. If then our faith is overcome, and our adversary prevails, our salvation will have been lost. For after this life there is no room for either repentance or reconciliation.

Therefore also this is certain, that our most gracious Redeemer, who willed that salutary remedies against all dangers to their salvation should at all times be in view for His servants, has not only prepared aid by which Christians may be preserved in grace while they live and are whole, but chiefly that at the end of their life, when the struggle is hardest and most perilous, they should be fortified and strengthened with firm defense and effective support for their tottering confidence, in order that they "may be able to withstand in the evil day, and having done all, to stand" (Eph. 6:13) and give thanks to God, who gives us the victory over death and its sting. (1 Cor. 15:56-57)

2 About these two points there is no controversy, for we loudly confess both. But the question is: What are the remedies and aids, or rather, the antidotes? For in order for these to be effective against death and its sting, it is necessary that they be not thought out or imagined by men but instituted and prepared by the Son of God Himself, who is the true Physician; and they must have added to them the promise of power and efficacy. Therefore these remedies and antidotes, which can give life in the midst of death, must be sought in His medical laboratory for souls, as Basil beautifully and truthfully calls Holy Scripture.

However, the division which the Tridentine decree seems to set down as its basis is false, namely, that Christ prepared one set of remedies and helps for salvation for the living and another for the dying, as though the means through which God confers grace on us while we live and are whole in this world, and preserves us in it, were no longer effective or sufficient when we have come to the end of this life and must now through death cross over into another life, but that we must then look around for other remedies and aids. Certainly Christ, who is the Resurrection and the Life, yes, the Death of death and the Antidote against death (as Irenaeus says concerning the word of the Gospel, through which this life is offered and communicated to us, and concerning faith, by which Christ our Life is grasped and accepted in the Word), attests that the power and efficacy of the Gospel is able to save not only while we live here, but He expressly includes also the hour of death, the resurrection of the dead, and the life of the world to come.

3 John 5:24-25: "Truly, truly, I say to you, he who hears My Word and believes Him who sent Me has eternal life; he does not come into judgment, but has passed from death to life." Likewise: "The dead will hear the voice of the Son of God, and those who hear will live." John 6:50: "This is the bread which comes down from heaven, that a man may eat of it and not die." John 8:51: "Truly, truly, I say to you, if any one keeps My Word, he will never see death." John 11:25-26: "He who believes in Me, though he die, yet shall he live; and whoever lives and believes in Me shall never die." You hear that everywhere no other Word and no other faith is set forth for the dying than for the living, but He declares that the same Word we apprehend by faith while we live has and exerts power for life in death itself; in fact, we lay hold of that Word while we live, in order that in the hour of death we may by its power pass over to life. For if we were to have hope in Christ in this life only, we would be of all men most miserable (1 Cor. 15:19). Therefore Paul has the custom in his epistles of praying that the believers may be preserved and confirmed in what they accepted in this life until the day of Christ (1 Cor. 1:4-8). And Phil. 1:6: "I am sure that He who began a good work in you will bring it to completion at the day of Jesus Christ." Eph. 4:30: You were sealed by the Holy Spirit for the day of redemption. Heb. 3:14: "We share in Christ, if only we hold our first confidence firm to the end." Rev. 2:10, 25: "Be faithful unto death." Likewise: "Only hold fast what you have, until I come." 1 Cor. 3:22: If you are Christ's, then all things are yours, whether life or death. Rom. 8:33-34, 38: God justifies; Christ who died and was raised again intercedes for us; therefore neither death nor life will separate us, etc.

4 Therefore no other remedies or aids for salvation are to be sought in death than those offered in the Word in order to be accepted by faith while we are living. For the one and only true and sufficient antidote against death is Christ, our Life. He offers and imparts Himself to us, together with all His benefits, in the word of the Gospel; and through faith He is not only accepted but dwells in our hearts (Eph. 3:17). The word of the Gospel is, however, found not only in the simple or bare promise but also in those sacraments to which, by the divine Word and institution, the promise of grace is attached. And for the strengthening of faith amid the terrors of death there is the greatest need for this application and sealing of the promise of grace which is offered to every individual believer when he uses the sacraments. Thus Baptism, once received, furnishes consolation in death itself. For this reason some in ancient times were baptized over the dead (1 Cor. 15:29). And 1 Peter 1:3-5: "He has regenerated us to a living hope . . . to an inheritance which is imperishable . . . kept in heaven for us who by God's power are guarded through faith for salvation." In Eph. 6:11 ff. Paul describes the whole armor of God, by which we are able to stand against all the ambushes of Satan in every evil day—truth, righteousness, the Gospel, faith, salvation, the Word of God, prayer and supplication. And in 1 Thess. 5:8, 10 he says that the usefulness of this armor is "that, whether we wake or sleep, we may live with Him." In Phil. 1:19-21 he adds the common prayers of the church: "Through your prayers and the help of the Spirit of Jesus Christ this will turn out for my deliverance . . . that . . . as always Christ will be honored in my body, whether by life or by death. For to me to live is Christ, and to die is gain."

5 To these things comes also the custom of the ancient church, which was wont to comfort the sick, reminded of sin and the wrath of God, with the word of the Gospel and to pray for their deliverance. It also set before them and applied to them absolution through the word of the Gospel, and the Communion of the body and blood of Christ. For in these ways, according to the teaching of Scripture, the promise of grace, of remission of sins, of salvation and eternal life is, through the effectual working of the Son of God, applied and sealed to every individual believer for the sustaining and strengthening of his faith against all temptations. Thus Dionysius the Corinthian, in Eusebius, Bk. 6, Ch. 34, says that he had ordered that these remedies and aids should be applied also to lapsed persons who were dying, if they requested it, in order that they might be able by these aids to depart this life in good hope. He mentions remission of sins or absolution, and the Communion of the body and blood of Christ.

A canon of Nicaea says: "With respect to those who are departing from their bodies, the rule of the ancient law shall be observed that, if someone is by chance departing from his body, he shall not be defrauded of the viaticum,[1] which he needs for his journey. The Fourth Council of Carthage explains this as follows: "If it is believed that the person will die forthwith, let him be reconciled through the laying on of hands, and let the Eucharist be poured into his mouth." A canon of Orange says that

---

[1] The term "viaticum," which in Latin means literally "provision for the journey," has passed into the English language. It is used particularly in the Roman Catholic Church for the Eucharist which is given on the deathbed as provision for the journey into eternity.

Communion has fitly been called "viaticum" in the case of those departing this world. See a number of statements of this kind, 26, quest. 6. In his *Epistle to the Ephesians* Ignatius with the most comforting words calls the Lord's Supper "a medicine of immortality, an antidote, that we may not die but live in God through Jesus Christ, a cleansing medicament that turns aside and wards off evils."

6 These remedies and aids for the hour of death have a command and promise of God, and there is no doubt that the Son of God is present in them with His efficacy, so that they are a power and force of God for salvation to everyone who believes. And because the Son of God, the Mediator, offers and communicates Himself wholly, together with all His benefits, to faith through these means, and seals their application to every individual believer, therefore faith has in their use enough aid and support even in the hour of death; for it has the whole armor of God, by which it is able in the evil day, in the death struggle against spiritual wickedness and against the ambushes of the devil, to resist "and, having done all, to stand" (Eph. 6:11-13). And thus our most gracious Redeemer wanted His church at all times, most of all, however, when the most grievous peril rushes in, about the time of the end of life, to be provided with salutary remedies against all weapons of all enemies; and He fortified the end of life with sufficiently strong protection.

7 But they say: What if Christ, who judges the extreme danger to our souls in the agony of death better than we, had wanted to institute a special sacrament over and above the remedies mentioned, by which He would, as by the strongest defense, firmly and effectively protect the end of our life against the attacks of Satan, which are then more violent than usual, and against the terror of death? I answer: If the Son of God, our Physician, had judged this to be useful and necessary, He would without doubt have instituted a special sacrament for those who are about to die. For those whom He loves, He loves to the end (John 13:1). Now if it were established from the Word of God that Christ had instituted such a sacrament, with a certain form prescribed, and had given an express command, with a special promise added, generally for all the faithful until the end of the world, to be administered at the time of death, then the obedience of faith would altogether require us to receive and use it with faithful reverence and devout gratitude.

8 And, indeed, the papalists firmly declare that extreme unction is such a sacrament. But this, precisely, is the question which is in controversy in this dispute: whether Christ instituted this anointing in order that it should be such a sacrament.

9 Now in order that it may be possible to determine and decide this question more simply, clearly, and surely from the Word of God, we must briefly repeat how the papalists describe the sacrament of their Extreme Unction. For in this way the inquiry, whether such a sacrament was instituted by Christ and handed down to the church by the apostles, will be simpler.

First: They say that the material of this anointing must be oil, not common or ordinary, but oil which has first been consecrated, not by just any priest but only by a bishop, and that on a certain day of the year, namely, on Thursday of Holy Week, and with certain exorcisms, namely, that he exorcise the vessel with the oil for the sick as follows: "I exorcise you, most unclean spirit, and every assault of Satan, and every specter, in the name of the Father and the Son and the Holy Spirit, that you depart from this oil, that it may be able to become a spiritual anointing, that it may invigorate the temple of the living God, in order that the Holy Spirit may be able to dwell in it, through the name of God the Father almighty and of His Son," etc. Thereafter he blesses the oil itself with these words: "Send, O Lord, we pray, the Holy Spirit, the Paraclete, from heaven into this fatness of the olive tree, which Thou has deigned to bring forth from the green wood for the refreshing of mind and body, that it may by Thy holy blessing be to everyone who is anointed with this ointment of the heavenly medicine a protection of mind and body, to drive out all pain, all infirmities, and every sickness of mind and body," etc. Unless the oil has been exorcised and consecrated by the bishop in this way, say they, it cannot be the material of this sacrament.

Second: They teach that with this oil those members are to be daubed and anointed which are the organs of the five senses, such as the eyes, ears, nostrils, lips, hands, feet, and loins.

Third: Not all are agreed with respect to the form of this sacrament. For some teach that these words are the form: "May the Lord through this sacred anointing and through His own tender mercy forgive you whatever fault you have committed with your eyes, in the name of the Father," etc. And so with respect to the other senses. Others use this formula: "In the name of the Father, Son, and Holy Spirit I anoint you with the hallowed oil, that through this anointing you may receive full remission of sins."

Fourth: The Tridentine decree says that the effect of this anointing is the grace of the Spirit, whose unction cleanses away the faults, if there are any which are still to be expiated, and the remnants of sin, alleviates and strengthens the mind of the sick person, etc. Canon 2 says that this anointing confers grace and remits sins.

Innocent says of the sacred unction that this outward anointing, if it is worthily received, either brings or increases the grace of the Holy Spirit; this is the invisible unction. Aureolus[2] posits seven fruits of this unction: (1) the cancelling of venial sins; (2) the lessening of the punishment owed to mortal sin; (3) the increase of grace, which is increased by the power of this anointing, not only by the devotion of the ministrant and the recipient but also in virtue of the work which is performed; when grace is increased, then also glory is increased; (4) firmness against the wiles of the devil; (5) a lessening of the power of the devil, which is not so strong when this sacrament has been received; (6) healing of the body, if this is expedient; (7) a declaration of the dying person that he has remained in the faith of the church. Thomas adds an eighth effect—cancelling of mortal sin so far as its guilt is concerned.

Fifth: They teach that this unction is to be applied to those who are so dangerously sick that they seem to be about to depart this life, wherefore it is called the sacrament of the departing. Therefore the Tridentine decree agrees with others who say: "This unction is not to be given to all the sick but only to those who are in danger and at the point of death, about whom there is reasonable doubt that they will live." Yes, the Council of Florence decrees that this extreme unction should be given only to a sick person of whom one fears that he will die.

10 These are the chief traditions of the papalists about extreme unction, enumerated in the Tridentine decree, about which there is controversy. Now we must see whether such an unction was instituted by the Son of God in order that it should be such a sacrament. The scholastics argue that, because none of the evangelists says that Christ instituted this extreme unction, it is more probable that it was instituted by the apostles and that, because the apostles were not able to hallow the material, therefore it ought not to be a simple element, but oil which has been exorcised and consecrated. Eck indeed judges that it is not absurd to believe that the apostle James instituted this sacrament by the authority of Christ and at the command of the Holy Spirit. But the scholastics themselves confess that the authority to institute sacraments belongs to Him who is able to bestow efficacy on them. To this comes the fact that the Epistle of James does not have so great authority that it can, without other testimonies of the canonical Scriptures, institute a new sacrament for the church. For it is known that Jerome wrote that the ancients judged that this epistle was not written by the apostle James but was published under his name by some other person. Eusebius also says concerning it: "One must know that it is deemed spurious." Therefore others said that

---

[2] Peter Aureoli, 1280–1322, French Franciscan philosopher and theologian.

extreme unction was only promulgated to the church by James but that it was instituted by Christ Himself. Some of those who think thus say that Scripture does not tell where, when, and how Christ instituted extreme unction but that it is one of the secret traditions. Neither of these opinions is approved by the Synod of Trent. For the ancients assert that the unction in Mark and in James are one and the same thing. Therefore the Tridentine chapter says that the anointing of the sick, as truly and properly a sacrament of the New Testament, was alluded to by Christ our Lord in Mark.

We have, therefore, the passage in Scripture about which this dispute revolves. Now it will not be difficult to settle the question whether extreme unction as described and practiced by the papalists was instituted by Christ as a sacrament of the New Testament. For it is necessary for the institution of a sacrament that the material, form, action, and efficacy of the sacrament be prescribed by the Word of God by way of command and promise, and that in such a way that it is ot something for a certain person or time but that the command to do a certain thing and the promise of efficacy pertain to the whole church of the New Testament for all time, even to the end of the world, when Christ comes to judgment. For that is how it is with Baptism and the Lord's Supper. Thus circumcision indeed has a divine command and promise, but these do not apply to us. The apostles had a command about laying hands on the sick, and a promise that they would be restored to health. Christ put clay on the eyes of the blind. Paul lay down on a dead person. Handkerchiefs of his were laid on the sick, etc., but these things were for particular persons and times and are not to be applied to us as an example to imitate without a special Word pertaining to us.

11 Now the passage on which the sacrament of extreme unction needs to be grounded is Mark 6:12-13, and reads as follows: "So they went out and preached that men should repent. And they cast out many demons, and anointed with oil many that were sick and healed them." We shall hold the description of papalist unction against this passage point for point, for in this way what we are seeking will stand out plainly. For it is a very great thing to put forth and regard something as a sacrament of the New Testament, especially in the supreme crisis of imminent death—that then one departs from the Word and the other sacraments and places one's ultimate aid at the departure from life in extreme unction.

First: We shall see whether the apostles conferred this unction on those who were about to die, for this end and use that through this, as the strongest protection, the end of life might be fortified against sins, the devil, and death. But it is certainly clear from the descriptions of the evangelists what kind of unction Mark writes about. Matthew says: "He gave them authority . . . to heal every disease and every infirmity" [Matt. 10:1]. Luke says: "He gave them power and authority . . . to cure diseases" [Luke 9:1]. Mark himself also says (3:15): "He gave them authority to cure diseases and to cast out demons."[3] And in Mark 6:13 nothing else is described except what the apostles already did the first time they were sent out, namely, how they healed the sick, applying the outward sign of anointing with oil. Therefore Mark does not at all say in this passage that the apostles anointed those who were in their death struggle, in the belief that in this unction they would have the highest and firmest aid against sins, the devil, and death. Much less does he prescribe that this anointing with oil should be performed and preserved in the whole church of the New Testament at all times until the end of the world, but he is describing the gift of healing; it is plain that this, even as other gifts of performing miracles, was temporary and that it ceased after the Gospel had been proclaimed throughout the world.

Second: Mark does not say of this gift of healing that Christ prescribed the material of oil in His command to the apostles as something necessary to be applied in all healings of the sick. He says only that Christ gave them authority and power to heal the sick, but that they themselves added the outward symbol of anointing with oil. However, the apostolic history testifies that they did not always employ the same external signs in healing, for we read that for healing the sick they sometimes used only a word, sometimes the laying on of hands, sometimes a touch, a shadow, handkerchiefs and girdles. I do not think that Mark means that the apostles during their first mission healed no one unless they had first anointed him with oil, for he says: "They anointed with oil many that were sick".

And even if, in that first mission, this external symbol of the gift of healing had been general, Christ certainly does not, after His resurrection, say in Mark 16:18: "They will anoint the sick with oil, and they will be healed," but: "They will lay their hands on the sick, and they will recover." Therefore the anointing with oil was not a general and necessary sign of healing at the time of the apostles. But in Ch. 6, at the first mission of the apostles, when they were sent only to Judaea, in which mission there were many things which were temporary and concerned only certain persons, Mark puts down an account of what was done by only the 12 apostles, namely, with what outward sign they administered

---

[3] Chemnitz is following the Vulgate, which has *curandi infirmitates*. These words are missing in the most ancient manuscripts.

the gift of healing. But in Ch. 16, when they are commanded to go into all the world and to preach the Gospel to every creature, Christ is speaking not only of the apostles but also of those who would believe, when He says: "They will lay their hands on the sick," etc. Why do we not therefore rather make a general sacrament for the sick of the laying on of hands, which has a word of Christ that pertains not only to the apostles but also to the believers? The answer is easy: Because He speaks of signs, that is, of gifts of miracles which were temporary. And yet not even then, when the gift of miracles was thriving greatly, did the apostles generally, always, and of necessity apply the imposition of hands in the gift of healing. Therefore this answer will have much more force in the matter of the anointing with oil in the first mission of the apostles, of which we read that it was not so much expressly commanded by Christ as done by the apostles.

Third: The evangelist says nothing either about a command of Christ or about an act of the apostles to the effect that the oil in this unction must first be exorcised and consecrated with a set form of words.

Fourth: We do not read that the apostles anointed those of whom they anticipated with good reason that they would soon die, but with their anointing they healed the sick, lest they should then and there die through that illness.

Fifth: Of the form of words which the papalists prescribe not one letter or syllable is found in the history of the evangelists.

Sixth: We read nothing either of a command of Christ or of an action on the part of the apostles to the effect that they anointed the organs of the five senses.

Seventh: Mark does not say that the purpose and effect of this unction was that through it sins would be blotted out, the wiles of the devil suppressed in those about to die, etc., but that they should with this outward sign administer the gift of bodily healing. Therefore it is as plain as can be from this one comparison that Christ in Mark 6:13 neither instituted nor alluded to (as the Tridentine chapter expresses it) such an unction in order that it should be such a sacrament for those who have come to the end of their lives, as the description and practice of the papalists holds. And because the Tridentine decree appeals to Mark 6, we have already shown that the papalist unction has in that passage neither institution nor command nor promise nor example so that it could be a sacrament of the New Testament, as their description has it.

12 But because the description in Mark is somewhat obscure (for it only tells us what the apostles did, but does not quote a command of Christ on the basis of which they did it), they say that its fuller explanation must be taken from James, about whom there is no doubt that as an apostle, and indeed a brother of the Lord, he knew perfectly what Christ had instituted with respect to unction—what, how, and for what purpose the apostles did it. Let us hear, therefore, whether James asserts that Christ instituted such an unction, that it should be such a universal sacrament for those who are about to die, as the papalist description has it.

The papalists have indeed tried to demonstrate this in this way, that the word *allevare,*[4] which the ancient translator had used, was changed by monks to *alleviare,*[5] which they afterward explained as referring to the terrors excited by Satan and death in the hour of death. Likewise, because James says *ut salvemini,*[6] as the translator rendered it, therefore they contend that James understood his unction not of bodily healing but of salvation in the hour of death. But the ancient interpreters say, and indeed also the Tridentine decree admits this, that James is not speaking about a different anointing but about the very same one described in Mark 6:13. That this refers to the gift of healing the evangelists plainly show. Grammar also shows that the interpretation of the papalists is false. For James uses two words which without question refer to bodily healing. The first is *egeirein,* which Christ uses when sick persons, who are bedfast, are restored so that they can arise and walk (Matt. 9:5-6; Mark 1:31; 9:27; John 5:8). This the ancient translator rendered *allevare,* which they later changed to *alleviare.* The other word is *iasthai* [James 5:16], which is used very frequently of healings; indeed, the gift of healing which was found in the primitive church is described by this very word in 1 Cor. 12:9, 28, 30. From this we can also understand that the third word, *soozesthai,* must be understood, as it is frequently used, of bodily healings (Matt. 9:22; Mark 5:34; 6:56; Luke 8:48). Therefore James, even as also Mark, is speaking of the gift of healing which is also described in 1 Cor. 12:9, 28, 30, and indeed with the same word James uses.

Neither was it lawful for James as an apostle to transfer this unction to another action, another purpose, use, and effect than the one that had been alluded to by Christ (Mark 6:13) and employed by the apostles. But you say: James is not here prescribing anything to the apostles, who had the gift of healing, but to other presbyters of the church; and indeed, he makes express mention there of the remission of sins. I answer: When Christ (Mark 16:17-18) speaks of the signs which will follow the proclamation of the Gospel, He ascribes these gifts not only to the apostles but also to other believers. Therefore at that time, when the gift of healing in

---

[4] *Allevare:* "to raise up," e.g., from a sickbed.
[5] *Alleviare:* "to lighten, relieve."
[6] *Ut salvemini:* "in order that you may be saved."

the church was no longer in possession of the apostles only, but also of other presbyters, James prescribed to them how they ought to use this gift piously, salutarily, and for edification, both those who administered it and those who received it, as long as this gift would remain in the church. Therefore no universal and perpetual precept must be constructed from this about applying unction also after the gift of healing, the sign of which was unction, had ceased, as can be understood from 1 Cor. 14. Certain persons were misusing the gift of tongues and of prophecy. For this reason Paul prescribes as a manner and form how these gifts, as long as they were present in the primitive church, should be used in a salutary manner and for edification. But these have now ceased. Thus, since many were either misusing or at least not rightly using the gift of healing, which was at that time present in the primitive church, James prescribes a manner and form, how this gift is to be used piously, salutarily, and for edification, namely, lest it be used like some surgical or medical skill, but that it might lift up the mind to a consideration of our sin and misery, that is, to repentance and recognition of the spiritual benefits of the Son of God. For this was the right use of all miracles. Therefore James teaches that when a sick person was to be healed through unction, he should be reminded of the cause of illness, in order that he might acknowledge his sins. He also wants this to be taught about faith, that through remission of sins the cause of illness, that is, sin, is taken away. To this he also wants joint prayers added that also the sick person himself should at the same time pray from faith; for the sins of an unbeliever or a reviler are not forgiven when others pray for him. He shows that in this way the gift of healing, in which the external sign of unction was added, could be used in a salutary manner. However, he clearly ascribes the remission of sins not to the outward sign of unction but to the prayer of faith. This also Lyra understood. And a little later he shows by the example of Elijah that miracles, such as the gift of healing at that time, are often done through the prayers of the righteous.

This is the sum of the statement of James. And if the gift of healing were still found in the church today, this teaching and rule of James would be useful and altogether necessary to observe. But because it is evident and well known that this gift has now ceased in the church, the question is whether the outward sign, now that the thing signified, namely, the restoration of health through a miracle, is no longer present in the church, should be retained and used in the church, and indeed in such a way that it is transferred to an action of another kind, to another purpose, use, and effect, namely, that through this unction those about to die should obtain remission of sins, be protected from the wiles of the devil and from terrors of death, in order that they may die in the Lord. Surely, James does not say either that this unction was instituted for those about to die, or that it is to be used at the point of death, in order that the end of life may be fortified by some special protection and whatever other causes and effects the papalists ascribe to their unction. But he says that it is applied for restoring wholeness through the gift of healing.

By what commandment, therefore, by what promise is that unction, to which the gift of healing is now no longer joined, transferred to another purpose, to another use and effect? For the command and promise which that unction had pertains according to both Mark and James to the gift of healing. It is just as if I now wanted to apply the anointing of priests and kings, which in the Old Testament had command and promise, to those who are about to die. Therefore, because papalist extreme unction is transferred to another use after the gift of healing has ceased, it has neither a divine command nor promise, yes, not even an example in either Mark or James.

13 Neither does the material nor the form nor the action of the papalist unction have the descriptions of either Mark or James as authors. For James says nothing about oil that has been charmed by exorcisms and consecrated with a set formula; he says nothing about anointing the external organs of the senses. Moreover, James does not prescribe the form of words which papalist unction uses. James applies unction in order that the sick person may, through the gift of healing, be restored to good health. However, the papalists forbid anointing a person of whom there is still some hope of life; but when it is presumed that he is already departing this life, and about to die, then he is anointed, not in order that he may recover (except by accident) but that he may die well. Therefore the extreme unction of the papalists is not the one of which Mark speaks, nor is it the one which James describes, whether you look at the material or the form or the action or the use, purpose, and effect.

Neither has the prayer of faith of which James speaks any part in the unction of the papalists. For they pray that through this unction full remission of sins may be given, although there is no divine promise of this. And because there is no faith without a promise, therefore there can be here no prayer of faith. They also employ the invocation of the dead; Because this has no command and promise from God, it cannot be a prayer of faith. Therefore it is rightly said that this extreme unction is a human invention which has neither a command from God nor a promise of grace. For what belongs to the gift of healing must not, without a special Word, be transferred to other uses. False is also what Andrada says, namely, that without the anointing with oil faith and prayer avail nothing in the case of the sick. For that was not even true when the gift of healing was still found in the church. For we read that the apostles healed many through prayer, without unction with oil. And James does not want either healing or the forgiveness of sins to be ascribed to unction with oil, even when it was employed as an outward sign of the gift of healing, but he ascribes these gifts to faith and prayer.

Now we shall at once be ready with the answer to the following argument, which has some show of validity: The rite of anointing the sick has a word of God and the promise of grace (Mark 6:13; James 5:14-15). Therefore on the basis of the section on definitions it is truly and properly a sacrament of the New Testament. I answer: Insofar as unction is the external sign of the gift of healing, to that extent it has God's Word and promise. We do not, however, have a command of the Word of God that after the cessation of the gift of healing the external sign of unction should either be retained and used without purpose in the church or be transferred to another purpose and use. Neither do we have a promise that it will effect grace if this unction is changed into another action and to another use, as we have shown is done with the papalists. Therefore the extreme unction of the papalists is not truly and properly a sacrament of the New Testament. For when the thing itself, the gift of healing, ceases, then also its external sign, namely anointing with oil, deservedly ceases. Nevertheless, whatever belongs to the Word remains meanwhile in the illnesses of Christians—acknowledgment of sins, faith, prayer, and remission of sins. Now that the gift of healing has ceased, these things are not bound by any command of God to unction; yes, not even the gift of healing itself was tied, even at that time, to unction, as all examples of healing in the Acts of Apostles testify, in none of which we read that anointing with oil was employed.

But if the objection is raised that the ministry of the apostles was not something medicinal or corporal but spiritual, and that therefore this anointing did not pertain only to the gift of healing, I answer: External or bodily miracles were employed in order that the teaching of the spiritual benefits of Christ might be confirmed by them and that they might be a discipline for acknowledging, considering, seeking, and embracing the spiritual and eternal blessings offered in the Gospel. All the while outward miracles were shown to many who did not accept the spiritual benefits of Christ, just as on the other hand many in whose bodies no sign was performed accepted the grace of God by faith in the word of the Gospel. Neither were outward miracles the instrument through which the spiritual blessings were offered and bestowed, but they only prepared the way for the Gospel, which is the ministry of the Spirit, in which faith seeks and receives grace, forgiveness, etc.

14 Therefore, [first], the apostles employed the external sign of anointing with oil in the gift of healing, not because either the oil itself or the action of anointing held or brought any power and efficacy for healing (which was a miraculous thing), and much less for the remission of sins, which James ascribes to the prayer of faith—but because it was at that time customary, and known from the Old Testament, that oil symbolized supernal and celestial gifts, therefore they employed anointing with oil in the gift of healing in order that the external sign might remind people that these healings were not conferred either in a human or in some magical manner but that they were heavenly gifts by the power and working of God.

Second, because in Scripture oil signifies the spiritual benefits of God, therefore they employed anointing with oil in the gift of healing, in order to remind those who were healed by this outward sign that they ought not to stop with these physical benefits but should lift up the mind to recognize, seek, and accept the spiritual benefits of Christ the Mediator, to which they were being invited and led through these miracles in their bodies.

Third, the oil in those regions was of most excellent quality, and in daily use, not only for food and for merriment (2 Kings 4:2-7; Ps. 104:15) but also for healing (Is. 1:6; Ezek. 16:9; Luke 10:34). Therefore, as Isaiah took figs to heal the disease of Hezekiah [2 Kings 20:7; Is. 38:21], so the apostles, lest they should seem to be practicing magic, applied oil for healings, which however far exceeded the natural power and efficacy of the oil, for they were miracles. And thus, after that gift of healing ceased, the passage in James could in a godly and useful manner be accommodated to the use of medicines in the illnesses of Christians, namely, that they should first be instructed about the cause of illness, that is, that they should learn to acknowledge their sin, be reconciled to God by faith, and commit the state of their health to God in prayer. Thereafter they would be able to use remedies in a godly manner, having called on the name of God and added also the common prayers. These things can be considered with profit in connection with the causes for the application of oil in the miraculous healings of the apostles.

15 Therefore the extreme unction of the papalists was neither instituted nor promulgated because Mark and James say that the apostles anointed the sick with oil. For neither the material nor the form nor the action of the papalist unction can be proved from the apostolic unction.

But the use, purpose, and effect which the papalists ascribe to their unction is clearly different and another from the apostolic unction, as the comparison shows.

16 To this comes the fact that in the true and purer antiquity nothing is read about this sacrament of the departing. We find with the ancients descriptions of visits to the sick; we have accounts how many godly persons fell happily asleep in the Lord. There are ancient canons which tell with what aids those who are departing this world should be fortified, with what provisions for the journey they should be supplied in order that they may, as Dionysius the Corinthian says, "depart hence happily and with good hope." They enumerate comfort of the Word, faith, prayer, absolution, and Communion of the body and blood of the Lord. No mention is made that there is in the church a special sacrament of unction for those who stand at the end of life and must journey hence through death, and that this unction is the strongest aid at the moment and crisis of death against sins, against the infirmity of the flesh, against the terror of death, against the wiles and power of the devil, in order that, fortified by this unction, we may be able to pass through death to life—this, I say, cannot be shown in all the history of the true and purer antiquity. For we are not now speaking of the Roman pontiffs.

17 But they object: Certainly Jerome furnishes a testimony for this unction in his comments on Mark 6:13. But who is that Jerome? They themselves know that the commentary on Mark is not by the famous Stridonian[7] but that it was written long after his time.

Thus they also declare: Does not Augustine expressly number unction among the necessary consolations of those who are departing this world? But where does he do this? They say: In Bk. 2, *De visitatione infirmorum;* likewise, *De rectitudine catholicae conversationis.* But they themselves are not ignorant of the fact that these books are not by Augustine but were written by others after his time; afterward these began to be falsely ascribed to Augustine. From this the reader can assuredly judge how the case of this extreme unction stands, for whose proof witnesses must be begged from spurious writings. Nevertheless, at the time these books were written the anointing of the sick did not yet have the accretions which are now the substance and, as it were, the very soul of papalist unction.

There is no command to anoint the organs of the five senses, nor do these books teach that through this unction sins are forgiven; they do not teach that this unction is the strongest aid to the dying against death and

---

[7] St. Jerome was born at Stridon, a city in northeastern Italy, about A.D. 345.

the devil; not yet in use in unction at that time was the invocation of angels, patriarchs, prophets, apostles, martyrs, virgins, widows, etc., which is now an important part of the action in extreme unction. But at that time the sick were still led to Christ the Mediator. And in Bk 2, ch. 2, these most comforting words are found: "I speak with greater safety and joy to my Jesus than to any one of the spirits of the saints of God; Christ has a greater obligation to me than to any one of the heavenly spirits. God deigned to become what I am; He did not take on the nature of angels. Your God, your Man, went before the court of His God and your God, clothed in your garment of damask; He prays for us without ceasing. Whom therefore you have as Intercessor, Him you have as Mediator; make Him your gracious Advocate. And if God is for you, who can be against you?" And in Bk. 1, ch. 6, there is recorded this prayer of one about to die: "My God, my Mercy, my Refuge, Thee I desire; to Thee I flee; I hasten to come to Thee; do not spurn me as I come under Thy fearful judgment; let Thy gracious presence be with me in these my great necessities; I cannot redeem myself with my works, but do Thou redeem me and take pity on me; I have no confidence in my merits, but trust in Thy mercies, and I trust more in Thy mercies than I despair on account of my evil deeds. Thou art my Hope, my God; against Thee, Thee only have I sinned; because I was precious enough that Thou hast redeemed me, I am not so vile that I must perish. And now I come to Thee, who forsakest no one; I desire to be loosed and to be with Thee. Into Thy hands, Lord, I commend my spirit; look upon me, Lord God of truth, that I may sleep in peace and be at rest." I have copied these things in order that the reader may consider how recent is the drama of the papalists in extreme unction.

But they also trot out Theophylact, who took his interpretations from the ancient Greeks. But what does he say? Does he say that in the Greek church unction was the special sacrament of the departing, so that those who stand at the end of life may, if they are anointed with oil in the organs of the five senses, have the strongest aid against sins, death, and the devil? Certainly he says none of these things. But in his explanation of Mark 6:13 he says that the apostles anointed with oil those whom they cured through the gift of healing. And he adds that also James says the same thing in his epistle. And immediately he adds the reason why the sign of the oil was employed, namely, as the outward sign of the gift of healing, because it signifies the mercy of God and the grace of the Spirit, through which we are freed from distress and receive spiritual light and joy.

Thus Oecumenius, in explaining the passage James 5:14-15, says nothing else than that also the apostles did this when the Lord was still walking among men, when they anointed the sick with oil and healed them.

Therefore unction was not a sacrament for the departing in the Greek church. But Lindanus says that Chrysostom, Bk. 3, *De sacerdotio,* interprets the passage in James as pertaining to this sacrament of extreme unction. But how so? Does he say that at his time there was in the church a special sacrament of unction for those about to die, with this material, form, and action, administered for the same purpose, use, and effect as the description of papalist unction has it, that it should be for those departing this life a fortress and defense against sins, death, and the devil? Certainly Chrysostom says none of these things, but in setting forth the prerogatives of a Christian priest he enumerates the preaching of the Gospel, the administration of Baptism and the Lord's Supper, and the power to remit sins through absolution.

However, he adds also that in illnesses priests do more good than the natural parents. He explains this by a division: "1: Often they restore a person to health who is already struggling and near death; 2. They have rendered the torment of the illness less severe; 3. They have preserved some persons in the very beginning lest they fall into the scourge of illnesses, which are punishments of sin." This is how this passage in Chrysostom must be rendered, which the translator gave an altogether foreign sense.

But how do priests bring this about in illnesses? Chrysostom answers: "Because not only when they regenerate us, but also afterward they have the power to remit sins." What and what kind of power that is he explains in the foregoing, namely, the power described in John 20:22-23. He also adds that the priests bring about what he says they do for the sick by teaching and admonishing, and with the aid of prayer. And after these things he adds the passage James 5:14-15. He does not, however, say clearly that the external unction was then customarily applied, but makes mention of teaching, admonition, prayers, and absolution.

Even if he had clearly said that external unction was applied, nevertheless this passage would give no support to the extreme unction of the papalists. For he is not arguing about the aid with which the dying must be fortified in order that they may be able to fall asleep in the Lord, but he is expressly treating of preservation in, mitigation of, and liberation from bodily illnesses, as is clear from the Greek text. Therefore neither the material nor the form nor the action nor the purpose, use, and effect of the extreme unction of the papalists can be proved from this passage in Chrysostom. For it is not sufficient for the proof of papalist unction to have shown that the ancients make mention of the unction which is described in Mark and James, but it must be shown that the ancient church acknowledged and used unction as a special sacrament for those who were departing this life, with the kind of material, form, action, understanding, and for that purpose and use which the papalists teach about their extreme unction. This indeed they are not able to teach on the basis of any writing of the true antiquity which is worthy of credence.

18 This, however, can be shown, that not long after the time of the apostles the apostolic unction of the sick was transformed to a different use, apart from the gift of healing, and corrupted by heretics. For Irenaeus says, Bk. 1, ch. 13, that some of the Valentinians[8] anointed their dying ones at the very end by pouring oil and water on their heads, along with invocations, in the belief that they were redeemed by that anointing. The account is noteworthy in that the action of apostolic unction apart from the gift of healing began to be transferred to the dying by heretics, in the belief that the dying would at the moment of death be redeemed by this unction. This was however reckoned among the heresies at the time of Irenaeus. But let the reader consider how greatly the description of Irenaeus differs from the extreme unction of the papalists. In ch. 7 of his *Hierarchia,* Diogenes pours oil on a dead person who is about to be buried, something which was simply taken over from a custom of the Gentiles, as Vergil says:

They wash the stark corpse and anoint it.

Familiar is the line from Ennius:

The good woman washed and anointed the corpse of the fallen Tarquin.

Apuleius, *De asino aureo,* Bk. 9, calls this the final bath. These items from history need to be observed in order that we may consider that at an early time superstitions crept into the church with respect to anointing the dying and the dead. But at the time of Irenaeus such anointings were rejected as heretical. Indeed, the church did not accept Dionysius' anointing of the dead, a leftover from heathen superstitions.

19 It is also useful to observe how the church finally arrived at the extreme unction of the papalists for the dying. As long as the gift of healing was present in the church, the custom of anointing with simple oil also remained. Later some related miraculous healings with hallowed oil, as Rufinus writes about the disciples of Antonius in *Historia Ecclesiastica,* Bk. 11, ch. 4: "When a man was laid before them who was already dried

---

[8] The Valentinians: a Gnostic, and therefore heretical, sect that flourished in the second century.

up in all his members, particularly his feet, they anointed him with oil in the name of the Lord, and immediately his feet were strengthened." Sulpicius Severus writes, ch. 21, that St. Martin restored to health with hallowed oil a certain girl who was so drawn together by paralysis that she performed no function of the body for human uses. In *Tripartita,* Bk. 8, ch. 1, Socrates writes that the monk Benjamin had the charismatic gift of healing the sick with the touch of the hand only, or with oil. But when miracles no longer followed upon the use of hallowed oil, Felix IV around A.D. 528 ordered that, lest there should no longer be any use for it, the sick should be anointed with oil before they died. Afterward, as time went on, more and more other things were added until finally this sacrament of the papalists with all that goes with it was constructed, which is now sold very dearly as alluded to by Christ and promulgated by the apostle James, so that it is asserted that it cannot be spurned without a heinous crime and an insult to the Holy Spirit Himself.

Ninth Topic

CONCERNING HOLY ORDERS

From the 23rd Session
of the Council of Trent

SECTION I
Concerning the Sacrament of Order, etc.

Chapter I

Sacrifice and priesthood are by the ordinance of God linked together in such a way that both have existed under every law. Since therefore the Catholic Church has in the New Testament received from the institution of the Lord the holy, visible sacrifice of the Eucharist, one must also confess that there is in her a new visible and external priesthood, into which the old has been changed. And the sacred writings show, and the tradition of the Catholic Church has always taught, that this was instituted by the same Lord, our Savior, and given to the apostles and their successors in the priesthood for consecrating, offering, and administering the body and blood and also for remitting and retaining sins.

CANON I

If anyone says that there is not in the New Testament a visible and external priesthood, or that there is no power of consecrating and offering the body and blood of the Lord and of remitting and retaining sins, but only an office and bare ministry of preaching the Gospel, or that those who do not preach are not priests at all, let him be anathema.

Examination

1 The explanation is short and easy once it is shown what the controversy is about. They shout loudly that those who do not approve the priesthood of the papalists take away all order out of the church, that with infinite confusion they prostitute the ministry to any one of the common people and (something which Tertullian ascribes to the heretics) make laymen out of priests and enjoin priestly functions to laymen, with the result that there is neither any authority nor dignity of the ministry, etc. Therefore this slander must first of all be removed.

Now the Anabaptists and Enthusiasts are rightly disapproved, who either take the use of the external ministry of Word and sacrament entirely out of the church, or imagine that it is useless and unnecessary. For they teach that new and special revelations should rather be sought and expected from God without the use of the external ministry of Word and sacrament, and that this kind of calling, illumination, and conversion is much more excellent and worthy of honor than if we use the voice of the ministry. And indeed, it is God by whose power, working, efficacy, impulse, and inspiration whatever pertains to calling, illumination, conversion, repentance, faith, renewal, and in short, to the business of our salvation is begun, effected, increased, and preserved in men. But God arranged by a certain counsel of His that He wills to dispense these things, not by infusing new and special revelations, illuminations, and movements into the minds of men without any means, but through the outward ministry of the Word. This ministry He did not commit to angels, so that their appearances are to be sought and expected, but He put the Word of reconciliation into men, and He wills that the proclamation of the Gospel, divinely revealed, should sound forth through them.

2 All Christians are indeed priests (1 Pet. 2:9; Rev. 1:6), because they offer spiritual sacrifices to God. Everyone also can and should teach the Word of God in his own house (Deut. 6:7; 1 Cor. 14:35). Nevertheless, not everyone ought to take and arrogate to himself the public ministry of Word and sacrament. For not all are apostles; not all are teachers (1 Cor. 12:29), but those who have been set apart for this ministry by God through a particular and legitimate call (Acts 13:2; Jer. 23:21; Rom. 10:15). This is done either immediately or mediately. Paul prescribes a legitimate manner of calling which is made through the voice of the church (1 Tim. 3:2-7; and Titus 1:5-9). Christ Himself indeed called certain men to this ministry immediately, in order to show that He approves the ministry of those who are chosen and called by the voice of the church according to the rule prescribed by the apostles, as will be explained more fully later. There is added also the promise that God will truly work effectively through the ministry of those who teach the Gospel, which the Son of God wills to preserve in the church through perpetual calling, as Paul says in Eph. 4:8 ff.: He ascended; He gave gifts to men; and He gave some to be apostles, some prophets, others evangelists, others however pastors and teachers for perfecting of the saints in the work of ministry, in edification of the body of Christ. To this use of the ministry, which God both instituted and preserves in the church, men must therefore be guided, and taught that through this ministry there are offered to us eternal blessings, and indeed that God in this way receives us, rescues us from sin and the power of the devil and from eternal death, and restores to us righteousness and eternal life.

3 This ministry does indeed have power, divinely bestowed (2 Cor.10:4-6; 13:2-4), but circumscribed with certain duties and limitations, namely, to preach the Word of God, teach the erring, reprove those who sin, admonish the dilatory, comfort the troubled, strengthen the weak, resist those who speak against the truth, reproach and condemn false teaching, censure evil customs, dispense the divinely insti-

tuted sacraments, remit and retain sins, be an example to the flock, pray for the church privately and lead the church in public prayers, be in charge of care for the poor, publicly excommunicate the stubborn and again receive those who repent and reconcile them with the church, appoint pastors to the church according to the instruction of Paul, with consent of the church institute rites that serve the ministry and do not militate against the Word of God nor burden consciences but serve good order, dignity, decorum, tranquillity, edification, etc. For these are the things which belong to these two chief points, namely, to the power of order and the power of jurisdiction.

4 We are not fighting about words. Paul, with a general term, calls teachers and pastors "ministers." In the Scripture of the New Testament the terms "priests" and "priesthood" are nowhere applied to the ministry of the New Testament. But in the use of the ecclesiastical writers a strong trend developed to call the ministry "priesthood" and the ministers "priests." Thus Chrysostom calls whatever pertains to the ministry of the New Testament "priesthood." Augustine, *De civitate Dei,* Bk. 20, says: "Bishops and presbyters are now properly called priests in the church." Now, if the papalists wanted only this, that there is in the New Testament an external priesthood, that is, an external ministry of the Word and the sacraments, as we have already explained, there would be no controversy, neither would disturbances arise on account of the term "priesthood" so long as matters which are true and necessary were inviolate.

5 But there is no obscurity about what they want and seek. For in this first canon they say expressly that by the priesthood for which they are contending they do not understand the office and ministry of preaching the Gospel, but declare in the first chapter that they are fighting in behalf of the sacrifice of the Mass, about their external and visible priesthood, which they define as being chiefly the power of sacrificing Christ in the Mass. And they think that such a priesthood is necessary in order that the church may have mediators who can plead their cause before Christ, the supreme Judge, and by this act of sacrifice placate the wrath of the Father and obtain for the church propitiation and other gifts, both such as are spiritual and necessary for salvation and also bodily gifts that pertain to this life, yes, the liberation of souls from purgatory.

6 But we have shown above, under the topic of the Mass, that this sacrifice is not only fabricated but injurious to and blasphemous against Christ. There is therefore no need to undertake a special refutation at this point. For such as the sacrifice is, such also is the priesthood. I shall only add this reminder, that the first canon devotes their priesthood to sacrifice in such a way that it frees it from the ministry of the Word. This they profess much more openly elsewhere, namely, that the ministry of teaching, the dispensation of Baptism, and the distribution of the Eucharist, which can be done through deacons, is not part of the substance of the papalist priesthood.

Therefore let a comparison be made! Christ says: "Go, teach, preach, baptize" (Matt. 28:19-20; Mark 16:15). Paul says: "A bishop must hold firm to the sure Word as taught, so that he may be able to give instruction in sound doctrine and also to confute those who contradict it" (Titus 1:9). He must be an apt teacher (1 Tim. 3:2), must attend to reading and teaching (1 Tim. 4:13), must rebuke those who sin, in the presence of all (1 Tim 5:20), etc. Therefore the apostles unburdened themselves of other duties, in order that they might be able to devote themselves to teaching and prayer (Acts 6:4). Paul says: "Christ did not send me to baptize but to preach the Gospel" (1 Cor. 1:17). These things, which Christ and the apostles declare to belong to the ministry of the Word, that is, the priesthood, the papalists remove from the substance of their priesthood. Also they do not want the dispensation of Baptism and the distribution of the Eucharist to belong properly to their priesthood. Therefore the papalists remove and separate from their priesthood all the things of which, according to the teaching of Scripture, the ministry of the New Testament consists. They establish as the essence of their priesthood the sacrifice of the body and blood of Christ in the Mass, which was brought into the church without, yes, contrary to Scripture, as was shown under the topic concerning the Mass.

They add also the remission and retention of sins. But this they are unwilling to have happen through the voice and proclamation of the Gospel, as Christ instituted it, but by that judicial act of which we spoke under a previous topic. Therefore the papalist priesthood is not the ministry of the New Testament but truly an abomination of Antichrist, standing in the holy place.

The ancients do, indeed, at times say that it is the duty of priests to offer the body and blood of Christ, but we have shown above, under the topic of the Mass, that they understand this of the administration of the Lord's Supper according to Christ's institution. For Paul also calls the preaching of the Gospel a sacrifice. Many among the papalists who heretofore displayed a certain degree of moderation indicated that they desired a reformation of the priesthood in which the ministry of teaching, which according to the heritage of Scripture belongs to the ministry of the New Testament, might again be enjoined to the care of the priests. But the Council of Trent simply defines the priesthood as the action of sacrificing, and Canon 1 pronounces the anathema on anyone who says that those who do not exercise the ministry of the Word and the sacraments are not priests.

7 They have only one argument, namely, that in the Old Testament there was a priesthood for offering sacrifices and that there is in the New Testament a fulfillment of the shadows of the Old. But you cannot construct the priesthood of the papalists from this. For the Epistle to the Hebrews teaches at great length that the sacrifices of the Old Testament have been fulfilled and completed in the New by the one sacrifice of Christ, our true High Priest. But they say: Yet Paul argues (2 Cor. 3:7-11) that if the ministry of the Old Testament had its own splendor, the splendor of the ministry of the New Testament will be much greater. I answer: What this ministry of the New Testament is and what duties belong to it must not be established by a bad imitation of the ceremonies of the Old Testament but must be learned from the description of Christ and the apostles in the New Testament.

SECTION II

[Concerning the Seven Orders]

Chapter II

Since, however, the ministry of the sacred priesthood is a divine thing, it was fitting, in order that it could be exercised more worthily and with greater reverence, that there should be in the church by a most well-ordered arrangement more and diverse orders of ministers who would by virtue of their office serve the priesthood, distributed in such a way that those who have already been marked by the clerical tonsure should ascend through the minor orders to the higher. For the sacred Scriptures openly make mention not only of priests but also of deacons, and teach in the weightiest words what things are most of all to be attended to in their ordination; and from the very beginning of the church the names of the following orders and the proper ministrations of each of them, namely subdeacon, acolyte, exorcist, lector, and doorkeeper, are known to have been in use, although they were not equal in rank. For the subdiaconate is classed with the major orders by the fathers and the sacred councils, in which we very frequently also read of the other, lower orders.

CANON II

If anyone says that there are not in the Catholic Church other orders, both major and minor, beside the priesthood, through which as by certain steps advance is made toward the priesthood, let him be anathema.

Examination

1 In this topic the papalists fight about the seven orders, that is, about the shadow, or rather about the mask, of empty titles, while the things themselves neither exist nor are any longer present in their church. Nevertheless, they do not do this for nothing, but on account of the fat allowances which were annexed to these titles at the time when genuine functions of the ministry were still connected with them. In order that they might be able to retain the benefits of these allowances with some show of right when these offices had broken down and been discontinued, they made so many sacraments of empty titles, and for this reason they fight for this their Helen.

2 The fact of the matter is this: Because many duties belong to the ministry of the church which cannot all conveniently be performed by one person or by a few, when the believers are very numerous—in order, therefore, that all things may be done in an orderly way, decently, and for edification, these duties of the ministry began, as the assembly of the church grew great, to be distributed among certain ranks of ministers which they afterward called *taxeis* (ranks) or *tagmata* (orders), so that each might have, as it were, a certain designated station in which he might serve the church in certain duties of the ministry. Thus in the beginning the apostles took care of the ministry of the Word and the sacraments and at the same time also of the distribution and dispensation of alms. Afterward, however, as the number of disciples increased, they entrusted that part of the ministry which has to do with alms to others, whom they called deacons. They also state the reason why they do this—that they might be able to devote themselves more diligently to the ministry of the Word and to prayer, without diversions. (Acts 6:1-4)

3 This first origin of ranks or orders of ministry in the apostolic church shows what ought to be the cause, what the reason, purpose, and use of such ranks or orders—that for the welfare of the assembly of the church the individual duties which belong to the ministry might be attended to more conveniently, rightly, diligently, and orderly, with a measure of dignity and for edification. And because the apostles afterward accepted into the ministry of teaching those from among the deacons who were approved, as Stephen and Philip, we gather that this also is a use of these ranks or orders, that men are first prepared or tested in minor duties so that afterward heavier duties may more safely and profitably be entrusted to them. That is what Paul says in 1 Tim. 3:10: "Let them also be tested first, and so let them minister." Likewise: "Those who serve well as deacons will gain a good rank for themselves."[1] Thus there were in the worship service of the church at Antioch (Acts 13:1) prophets and teachers, of whom the former either prophesied of future events or interpreted the more difficult passages of Scripture (1 Cor. 14:29-32), while the latter set forth the elements of Christian doctrine to the people (Heb. 5:12-14). Paul and Barnabas receive Mark into the ministry (Acts 13:5) not merely in order that he might render bodily services to them but so that they might be able to entrust some parts of the ministry of the Word to him, as Paul expressly says (Acts 15:38). There were in the church at Corinth apostles, prophets, and teachers; some spoke in tongues, some interpreted, some had psalms, some prayers, benedictions, and giving of thanks, not in private exercises but in public assemblies of the church. (1 Cor. 12:28-30; 14:26-27)

---

[1] Chemnitz follows the Vulgate reading in 1 Tim. 3:13: *gradum bonum sibi acquirent.*

In Eph. 4:11 the following ranks of ministers are listed: (1) apostles, who were not called to some certain church, and who had not been called through men, but immediately by Christ, and had the command to teach everywhere, and were furnished with the testimony of the Spirit and of miracles, that they might not err in doctrine but that their doctrine might be divine and heavenly, to which all the other teachers should be bound; (2) prophets, who either had revelations of future events or interpreted tongues and the Scriptures for the more advanced, for these things are ascribed to the prophets of the New Testament in 1 Cor. 14; (3) evangelists, who were not apostles and yet were not bound to some one certain church but were sent to different churches to teach the Gospel there, but chiefly to lay the first foundations; such an evangelist was Philip (Acts 21:8), and Timothy (2 Tim. 4:5), Tychicus, Sylvanus, etc.; that there were such evangelists also after the times of the apostles Eusebius testifies, Bk. 3, ch. 37, etc.; (4) pastors, who were placed over a certain flock, as Peter shows (1 Peter 5:2-3), and who not only taught but administered the sacraments and had the oversight over their hearers, as Ezekiel (34:2 ff.) describes the pastoral office; (5) teachers, to whom the chief governance or oversight of the church was not entrusted but who only set the doctrine before the people in a simple manner, such as the catechists were later; thus Paul (Rom. 2:20) speaks of "a teacher of children," and the word "teach" is expressly used in this sense in Heb. 5:12. All these ranks the apostles include under the terms "presbytery" and "episcopacy." Sometimes they also call those to whom the ministry of Word and sacrament has been committed by the term "minister" ("servant"). (Col. 1:7, 23; 1 Thess. 3:2; 2 Cor. 3:6; 11:23; Eph. 3:7)

Also Paul himself sometimes performed the ministry of the Word in such a way that he entrusted the administration of the sacraments to others. 1 Cor. 1:17: "Christ did not send me to baptize but to preach the Gospel." And in 1 Tim. 1:17 he mentions two kinds of presbyters, of whom some labored in preaching and teaching, while others had been placed in charge of ecclesiastical discipline. Tertullian also mentions this kind of presbytery, *Apologeticus*, ch. 39. This about completes the list of ranks into which we read that the ecclesiastical ministry was divided at the time of the apostles.

4 This division has examples also in the Old Testament. For David, according to 1 Chron. 23 ff., divided the ministry of the temple into certain ranks or orders. Also in the synagogue there were readers, who only read the Scripture text. There were, besides, also teachers who interpreted the Scripture and applied the text for the purpose of exhortations (Luke 2:46; Acts 15:30-35). And this was the difference between the scribes and Pharisees.

5 However, because of the present dispute, the following reminder must be added: (1) that there is no command in the Word of God, which or how many such ranks or orders there should be; (2) that there were not at the time of the apostles in all churches and at all times the same and the same number of ranks or orders, as can be clearly ascertained from the epistles of Paul, written to various churches; (3) that there was not, at the time of the apostles, such a division of these ranks, but repeatedly one and the same person held and performed all the duties which belong to the ministry, as is clear from the apostolic history. Therefore such orders were free at the time of the apostles and were observed for the sake of good order, decorum, and edification, except that at that time certain special gifts, such as tongues, prophecies, apostolate, and miracles, were bestowed on certain persons by God. These ranks, about which we have spoken until now, were not something beside and beyond the ministry of the Word and sacraments, but the real and true duties of the ministry were distributed among certain ranks for the reasons already set forth.

6 This example of the apostles the primitive church imitated for the same reason and in similar liberty. For the grades of the duties of the ministry were distributed, not however in identically the same way as in the church at Corinth or in that at Ephesus, but according to the circumstances obtaining in each church. From this one can gather what freedom there was in the distribution of the ranks.

Dionysius, *Hierarchia*, ch. 5, expressly names only three orders: (1) that of the "chief priest,"[2] to whom he ascribes the highest and most complete office of teaching, explaining all mysteries of Christ, and administering the sacraments; (2) that of "the priests," who more fully taught those who had been instructed as catechumens, led them to the bishop and assisted in matters belonging to the administration of the sacraments; (3) that of "the liturgists,"[3] to whom he assigned the duty of purifying and preparing those who were to be initiated, that is, to be instructed in the rudiments. And in ch. 3 he says: "Through the office of ministers[4] the reading of sacred Scripture is recited in its place." Like-

---

[2] In classical Greek, the one who presided at sacred rites.

[3] In classical Greek, those who perform public duties; then also, ministers of God.

[4] "Ministers" here refers to the lowest rank of clergy, perhaps the equivalent of the subdeacons in the Western church.

wise: "Some of the ministers stand ready to close the forecourts of the temple when the catechumens, the penitents, and the possessed are put out; others have another duty—they disrobe the person to be baptized," etc. You see that he enumerates many duties of the ministry but nevertheless does not ascribe special orders to each one, but names only three orders. The *Canones Apostolorum* name bishop, presbyter, deacon, lector, and cantor. However, no mention is made of the doorkeeper, exorcist, or acolyte. Ambrose, on Eph. 4, in describing the ranks of offices of the ministry in his time, enumerates bishops, presbyters, deacons, lectors, exorcists. In a booklet about the seven ranks of the clergy which is ascribed to Jerome, exorcists and acolytes are not enumerated. Therefore the assertion about these seven orders is not a catholic dogma. Indeed, some of the ancients enumerate more than these seven orders. The epistle of Ignatius adds *tous kopioontas,* whom Epiphanius calls *kopiazontas.*[5] The booklet of Jerome calls them *fossores* (diggers), namely, men who took care of funerals and buried the dead. The Greeks had the peculiar office of the *syngeli.*[6] Ignatius adds to the orders "confessors", Clement adds "catechists." The canonists count nine orders, for they add psalmists and bishops.

From this there afterward arose the multiplication of ecclesiastical orders. For Cyrian, Bk. 3, Letter No. 22, shows that the discipline was such that nothing which had to be done in the church and in church matters could be done by any save clerics, even if it did not properly pertain to the ministry of the Word. And therefore it was necessary that the footmen or servants of bishops and presbyters be clerics. From among the clerics there were afterward taken stewards, guards, chief stewards, and majordomos. Therefore clerics were persons who by a special and rather strict training were formed and prepared for service to the church. And these were first employed in certain lesser duties, in order that their zeal, diligence, faithfulness, and dignity might be tested, to see whether they would in future be fit for greater and more important duties of the ministry. And in the more populous churches, especially when people had to assemble from all sides, from the country, from the villages and small cities, to a metropolitan church, especially at the more solemn feasts, as many ancient canons teach, one or even a few were not able to perform all individual duties of the ministry.

7 Therefore the ranks or orders were distinguished, not by empty titles but according to certain duties that belonged to the ministry of the

---

[5] Both terms signify such as perform hard physical labor.

[6] Chemnitz does not explain this office, and the dictionaries do not list the term.

church. The bishop taught the Word of God and had charge of the church's discipline. The presbyters taught and administered the sacraments. The deacons were in charge of the treasuries of the church, in order from them to provide sustenance for the poor and in particular for the ministers of the church. Afterward the deacons also began to be employed for assisting with a certain part of the ministry of the bishop and the presbyters, as also Jerome testifies, *Ad Rusticum,* such as for reading something publicly from the Scriptures, for teaching, exhorting, etc., admonishing the people to be attentive, to turn their hearts to the Lord, to proclaim peace, to prepare the things which belong to the administration of the sacraments, distribute the sacraments to the people, take those who are to be ordained to the bishop, to remind bishops about matters which pertain to discipline, etc. However, Jerome complains, *Ad Rusticum Narbonensem,* that so many such things had been laid on the deacons, especially in the Roman church, which were outside of the apostolic discipline and the custom of the other churches, that among the deacons the first and true duty of deacons had been all but forgotten. For because the deacons were occupied with these new duties, subdeacons were placed under them; they collected the offerings of the faithful which were contributed for the sustenance of the poor and the ministers.

Besides these there were lectors, who read publicly to the people from the Scriptures, especially from the Old Testament, for the reading of the New Testament was thereafter given to the deacons. There were psalmists or cantors, who sang first what the whole assembly was accustomed to sing. There were doorkeepers, who at the time of the sacrament, after the announcement by the deacon, put out of the church the Gentiles, catechumens, penitents, the possessed, heretics, and persons who had been excommunicated, for thus Dionysius describes this office. Bishops, presbyters, and deacons had their *famuli,* servants, companions, or followers, whose services they used when necessity demanded it, as Paul had used the services of Onesimus. They called these men acolytes.[7] From this the ignorant afterward made candle bearers. Besides these there were exorcists, who had the gift of casting out or restraining demons.

8 This distribution of ranks in the more populous churches was useful for the sake of order, for decorum, and for edification by reason of the duties which belong to the ministry. In the smaller or less populous churches such a distribution of ranks was not judged necessary, and also in the more populous churches a like or identical distribution of these

---

[7] According to the Greek word from which the term *acolyte* is derived it should mean "follower." But note Chemnitz' comment.

ranks was not everywhere observed. For this reason, for this use, and with this freedom many of these ranks of the ancient church are preserved also among us.

9 I have related these things that it may be possible more readily to show what has come into controversy in this chapter about the ecclesiastical ranks or orders. For we do not outrightly reject or condemn the distribution of these ranks, such as it was in the apostolic and in the ancient church, but use them in our own churches where necessary and for edification, in the way we have said.

But this we justly and deservedly rebuke in the papalist orders: 1. They retain and usurp titles without the reality, and the benefits of the titles without the duties; for when they had thrown the duties of the canonical ministry of the Word and sacraments out of their great churches into the small and lowly chapels in the parishes, where one or two were compelled to perform all duties of the ministry, they themselves retained the empty titles without[8] the duties of the ministry. Nevertheless they did not retain them as empty titles, but retained the names of the orders on account of the fat allowances. Bishops no longer taught, presbyters did not administer sacraments to the people, offerings were no longer contributed since the churches were sufficiently endowed. What need was there then for either deacons or subdeacons? The custom of putting out the catechumens, the penitents, and the possessed had already long lapsed. What is the use, therefore, of doorkeepers? There is no need of a special sacrament of order for shutting the doors of the church, chasing out dogs, and sweeping the floor. The readers do not read in order that people may understand; the cantors do not lead in singing in order that people may sing along. Therefore they do not have the kind of readers or cantors which were in the ancient church. They do not have the gift of casting out demons; what therefore is the order of exorcists among them? The servants of the bishops and priests are horsemen and soldiers; nevertheless they argue much about the sacrament of the order of acolytes. Therefore not a single rank or order of the true ecclesiastical ministry is found in that office among the papalists, such as were in the apostolic and ancient church, but they have only the empty titles.

Moreover, they have made a mockery also of this, that according to the old canons no one is to be received to the higher orders unless he has first been proved in the lower. For they confer all the minor orders either simultaneously or after a very short interval, and in these orders they

---

[8] The Latin text, which has *quia si,* is evidently corrupt here. Ed. Preuss has substituted *in* for *quia si.* More satisfactory seems the emendation of Nigrinus, who has *ohne,* which our translation follows.

nevertheless exercise no true functions of the ministry by which they could be prepared for the ministry of the Word and sacraments.

10 2. Under these titles they have fraudulently substituted false duties, after rejecting the true and lawful ministry of the Word and sacraments. For of the office of bishop they have made unrestricted political dominion; of presbyters they have made sacrificers; of acolytes they have made candle bearers, namely, because the ancients somewhere say that they were servants of the lamps at nocturnal meetings. The papalists imagined that acolyte meant to the Greeks what Latins call *caeroferarius* (candle bearer), who illuminates the sun with torches in broad daylight. This interpretation is totally false, inept, and barbarous. Out of doorkeepers they have made treasurers. How far readers and cantors have degenerated from the form of the ancient church one single comparison shows. At last all the orders, both major and minor, were transformed into readers and cantors. For what else do they do every day? This is contrary to the canons themselves, dist. 92, *In sancta Romana.* The exorcists they have transformed into magical enchanters. For at one time it was a special gift with the human voice and with divine power to scourge, harass, torture, and cast the devil out of bodies, or at least to control him. Tertullian, in *Apologeticus,* testifies that in his time this gift was still in the church. And Cyprian says, Bk. 4, Letter No. 77: "This is done also today through exorcists." Also Ambrose, Bk. 1, ch. 4: "Another is more concerned to exorcise those who suffer from an evil spirit." That this gift was still present also at the time of Augustine is gathered from *De civitate Dei,* Bk. 10, ch. 22. Indeed, in the age of Chrysostom and Prosper possessed persons were brought into the church and often were set free by the communal prayers of the church.

Afterward, when this gift ceased, in order that the rank of exorcists might nevertheless be retained, another duty was invented which might be assigned to them, namely, to prepare the catechumens, who were to be baptized, with exorcisms and by blowing on them for Baptism, as the book *De Ecclesiasticis dogmatibus,* ch. 51, testifies. And Gregory of Nazianzus says: "Do not be discouraged with the rather long discipline of exorcism, and do not grow weary on account of its length." But such a peculiar action of exorcising was not found in the apostolic church, nor was this the office of the exorcists in the ancient church, and now it is not even observed among the papalists. However, this example shows what a bad imitation accomplishes. When the gift of casting out demons had ceased, and they wanted nevertheless to retain the order of exorcists, a different and new duty was invented which could be assigned to them. Some indeed retained the recitation of exorcisms, although they did not have the gift of casting out demons. From there the bad imitation finally passed over to superstitious exorcisms and to more truly magical incantations. And since the demons scoff at these exorcisms, there is now nothing left with the papalists of the office of exorcists except the bare title, for those who practice exorcisms among them are not the persons who have been especially ordained for this. How then do the Tridentine fathers promise to restore the function of exorcists the way it was in the ancient church, since they do not have and are not able to bestow the gift of casting out demons? In the ancient church there were prophets or seers, and also evangelists, as Eusebius testifies, Bk. 3, ch. 37. How silly it would be to make particular orders in the church of these offices, although these gifts have ceased! That is also how matters stand with the exorcists.

11 3. We disapprove in the papalist doctrine about orders that they pretend it is necessary on account of an institution and command of Christ, and from apostolic tradition, that there be just so many orders in individual churches. For we have before shown the contrary from the apostolic history. And the fathers at whose time there was such a distribution of ranks of the ecclesiastical ministry say expressly that these were not by divine command or by apostolic tradition. For Ambrose, on Eph. 4, when he had enumerated the orders of his church, added that at one time the bishop had performed all the duties of the church in its ministry to the faithful, but that after churches had been established in all localities, and the duties ordered, the matter had been ordered differently than it had begun. And he adds at once: "Therefore the writings of the apostles do not agree in everything with the ordination which is now in the church, because all this was written when things were in their beginnings." Hugo says that these orders were arranged in different places not only by the voluntary regulation of the spiritual fathers but also on the basis of the custom of each tribe, a suitable reason being assumed.

What a beautiful invention it is, therefore, that Christ Himself passed through all these orders; that He was a doorkeeper when He drove those who bought and sold out of the temple, a reader when He read out of the Book of Isaiah, an exorcist when He cast out demons, an acolyte when He said, "I am the Light of the world," a subdeacon when He washed the feet of the disciples, a deacon when He distributed the Eucharist, a presbyter when he offered Himself up on the altar of the cross and when He consecrated the Eucharist!

Finally, the papalists fight for these orders in order that they may make sacraments of each one of them, even if only empty titles are brought forward. However, the title of sacrament is venerable in the church; it is not to be prostituted that it is applied to candle bearers or to those who now chase dogs out of the church.

SECTION III

[Whether Order Is Truly a Sacrament]

Chapter III

Since it is clear from the testimony of Scripture, from apostolic tradition, and from the unanimous consensus of the fathers, that through sacred ordination (which is performed through words and outward signs) grace is conferred, no one ought to doubt that order is truly and properly one of the seven sacraments of holy Church, for the apostle says: "I remind you to rekindle the gift of God that is within you through the laying on of my hands; for God did not give us a spirit of timidity but a spirit of power and love and self-control."

CANON III

If anyone says that order or holy ordination is not truly and properly a sacrament instituted by Christ the Lord, or that it is some human invention, thought out by men inexperienced in ecclesiastical matters, or that it is only some rite for choosing ministers of the Word of God and the sacraments, let him be anathema.

CANON IV

If any one says that the Holy Spirit is not given through holy ordination and that it is therefore in vain that the bishop says, "Receive the Holy Spirit," or that through it a character is not imprinted, or that he who was once a priest can again become a layman, let him be anathema.

CANON V

If anyone says that the sacred anointing which the Church uses in holy ordination not only is not required but is despicable and destructive, and other ceremonies of order likewise, let him be anathema.

Examination

1 Here this question is being argued, whether ordination is truly and properly a sacrament of the New Testament. We must first speak about the thing itself, in order that we may be able afterward to decide more easily and correctly about calling it a "sacrament." Now there is no doubt that the ministry of the Word and the sacraments as we have described it above was instituted by the Son of God also in the New Testament. For the church has a command about calling and appointing ministers. And the promise is added: 1. God approves the ministry of those who have

691

been called and set apart for the ministry by the voice of the church. Thus Paul says (Acts 20:28), of those who had been called mediately, that the Holy Spirit had made them guardians to feed the church of God. And in Eph. 4:11 it is written that the Son of God gave as gifts not only apostles but also pastors and teachers, who are called mediately. 2. The promise is added that God will give grace and gifts by which those who have been legitimately called will be able rightly, faithfully, and profitably to do and perform the tasks which belong to the ministry. John 20:22: "Receive the Holy Spirit." Likewise [Luke 24:45]: "Then He opened their minds to understand the Scriptures." Matt. 28:20: "Lo, I am with you always," etc. 1 Tim. 4:14: "Do not neglect the gift you have, which was given you by prophetic utterance when the . . . elders laid their hands upon you." 2 Tim 1:6: "Rekindle the gift of God that is within you through the laying on of my hands." Luke 21:15: "I will give you a mouth and wisdom." Matt. 10:19-20: "What you are to say will be given to you in that hour; for it is not you who speak, but the Spirit of your Father speaking through you."

3. This promise is also added, that God is present with the ministry, that by His blessing He gives the increase to its planting and watering, and that He is truly efficacious through the ministry to call, enlighten, convert, give repentance, faith, regeneration, renewal, and, in short, to dispense through the ministry everything that pertains to our salvation. Matt. 28:20: "Lo, I am with you always." John 20:22-23: "Receive the Holy Spirit. If you forgive the sins of any," etc. Matt. 16:19: "I will give you the keys of the kingdom of heaven . . . and whatever you loose on earth shall be loosed in heaven." According to 2 Cor. 3:6 ff. it is a ministry not of the letter but of the Spirit, who gives life and takes away the veil from men's hearts that they may be converted and set free, so that "with unveiled face, beholding the glory of the Lord, they may be changed into His likeness." 2 Cor. 5:19-20: "He has entrusted to us the word of reconciliation. So we are ambassadors for Christ, God making His appeal through us." 2 Cor. 13:3: "Are you seeking proof of Him who is speaking in me, namely Christ?" Eph. 4:8, 11-14: "He gave gifts to men . . . apostles, pastors, teachers, for the equipment of the saints, for the work of the ministry, for building up the body of Christ, until we all attain to the unity of the faith and of the knowledge of Christ, so that we may not be . . . driven hither and thither, and carried about with every wind of doctrine," etc. 1 Cor. 3:6: "God gave the growth." 1 Cor. 15:58: "In the Lord your labor is not in vain." Rom. 1:5, 11, 16: "He gave me grace and apostleship to bring about the obedience of faith . . . . That I may impart to you some spiritual gift . . . . The Gospel is the power of God for

salvation to every one who has faith." 1 Tim. 4:16: "Attend to teaching, for by so doing you will save yourself and those who will hear you." 1 Cor. 4:15: "I became your father in Christ through the Gospel."

2 These very great and comforting promises concerning the ministry ought to be displayed, as it were, in a prominent place in the church, in order that the dignity of the ministry might be extolled against the fanatics, and that those to whom the ministry has been committed may go about their labors and bear their difficulties with greater eagerness, and that men may learn to use the ministry reverently. For without the preaching and hearing of the Word there is no faith, no calling on God, no salvation (Rom. 10:14). However, no one is able to preach in order that faith may follow hearing unless he be sent (Rom. 10:15) Moreover, this also is certain, that the call to the ministry of the Gospel ought to have the public testimony and the public attestation of the church, on account of those who run although they were not sent (Jer. 23:21). Therefore the apostles with some public testimony and public attestation of the church announced and as it were pointed out the call of those who had been legitimately chosen for the ministry of the Word and the sacraments. For the Holy Spirit willed that also Paul, who had been called immediately, should be declared and designated as the one who should be the apostle of the Gentiles. In that public approbation, attestation, or announcement, since it was a public action, the apostles employed the outward rite of the laying on of hands, which was customary at that time with those people, in part on account of the public designation of the one called, in part on account of the prayers and supplications which were made by the whole church in behalf of the person called.

The rite of laying on hands was extraordinarily suited to this process:

1. That the person in question might be publicly pointed out to the church and declared to be legitimately chosen and called. For by this rite Moses points out and declares to the people the calling of Joshua, his successor. (Deut. 34:9)

2. That by means of this rite the one who had been called might be given full assurance about his legitimate and divine call and might at the same time be admonished to devote, give, and as it were vow himself to the service and worship of God. Thus hands were laid on sacrificial animals and in this way Joshua was confirmed in his call.

3. That it might as it were be a public and solemn declaration of the church before God that the model and rule prescribed by the Holy Spirit had been observed at the election and calling. Therefore Paul says (1 Tim. 5:22): "Do not be hasty in the laying on of hands, nor participate in another man's sins."

4. That it might be signified by this visible rite that God approves the calling which is done by the voice of the church, for just as God chooses ministers by the voice of the church, so He also approves the calling by the attestation of the church. Thus the calling of the deacons was approved (Acts 6:6). And thus it comes about that God bestows grace through the laying on of hands.

5. During the prayers, when the name of God was especially invoked over a certain person, it was customary to employ the imposition of hands, by which that person was as it were offered to God and set in His sight, with the request added that God would deign to shower His grace and blessing on him. Thus Jacob placed his hand on the lads whom he blessed (Gen. 48:14 ff.); thus the elders pray over the sick (James 5:14-15); thus Christ blessed little children, laying on His hands (Mark 10:13-16). Now the prayer of a righteous man avails much if it is *energoumenee*, that is, full of activity or earnestness. In order, therefore, that men may consider how necessary the special divine grace and blessing is in view of the usefulness and difficulty of this gift, in view also of the hindrances laid in its way by Satan, the world, and the flesh, and that thus the prayer of the church may come to its aid and be, according to James, rendered full of activity or earnestness, therefore the outward rite of the laying on of hands was employed.

Fasting was also added to the prayer (Acts 13:2). And this earnest prayer at the ordination of ministers is not without effect, because it rests upon a divine command and promise. This is the meaning of Paul's words: "The gift . . . that is within you through the laying on of . . . hands."

3 If ordination is understood in this way, of the ministry of the Word and the sacraments, as already the Apology of the Augsburg Confession explained the position of our churches, then we have no objection to calling ordination a sacrament. And there the words are added, "We shall not object either to calling the laying on of hands a sacrament."[9] For that the term sacrament covers a wide range of meanings we have shown above. Thus Augustine says, Bk. 2, *Contra Parmenianum*, that ordination is a sacrament because it is conferred upon a man by some kind of consecration.

4 This reminder must, however, be added, that the rite of ordination must be distinguished from the ceremony of Baptism and the Lord's Supper, for ordination is not a sacrament in the same way as Baptism and the Lord's Supper. The difference is plain. Baptism and the Lord's Sup-

---

[9] Apology of the Augsburg Confession, Art. XIII, par. 12 (Tappert edition, p. 212).

per are means or instruments through which God applies and seals the promise of reconciliation or forgiveness to individual believers who use Baptism and the Lord's Supper. Ordination is not such a means or instrument, neither are all to be ordained who desire and ask that forgiveness of sins be applied and sealed to them. Many also, like Judas, indeed receive and have the grace of ordination but do not have the grace of reconciliation or the forgiveness of sins. There is therefore a difference between the promises which are added to ordination and those which are added to Baptism and the Lord's Supper. Besides, there is also a difference in the ceremony or external rite. For in Baptism and the Lord's Supper the Son of God Himself prescribed and commanded a certain external element, a certain ceremony or rite. In ordination, however, such as we now understand it, Christ Himself applied an external sign just once, when on the day of His resurrection He breathed on His disciples (John 20:22). He did not, however, add a command that the church should imitate that rite of breathing upon the ministers at their ordination. And in Mark 3:14; Matt. 10:1; Luke 9:1 ff.; 10:1 ff. He gave authority and power to the apostles and to the 70 disciples when He committed the ministry to them, but we do not read that He used any external sign or symbol or rite for this bestowal. Before His ascension, in Galilee, when He says: "Go into all the world, preach, baptize," etc., He indeed adds the promise: "I am with you," but He does not use any visible sign or external rite (Matt. 28:19-20; Mark 16:15-16). Thus at the Last Supper, when He says: "Do this," we do not read that He applied any external rite of ordination.

It is also worthy of consideration that when the apostles wanted to apply some outward rite in ordination, they did not take the visible sign of breathing on the ordinand, which Christ had used—lest people think that Christ had given a command about using the rite of breathing on them. Therefore they took another rite, one indifferent and free, namely, the rite of laying on of hands, for they did not want to impose something on the church as necessary concerning which they did not have a command of Christ.

Now the ministry of the Word and the sacraments has divine promises, and the prayer at ordination rests on these, but these promises are not to be tied to the rite of the imposition of hands, about which there is neither a command of Christ nor such a promise as there is about Baptism and the Lord's Supper. This reminder must be added, because the papalists contend that ordination is truly and properly a sacrament of the New Testament, just as are Baptism and the Lord's Supper.

5 I wanted to explain this opinion in order that it might be manifest what the Augsburg Confession holds about the ordination of ministers of the Word and the sacraments.

Now [first], the assembly at Trent says expressly in the third canon that they do not take the ordination about which they contend to mean the rite of choosing ministers of the Word and the sacraments, that is, the papalists do not understand the sacrament of order as referring to the ministry of the Word and the sacraments in the way we have just set forth the teaching of Scripture, but they take it as referring to a sacrifice for the living and the dead through which the priests procure the grace of God and all necessary gifts for the living, and liberation from purgatory for the dead. This is what they are after when they argue that grace is conferred and the Holy Spirit given in ordination.

Second, to these external signs and rites, about which there is neither a command nor a promise of God, they tie the grace of God in such a way that they imagine that anyone to whom not all the rites of papalist ordination have been applied cannot have the grace necessary for the ministry, is not able to forgive sins, nor to consecrate the sacrament of the body and blood of Christ, but that whoever has been ordained with these rites, even if he never exercises or intends to exercise the ministry of the Word and the sacraments, nevertheless on account of these rites has forever impressed upon him the grace of order and the Holy Spirit.

Third, they have in these same external rites of ordination departed far from the example of the apostles. We have spoken of the moderation of the apostles, that they were unwilling to use the symbol of breathing on the ordinand in ordination since they did not have a command of Christ, although Christ Himself had used it, and that they did not want to adopt this without a divine promise, as though they could with their breathing confer the Holy Spirit. But with the papalists the suffragan of the bishop arrogates this to himself without shame. For as he breathes upon the ordinand he says: "Receive the Holy Spirit." But where is the command? Where the promise? It is blasphemy to pretend that the Holy Spirit is enclosed in the foul exhalation of the suffragan, so that he is able to say as he breathes on the ordinand: "Receive the Holy Spirit." In the Fourth African Council the rites are described, how by outward delivery of certain insignia along with words of admonition they were at that time accustomed to commit the grades of the ecclesiastical ministry to those who were called. It was a useful discipline to bring their duty to the remembrance of those who were called. But to interpret this in such a way that when these words come to these rites it becomes, without a command and promise of God, such a sacrament as when in Baptism and the Lord's Supper the Word comes to the element and it becomes a sacrament, this surely amounts to a profanation of the name and actions of the New Testament sacraments, which are based on the command and promise of

God. In 2 Chron. 23:11 Joash is ordained king with a beautiful rite accompanied by prayers. In the universities, when degrees are conferred, external rites are employed together with some words. Will these therefore be sacraments?

6 It is the anointing, however, about which the papalists contend most of all when they argue about the sacrament of order. This they do not try to hide in Canon 5. However, it is crystal clear that neither Christ nor the apostles employed external anointing in the ordination of ministers of the Word and the sacraments. Dionysius says in his *Hierarchia* that the bishop indeed uses ointment for nearly every function of the priestly office, but makes no mention of ointment in ordination. He uses only the rite of laying on of hands, as is clear from ch. 5. Ambrose, *De dignitate sacerdotali,* ch. 5, does not mention unction—only the laying on of hands: "Man lays on hands; God bestows grace. The priest lays on his right hand in supplication, and God blesses with his powerful right hand."

Also in the time of Augustine, in the African Council, where the rites of ordination are described, no mention is made of unction, but only of the imposition of hands and of other rites. And in the whole history of the church, also in the *Tripartita,* where many examples of ordination are described, mention is never made of unction as being employed in ordination, but only the imposition of hands.

7 But they oppose to us Cyprian, who in a discourse on the chrism says that, when the other rites of the Old Testament were rejected, the honor of anointing remained for kings, for priests, and for all the people. Let the reader conclude from this how sincere the papalists are in the way they adduce the testimonies of the ancients! For they know that this discourse about the chrism is not by Cyprian, and yet they try to deceive the simple with an appeal to Cyprian, since they are without testimonies of the true antiquity. For what they bring forward from forged epistles of Roman pontiffs we leave to the authors of falsehoods. Although Cyprian himself speaks a number of times of ordination in his genuine writings, he does not mention unction as having been applied. Yes, Innocent, *De sacra unctione,* acknowledges that around A.D. 1200 the custom of anointing at the ordination of presbyters and the consecration of bishops was not yet found in the Greek church. Indeed, he adds that there were some ancients who said that the church Judaizes when it practices the sacrament of unction.

Concerning this unction in ordination, which is without testimonies of Scripture and of the true antiquity, the Tridentine canon brings as proof only the anathema: "If anyone says that the sacred anointing is not required in ordination, let him be anathema." Lombard says it was taken from the fact that we read that in the Old Testament unction was employed in the ordination of priests. Why do we not therefore restore the whole Levitical worship? Scripture certainly teaches clearly about the abrogation of the Levitical ceremonies. Therefore nothing about which there is no command of Christ or example and tradition of the apostles ought to be brought into the church of the New Testament from Levitical ceremonies.

8 It is worth the trouble to hear what Pighius answers to this objection that we do not read in the apostolic letters that anointing with chrism was employed in the ordination of ministers, but only the laying on of hands. He says this: "In the rude beginning of Christianity, when the hierarchy and ecclesiastical discipline had not yet been ordered and established, very many things were performed perfunctorily by the apostles from a certain direction of the Spirit, things which later received a prescribed and certain form." Of this unction a forgery attributed to Anacletus says that those who are ordained should be anointed because the invisible power of the Spirit is mixed into the sacred chrism. What other things they ascribe to this unction the consecration, or rather the enchantment, of the chrism shows. Therefore it is rightly said that this unction is not only to be despised but that it is also harmful. Nor is it sufficient that they set against us only the rumbling of the anathema without any proof, as the Tridentine canon does.

SECTION IV

[Concerning the Ecclesiastical Hierarchy and Ordination]

Chapter IV

Since, in the sacrament of order, just as in baptism and confirmation, a character is imprinted which can be neither obliterated nor taken away, the holy synod deservedly condemns the opinion of those who assert that priests of the New Testament have only a temporary power and that those who have once been rightly ordained can again become laymen if they do not exercise the ministry of the Word of God. But if anyone asserts that all Christians without distinction are priests of the New Testament or that all are mutually endowed with equal spiritual power, it is clear that he does nothing but throw into disorder the ecclesiastical hierarchy (which is set in order as a battle line before a camp), as though contrary to the teaching of blessed Paul all were apostles, all prophets, all evangelists, all pastors, all teachers. Accordingly the most holy synod declares that, beside the other ecclesiastical ranks, the bishops, who succeeded to the place of the apostles, belong chiefly to this hierarchical order and that they are placed there, as the same apostle says, by the Holy Spirit to rule the Church of God, that they are superior to priests, and confer the sacrament of confirmation, ordain ministers of the church, and that they are able to perform very many other functions which the rest, who are of an inferior order, have no power to perform. The most holy synod further teaches that in the ordination of bishops, priests, and the other orders the consent, call, or authority either of the people or of any secular power and magistrate is not required in such a way that without it the ordination is invalid; rather, it decrees that those who, called and appointed only by the people or by a secular power and magistrate, ascend to the exercise of these ministries and those who have taken them to themselves by their own rashness are all to be considered not ministers of the church but thieves and robbers who have not entered by the door. These, in general, are the things which it seemed good to the sacred synod to teach the faithful of Christ about the sacrament of order.

CANON VI

If anyone says that there is not in the Catholic Church a hierarchy, instituted by divine ordination, which consists of bishops, presbyters,[10] and ministers [or deacons], let him be anathema.

---

[10] The Greek word *presbyteros* (*presbyter* in Latin) first meant "elder" and later "priest." We have translated it "presbyter."

CANON VII

If anyone says that bishops are not superior to presbyters, or that they do not have the power of confirming and ordaining, or that the power they have is common to them together with the presbyters, or that orders conferred by them without the consent or call of the people or of the secular power are invalid, or that those who have neither been validly ordained nor sent by ecclesiastical and canonical power, but have come from elsewhere, are lawful ministers of the Word and the sacraments, let him be anathema.

CANON VIII

If anyone says that bishops who are obtained by authority of the Roman pontiff are not legitimate and true bishops but a human creation, let him be anathema.

Examination

1 I shall record nothing here about the things treated in the first part of this chapter—about the character which is said to be imprinted in the sacrament of order and about the priesthood which all Christians have in common. For of the character imprinted in the sacraments we have spoken in connection with the ninth canon under "Concerning the Sacraments in General" [pp. 92-97]. That not any and every Christian should rashly, without a lawful call, take the ministry of the Word and the sacraments to himself, even though all are spiritual priests, we have explained in connection with the 10th canon under "Concerning the Sacraments in General" [pp. 98-100] and in the first section of this topic [pp. 677-678]. There remain, therefore, two questions: about bishops, and about what is a legitimate call. About these questions certain things must be said.

2 Now in order that what is judged here about bishops may be more rightly understood, certain things from Scripture and from testimonies of the true antiquity must first be repeated. The terms *episkopos* [bishop] and *episkopee* [office of bishop] are found used of the ecclesiastical ministry in the apostolic writings (Acts 1:20; 20:28; Phil. 1:1; Titus 1:7; 1 Tim. 3:1-2; 1 Peter 5:2). These terms were, however, taken from the use of everyday language and were adapted to the ministry of the church because it has the duty of administration and inspection. Suidas[11] says that in the Athenian republic those were called *episkopoi*, and "guards," who were sent to territories which were subject to them, not in order that they might preside with naked power, as Lindanus interprets, but to look into the affairs of each, that is, as Budaeus translates it from Livy, to look into the affairs of their allies. Plutarch says, on Pericles: "Phidias was *episkopos*, that is, inspector of all works." In Homer's *Iliad*, 9 and 24, Hector

---

[11] Byzantine lexicographer c. A.D. 1000.

is called *episkopos* of the city. With Demosthenes, in verses of Solon, Pallas is called *episkopos* of Athens. In Plutarch, on Numa, he is called *episkopos* of the vestal virgins. In the same place Venus is *episkopos* over the dead. Cicero, *Ad Atticum*, Bk. 7: "Pompey wants me to be the one whom the whole Campagna and the people of the maritime districts have as *episkopos*, to whom all the recruiting and the revenue is committed." In *Pandectis*,[12] *episkopoi* are people placed over things offered for sale.

3 The apostles accommodated these words more willingly to the ecclesiastical ministry because they were at that time generally known from the Greek version of the Old Testament. For the words *paqad*, *pequdah*, and *pequdim*, which mean visitation, inspection, office, care, administration committed to someone, a duty demanded—these the Greeks translated *episkopein*, *episkopee*, and *episkopos*. In Num. 31:14 the officers of the army are called *episkopoi*; in Judges 9:28[13] Abimelech had Zebul as his *episkopos*. 2 Kings 11:15 speaks of the captains who are *episkopoi* over all the army. There also guards were placed over the house of the Lord [2 Kings 11:7]. This is explained thus by the Greeks: He placed *episkopos* over the house of the Lord. In 2 Chron. 39:12 the inspectors of works are called *episkopoi*. Num. 4:16: The office or duty of Eleazar in the tabernacle of God is called *episkopee*. Thus in Ps. 109:8 the office of Judas is called *episkopee*. I have noted down these examples which I had observed, in order that consideration might be given to the source from which the apostles took this term, the peculiar emphasis of which can also be gathered and understood from these passages. Jerome translated it *superattendens* (superintendent), Ambrose *superinspector* (overseer).

4 The question, however, is what rank in the ecclesiastical ministry the office of bishop is and what the duties of a bishop are. We can complete the explanation of this question more briefly because it has been treated *ex professo* by Jerome. He shows and proves that at the time of the apostles, bishops and presbyters were one and the same, or that one and the same person was both presbyter and bishop, one of these being a term for his office and dignity, the other for his age. For Paul says (Phil. 1:1) that in that one church there were bishops and deacons. In Acts 20:17 Luke says that the presbyters of the church at Ephesus were called out. When Paul has assembled them, he calls them bishops ["overseers," KJV and RSV; Acts 20:28]. In Titus 1:5 ff. Paul speaks of appointing presbyters in every town. And as he explains what kind of pres-

---

12 An early kind of encyclopedia.
13 The text erroneously has Judith 9.

byter ought to be ordained, he says: "For a bishop must be blameless." In 1 Peter 5:1-2 Peter, addressing the presbyters calls himself a fellow presbyter and ascribes to the office of presbyters *to episkopein* ["oversight," KJV]. That the same ordination was common to [bishops and] presbyters Jerome shows from 1 Tim. 4:14, which speaks of the laying on of hands of the presbyters.

This opinion did not fall from the lips of Jerome accidentally while he was concerned about something else, but he argues it *ex professo* and repeats it in a number of places, e.g., on the Epistle to Titus, in his Letter to Evagrius, likewise to Oceanus. Ambrose follows this opinion, likewise Bede in the chapter on Philippians, likewise Isidore, dist. 21, ch. *Cleros*. The same Jerome also explains what was the cause and origin of the difference which was later made between a bishop and the presbyters, why and for what use this difference was accepted by the church. Thus he says, on Titus 1: "Before, by an impulse of the devil, a zeal in religion developed and it was said among the people, 'I belong to Paul; I to Apollos; I to Cephas,' the churches were governed by the common counsel of the presbyters. But after everyone thought that those whom he had baptized were his, not Christ's, it was decreed that in the whole city one who was elected from among the presbyters should be placed over the rest, to whom the care of the whole church should belong, and the seeds of schisms would be removed." Likewise: "With the ancients, presbyters and bishops were one and the same. But little by little, in order that the seedbeds of dissensions might be rooted out, the whole responsibility was conferred on one." The same says in the Letter to Evagrius (and this is quoted in dist. 93, ch. *Legimus*): "However, that later on one was elected who was placed over the rest, this was done as a remedy against schisms, lest everyone draw the church of Christ to himself and split it. For also at Alexandria, from the time of Mark the Evangelist until Dionysius, the presbyters always chose one from among themselves and placed him in a higher rank. Him they called *episcopus,* just as if the army would make a commander-in-chief for itself," etc.

Moreover, a little before the time of Jerome, Aerius began to urge this equality of presbyters and bishops, which existed at the time of the apostles, in such a way that he simply condemned the custom of the church which made the bishop superior to and placed him over the presbyters and gave him the supervision of the whole church as a remedy against dissensions and for the sake of order and harmony. However, when this opinion of Aerius was seen to give occasion for confusion and dissensions, it was rejected and disapproved. Then the bishops grew arrogant, despised the presbyters, and thought this prerogative was due them by divine right.

Because these controversies were still raging in his time, Jerome, as he himself declares, interposes his opinion from Scripture and shows that at the time of the apostles and with the ancients there was no distinction, but that presbyters and bishops were one and the same and that the churches were governed by their common counsel. Then he explains for what reason, for what purpose and use one bishop was placed over the others as head, namely, to remove the seedbeds of dissensions and schisms. To this extent Jerome approves this arrangement. But the pride of the bishops he curbs with these words: "Therefore as the presbyters know that, from the custom of the church, they are subject to the one who has been placed over them, so the bishops should know that they are greater than the presbyters more by custom than by the truth of an arrangement of the Lord, and that they ought to govern the church in common." Of the office of bishops Jerome says to Evagrius that the bishop does the same thing a presbyter does. Therefore the ministry of the Word and the sacraments and the care of ecclesiastical discipline were at that time the joint duty of the bishop and the presbyters. So far were bishops removed from shrinking back from the ministry of the presbyters that Jerome complains, *Ad Rusticum Narbonensem,* dist. 93, ch. *Diaconi:* "The bishop alone uses the ministry; he alone claims everything for himself; he alone invades areas belonging to others."

At that time ordination was specifically the duty of the bishops, as Jerome says: "What does a bishop do that a presbyter does not do, ordination excepted?" And Chrysostom says, on 1 Timothy, that a bishop is greater than a presbyter only in that he performs ordinations. Afterward more special duties began to be assigned to the bishops, as Leo lists them in dist. 98: the ordination of clerics, the arrangement, blessing and anointing of an altar, the consecration of a church, the reconciliation of heretics and penitents through the laying on of hands, preparing the chrism, marking the forehead with chrism, sending out prepared epistles, etc. As they gradually relaxed the ministry of the Word and the sacraments, the bishops began to devote themselves entirely to these actions. Finally, after they had cast off the ministry of the Word and the sacraments, also these small duties were relegated to the subsidiary bishops, and the episcopal offices were turned into overlordships.

Such are now the bishops who are created by the Roman pontiff, of whom it is rightly said that they are not true and lawful bishops but a human invention, because they have entirely cast off from themselves the episcopal office as it was at the time of the apostles, at the time of Jerome, and even at the time of Leo, and have become chiefs of peoples, who rule because, while Christ said to the apostles, "It shall not be so among you" [Matt. 20:26], perhaps He said to the successors of the apostles, "It shall be so among you." And although these things ought to have been re-formed at the council, the Tridentine canon only declares: "If anyone says that bishops who are obtained by authority of the Roman pontiff are not legitimate and true bishops but a human creation, let him be anathema." And so the order of bishops has been duly reformed!

5 Now that these things have been explained, it will be clear what the Council of Trent establishes about bishops. For when they reckon the bishops over and above the other ecclesiastical ranks, they appear to want to terminate the controversy which is going on between the scholastics and the canonists about the ecclesiastical orders or ranks, where the latter forge a special order for the bishops while the former count the bishops as belonging to the order of presbyters. If, when they say that the bishops are superior to the presbyters, they were speaking of true bishops and would understand this as Jerome explains it, it could be tolerated. But the sixth canon asserts that the hierarchy, which consists of bishops, presbyters, and ministers [or deacons], was instituted by a divine decree. And they pronounce the anathema on anyone who holds otherwise. But we have already reported what Jerome, whom the other ancients follow, states about this question from Scripture. Therefore the Council of Trent pronounces the anathema on them.

6 This is truly a strange artifice, that when they need to speak about the power of the bishops, they make no mention whatever of the ministry of the Word and the sacraments, but, after mentioning the anointing with chrism, and ordination, they add by means of a general conclusion that the bishops are able also to do many other things, namely maintain horses and dogs, if not also harlots, exercise royal dominion, and similar episcopal duties. They pronounce the anathema if anyone holds that the power to ordain is held by the bishops in common with the presbyters, although Jerome, *Ad Evagrium*, proves this from Paul, who says in 1 Tim. 4:14 that Timothy was ordained through the laying on of the hands of the presbytery. So great is the Tridentine outpouring of anathemas!

7 The final question of this chapter is: What is a legitimate call of ministers of the Word and the sacraments? With this supplement they try openly, not so much to beat our churches but to cut their throat once and for all and to overthrow them utterly. With this supplement they wanted to strengthen the cries of those who contend that there is no true and lawful ministry of the Word and the sacraments in our churches, that God does not work through our ministry, that there is no true absolution or forgiveness of sins in our ministry, that our churches are not able to have a true sacrament of the body and blood of Christ, but that all who discharge the ministry of the Word and the sacraments in our churches are thieves and robbers who have not come in through the true door. Surely, a fearful threat! But they add no other reason for this than that the ministers of our churches have not been called, sent, ordained, shaven, and anointed by papalist bishops.

8 Now, because the ministry of the Word and the sacraments is the ordinary means or instrument which God employs in matters pertaining to the dispensation of salvation, it is absolutely necessary to show to the church sure and firm arguments from Scripture in this question, namely, what is a true, lawful, orderly, and therefore divine call of ministers of the Word and the sacraments. Therefore we shall briefly draw them together as called for by our purpose.

9 To begin with, it is certain that no one is a legitimate minister of the Word and the sacraments—nor is able rightly and profitably to exercise the ministry for the glory of God and the edification of the church—unless he has been sent, that is, unless he has a legitimate call (Jer. 23:21; Rom. 10:15). The nature of this call is not, however, the same as when political or domestic offices are established either by the head of a family or by those who have the highest power in the state, that those who take onto themselves the rule in the church also do it in the same way and are able to order the ministries of the church according to their own will and by their own authority. But God, the author, preserver, governor, and (if I may use this term) husbandman of the ecclesiastical ministry, has reserved for Himself the right and authority of calling and sending those whom He wants to receive as co-workers in this ministry, and wants it to belong to Himself as Lord of the harvest. Therefore Christ says in Matt. 9:38: "Pray the Lord of the harvest to send out laborers into His harvest." Jer. 23:21: "I did not send the prophets, yet they ran." Eph. 4:11: Christ gives apostles, evangelists, pastors, teachers. Acts 20:28: "The Holy Ghost has made you overseers to feed the church of God." Acts 13:4: "They were sent out by the Holy Spirit." Therefore it is necessary for a legitimate call to the ministry of the church that the person who is to be a legitimate minister of the Word and the sacraments be called and sent by God, so that both the minister and the church can truthfully declare, as it is written in Is. 59:21: "I have put My words in your mouth." 2 Cor. 5:19-20: "He has entrusted to us the message of reconciliation. So we are ambassadors for Christ, God making His appeal through us." Luke 10:16: "He who hears you hears Me." John 20:21: "As the Father has sent Me, even so I send you."

10 These things must be considered in a call of the church, in order that both the minister and also the church can state with certainty that God is present with this ministry and works through it, as He says in Matt.

28:20: "I am with you." John 20:22: "Receive the Holy Spirit." 2 Cor. 3:6: "He has qualified us to be ministers . . . not of the letter but of the Spirit." 1 Cor. 3:5-9: "You are God's field, God's building." "We are God's assistants." "Paul plants; Apollos waters; God gives the growth." John 20:23: "If you forgive the sins of any, they are forgiven; if you retain the sins of any, they are retained." Matt. 16:19: "I will give you the keys of the kingdom of heaven, and whatever you loose on earth shall be loosed in heaven, and whatever you bind on earth shall be bound in heaven." Therefore Paul says in Rom. 10:14 ff. that those who are not sent by God cannot preach in such a way that faith is received from that preaching—faith which calls upon the name of God, so that we are justified and saved. These things are certain from Scripture.

11 Now when God Himself speaks immediately to men and with His own voice makes known His will, as He often did in the Old Testament, and as later, in the time of the New Testament, He spoke through a Son (Heb. 1:2), then there is no doubt about the efficacy of the Word. However, God did not always want to set His Word before the church without means, with His own voice, but determined by sure counsel to use the voice of the ministry as His ordinary means or instrument. Nevertheless there remains also in this medium what is appropriate to the prophets: "Thus says the Lord: . . . because I have put My words in your mouth . . . [Is. 59:21]. " . . . God making His appeal through us" [2 Cor. 5:20]. "Do you seek proof that Christ is speaking in me?" (2 Cor. 13:3). That these things are right and proper in those who are called immediately by the divine voice, not through men but by God Himself, as were the prophets in the Old Testament and the Baptist and the apostles—this no sane person is able to doubt.

But God called few men in this immediate manner. For those who at the time of the apostles were prophets, evangelists, pastors, teachers, bishops, presbyters, and deacons were called to the ministry not immediately but by the voice of the church. Now are the things which Scripture teaches about the presence and efficacy of God through the ministry doubtful, uncertain, or false in the case of a mediate call? Surely, this is a very great and comforting promise, that Scripture declares that also that call which is issued by the voice of the church is divine, or from God. Eph. 4:11: The Son of God gives pastors and teachers, who certainly were not, like the apostles, called immediately. And in Acts 20:28 Paul addresses the presbyters, who had been appointed either by Paul or by Timothy, thus: "The Holy Spirit has made you overseers." Therefore Paul, in the signature of 1 Corinthians, links Sosthenes to himself; in 2 Corinthians, Timothy; in 1 Thessalonians, Sylvanus. Therefore Paul applies the sayings: "We are God's fellow workers" [1 Cor. 3:9]; "He has entrusted to us the message of reconciliation . . . God making His appeal through us" [2 Cor. 5:19-20], also to those who had been called mediately. Likewise, he declares that God works efficaciously also through the ministry of those who were called through the voice of the church: "Apollos waters; God gives the growth" [1 Cor. 3:6]. And in 1 Tim. 4:16 he says to Timothy: "You will save both yourself and your hearers." Eph. 4:11 ff.: He gives teachers for building up the body of Christ, that we may attain to unity of faith, and doing the truth may grow in Christ. The promises are most delightful, and very necessary, namely, that the call also of those who have been called by the voice of the church is divine, that God is present with and works effectively through their ministry. Therefore Paul says that there is in Timothy a grace and a gift through the laying on of hands. He does not say only, "of my hands" [2 Tim. 1:6], but adds, "when the . . . elders laid their hands upon you" (1 Tim. 4:14), lest it be thought that it makes a difference whether a person is ordained by apostles or by presbyters.

12 However, in order that this mediated call may enjoy these privileges, it is necessary that it be legitimate, i.e., that it be made in the manner and by the persons prescribed by Scripture. With respect to the kind of persons who should be called to the ministry a certain rule has been prescribed (Acts 6:3; Titus 1:6-9; 1 Tim. 3:2-13). But the question here is by whose voice and vote this election and call ought to be made in order that it may be possible to declare that it is divine, that is, that it is God Himself who through these means chooses, calls, and sends laborers into His harvest.

Of this there are sure and clear examples in Scripture. In Acts 1:15-26, when another person had to be substituted in place of Judas, Peter laid the matter not before the apostles alone, but also before the rest of the disciples, for that is how the believers were at that time called, their number, gathered together, being about 120. There Peter set forth from Scripture what sort of person it should be and how they ought to choose him, to which they added their prayers. Lots were cast because the call was not to be simply mediated, but apostolic. For this reason lots were not used in calls thereafter.

In Acts 6:2-6, when deacons are to be chosen and called, the apostles are not willing to arrogate the right of calling to themselves alone, but they call the church together. They do not, however, wholly renounce oversight over the calling and commit it to the pleasure of the common people or of the blind and confused crowd, but they are as it were steersmen and directors of the election and calling, for they set forth the principle and rule as to the sort of persons they should be and how they should be chosen. The men are placed before the apostles in order that the election might be examined, to see whether in their judgment it has been rightly made. They prayed, and approved the election by the laying on of hands.

In Acts 14:23 Paul and Barnabas appoint elders in all churches to which they had preached the Gospel. However, they did not take the right and authority of choosing and calling to themselves alone. Luke uses the word *cheirotoneesantes,* which in 2 Cor. 8:19 is used of an election which is made by the voice or votes of the church, for it is taken from the Greek custom of voting with uplifted hands, and signifies to create or designate someone by vote or to show agreement. Therefore Paul and Barnabas did not force presbyters on unwilling people, without the consent of the church. And in Acts 15:22, when men had to be elected who were to be sent to the church at Antioch with commands, Luke says: "It seemed good to the apostles and the elders, with the whole church, to choose . . . Barnabas and Silas."

It is useful to observe in the apostolic history that sometimes both the ministers and the rest of the congregation jointly proposed and chose those whom they considered suitable (e.g., Acts 1:23). At other times the church proposed and chose; however, the election was submitted to the judgment of the apostles for their approval (Acts 6:3-6). Thus Paul sends to the churches Timothy, Titus, Sylvanus, etc. In Acts 14:23 presbyters were proposed, whom the church accepted by raising of hands. Meanwhile some also offered their services to the church, 1 Tim. 3:1: "If any one aspires to the office of bishop, he desires a noble task." Always, however, in a legitimate call at the time of the apostles the consent of the church and the judgment and approval of the presbytery was present and required.

Thus Titus was put in charge of guiding and moderating the election of presbyters on Crete, in order that it might be done rightly and that he might by means of ordination approve it and confirm the rightly performed election. For in Titus 1:5, in speaking of appointing elders, Paul uses the same word which is found in Acts 14:23, where likewise both *cheirotonia* and the appointing of elders are mentioned. And he instructs Titus that he should rebuke sharply those who are not sound in doctrine nor teach what they should, that is, as he says more clearly in 1 Tim. 5:12: "Do not be hasty in the laying on of hands, nor partake in another man's sins," namely, by approving an election or call which was not rightly done.

13 These examples from the apostolic history show clearly that election or calling certainly belongs in some way to the whole church, so that in their choosing and calling both presbyters and people are partners. This apostolic manner of choosing and calling was retained and practiced in the church also later on. Dist. 24, Canon 3, of a Council of Carthage says: "No cleric shall be ordained unless he has been tested either by examination of the bishops or by testimony of the people." Leo says, Dist. 62: "No reason allows that any should be accounted as bishops who have neither been elected by the clergy nor desired by the people nor consecrated by the provincial bishop in accord with the judgment of the metropolitan." Dist. 67: "The other priests shall be ordained by their own bishop in such a way that the citizens and the other priests may give their assent." Dist. 24, from the Fourth Council of Carthage: "The bishop shall not ordain clerics without the counsel of his clerics, in order that he may seek the agreement and testimony of the citizens." Dist. 23, from the same council, ch. *Qui episcopus:* "When the person examined shall have been found fully instructed in all these things, then he shall with the total consent of clergy and laity, and with the agreement of the bishops of the whole province, and most of all either by order or in the presence of the metropolitan, be ordained a bishop."

VIII.[14] Quest. 1 is quoted as from Jerome, but it is from Origen, ch. *Licet:* "Therefore in the ordination of a priest the presence of the people is also required, in order that all may know and be certain that he who is the most outstanding among all the people is chosen for the priesthood, and that in the presence of the people, lest there remain later on a reconsideration or some doubt in anyone's mind." Dist. 65, ch. *Plebs:* "It is necessary that you bishops should frequently call together the presbyters, deacons, and the whole multitude in order that they may, not according to everyone's whim but with one mind, with your admonition, seek out such a person whom no opposition can keep back from the written decisions." Likewise: "You are not to consecrate bishops through Emilion except after election or consent of clergy and people." Ch. *Metropolitano:* "After the will of all the clerics and citizens has been discussed, let the best one be ordained." Ch. *Si in plebibus:* "The archdeacon together with the clerics and people of his community shall do the choosing." Ch. *Sacrorum canonum:* "The emperors Charles and Louis decree that bishops are to be chosen through an election by the clergy and the people, according to the statutes of the canons."

Jerome, *Ad Rusticum monachum:* "So live in the monastery that you may deserve to be a priest. When you shall have arrived at a mature age,

---

[14] We are uncertain as to what this refers to.

and either the people or the bishop elect you to the priesthood, then perform the duties of a priest." Ambrose, Bk. 10, Letter No. 82: "He has deservedly become a great man whom the whole church has chosen, and it is rightly believed that he whom all the people requested has been elected according to the judgment of God."

14 Later on, when emperors and kings had embraced the Christian religion, their will, judgment, and authority also began to be brought to bear and to be requested in the matter of electing and calling, because they ought to be nurses of the church and according to the examples of Jehoshaphat, Hezekiah, and Josiah the oversight was committed to them in order that the ministries of the church might be rightly set up and administered. There are many canons about this matter, dist. 63. According to Sozomen, Bk. 7, ch. 7, the emperor gives the first place at the synod to Gregory of Nazianzus, and all the bishops support him. A very beautiful example of modesty is described in ch. *Valentinianus,* where the synod asks that the emperor, as a wise and pious man, should choose or propose someone. The emperor, however, answers: "The election is up to you. For you, possessing divine grace, and shining with such splendor, are better able to choose." Afterward he gave his assent to the election.

15 The fact that certain examples of the ancient church seem to deviate somewhat from this format is due to the following cause. This glorious harmony of bishops, clergy, the Christian magistrate, and the people in choosing and calling ministers of the church was very often disturbed. Clerics who were either heretics or schismatics, or were corrupted by other ignoble passions, often abused the right of election or arrogated it to themselves alone. In that case both the magistrates and the Christian people were compelled to interpose themselves. Thus, when after the death of Aelurus the clergy on their own authority had elected Peter Mongo as bishop, Emperor Zeno was so angry that he even caused some to be punished, Evagrius, Bk. 3, ch. 11. When at Antioch, in the absence of the people, Porphyry had been ordained as bishop by a few bishops, a frightful tumult followed, Nicephorus, Bk. 13, ch. 30. Courtiers also repeatedly abused this, as though in their own right. In that case the clergy opposed them. A number of statutes of this kind are found in dist. 63. The most discreet regulation of all is that of Charles and Louis, which reads thus: "Mindful of the sacred canons, in order that the holy church may more freely possess her honor in the name of God, we proffer our assent to the ecclesiastical arrangement that bishops shall, according to the rules of the canons, be chosen by election of clergy and people."

16 Also the people very often abused their right in a way that led to tumults, dissensions, and all kinds of disorder. There bishops and Christian governments stepped in, as in the election of Ambrose. As a result a Laodicean canon says: "It must not be permitted to bring about by tumult[15] the election of those who are to be advanced to the priesthood." According to Sozomen, Bk. 7, ch. 8, when the votes of the bishops and those of the people were against each other, the emperor chose Nectarius, and this election was afterward held valid by a synod. But the people or the Christian magistrates were not for this reason simply excluded from choosing and calling, but this moderation was added, dist. 62: "The people must be taught, not followed. We also ought to inform them, if they do not know what is lawful or what is not lawful, not give them our consent." A decree of Leo says: "Let the desires of the citizens, the testimonies of the people, the will of those who are respected, and the choice of the clerics be determined in the ordination of priests." Likewise: "Let those who are to become priests be asked for peaceably and quietly; the election must have the subscription of the clerics, the testimony of those who are respected, the consent of the order and of the people." Likewise: "Let the consent and desire of the clergy and of the people be sought." And in ch. *Nosse:* "When clergy and people have been summoned, let such a one be chosen whom the sacred canons do not make ineligible. For it is in fact an election of priests, and the consent of the faithful people must be added, because the people must be taught, not followed." In the *Historia tripartita* the common people were able to choose and to offer someone with their petition.

Being a bishop, Cyprian, Bk. 3, Letters, and Bk. 4, proposes Saturus, Optatus, and Celerinus to the church. Valerius, desiring Augustine as his assistant and successor, proposes this to the people. And Augustine himself, Letter No. 110, in a lovely plea informs the people that he desires Eradius as his successor, "Because I know," says he, "that the churches are usually troubled after the death of bishops by ambitious and contentious men, and I ought, as far as I am able, to take forethought for this city, that this may not happen." This choice of Augustine is confirmed by the people, and this is made known to the Emperors Theodosius and Valentinian. Augustine also relates the example of Severus of Mileve, who had thought it sufficient to point out his successor to the clergy and had therefore not spoken before the people. As a result a disturbance arose afterward. Augustine says about this: "However, somewhat too little had been done."

---

[15] The Latin word is *turbis,* which may also be translated "crowds" or "mobs." Nigrinus so understands it, and translates: *Es ist dem gemeinen Volk nicht zuzulassen,* etc.

Cyprian describes the manner of election in use at his time thus, Bk. 1, Letter No. 4: "Therefore the people, in obedience to the Lord's commands and in the fear of God, ought to separate themselves from a sinner who is placed over them, nor to attend the sacrifices of a sacrilegious priest, since they especially have the power either to choose worthy priests or to refuse unworthy ones. For we see that also this comes down to us by divine authority, that a priest should be selected in the presence of the people, before the eyes of all, and be approved as worthy and fit by public judgment and testimony." And a little later: "God commands that a priest should be appointed before the whole assembly, i.e., He teaches and shows that it should not be done except with the knowledge of the people who assist, so that either the misdeeds of the wicked may be revealed or the merits of the good made known in the presence of the people; and let that be a just and lawful ordination which has been examined by the vote and judgment of all, and let this be observed in action afterward according to the divine instructions." In the same place: "We sometimes see unworthy persons ordained, not according to the will of God but by human presumption. That whatever does not proceed from a legitimate and just ordination is displeasing to God, God Himself shows through the prophet Hosea, when he says: 'They made kings, but not through Me' (Hos. 8:4). Therefore the divine teaching and the apostolic custom must be diligently preserved and adhered to, which is held also among us and throughout nearly all the provinces, that for rightly conducted ordinations the five closest bishops of that province come together to the people for whom an overseer is to be ordained, and a bishop be chosen in the presence of the people who know the life of the individual candidates well and have insight into the actions and way of life of each," etc. The same says, Bk. 1, Letter No. 3, that the vote of the people and the consensus of fellow bishops is a divine judgment.

17 However, because it was not convenient for the whole multitude of the people always to be called together, and to ascertain the vote of every individual, the custom was observed among Christians, as Lampridius reports in a biography of Alexander, that the names of those who had been proposed for choosing and calling were openly published before the ordination, and the people were admonished that if anyone had anything against a man who was to be ordained, he should bring it up and set it forth. And in short, according to the statement of Gregory, it was always judged a grave abuse if anyone was given to such as were unwilling and did not ask for him.

18 This is the opinion of the primitive apostolic and ancient church about the lawful election of ministers of the Word and the sacraments,

which opinion is followed in the churches which have now been ordered according to the Word of God, where there is a presbytery which embraces the faithful Word as taught, a godly government, and people who know the doctrine and love godliness. But where there were at the time of the apostles idol priests, wicked rulers, people who walked in darkness, there at first the ministry could not be established through such an election, but there the apostles either went themselves or sent others who had been rightly elected elsewhere, that they should first lay the foundations. Thus (Acts 13:2-3) Paul and Barnabas are sent to the Gentiles. And thus (Acts 11:19) the Gospel was spread all the way to Phoenicia and Cyprus, and indeed thus it was first proclaimed to the Gentiles at Antioch. Thus Paul had many around him whom he sent here and there to the churches. But where the churches had been in a measure grounded, the ministries in the churches were soon ordered in the manner we have described (Acts 14:23). And although there the magistrates and priests continued in idolatry, the calling which was done by pure teachers together with faithful people was nevertheless lawful. Thus when the chief priests and priests had in part given up, in part devoted themselves to groves and high places, etc., and the people walked in darkness, Jehoshaphat himself set up ministries. (2 Chron. 17 and 19)

19 I undertook this report in order to show that our churches have restored the true and lawful manner of choosing and calling, which was in use in the apostolic, primitive, and ancient church, and that from the contrast it might be seen more clearly what kind the ordination that of the papalist church is.

From the things we have said until now, the examination of the Tridentine decree concerning the lawful calling and sending of ministers of the Word and the sacraments will be easy. For the fourth chapter and the seventh canon declare that those are lawful ministers of the Word and the sacraments who have been called, ordained, and sent by the papalist bishops and their subordinates alone, and that neither the consent nor the call and authority of the faithful people or of a pious government are required. Yes, they pronounce the anathema on anyone who says that for a legitimate call the consent of the faithful people or of a pious government is required. But we have already clearly shown that the manner of a lawful election or call which the men of Trent condemn with the anathema is the manner of the apostolic, primitive, and ancient church. But we must remember that the concern which was laid on the Tridentine fathers by the Roman pontiff was not that they should restore the custom of the apostolic and ancient church but that they should preserve and strengthen the present state of the papalist kingdom in any way they could. What therefore they have until now practiced they want to have permitted to them with impunity hereafter, namely, that they be able to place over the churches any and all men who have been rendered suitable by partiality, request, or bribery, without a petition, consent, or vocation either of the faithful people or of a pious government, and to foist unknown men on the people. The assistants to the bishops do not even see fit to ask questions about the call so long as a person provides them an allowance and offers them money for the ordination. And the good fathers are not ashamed to establish with no more than a word things which clearly and diametrically are opposed to Scripture and to the true antiquity, and at once to append the anathema.

20 In our churches, however, the ministers of the Word and the sacraments are not only called and placed into office by the people and the secular government, as the Tridentine chapter imagines, but there comes to these the very weighty judgment, examination, and approval of the true presbytery. That this is a legitimate call we have already abundantly shown.

21 But why, they ask, do you not seek ordination from our bishops? I answer: if they were true bishops, and professed sound doctrine, they would rightly claim this for themselves. But now they are enemies and persecutors of the true doctrine. Does a shepherd ask that the care of a flock should be entrusted to him by a wolf? And they are not willing to ordain anyone who adheres to sound doctrine unless he first rejects and abjures it. Neither do they admit to ordination those who have been legitimately called according to the apostolic manner, lest damage arise from this for their kingdom. Nor do they ordain their priests to the ministry of the Word and the sacraments, but to the impious sacrifice of the Mass. They also ensnare those whom they ordain in ungodly obligations, and apply their blasphemous chrism. Therefore we have the most weighty and just causes why we do not ask ordination from the enemies of the sound doctrine.

22 But they say: "Those who have not been called, ordained, and sent by the usual ecclesiastical authority are thieves and robbers." That will make thieves and robbers of the apostles, evangelists, pastors, teachers, presbyters, and deacons of the apostolic church, who were not ordained by the chief priests, who at that time had the regular ecclesiastical power. That is the same question with which the chief priests once attacked the ministry of the Baptist (John 1:19-25) and of Christ Himself, (Matt. 21:23): "Who gave You this authority?"

Tenth Topic

CONCERNING MATRIMONY

Session VIII Under Pius IV
[24th Session of the Council of Trent]
1563

[SECTION I]

[Whether Matrimony Is a Sacrament]

The first father of the human race under an impulse of the Spirit of God pronounced matrimony a perpetual and indissoluble bond when he said: "This at last is bone of my bones and flesh of my flesh. . . . Therefore a man leaves his father and his mother . . . and they become one flesh." However, that by this bond two only are united and joined together Christ our Lord taught more openly when, referring to these last words as having been spoken by God, He says: "Therefore they are now no longer two but one flesh," and at once confirmed the endurance of this bond which had been proclaimed by Adam so long before with these words: "What therefore God has joined together, let no man put asunder."

Christ Himself, the Institutor and Perfecter of the venerable sacraments, by His suffering merited for us the grace which can perfect that natural love, confirm the indissoluble oneness, and sanctify the spouses. This the apostle Paul intimates when he says: "Husbands, love your wives, as Christ loved the Church and gave Himself up for her," and presently he adds: "This is a great sacrament.[1] However, I speak in Christ and in the Church."

Since therefore in the evangelical law matrimony excels the ancient marriages in grace through Christ, our holy fathers, the councils, and the tradition of the universal Church have at all times taught that it is deservedly to be reckoned among the sacraments of the New Law. Raving against this, ungodly men of this age not only have thought wrongly about this venerable sacrament but after their manner, under pretext of the Gospel introducing fleshly license, have in writing and orally asserted many things that are alien to the understanding of the Catholic Church and to the custom approved from the times of the apostles, and that not without great loss to faithful Christians. Wishing to oppose the rashness of these men, the holy and ecumenical synod thought fit, lest their destructive contagion draw more to itself, that the more outstanding heresies and errors of the aforementioned schismatics should be exterminated by decreeing anathemas against these heretics and their errors.

CANON I

If anyone says that matrimony is not truly and properly one of the seven sacraments of the evangelical law instituted by Christ the Lord, but that it has been brought into the Church by men and that it does not confer grace, let him be anathema.

---

[1] In Eph. 5:32 the Vulgate translates *mysteerion* with *sacramentum*.

Examination

1 The chief question in this decree is whether matrimony is a sacrament of the New Testament. Now the simplest and most correct way to explain a matter is to speak first of the thing itself. For after that it will be easy to agree about the name. But it is strange that the papalists want to appear to honor the conjugal estate more than we, on account of the appellation "sacrament," which they contend should be given to matrimony just as to Baptism and the Lord's Supper, although their complaints and accusations are public over the fact that matrimony is extolled with too great praise by men on our side. They on their part do not hesitate to apply these statements to wedlock: "Those who are in the flesh cannot please God." Therefore they imagine that the Holy Spirit cannot bear an honorable marriage in ministers of the Word and sacraments, namely, because it is written: "You shall be holy, because I am holy." Likewise: "Cleanse yourselves, you who carry the vessels of the Lord." And yet they argue valiantly that matrimony is one of the seven sacraments. Such protectors of its dignity has matrimony been allotted who would rather, as a man at Cologne says, grant their priests 100 prostitutes, although successively, than one lawful spouse!

2 Because they allege that they number matrimony among the sacraments of the church for the purpose of asserting and illustrating its dignity and sanctity, I will briefly recite the chief points concerning its dignity and sanctity which our churches both learn and teach from the Word of God.

[1.] Wedlock existed also among the Gentiles, just as there is true marriage also today among unbelievers, but they think it is only a civil arrangement, although the law of nature, demonstrating that promiscuous copulation, lewdness, and adultery are against nature, shows, although very obscurely, that it is something greater than a human invention. The church, however, learns and understands from the Word of God that God Himself is the Author of wedlock, because He instituted it in paradise before the fall, when human nature was still without sin and troubles, whole and happy. He repeated this institution and its blessing immediately after the fall, and again after the flood, and established it also for fallen nature (Gen. 4:1, 25-26; 9:7). Moreover, in the New Testament the Son of God does not abrogate or change this first institution, but repeats and confirms it, not in words only (Matt. 19:5-6) but also by His presence and first miracle at a wedding, as told in John 2:1-11. The apostles explained this teaching in many statements and discourses.

3 2. God not only instituted matrimony in order that men might of their own accord join themselves in this conjugal union, but even as God was the first bridesman, who brought Eve to Adam, and Himself joined the first spouses together (Gen. 2:22), so Christ affirms that today also it is God who joins spouses together in lawful matrimony and unites them when they come together according to His Word. He says: "What God has joined together, let no man put asunder." He uses a word which is properly spoken about the joining of spouses. Thus in Tobit 7 Raguel, in giving his daughter to Tobias, says: "May the God of Abraham, Isaac, and Jacob join you together and fulfill His blessing in you." And in Gen. 24:7, when Abraham sent his servant that he might fetch a wife for Isaac, he says most charmingly: "The Lord of heaven and earth, who spoke to me, etc., will send His angel before you, and you shall take a wife for my son from there." Later the servant prays: "Lord God of my master Abraham, come, I pray, to meet me today; be merciful, and show whom Thou hast appointed for Thy servant Isaac," etc.

These things must be set forth in the church in order that marriages may be contracted in the fear of God, with faith and prayer to Him, because God is not only the author but also the promoter of matrimony. Thus Prov. 19:14 says: "House and wealth are inherited from fathers, but a prudent wife is from the Lord." And Sirach 26:3: "A good wife is a good fortune; she falls to the lot of those who fear the Lord." V. 14: "A good wife is a gift of God," etc. Eccl. 7:26: "I have found a woman more bitter than death . . . he who pleases God shall escape her, but the sinner is taken by her." In Mal. 2:13 ff. He admonishes spouses most earnestly on this basis about the duty they owe: "I will not receive any peace offering at your hands. Why does He not? Because the Lord was witness to the covenant between you and your wife, your companion, and the wife of your covenant." Now 'ud[2] means to confirm and establish something by witnessing to it. Therefore not any and every union is lawful and pleasing to God, but one which does not militate against the Word of God. Thus in Lev. 18:6 ff.; Gen. 6:2 ff.; Ezra 10:2 ff.; Neh. 13:23 ff.; Luke 17:26-27; and Mark 6:17-18 conjugal unions which are not lawful are disapproved.

4 3. Because of this divine joining together, marriage is not like other civil associations, which, just as they are entered into by mutual consent, are also dissolved by mutual consent; but it is an indivisible connection and an indissoluble union. For what God has joined together man must not put asunder. Indeed, Scripture asserts that it is a much closer union than that of parents and children, for it says: "A man will leave his father and mother, and cleave to his wife, so that those who are

2 Ed. Preuss has corrected this.

two become one flesh." The word *dabaq* signifies an adhering or joining which comes about through an embrace with the most ardent emotion of love, as is said in Gen. 34:3 of Sichem's love for Dinah, in 1 Kings 11:2 of the love of Solomon, in Ps. 63:8: "My soul clings to Thee." This word is properly used of the union of the skin, flesh, and bones. Job 19:20: "My bones cleave to my skin and to my flesh." Job 29:10: "Their tongue cleaved to the roof of their mouth." Ps. 102:5: "My bones cleave to my flesh." From this meaning of the word it is possible to understand what God asserts such cleaving to be, namely, that the two become one flesh. And Paul says: "No one hates his own flesh" [Eph. 5:29]. The Lord says (Jer. 13:11): "As the waistcloth clings to the loins of a man, so I shall make the whole house of Israel . . . cling to Me." But God did not form the woman from Adam's girdle but from his side, in order that the closest possible union might be indicated. Solomon says (Prov. 16)[3] that a friend often "sticks closer than a brother." But in wedlock there is a closer connection than that of parents and children. For "a man shall leave father and mother," etc. The Septuagint renders this word with *proskollasthai* (to fasten on to), which is used when two things are joined together by glue in such a way that they are, as it were, one thing. So it is used in Is. 41:7. Therefore Paul teaches that neither spouse has power over his own body (1 Cor. 7:4). Likewise: "He who loves his wife loves himself." [Eph. 5:28]

5 4. Scripture also explains for what causes God instituted this conjugal union. For while He founded the angel hosts all at one and the same time, He willed according to His sure counsel that the preservation and multiplication of the human race should take place through propagation by generation, that in it we might perceive His presence, wisdom, and goodness. He willed also that the first nursery of the church should be in the pious rearing of children, wherefore churches are in Paul called households. He willed that the exercise of faith, prayer, love, patience, and all godliness should in their beginnings be practiced in the family circle, and be from there propagated more widely. "For if a man does not know how to manage his own household, how can he care for God's church?" (1 Tim. 3:5). Likewise: "If any one does not provide for his . . . own family . . . he is worse than an unbeliever." [1 Tim. 5:8]

By the institution of wedlock God shows that He is a pure Spirit and that He hates roving passions. Therefore He gave and prescribed certain laws about wedlock for those who do not have the gift of continence. Then God Himself, in the most beautiful words, sets forth another reason

---

[3] The reference is to Prov. 18:24.

for the institútion of wedlock (Gen. 2:18): "It is not good that the man should be alone; let us make for him a helper who shall be, as it were, before him and around him." All the animals had indeed been created for the service of man; but there was not found a helper who might be before him. Therefore God instituted wedlock for mutual indulgence and help, in order that all things might be shared, whether joyous or sad.

Eph. 4:[4] "Two are better than one, because they have a good reward for their toil . . . . Woe to him who is alone when he falls and has not another to lift him up." Eccl. 9:9: "Enjoy life with the wife whom you love all the days of your vain life . . . because that is your portion in life and in your toil which you toil under the sun." Sirach 26:13: "The grace of a wife delights her husband, and her knowledge fattens his bones." Gen. 3:16: The desire of the wife is for her husband. Eph. 5:33: The husband loves and cherishes his wife, and the wife respects her husband.

Finally, God also willed that wedlock should be used in our fallen state as a remedy against incontinence. 1 Cor. 7:2 ff.: "Because of the temptation to immorality each man should have his own wife and each woman her own husband." Likewise: "Lest Satan tempt you through lack of self-control." . . . "If they cannot exercise self-control, they should marry. For it is better to marry than to be aflame with passion." This is what the ancients mean when they say that matrimony was instituted before the fall to be a service to man; that it was given after the fall as a remedy. Augustine says: "What is for a service to those who are well is for a remedy to those who are sick."

6 5. This also is certain, and known from Scripture, that in a chaste and godly marriage God is present with His blessing and with various gifts of grace, as Paul speaks of grace in Rom. 12:6 ff. For whom God joins together, them He blesses (Gen. 1.28). For the blessing was not promised to marriage only when nature was whole, but it was repeated and confirmed also to fallen nature (Gen. 9:1 ff.) This blessing embraces first fruitfulness and generating, according to the word: "Be fruitful and multiply," and secondly the happy state of wife and children. Ps. 128:3-6: "Your wife will be like a fruitful vine . . . your children like olive shoots. . . . Lo, thus shall the man be blessed who fears the Lord. . . . May you see your children's children." Also Ps. 127:3-5: "Lo, sons are a heritage from the Lord. . . . Happy is the man who has fulfilled his desire[5] by means of them! He shall not be put to shame when he speaks with his enemies in the

---

[4] A misprint for Eccles. 4:9-10. So corrected by Nigrinus.

[5] Chemnitz is following the Vulgate which follows the text of the Septuagint, which has the word for "desire." Modern English versions follow the Hebrew and translate: "Happy is the man who has his quiver full of them."

gate." Thirdly, the blessing includes success in home and community. Ps. 128:2-6: "You shall eat the fruit of the labor of your hands; you shall be happy, and it shall be well with you. . . . Lo, thus shall the man be blessed who fears the Lord. . . . May you see the prosperity of Jerusalem all the days of your life. . . . Peace be upon Israel." Ps. 127:5: "He shall not be put to shame when he speaks with his enemies at the gate." This is what the first blessing (Gen. 1:28) means: "Subdue the earth, and have dominion . . . over every thing that moves upon the earth." In the fourth place, admixed with this blessing on account of the fall there is some difficulty and pain of the cross (Gen. 3:16-19), even as in remedies, such as wedlock has become after the fall, certain troublesome and painful things are generally mixed in. But for those who fear God this pain is mitigated by patience, comfort, aid, and divine liberation, even as the presence of Christ at the wedding (John 2:1-11) shows both the cross and the comfort.

Marriage has besides, from its divine institution, also this privilege, or this grace, that it is a holy kind of life and pleasing to God. And although copulation outside of marriage is abominable in the sight of God (for the Lord will judge whoremongers and adulterers), in wedlock intercourse is honorable among all, and the marriage bed undefiled (Heb. 13:4). "If you marry, you do not sin, and if a girl marries, she does not sin" (1 Cor. 7:28). Rather, in a marriage of the godly this is called sanctification and honor (1 Thess. 4:4). Thus in 1 Tim. 2:15 sanctification and chastity are ascribed to women who bear children. And in Titus 2:4-5 women who love their children are called chaste. In 1 Peter 3:5 women who are submissive to their husbands are pronounced holy and hoping in God. In 1 Cor. 7:13-14 cohabitation of a believing woman with an unbelieving husband is pronounced holy, and there [Paul] says that begetting of children, which would under other circumstances be something unclean, is holy in wedlock, especially in the case of believers. In 1 Tim. 2:15 he asserts that a woman will be saved through bearing children, if she continues in faith.

This also is a grace of God in marriage, that God joins the minds of spouses so that they both will and are able to cultivate this indivisible partnership of life, to preserve conjugal faithfulness, and to remain in this indissoluble union, so that the loving embrace between spouses becomes closer and more fervent than between parents and children, according to the saying: "He will leave father and mother, and will cleave to his wife so that they are, as it were, one flesh. . . . What therefore God has joined together, let no man put asunder." [Matt. 19:5-6; Mark 10:7-9]

God also bestows this grace on spouses who fear God and walk in His ways, that the man loves, cares for, cherishes, and gives honor to his wife as to the weaker vessel (Eph. 5:25 ff.; 1 Cor. 3),[6] that the desire of the wife is for her husband (Gen. 3:16), that she is respectfully subject to her husband (Eph. 5:21 ff.), is a helper to her husband (Gen. 2:18), and gladdens the heart of her husband (Sirach 26:2, 13; Prov. 31:28-29). In short, there is need for the guidance of the Spirit of God for a godly marriage, in order that both may perform their proper duties, bear one another's infirmities, sustain one another in their common difficulties, train their children in a godly manner, govern the household, perform domestic tasks, patiently bear the cross, and that their dwelling together may be with consideration (1 Peter 3:7) and in the Lord (1 Cor. 7:39). For these things godly spouses pray God, and there is no doubt that God abundantly bestows this grace on those who ask for it.

7 Finally, marriage is a most beautiful picture of Christ and His church, as Paul explains this in Eph. 5:21 ff.: "Husbands, love your wives, as Christ loved the church." "Wives, be subject to your husbands . . . as the church is subject to Christ." The fact that Eve was formed out of the side of the sleeping Adam in order that she might be bone of his bones, flesh of his flesh—this the ancients interpret beautifully as signifying and foretelling that it would come to pass that the Son of God would leave His Father, descend from heaven, assume our nature, become flesh of our flesh, taking on the form of a servant, that He should be made in the likeness of men, in order that by His life He might condemn sin in the flesh; and again, that from sleep, that is from the suffering and death of Christ, the church might be born, when the sacraments flowed from His side, by which she is begotten, built up, and united with Christ by faith in such a way that we are members of His body and of His bones.

The fact that Adam says: "This is now bone of my bones. . . . For this reason a man will leave his father and mother, and will cleave to his wife, and the two will become one flesh"—this Paul declares to be a great mystery in Christ and in the church. Therefore there is set before us in wedlock a most beautiful image of redemption. And what could possibly be a more pleasing picture of how holy and pleasing to God are the obligations of spouses than when Paul declares that a husband's love for his wife is like Christ loving, redeeming, and sanctifying the church, and that a wife who is subject to her husband imitates and expresses an example of the church being subject to Christ?

8 This glorious teaching about the dignity and sanctity of marriage is diligently set forth and inculcated in our churches from the Word of God.

---

[6] The reference should be 1 Peter 3:7.

This teaching I wanted to repeat briefly here, lest anyone should suppose that we think less honorably of wedlock or that we want anything taken away from its dignity when we contend that it is not truly and properly a sacrament of the New Testament as are Baptism and the Lord's Supper. If therefore the argument revolved only about this point, that the name "sacrament" should be applied to matrimony for this reason only, that it might be a reminder of this whole teaching about the dignity of matrimony, about which we have spoken until now, and that, against all doctrines of demons, the name "sacrament" might place wedlock on a high pedestal and remind us that in the church we must think and speak more clearly and reverently about wedlock than is done among the Gentiles, to whom the teaching of the Word of God was unknown, and in order that it might admonish those who are married of their duty and show the comfort under the cross—if this were all, I say, that is sought and discussed by the papalists in this dispute, it would be easy to agree on the term. The term "sacrament" is not found in Scripture and may be used in a wide range of meanings, as we have shown in the proper place [pp. 23-40]. Therefore the Apology of the Wittenberg Confession says: Because matrimony is a holy way of life, divinely instituted and commanded, we gladly call it a sacrament. But in this way many more things than seven will have to be counted as sacraments. For also other godly ways of life have a commandment and promise from God.[7] For also in those ways of life the godly walk differently from the Gentiles. Who would want for this reason to contend that farming, livestock breeding, etc., should also be numbered among the sacraments of the church?

Nor indeed was matrimony first instituted in the New Testament; rather, Christ expressly takes His teaching about matrimony back to that first institution: "Have you not read," says He, "that He who made them from the beginning," etc [Matt. 19:4-8]. And in connection with the question of polygamy and of Jewish divorces Christ did not institute anything new, but restored the doctrine to its first institution. "From the beginning," says He, "it was not so" as it was later done in polygamous marriages and rash divorces. It is certain also that that grace of matrimony of which we have said Scripture speaks was not[8] wanting in the godly marriages of the ancients. Neither is there any doubt that in the church marriage always was the mystery of the union of Christ with His church, also at the time of the Old Testament. For the Lord says (Hos.

---

[7] Seemingly a summary of statements in the Apology of the Augsburg Confession, XIII, 14-15.

[8] The Latin omits the word *non*, which the context requires. Nigrinus supplies it, and translates; *Dass die Gnad nit gemangelt hab.*

2:19-20): "I will betroth you to Me for ever . . . in righteousness and in justice, in steadfast love and in mercy . . . in faithfulness." And Solomon specifically wrote a nuptial song about this marriage referring to Christ and the church. For Paul declares (Eph. 5:31-32) that what Adam says about his marriage in the beginning of the creation (Gen. 2:23-24) is that great mystery referring to Christ and the church.

9 Therefore it is without foundation to say that matrimony is a special sacrament of the New Testament. For everything which is considered to belong to the nature of a sacrament is present in the marriages of the godly also in the Old Testament. For the things that were practiced by some in polygamy and in divorces Christ declares to have been done contrary to the original institution, for He says: "In the beginning it was not so." Neither were all the saints in the Old Testament living in polygamy. And yet Augustine, *De bono conjugali,* ch. 18, seeks the mystery of Christ and the church even in the polygamy of the ancients. Therefore no matter how the term "sacrament" is used generally, so that whatever signifies something sacred and has a command and promise from God is called a sacrament, this much is certain and clear, that matrimony is not truly and properly a sacrament in the same way as are Baptism and the Lord's Supper. This distinction is altogether necessary in the church, lest the sacraments which were divinely instituted to be means or instruments for applying and sealing the promise of forgiveness and eternal life be confused with other rites.

For Baptism and the Lord's Supper have connected with them a promise of the application and sealing of gratuitous reconciliation and remission of sins to everyone who uses the sacraments in faith. Such a promise wedlock certainly does not have. Neither is there need that one who desires that the sacrament apply and seal the gratuitous reconciliation with God to him should take a wife. Also, many who are not reconciled to God do take wives. In short, marriage is not an instrument instituted by God in order that the gratuitous reconciliation with God might be applied and sealed through it. This distinction is clear and must of necessity be retained.

10 The very definition of a sacrament, which calls for an external, material, and visible symbol, cannot fit matrimony. For the scholastics can hardly, with all their contriving, figure out what they want to designate as the material in the sacrament of matrimony. Richard says that the word which is first spoken (as: I take you as my wife) is the material and the word spoken next (as: I take you as my husband) is the form, or conversely, that the word of the man is sometimes the material, at other times the form. What could possibly be said more ineptly when men argue about the material of the sacraments? The canonists argue that the consent is the material, and that the words which express the consent are the form. Some want that as in penance the acts of the penitent are the material, so also the acts of those who make use of marriage should be the material, and the consent should be the form. But what monstrous opinions arise from the fact that, on account of the preconceived opinion that marriage is a sacrament, they try to apply the definition of a sacrament to matrimony!

Gropper has noticed this; therefore he argues that the form of the sacrament of matrimony is this word: "Whom God has joined together," etc., and that the visible element are the outward gestures and acts by which the spouses are joined together in the name of the Lord and by which, during the marriage ceremony, they promise that they will in future be one flesh. This is less absurd than the arguments of either the scholastics or the canonists. But in order that something should be a sacrament it is not sufficient that some external gestures and actions be present and employed. For such external signs are employed also when kings are crowned, when princes receive fiefs, in schools when degrees are conferred, yes, also when cobblers receive someone into their guild. Shall all of these now be made into special sacraments? Now for something to be a sacrament it is required that a material element or external symbol have been instituted, prescribed, and commanded by God and that a promise have been attached to its use. This Gropper will not be able to show with respect to the external rites in the marriage ceremony.

Although that is how matters stand, the Synod of Trent boldly asserts even to the point of pronouncing the anathema, that matrimony is truly and properly one of the seven sacraments of the evangelical law. But what either the material or the form of this sacrament may be it does not mention with even one word, although they did this in the case of the other sacraments. Therefore they are either uncertain with respect to the material and form of this sacrament, or they wanted to leave everyone free to devise whatever material or form he would, so long as he believes that matrimony is a sacrament of the new law. Let the reader consider this stratagem well!

11 But the Tridentine chapter says that Paul numbers matrimony among the sacraments of the church. For Paul says: "This is a great sacrament . . . in Christ and in the church" (Eph. 5:32 [Vulgate]). I would have thought that it had been enough that the scholastics, on account of their ignorance of the languages, had erred in this passage in Paul. But, as I see, the Tridentine fathers are ashamed of nothing which helps to preserve the state of the papalist kingdom. Therefore, because the ancient translator in this place has the word "sacrament," and the words "in the church" follow, they at once conclude that matrimony is a sacrament of the church or of the New Testament. But Paul has the word *mysteerion*, which the translator often retained as *mysterium* but sometimes rendered *sacramentum*. Now *mysteerion* signifies either the spiritual and hidden thing itself, or the outward sign which signifies something hidden. Shall we now count as many sacraments as things to which the term "mystery" is applied in Scripture? The decree of redemption is called a mystery (Eph. 2),[9] the calling of the Gentiles (Eph. 3:9), the resurrection of the dead (1 Cor. 15:51), the conversion of the Jews (Rom. 11:25), the mystery of the seven stars and lampstands (Rev. 1:20), yes, the mystery of lawlessness that sits in the temple of God (2 Thess. 2:7), yes, the mystery [translated *sacramentum* in the Vulgate] of the Babylonian harlot. (Rev. 18)[10]

Therefore Paul is saying nothing else than that the conjugal union which Adam describes in words is a great mystery, not in itself but because it signifies and bears the image of the hidden union of Christ and the church; that which Adam says about the conjugal union is this great mystery: "I say in Christ and in the church" [Eph. 5:32 Vulgate]. For here two statements are being placed side by side for comparison, both what Adam said about the conjugal union and what Paul says about the hidden union of Christ and the church.

Thus Augustine says, *In Evangelium Johannis tractatus*, 9: "Lest someone understand this greatness of the sacrament to refer to any and all men who have wives, he says: 'I say in Christ and in the church.' What is this great sacrament? Two shall be one flesh. Therefore Christ cleaves to the church in such a way as two would be in one flesh."

Now if matrimony must be numbered among the sacraments of the church for this reason that it is a mystery, then all the works which the Holy Spirit sets before us and uses as some kind of similitude and image of Christ must be placed in the number of the sacraments.

How frequently Scripture uses the image of shepherd and sheep, and how comforting is its application to Christ and the church! Shall livestock breeding, as a holy and blameless way of life, therefore be a sacrament of the New Testament like Baptism and the Lord's Supper? The kingdom of David was an image of the spiritual kingdom of Christ, but it is not for this reason numbered among the sacraments. Neither is anything and everything which contains either a mystery or a mystical meaning at once a

---

[9] The reference should be Eph. 1:9.
[10] The reference should be Rev. 17:7.

sacrament of the New Testament as are Baptism and the Lord's Supper.

This contention that matrimony is a sacrament of the New Testament like Baptism and the Lord's Supper was wholly unknown to the ancient church. When Augustine was about to defend matrimony against the calumnies of Jerome, he argued that there are three benefits of wedlock—offspring, faithfulness, and *sacramentum*. However, he understands by *sacramentum* the mystical denoting of the union of Christ and the church. And on account of this *sacramentum* he says that in the New Testament polygamy is not permitted, but that lawful marriage is the indissoluble union of one man and one woman. Thus he says, *De fide et operibus*, ch. 7: "In the church not only the bond but also the *sacramentum* of wedlock is commended in such a way that it is not lawful for a woman to give her husband to another woman." He also says, *De bono conjugali*, ch. 18: "In the marriages of our women the sanctity of the sacrament counts for more than the fruitfulness of the womb." And how modestly he speaks when he says: "What in Christ and in the church is a great *sacramentum*, that is in all men and their wives a very small *sacramentum*, but it is nevertheless the *sacramentum* of an inseparable union." In this way and in this sense Augustine declares that also the polygamy of the ancients was a *sacramentum*, *De bono conjugali*, ch. 18: "Just as the *sacramentum* of the polygamous marriages of that time signified that in future a multitude among all nations on earth would be subject to God, so the *sacramentum* of the monogamous marriages of our time signifies that the unity of all our people will be subject to God in one heavenly community." Therefore Augustine has a far different understanding when he speaks of the sacrament of matrimony than when the papalists argue that matrimony is truly and properly one of the seven sacraments of the New Testament as are Baptism and the Lord's Supper. Therefore the papalists are selling smoke when they prove their contentions about the sacrament of marriage from Augustine, just because he called matrimony a *sacramentum*. Indeed, it is an even greater piece of shamelessness on the part of the Tridentine chapter that it imagines that all the fathers have always taught thus, although it cannot easily be shown that the generic term *sacramentum* was ascribed to matrimony before the age of Augustine.

Among the scholastics Durandus argues that matrimony is not a sacrament in the same sense as other sacraments of the new law, and he concludes that strictly and properly speaking it is not a sacrament.

12 Of the same kind is what the Tridentine chapter says, namely, that the councils always taught thus. Which councils, we ask? Was it the apostolic or the Nicene or that of Ephesus? etc. Certainly, they cannot name any of the more ancient councils. But they trot out the Councils of

Constance and of Florence. Vincent of Lerins[11] teaches that that is catholic which has been observed always, everywhere, and by all. But, as I see, for the Tridentine fathers a thing is catholic if it has been a rule for no more than 100 years.

What do you suppose is the reason why the papalists argue so strongly that matrimony is to be numbered among the sacraments of the new law? Are they so friendly to matrimony? Are they so greatly inclined to honor its worth? By no means! They forbid wedlock to their holy men, and that for this reason, that they may be able to be pure. For they are not afraid to interpret of wedlock what Paul says: "Those who are in the flesh cannot please God" (Rom. 8:8). Do they then make a sacrament of matrimony without cause? No, they have many causes, namely, that matrimonial matters may be made subject only to ecclesiastical judges in order that they may be able to impose their prohibitions and their implementation as snares on the consciences of men; that they may sell dispensations all the more dearly; that it may not be permitted to the innocent party after a divorce again to contract a marriage permitted by divine right; that they may be able to teach that a blessing is not to be given a second marriage, because it lacks the sacrament, that is, because second marriages are really a kind of fornication and prostitution. For so the decree says, 31, quest 1, ch. *Hac ratione* and *Quomodo*. These are the true causes which among the papalists make matrimony a sacrament.

---

[11] A Gallic theologian, died c. A.D. 450.

[SECTION II]
[Concerning Polygamy]

If anyone says that Christians are permitted to have a number of wives at one and the same time, and that this is not forbidden by any divine law, let him be anathema.

Examination

Whatever the case may be with respect to the dispensation and permission or the toleration by God of the polygamy of the ancients, so much is certain, that wedlock from its first institution was the union of one husband and one wife. For Christ did not lay down some new law, but recalls to the first institution the matrimonial cases among the Jews which had departed from the earliest rule. He says: "From the beginning of the creation it was not so." And He learnedly shows from that first institution that marriage is a divine union between two, namely, one husband and one wife. For God did not in the beginning create one male and a number of females, but one husband and one wife. Between these two He instituted marriage. Neither did He say: "He will cleave to his wives," for there was at the time only one woman, but "to his wife," namely, to the wife brought and joined to him by God. It is worthy of note that although in Gen. 2:24 it only says: "They shall be one flesh," Christ adds the explanation: "And the two shall be one flesh." He takes this explanation out of the circumstances of the text. There were at that time no more than two, namely, one man and one woman. What follows (Gen. 2:25): "However, those two were both naked," Christ also refers to the preceding statement: "And the two shall be one flesh." For the sake of greater emphasis He adds the article "the" two. And He repeats: "Therefore they are no longer two, but one flesh." Thus in what follows: "What God has joined together," the "what" refers to the "two," namely, one husband and one wife.

With respect to whatever was done differently by the ancients Christ answers: "From the beginning it was not so." Therefore Moses explains that Lamech, with his polygamy, was the first author of the departure from the rule of the first institution of marriage. That examples of polygamy are reported of some fathers in the Old Testament must be attributed to a dispensation of God, as Augustine argues in *De bono conjugali,* on account of the blessed Seed which was to be born of that nation, or to signify a future union of Jews and Gentiles in the church of Christ, or it may be ascribed to the toleration of God, for the fathers were not free from all faults, and God tolerates many things in His saints. Whichever of these possibilities is correct, Christ declares that examples ought not to prescribe to the divine institution. He also shows plainly that those things which God for a time tolerated in the Jewish state, although they differed from the original institution, are abrogated in the time of the New Testament, in order that matters of marriage may be brought back to the original institution. Thus also Paul says (1 Cor. 7:2, 4): "Each man should have his own wife and each woman her own husband. . . . The wife does not rule over her own body, but the husband does; likewise the husband does not rule over his own body, but the wife does."

Therefore Christians are not permitted to have a number of wives at one and the same time, and that not as though Christ had instituted a new and special sacrament of matrimony in the New Testament, but because God established it thus at the beginning of the creation, when He first instituted marriage. And Christ recalls and restores matrimonial matters in the New Testament to this rule of the original institution, thus abrogating the exceptions which Moses had permitted. Therefore the Anabaptists and all others who, contrary to the norm of this institution, taught by God in the beginning of the creation and afterward repeated and confirmed by Christ, attempt either to introduce or to defend polygamy in the New Testament are rightly condemned.

[SECTION III]

[Concerning Prohibited Degrees]

CANON III

If anyone says that only those degrees of consanguinity and affinity which are described in Leviticus are able to hinder matrimony from being contracted, and to dissolve it where it has been contracted, and that the Church cannot grant dispensation in the case of some of them, or decree that more degrees may hinder and dissolve it, let him be anathema.

Examination

1 The first part of this canon speaks about degrees which are divinely prohibited. For in order that matrimony may be a lawful or, rather, a divine union, God decreed a certain order of persons or degrees in which God wanted the union to be forbidden after the human race had multiplied. In the beginning only cohabitation with parents was forbidden, according to the word: "A man will leave father and mother and will cleave to his wife." For at that time brothers were married to their sisters of necessity and by divine dispensation. Augustine rightly says, *De civitate Dei,* Bk. 15, ch. 16: "By how much that is more ancient when necessity compelled, by so much is what is false later the more damnable when religion prohibits it, so that if it were not necessary that it be done, it would be criminal if it were done." That the prohibition of marriage between brothers and sisters is part of the law of nature Augustine proved from the fact that, now that the human race has multiplied, it is observed even among idolaters, and he adds: "Even though in some places brother and sister marriages are permitted by wrong laws, nevertheless the better custom prefers to abhor this freedom." And indeed, even before Moses certain other degrees beside father and mother were held to be unlawful on the basis of natural law. Thus when Abraham said that Sarah was his sister, and Isaac said the same of Rebecca, also the heathen thought that therefore she could not be his wife. Jacob curses Reuben because of intercourse with his stepmother. Judah does not want to have intercourse anymore with Tamar, his daughter-in-law. Therefore he judged that that intercourse was sinful.

732

2 Afterward, when the human race had multiplied, when the law of nature had been in part obscured, in part perverted, God Himself with His own voice made known and established what prohibitions should be observed by natural and divine law (Lev. 18 and 20; Deut. 27). Moreover, that the laws about prohibited degrees (Lev. 18) are not merely ceremonial laws which pertained only to the commonwealth of Israel and to that people, but that they are natural demands which pertain to all men and all times as immutable rules of righteousness in the divine mind and will, God Himself shows clearly in the promulgation of these laws. For He declares first that He punishes the nations which are outside the commonwealth of Israel on account of these incestuous unions; secondly, He says that such intercourse was an abomination in the sight of God also among the heathen before the Mosaic law was promulgated (Lev. 18 and 20). It seems that among the Corinthians, among other arguments about liberty to the effect that in the New Testament all things are permitted to Christians, because they are free from the Law, there was also this, that together with other Levitical laws also the law about the degrees prohibited in Leviticus has been abrogated. For under pretext of this liberty a certain man had married his stepmother. But when Paul says (1 Cor. 5:1) that such intermingling is not found even among pagans, he shows that these laws about prohibited degrees are not ceremonial but are commandments of the law of nature which pertain to all men and all times. The strongest argument that these laws in Leviticus belong to the law of nature is the fact that pagan legislators, to whom the divine law was unknown, list the prohibited degrees in almost the same way. Also John the Baptist, whose ministry signaled the end of the Law, confirms these prohibitions. For He says to Herod: "It is not lawful for you to have your brother's wife."

In order that men might understand that God is in earnest when He forbids marriages in these prohibited degrees, He adds threats of various punishments, such as: [1]"He shall be cut off from among the people." This is to be understood of the punishments inflicted by God, such as this: "The land vomited out its inhabitants" (Lev. 18:25), likewise: "They shall die childless" (Lev. 20:20-21). 2. They are commanded to be punished publicly before the people by stoning, burning, being struck down. 3. A bastard, i.e., one born of these forbidden marriages, shall not enter into the congregation until the 10th generation, Deut. 33,[12] that is, no marriages are to be made with them, no contracts entered into, they are not to be admitted to inheritances, public offices, etc. For that is how they

---

[12] The reference should be Deut. 23:2-3.

dealt with Ammonites and Moabites, who are mentioned together with those who committed incest, as is clear from Ezra and Nehemiah. From this one may gather what it means not to come into the congregation. Perhaps Paul had reference to this when he says (1 Cor. 7:14): "Otherwise your children would be unclean." 4. Cutting off includes not only outward, corporal punishments but also spiritual and eternal, as in circumcision. Therefore Paul excommunicates the incestuous person and delivers him to the devil (1 Cor. 5:5). In this way, therefore, we think and teach about the divine prohibitions. How the persons are listed in such a way in Leviticus that certain degrees of prohibitions can be learned and established from there is explained elsewhere.

3 What dispute is there, then, between the papalists and us about this question? I answer: It is this, that in the matter of these divine and natural prohibitions the papalist church takes to itself the right, authority, and power of dispensation, that is, that it is able, by its authority and power, to relax and dissolve divine prohibitions. Therefore the Tridentine canon pronounces the anathema if anyone says that the church cannot dispense in some of these degrees, which are divinely prohibited. The canonists argue that some such case could happen in an already contracted marriage where for conscience' sake one might have to consider a dispensation, but that in contracting a marriage no dispensation would be valid. But the Tridentine canon does not add this distinction, for they want license to do both with equal power.

4 The other question in this canon concerns human prohibitions which are added to the divine with respect to the closest degrees, with the intent that the divine prohibitions may be observed with the greater reverence. Since this intent is not dishonorable or wicked, it is therefore not simply to be disapproved and condemned. The origin of the human prohibitions seems to have been what Augustine describes in *De civitate Dei*, Bk. 15, ch. 16. He says: "We have experienced in the marriages of first cousins also in our times, on account of the closeness of the degrees nearest to the degree of brother, how rarely that was done by custom which was permitted by the laws because the divine law did not prohibit it and human law had not yet prohibited it. However, also the lawful deed was abhorrent on account of the closeness," etc. What was done with a first cousin almost seemed to be done with a sister. From this spontaneous refraining from marriage with first cousins there later followed for honorable reasons the prohibition. For Augustine says: "The ancient fathers loved to take wives from their own relationships. Yet who would doubt that in our times it is more honorable that also marriages of first cousins are prohibited, not only on account of the multiplication of affinities but

also because there is somehow something natural and laudable in human modesty, so that it deters sexual desire from any woman to whom modest honor is due on account of near relationship; we see that also conjugal modesty is ashamed of this."

5 Ambrose writes, Letter no. 66, that Theodosius prohibited marriages of first cousins. Yet it is worthy of note that that prohibition either was not universal or that it was soon afterward amended, as one gathers from the law of the emperors Arcadius and Honorius about marriages, where unions of first cousins are permitted, as also Justinian, *Instit. de nuptiis,* later concedes the same. Therefore the ancients did not consider the human prohibitions to be as fixed, sure, and immovable as those which are by divine and natural law. Ambrose tells, Bk. 8, Letter No. 66, that Paternus wanted to unite a granddaughter by his daughter to his son. Ambrose declares that this was not lawful, because that degree is prohibited by divine law.

At the Synod of Tours, about the year 560, the statements of Scripture and of earlier synods about prohibited degrees are recited. From this recitation one gathers that until that time very few human prohibitions had been added to the divine, such as, that no woman should marry the husband of her sister after that sister's death, or that no man should marry the sister of his wife after that wife's death, likewise, that no surviving brother should approach the couch of his deceased brother. At that time also the marriage of first cousins was prohibited, also that one would marry the widow of his paternal or maternal uncle, etc. These same things are clearly repeated at the Synod of Paris about the same time, except that there the prohibition is added about the paternal aunt of a stepdaughter and of the daughter of a stepdaughter.

6 What the prohibited degrees were in the state through 500 years after the birth of Christ is clear from Justinian. For his prohibitions extend to the grandson or granddaughter, whether from a brother or from a sister, that is, to the third degree in an indirect line, yet in such a way that in the second degree in a direct line marriage is permitted. However, the whole of the ecclesiastical prohibitions, as one may gather from the Council of Tours, at that time went no farther than to the second degree in a direct line and to the third degree in an indirect line, for that is how I understand the matter about first cousins. It certainly did not go beyond the third degree in a direct line.

7 The Roman pontiffs, however, extended these prohibitions much farther, some to the fourth, others to the fifth, still others to the sixth, and many to the seventh degree, as these things are told in the *Decrees, causa* 35. The Second Council of Toledo, ch. 5, declares that no one should desire to unite to himself in matrimony any blood relative so far as he knows the lines of affinity in his relationship in their order. The Canon of Worms, *causa* 35, says: "As long as the descent is known by recollection or retained in memory." Finally, after long, unbearable variations, at the Lateran Council, around A.D. 1200, the prohibitions were reduced down to and including the fourth degree.

8 I have recited these things so that it might be borne in mind that the human prohibitions which were added to the divine were not always and everywhere similar and equal, but that they varied according to place and time and that for edification these prohibitions were, on account of circumstances, either extended or restricted, often even abrogated. Moreover Christian emperors like Theodosius, Honorius, Arcadius, and Justinian judged that also this matter belonged to their responsibility, for they promulgated laws about these degrees.

9 With respect to such human prohibitions that are added to the divine, I judge that they should not be rashly or out of hand disapproved and condemned if they are made with honorable and godly intent, namely, that the divine prohibitions may be observed with greater reverence, provided that they are made with respect to the degrees nearest to those which are divinely prohibited, and by those to whom this responsibility belongs, according to the circumstances of place, time, and persons, without snares and enslaving of consciences.

10 Therefore the churches in every nation that have a godly government have this liberty or power which was found in the ancient church, that they establish, according to the circumstances of the peoples, places, and times, rules about these degrees which are not contrary to the Word of God and are useful for edification. For the ancient church did this time and time again.

11 Now the Roman pontiff alone arrogates to himself this universal power over all the churches, and indeed in such a way that, on account of the fullness of his power, he wants consciences bound no less by papal prohibitions than by the divine. Often the pontiff dissolves and separates marriages which God Himself has joined, since they do not militate against the divine prohibitions, although this bond is exceedingly strong: "What God has joined together, let not man put asunder."

There are weighty reasons for the papalist prohibition by which they seek to cast snares on consciences, namely, because there are four fluids in the human body, which correspond to the four elements.[13] Therefore

---

[13] Four elements, air, water, fire, and earth, were formerly believed to make up the physical universe. Chemnitz' point here is obscure.

those who are not willing to acknowledge the papalist tyranny of Antichrist against the church and pious consciences rightly demonstrate their liberty by examples, since in the Roman curia no prohibitions stand in the way, not even the divine, provided their queen, money, intercedes.

[SECTION IV]
[Concerning Impediments]

CANON IV

If anyone says that the Church could not establish impediments that dissolve marriage, or that it erred in establishing them, let him be anathema.

CANON VI

If anyone says that a marriage which has been contracted but not yet consummated is not dissolved through the solemn profession of religion on the part of one of the spouses, let him be anathema.

Examination

There is a long dispute about impediments which dissolve a marriage, either when it is being contracted or has already been contracted. It is not our purpose to explain this in its entirety. So far as the examination of this fourth canon is concerned, the arguments, which are sure and strong, can be shown in a few words. It is absolutely necessary that the decree of the Son of God remain firm, fixed, and immutable when He says: "What God has joined together, let not man put asunder." But in order that it should be such an indissoluble bond and inseparable union, it is necessary that it be a divine union, that is, that it not be in conflict with the teaching of the Word of God about the essence of marriage. For these two things hang together: Let not man separate what God has joined together! It is possible, therefore, that impediments occur which are of such a nature that they militate directly against the institution of marriage. In the case of such impediments man is not separating what God has joined together, but the church shows that such a union is not a legitimate or divine union because it is in conflict with the divinely taught norm of marriage—for instance, if there is an impediment in the degrees either of consanguinity or of affinity which God in His own Word strictly prohibited; if a person had another lawful wife beforehand; if the consent was not freely and expressly given; if the kind of error with respect to the person entered in which happened to Jacob with Leah; if a person's nature is simply not fit for marriage, etc. Such impediments have not been laid down by the church by its own private or particular authority but have

738

been pointed out by God Himself when He instituted marriage. Moreover, they do not separate a marriage that has been divinely joined, but show that it is not a lawful or divine union. About these things there is no controversy, because they have a basis in the Word of God.

Beside these there are other impediments, established by men, which do not[14] contradict the Word of God about matrimony, like the fiction about spiritual kinship. For that such a kinship dissolves a marriage either when it is to be contracted or has already been contracted is wholly unknown both to Scripture and to the true antiquity, for otherwise no marriage could exist among Christians, for we are all brothers and sisters. Scripture also knows nothing of this, that the vow of chastity dissolves an already contracted marriage. And men are rightly admonished that they should not contract marriage with such as are of a different and false religion. Nevertheless, difference in religion does not dissolve a marriage (1 Cor. 7:12-14). Therefore whatever impediments have been established by men, which do not contradict the divine union which exists in a marriage according to its institution, these are justly and deservedly censured. For in that case man separates what God has joined together, when impediments that dissolve a marriage are instituted by human authority even though they do not contradict the Word of God about the marriage union. For it is the same as if I were to say: Even though it is a lawful and divine union, men can nevertheless set down some impediments by which it is separated and dissolved. On the basis of this distinction between impediments, which is both true and clear, the things which are being argued at great length about impediments to marriage can be rightly explained, impediments which in this canon are all without distinction approved and confirmed.

---

[14] Nigrinus ignores the "not" and translates: *Welche straiten mit dem Wort Gottes.* Chemnitz' meaning is clear, however. He is opposed to letting manmade rules dissolve marriages which are not against the Word of God.

[SECTION V]
[Concerning Divorce]

If anyone says that the bond of marriage can be dissolved on account of heresy, or on account of irksome cohabitation, or on account of studied absence from one's spouse, let him be anathema.

Examination

1 The question about divorce has at all times been argued with great contention—not, however, at all times in the same manner. For it is a great and difficult thing to dissolve the bond of matrimony by repudiation, since it appears that the divine decree stands in the way: "What God has joined together, let not man put asunder." On the other hand, if second marriages are forbidden to those who have been separated, what Paul says in 1 Cor. 7 cries out against it, namely, that rules about matrimonial matters should be moderated in such a way that snares may not be laid on consciences and that one who does not have the gift of continence may not be exposed to the temptations of Satan and to burning desires, for it is better to marry than to be aflame with passion. Also, in order to avoid fornication each man should have his own wife. Because these regulations were considered in different ways, it came about that some leaned to this side, others to that. We, however, shall note down only what shall seem necessary for the explanation of these canons.

2 For the sake of explanation I shall make a distinction between genuine impediments, which dissolve a marriage which is either being contracted or has been contracted, and divorce. For we speak of impediments when a union which is not legitimate is dissolved, and in particular when the marriage has not yet been consummated.

Divorce, however, takes place in a marriage that was lawfully contracted, and especially when it has already been consummated. Thus Moses (Deut. 24:1), when he is about to describe divorce, says: "When a man takes a wife and marries her." But in Ezra 10 the separation from the foreign-born women is performed without a bill of divorce, because they had been married contrary to the divine command, although this difference is not observed everywhere by all. For some number among the causes for divorce also the prohibited degrees, which properly belong to the impediments to matrimony.

3 Therefore the first question is: For what causes is divorce lawful and permitted in the New Testament? Now there is no doubt that Moses allowed a number of reasons for divorce on account of the hardness of heart of the Jews. For he says (Deut. 24:1): "If then she finds no favor in his eyes because he had found some indecency in her." Mal. 2:16: "If you hate her, dismiss her."[15] Later on divorce among the Jews degenerated to such licence and frivolity that they dismissed their wives for any and every cause. Matthew says, "for any cause" (Matt. 19:3), that is, whatever it might be of which they could plausibly accuse their wives—they at once asked for a divorce. Now because such levity in repudiating their wives for any and all causes was displeasing to wise and earnest men, they proposed the question to Jesus whether divorce is possible for any and every cause. The question at the same time asks what are the true causes for a legitimate divorce. Christ accepts only one cause, namely fornication; concerning all other causes He says: Whoever, having dismissed one, marries another, and whoever marries one who has been dismissed, commits adultery.

4 Adultery, however, cannot be committed unless both or at least one of the persons is bound by the bond of matrimony. Therefore Christ declares that besides fornication there is no other cause which is able to bring about the kind of divorce by which the bond of matrimony is dissolved, so that the spouses can be truly and legitimately separated. He declares that in all other cases, fornication excepted, the divine decree remains: "What God has joined together, let not man put asunder."

I know that there have been those who argued that fornication is not to be understood as the sole cause in the statement of Christ, although it is the only one expressed in so many words, but that under this also other causes are comprehended, which are either equally weighty or even more weighty than fornication, for it is the custom of Scripture to set forth some one thing as an example, and to express it clearly, under which other things of the same kind are comprehended; thus under the example of helping the ass of an enemy to rise, all acts of love are comprehended by which one may avert some harm from his enemies. Thus the example about turning the other cheek embraces affronts of every kind, and the example of the ax-head springing from the handle embraces all cases of involuntary homicide.

---

[15] Chemnitz follows the text of the Vulgate and of the Septuagint, as does also Luther, who translates: *Wer ihr aber gram ist, der lasse sie fahren.* The RSV translates according to the Hebrew text: "For I hate divorce."

However, I judge that the statement of Christ does not admit of such an explanation, because the scope of the answer must be determined by the question it addresses. Now the question which was proposed is whether it is lawful to divorce a wife for any and every cause. In answering this question Christ does not say that it is lawful for any and every cause; also He does not say that it is lawful for no cause whatsoever. But when He wants to explain for what causes it is lawful and for what causes it is not, He lists only the cause of fornication; for other causes, whatever they may be, He declares that the bond of marriage is not dissolved, but that if intercourse takes place with another person adultery is committed. This opinion is safest for consciences, for it is clear and certain from the words of Christ.

Nevertheless the following, which is worthy of note, can be added to this, as the common saying is, that there is one law for the stranger, another for the citizen, and that the secular court is one thing, the forum of the conscience another. For Theodosius and Valentinian, Christian emperors, published a decree about divorces under very learned and watchful bishops, such as Ambrose, in which they allow more causes of divorce, such as cruelty, sorcery, plots against a spouse's life, etc. For political regulations must be so moderate that not only the good and the curable are governed according to the rule of a good conscience, but that also the wicked, the inflexible and stubborn, who are not willing to be ruled by just admonitions, may be held in check and coerced, lest they disturb the peace of the rest. And since it is not possible by means of political laws to guard against all things which do not fit the exact norm of justice, therefore, when two misfortunes threaten, in order that the lighter of the two may be chosen, limits are set up, as much as can be granted without disturbing the commonwealth and where the civil sword may repress the obstinancy of the wicked. Thus when God set up the commonwealth of Israel He Himself set forth the rule for the institution of wedlock. But because many, on account of the hardness of their heart, were not willing to be ruled by that norm, Moses, as a political lawgiver, made a political decree about the mode and limits of divorce, lest domestic tranquillity be totally disturbed and destroyed.

Nevertheless, the word of the teaching always says to consciences: "From the beginning it was not so." "What God has joined together, let not man put asunder." Similarly Ambrose, who instructed consciences concerning divorce according to the teaching of Christ, was not ignorant of this civil decree of his emperor, Theodosius, but he did not condemn it just because it had been published with this political purpose. Nevertheless, he did not teach that godly persons could and should do this before the forum of the conscience, as this can be beautifully seen from what he wrote on Luke 16:18: "Every one who divorces his wife and marries another commits adultery." "Hear," he says, "the law of the Lord, which also those who produce the laws obey." Likewise: "So you divorce your wife as though by right, without an offense on her part, and you think you are free to do this because man's law does not prohibit it; the divine law, however, does prohibit it."

5 Thus Christ does not approve each and every kind of cause for divorce. But neither does He allow no cause at all for divorce, but excepts the cause of fornication from all other, illegitimate, illicit, and insufficient, causes of divorce. Therefore a true and lawful divorce can be performed on account of adultery. Such a divorce does not militate against the divine decree: "What God has joined together, let not man put asunder." For there it is not man but God Himself who separates. For what the Word of God does must be judged as having been done by God Himself.

6 It is a different thing to speak of the case of desertion, of which Paul speaks in 1 Cor. 7:12-15: "If the unbelieving partner desires to separate, let it be so." For the question about divorce is set forth this way: For what causes may a man or a woman repudiate and cast off a wife or husband who was lawfully wedded? This question is rightly answered with the words of Christ, that it is only on account of adultery. Neither does Paul grant a believer an exception over and above the one granted by Christ, so that he may divorce an unbeliever on account of the disparity in religion, as the Anabaptists imagine, that one may at once divorce the other spouse if he is unwilling to embrace their sect. For Paul says expressly: "If the unbelieving spouse consents to live with him, he should not divorce her. . . . But if the unbelieving partner departs, let it be so; in such a case the brother or sister is not bound."

You hear Paul speaking distinctly. 1. He does not permit a believer either to seek or to procure a divorce on account of a difference in religion. For he says: The believer should not divorce the unbeliever. 2. If, however, the believer is unjustly deserted and cast off by the unbeliever—in this case of desertion, if the unbeliever cannot be induced to dwell with his spouse, and the believer does not have the power of continence, Paul says that the believer is not slavishly bound to the deserter, but is free. For slavery and freedom are opposites. And the expression of Paul "is not bound" can best be understood from what he writes in Rom. 7:2: "A married woman is bound . . . to her husband." Likewise: "She is free from the law concerning the husband, so that she is not an adulteress if she marries another man." Thus Ambrose interprets this statement, that it is no sin for one who is cast off on account of God, if he marries another, and that a woman who has been deserted is not accused if she is wedded to another. However, the unbeliever who departs is recognized as one who sins both against God and against marriage. And a little later: "If Ezra compelled unbelieving wives and husbands to be dismissed in order that God might be propitious and not angry if they married others of their own people (for they were not commanded to marry no others after these had been put away), how much more will a believing wife whose unbelieving spouse has forsaken her be free to marry a man of her own faith if she chooses." So says Ambrose. Phoetius writes thus: "If an unbeliever brings about a divorce, the believer is not subject to servitude so that he could not also be divorced." However, he interprets the word *choorizesthai* not simply as "depart" but "to separate himself" or "to procure a divorce," as the word is used in the statement: "Let not man put asunder."

7 Therefore we have two causes in Scripture by which the bond of matrimony is dissolved, so that spouses are separated, not only by men but by God Himself. 1. On account of adultery a man may lawfully, rightly, and without sin repudiate his wife. 2. If an unbeliever is not willing to live with a believing spouse, but deserts, dismisses, repudiates her without the guilt of adultery, only because of her faith, the unbeliever indeed is sinning both against God and against the law of marriage, but the innocent spouse, who has been deserted, is not subject to servitude but is free from the law concerning the husband, so that she is not an adulteress if she is lawfully joined to another man. Also Chrysostom notes these two cases, writing on 1 Cor. 7. He says: "The unbeliever furnishes a cause, as does fornication."

[SECTION VI]

[Concerning the Remarriage
of Divorced Persons]

CANON VII

If anyone says that the Church erred when it taught and teaches (in accord with the teaching of the Gospels and of the apostles) that the bond of matrimony cannot be dissolved on account of the adultery of one of the spouses, and that both, or even the innocent party, who did not give occasion for adultery, cannot contract another marriage as long as the other spouse lives, and that he who after divorcing an adulteress marries another commits adultery, as also the woman who marries another after divorcing an adulterer, let him be anathema.

Examination

1 Here that papalist law is repeated and bolstered which does not allow the innocent party, which has been separated by a legitimate divorce from a spouse that is either an adulterer or an adulteress, for any reason to contract another marriage as long as the guilty party still lives. Many, indeed, had hoped for some mitigation of this harsh law for the reason that its inhuman severity not only deprives the innocent party of its right without any guilt on its part, a thing which is against all rules of justice, but also casts the most perilous snares on consciences. For if after a legitimate divorce, lawfully gotten, the innocent party does not have the gift of continence, and yet is unable to contract a second marriage, he or she is compelled either to live with constant burning by which prayer is disturbed and quenched, or in fornication, which excludes from the kingdom of God—and that not through their own guilt, but through that of another. And so the divorce permitted by the Son of God on account of adultery will be to the innocent party nothing but a snare by which he is cast into burning, into fornication, and finally into the wrath and judgment of God. Therefore Christ would have counseled His church better if He had simply allowed no divorce at all, even on account of adultery. For thus the innocent party would have retained the ability to use the remedies divinely granted against fornication.

But the Council of Trent is not concerned about how it may counsel consciences, for even as they do for priests, perhaps so they also rather grant divorced persons a hundred concubines than one lawful wife. Thus the seventh canon forbids under the anathema that an innocent spouse who gave no cause for adultery should contract another marriage as long as the other spouse lives, and declares that anyone who after a lawful divorce, legitimately performed, marries another after the adulteress has been dismissed commits adultery. For it contends that the bond of matrimony cannot be dissolved by divorce even if it is done lawfully on account of adultery.

2 I am not ignorant of the fact that Augustine and those who follow him savagely and harshly debate and explain this question. But if the prejudices and preconceived notions of men are laid aside, and this question is decided on the basis of the very words of Christ, the matter is certainly plain and clear. A question is laid before Christ by the Pharisees about divorce or repudiation, that is, about dismissing one's wife or separating from her. Now one must establish before all else what is the definition of the kind of divorce about which the Pharisees are asking. That definition is certain and clear from Deut. 24:1-4, which the Pharisees adduce. For there Moses says that through divorce a woman is sent away from the house of her husband, and sent out in such a way that she can be married to another husband. And in Lev. 21:7 and Ezek. 44:22, a priest, even as he is forbidden to marry a widow, so also a divorced woman. In Jer. 3:1 it is adduced as common knowledge that after divorce a person is at liberty to go to another spouse. Therefore the repudiation or divorce about which the question of the Pharisees speaks is not only a separation from bed and board but is a dissolution of the bond of wedlock, so that after a legitimate divorce lawfully accomplished another marriage can be contracted, not only after the death of the prior spouse but while he lives. For that is explicitly laid down in Deut. 24:1-4. And the word *karath,* by which the Hebrews express repudiation or divorce, means "to cut off" or "to tear off," which fits well to the dissolution of the conjugal bond. Thus the conjugal bond does not remain between the former spouses after a divorce, as Deut. 24:4 and Jer. 3:1 declare that it is an abomination if a man wanted to marry his divorced wife after the death of the other man.

Dietenberger[16] objects that the Jews were permitted to marry another wife after a divorce, not by reason of the divorce but because at that time it was permitted to have a number of wives simultaneously. It is certain that this reason is vain and false, for also a repudiated woman

---

[16] Johann Dietenberger: Roman Catholic theologian, teacher, and writer, 1475-1537

could be married to another (Deut. 24:2; Lev. 21:7; Ezek. 44:22; Jer. 3:1). Therefore it is certain and clear what the question of the Pharisees understands by the term "divorce." Also the wording of the bill of divorcement, which is still customary with the Jews today, bears this out. For in it there is found this clause: "I grant her the liberty and power to go freely wherever she will, and she can be married to any man; neither let any man presume to forbid her."

3 Let us see further what Christ Himself in His response understands by divorce or repudiation. In Matt. 19:9; Mark 10:11; Luke 16:18 He links these two: to put away his wife, and after the divorce to marry another. Therefore the definition of divorce is the same in the question of the Pharisees and in the answer of Christ. We shall apply this meaning of divorce to the question itself and to the answer. For the Pharisees are asking for what causes a divorce may be permitted. Here I freely confess that if Christ had answered only what Mark and Luke describe, the sense would simply be this, that such a divorce is not lawful for any cause whatsoever, but that, no matter what befell, it is not permissible for the bond of marriage to be dissolved except through death. For the words read thus: "Whoever divorces his wife and marries another commits adultery." But because it is a universal and necessary rule in reading the evangelists that the true interpretation and meaning must be sought and taken from a comparison of the descriptions found in the other evangelists, for they render each other aid in this way, that what one stated more briefly and obscurely the other complements and explains more clearly— therefore also the description of Matthew must be compared, which testifies, not once but in two places, that Christ, on different occasions, when He treated the matter of divorce, expressly added as an exception the cause of fornication (Matt. 5:32; 19:9). Therefore the statement of Christ in Mark and Luke are not simply universal but are to be taken with the exception which the apostle Matthew, who was present at these discourses, adds in two places.

Now because it is a wholly true rule that something is taken away from a general statement by a particular case, the meaning of Christ's answer, according to a comparison of the evangelists, will be this, that only in the case of fornication is a divorce, such as we have described above, lawful and that in all other cases it is not lawful that a man should send away his wife and marry another. And because He declares that adultery is committed if someone marries another, He shows that in all other divorces, for whatever causes they are performed, the bond of matrimony remains— with the exception of that divorce which is made on account of fornication. For the arguments taken from the contrary sense are of all arguments both the clearest and strongest. Therefore because Christ says: "Whoever divorces his wife, except for the cause of fornication, and marries another commits adultery," therefore, from the contrary sense, whoever divorces his wife for the cause of fornication and marries another does not commit adultery.

4 This is certainly clearer than the light of noon, and this clear simplicity is strongly confirmed by the fact that Augustine cannot protect his different understanding in any other way than by twisting the words of Christ, "except for fornication," miserably and contrary to what the simplicity of the context can bear. For he says that the meaning of the exception is that those who divorce their wives without the cause of fornication sin even more grievously, but that nevertheless also those who divorce their wife for the cause of fornication and marry another are nevertheless guilty of adultery.

But only let the text be examined, and it will be clear that Christ does not say this, for the question which had been proposed to Him was not whether illegitimate divorces are a graver sin, but the question was about legitimate causes of divorce. The Pharisees indeed were of the opinion that any and every cause was sufficient. Christ, however, answers that with the exception of the cause of fornication there is no other cause which can dissolve the bond of matrimony. But let the definition of divorce always be recalled to mind. For the Pharisees are raising a question about something which has been defined; they are asking about causes for divorce. Now Christ, in His answer, uses this definition of divorce, namely, to send away one's wife and to marry another. And this definition He ascribes to no cause except the cause of fornication. For the little words *parektos* and *ei mee* do not permit Augustine's contortion. The translators of the Septuagint render 1 Sam. 20:39 *parex:* "The lad knew nothing; only David and Jonathan knew. 1 Sam. 21:9: "There is here no other sword except this." 1 Kg. 3:18: "No one was present except we two." Acts 26:29: "I wish that all would become such as I am except for these chains." In these statements the interpretation about greater and lesser would certainly be most unfitting, since the exceptions are simply exclusive, as is also the word "except," which is used in Matt. 19:9. Examples of this are found everywhere.

5 Therefore Christ's meaning is plain. But two statements of Paul are quoted in opposition. There is no doubt that Paul, of all men, understood the meaning of Christ most correctly. Therefore we shall show briefly that these do not remove the exception of Christ about the cause of fornication. In Rom. 7:2 he says that "a woman is bound by law to her husband as long as he lives . . . so that she will be called an adulteress if she lives with another man while her husband is alive." This the papalists interpret as though Paul wanted to teach that not even after a legitimate divorce, lawfully procured on account of fornication, could another marriage be allowed as long as the other spouse still lives. But Paul is not, in this passage, professedly treating of divorce, but is taking an analogy from the institution of matrimony inasmuch as it is an indissoluble union, insofar as it fits his purpose. There is no doubt that matrimony per se, according to its institution, is such a union, as Christ says: "They are no longer two, but one flesh." Likewise: "What God has joined together, let not man put asunder." In this way, according to its institution, matrimony is not dissolved except by death. Up to this point the picture served Paul's purpose. The other question, however, is about divorce, the picture of which Paul does not add because there was no need of it for what he was treating of at that point. However, Christ (Matt. 19:9) at the same time both teaches the law of the indissolubility of marriage on the basis of its institution and adds the exception about divorce on account of fornication. Therefore it must not be supposed that Paul either removed or abrogated that exception of Christ when he quotes the law of the institution about the indissolubility of the marital association. And, in order that there may be no need for conjectures, we will let Paul himself be his surest interpreter. For he says that he is speaking to people who know the law. But it is very certain that the law allows second marriages after a legitimate divorce (Deut. 24:1-4; Lev. 21:7; Jer. 3:1; Ezek. 44:22). Therefore Paul is speaking in this particular passage of the marriage bond as it is per se, apart from the case of divorce. For he himself also (1 Cor. 7:15, 39), where he repeats the statement found in Rom. 7:2-3, releases a believer from bondage in case of desertion and claims liberty for her from the law of the unbelieving husband while he yet lives.

6 Paul's second statement in 1 Cor. 7 (vv. 10-11) seems to press harder. For he says by way of introduction that he is repeating a precept of the Lord about divorce. He says simply without exception that it is a command of the Lord that a woman should not be separated from her husband; if, however, she is separated, that she should remain single or that she be reconciled to her husband, and that the husband should not divorce his wife. Let us look at this statement of Paul somewhat more closely, most of all because he says that he is repeating a precept of the Lord about divorce. However, Christ embraces two things in this His precept: (1) for what causes divorce is not lawful so it would be possible to contract another marriage; (2) he adds the exception about the cause of fornication. Let us now see whether Paul includes both parts of the precept of Christ, or whether He speaks only of the one part. We shall not resort to divination but base our judgment on Paul's own words.

First we shall take what is certain also according to the admission of our adversaries. For although they do not, after a divorce, permit another marriage, they nevertheless confess that a man is permitted to dismiss his wife, and a wife her husband, on account of fornication. For other causes, however, outside of fornication, Christ declares such dismissing is not permitted. For in Matt. 5:32 He is not speaking of a second marriage on the part of a man after he has dismissed his wife, but about divorce itself: "Every one who divorces his wife, except on the ground of unchastity, makes her an adulteress." However Paul in 1 Cor. 7:10 says: "I give charge, not I but the Lord, that the wife should not separate from her husband . . . and that the husband should not divorce his wife." You hear that Paul is speaking about that part of the Lord's precept which prohibits divorce itself for other causes, outside of the cause of fornication. And he rightly says that in those cases a second marriage cannot be contracted, because that is adultery, because the marriage bond has not yet been dissolved. However, the Lord's commandment is not that a man neither should nor can divorce his wife on account of fornication. Therefore the words, "except for the cause of fornication," are not contained in Paul's statement, because he expressly declares that he is speaking about those causes for which divorce is not permitted. However, the fact that he adds: "If the unbelieving partner desires to separate," etc., shows that many things are in fact done which by right are not permitted.

Second, the words about being reconciled show that Paul is not speaking about the cause of fornication. For when it is said in Scripture that one is reconciled to another, this is properly understood not of the innocent party but that the party which offended is reconciled to the other, as is shown in Rom 5:10: "While we were enemies we were reconciled to God." Matt. 5:23-24: If your brother has anything against you, go and be reconciled to your brother.

If therefore Paul here understood the departure of the woman to be on account of fornication on the part of the husband, he would not recommend reconciliation to the woman as the innocent party but to the husband as the party who had offended. But because he says: "Let the wife reconcile herself to her husband," he understands a separation which takes place not on account of fornication but for other causes. Therefore the exception posited by Christ remains in force.

Third: Paul himself does not at once propose to the believing partner who has been deserted the command: "Let her remain single," but declares her to be free. Therefore Paul himself shows that the earlier statement is not to be understood as being without exception.

Fourth: The Greek interpreters expressly add the exception of the cause of fornication in their explanation of this Pauline statement. Chrysostom says that a woman should not leave her husband unless there is fornication, and adds that this is Paul's meaning. He also adds that because it happens that divorces take place for reasons other than fornication, it is better that they should not happen at all, but if they do happen, that the parties remain unmarried or be reconciled.

Theophylact repeats the same explanation. Oecumenius says: "The law of God is that there should be no divorce except for fornication." Likewise: "Let not the husband divorce his wife except only on account of fornication, for this is the law of Christ."

Ambrose also says: "If she leaves her husband because he is hard to live with, let her remain unmarried thereafter."

Thus the question of the Corinthians was not about legitimate divorce, which is procured because of fornication, but about the kind of divorces which, by reason of the fickleness of the Greeks, were customary among them for all kinds of causes. Therefore the decision with respect to this question, as far as the statement of Scripture is concerned, is plain. And pious minds ought to acquiesce when they have the simple and genuine meaning of the divine will revealed in Scripture.

7 However, among ecclesiastical writers this question has not been defined in the same way. For to the extent that conscience can bear, one must strive that also legitimate divorces may be avoided and the marriage either be preserved indissolubly or, if it has been interrupted, be restored. Therefore the ancients earnestly admonished and exhorted men that they should allow adulterous wives to be reconciled to themselves if they repented and showed hope of betterment, especially since we Christians ought to consider that the spiritual covenant of marriage between Christ and the church is often violated by us through spiritual fornication. We, however, would not be willing to have God deal with us so harshly that He would on this account cast us off from Himself forever without hope of reconciliation. But let us, as is right, praise the mercy of God which is most beautifully described in Jer. 3:12-18. Therefore it is just that also we should show the same kindness and mercy to the fallen party, lest we fall under the judgment: "The measure you give will be the measure you get back," especially because Christ gently received the adulterous woman who returned to her senses (John 8:11). Augustine tells us that rigorous men, driven by great hatred, expunged this passage from its place.

To this comes the fact that a second marriage has its problems on account of the children from the prior marriage. Also the fallen party will find greater difficulty in coming to repentance when she is cast off without any hope of being received back, but will, from desperation, sully herself with other even more atrocious and shameful deeds. Jerome quotes a certain statement of Solomon's from Prov. 18, which is not found in the Hebrew text: "He who keeps an adulteress is foolish and ungodly." From Chrysostom is quoted 32, quest. 1: "Whoever retains a harlot is foolish and unjust, for he is a protector of infamy who hides the misdeed of his wife."

However, it does not militate against godliness to receive back an adulteress who returns to her senses. Thus David again received his spouse Michal, who had been joined to another.

8 These and other arguments by which the feelings of a husband can be persuaded and mollified are found with Augustine. And it is approved by all pious consciences that one does not at once hasten to procure a divorce but that first everything be tried which can serve reconciliation and restoration. For Paul says: "All things are lawful for me, but not all things are helpful and edify."

9 Therefore, in order that they might the more effectively influence the minds of husbands, the ancients taught that it is more right, more excellent, more perfect if also a person who is separated from an adulteress either remains unmarried or again takes back his reconciled wife. And they reprimanded second marriages after divorce also with a certain amount of public censure, in order that they might the more easily bend minds toward reconciliation. They were not, however, so harsh, hard, savage, and inhuman that they preferred to cast the consciences of those who were separated into eternal ruin by traditions of this kind, snares of passionate burning and fornication, rather than to grant another marriage.

Thus Origen says, on Matt. 18, that such marriages are indeed outside of Scripture and against what is written in Rom. 7:2-3 and Matt. 18; nevertheless he adds: "I know that some who are in charge of churches have permitted some woman, outside of Scripture, to be married while her former husband is still alive. And although they acted contrary to Scripture (Rom. 7:2-3), nevertheless they did not permit this altogether without cause. For perhaps they permitted things which are bad by comparing them with things which are even worse, in view of the kind of infirmity found in persons who cannot practice continence." He says that such permission is not according to exact justice but according to the hardness of carnal people. However—and this must be diligently noted—he compares this permission[17] with what is found in 1 Cor. 7:1-2, 5-6: "It is well for a man not to touch a woman. But because of the temptation to immorality, " etc. Likewise: "Come together again, lest

Satan tempt you. . . . I say this by way of concession, not by command."
Therefore he does not understand permission to commit a mortal sin
which destroys the conscience and makes a person fall from grace. And if
Cajetan, Erasmus, and Catharinus hoped for nothing more they certainly
hoped that now at last there would be such a permission[18] or indulgence in
the council—but in vain, as is now apparent.

In this way learned men understand the seventh canon of Neocaesarea about this kind of second marriages, and indeed, in my judgment,
rightly. For it declares that a presbyter ought not be present at weddings
of persons married for a second time, lest by his presence at the banquet
he appear to approve of such marriages. And the reason is added: Because the command is to impose penance on second marriages. Therefore
second marriages after a divorce were marked by some public disappro-
val on the part of the church; however, they were not completely condemned or prohibited or rescinded.

Thus Jerome tells that Fabiola, who after a legitimate divorce, while
her former husband still lived, was married to another, did public penance such as the seventh canon of Neocaesarea speaks of, because it was
against the strict understanding of the Gospel, which cuts off from women
every excuse for marrying as long as their husbands live. Nevertheless, he
adds that she had done this not as a mortal sin, nor had she merely
followed the laws of Papinian, but she had done this according to the
saying of Paul: "It is better to marry than to be aflame with passion."
Likewise: "I would have younger widows marry, lest they stray after
Satan." Neither did the public penance of Fabiola make her sin downright mortal and damnable, for at that time a penance of two or three
years was imposed on those who retained an adulterous wife without
divorcing her, ch. 32, quest. 1.

The ancients were very hard toward women in order that no second
marriage might be allowed them after a divorce, as Ambrose says on 1
Cor. 7: "A woman is not permitted to marry if she divorced her husband
because of fornication." However, he thinks that Paul did not say about
the husband: "Let him remain single," because, says he, "the man is
permitted to marry another if he has divorced a wife who sinned." Other
divorces Ambrose both censures and condemns, on Luke 16. But he says
expressly that after a divorce because of fornication it is lawful for a man
to take another wife, and declares that he can do this not on the basis of

---

[17-18] The text has *promissionem* in both places. Nigrinus evidently read *permissio-
nem,* which fits the context. We have so translated it.

civil law, as Lindanus imagines, but on the basis of Paul's statement. From this passage of Ambrose one gathers that the public reproofs which are found in Origen and Jerome were formulated chiefly against the second marriages of women. For Ambrose openly declares that this was permitted to men.

Around the time of Augustine this question began to be debated more harshly, namely, that marriages contracted, whether by men or by women, even after a legitimate divorce lawfully performed on account of fornication, were simply adulterous. However, that this dogma was not universal is clear from the fact that there were at that time those who spoke against the opinion of Augustine, as for instance Pollentius. But on the authority of Augustine it was brought about that at the Council of Mileve the 17th canon about this matter was stated thus: "It pleases us that in accord with the evangelical and apostolic teaching a woman dismissed by her husband shall not be married to another, but remain single, or be reconciled to him. But if they disregard this, they shall be brought to repentance." But this canon is not speaking of the innocent party, which divorced the party that sinned on account of fornication; rather it is speaking of those who have been dismissed, that is, of the guilty party. It indeed is worthy of note that this canon adds that an imperial law should be asked for in this matter. Therefore, until those times, also under Christian emperors, there was no law or regulation which prohibited such marriages. Neither did they obtain such a law afterward from Christian emperors, as is clear from the code of Justinian. Also after that time such marriages were not simply rescinded in the church, as being worthy of condemnation. For Leo, Letter No. 85, speaks of a certain priest who, after divorce from his wife, had married another. He only removes this man from the ministry; he does not, however, rescind this second marriage; neither does he excommunicate him from the church.

10 And, granted that after these times even harsher regulations were made concerning this matter, nevertheless some regulations and examples retained the gentleness of the ancient church. Thus, ch. 32, quest. 7, a canon of a certain council is quoted: "A certain woman slept with the brother of her husband; it was decreed that the adulterers should never be married; but to the man whose wife had been debauched a lawful marriage was not denied." Likewise from a decree of Zacharias: "If you have had intercourse with the sister of your wife, thus you have done; you shall have neither; and if she who was your wife did not know about the crime, and does not want to remain continent, let her marry in the Lord; however, you and the adulteress shall remain without hope of marriage."

From the Concilium Triburiense:[19] "If anyone has had intercourse with his stepmother, neither one of them can enter matrimony, but her husband can, if he cannot remain continent, take another woman if he will." And Gregory writes to Boniface: "In answer to your question, what a married man is to do if his wife, seized by illness, cannot render him the conjugal debt: It would be good if he remained thus and maintained abstinence; but because this is a difficult thing, let him who cannot be continent rather marry."

11 I have related these things so that the reader may more correctly weigh what kind of anathema that is which the men of Trent pronounce in this seventh canon, chiefly however in order that the reader might consider for what causes and reasons the gentleness of the ancient church sometimes allowed marriage after a divorce. If a judgment of the magistrate would follow the adulterer and adulteress (Deut. 22:20-22; Ezek. 16:38, 40; 23:45, 47), there would be no need for the question which troubles consciences. But because the magistrate does not act, therefore consciences must be counseled from the Word of God, as Paul counsels the deserted person on the basis of this rule: "God has called us to peace" (1 Cor. 7:15). Likewise 1 Cor. 7:35: "Not to lay any restraint upon you."

---

[19] A council of German bishops held A.D. 895.

[SECTION VII]

[Concerning Separation]

If anyone says that the Church errs when it decrees that separation of spouses so far as bed and cohabitation are concerned, for a definite or indefinite period of time, can take place for many causes, let him be anathema.

Examination

[First:] This is not a new definition of divorce, namely, that it is only a separation from bed and cohabitation between spouses, while the marriage bond remains between those who are separated. Such a separation was first taken from the statement of Paul (1 Cor. 7:11): "If she separates, let her remain single or else be reconciled to her husband," namely, when there was no legitimate cause for divorce. However, certain other, more serious disagreements happened. Then, since divorce was not possible, a separation of some kind took place; afterward, through a reconciliation, cohabitation was restored. From that separation a definition of divorce was afterward made, although Paul expressly testifies that he is not speaking about a true divorce, that is, about the kind of dismissal and separation which is granted by the precept of the Lord, for he says: "To the married I give charge, not I but the Lord, that the wife should not separate from her husband . . . and that the husband should not divorce his wife" [1Cor. 7:10-11]. Therefore what Paul adds: "If she separates, let her remain single or else be reconciled to her husband," does not belong to a true and legitimate divorce such as Christ speaks of. Yet the papalists fabricate the definition of a true and legitimate divorce from this passage.

Second: Christ pronounces separation from a spouse illicit and unlawful unless it is done on account of fornication (Matt. 5:31-32): "It was said to the men of old: Whoever divorces his wife, let him give her a certificate of divorce. But I say to you that every one who divorces his wife, except on the ground of unchastity, makes her an adulteress." Against this statement of Christ the papalists decree that there are many other causes beside fornication on account of which a lawful and legitimate separation of spouses can take place.

Third: The kind of separation or divorce which is described in 1 Cor. 7:11, outside the cause of fornication, Paul neither recommends nor decrees, but teaches that it militates against the command of Christ, who teaches that one should not separate. When spouses for reasons of private obstinacy do separate contrary to the teaching and admonition of the apostle, then Paul recommends that they be reconciled or, if they are unwilling to do this, that they should remain single. But this eighth canon says that the church can decree a separation for many causes beside fornication.

Fourth: Christ (Matt. 5:32) disapproves the dismissal or separation of spouses which takes place apart from the cause of burning passion, fornication, and adultery. "He makes her," says He, " an adulteress." But the papalists are not concerned about these dangers, for they freely decree a separation for a definite or an indefinite time.

Fifth: They contend that it should be the kind of divorce in which the marriage bond nevertheless remains undissolved. However, in this papalist separation the marriage bond is dissolved and disrupted in many and various ways. For to the marriage bond belong these statement: "He shall cleave to his wife"; "I will make him a helper fit for him"; "the wife does not rule over her own body, but the husband does"; "come together again, lest Satan tempt you through lack of self-control"; "so they are no longer two but one flesh." Moreover, marriage is defined as an indissoluble union for life. Now these bonds of marriage are dissolved and disrupted in the papalist separation so far as bed and cohabitation are concerned: therefore men are, contrary to the divine decree, separating what God has joined together.

[SECTION VIII]

[Concerning the Prohibition of Wedding Celebrations at Certain Times of the Year]

CANON XI

If anyone says that the prohibition of wedding celebrations at certain times of the year is a tyrannical superstition, derived from the superstition of the heathen, or condemns the benedictions and other ceremonies which the Church uses in them, let him be anathema.

Examination

Formerly at Christmas, at Easter, and at Pentecost a great and solemn Communion of the whole populace was celebrated. In order that preparation for worthy Communion might not be disturbed or hindered by wedding banquets and other displays, it was wisely decreed that on those festivals and on the nearest days before them the displays of weddings should not be celebrated. Later, when the custom of a solemn Communion on those festivals had fallen into disuse, that is, when the cause, purpose, and use of this statute had ceased, the statute itself was nevertheless retained. And a new opinion began to be attached to it, as though the sanctity of those times could not bear the mingling of the flesh in the conjugal bond, as once upon a time the married women were compelled to sleep alone at the time of the rites of the Bona Dea.[20] This opinion we criticize and rebuke. For Scripture declares that the marriage bed is undefiled, likewise that it is true chastity and sanctification.

---

[20] The Bona Dea was a Roman goddess worshiped exclusively by women. Men were strictly barred from the rites which were annually observed in her honor.

[SECTION IX]

[Concerning Jurisdiction in Matrimonial Cases]

If anyone says that matrimonial cases do not belong before ecclesiastical judges, let him be anathema.

Examination

Because marriage in the church has as its norm the Word of God itself, there occur in matrimonial matters also many cases involving consciences. Therefore the church cannot simply refuse entirely to deal with matrimonial cases and simply throw them to the civil magistrate, as is done in cases involving inheritances, successions, and similar matters. For Christ, who completely refused to deal with a case of dividing an inheritance (Luke 12:13-14), does not in the same way reject the question about divorce but shows from the Word of God what agrees with the norm of the institution and what militates against it. Thus Paul (1 Cor. 7), when he had been consulted about matrimonial matters, does not throw the whole business to the civil magistrate but instructs consciences from the Word of God. Thus Ambrose answers in a matrimonial question about the forbidden degrees, Bk. 8, Letter No. 66. We also read certain rules about matrimonial cases in the ancient councils.

However, the ancient church at no time transferred matrimonial matters to its own court in such a way that it entirely excluded the civil magistrate, particularly if he was a Christian. For it belongs to the duty of the magistrate to declare laws. Thus it was not the bishops but Emperor Theodosius who declared the law about the marriage of first cousins, Augustine, *De civitate Dei*, Bk. 15, ch. 16. Thus the Council of Mileve judges that it needs an imperial law for a rule about divorce. Such was at that time the union between the ministry of the church and the civil magistrate in matrimonial matters. Afterward the pope and the bishops entirely grasped these things for themselves, simply excluding even a Christian magistrate.

[SECTION X]
Concerning Clandestine Marriages

Although it is not to be doubted that clandestine marriages made with the free consent of those who contract them are valid and genuine marriages as long as the Church has not made them invalid, and that in consequence those who deny that they are true and valid are justly to be condemned, even as the holy synod condemns them with the anathema, also those who falsely assert that marriages contracted by children without the consent of the parents are invalid and that the parents can make them valid or invalid; nevertheless the holy Church of God has for the justest of all reasons at all times detested and prohibited them, etc.

Examination

1 The more sensible among the papalists acknowledge and confess that marriages contracted without the knowledge and against the will of parents are not a lawful or a divine union. For Gropper, in the *Institutio Coloniensis,* says very severely: "We would wish that the clearly very holy canon of Evaristus[21] might be brought back into the church by a general council, in order to do away with these clandestine marriages, which are now here and there being joined by male and female procurers, not openly but furtively, between boys and girls, without the consent of their parents, or which are joined between fools or drunk persons, solely in the interest of passion, without regard for God, but at the instigation of the devil, and that very often without their considered consent. For who would rightly call that consent which was brought about not by deliberation but by either youthful ignorance or by a drunken state or by a trap or by lust? Who does not know how much opportunity for lewdness, for perjury, and for other crimes of this kind, and for innumerable ills these clandestine marriages give rise to?" And afterward: "We know that the church has for a long time borne these marriages and that it did not lightly annul them, lest their simplicity cause the injured maidens to be cheated and the young men go scot-free, seeing they have brought disgrace on the maidens. Now, because experience teaches that this indulgence of the church offers opportunity for many evils through the fault of those who

---

[21] Evaristus was bishop at Rome from A.D. 99 to about 107.

abuse it, who could fail to see that it would be far more satisfactory that these clandestine marriages, which totally lack the nature of a sacrament, should be removed from the church, or at least it were decreed that they should not be regarded by the church as having the durability of marriage unless the strength of a new consent comes to it?" etc. So we read there.

2 This opinion surely has the most weighty proofs and a firm basis in divine law, natural law, civil law, and in the regulations of the ancient church.

First: The church holds and declares that marriage is a union whose Author, Joiner, and Promoter is God Himself. In order, therefore, that spouses may be certain that they have been joined together by God, and that they may hope and seek Him with His blessing for the future, once they have entered wedlock, they must be taught not to enter matrimony contrary to the Word and commandments of God. For God will not be the Promoter of a union which is established contrary to His Word. Now indeed paternal authority is not only grounded in civil law, but the divine command subjects children to the authority of parents, that they should obey them in all things in the Lord. How then can that be a legitimate and divine union which is entered into in violation of the obedience and respect which children owe their parents on the basis of the divine command?

Certain of the canonists complain loudly that we add this to the Fourth Commandment, that paternal power has, by divine right, authority over children in the matter of contracting marriages, although matrimonial matters seem to be exempted from the Fourth Commandment by the statement: "Therefore a man leaves his father and his mother and cleaves to his wife." But this statement speaks, not about a betrothed woman but about a wife, that is, about a marriage already lawfully contracted. However, Scripture, both by precept and example, includes the contracting of marriages of children under the Fourth Commandment. For it commands parents to give their daughters in marriage or to take wives for their sons (Deut. 7:3; Jer. 29:6). And Abraham, by virtue of his power as father, decrees by a testament as it were what kind of wife he wills to accept for his son and what kind he does not want his son to marry. And in the New Testament (1 Cor. 7:25-38), where Paul argues about either preserving girls as virgins or giving them in marriage, he prescribes this advice to parents. Therefore divine law gives to paternal power the authority over children, not only in the matter of civil contracts but expressly also in the contracting of marriages. Therefore the Fourth Commandment, which deals with the respect and obedience of children toward parents, expressly and specifically includes also the contracting of marriage. And that the power of the father is able to make marriages contracted without consent of the parents either valid or invalid, God shows expressly in His law. For in Deut. 22:28-29 there is this divine law: "If a man has ravished a virgin, he shall give her father so and so many shekels, and shall have her for wife; he cannot divorce her as long as she lives." You hear that by law he must take her to wife if her father consents. But according to Ex. 22:16-17 this can, through the intervention of paternal power, become either valid or null and void. For if the father of the maiden is not willing to give her to the ravisher, he cannot have her as wife. Yes, if a maid who is still in the power of her father vows something to God Himself, the vow can be rendered null and void if the father objects to it (Num. 30:3-5). Much more therefore will the power of the father have authority in the case of a promise of marriage made without consent of the parents.

Now because it is a difficult thing to make a marriage contract in such a way that God Himself binds them together, joins and unites them, we may ask how God does this. He does not do it without means, as He Himself conducted Eve to Adam, but through specific and lawful means. What these are He Himself shows in the explanation of the Fourth Commandment. Therefore when these means are spurned and trodden underfoot when a marriage is being contracted, will anyone say that it is a legitimate and divine marriage? This is surely a most weighty argument, taken from divine law.

3 Second: That this is the opinion not only of the civil law but also of the natural law, the civil laws show, as in *Digestis de ritu nuptiarum:* "A marriage cannot take place unless all parties consent, that is, those who are being married and those under whose authority they are." Also *Codex de nuptiis:* "If you have observed the precepts of the law, you will not be hindered from marrying the woman of your choice; however, in such a way that the consent of your father is given to the marriage you are contracting." And in the regulations *De nuptiis:* "Those Roman citizens contract lawful marriages among themselves who marry according to the precepts of the laws, namely, adult males and marriageable females, and who have the consent of the parents in whose power they are." That this is how it should be is urged to such a degree by both civil and natural reason, that the command of the parents should go before.

4 Third: The regulations of the ancient church uphold the same opinion, and that indeed with great earnestness. We have a regulation of Evaristus, published about A.D. 100, which says: "A marriage is not legitimate unless the woman is requested from those who appear to have power over her and by whom she is guarded and she is betrothed by her parents and kinsmen," etc. "When it is done in this way, know that it is a legitimate marriage; otherwise, if she is taken beforehand, then there is no doubt that it is not a marriage but adultery or concubinage or debauchery or fornication rather than a legitimate marriage, unless her own will has agreed and legitimate vows have come to its aid." Evaristus adds: "So we have received it from the fathers and have found it taught by the holy apostles and their successors."

What the opinion of the church about this question was around A.D. 390 we learn from Ambrose, who says of the story of Rebekah in his book *De patriarchis:* "Rebekah is not consulted about her betrothal, for this awaited the judgment of her parents. For it is not in harmony with maidenly modesty to choose her own husband. She is, however, consulted about the date of her departure." And Ambrose adds that this sentiment comes from natural law. "Very many," says he, "admire it when in a play of Euripides a woman says when she was sought for a second marriage: 'My father is in charge of my betrothal for this does not belong to me.' Therefore, maidens, observe that which also philosophers admired, and not only maidens, but also if a widow wants to marry, let her marry in the Lord in such a way that she leaves the choice of a husband to her parents," etc.

The Fourth Synod of Carthage shows that around the year 436 it was customary that bridegroom and bride were presented by their parents to the priest who blessed the marriage, to bear witness that the parents had given their consent. Around A.D. 450 Pope Leo decreed that it would be clear that a wife was being taken in harmony with the Law and the Gospel if the bride were given to the groom in marriage at a public ceremony. The same Leo says: "Women united with their husbands by the will of the father are guiltless."

At the Fourth Council of Toledo, around A.D. 630, it was decreed that maidens should not be compelled to accept husbands against the will of their parents or against their own will. And around the year A.D. 865, when the Bulgars had recently been converted to the faith, Nicolaus writes concerning the custom of the Roman church as follows: "With our countrymen covenants of betrothal, which are a promise of future marriage, are solemnized by the consent of those who contract them and of those in whose power they are." These things are found in the Decrees, *causa* 30, 32, which I have distributed in the order of the years, in order that it may be seen all the more clearly that the papalist regulation about considering clandestine marriages valid is of recent date and that it disagrees with the opinion of the ancient church.

Here also what is written in 36, quest. 1, 2, fits in, about abductors who forcibly abduct a girl from the house of her father in order that they may have the injured one to wife. For there it is decreed, from the Synod of Orleans, that although the girl is in agreement with her abductor, she is nevertheless to be returned to the power of her father. And Gregory says: "When the abducted girl has been restored to the power of her father and the abductor has done penance for his robbery, and when the will of the parents of both parties has come to an agreement, they are not prohibited from marrying each other."

5 These things must be understood especially of cases where the matter is still whole. For when the marriage has been consummated and intercourse has taken place, then, to avoid even greater offense and that no harm may be done to the violated and deserted woman, the dispensation may be observed which is found in Deut. 22:29: "She shall be his wife." Thus Ambrose counsels Sisynnius, the father; nevertheless he confesses at the same time that the son is at fault. Bk. 6, Letter No. 43. Yes, even Isaac tolerated this in the case of Esau.

6 If, however, either the negligence or the insensibility of the parents should abuse this power of theirs, and should be unwilling to provide for the marriage of their children or should attempt to hinder honorable marriages, or to compel unwilling children to enter unions that are disagreeable to them, certain legal remedies are set up against such abuse, and other remedies can be brought to bear against them.

7 But hear what contradictory things the Synod of Trent sets down about this question! It declares that the church has at all times detested and prohibited such clandestine marriages, and yet it at the same time condemns with the anathema those who deny that these are true and valid marriages. Can therefore a detestable and forbidden union make a true marriage? That is: According to the Council of Trent a detestable and forbidden union is a legitimate and divine union. But 1,450 years earlier Evaristus, a Roman bishop, declared that they are not true marriages, and this on the basis of apostolic tradition. Therefore the Tridentine Synod condemns the apostles themselves with the anathema. The council, however, adds that the church, that is, the pope with his prelates, can make such marriages invalid; however, as long as the church has not done this, all who, on the basis of the Word of God, natural law, and the regulations of the ancient church, deny that they are true and valid marriages are to be condemned with the anathema. Judge from this the character of the anathemas of the Council of Trent! For they show plainly why they contend for clandestine marriages—not because they are in agreement with either the Word of God or the regulations of the ancient church but only in order to retain and strengthen the tyranny of the papalists. For they confess that if only they wanted to, they could make such marriages invalid; but as long as they are unwilling to do this, all who think otherwise should be anathema. And that is all the papalist dominion finds necessary.

[SECTION XI]
[Concerning Virginity and Celibacy]

CANON IX

If anyone says that clerics who have been placed in sacred orders or that regulars who have solemnly professed chastity are able to contract marriage, and that the contracted marriage is valid, ecclesiastical law or vows notwithstanding, and that to say the contrary is nothing else than to condemn marriage, and that all who do not feel that they have the gift of chastity (even though they have vowed it) can contract marriage, let him be anathema, since God does not deny this gift to those who rightly ask for it, and does not let us be tempted beyond our strength.

CANON X

If anyone says that the married state is to be preferred to the state of virginity or celibacy, and that it is not better and more blessed to remain in virginity or in celibacy than to be joined in marriage, let him be anathema.

Examination

The dispute about virginity and about the celibacy of clerics cannot be resolved in a few words. Moreover, there still remain from the ninth session [Session 25 of the Council of Trent] the topics of purgatory, relics, images, the invocation of saints, indulgences, the choice of foods, fasting, and festivals. But because this second part of our examination has grown longer than I had expected, and also for other reasons, I cannot at this time continue. Therefore we shall explain the remaining things at some future time in a special treatise if it pleases God and the welfare of the church seems to demand it.

The End of the Second Part of the
Examination of the Decrees of the Council of Trent

Subject Index

Absolution
comprehensive treatment 620 ff.
lay 621
minister gives 623
nature and effects 622
papalist 575, 621, 623 f., 627
private 557, 562
scholastics on 624

Acesius
denied priests can forgive sin 554

Acolytes
origin of 687, 689

Adiaphora
ceremonies 117
power of church in matters of 90

Anabaptism
repetition of Baptism 135

Anabaptists
reject papal baptism 141
remove external ministry from church 677
renew error of Donatists 107

Anathema
great and difficult thing to pronounce 90
Trent pours out 215, 704
used without firm arguments 24, 152

Ancient church
Lutherans hold it in honor 198
opposes papalist antithesis between Baptism and chrismation 201

Andrada
interpreter of Council of Trent 17, 402

Antichrist
Mass is his stronghold 41
tyranny of strengthened by denial of cup 60

Apostolic tradition
how papalists define 385

Aquarians
administered Lord's Supper with water 51

Articles of faith
cannot be established by allegories 465
established only from clear testimonies of Scripture 262, 465

Attrition
imperfect contrition 580
Luther on 587

Augsburg Interim 574

Baptism
See also Baptism of John; Infant baptism
binds to commandments of God but not to human ordinances 147 ff., 151
catechumen or lay person administering 209
corrupted 139
Cyprian sometimes Montanized concerning 200
efficacy of 156 f., 207
first door to church 157
grace of 143 f., 158
heresy or schism and 208 f.
heretical or evil ministers administering 70
Novatus' 210
of Spirit and blood according to ancients 67
promise of 145
proper time for 163
remembrance of 155
second plank and 139
sins committed after 155
unrepeatable 160 f.
use and power endures throughout life 139
validity of 102

Baptism of John 121 ff.
Ambrose on 123
Augustine on 122, 126 ff.
Baptism of Jesus and 125 ff.
Basil on 128
Chrysostom on 122
Cyprian on 121
Cyril on 128
efficacy of 123 ff.
Gabriel on 122
Gregory of Nazianzus on 128
Lombard on 121, 129
temporary 121
validity of 127 ff.

Baptizein
definition 394

Bishop
bishops and presbyters identical in Scripture 215, 701
duties of 703 f.

767

Scripture Text Index

(This index lists many Scripture passages quoted or referred to by Chemnitz without indication of chapter and verse numbers.)

Old Testament

Apocrypha

New Testament